THE
EARNHARDT
COLLECTION

TRIUMPH
BOOKS
CHICAGO

THE FIRST DECADE

All photos by David Chobat and NWCS Archive

Copyright © 2003 by Street and Smith's Sports Publications

No part of this publication may be reproduced, stored in a retrieval system, or transmitted, in any form by any means, electronic, mechanical, photo-copying, or otherwise, without prior written permission of the publisher, Triumph Books, 601 S. LaSalle St., Suite 500, Chicago, Illinois 60605

ISBN 1-57243-613-1

This book is available in quantity at special discounts for your group or organization. For further information, contact:
Triumph Books, 601 S. LaSalle St., Suite 500, Chicago, Illinois 60605
Phone: (312) 939-3330   Fax: (312) 663-3557
Printed in China

Street & Smith's
SPECIALTY PUBLICATIONS
120 W. Morehead St., Suite 240
Charlotte, N.C. 28202
704-973-1621

TRIUMPH
BOOKS
CHICAGO

CONTENTS

THE SECOND DECADE
AND BEYOND

DALE EARNHARDT

Earnhardt's

DATE	EVENT	TRACK
4/1/79	Southeastern 500	Bristol
2/10/80	Busch Clash	Daytona
3/16/80	Atlanta 500	Atlanta
3/30/80	Valleydale SE 500	Bristol
7/12/80	Busch Nashville 420	Nashville
9/28/80	Old Dominion 500	Martinsville
10/5/80	National 500	CMS
4/4/82	CRC Chemicals Rebel 500	Darlington
2/17/83	UNO 125-Mile Qualifier	Daytona
7/16/83	Busch 420	Nashville
7/31/83	Talladega 500	Talladega
7/29/84	Talladega 500	Talladega
11/11/84	Atlanta Journal 500	Atlanta
2/24/85	Miller High Life 400	Richmond
4/6/85	Valleydale 500	Bristol
8/24/85	Busch 500	Bristol
9/22/85	Goody's 500	Martinsville
2/9/86	Busch Clash	Daytona
2/13/86	7-Eleven Twin 125-Mile Qualifier	Daytona
4/13/86	TranSouth 500	Darlington
4/20/86	First Union 400	N. Wilkesboro
5/25/86	Coca-Cola 600	CMS
10/5/86	Oakwood Homes 500	CMS
11/2/86	Atlanta Journal 500	Atlanta
3/1/87	Goodwrench 500	N.C. Speedway
3/8/87	Miller High Life 400	Richmond
3/29/87	TranSouth 500	Darlington
4/5/87	First Union 400	N. Wilkesboro
4/12/87	Valleydale Meats 500	Bristol
4/26/87	Sovran Bank 500	Martinsville
5/17/87	The Winston	CMS
6/28/87	Miller American 400	Michigan
7/19/87	Summer 500	Pocono
8/22/87	Busch 500	Bristol
9/6/87	Southern 500	Darlington
9/13/87	Wrangler Indigo 400	Richmond
2/7/88	Busch Clash	Daytona
3/20/88	Motorcraft 500	Atlanta
4/24/88	Pannill Sweatshirts 500	Martinsville
8/27/88	Busch 500	Bristol
4/16/89	First Union 400	N. Wilkesboro
6/4/89	Budweiser 500	Dover
9/3/89	Heinz Southern 500	Darlington
9/17/89	Peak Performance 500	Dover
11/19/89	Atlanta Journal 500	Atlanta
2/15/90	Twin 125-Mile Qualifier	Daytona
3/18/90	Motorcraft Quality Parts 500	Atlanta
4/1/90	TranSouth 500	Darlington
5/6/90	Winston 500	Talladega

EARNHARDT

Wins By Date

DATE	EVENT	TRACK
5/20/90	The Winston	CMS
6/24/90	Miller Genuine Draft 400	Michigan
7/7/90	Pepsi 400	Daytona
7/29/90	DieHard 500	Talladega
9/2/90	Heinz Southern 500	Darlington
9/9/90	Miller Genuine Draft 400	Richmond
11/4/90	Checker 500	Phoenix
2/10/91	Busch Clash	Daytona
2/14/91	Gatorade 125-Mile Qualifier	Daytona
2/24/91	Pontiac Excitement 400	Richmond
4/28/91	Hanes 500	Martinsville
7/28/91	DieHard 500	Talladega
9/29/91	Tyson Holly Farms 400	N. Wilkesboro
2/13/92	Gatorade 125-Mile Qualifier	Daytona
5/24/92	Coca-Cola 600	CMS
2/7/93	Busch Clash	Daytona
2/11/93	Gatorade 125-Mile Qualifier	Daytona
3/28/93	TranSouth Financial 500	Darlington
5/22/93	The Winston	CMS
5/30/93	Coca-Cola 600	CMS
6/6/93	Budweiser 500	Dover
7/3/93	Pepsi 400	Daytona
7/18/93	Miller Genuine Draft 500	Pocono
7/25/93	DieHard 500	Talladega
2/17/94	Gatorade 125	Daytona
3/27/94	TranSouth Financial 400	Darlington
4/10/94	Food City 500	Bristol
5/1/94	Winston Select 500	Talladega
10/23/94	AC-Delco 500	N.C. Speedway
2/12/95	Busch Clash	Daytona
2/18/85	Gatorade Twin 125-Mile Qualifier	Daytona
4/9/95	First Union 400	N. Wilkesboro
5/7/95	Save Mart 300	Sears Point
8/5/95	Brickyard 400	Indianapolis
9/24/95	Goody's 500	Martinsville
11/12/95	NAPA 500	Atlanta
2/15/96	Gatorade 125-Mile Qualifier	Daytona
2/25/96	Goodwrench Service 400	N.C. Speedway
3/10/96	Purolator 500	Atlanta
2/13/97	Gatorade 125-Mile Qualifier	Daytona
2/12/98	Gatorade 125-Mile Qualifier	Daytona
2/15/98	Daytona 500	Daytona
2/11/99	Gatorade 125-Mile Qualifier	Daytona
4/25/99	DieHard 500	Talledega
8/28/99	Goody's Headache Powder 500	Bristol
10/17/99	Winston 500	Talladega
3/12/00	Cracker Barrel Old Country Store 500	Atlanta
10/15/00	Winston 500	Talladega

dale earnhardt

Earnhardt
Wins Southeastern 500

First Rookie Winner Since Ross' 1974 Martinsville Victory

By STEVE WAID

They have been saying that rookie driver Dale Earnhardt (Kannapolis, N.C.) will someday reach the pinnacle of NASCAR Grand National racing.

He got there sooner than expected.

Driving the Jake Elder-prepared, Rod Osterlund Monte Carlo, Earnhardt more than fulfilled his promise Sunday by winning the Southeastern 500 at Bristol International Raceway.

In doing so, Earnhardt became the first rookie to win a Grand National Race since Earl Ross' victory in the 1974 Old Dominion 500 at Martinsville – some 132 races ago.

"I'll probably believe it in the morning," said the excited Earnhardt. "This is a bigger thrill than my first-ever racing victory. This

was a win in the big leagues, against the top-caliber drivers. It wasn't some dirt track back at home."

A combination of hard driving, excellent pit work and a smooth-handling car gave Earnhardt a triumph in only his sixteenth Grand National start. Earnhardt was quick to praise the skill of crew chief Elder and the Osterlund pit crew for his 2.7-second win over Bobby Allison's Bud Moore Thunderbird.

"The pit crew got me the win," said the 27-year-old Earnhardt. "When I was racing Darrell (Waltrip) at the end, they got me out ahead of him. I could build up a lead through the traffic, and I could tell I was

getting farther ahead. After a while, I stopped looking in the mirror for him. I didn't look at nothing until the checkered flag.

"I kept thinking, 'This has got to be it.'"

Elder, who joined the Osterlund team just three races ago in Atlanta, said, "The boy (Earnhardt) ran a hard race. We had a few handling problems at the start, but we added wedge to tighten the car. Dale said he could live with it and it was the only change we made all day.

"The car ran beautiful, but Dale run good, too. There's no doubt that the boy is a race driver."

Starting ninth was a bit of a disappointment for Elder and Earnhardt, but it was clear after the race started that the Osterlund Chevy was the fastest car on the high-banked, half-mile track.

Earnhardt continued to improve his position and was left with only a challenge from defending Southeastern 500 champion Waltrip after a wreck put polesitter Buddy Baker out of the race. Baker led the first 138 laps.

Baker's W.I.N. Inc., Monte Carlo collided with Cale Yarborough's Junior Johnson Olds coming out of the fourth turn on lap 210. A bent rear end housing forced Baker

EARNHARDT HOISTS HIS FIRST GRAND NATIONAL TROPHY AFTER TAKING THE CHECKERED FLAG AT THE SOUTHEASTERN 500.
DAVID CHOBAT PHOTO

out of the race while Yarborough's crew made hasty repairs to the front suspension. Yarborough could complete only six more laps before having to retire.

That left the race to Earnhardt, Waltrip and Allison. Waltrip had command at first, but then a couple of fine pit stops helped turn the tide in favor of Earnhardt.

Twice he beat Waltrip down pit road. The

final time, which came after a caution on lap 473, put Earnhardt in the lead to stay for the final 23 circuits. Waltrip lost ground and was passed by Allison on lap 496 and relegated to third place.

"Dale ran good, really good," said Waltrip, who was one of several top drivers to compliment Earnhardt. "He was the only one to beat but I couldn't do it. I got a bad set of

tires on the last stop and couldn't run as well as I did earlier. But give Dale credit. He did the job."

"I've received a lot of help from Bobby Allison, Richard Petty and a lot of the guys who have been racing in Grand National," said Earnhardt, the son of legendary short-track racer Ralph Earnhardt. "I sure would like to thank them for taking time to talk to me and teach me things. Thing of it is, I kinda wonder if they'll hush up now."

Earnhardt's victory not only earned him $19,800, it also put the Osterlund team on NASCAR's "Winner's Circle" program, which is designed to pay out appearance money to seven winning teams.

ROOKIE GRAND NATIONAL DRIVER EARNHARDT IS JUST HAPPY TO FIND A PLACE TO SIT AND GET READY FOR THE RACE AT BRISTOL.
DAVID CHOBAT PHOTO

"If he don't get hurt, **he's got at least 12 good years** ahead," says Jake Elder, Earnhardt's crew chief.

At a rate of $3,700 for a superspeedway race and $2,700 for a short-track event, that means the Osterlund team will net about $200,000 through the remainder of this season and all of next year.

"When we qualified ninth for this race, we didn't win tires or nothing," said Elder. "Now we can go out and buy all we need."

Richard Petty finished fourth, two laps down in his Olds. Three laps down and finishing fifth was Benny Parsons in the M.C. Anderson Monte Carlo. Donnie Allison wound up sixth in the Hoss Ellington Chevrolet. Rounding out the top 10 were rookie Terry Labonte in a Chevy, rookie Joe Millikan in a Chevy (Millikan got an object in his eye while racing and was taken to the hospital; J.D. McDuffie drove for him), James Hylton in a Chevy and Ricky Rudd in a Ford.

Earnhardt, who won with an average speed of 91.033 mph before a crowd of 26,000 led three times for 164 laps – more than any other driver.

"I really believe this is only a start," said Elder. "I think you will see the boy win some more short-track races, and I'm even looking at a couple of superspeedway wins. He's young and he's good. If he don't get hurt, he's got at least 12 good years ahead."

Twelve more years can mean many more victories for Dale Earnhardt. ∎

dale earnhardt

50 Miles, 20 Laps Later –

Earnhardt Best in Busch Clash

By STEVE WAID

Dale Earnhardt might be just a second-year man on the NASCAR Grand National circuit, but he proved today at Daytona International Speedway that he's ready to give lessons instead of taking them.

Using a bold, calculated move, Earnhardt, the 1979 Rookie of the Year, won the second annual Busch Clash. In doing so, he emerged as the best in a 12-car field of the finest drivers in stock car racing.

The 50-mile, 20-lap race among the dozen drivers who won pole positions in 1979 was as tense as one might expect. Earnhardt was in the midst of the brief battle (15 minutes, 39 seconds) throughout, choosing to remain in second or third place until the final lap.

At that point, Earnhardt pushed his Rod Osterlund Oldsmobile to the outside of Darrell Waltrip's DiGard Olds as the two went down the final portion of the backstretch.

Earnhardt broke away from the field and held on for the victory, worth $50,000. Neil Bonnett, driving the Wood Brothers' Mercury, finished second, while Cale Yarborough was third in the Junior Johnson Olds and Bobby Allison fourth in the Bud Moore Mercury. Waltrip drifted back to fifth place.

"Coming down the backstretch, I sort of went to the inside of Darrell," said the 28-year-old Earnhardt, who won with a speed of 191.693 mph. "When he moved inside to block me, I went on to the outside. When I went by, it sort of slowed all the others up and I got away from 'em a bit."

The move was uncharacteristic, since most passing at Daytona is done on the inside. The low groove is the quickest route around the track. Earnhardt admitted as much, but he had learned some lessons in 1979.

"They say I'm inexperienced, but I got some experience racing with these guys last year," Earnhardt said. "They would not only talk to me, but I'd also learned from them while we were on the track."

Earnhardt had also watched video tapes of last year's Daytona 500, in which Donnie Allison and Yarborough crashed on the backstretch while battling for the lead on the final lap.

"I'd made up my mind I wasn't going to get into that predicament," Earnhardt said. "I wasn't going to get into trouble fighting for the inside. If Darrell had taken me to the third

> "Yeah, there might be a trick or two Richard (Petty) and Bobby (Allison) haven't shown me," Earnhardt said, "but **I know I can run with the best of 'em.**"

EARNHARDT POPS THE CORK ON HIS FIRST WIN OF 1980 AFTER EDGING NEIL BONNETT AND CALE YARBOROUGH IN DAYTONA'S BUSCH CLASH.
DAVID CHOBAT PHOTO

corner on the inside, well, I would've been leery of going to the outside and getting too high, but I was passing him before we got there."

The Kannapolis, N.C., driver said that he was content to stay in second or third place until the final lap because "there wasn't much room out there. Everyone wanted to be up front and things tightened up. I thought I was in the best place I could be."

Buddy Baker broke into the lead from his No. 2 starting position on the first lap. However, the pre-race favorite and 1979 winner led only three laps before falling back to sixth because of handling problems.

"I got so loose, I couldn't do anything," he said. "I had to drop back because it was all I could do to hold on." He finished seventh.

Bonnett and Waltrip then took turns leading the eight-car pack that had split from tailenders Harry Gant, Richard Petty and Joe Millikan, who finished 10th through 12th, respectively.

Waltrip was in front of Earnhardt on the final lap, only to be passed. "Boy, I was between a rock and a hard place," he said. "When Dale went by, he just pulled everybody else along with him. My car hasn't run as good as it should since we got here."

Maybe not. But the DiGard crew replaced the engine in Waltrip's car prior to the race and the Franklin, Tenn., driver led 11 laps, most of anyone in the race.

"Whew!" sighed Bobby Allison. "It was a wild finish, wasn't it? Earnhardt went high and Darrell went low and it was really wild from there to the finish line."

Bonnett earned $18,000 for his second-place finish, while Yarborough received $14,000, Bobby Allison $13,000 and Waltrip $12,000.

Benny Parsons finished sixth, followed by Baker, David Pearson and Donnie Allison, who would up ninth.

The victory was a sweet start to the 1980 season for Earnhardt, who recently signed a five-year contract with Osterlund. If nothing else, it proved that he can run with – and beat – the veterans.

"Yeah, there might be a trick or two Richard (Petty) and Bobby (Allison) haven't shown me," Earnhardt said, "but I know I can run with the best of 'em."

John Rezek of Alvin, Texas, won the Auto Racing Club of America (ARCA) 200 Sunday in an Oldsmobile, his first major racing win. Rezek edged Chevy-driving Lake Speed of Jackson, Miss., the only other driver to finish on the same lap. ∎

EARNHARDT HOISTS THE VICTOR'S TROPHY ALONGSIDE FUTURE WIFE, TERESA.
DAVID CHOBAT PHOTO

EARNHARDT TAKES THE INSIDE LINE AND PASSES CALE YARBOROUGH ON HIS WAY TO WINNING THE ATLANTA 500.
DAVID CHOBAT PHOTO

Earnhardt On Top
in Points

Earnhardt Surprise Winner of Atlanta 500

By LYNN GYNTHER

Dale Earnhardt has shed his rookie stripes as smoothly as a snake sheds its skin.

The 1979 NASCAR Rookie of the Year came from a 31st starting position to win the 21st annual Atlanta 500 today at Atlanta International Raceway – his first superspeedway win and the second Grand National victory of his brief career. And the 28-year-old driver from Mooresville, N.C., continues to dominate the Winston Cup point standings with his fifth top-five finish in five starts.

The scenario didn't read so well for Earnhardt earlier in the week, however. Engine trouble during first-round qualifying prevented the team from gaining a top starting spot, and while the Osterlund Chevrolet Monte Carlo clocked the fastest time in the second session, Earnhardt's speed of 161.934 mph was still almost a full second slower than that of polesitter Buddy Baker.

"It looked bad to start with. We had problems, but we worked hard all week and overcame those problems," said Earnhardt. "I was still a little down in horsepower, but my car worked well in the corners."

Earnhardt was the fourth driver ever to win a race in his rookie year when he won the 1979 Southeastern 500 at Bristol, Tenn., a 0.533-mile track. But the win here today was particularly satisfying.

"My two favorite places are Atlanta and Charlotte, so it's good to win one here," he said. "Superspeedways are a little more prestigious and harder to win on."

The real surprise of the race was the runner-up, as the second-place money went to another 1979 Rookie of the Year – Rusty Wallace, who won that title on the USAC stock car racing circuit. Wallace, 23, was driving in his first Grand National event and his first 500-mile race ever when he brought the Penske Racing Chevrolet Caprice in nine seconds behind the Osterlund Chevy.

"I never thought that we could take a brand new car and a brand new driver and do that well. But every race I go to I try to win," said Wallace, who hopes to compete for the NASCAR Winston Cup Rookie-of-the-Year award in 1981.

"I believe if it wasn't for Donnie Allison giving me a little speech before the race I might have had problems. He told me that the car would have a tendency to break loose in the fourth turn and I needed to keep full control. He really helped me out," said Wallace. "I could make all my time in three-four."

Wallace, like Earnhardt, also had some trouble with the engine. "We had oil temperature problems. We thought the motor was bad, but the motor we put in today had the same problem. It was reading 270 degrees," he said. "That's too hot to run, but it lasted 500 miles."

Bobby Allison brought the Hodgdon/Curb Ford in third, and Dave Marcis, driving the Hudson Chevy Olds, finished fourth, one lap down. Dick Brooks came under his first checkered flag of the season as he finished fifth in the Sanyo Chevrolet, three laps off the pace.

Baker, who won last year's Atlanta 500 from the pole, set a new race record in qualifying Friday with a speed of 166.212 mph around the 1.522-mile speedway. The NAPA/Regal Ride Olds wasn't handling today, though, and Baker led only the first two laps before Cale Yarborough took over the front position. Baker quickly dropped out of contention.

For most of the race, Yarborough looked like a sure bet to become the first driver to win this event from a third-place start. Despite 27 lead changes among 11 drivers, the Junior Johnson-prepared Busch Chevrolet was the major force in the field, and Yarborough led 183 of the 328 laps to collect an extra $10,000 for leading the most circuits.

Seven caution periods for 45 laps allowed most of the scheduled pit stops to be staged under the yellow flag. The lead swapped hands swiftly as the frontrunners pitted, but Yarborough would soon work his way back into the front position on the restarts, stretching out to a full straightaway lead several times.

As the race wore on, the number of cars battling behind Yarborough was gradually reduced. Richard Petty, whose STP Chevy was running particularly smooth, was sidelined after 117 laps with engine failure – his first in 35 races. Benny Parsons parked his Melling Tool Chevy three laps before the halfway mark when the clutch went out. Darrell Waltrip, running third at 192 laps, was black-flagged and sent behind the wall when the engine bearing seal broke in his Gatorade Chevy.

Donnie Allison, whose last win was here in the 1978 Dixie 500, had taken the lead on lap 169 and doggedly held off the assaults on his position. His Hawaiian Tropic Chevy was running strong, and it looked as though the Hueytown, Ala., driver might have a chance at victory.

Yarborough was right on Donnie's tail when Earnhardt and Terry Labonte hooked up and moved in on the leaders. The four edged into tight formation as they dueled for the lead. Yarborough, trying to inch past Donnie, was leading Earnhardt along the inside grove, while on the outside, Donnie was clinging tenaciously to the front spot, followed by Labonte.

> ## "Every race I go to
> # I try to win,"
> said surprise second-place
> finisher, Rusty Wallace.

Then on the 202nd lap, Labonte and Donnie tangled in the fourth turn. Hitting the outer wall, the two spun back down onto the apron, bringing out the final caution of the race. They recovered quickly and both crossed the start-finish line, Donnie from behind the pit wall, but mechanical injuries doomed their efforts.

Donnie was forced to drop out only a few laps later with a damaged rear end, a 26th place finish was all he had to show for his pains. Labonte, who broke a rotor button, lost several laps repairing the Stratagraph Chevy. He returned to the race, out of contention, to finish 15th.

Yarborough rapidly began to run away with the race on the restart. As he gained ground, Earnhardt, Bobby Allison, Wallace and Marcis shuffled positions between them.

With slightly more than 50 laps remaining, the leaders came in for their final pit stops. Yarborough took on four new tires, confident on the strength of his car to compensate for the extra time in the pits. Bobby Allison was able to assume a healthy lead.

Yarborough, running fifth, quickly moved into third behind Earnhardt. The two hooked up in a draft and started gaining on Allison. Closing in on the leader as they entered the third turn, Yarborough suddenly slowed and headed to the pits. Earnhardt continued his charge and swung past Allison as they crossed the start-finish line on lap 300.

Allison, falling back with a badly misfiring engine, was unable to challenge, and Earnhardt sailed to an easy win.

"Cale was pulling me up to Bobby, and all of a sudden Cale pulled down with ignition problems. Bobby wasn't running good at all. They both had problems," said Earnhardt, obviously not feeling overly sorry for his competitors.

With the race in the bag and 28 laps to go, Earnhardt noted that he only had one thought in his mind. "Lordy, don't have a flat tire," he recalled with a grin.

Jody Ridley was the highest finishing rookie contender with a sixth-place finish, and Baker came in seventh, both three laps in arrears. Yarborough had to settle for eighth, J.D. McDuffie was ninth and Slick Johnson came in tenth.

The race was completed in 3 hours, 42 minutes and 32 seconds at an average speed of 134.808 mph. Only 21 of the 41 starters finished the race. ■

EARNHARDT LOOKS A LITTLE MORE AT HOME IN VICTORY LANE AFTER THIS, HIS SECOND NASCAR GRAND NATIONAL WIN.
DAVID CHOBAT PHOTO

dale earnhardt

Earnhardt Beats Bristol Again!

Second Straight Win For Osterlund Driver

By STEVE WAID

The "Sophomore Jinx," that strange malady which often strikes NASCAR race drivers, has been unable to infect Dale Earnhardt.

After six races into the 1980 Grand National campaign, the 1979 Rookie of the Year from Mooresville, N.C., seems to be immune to racing adversity.

Today at Bristol International Raceway, Earnhardt roared to his second straight victory of the year in the Valleydale Southeastern 500. It was also the second consecutive Southeastern 500 triumph for the 28-year-old driver, who was the winner of the March 13 Atlanta 500.

Earnhardt's victory solidified his lead in earnings and the Grand National point championship standings. Not counting the $50,000 he pocketed for winning the February Busch Clash at Daytona, Earnhardt has won $132,945 to date and has an 80 point lead over Bobby Allison (1,025-945) in the battle for the driving championship.

So much for your basic jinx.

"I love it, I love it," said the elated Earnhardt. "Let's do it all the time. Sure don't see any reason why I can't win the championship."

Driving a Rod Osterlund Monte Carlo prepared under the direction of crew chief Jake Elder, Earnhardt beat Darrell Waltrip to the finish line by 8.7 seconds. Earnhardt's car was competitive throughout the race, leading three times for 208 laps.

"The car was a little loose at the start of the race, especially when I went high," said Earnhardt. "But we kept making chassis adjustments in pit stops and the car ran better and better."

Perhaps the key to Earnhardt's victory – worth $10,025 – was a quick pit stop made under green on lap 363. On that stop, Earnhardt joined Waltrip's Caprice on pit road. But the Osterlund crew changed right side tires and refilled the gas tank in time to get its driver back on the 0.533-mile track well ahead of Waltrip. Earnhardt passed Cale Yarborough for the lead on lap 366.

"The crew did a fine job today; they all worked hard," said Earnhardt. "They get pumped up when we make a stop under green, and that one just put me that much farther ahead of Waltrip."

Waltrip never made up the distance. The Franklin, Tenn., driver, who has won two Bristol races over the last three seasons, felt that the damaged front end his car suffered after ramming Benny Parsons' Monte Carlo on pit road hampered his chances.

"Benny and I started down pit road," said

EARNHARDT SHARES THIS, HIS SECOND WIN IN AS MANY WEEKS, WITH CAR OWNER ROD OSTERLUND.
DAVID CHOBAT PHOTO

Waltrip, referring to the incident that occurred on lap 127, "and suddenly the official at the end of pit road flashed the stop sign. I ran right into Benny.

"After that, the car was squirrely when I was in traffic. It was all right when I was running by myself. Really, I thought I'd wrecked the car when I hit Benny – I had the fastest car on the track at the time."

Parsons finished fourth, while Yarborough wound up fifth. Yarborough, who started on the pole with a record speed of 111.688 mph, led five times for 187 laps and for a time appeared headed for his ninth Bristol win.

On lap 390, however, his Junior Johnson Monte Carlo began losing power. "We dropped a valve or a push rod," he said. "It was my race. It was no contest. When I got out front I would have lapped the field, but I finished on seven cylinders.

"That's two races in a row I've lost because something happened to my car. If things turn around, the rest of them better look out."

Joe Millikan, Harry Gant, Richard Petty, Dave Marcis and Terry Labonte rounded out the top 10, all driving Monte Carlos. Petty was relieved on lap 420 by Richard Childress.

"I really thought it
would take a year to win my first race,"
said Earnhardt.

"I was tired," explained Petty. "I've had a cold since Atlanta and that didn't help none. The car pushed real bad, then we changed tires and it ran a lot better. But we were out of it then."

"I could never let it hang out because I couldn't reach the pedals,' said Childress, who is considerably shorter than the lanky Petty.

Earnhardt started fourth and averaged a fast 96.977 mph as the race was slowed by only three caution flags for a total of 14 laps. The victory kept alive the Osterlund team's streak of not finishing out of the top five in any 1980 race.

"When I joined Osterlund, I really thought it would take a year to win my first race," said Earnhardt. "But then we won this race last year, and we'll win our share this year. I'll try to do my part. Jake has been talking to me and we learned a big lesson at Atlanta.

"You can't get down in the mouth. We started 31st there but with the help of the good Lord and just keeping our heads on, we learned you can come out all right."

Earnhardt was named the winner of the

Southeastern 500's Bobby Isaac memorial award for achievement. "I knew Bobby," said Earnhardt of the late Grand National driver from Catawba, N.C. "He used to talk to me and help me when I was racing Sportsman cars. I feel honored to win the award named after him."

No doubt Isaac would be pleased with Earnhardt – who, in only his second year, is clearly making his mark in Grand National racing. ■

EARNHARDT IS QUICKLY ESTABLISHING HIMSELF AS THE MAN TO BEAT IN 1980, MOWING DOWN THE COMPETITION AT BRISTOL. DAVID CHOBAT PHOTO

BUSCH NASHVILLE 420

EARNHARDT WAS ABLE TO HOLD OFF A FEISTY CALE YARBOROUGH AND STAY AHEAD OF RICHARD PETTY TO WIN HIS THIRD NASCAR GRAND NATIONAL RACE OF THE SEASON.
DAVID CHOBAT PHOTO

Yarborough
Fails To Rattle Sophomore
Dale Wins In Nashville

By GENE GRANGER

Dale Earnhardt was on the ropes twice in the waning laps, but the young driver from Mooresville, N.C., refused to bend on a Saturday night sizzler at Nashville Raceway.

Driving with the aplomb of a veteran of several hundred races, Earnhardt held off a furious charge by Cale Yarborough over the last 25 laps to win the 23rd annual Busch Nashville 420 by four car lengths on the 0.596-mile track.

Yarborough, who had won seven of the last 15 races here, bumped Earnhardt several times in a classic duel to the finish, but the 29-year-old sophomore driver refused to be intimidated.

Earnhardt, Yarborough and Benny Parsons had a full house of 16,700 fans on their feet for the final laps of the 250-mile race. It had been a mad dash throughout the race, but a caution flag with just 36 laps remaining set up the eventual showdown.

Bobby Allison, running on only seven cylinders since early in the race, spun out on the front straightway to bring out the only caution flag of the hot, muggy night.

Earnhardt, piloting the Osterlund Racing Chevrolet, and Yarborough changed all four tires under the caution while Parsons took on only right side tires.

Parsons, in the M.C. Anderson/Melling Tool Chevrolet, had the lead when the race was restarted on the 389th lap. But on the backstretch on lap 391, Earnhardt and Yarborough's Busch Chevy shot by Parsons, and the latter was never a factor again.

Yarborough's one major attempt to pass Earnhardt almost ended in an accident. He started around Earnhardt on the backstretch and almost bought a piece of the wall. After that, Earnhardt was in complete command, albeit Yarborough stayed within striking distance. Parsons wound up third, more than a half-lap behind in the 420-lap race.

"I didn't see him. I was the leader and I had the race track. I didn't think he would try to pass me on the outside. I know he wasn't alongside of me because I would have seen him," Earnhardt said of Yarborough's futile attempt to get by him.

Earnhardt averaged 93.811 mph in the race slowed only once for five laps. He earned $14,600 for his third win of the season and fourth of a 54-race career.

He also increased his lead to 48 points over Richard Petty in the battle for the Winston Cup championship. Petty, who required some relief driving from Harry Gant, finished fifth, four laps in arrears.

Petty came out of his car on the 347th lap. "I got cramps in my legs and had to get out," said Petty, who was fifth for the third race in a row.

Darrell Waltrip was fourth, one lap down in the DiGard Gatorade Chevrolet. He tagged Earnhardt on the 335th lap and almost spun both of them out. But they straightened their cars and kept going after the fourth-turn incident.

Six drivers called on relief. There probably would have been other calls, but only seven of the 30 starters fell out of the race. Gant was the busiest of the night. He first drove in relief of Don Sprouse after falling out, then jumped in Petty's STP Chevy.

Allison was sixth in the Bud Moore/Warner Hodgdon Ford and young Sterling Marlin was seventh in D.K. Ulrich's Waylon Jennings Chevy. Each was seven laps behind.

The 29-year-old sophomore driver
refused to be intimidated.

Yarborough led the first 150 laps. After the first series of pit stops, Parsons had a super quick tire change and took the lead on the 151st lap. Yarborough was to lead only one other lap. Parsons dominated the second third of the race, and Earnhardt was top dog in the final third, when it counted the most.

Yarborough led twice for 151 laps, Parsons set the pace four times for 137 laps, Earnhardt led three times for 103 laps, including the final 30 circuits. Petty led for 17 laps and Waltrip was in front the other two laps.

Waltrip and Petty were never seriously in contention. Petty's car wasn't running down the straights, while a long stop on lap 251 cost Waltrip a lap he wasn't to regain.

"I didn't have any close calls except there at the end with Cale. It was one of the most competitive races I've ever been in. It was a good feeling to win this one," Earnhardt said.

On the incident with Waltrip, he just grinned and said, "It was close, wasn't it?"

Asked about the stifling heat (it was 96 degrees at race time), Earnhardt said, "It was about as bad as Daytona. The hardest part

was the first 100 laps. I got in the car to run 420 laps, not any less."

After what appeared to be the final pit stops, Parsons ran down Earnhardt. He was riding his bumper, ready to make a pass, when the caution flag was waved.

"I was still in front of Benny and I was prepared to stay there. After the caution, I figured it would be a race between Cale and

EARNHARDT SHARES THE SPOTLIGHT WITH ENGINE BUILDER LOU LAROSA. DAVID CHOBAT PHOTO

I because we each changed four tires. I didn't think Benny could stay with us on just two new tires," Earnhardt said.

Earnhardt couldn't say enough about his crew, headed by 20-year-old Doug Richert. "Doug did a fine job in setting up the car. Doug has a lot to learn, just as I do. But we laugh, argue a little, put our heads together and make the car go fast," he said.

He also had words of praise for engine builder Lou LaRosa. "We had a rattle in our

engine Saturday, so we went to a good spare engine. Lou did a good job in making that engine run.

"We were a little loose at the beginning," Earnhardt continued, "but we added two rounds of bite and the car was handling perfectly at the end of the race.

"Goodyear also came with a harder compound, and we changed less tires than we did in May here. Goodyear is to be congratulated."

Earnhardt said his only goal this year was to win the championship, and he believes his "no name" team can do it.

"Not too many people knew any of us two years ago. But our team has it together. I'm proud of my team and I can't say enough good things about them boys," Earnhardt said. ∎

EARNHARDT'S CAR SHOWS THE SCARS OF A TOUGH WIN AT MARTINSVILLE.
DAVID CHOBAT PHOTO

Dale Wins In
Martinsville

Earnhardt Dominates The Old Dominion 500

By STEVE WAID

Dale Earnhardt of Doolie, N.C., enhanced what has already become a super sophomore season on the NASCAR Grand National circuit by winning the Old Dominion 500 today at Martinsville Speedway.

In capturing his fourth victory of the season – a record for a second-year Grand National driver – Earnhardt overcame a spin, a loss of brakes and Cale Yarborough to beat Buddy Baker to the finish line by 1.35 seconds.

It was a typically unpredictable Martinsville race, with numerous wrecks,

blown engines and assorted mechanical maladies bringing out a record 17 caution flags for 79 laps. Conversely, there were a record 21 lead changes among nine drivers.

Earnhardt took the lead for good on lap 488, just 12 circuits from the finish. Before that, it appeared Yarborough was headed for his fourth Martinsville win since 1976 behind the wheel of a Junior Johnson car.

Earnhardt took the lead in the Rod Osterlund Monte Carlo on lap 345 after John Anderson spun his Chevrolet in the second turn. Yarborough followed Earnhardt, who slowly but steadily pulled away.

But Yarborough seemed to get the break he needed on lap 448 when the long-suffering engine in Richard Petty's Caprice expired, bringing out the 16th caution of the day.

The Johnson team got Yarborough's Olds out of the pits ahead of Earnhardt, whose absence of brakes forced him to overshoot his pits, losing valuable time. Yarborough, now in command, began what he hoped would be a drive to victory.

But the final caution of the day, brought out by Terry Labonte's spin in the fourth turn on lap 481, gave Earnhardt a badly needed boost.

Both the Osterlund and Johnson crews elected not to pit their drivers. On the restart on lap 486, Yarborough suffered a cut-down right front tire in the first turn, and this allowed Earnhardt to break away.

Baker, who started on the pole, made the most of a right-side tire change on the Harry Ranier Monte Carlo during the last pit stop to breeze to second place. Yarborough fell to third, while Benny Parsons wound up fourth in a Monte Carlo and David Marcis was fifth in a Caprice.

Rounding out the top 10 were Donnie Allison in a Caprice, Labonte in a Monte Carlo, Buddy Arrington in a Dodge, Jody Ridley in a Thunderbird and James Hylton in a Caprice.

"At first I thought Cale was just pushing out into the second turn," said Earnhardt of the fateful final restart. "But then I saw his tire was flat. It was a pretty good break.

"I don't know if I could have caught Cale if we didn't have that last caution. My car wasn't running as well; the tires just weren't matched up. Cale would've probably beaten us.

"But then, if we hadn't had any cautions at all, we would've beaten him."

"We had three flat right-front tires today," said Yarborough. "I cut down the last one on the last restart. It was flat as I went into the first corner. I was just trying to get out of the way; Dale and I didn't touch.

"I had brake problems all day long. When I got the lead, I could keep air on them and keep them cool. I was all right then. But it was just rotten, rotten luck. I just can't get the monkey off my back."

"I went up alongside him (Marcis) and scolded him..."
—Earnhardt

Earnhardt's win, worth $24,375, strengthened his position as leader in the NASCAR Grand National points championship. He came into the Old Dominion 500 leading Yarborough by 90 points. He now holds a 105-point lead (4,032-3,927).

"I don't feel any more comfortable with that lead," said the 29-year-old Earnhardt. "I've had bigger leads than that and something has happened. Sure, I'd like to keep score all day long, but you can't. It didn't cross my mind all day where Cale and Richard were.

"I was trying to win the race. I've never won at Martinsville and a lot of other places, too. The others need to do the worrying now. They're behind me."

On lap 218, Earnhardt's car was knocked in the side on the backstraight by Marcis and sent for a loop, nearly removing him from the competition.

"It was almost a helluva wreck," Earnhardt said. "It scared me. The car turned around, I saw the inside wall, the outside wall and then the racetrack. I shoved it into third gear and kept going.

"I said, 'Thank you, Lord.' Skill? I was

EARNHARDT'S BATTLES AREN'T LIMITED TO THE TRACK. HERE, HE CLOWNS WITH DRIVER TERRY LABONTE BEFORE THE RACE.
DAVID CHOBAT PHOTO

very skillful. I had my foot on the brake and my hands on the wheel. I went up alongside him (Marcis) and scolded him, but later I came up on him again and apologized after I had cooled down."

With only 14 of 31 cars running at the finish, mechanical difficulties were plentiful. Blown engines eliminated Harry Gant, Lennie Pond, Bobby Allison, Neil Bonnett, Petty and Darrell Waltrip. Waltrip, who has won at Martinsville twice in the last four years, was leading when his Monte Carlo's engine failed on lap 308.

By leading four times for 174 laps, Earnhardt, who averaged 69.728 mph today, pocketed a bonus of $3,000 – part of Martinsville's $5,000 lap battle. Baker and Waltrip each won $1,000.

Beginning with the National 500 at Charlotte Motor Speedway, Earnhardt has four races in which to win the Grand National title – or lose it.

"We're going out to win," Earnhardt emphasized. "We aren't going to stroke for points. Cale, Benny and the others don't stroke, so why should we?"

So far, that strategy has paid off very well in 1980 for Dale Earnhardt. ∎

SECOND-YEAR DRIVER, EARNHARDT DEBUTED A NEW LOOK IN MARTINSVILLE.
DAVID CHOBAT PHOTO

SIDE-BY-SIDE WITH RICHARD PETTY, EARNHARDT LOOKS LIKE HE BELONGS AMONG THE BEST.
DAVID CHOBAT PHOTO

Earnhardt
Wins The National 500

Dale Earnhardt Wins One For The Hometown Fans

By GENE GRANGER

Dale Earnhardt proved today at Charlotte Motor Speedway that dreams can come true.

Ever since he was a kid growing up some 12 miles from the 1.5-mile track, Earnhardt dreamed of winning a NASCAR Grand National race there before a cheering throng of friends and neighbors.

Combining his own driving skill with that of his Osterlund Racing pit crew – led by 20-year-old Doug Richert and team manager Roland Wlodyka – Earnhardt made his dream a reality by winning the National 500.

Earnhardt and his crew won not only the race, but also almost every special incentive award that went with it. By being the quickest in the pits, the crew was given first place in the Sears Pit Crew Championship. By leading 14 times for 148 laps, including the last 47, Earnhardt was given the Lead foot Award. And the Osterlund team joined forces with rookie Lake Speed, who finished seventh, to win the $25,000 first prize in the much publicized Buck Stove $50,000 Team Challenge.

It was, to say the least, a near perfect day for Earnhardt, whose victory also intensified his relentless drive to the Grand National driving championship. He now has 4,217 points and is the current points leader by 115 over Cale Yarborough.

Ironically, it was Yarborough whom Earnhardt beat to the finish line by 1.83 seconds. "All of the wins are great," said the 29-year-old Earnhardt, who earned $49,050 today. "I guess I can really savor my first one (at Bristol, Tenn., in the spring of 1979) because it was my first Grand National win. But winning at Charlotte is something I have wanted to do for a long, long time. It happened in front of the hometown people, and it was something I knew I could do.

"It's got me as high or higher than I was after my win at Bristol."

The victory was Earnhardt's second in a row after his win in the Old Dominion 500 at Martinsville (Va.) Speedway last week. It was also his fifth of the season, which ties him with Darrell Waltrip for the most victories this year.

Earnhardt was helped tremendously by an excellent pit stop under green on lap 280, the last scheduled stop for the Osterlund team. Yarborough, driving the Junior Johnson

Monte Carlo, was leading the race as Earnhardt took on right side tires and a tank of gas in 13.1 seconds.

Just four laps later, Yarborough pitted for 17.1 seconds and came out third, behind Buddy Baker, who trailed Earnhardt's Monte Carlo by 5.3 seconds.

Yarborough passed Baker for second place on lap 309 – just 25 circuits from the finish – and very slowly made up ground on Earnhardt. But he ran out of time.

Baker made a courageous effort to overtake Yarborough, but on the last lap, he got sideways in the fourth turn as he tried to pass on the high side. He kept the car under control, dashed into pit road and across the grassy area between the road and the racing surface to cross the finish line ahead of fourth-place Ricky Rudd.

Rudd, driving his own Monte Carlo prepared under the guidance of veteran mechanic Harry Hyde, turned in his best performance of an abbreviated season. He was given a $5,000 bonus as the top-finishing driver who had not won a Grand National race.

Donnie Allison finished fifth, followed by Bill Elliott, Speed, Jody Ridley, Kyle Petty and Dick Brooks.

"Winning at Charlotte

is something I have wanted to do for a long, long time."
—Earnhardt

"Doug Richert and Roland planned that last pit stop strategy," Earnhardt said of the fateful final stop. "They decided we would pit ahead of the other guys, and they got me in and got me out. I can drive the car as hard as it can go, but they're the guys who have to get the job done in the pits. They did."

"We just planned on getting him in and out as quickly as possible," said Richert. "We knew how far we could go on the fuel we could hold and we were pushing it to the limit, so it was a scheduled stop."

Earnhardt's plan afterward was to drive as smoothly as possible, avoid mistakes and hope that was enough to beat Yarborough, the defending National 500 champion.

"I was just going 'round and 'round, making the car do what I wanted," Earnhardt said. "I felt I had enough laps just to ride and beat him, but I wanted to make every lap count. I was contemplating what would happen if I ran too hard, messed myself up and

let him have a chance to catch me. I just concentrated on running smooth, and I thought that was enough to beat him."

It was. "Yep," said Yarborough, "just say we got beat. We had some tough breaks, but we just got beat. Two things happened on my pit stop at the end. I ran out of gas and had to coast in. Then I put the gear in low, and it fell into reverse. That sounds funny, but it

CHARLOTTE MOTOR SPEEDWAY PRESIDENT BRUTON SMITH IS PLEASED TO PRESENT THE NATIONAL 500 TROPHY TO LOCAL DRIVER, EARNHARDT
DAVID CHOBAT PHOTO

happened another time, too.

"After my crew made chassis adjustments on the next to last pit stop, we were really running. I was running Earnhardt down. But it was just a matter of time and we didn't have enough of it. Just say we got beat."

The pace set by most of the leaders through two-thirds of the race was hectic and, as could be expected, it took its toll. Eliminated from the competition because of wrecks were Benny Parsons (who tangled

with Waltrip on lap 168 and thus lost all hope of collecting the $100,000 bonus offered him if he won the race), Neil Bonnett, Terry Labonte and Bobby Allison. Blown engines sidelined Waltrip (on lap 322) and Petty (on lap 252). A fouled ignition put David Pearson out of the race on lap 66.

For Earnhardt, who lives in Doolie, N.C., just 21 miles from the speedway, the win solidified his position as the hottest driver on the Grand National circuit. He has earned $432,675 this season, and with three races remaining, he has an excellent chance of becoming the first driver to earn $600,000 in one season.

No doubt he is aware of that. But he probably didn't think about it as he accepted the congratulations of his friends and neighbors. Foremost on his mind was the fact that, finally, he had won at Charlotte. ∎

EVEN AFTER A WELL-DOCUMENTED LOSING STREAK, EARNHARDT LOOKS RIGHT AT HOME IN VICTORY LANE.
DAVID CHOBAT PHOTO

Earnhardt
Wins The Rebel 500

Earnhardt Is A Winner Again

By STEVE WAID

Dale Earnhardt said repeatedly that his well-publicized losing streak in NASCAR Winston Cup racing would come to an end. It was just a matter of time.

Today at Darlington International Raceway, the time finally came.

By besting Cale Yarborough in an exciting, head-to-head duel over the final laps of the CRC Chemicals Rebel 500, Earnhardt earned his first victory since the 1980 National 500 at Charlotte Motor Speedway, 39 races ago. It was his first win in the Bud Moore

Thunderbird, which he began racing this season, and his first for Wrangler Jeans, which undertook its sponsorship at the start of the 1981 season.

More importantly for the relieved and happy Earnhardt, it put him back into the winning mold he had forged through 1979 and 1980, when he won successively the Champion Spark Plug Rookie of the Year and Winston Cup titles.

"Wrangler and a lot of people stood by me through some hard times," said the 30-year-old Earnhardt, a resident of Doolie, N.C., a community on Lake Norman.

"I kept saying we would win and they never doubted me. They said, 'We know. You just take it easy.'"

But throughout the early part of this season, Earnhardt never took it easy – his Thunderbird was powerful enough to make him a consistent race leader. He had led every previous race this season, winning the Gillette Atra Lap Leader award for leading the most laps three times – the third being today after he paced the field 10 times for 182 circuits.

But he finished only one race, earning second place in the Valleydale 500 at Bristol Raceway. A series of mechanical problems put him out of events and, of course, away from victory lane.

But he was continuously cast as a race favorite and for the CRC Chemicals Rebel 500, he lived up to the billing. He started fifth and had what his rivals admitted was the fastest car in the field.

That, however, did not make things easier. After dodging some near-disasters in the face of wrecking cars, Earnhardt had to hold off a determined challenge by Yarborough that covered the final 36 laps.

On lap 327, Kyle Petty's Pontiac smacked the fourth-turn wall on the tough 1.366-mile Darlington track and brought out the last caution of the day. Earnhardt, the leader, made his final pit stop, as did challengers Yarborough in the Valvoline Buick and Benny Parsons in the J.D. Stacy Pontiac.

Parsons was immediately put out of the competition when a cut tire forced him to the pits again, putting him nearly a lap down after running his most competitive and determined race of the year.

That left it to Yarborough and Earnhardt. Yarborough, seeking to win his second consecutive race this season, took the lead on lap 354 when he passed Earnhardt low in the third turn.

> "I got beat,
> didn't I?" said
> [Cale] Yarborough.
> # "Dale was tough."

But a lap later, Earnhardt retook the lead in the first turn and never gave it up. Still, it was a nerve-crunching finish.

On the 367th and final circuit, Yarborough rode Earnhardt's rear bumper until the cars came out of the fourth turn and headed toward the finish line.

Yarborough slung his Buick low down the straightaway in an attempt to win on the widest portion of the Darlington oval. His effort almost worked. Earnhardt crossed the finish line a mere half-car length ahead, thereby giving car owner Bud Moore his first triumph at Darlington since Darrell Dierenger won for him in the 1966 Southern 500.

"I knew Cale was gonna come to the inside," said Earnhardt, who won $31,450, including the $2,000 lap leader bonus from Gillette. "So I started to fade to the inside. I couldn't see Cale out of my left window, so I figured I had finished ahead of him."

"I got beat, didn't I?" said Yarborough. "Dale was tough. He drove a real good race and deserved to win. I had to go all out to pass Dale near the end just that one time, and he got back around me easily. So I knew it was going to be a one-shot effort to get by him.

"If I had passed him in turns one and two, he would have gotten by me in three and four. So I had to try him on four. It nearly worked. But I ran out of space."

Earnhardt's dominance of the race was obvious, as it has been before. He led 90 of the last 91 laps but the difference was that – finally – he got a dose of good luck.

"You don't ever figure you've won a race until the checkered flag falls," said Earnhardt.

"Until then, Cale could have beaten me. I got some good breaks. Earlier, it seemed that Cale was able to pull up on me whenever we got into traffic. But at the end, there was no traffic and that helped."

Earnhardt also admitted luck was on his side when he avoided a few incidents that, had he been involved, could have put him out of contention.

"Bonnett hit the wall and started to come back down on me and I didn't think I'd get through it. But then he turned back up toward the wall and that was lucky for me."

Earnhardt praised the Moore crew and said that the right tire combination enabled his Thunderbird to emerge as the race's most powerful car.

"We started the race on the tires we qualified on and took them off after our first pit stop," Earnhardt said. "We discovered that the set was the best we had and saved them until our final pit stop. We had to take only one round of bite out of the car and it ran tight all day."

Bill Elliott drove the Melling Thunderbird to a third-place finish – his best of the year – while Parsons finished fourth. Tim Richmond, driving the Stacy Buick vacated by Joe Ruttman, wound up fifth, one lap down.

Terry Labonte finished sixth in a Stacy

Buick and retained his Winston Cup point lead. He now leads Parsons by 59 points (952-893).

Mark Martin finished seventh in the Apache Stove Buick, followed by Buddy Arrington in a Dodge, Donnie Allison in the Simoniz Buick, and Lennie Pond in a Buick.

Darrell Waltrip, the defending CRC Chemicals Rebel 500 champion, was eliminated after a wreck in the first turn on lap 269. He was 15 laps in arrears at the time, after an extended pit stop to correct an engine disorder that arose on lap 177.

Engine failure also claimed the cars of Richard Petty, Ron Bouchard, Dave Marcis, Jody Ridley, Morgan Shepherd, Ricky Rudd and Bobby Allison. Harry Gant finished 19th after an extended pit stop to replace a broken A-frame. He also damaged his 7-Eleven/Skoal Bandit Buick on lap 148 after hitting the fourth-turn wall.

Pole winner Buddy Baker was eliminated after just three laps with a broken flywheel.

Earnhardt won with an average speed of 123.544 mph and the race took 4 hours, 3 minutes, 27 seconds to complete. There were eight caution flags for 53 laps. ∎

Earnhardt's Nifty Move Earns First in Qualifier

"Daytona Slingshot" Leaves Foyt Third

By **STEVE WAID**

EARNHARDT DOESN'T MIND SHARING VICTORY LANE WITH MISS HURST GOLDEN SHIFTER, LINDA VAUGHN.
DAVID CHOBAT PHOTO

After his victory in the first UNO 125-mile qualifying race for the Daytona 500 at Daytona International Speedway today, Dale Earnhardt managed to come out ahead financially.

His award for his exciting win in the Bud Moore/Wrangler Thunderbird amounted to $18,000, more than enough to compensate for the fine slapped on him by NASCAR because of his failure to heed the black flag in the Busch Clash here on Feb. 14.

The final assessment against Earnhardt amounted to $5,000 with $2,000 to be returned after 10 races if he conducts himself properly and according to NASCAR guidelines.

But in today's first 50-lap event on the 2.5-mile Daytona trioval, Earnhardt had no problems of any sort. He made a nifty slingshot pass by A.J. Foyt's Chevrolet Monte Carlo in the third turn and went on to win by a car length over Buddy Baker, who had followed him in his Valvoline Thunderbird.

The race was marred, however, by a terrible wreck on the seventh lap. Bruce Jacobi lost control of his Pontiac as it came out of the second turn and the car spun into the soggy infield grass along the back straight.

Caught in the strong wind, which buffeted the track, Jacobi's car flipped violently, shredding the roof and other sheet metal in a series of four somersaults. It then plowed into the embankment which separates the track from Lake Lloyd.

Jacobi was taken from the wreckage to the infield hospital and then transferred to nearby Halifax Memorial Hospital. There he underwent X-rays and a CAT scan, which surveys the entire body for internal injury, including the nervous system.

Later, Jacobi was moved into the intensive surgical care unit with a brain injury. His condition was changed to guarded, which means serious but stable. He remained in that condition as of Feb. 18.

The statement from Dr. Carl Schwenker, Daytona International Speedway's chief physician, on the condition of Mr. Jacobi as of 1 p.m. Feb. 18 was: "Mr. Jacobi has an acute brainstem concussion. Additionally, he has a minor eye laceration, which is sutured. He has no fractures. His condition is listed as critical and stable, with the outlook guarded."

Jacobi's condition at the end of the day was still critical. He is a 47-year-old driver from Indianapolis, Ind., who has competed on the NASCAR Winston Cup circuit on a very limited basis for several years. He also does work for ABC-TV during its racing broadcasts.

Earnhardt, from Lake Norman, N.C., made what has become a classic move from standard Daytona strategy to win. He tucked in behind Foyt on the 28th lap and rode in the draft until the final circuit, at which time he slipped by on the inside, being pushed along by the following Baker.

"I was exactly in the place I wanted to be," said Earnhardt. "I had no intention of making a move until the last lap. I was just hoping that none of the other guys could catch up and come alongside me, letting Foyt get away.

"He (Buddy Baker) kidded me after the race,

saying it would be different in the Daytona 500. I told him no way he was going to see the same thing again."
—Earnhardt

"I was worried that Buddy would try to make the same move I did, but he fell in behind me instead of trying to go under me. That really helped me. Then I looked in the rear view mirror and saw Buddy trying to cut under me so I moved down a bit to cut him off. He kidded me after the race, saying it would be different in the Daytona 500. I told him no way he was

going to see the same thing again."

Kyle Petty, driving the 7-Eleven Pontiac, managed to get under Foyt at the finish line to finish third. Joe Ruttman in the Levi Garrett Chevrolet Monte Carlo finished fifth.

"I knew Dale was going to make the move on the last lap," said Baker, whose runner-up finish gave the 1983 Thunderbird a one-two sweep of the race. "When he went around Foyt, I just followed. I planned to try and pass Dale in the fourth turn, but he saw what I was going to do and cut me off at the pass.

"Our car is really running and handling super. I wish we were running the Daytona 500 later today. That's how ready we are."

The Thunderbirds ran their second race equipped with a rear end spoiler four and one-half inches wide. They were given the increased size (up from three inches) on Feb. 12.

The Monte Carlos got an increase from NASCAR, also, when the sanctioning body ruled on Feb. 15 that they could run with spoilers four and one-quarter inches wide, up from four inches. The same day, the Pontiac LeMans was given a spoiler of three and three-quarters inches wide, up from three and one-half inches.

Darrell Waltrip's Pepsi Challenge Monte Carlo fell out of competition with ignition problems after 46 laps.

Ricky Rudd and Geoff Bodine won the top two starting positions in Feb. 14 qualifying runs. The top 14 finishers in each of today's two qualifying races completed the top 30 Daytona 500 starters with the final 10 being selected on the basis of qualifying speeds.

Because he failed to finish today's 125-miler, Waltrip will start 31st based on his qualifying speed of 196.271 mph.

Earnhardt's victory gave him the No. 3 starting spot in the Feb. 20 Daytona 500, the first NASCAR Winston Cup race of the season.

The race was slowed by two caution flags for 12 laps, the first for Jacobi's wreck.

The second caution came out on lap 19 when Mike Potter and Delma Cowart collided in the third turn.

The race took 18 minutes, 28 seconds and Earnhardt won with an average speed of 154.746 mph.

Rounding out the top 10 finishers were Harry Gant, sixth in the Skoal Bandit Buick; Rudd, seventh in the Piedmont Airlines Chevy; David Pearson, eighth in the Chattanooga Chew Chevy; Bill Elliott, ninth in the 1982 Melling Thunderbird; and Elliott Forbes-Robinson, 10th in the Yurika Foods Buick. ∎

...OR A PAIR OF UNOCAL GIRLS AND MISS WINSTON.
DAVID CHOBAT PHOTO

BUSCH 420

AFTER WINNING JUST ONE WINSTON CUP RACE IN 1982 AND NONE IN 1981, EARNHARDT IS JUST HAPPY TO BE BACK IN THE WINNER'S CIRCLE.
DAVID CHOBAT PHOTO

Earnhardt Wins At
Nashville

Earnhardt Rolls To Busch 420 Win

By JACK FLOWERS

Dale Earnhardt hopes his victory here tonight in the Busch 420 at Nashville International Raceway is a signal of his return to more prosperous days on the NASCAR Winston Cup circuit.

Certainly Earnhardt's first-place finish, 15.55 seconds ahead of Darrell Waltrip, was reminiscent of the days that carried the Lake Norman, N.C., driver to the Champion Spark Plug rookie title in 1979 and the Winston Cup points championship in 1980.

The years have been lean since.

After the 1980 season, when Earnhardt won five races, it required 37 events before Earnhardt was to win again – at the 1982 Rebel 500 in Darlington, S.C. Thirty-nine races were history before Earnhardt drove the Bud Moore-prepared Wrangler Ford Thunderbird to the winner's circle in the Busch 420.

It came with apparent ease and with some surprise, too, as Waltrip of nearby Franklin, Tenn., wasn't able to dominate the 0.596-mile raceway on which he had won the previous four Grand National stock car races.

"It's about time we won a race," Earnhardt said afterwards of snapping his slump. "We've

been working awful hard lately and we knew this was going to come sooner or later. I'm just glad it was sooner, not later."

Waltrip, driving the Junior Johnson Pepsi Challenge Chevrolet Monte Carlo, was the only driver on the same lap with Earnhardt at the end of the 250-mile race, which attracted a crowd estimated at 15,800.

Twenty-four of the starting 30 cars were running at the finish of the race, which was relatively trouble-free. There were only four caution flags for 25 laps and none of the incidents were of a serious nature.

Tim Richmond, a neighbor of Earnhardt's at Lake Norman, finished third in the Raymond Beadle/Old Milwaukee Pontiac, a lap down and ahead of fourth-place finisher Bobby Allison of Hueytown, Ala., in the Miller High Life/DiGard Buick. Ricky Rudd of Chesapeake, Va., was fifth in the Richard Childress/Piedmont Airlines Monte Carlo, but he was three laps behind.

Rounding out the top 10, in order, were Neil Bonnett of Hueytown, Ala., in the Warner Hodgdon/Rahmoc Monte Carlo, three laps down; Bill Elliott of Dawsonville, Ga., in the Melling Oil Pump Thunderbird; Harry Gant of Taylorsville, N.C., in the Skoal Bandit Buick; Dave Marcis of Skyland, N.C., in the Transmission Unlimited Monte Carlo; and Morgan Shepherd of Conover, N.C., in the J.D. Stacy/ACM Equipment Sales Buick. Elliott, Gant and Marcis each were four laps in arrears to Earnhardt and Shepherd was six laps behind the winner.

"The car wasn't working too well at the beginning of the race," said Earnhardt. "As we got into the race, we got it working better and better by making an adjustment here and an adjustment there. The further we went, the better the car would work.

"That's a tribute to how long and hard Bud (Moore) and the crew worked in getting prepared for this race. We were ready for this one.

"We even thought we had a shot at winning the pole for this one and were a little disappointed when we didn't."

Earnhardt was the third fastest qualifier behind pole-winner Ron Bouchard of Fitchburg, Mass., in the Jack Beebe Buick. After running among the top five for the first 148 laps, Bouchard was forced to retire with engine failure.

It was one of the most competitive races at Nashville International Raceway in some time, according to many observers. It might have been because Earnhardt, Waltrip, Bonnett, Marcis and Allison swapped the lead 12 times. Earnhardt led three times for 212 laps, earning him his first Gillette-Atra Lap Leader award of the 1983 season.

Earnhardt moved his Thunderbird around Waltrip on lap 216 and except for a couple of laps under caution when Marcis was out front, Earnhardt was the leader the rest of the way – steadily increasing his margin over Waltrip.

The caution came out on lap 274 when Geoff Bodine cut a right-rear tire and spun out in turn four in the Gatorade Pontiac. It was the fourth tire Bodine cut during the race, forcing him into the wall each time.

"It just seemed as the sun went down the better this car would run," said an obviously happy Earnhardt. "It kept getting cooler and running better.

"Certainly it has been a long time since that victory at Darlington and sometimes you have a chance to get a bit discouraged, but you just try to keep the right attitude about things, knowing and hoping things will get better. This win tonight is an indication of what I'm trying to say."

Earnhardt said he had some trouble with slower traffic, but no problems of any magnitude. "It was just a typical Saturday night short-track race," said Earnhardt. "I thought some of the cars out there that were a lap down at the time might have been running in

the wrong place at the wrong time."

Earnhardt admitted he was in favor of the recent NASCAR rules changes which took mushroom lifters and rev kits away from the Winston Cup teams, along with closing off the cowl induction system. However, the cowl induction was reinstated by NASCAR officials and allowed for the Busch 420. Cowls control the amount of air a car is able to intake.

"It definitely was cooler in the cockpit of the car," said Earnhardt. "I'm definitely in favor of the new rules.

"Ford has been helping us a lot more lately with the equipment we have needed and that has helped a lot, too. I think we definitely are turning things around in our favor."

This was Thunderbird's second straight victory on the Winston Cup circuit, with Earnhardt's coming on the heels of Buddy Baker's triumph in the July 4 Firecracker 400 at Daytona International Speedway.

Until Earnhardt's victory in the Busch 420, Waltrip and Allison had dominated the short-track races on the Winston Cup schedule this season – Allison winning at Richmond, Va., and Waltrip winning at North Wilkesboro, N.C., Martinsville, Va., Bristol, Tenn., and the May race here.

"We knew Waltrip was the one we had to beat here tonight and we did it," said Earnhardt. "I don't really think I was running

the car as well as it was capable of running at the finish. That's how strong it was."

This had to be one of the most satisfying races in some time for Richmond and Marcis, too. Marcis ran for a long spell on the lead circuit before being lapped by Waltrip on lap 167. Richmond battled Earnhardt for the lead in later stages of the race prior to the last caution flag which was brought out by Bodine's spin.

The Busch 420 was the first at Nashville since Warner Hodgdon of San Bernardino, Calif., assumed the sole ownership of this raceway and the one at Bristol a week ago from co-owner Gary Baker of Nashville.

"It seems like that every time Warner Hodgdon gets involved in something that something good happens to me," said Earnhardt.

"In 1980 when I won the championship, Hodgdon and Mike Curb sponsored our car.

"Now he buys the raceway here and I win. That's something, isn't it?"

Starting 13th and finishing third allowed Richmond to win an additional $1,000 for the Chameleon Sunglasses Award (for the driver who improves the most positions at the finish over his starting position). The Goody's Headache Award went to Bodine.

It took Earnhardt 2 hours, 55 minutes and 12 seconds to complete the race at an average speed of 85.726 mph. His winnings totaled $23,125. ∎

TO WIN THE NASHVILLE BUSCH 420, EARNHARDT TOOK TO THE INSIDE TO PASS THE COMPETITION.
DAVID CHOBAT PHOTO

PRECISE PIT STOPS KEPT EARNHARDT ON TOP AND IN THE LEAD 12 TIMES FOR 42 LAPS.
DAVID CHOBAT PHOTO

Last Lap
Showdown

Earnhardt Tames Talladega 500

By STEVE WAID

Dale Earnhardt made the most of the kind of opportunity he hadn't had in a long, long time.

With the aerodynamic slingshot pass that has been commonplace at the 2.66-mile Alabama International Motor Speedway, Earnhardt slipped past Darrell Waltrip on the 188th and final lap to win the Talladega 500 NASCAR Winston Cup race today.

The victory for the resident of Lake Norman, N.C., gave the race another new face – it's 14th different winner in 15 races, dating back to 1969.

More significant to Earnhardt was the fact the win was his first on a superspeedway since the 1982 Rebel (now TranSouth) 500 at Darlington, S.C.

"It was our plan to be around at the end and be in contention," said Earnhardt. "So many times in the past, we weren't able to do that. But today the car ran well all day. It was just my turn. I think we turned things around eight or nine races ago and I'm looking forward to the rest of the 1983 season."

Driving the 1983 Bud Moore/Wrangler Ford Thunderbird, Earnhardt made his dramatic last-lap pass on Waltrip's Junior Johnson/Pepsi Challenger Chevrolet Monte Carlo down the backstretch. He then held off his Franklin, Tenn., rival to take the checkered flag by a half-car length in front of 100,000 fans and a nationwide CBS-TV audience.

Waltrip, who led four times for 21 laps, had assumed the lead on lap 178 after Neil Bonnet, driving in relief for Tim Richmond in the Old Milwaukee Pontiac, pitted for gas. Bonnett had taken over for Richmond after the latter was forced to leave the car on lap nine because a foreign substance had blown into his eye.

Earnhardt, who had pitted for the final time on lap 162, tucked into second place while Ricky Rudd's Piedmont Airlines Monte Carlo held onto third.

Ignition problems on lap 179 put Rudd out of the hunt and the race to the checkered flag was left to Waltrip and Earnhardt.

Earnhardt seemed to be in the right position, as many drivers claim the ideal spot to be in the closing laps at AIMS is second place. That permits the slingshot pass.

There was some added drama. Bobby Allison's DiGard/Miller High Life Buick ran third behind Earnhardt but was running in ninth place, two laps back after making a pit stop on lap 164 that lasted 58.8 seconds because a cracked windshield had to be replaced.

Allison, however, was in a position to

assist Earnhardt by dropping behind him when the pass was made. This would theoretically propel Earnhardt's Thunderbird through the draft and by Waltrip.

"I had been studying Darrell for a long time, trying to determine where I could make the pass," said Earnhardt. "As we came out of the second turn and onto the backstretch, I saw the slower cars of Bobby Hillin and Kyle Petty ahead. I figured they'd be a factor as we got into the trioval so I thought I would go ahead and pass."

As he did, Allison joined him to the inside of Waltrip's Monte Carlo. "Darrell then did just what I would've done," said Earnhardt. "He tried to take up as much of the track as he could and sort of pushed me and Bobby to the infield. That was his option."

Earnhardt took the lead in the third turn and as he came out of the fourth turn and into the trioval, Allison dropped low to the inside out of the way. Waltrip still had an opportunity to make a pass of his own.

"I don't know if Bobby had helped me or not," said Earnhardt. "That's a big 'if.' I'm not sure I could've gotten completely around Darrell when I did without Bobby, but I do feel confident I could have drafted around him at any rate.

"I knew that when we got to the trioval Darrell was going to try and pass me. I just didn't know which direction he'd take. I was picking up on him pretty good because I was drafting on Hillin's car. Just as I came up on it I cut to the outside. I had plenty of room there.

"As I crossed the finish line, I looked over and saw Hillin's car but not Darrell's. I was tickled to death."

Waltrip, who was gunning for a second straight Talladega 500 win – he is the only man to win the race twice – claimed he had let Earnhardt pass.

"I let Dale get around me because I figured I could get back around him going into the trioval," said the defending Winston Cup champion. "But then we ran up on a slower car and that won the race for Dale. I'm thankful for that second-place finish, however. It helped us gain some ground in the point standings."

Waltrip now lurks in second place in the standings behind Allison with 2,782 points. Allison has 2,947 points with 11 races remaining in 1983.

Bonnett drove Richmond's car to a third-place finish while Richard Petty took fourth in the STP Pontiac. Harry Gant's Skoal Bandit Buick nipped Geoff Bodine's

Gatorade Pontiac for fifth place, while Dick Brooks finished seventh in the Donlavey/Chameleon Sunglasses Thunderbird, one lap

"As I crossed the finish line, **I looked over and saw Hillin's car** but not Darrell's. I was tickled to death." —Earnhardt

down. Taking positions eight through 10 were Bill Elliott in the Melling Oil Pumps Thunderbird, Allison and Mark Martin in the Jim McGill Monte Carlo.

Bonnett was available as a relief driver because his Hodgdon/Rahmoc Monte Carlo blew an engine after the first lap. That triggered the day's only accident, which involved eight cars and sidelined five.

Eliminated were the cars of Grant Adcox, Dick Skillen, Travis Tiller, Billie Harvey and Tommy Gale.

"My motor blew going into the third turn," explained Bonnett. "It just exploded, driving the crankshaft through the engine. My oil got all over the place and that's when everybody started spinning in the fourth turn."

Skillen's car plowed into the outside wall, while Adcox's was demolished when it collided with the inside wall and then was hit by other cars.

Terry Labonte left the race after 66 laps when the engine in his Hagan/Budweiser Monte Carlo blew, bringing out the only other caution of the day. The two cautions for just 16 laps allowed Earnhardt to win with an average speed of 170.611 mph, the second-fastest Talladega 500 ever. Lennie Pond won in 1978 with a speed of 174.700 mph.

Earnhardt's win – his second of the year – meant that Fords have now won three of the last four Winston Cup events. Prior to the streak, Ford's last win came in the 1982 World 600 at Charlotte, N.C., when Neil Bonnett drove a Wood Brothers Thunderbird.

There were 46 lead changes among ten drivers, with Earnhardt earning the Gillette-Atra Lap Leader Award by leading 12 times for 41 laps.

Pole winner Cale Yarborough left the race after 140 laps, the victim of a blown engine in his Ranier/Hardee's Monte Carlo. Buddy Baker, who led six times for 30 laps, retired on lap 69 after his brakes went out. David Pearson and Lake Speed also suffered engine failure, as did Benny Parsons. Twenty-one of the 40 cars that started the 2-hour, 55-minute, 52-second race were running at the finish. ■

AFTER EDGING RIVAL DARRELL WALTRIP DURING AN EXHILARATING LAST LAP, EARNHARDT CAN SMILE AND BREATHE A SIGH OF SATISFACTION, KNOWING HE IS BACK ON TRACK TO WIN MORE RACES.
DAVID CHOBAT PHOTO

WITH TERESA BESIDE HIM, EARNHARDT ENJOYS THE SATISFAC-TION, AND RELIEF, OF BREAKING A 30-RACE LOSING STREAK.
DAVID CHOBAT PHOTO

Earnhardt
Wins Talladega's Best

By STEVE WAID

N ASCAR Winston Cup driver Dale Earnhardt may be remembered best as the man who won what many consider the greatest race in stock car racing history.

The 33-year-old competitor from Doolie, N.C., ended a personal 30-race losing streak and became the 12th different winner during the 1984 season – thus tying the modern record established last year – when he beat Buddy Baker to the finish line by 1.66 seconds at the 2.66-mile Alabama International Motor Speedway.

Earnhardt became only the second man ever to win the Talladega 500 twice, joining Darrell Waltrip. But to do so, he had to contend with some of the stiffest competition seen at the speedway, which is noted for its dramatic, close racing at speeds in excess of 200 mph.

On the final lap, there were 10 cars in the lead pack and any of the first five could have won the race, as evidenced by the Talladega 500 record 68 lead changes among 16 drivers. Throughout the three hours, 12 minutes and four seconds of the race, the lead was never safe – until Earnhardt saw the finish line a few hundred yards away.

"It was the most exciting race I've ever been involved with here," said Earnhardt, driver of the Richard Childress-owned Wrangler Chevrolet Monte Carlo. "It seemed

I was always wondering what to do while everyone else was doing something. There were 10 or 12 cars always racing for the lead. I'd be racing with Cale (Yarborough) and then there'd come Darrell and (Harry) Gant would move up there and scrape some paint, too."

The finish was so close it required two photo finishes. But there was no doubt about the winner.

As the white flag flew to indicate the 188th and final lap, Terry Labonte's Piedmont Airlines Monte Carlo held the lead. On his rear bumper were Earnhardt and Baker in the Wood Brothers/Valvoline Ford Thunderbird.

As the three sped into the third turn, Earnhardt used the classic Talladega "slingshot pass" in the high-speed draft, but a bit differently. He went to the outside of Labonte rather than the inside and was helped considerably when Baker decided to follow.

Coming out of the fourth turn into the trioval, Earnhardt gained valuable distance as Baker and Labonte battled side by side. Only after NASCAR officials reviewed photos of the finish was Baker given second place – by inches. Photos were needed to determine that Bobby Allison's DiGard/Miller High Life

Buick finished fourth instead of Yarborough's Ranier/Hardee's Monte Carlo by a couple of feet. That's how close the conclusion was.

"Terry started slowing down the pace toward the finish," said Earnhardt, whose victory was worth $47,100. "I was having to lift going into the turns. I knew he was trying to cool his tires so he could try to run away from us.

"He went low into the first turn and I knew he was going to try to pull me off the second turn and down the backstretch. When he pulled low into the third turn, I figured it was too muddy to race in the infield, so I just held on and ran straight, which put me to the outside.

"My only worry was that Buddy would try something earlier, but he stayed in line and then gave me some help when he went to the outside with me.

"When I got by Terry, I looked in my rear view mirror and saw him and Buddy running side by side and I thought, 'Oh, Lord let me hold on. Let me hold on.' I knew I had it won. I was so excited. I started waving to the crowd as I went down the trioval."

The victory was Earnhardt's first of the season and his first with Childress' Winston-Salem, N.C., team. Ironically, his last win came in this race last year, when he drove a Bud Moore Thunderbird.

"You cherish all your wins," said Earnhardt. "I'll cherish the victory here last year because it was my last with Bud and I'll cherish this one because it is my first with Richard and the Chevrolet. I've won here in a Ford and a Chevrolet, so I guess I've proven I can be a winner in any car."

Baker's runner-up finish was his best of the season for the Wood Brothers/Valvoline team. His Thunderbird was one of a fleet of competitive cars and he led 16 times for 41 laps, more than any other driver.

"I never run so hard for so long in all my life, I don't think," said Baker.

"I thought we got Labonte there at the finish. I could run anywhere I wanted over the last 50 miles, in fact all day long, but I started pushing there at the end," said Earnhardt, who won with an average speed of 155.485 mph. "I was fortunate in that the car ran good enough and the engine ran good enough for me to be there. We pulled a higher gear than usual and that paid off.

"We had to make some adjustments during the race, too. It got a bit loose and we changed a few things, which helped us. Basically, the car ran consistent and that's what it took."

Twenty-four of the field of 40 cars were running at the finish, with a record 15 completing all 188 laps. Wrecks eliminated Trevor Boys, Dick Brooks, Eddie Bierschwale and Elliott Forbes-Robinson while Joe Ruttman, Morgan Shepherd, Sterling Marlin, Tim Richmond, and Geoff Bodine were victims of engine problems.

"I've proven I can be
a winner
in any car."
—Earnhardt

"I knew I was ahead of Terry, but I didn't want to say anything at the time," said Baker. "They had the camera on it. Terry's doorpost was behind mine at the end. I was worried that it took so long to decide (one hour after the race). I told myself that those Chevrolet nose pieces were longer than I thought.

"Anyone who says there isn't a driver in the No. 21 after today had better come and see me. I'll have a chat with him after a performance like I had today."

Rate Labonte's performance high, also. He led six times for 19 laps. "Dale was too strong and I figured that out before the last lap," he said. "Going into the last lap, I saw Buddy and Dale side by side behind me and I really thought things looked great. But then Dale came flying by me and that was it. He just ran me down. There were so many strong cars out there you really didn't know what to do."

Earnhardt, who led 13 times for 40 laps, led only the final lap following the day's final caution period, which ended on lap 161 after Boys' spectacular accident at the exit of turn four.

"We all stopped then and that took out any worries about gas mileage," said Earnhardt.

Over the last 17 laps, five different drivers took the lead – Waltrip, Baker, Ron Bouchard, Labonte and Earnhardt. Labonte slipped into the lead on lap 182 with Earnhardt and Baker following. The three ran that way until the final circuit.

"I had been formulating plans all day long, but I knew where I wanted to be at the end," said Earnhardt.

Richard Petty, winner of the Winston 500 at AIMS in 1983, lost 30 laps in the pits because of repairs to a broken transmission on his Curb/STP Pontiac. Petty's car went up in smoke as it exited pit road on lap 34 during the caution period for Forbes-Robinson's wreck. He returned to the race on lap 64.

Waltrip finished sixth in the Johnson-Hodgdon/Budweiser Monte Carlo while Gant took seventh in the Skoal Bandit Monte Carlo. Lake Speed finished eighth in the Ellington/Bull Frog Knits Monte Carlo while rookie Tommy Ellis wound up ninth in the Jim Magill Monte Carlo. Bill Elliott rounded out the top 10 in the Coors/Melling Thunderbird. Of the top 10 finishers, only Speed failed to lead a lap.

The character of the race was best described by Waddell Wilson, Yarborough's crew chief: "There wasn't any strategy. It was go like hell and hope you're first."

Earnhardt, who strengthened his hold on the Winston Cup points lead (he has 2,843 points to 2,778 for second-place Labonte), would agree.

"There was a lot of close racing and a lot of jumping around out there," he said. "There were times when a couple of us got sideways. But everybody in the lead pack did a super job of driving. It was a great show by the drivers." ∎

THE CHILDRESS RACING TEAM HADN'T FELT THE STING OF CHAMPAGNE IN THEIR EYES IN QUITE A WHILE.
DAVID CHOBAT PHOTO

EARNHARDT ISN'T GOING TO LET ANYBODY SNATCH THIS TROPHY FROM HIS HANDS.
DAVID CHOBAT PHOTO

Journal 500
Belongs to Earnhardt

Earnhardt Upstages Labonte, Gant

By STEVE WAID

Dale Earnhardt won the Atlanta Journal 500 today, but his accomplishment was nearly upstaged by the antics of Terry Labonte and Harry Gant and marred by the death of novice competitor Terry Schoonover.

Driving the Richard Childress-owned Wrangler Chevrolet Monte Carlo, Earnhardt earned his second victory of the 1984 NASCAR Winston Cup season by beating Bill Elliott's Coors/Melling Ford Thunderbird to the finish line by 0.57 second on the 1.522-mile Atlanta International Raceway.

The victory, worth $40,610, was the 11th of Earnhardt's career and his second at AIR, where he also won the 1980 Atlanta (now Coca-Cola) 500.

Even though the day belonged to Earnhardt – and deservedly so – fans were captivated by the drama played out by Labonte and Gant.

The two drivers are engaged in the duel for the 1984 Winston Cup championship and, today, each dodged a bullet. For the first time in months, each driver suffered mechanical maladies, marring their admirable record for high finishes.

First, Gant experienced trouble with a broken spindle and hub on his right-front wheel. Although repairs were made, Gant lost eight laps in the process and Labonte appeared to have a golden opportunity to expand his 49-point lead over Gant in the Winston Cup point standings.

But on lap 205 of the 328-lap race, the engine in Labonte's Hagan/Piedmont Airlines Monte Carlo blew, relegating the Trinity, N.C., driver to a 30th-place finish.

Gant now had the loaded gun. With Labonte out of the race, he had a chance to snatch the points lead away from Labonte or at the very least close the margin considerably.

But his gun didn't fire. By lap 241, his Skoal Bandit Monte Carlo developed engine problems and was smoking badly. He made a series of pit stops to try to correct the problem, but to no avail. On lap 315, his car gave up the ghost in a plume of smoke and Gant wound up with a 26th-place finish.

The outcome was that Gant managed to pick up just seven points on Labonte and still stands in second place as the season winds down to its final event, the Nov. 18 Winston Western 500 at Riverside, Calif. Labonte has 4,338 points; Gant, 4,296.

Of the Labonte-Gant follies, Earnhardt said, "I didn't pay any attention to them. I am out of that points thing; that's their worry. I wanted to win the race."

The 33-year-old Earnhardt was at the front of the field most of the day and led five times for 48 laps. On a chilly, cloudy day, the field was very competitive as 11 drivers swapped the lead 25 times. But many fell victim to mechanical failure.

One of them was Geoff Bodine, driver of the Northwestern Security Life Monte Carlo, who was trying to win the first superspeedway race of his Winston Cup career. Bodine made a noble effort. He led six times for 125 laps and earned a $10,000 bonus from AIR for leading the most laps.

By lap 276, he was in command of the race as it settled down to a three-man battle among himself, Earnhardt and Elliott. Earnhardt was the leader at that point, but Bodine took over on lap 278 and seemed to have control of the situation. But on lap 292, the engine blew in Bodine's Monte Carlo and he was out of it.

"It was the race of my life on a super-speedway and then this had to happen," said Bodine, a winner at Martinsville, Va., and Nashville, Tenn., this year. "I don't know what happened to the engine, but with water coming out the exhaust, it was obviously blown. I can't complain, though. The car ran comfortably all day and I was in a position to win. I won't say we had 'em covered, but we would have been there at the end."

With Bodine gone from the competition, the tussle for victory was left to Earnhardt and Elliott. Earnhardt took the lead when Bodine left and never relinquished it.

But he had some anxious moments. "I was just trying to run a steady pace at the end," explained the resident of Lake Norman, N.C. "I watched Bill for several laps and it looked like his car got loose out of the fourth turn whenever he ran hard through there.

"So I wanted to run steady because if he found enough to get to me, I would still have enough in my tires to get away from him."

Earnhardt's plan worked, but it wasn't without difficulty.

"With about 19 laps to go, a piece of one of my header pipes flew off and it busted a hole in the oil pan," said Earnhardt. "It was just a small hole, not enough to force a big leak but I figured the car could have run only 30 or 40 more laps. When the header pipe piece flew off, it caused sparks to fly and I saw smoke coming out of the car. For a minute, I thought it was going to blow up.

"Bill saw it, too, and he backed off a bit. I ran really cautious for the next few laps and then when I saw the car was going to run OK, I got back on it again. Oh, the alternator went out, too, but that doesn't affect your speed any. It just puts a drain on your battery."

Elliott of Dawsonville, Ga., and the hometown favorite, won the pole Nov. 1 with a record speed of 170.198 mph. He, like the rest of the competitors, was unable to

> "I didn't know he [Schoonover] died until the race was over.
> ## We try hard not to think about those things in racing."
> —Earnhardt

compete on the race's original date of Nov. 4 because rain postponed the event one week.

The time lapse made no difference in Elliott's pre-race standing. He was a heavy favorite. He ultimately led four times for 54 laps and, like Earnhardt, was never out of the lead pack.

But in his final confrontation with the eventual winner, Elliott had problems. "I never had a chance to overtake Earnhardt," he said. "With maybe 25 laps to go, his car started to throw oil. It got all over my windshield and I couldn't see. I couldn't judge distance and had to feel my way through the corners.

"I kept waiting for something to come from under his car but it never did. But give Dale credit. He won and I didn't. He drove a good race.

"Also, Geoff Bodine had one strong car. He would have been hard to deal with there at the end, had he been there."

There were seven caution flags for 44 laps, many of which were brought out by spins or wrecks. However, no one was injured other than Schoonover.

A 32-year-old from Royal Palm Beach, Fla., Schoonover was involved in a single-car incident on lap 129. His Monte Carlo went out of control in the second turn, smacking the outside wall. It careened down the back straight before pounding into a dirt embankment in the grass at the third turn.

Rescue crews had to cut through the roof of Schoonover's car to retrieve the already fatally injured driver. He was taken to the infield medical facility before being transferred to Grady Memorial Hospital in Atlanta where, at 4:27 p.m., he was pronounced dead due to massive head and internal injuries.

Earnhardt expressed sorrow over Schoonover's death and said he didn't know the fledgling driver.

"I am very sorry that it happened," he said. "I didn't know he died until the race was over. We try hard not to think about those things in racing."

In spite of the caution flags, the race was very competitive. "With the cool weather there was a real fast pace," said Earnhardt,

who averaged 134.610 mph over the three-hour, 42-minute and 31-second race. "I think it was a close race all the way, and I think it would have been really close among three or four of us at the end – but then Bodine blew and left us.

"Goodyear did some testing and came up with a tire for this race that allowed all of us to run very consistent. I think all of us who started up front pretty well stayed there, except for those who had trouble."

Another front-runner to experience problems was Cale Yarborough, who led three times for 56 laps. Yarborough, in fact, was the leader on lap 164 – the halfway point of the race – and thus won a $10,000 bonus from Barclay's American.

But Yarborough soon fell off the pace, the victim of a broken A-frame. He finished 11th.

Winding up in third place, 10 seconds behind Elliott, was Ricky Rudd in the Moore/Wrangler Thunderbird. Benny Parsons finished fourth in the Hayes/Copenhagen Monte Carlo and was the last driver to complete all 328 laps.

Rounding out the top 10 were Bobby Allison, fifth in the DiGard/Miller High Life Buick; Darrell Waltrip, sixth in the Johnson-Hodgdon/Budweiser Monte Carlo; Lake Speed, seventh in the Ellington/Bull Frog Knits Monte Carlo; Richard Petty, eighth in the Curb/STP Monte Carlo; Sterling Marlin, ninth in the Elliott and Associates Monte Carlo; and Dave Marcis, tenth in the Rahmoc Monte Carlo. ■

IT HAS BEEN A LONG SEASON FOR THE NO. 3. STAYING AHEAD OF THE PACK AND WINNING THE ATLANTA JOURNAL 500 GIVES THE TEAM SOMETHING TO BUILD ON.
DAVID CHOBAT PHOTO

EARNHARDT TOOK THE MILLER HIGH LIFE 400 FROM TIM RICHMOND AFTER A CAUTION IN THE CLOSING LAPS AND NEVER LOOKED BACK, NOT EVEN TO CHECK OUT THE CHARGING GEOFF BODINE AND DARRELL WALTRIP.
DAVID CHOBAT PHOTO

Earnhardt Does It At
Richmond

A First For Earnhardt At Richmond

By GARY McCREDIE

Following what some would call a "bold yet storybook move," Dale Earnhardt, driver of the Childress/Wrangler Chevrolet Monte Carlo, landed in victory lane at Richmond Fairgrounds Raceway today for the first time.

In winning the Miller High Life 400 – his 12th career NASCAR Winston Cup victory – Earnhardt survived a metal-crunching race that featured 10 caution flags for 74 of its 400 laps and also put to use his long apprenticeship on the dirt and asphalt "bullrings" of the Southeast.

The scene for Earnhardt's win was – in a way – set by the race's final four caution periods that came within 52 laps of each other, commencing on lap 335 and ending on lap 386.

On the 334th lap, Bill Elliott crashed into the fourth-turn wall when a right-front tire blew on his Coors/Melling Ford Thunderbird. Earnhardt, who was leading, pitted for fresh left-side tires, as did Harry Gant, while Tim Richmond, Geoff Bodine and Ron Bouchard opted for right-side tires.

Following the green flag on lap 340, Earnhardt pulled away from Richmond's second-running Blue Max/Old Milwaukee Pontiac and the third-place Johnson/Budweiser Monte Carlo of Darrell Waltrip. By the 366th lap, he had a 2.41-second lead on Richmond and Waltrip.

The race, however, was slowed on the next lap when Clark Dwyer crashed his Langley/Sunny King Thunderbird in turn three. Earnhardt pitted again for right-side tires; Waltrip, Bouchard and Geoff Bodine in the Hendrick/Levi Garrett Monte Carlo went in for left-side tires. Richmond chose not to pit and remained on the track, thus assuming the lead on lap 369.

The race resumed on lap 373 but was immediately curtailed once more when Bouchard spun out in the third turn. He, along with Waltrip and Kyle Petty in the Wood Brothers/7-Eleven Thunderbird, made stops for tires and the race went back to green on lap 377.

There was more action in turn three two laps later when the Hamby/Skoal Bandit Monte Carlo driven by Phil Parsons spun around, but almost no one made another pit stop.

When the green flag came out for the final time on lap 387, Earnhardt shot around Richmond on the inside going into the first turn as the pack roared down the front straightaway. Bodine passed Richmond on the outside, dropping Richmond back to fifth.

A crowd estimated at 27,500 (that filled the 0.542-mile speedway to capacity) watched Earnhardt scoot across the start/finish line three tenths of a second in front of Bodine. Waltrip was third; Bouchard, fourth; and Harry Gant was fifth, a lap down in the Skoal Bandit Monte Carlo. Richmond, who pitted for outside tires on lap 390 was ninth, also a lap behind.

"It was a helluva race wasn't it," said Earnhardt. "I felt Darrell would be the one to beat. I felt like we could lap the majority of the field.

"We had to make something happen," he said of the move around Richmond that was especially daring on the tight little short track. "Tim wasn't going to let me by. It worked out, not for him, but for me.

"But that's racing. I think he'd try and do the same thing. Anybody would. If they say they wouldn't, they're lying (because) we're all out there to win the race."

Earnhardt also said he thought that the sealant that had been applied to the track late last year helped him to the win. And, too, there was a new tire compound developed by Goodyear, as well as the new tire rule instituted by NASCAR permitting teams to change only two tires on caution-lap pit stops.

"For the first time out, it (the rule) seemed to work. It saved everybody some money and it kept the competition pretty equal," said Earnhardt. "The tires were a big help. They came up with a new compound and it seemed to be a well-balanced combination.

"The car worked better with some new lefts. We might have learned something today because we usually change the rights."

And as to why he decided to pass Richmond on the inside, Earnhardt said he thought the low groove was, for him, the fastest route to take. Obviously, it was.

"I figured he'd (Richmond) try to squeeze by me, but he didn't have the new tires on," said Earnhardt. "He was trying to play his strategy, but it didn't work."

Earnhardt experienced two close calls in the race, and each involved the Johnson/Budweiser Monte Carlo of Neil Bonnett. Following the third caution on lap 91, the field pitted and in trying to avoid Bonnett, Earnhardt swerved and came in contact with Terry Labonte's Hagan/Piedmont Airlines Monte Carlo.

The incident fouled up the toe-in on Earnhardt's car and also bent the right-front fender, causing the metal to rub on the tire. Earnhardt pitted twice more under caution to have the fender pulled away from the tire and

the car's steering mechanism was also adjusted.

"I don't know why Neil didn't pit real well. I had to get around him," said Earnhardt. "It was just a tight situation down there at the end of pit road (and) I was lucky to survive it.

"It knocked the fender down and by NASCAR's rule, if we had changed the tire it would have knocked us down two laps. But it's the same rule for everybody.

"The car wanted to push in the corners and it gave you a false feeling for about 25 laps.

"It was sort of odd because Neil and Tim Brewer (Bonnett's team manager) were kind of getting on me before the race. We pitted next to them and they didn't want me to run into them," said Earnhardt. "Then they get in my way."

Bonnett took the lead on lap 156, but that came to an end on lap 239 and on lap 240 he crashed hard into the outside guardrail on the backstretch coming out of the second corner. That brought out the day's sixth caution and the race was then stopped completely for about 15 minutes while the railing was replaced.

"I was really closer (to Bonnett) than I wanted to be, but I didn't hit anybody," said Earnhardt, who was running fourth at the time. "He took a pretty hard lick."

"It would be nice if they had a more sturdy barrier around this place."

"I really needed those last couple of caution flags. I had to change tires and the setup," said Bodine, who was not among the race's six leaders.

"I was really proud of the way the car ran, but Dale was awfully strong. I tried everything I could at the end, but Darrell was right behind me, so I had to be a bit careful.

"Dale was just – as they say – one tough customer," added

Bodine. "By the way, I enjoyed the halftime (red flag). The engine was running hot and I was hot, too. I liked the break."

Pole winner Waltrip led the first 110 laps but following the fourth caution that came out on lap 109 fell back into the field. Later, Waltrip regained his strength and was in contention during the event's later stages.

"When my car got into traffic, it just wouldn't run good. You might say I was scared," said Waltrip. "We had the car set up to run under the green and not change many tires.

"All those caution flags during the middle of the race messed us up. And the sealer didn't wear off like we thought it would.

"We just missed on a couple of things we thought would work. I could run with them at the end one on one, but in bunches, it just wasn't any good," said Waltrip.

The race was only a lap old when Rich Newsome crashed and brought out the first yellow flag. Ronnie Thomas wrecked into the second turn on lap 15 to bring out the second caution and the third caution came on lap 91 when Rusty Wallace also pasted the wall in the second corner.

Caution No. 4 occurred, also in turn two, when Ricky Rudd, the race's defending champion, lost the engine in his Moore/Motorcraft Thunderbird. Also involved were the cars of Richard Petty and Labonte. And the fifth yellow was instigated by Newsome, who spun out in turn three.

Sixteen of the race's 30 starters took the checkered flag behind Earnhardt, who finished the event in three hours, 11 minutes and 27 seconds at an average speed of 67.945 mph.

Earnhardt won $33,625, while Waltrip assumed the lead in Winston Cup points. He has 340 to 316 for Bodine, 309 for Lake Speed, 282 for Elliott and 268 for Bobby Hillin Jr. ∎

DESPITE A FEW BATTLE SCARS, THE NO. 3 CAR MANAGED TO AVOID THE TROUBLE THAT MARKED THE MILLER HIGH LIFE 400.
DAVID CHOBAT PHOTO

VALLEYDALE 500

EARNHARDT AND RICKY RUDD RUBBED AND SCRAPED THROUGH THE FINAL THREE LAPS.
DAVID CHOBAT PHOTO

Earnhardt Survives
At Bristol

Earnhardt 'Muscles' Way To Victory

By GARY McCREDIE

Dale Earnhardt lived up to his reputation as a rugged, no-quarter-given race driver today as he manhandled a car which had lost its power steering to victory in the Valleydale 500 NASCAR Winston Cup race at Bristol International Raceway.

With 100 laps gone in the 500-lap event, Earnhardt's Childress/Wrangler Chevrolet Monte Carlo changed from a quick-steering, smooth-handling speedster into an uncooperative brute. However, it handled well enough for Earnhardt's strength to force it into the lead seven times for 213 laps.

But only after a critical pit stop during the day's 15th caution period (a record at BIR) was Earnhardt able to get the measure of Moore/Motorcraft Ford Thunderbird driver Ricky Rudd and take the victory by 1.14 seconds.

With the win, Earnhardt joined Bill Elliott as the only drivers to win twice this year. Earnhardt has claimed victory at the only two short-track events run so far this season, having also won the Feb. 24 Miller High Life 400 at Richmond, Va., before winning on the 0.533-mile Bristol track for the third time in his career.

There can be little doubt that today's win was his toughest ever.

"I've never driven a car which had lost the power steering, and I hope I never do it again," said Earnhardt, a resident of Doolie, N.C., on the shores of Lake Norman. "It was like having someone in the car holding the

wheel, trying to keep you from turning it. You had to fight all the time.

"Drove the last 400 laps without the power steering. I don't know what happened but, fortunately, the whole thing didn't give out. I had to pull on the wheel so much my right hand and arm went to sleep. When I could, I tried to steer with one hand so I could work my right arm and try to get it to recover a bit."

Earnhardt added that only the superior handling of the car allowed him to finish.

"If the car hadn't handled so good, even with the power steering gone, I would have never finished the race. But it did get to hurting me so bad that I radioed (team owner Richard Childress) and told him to go find someone just in case I gave out or something," he said.

Darrell Waltrip, knocked out of the race because of a blown engine in his Johnson/Budweiser Monte Carlo, stood by to drive relief but was never utilized.

"We decided to play it lap by lap," said Earnhardt, who won $31,525 for his 13th career victory. "I got a break because of all the cautions, but it got tough even with them after a while."

The race was characterized by yellow flags. The 15 that flew bettered the old Bristol record of 12 set last spring and was just two short of the modern day NASCAR record of 17 set in the Old Dominion 500 of 1980 at Martinsville (Va.) Speedway.

It reached the point where most of the cars in the field looked like refugees from a junkyard. Many drivers were involved in more than one incident and by just the 55th lap, eight of the more competitive cars were either laps in arrears or out of the event completely. More would follow.

Earnhardt escaped the carnage, even though his power steering had given out.

"I reckon there were just a wild and crazy bunch of guys out there," he said. "You had to pay attention. I started 12th and right away I started worrying about what might happen ahead of me. Sure enough, we hadn't gone far (eight laps, to be exact) before Lake Speed and a bunch of others got into it and started tearing things up. It was senseless that it happened that early and it involved a lot of good cars.

"I guess it was one of those days at Bristol. It's an exciting place to race and it's exciting for the fans to watch. But they work us to death here putting on the show."

Earnhardt added he had his share of close calls as the race wore on. On lap 362 he lost his lead to Rudd after he rubbed a slower car while passing in the third turn.

"That one got me sideways and I locked it up," Earnhardt said. "With the power steering out, I have no idea how the car got straight again, but it did."

Rudd maintained his lead as Earnhardt gave chase. Try as he might, however, it appeared that Earnhardt had only the slightest chance of catching his Thunderbird-driving rival, who was gunning for his first victory of the 1985 season.

"I had a tire problem," said Earnhardt. "I had blistered the left rear tire and the car was working as well off the corners as it could have. I got some good laps in on Ricky, but in the traffic he could pull away. If it had kept on that way, I think he would have beaten me. He was awful strong."

But fate gave Earnhardt the chance he needed. On lap 477, the day's final yellow flag flew when rookie Don Hume spun in the second turn. Earnhardt seized the opportunity to take on much-needed left-side tires. Rudd pitted for right-side rubber.

When the green flag came out on lap 480, Rudd and Earnhardt began racing side by side, rubbing metal at least a half-dozen times before Earnhardt's blue-and-yellow Monte Carlo took the lead on the frontstretch on lap 483.

"We were lucky," said Earnhardt, "because we had changed right-side tires on our last stop and planned to change the left-side tires when we made that final stop. As it happened, that is exactly what we needed. I know I got

into Ricky but, with the power steering gone, I needed more lanes out there."

"Bud (Moore, team owner and crew chief) wanted to change left-side tires but I wanted the right-sides," said Rudd, "and I guess that was a bad decision. It made us run a little too tight and the car was pushing. After the tire change, there was no way I could run with him. If I could have kept Dale on hot tires, I could have run even or ahead of him.

"But this was a good finish and a good lift for the team." Rudd led twice for 163 laps and won $18,050 for his runner-up finish.

By lap 204, well under the halfway point of the race, 10 caution flags had flown. It was so hectic that, prior to that, the longest stretch run under green had been 49 laps. For the race, the longest green flag period was 80 laps. Several drivers were involved in more than one accident, among them Neil Bonnett (eventually knocked out on lap 137 after clobbering the frontstretch pit wall), Harry Gant (who limped home 20th), Bill Elliott (who wound up 11th, 15 laps down), Lake Speed (who was seventh, five laps down) and Waltrip, the 23rd-place finisher.

In all, 20 different cars were involved in accidents.

"Overall, I was driving pretty cautious, but I was lucky to get by it all," said Earnhardt. "I was, as I said, concerned about starting back there in 12th place. We had missed it in qualifying (March 30). I scuffed up some tires for it, but we thought new ones would be the way to go so that is what we did. But that messed us up. We should have started fourth or fifth, we were lucky to get through it all."

Earnhardt, who won with an average speed of just 81.790 mph, said that some intense preparation on the part of his team for the short tracks benefited him today.

"During the winter, Kirk (Shelmerdine, crew chief) and I worked hard on the setups," he said. "Last year we were torn on it with power steering and setting caster and camber, stuff like that. We changed a lot during the season. But then, for this year, we worked on the basics, going about getting the settings we'd use all year. It seems to have worked for us.

"Like I said, it was very, very tough without power steering but, if the car hadn't handled the way it did, it would have been much worse."

Terry Labonte finished third, two laps down in the Hagan/Piedmont Airlines Monte Carlo, and assumed the Winston Cup points lead. He is the fifth different leader through the first five events of the season. He was involved in the first incident of the day (along with four other cars), and lost his laps when he took a two-lap penalty to change all four flat-spotted tires during a caution period. The penalty is enforced under the NASCAR rule which permits only two-tire changes during the yellow flag. A four-tire change brings a two-lap penalty.

Buddy Baker finished fourth, also two laps down, in the Bull Frog/Liquid Wrench Oldsmobile, a fine showing for the driver, who does not favor the short tracks. Rusty Wallace was fifth in the Stewart/AluGard Pontiac, three laps back, while Kyle Petty took sixth in the Wood Brothers/7-Eleven Thunderbird, five laps down.

Speed was seventh, followed by Richard Petty, Bobby Hillin and rookie Ken Schrader.

The race, which was run after a six-day postponement following rain on March 31, took three hours, 15 minutes and 30 seconds to complete.

Earnhardt's arms and back, however, are expected to be sore for a considerably longer time. ■

THE EARNHARDTS, ONCE AGAIN, GRACE VICTORY LANE.
DAVID CHOBAT PHOTO

EARNHARDT SOME-
HOW SURPRISES
MISS WINSTON WITH A
CELEBRATORY SPRAY.
DAVID CHOBAT PHOTO

Earnhardt Gets
Another
At Bristol

Earnhardt Outmuscles 'em at BIR

By STEVE WAID

Using the aggressive, daredevil style that he honed during his days as a dirt-track racer, Dale Earnhardt won the exciting – and sometimes confusing – Busch 500 NASCAR Winston Cup race tonight at Bristol International Raceway.

In his Childress/Wrangler Chevrolet Monte Carlo, Earnhardt led seven times for 343 of the race's 500 laps, held off a furious challenge from Darrell Waltrip and passed Tim Richmond with just 18 laps remaining to record his third win of the 1985 season. It was also his second-straight win on the 0.533-mile BIR track this year and the 14th of his career.

"A lot of drivers don't like this old track because it wears you out," said the 34-year-old

Earnhardt. "But it's been good to me. I earned my money tonight, though.

"Darrell and I were racing back and forth for a while and then at the end Tim raced me real hard. He didn't give me anything and if there could be two winners, he'd be one of them. He deserved it."

Earnhardt, who started on the pole with a track-record speed of 113.586 mph, quickly showed his strength by leading 114 of the race's first 125 laps. But he was pushed mightily by Waltrip in the Johnson/Budweiser Monte Carlo. Waltrip roared from his 10th-place starting position to Earnhardt's rear bumper – even taking the lead for 11 laps.

The race remained mainly a two-car duel for the next 220 laps, although Bobby Allison, Terry Labonte and Neil Bonnett took turns pacing the field.

By lap 261, Earnhardt was in command again and would stay there for a whopping 186 laps. But Waltrip was never far away, harassing Earnhardt's Monte Carlo continuously.

But that changed on lap 364. While pressing Earnhardt for the lead, Waltrip spun in the third turn. He recovered nicely, but two laps later he was the victim of a cut right-rear tire and looped his car again in the fourth turn. This time the mishap cost him a lap.

"Yeah, it was an aggressive race," said Waltrip later. "I guess I got a bit overaggressive a couple of times."

After Waltrip's mishap, Earnhardt had a full-lap lead on the field. But it wasn't to last. When Kyle Petty's Wood Brothers/7-Eleven Ford Thunderbird clobbered Allison's DiGard/Miller American Buick in the second turn on lap 433, bringing out the 12th caution of the night, Waltrip, Richmond and Bonnett beat Earnhardt out of the pits and put themselves back on the lead lap.

"I guess it was all too good to last," said Earnhardt. "My car was working so well all night but then, unfortunately, those guys got the lap back. I knew it wouldn't be that easy."

When Petty spun again between the first and second turns on lap 446, it precipitated a brief scoring confusion. Waltrip, Bonnett, Richmond and Earnhardt pitted – all too early as it turned out – because the pace car had not yet come onto the track. Bonnett and Richmond were quickly waved through pit road by their crews, but Waltrip and Earnhardt stopped.

It appeared at first glance that the field lineup behind the pace car should have had Earnhardt in the lead, with Waltrip, Richmond and Bonnett in tow. However, Richmond was listed as the leader because he did not make a pit stop, with Earnhardt in second place, Bonnett in third and Waltrip fourth, nearly a lap down.

This set up the final battle between Richmond and Earnhardt.

"I don't know what happened but there was some confusion there," said Earnhardt. "But it didn't matter much to me because Richard (Childress, team owner) told me just to go out there and race and bring home the trophy."

> "Of course,
> **he used one
> of his normal
> tactics**
> in getting around me."
> —Tim Richmond

That's exactly what Earnhardt did. When the final green flag flew on lap 460, he began to chase Richmond. He caught him in the fourth turn on lap 483, nudged him out of the way and went on to win by three car lengths.

"It was a good race but, unfortunately, it ended the wrong way," said Richmond, who is still searching for his first win of 1985. "Dale has got to quit making me the second-place guy. He did it first in qualifying (Richmond started in the No. 2 position) and now he does it in the race. Maybe I can pay him back at Darlington (S.C., in the September 1 Southern 500).

"I made an adjustment on the car on the last pit stop and it was the wrong way to go. I had to use up too much of my car getting around Earnhardt. Of course, he used one of his normal tactics in getting around me. I just had to hustle the car all day and use too much of it. I didn't have enough left at the end."

Bonnett wound up third in a Johnson/Budweiser Monte Carlo, while Waltrip was

fourth. Fifth place, one lap down, was Bill Elliott in the Coors/Melling Thunderbird.

Elliott's finish, coupled with a five-point bonus for leading the race (once for 16 laps) meant that he retained much of his lead over Waltrip in the Winston Cup point standings. Waltrip gained only five points, as Elliott leads by 138 points (2,996 – 2,858).

Harry Gant was sixth, two laps back, in the Skoal Bandit Monte Carlo; Ron Bouchard was seventh, three laps down, in the Beebe/Valvoline Buick; Richard Petty was eighth, four laps down, in the Curb/STP Pontiac; Ricky Rudd was ninth, five laps in arrears, in the Moore/Motorcraft Thunderbird; and Lake Speed – with relief from Geoff Bodine – wound up 10th, 10 laps back, in the Rahmoc/Nationwise Pontiac.

Earnhardt, who collected $34,675, has now won three of the five short-track races run this year, two at Bristol and one at Richmond.

"I think this win will give us momentum for the rest of the year," he said. "We have had our problems this year, especially on the superspeedways. We lost a windshield at Talladega (Ala.), for example, and Michigan wasn't too good for us either.

"The crew has worked very, very hard and our sponsors have been very patient with us. This win was important for those reasons and we have the feeling that we can win on the superspeedways.

"That is a good feeling to have, particularly when you are headed to Darlington and the Southern 500."

An earlier rain had soaked the track and the first five laps were run under caution. Because of the race's 13 caution flags for 85 laps, most of which were caused by accidents, Earnhardt's average speed was reduced to 81.388 mph. ∎

EARNHARDT PASSES TIM RICHMOND FOR THE LEAD, AND THE WIN, WITH JUST 18 LAPS REMAINING IN THE RACE. DAVID CHOBAT PHOTO

dale earnhardt

EARNHARDT TAKES THE CHECKERED FLAG IN THE GOODY'S 500.
DAVID CHOBAT PHOTO

Battered, But Not Beaten,
Is Earnhardt at Martinsville

Earnhardt's 'Touch' Is A Winner

By GARY McCREDIE

Dale Earnhardt used the years of experience he gained running on the dirt and asphalt "bull-rings" of the Carolinas to pull a gutsy move that resulted in his winning today's Goody's 500 NASCAR Winston Cup event at Martinsville Speedway.

In a typical Martinsville race that several competitors called "physical," Earnhardt, driving the Childress/Wrangler Chevrolet Monte Carlo, bullied his way alongside the Blue Max/Old Milwaukee Pontiac of race leader Tim Richmond coming out of the fourth turn on the 443rd lap. Richmond tried hard to keep the lead; the duo swept down toward the pit road wall on the front straightaway and as they entered the first corner they were still battling fiercely for the No. 1 position.

Just then, Greg Sacks' DiGard/Miller American Buick made contact with the Coors/Melling Ford Thunderbird of Bill Elliott and Elliott spun out in the second turn. Earnhardt, in avoiding Elliott, darted to the inside, took the lead going into the backstretch and kept it from there on out.

Richmond, who had led twice for 159 laps (the most of anyone) later experienced troubles on a pit stop when a lug nut got behind a wheel and jammed the brake rotor. He had already changed two tires, had to pit again for another fresh right-front tire when the wheel froze up, thereby violating the NASCAR rule stating no more than two tires may be changed on a yellow-flag pit stop and he ended up finishing seventh, two laps off the pace.

The race's defending champion, Darrell Waltrip, then took over second place and began to dog Earnhardt. On lap 453, his Johnson/Budweiser Monte Carlo and Earnhardt's car made contact in the first corner as the two fought for supremacy.

By lap 478, Earnhardt was almost two seconds in front of Waltrip. He stretched his advantage to 2.6 seconds by lap 481 and by the time the 489th of 500 circuits around the 0.526-mile flat track had been completed the Wrangler driver's advantage over Waltrip was 3.2 seconds.

The last of a dozen yellow flags for 65 laps came out on lap 494 when Bobby Hillin spun his Trap Rock Industries Monte Carlo out in the third corner. Both Waltrip and Harry Gant, who was running third in the Skoal Bandit Monte Carlo (and the last car on the lead lap), pitted for left-side tires while Earnhardt did not.

The green flag was waved for the last time on lap 497 and Gant ducked back into his pit for right-side rubber, going a lap down.

"He pulled the same stunt again.

We ain't even yet."
—Tim Richmond

Waltrip made one last attempt to pass Earnhardt in the third turn on the next lap, but it was to no avail and he finished two car lengths behind the winner.

Gant finished third. Fourth, and a lap down, was Ricky Rudd in the Moore/Motorcraft Thunderbird, while Kyle Petty took fifth in the Wood Brothers/7 Eleven Thunderbird, two laps off the pace.

"That was a pretty close call on that last stop. To get tires or not to get tires," said Earnhardt of his decision not to pit. "If I had pitted first, Darrell wouldn't have.

"I hadn't got the caution flag yet and I had a lap to think about it. It was a gamble and when Richard (car owner Childress) asked, 'What do you want to do?' I said, 'Let's go for it!'"

Earnhardt explained that when new tires are put on a car, "They're good, but not as good as they're going to be." It takes a few laps for them to effect maximum gripping power and had the caution come earlier or the race run longer, Waltrip and perhaps even Gant may have been able to pass him.

In fact, when the final caution flag flew, Earnhardt, who has now won four races this year (all on short tracks), admitted to being startled.

"Oh s---, what am I going to do now? Am I going to pit? My mind was going yes and no, yes and no," said Earnhardt. "And when Darrell pitted that decided it. I was going to gamble."

Thirty-one cars started the 263-mile race and 21 finished. Eight of the 12 cautions were for wrecks or spinouts.

The "one-groove" track took its toll on sheet metal and suspension parts and just after the checkered flag fell, Richmond was prompted to accuse Earnhardt of rough driving. That was something the race winner denied.

"He pulled the same stunt again. We ain't even yet," said Richmond, alluding to the fact that for the third time this year he was a victim of Earnhardt's driving style on the short tracks on which Earnhardt had won.

"We've got a long way to go. (But) he can get away with it as long as it sells tickets, I guess.

"They can't allow him to continue to do it," said Richmond.

Waltrip was more subdued, saying, "I don't

want to get into that." But when asked when competitiveness ended and overly-aggressive driving took over, he said, "You just witnessed it."

Earnhardt admitted to making contact with Richmond but said it wasn't intentional. He noted that metal-to-metal contact is required at Martinsville because of the track's configuration and added that he had driven carefully most of the way in order to conserve his car for the final late-race charge.

"I bumped him a little in the corner and he backed off a little bit," said Earnhardt. "He gave me a shot and let me know he didn't like it.

"That's Martinsville, I guess, and I must have gotten hit 100 times. At Martinsville you've got to run 500 laps and brakes are key to being competitive.

"I ran conservative, and when 60 laps to go came, it was time to go," said Earnhardt. "We pitted that time (on the 11th caution) and got lefts. Darrell got rights and I think that was the key to the win."

However, the event was something of a barnburner in style not found on the super-speedways. Pole winner Geoff Bodine shot into the lead and led the first 62 laps in the Hendrick/Levi Garrett Monte Carlo. He kept the front spot until the first yellow flag on lap 62. He came back to lead laps 64–119, 121–129 and 175–202 but dropped out at 288 laps with engine failure.

Morgan Shepherd and Ron Bouchard each led a single lap. Gant went to the front once for five laps. Waltrip paced the field twice for 121 laps and Earnhardt led the final 58.

The caution flag came out twice because of debris on the track, two more times due to blown engines, five more times because of single- or multi-car spinouts and three additional times for accidents.

The worst – and one that further tightened the points between Waltrip and Elliott for the Winston Cup crown – occurred between turns one and two on lap 342 when Waltrip and Elliott, along with Rudd, Richard Petty, Kyle Petty and Bouchard all either piled into each other or the wall.

Waltrip ended up on the infield grass, Elliott came to rest against the wall, and Petty's car was too badly damaged to continue on. Waltrip was the luckiest, with no serious damage to his Monte Carlo. Bouchard's Buick was mangled, but he kept going and completed 498 laps to finish sixth, while Elliott had to go behind the wall. Among other things, the steering linkage on his car was completely broken.

Elliott reentered the race on lap 365 but was black-flagged three laps later. The toe-in on his car was off kilter and could have caused

CHOOSING AN INSIDE LINE, EARNHARDT BLOWS PAST RIVAL AND FRIEND NEIL BONNETT.
DAVID CHOBAT PHOTO

a tire to blow, thus possibly precipitating another accident.

He rejoined the event on lap 372 but could muster only a 17th-place finish, 33 laps down. While he still leads in points, the deficit between him and Waltrip was whittled down to 23 points, 3,523 to 3,500.

"It was a very tough race. This is a hard track to pass on," said Waltrip. "We had some trouble up there in turn two.

"Somebody hit me and I don't know who it was. I was lucky to get out of it.

"That's more important than anything. We're going to win that championship," he added when told that he was that much closer to Elliott.

And for Earnhardt's goals for the year? It's to bounce back from early and mid-season misfortunes, win more races and complete the season with a top-10 points finish. He is not in the chase to the championship.

"We ran a good, smooth, conservative race and saved the car to the end," said Earnhardt. "I think Darrell and Harry did, too.

"Darrell is a tough person to beat here, or Tim, or Harry, or any of them. And when they got tires at the end, I knew it would be tough as hell to beat them.

"(The goal) is to try and win more races and get back in the top 10 in points," he said.

By finishing eighth, five laps back, in the

Trap Rock Industries Monte Carlo, Bobby Hillin Jr., posted his third top-10 finish of the year. Neil Bonnett was ninth, also five laps down, in the Johnson/Budweiser Monte Carlo and Bobby Allison completed 494 laps to finish 10th in his own Miller American Buick.

The victory was Earnhardt's second at Martinsville, ninth on a track of less than a mile in length and 15th overall, tying him with Bonnett for 25th place on the all-time win list. He completed the race in three hours, 43 minutes and 13 seconds at an average speed of 70.694 mph and won $37,725 in front of a crowd estimated at 37,000 – a record for the Goody's 500. ■

Steve Waid reflects on the
1985 NASCAR Season

Although no one knew it at the time, Dale Earnhardt's victory in the Goody's 500 would be his last of the season.

His second full season with team owner Richard Childress was not as productive as the first.

In '85, Earnhardt won four races - all on short tracks. He swept the Bristol events and won at Richmond and Martinsville. He finished seventh in the final Winston Cup point standings and earned $546,596.

By comparison, Earnhardt won only twice in 1984, on the super-speedways at Talladega and Atlanta. But with more finishes among the top five (12) and the top 10 (22) he wound up fourth in points. His earnings approached $635,000.

The short-track wins in '85 cemented Earnhardt's reputation as a master of NASCAR's "bull rings." The rough-and-tumble style he used to win the Goody's 500 (and upset Tim Richmond in the process) would be used repeatedly in the coming years. Competitors came to expect it, even if they didn't like it. Some fans felt Earnhardt was too aggressive, while many others came to view him as the ideal stock car driver, a man who gave no quarter and asked none.

Earnhardt never made any apologies for his style. He said repeatedly that he had learned it by watching his father, Ralph, race against some of the toughest drivers Southern stock car racing had to offer.

> Earnhardt never made any apologies for his style.

Although Earnhardt certainly drew his share of attention in 1985 - and would continue to do so throughout his career - the season's news was dominated by Bill Elliott.

Elliott won an astounding 11 superspeedway races and, with his triumph in the Southern 500 at Darlington, claimed the first Winston Million bonus. Ironically, Earnhardt led the most laps in the race, but with less than 200 miles to go he hit the wall in the second turn. Elliott narrowly missed him.

Elliott was in command of the points race, and with eight races to go it seemed the Winston Cup championship was his. However, Darrell Waltrip staged a late-season charge that eradicated Elliott's lead. At Riverside, Calif., in the last race of the year, Waltrip cruised to a seventh-place finish, while Elliott, who suffered a sheared bolt off his transmission, wound up 31st.

Waltrip won the title, his third and last with legendary team owner Junior Johnson, by 101 points. Earnhardt and Childress figured they could win the 1986 Winston Cup championship if they could maintain their form on the short tracks and improve on the superspeedways.

Oddly enough, in '86, Earnhardt won only one short-track race - at North Wilkesboro, N.C. However, he won four times on superspeed-ways, highlighted by a sweep of Charlotte's two events. Earnhardt also won the spring race at Darlington. And with his convincing victory at Atlanta in November in the next-to-last race of the year, he claimed the championship.

It was the second of his career and his first with Childress in only his third full season with the Richard Childress Racing team.

—Steve Waid
VP Editorial Development
NASCAR Scene and Illustrated

Earnhardt Outruns 'Em in Busch Clash

Earnhardt Whips Field In Busch Clash

By STEVE WAID

Dale Earnhardt's savvy on the track merged well with his Childress/Wrangler team's preparation to produce a victory today in the Busch Clash at Daytona International Speedway.

Behind the wheel of the Wrangler Chevrolet Monte Carlo SS, Earnhardt won the 20-lap, 50-mile chase around the 2.5-mile Daytona trioval for the second time in his career. He won The Clash the first time in 1980, the year he went on to claim the NASCAR Winston Cup championship.

Earnhardt, who started fourth in the eight-car field reserved for 1985 Busch Pole winners, fashioned his victory by snatching the lead away from Neil Bonnett in the Johnson/Budweiser Chevrolet on the sixth lap and holding it for the remainder of the race. He was, however, challenged by Bill Elliott's Coors/Melling Ford Thunderbird as the race came to its conclusion.

But, it was obvious that Elliott, the dominant winner in 1985 with 11 victories, would not get around his rival. Earnhardt's Chevrolet was handling particularly well in the corners, where Elliott's Ford was not.

There was a reason for that, according to Earnhardt.

"We tested here in January with this car and we got it running as good as we could," said the 34-year-old driver from Doolie, N.C. "It's the same car that had a driveshaft go through its windshield at Talladega (Ala.) last year.

"We weren't sure if we'd like it, but we tested it along with two others and by the time we checked the facts and figures, we thought it would be the best car. We made it race ready and although we haven't had much practice in the draft here, it proved to be as good as we expected."

Elliott started fifth and moved by Bonnett into second place on the 12th lap. He and Earnhardt slowly pulled away from the rest of the field, but it soon became evident that Elliott's Ford could not match the strength of Earnhardt's Chevrolet in the turns – especially in turn No. 3.

"I knew that I could beat Bill in that corner because he'd come up on me and then I could pull down and away from him," said Earnhardt. "But I didn't know if he was playing with me, setting me up or giving his all to it. I thought maybe I would let him by, but I got to thinking about the guys behind him and thought, 'No way.'

"Then, he tried me again in the third turn on the last lap and once we got there, I knew I had him. He just couldn't get through there as good as I could. His car would drift up and away."

"We were strong down the straights on the last four laps, but I'd turn the wheel and the car would still wash up the race track in the turns," conceded Elliott. "We made a wild guess at the suspension settings under the car this morning and we turned out pretty close. But that wasn't good enough.

"Dale really had our number when it came down to showtime during those last few laps. Me, I'm fighting the flu and I'm pretty woozy, but we're going to work to change the engine and springs for practice today and (Daytona 500) qualifying tomorrow."

Earnhardt said he tried to negate Elliott's strength on the backstretch by running a curved line from turn two to turn three.

"I'd run high up against the wall, then drift down low before going into the third turn," he explained. "I wasn't playing any games. When you run that way, you create curvy air behind you and it is much more difficult to pass in that than it is in straight air.

"I wanted to make it as hard as possible on Bill."

Earnhardt won a record $75,000 for his victory, which took just 15 minutes, 19 sec-

THE LAST TIME EARNHARDT TOOK THE TROPHY IN THE BUSCH CLASH, HE WENT ON TO WIN THE POINTS CHAMPIONSHIP.
DAVID CHOBAT PHOTO

EARNHARDT RUNS ALONE, AND UP FRONT IN THE BUSCH CLASH AT DAYTONA
DAVID CHOBAT PHOTO

onds to accomplish. That meant he made nearly $5,000 per minute.

Bonnett was third, some four car lengths behind Elliott. "Bill got into second ahead of me a lot quicker than I thought he would in those closing laps," said Bonnett. "My car was a bit loose and I really wanted to be second on the last lap because I had something I thought I might try against Dale. Even from third, with the car running as strong as it did on the back straight, I felt I still had a chance."

Geoff Bodine finished fourth in the Hendrick/Levi Garrett Chevrolet, a creditable accomplishment considering his early difficulties. He had charged from seventh to second place during the first two laps, but on the fifth lap he spun his car between the third and fourth turns, bringing out the race's lone caution flag. Since caution flags are not counted in the Busch Clash, Bodine rejoined the rear of the field after a pit stop to change all four tires.

"Wow! I'm still shaking!" said Bodine. "I was trying to move up and stick in there behind Earnhardt (then in second place) but the car just got loose. I tried to save it and nearly hit Earnhardt. After that, all I could do was hang on because you can only do so much in that kind of situation.

"The front spoiler was damaged after that so the car was pushing. But it ran pretty good so we know now that if we can keep the front spoiler on, we'll be all right

for the rest of the week."

Fifth place went to Terry Labonte in the Hagan/Piedmont Airlines Oldsmobile Delta 88, sixth to Rusty Wallace in the Blue Max/AluGard Pontiac Grand Prix 2+2, seventh to Harry Gant in the Skoal Bandit Chevrolet and eighth to Darrell Waltrip in the Johnson/Budweiser Chevrolet. Waltrip's car was never a factor, running in last place for nearly the entire event.

"Well, that was 20 laps of practice for us," quipped Waltrip, the defending Winston Cup champion. "Everyone said that the new rear window would make a lot of difference, but we had to see for ourselves. We set the car

"I ain't gonna change."
—Earnhardt on his aggressive style

up the way we raced last year and, by doing so, we flat screwed up. It was a shot in the dark and now we know what to do."

Observers were anxious to see how the new sloped-back General Motors cars would fare against the Fords but, if average speed means anything, little was proved. Earnhardt won with an average speed of 195.865 mph.

"For most of us, this was the first time to test the cars in the draft," said Earnhardt. "So a lot of us used the same setups we had last year. Some pushed and some were loose. We were lucky in that we could even up our car with its new rear window by using the right spring setup.

"But I don't think we will use this car in Daytona 500 qualifying or for the race (scheduled for Feb. 16). We'll probably run another one."

Elliott received $21,000 for second place while Bonnett earned $26,000 for third place, which included bonus lap leader money. Bodine pocketed $13,000, Labonte $12,000, Wallace $11,500, Gant $11,000 and Waltrip $10,000.

Earnhardt, who won four short-track races last season, admitted he's a no-holds-barred driver from "the old school."

"I learned by watching my daddy (the late former national Sportsman champion Ralph Earnhardt) load his car on the truck and go out there against Tiny Lund and Junior Johnson. They didn't know how to run any other way and I don't either. I ain't gonna change.

"And the last time I won this race, I won the championship. This year, we're prepared. We don't have any special tricks for our cars; we're just thinking positive and we'll go out and try to win every race we enter." ∎

dale **earnhardt**

HAVING WON THE BUSCH CLASH (2/9/86) AND ANOTHER 125-MILE QUALIFIER, EARNHARDT CERTAINLY LOOKS LIKE THE NO. 1 GUY HEADING INTO THE DAYTONA 500.
DAVID CHOBAT PHOTO

7-Eleven

Earnhardt Makes It Look Easy 125 Mile Qualifiers

By GARY McCREDIE

Ten laps after the second of two caution flags was displayed, Dale Earnhardt, in the Childress/Wrangler Chevrolet Monte Carlo SS, swept into the lead and at the finish held off Geoff Bodine's Hendrick/Levi Garrett Monte Carlo to win the second 7-Eleven Twin 125-mile qualifying race for the Daytona 500.

Earnhardt sped to his second career qualifying victory (he also won in 1983) by a comfortable one-second margin of victory over Bodine. Finishing third was Darrell Waltrip in the Johnson/Budweiser Monte Carlo, Morgan Shepherd took fourth in the Race Hill Farm Buick LeSabre and fifth went to Rusty Wallace in the Blue Max/AluGard Pontiac Grand Prix 2+2. They, along with the next 12 finishers, all completed the full 50-lap distance.

This event and its companion race are run to determine starting positions 3-30 in the season-opening NASCAR Winston Cup 500-miler on the 2.5 mile trioval. Those who ran first and second fastest in an initial round of qualifying (in this case Bill Elliott and Bodine) automatically earn the first two starting spots for the race, while positions 31-40 are filled on the basis of earlier time trial speeds with spots 41 and 42 being reserved for provisional starters.

"This is a brand-new car. Basically, it's like the car we ran Sunday (Feb. 9 in the Busch Clash which he won), but it's about an inch narrower," said Earnhardt. "But, really, I wouldn't toss a coin for the difference."

While Elliott, driving the Coors/Melling Ford Thunderbird, handily bested Bobby Allison's Buick on a last lap pass in the first race, Earnhardt said the improved design of the 1986 Chevrolet (and other General Motors makes) would definitely make this year's 500 more competitive than the '85 version. In the '85 event, Elliott lapped all but the second-finishing car at least once and won by a seven-car-length margin of victory.

"The (GM) cars are harder to draft with than last year. The flow of air over our cars is better," he said. "It will cause him (Elliott) problems.

"My car has been stable all week," said Earnhardt when he was told several other GM drivers had been complaining of handling problems in practice. "The guys are now having to work out the spring setups because of the (sloping) back glass.

"They've got to work on all four springs."

Bodine started on the pole and led the first six laps, but the event was only two circuits old when Phil Barkdoll crashed his Helen Rae Special Ford into the wall coming into the trioval, which brought out the first of two yellow flags for a total of 10 laps. Cale Yarborough, who started 30th in the Ranier/Hardee's Ford Thunderbird (he crashed earlier this week while practicing and was forced to run a backup car) immediately pitted for right-side tires. His car had also been hit in the rear end during the Barkdoll incident but suffered no major damage.

Buddy Baker led lap seven in the Baker/Crisco Oldsmobile Delta 88. Bodine led lap eight, Baker lap nine and then Earnhardt went into the lead for the first time on the 10th circuit and led through lap 29 until the second yellow was displayed.

That occurred when a tire popped on Tim Richmond's Hendrick/Folger's Coffee Chevrolet, sending him into the fourth-turn wall. Richmond was taken to Halifax Hospital, and diagnosed as suffering a bruised knee and swelling of the rib cage but was later released.

The field immediately pitted for fuel and tires; Harry Gant took the lead under caution in the Skoal Bandit Chevrolet but, when the green came out on the 35th lap, Benny Parsons headed the race in the Precision Products/Copenhagen Oldsmobile. Bodine snatched the lead away, however, on lap 36, but two laps later Earnhardt had taken the lead for good.

"Dale was blowing some oil and my windshield was covered, but I could see. I have no excuses," said Bodine. "I backed off and tried to get a run on him, but I laid off too long. I didn't have enough.

"I think I learned something today. Dale was real strong in turns one and two. I was getting through three and four.

"We've got to work on getting through one and two. No excuses," Bodine said.

Gant, who finished eighth, also said that "oil was coming from somewhere, from Dale's car or somewhere on the race track," but Earnhardt said he knew nothing about it and was not told of any problems by his crew.

"I just hung in there and moved up," said Waltrip, who started 16th. "I got hung up there a couple of times between Cale and Rusty. If I could have avoided those problems, I think I could have won.

"The car may not be the fastest, but it handles."

Shepherd, Wallace and Dave Marcis, all driving either for new teams or with an infusion of "new" money this year, all said they were pleased with their runs today, but Yarborough was definitely unhappy. He admitted that he was hampered by not being able to run his superspeedway car that had been damaged beyond repair.

"It (the car) just don't work good at all," he said. "We put a lot of work into our new car to run in the 500. Running our backup car is kind of like running a short-track car.

"It doesn't handle, run or cut through the wind like the other car. We got our work cut out."

The first 15 finishers today are guaranteed starting spots in the 500. They, position six on down, are: Marcis, Pontiac; Gant; Baker; Trevor, Chevrolet; Tommy Ellis, Chevrolet; Larry Pearson, Chevrolet; Bobby Hillin Jr., Chevrolet; Jim Sauter, Pontiac; and Pancho Carter, Ford.

"They must have put a time machine on this piece," said an ebullient Hillin, who also wrecked his '86 Miller American Buick in a Feb. 11 accident during practice when his engine blew. His Stavola Brothers crew worked around the clock on preparing an '85 Chevrolet, which the team had originally brought to Daytona to sell.

"They made it into '86 overnight," he said. "They put in the new rear window, painted it white and got Miller and all the associate sponsors on it. Just amazing!"

There were eight lead changes among five drivers and Earnhardt led twice for 33 laps. He completed the event in 48 minutes and 56 seconds at an average speed of 153.270 mph and won $22,000. ∎

ALTHOUGH HE WHIPPED THE COMPETITION, EARNHARDT FEARED ANOTHER LATE-LAP COLLAPSE THAT WOULD STEAL VICTORY FROM HIS GRASP.
DAVID CHOBAT PHOTO

Earnhardt **Whips Darlington** Field

It Was Earnhardt All The Way

By STEVE WAID

In the words of one down-home Southern boy, "This one was an old-fashioned fanny kicking."

Perhaps nothing could describe Dale Earnhardt's dominance of the TranSouth 500 NASCAR Winston Cup race at Darlington International Raceway better.

In a Childress/Wrangler Chevrolet Monte Carlo SS, which performed flawlessly, Earnhardt led a whopping 335 of the race's 367 laps to record his first victory of the season in convincing fashion. He became the sixth different winner of 1986 and, in doing so, maintained NASCAR's current streak of 11 different winners in 11 races on the elite stock car-racing tour.

Although it was Earnhardt who started the streak with his victory in the Goody's 500

last September in Martinsville, Va., the streak is still alive as it now simply dates back to Harry Gant's win in the Holly Farms 400 at North Wilkesboro, N.C., the week after the Martinsville event.

That probably means little to Earnhardt, whose win ended a more personal streak of frustrations, which had plagued him since the start of the year.

In many ways, he has been the dominant driver of the season, but late-race tactical errors and just plain running out of luck had robbed him of victory – until this event. In nearly every case, misfortune struck him with four or fewer laps remaining.

"We had that last caution with five laps left in the race (caused when Richard Petty hit the second-turn wall and was sent spinning

after being tagged by Bill Elliott). My boss, (Richard Childress) came on the radio and said, 'Oh, no, here's that three-lap deal bugging us again,'" said Earnhardt. "I said, 'Don't worry, we've got 'em covered.'"

Which was true for the entire day.

It was the type of domination some long-time Darlington observers said they hadn't seen since Fireball Roberts won the 1963 Southern 500, when he led every lap of a race run free of caution periods.

Earnhardt didn't lead every lap, but he was never passed for first place under the green flag. Save for the first five laps of the race, which were led by Tim Richmond, Earnhardt gave up his advantage only during caution periods.

"I don't recall when I've been able to lead almost a whole race and been the one to beat for the whole day,' said Earnhardt, whose victory today was the second of his career at the venerated 1.366-mile Darlington track. He won the 1982 TranSouth 500 while driving a Bud Moore-owned Ford Thunderbird.

"I've always had competitive cars in my Winston Cup career, but any time you beat this old track, come here as the man to beat and hold off the competition, you've done something."

Earnhardt took command after the fifth lap and proceeded to make shambles of the rest of the field. His only real concerns were avoiding any problems and maintaining his own comfortable – yet strong – pace.

"Well, I think every time I went into the

first turn I got sideways. Did you see that?" said the 34-year-old Earnhardt. "I remember once I lost it here trying to beat Cale (Yarborough) and Bill (Elliott) one time.

"Richard talked about slowing down the pace but, every time I did, I lost my line around the track. So, I decided to keep up the old pace all day."

Earnhardt's only sustained challenge came from Harry Gant, driver of the Skoal Bandit Chevrolet. Gant, who led only once for 10 laps, was in a position to contest the day's dominant driver midway through the race until an accident took him and third-place runner Ricky Rudd in the Moore/Motorcraft Ford out of contention.

Following the day's sixth of 11 caution periods on lap 202, caused when Tommy Ellis clobbered the fourth-turn wall in his Freelander Chevrolet, Gant moved into second place and was ready to pursue Earnhardt.

But just four laps later, Gant clipped Mark Stahl's Ford in the first turn and was turned sideways. Rudd, close behind, unavoidably T-boned Gant's car and thus the two strongest contenders were eliminated from the event.

"I had been watching Harry in my rear view mirror," said Earnhardt, whose win earned him $52,250. "I knew he had always run good at this race track. But I was going to set my own pace, no matter if he was behind me or ahead of me. When he and Ricky went out of the race, I knew then if I stayed cool and ran my own race, we'd have the day."

It then evolved that Bobby Allison moved into second place in his Stavola/Miller American Buick LaSabre, with Joe Ruttman third in the Bernstein/Quaker State Buick. But the lineup was shuffled following the ninth caution period, created when Morgan Shepherd hit the second-turn wall on lap 240 in his Beebe/Race Hill Farm Buick, ultimately eliminating Ruttman, who was also involved in the incident.

Waltrip, driving the Johnson/Budweiser Chevrolet, was the leader when the green flag flew on lap 245, but he surrendered it to Earnhardt just two laps later when he tapped the second-turn wall. He had been plagued by a rear-end problem that necessitated his crew to inject fresh supplies of grease during previous pit stops.

With 100 laps to go, Earnhardt had built a 7.88-second lead on Waltrip. By lap 300, that had expanded to 22.51 seconds and just eight laps later, Earnhardt passed third-place runner Neil Bonnett in a Johnson/Budweiser Chevrolet to make it just two cars – his and Waltrip's – on the lead lap.

Earnhardt's advantage remained the same until the 10th caution period and was bolstered

after Bobby Wawak spun his Superior Piping Buick in the third turn. Both Earnhardt and Waltrip took on four fresh tires but, when the green flag flew on lap 357, Earnhardt quickly pulled away. Only Petty's spin closed the gap.

"Darrell ran a good race but, if there hadn't been cautions, I would have lapped him," said Earnhardt. "I know he had rear-end problems and wasn't running as good as I was, but he ran a good race today."

"We gave it all we had, but it just wasn't enough," said Waltrip. "Dale ran a great race and deserved to win. I would like to thank my crew for doing a good job just to keep me in the race. We at least had a shot at winning the race.

"We used up all our buffed-in tires before my last stop and we had to use new tires. That tightened the car so much I didn't have any chance to run down Dale. I'm not sure we could have beaten him under any circumstances. He dominated the race from start to finish in a great performance.

"I'm just happy that we could run 500 miles and finish second," he said.

Waltrip retained his lead in the Winston Cup point standings with 1,000 points. Earnhardt, though, moved into second with 952.

"We are working for the Winston Cup championship," said Earnhardt, who won the title in 1980. "We are also looking for that half-season bonus ($150,000). We feel that, if we can continue to race good, either win or finish second or third every time we go out, we can do what we want."

Earnhardt, who has now led nearly half the laps run this year, beat Waltrip to the finish line by three car lengths – but the margin of victory wasn't really that close. Third place went to Allison, who was one lap in arrears. Bonnett took fourth place, one lap down, while Richmond was fifth, three laps down in the Hendrick/Folgers Chevrolet.

Sixth place went to Rusty Wallace in the Blue Max/AluGard Pontiac Grand Prix 2+2, also three laps down. Richard Petty finished seventh, three laps down in the STP Pontiac. Eighth place went to Elliott, five laps back in the Coors/Melling Ford, ninth to Kyle Petty, six laps down in the Wood Brothers/7-Eleven Ford and 10th place to Ken Schrader, 11 laps back in the Donlavey/Red Baron Ford.

Earnhardt won with an average speed of 128.994 mph and the race took three hours, 53 minutes and 11 seconds to complete. The 11 caution flags of the day slowed the race for 54 laps. ■

DATING BACK TO LAST SEASON, EARNHARDT IS THE 11TH DIFFERENT DRIVER TO WIN IN NASCAR WINSTON CUP RACING'S LAST 11 EVENTS.
DAVID CHOBAT PHOTO

FIRST UNION 400

FOR THE SECOND TIME IN AS MANY WEEKS, EARNHARDT EMERGED VICTORIOUS, SOLIDIFYING HIS STATUS AS THE HOTTEST DRIVER ON THE WINSTON CUP CIRCUIT.
DAVID CHOBAT PHOTO

Earnhardt Makes It
Two For Two

Earnhardt Prevails For Second Win

By STEVE WAID

The 1986 NASCAR Winston Cup season has been called "The Year Of Dale Earnhardt," and in the First Union 400 at North Wilkesboro Speedway, he gave ample evidence of that phrase.

Behind the wheel of his Childress/Wrangler Chevrolet Monte Carlo SS – which has been formidable at every race this year – Earnhardt raced to his second straight victory of the season and the first of his career in 16 starts on the 0.625-mile North Wilkesboro track.

He scored a two-car-length win over Ricky Rudd in the Moore/Motorcraft Ford Thunderbird to become the first two-time winner of the young season, which has gone seven races. Earnhardt was an easy winner

April 13 in the TranSouth 500 at Darlington (S.C.) International Raceway.

But at North Wilkesboro, the run to the checkered flag was considerably more difficult. Rudd, trying desperately to win his first race of the season pressed Earnhardt hard over the last 39 laps of the 400-lap race. He, in turn, was challenged for a time by the trio of Geoff Bodine in the Hendrick/Levi Garrett Chevrolet, Darrell Waltrip in the Johnson/Budweiser Chevrolet and Joe Ruttman in the Bernstein/Quaker State Buick LeSabre, who ultimately finished third through fifth, but nearly three seconds behind Earnhardt. "It was a hard race all day," admitted Earnhardt, a resident of Doolie, N.C., a community of Lake Norman. "But what made the difference was the last pit stop. The crew did a great job in getting

me out first, ahead of Ricky. Also, we had a good set of tires (matched correctly for stagger) on the car.

"I knew all I had to do was run the car smooth and I could stay ahead because the top five or six cars were so competitive, so close, that it was simply a matter of whoever the guy was in front, that's the guy you had to race."

Earnhardt, who led three times for 195 laps, was in third place when Rudd was afforded the lead on lap 251 – a lead he might well have kept had the race been completed caution-free. He stayed out on the track while the leaders pitted under the day's sixth caution, brought out when Willy T. Ribbs spun in his Red Roof Inns Chevrolet in the second turn.

Rudd held sway over second-place Bodine while Earnhardt stayed close in third place. Over 100 laps later, however, things changed.

Dave Marcis slammed into the second turn wall in his Helen Rae Special Chevrolet to bring out the day's eighth and final caution on lap 352. It was a caution that Rudd could ill afford. Until then, his only real concern had been retaining enough fuel to finish the race. But he, along with the rest of the leaders, pitted for four fresh tires and fuel. While Earnhardt darted out in first place, Rudd was hampered when an air wrench did not work properly, costing him valuable seconds in the pits. He did manage to come out behind Earnhardt, with Bodine, Bobby Allison in the Stavola/Miller American Buick, Ruttman and Waltrip in tow.

"When we got that last caution we were fortunate," said Earnhardt. "Before that, I had been racing with Bodine and was hoping that Ricky might not have enough gas to finish the race. The way things were then, I don't think there was any way I could have beaten him. And if he had gotten out first after that last stop, I still don't know if I could have beaten him.

"But when we got out first after the last caution, it helped me and hurt Ricky. He made a real dogfight out of it, but when you are in front of a guy, you can make him do things he doesn't want to while he's trying to catch you."

"We desperately need acceleration off the turns," said Rudd, who has now finished second twice this year, the first coming in the April 6 Valleydale 500 at Bristol, Tenn. "My car was running fairly well and handling great, but you can't win here unless you get off the corners.

"We had been making four-tire pit stops in 22 seconds all day until that last one, and that hurt us. Dale got the lead and I really overdrove it in the corners, hoping to get close to him and maybe give him a little 'Dale Earnhardt' in the rear bumper. But I couldn't do it."

On lap 377, Ruttman slid high in the fourth turn, which allowed Waltrip to take over fourth place. Waltrip, third place Bodine and Ruttman ran in a tight line but could make up no ground on Earnhardt and Rudd, who pushed away to a several-car-lengths lead and held it until the end of the race.

Earnhardt, who led the last 46 laps and earned $38,550, had been pegged as a race favorite because of his record this year. He was in a position to win both the Feb. 16 Daytona 500 and the Miller 400 a week later at Richmond, Va., until he ran out of gas and wrecked with Waltrip, respectively. In both cases, there were just three laps remaining.

He was also among the leaders at each succeeding event in Rockingham, N.C., Atlanta and Bristol until he finally overcame his late-race woes with his convincing win in the TranSouth 500, in which he led 335 of the 367 laps.

"I don't know that our team has the car to beat, but I do think that every time out we're capable of winning or at least finishing among the top five," said Earnhardt. "Our car has been competitive all year. It was our game plan to run more consistent, to lead laps and win races if we could.

"Dale got the lead and I really overdrove it in the corners, hoping to get close to him and maybe give him a little **'Dale Earnhardt' in the rear bumper.**"
—Ricky Rudd

"But above everything else, we wanted to be in a position to win the Winston Cup championship."

Earnhardt retained second place in the Winston Cup point standings. He has 1,137 points, just 23 fewer than the leader, Waltrip. Although he has yet to win in 1986, Waltrip has built his lead on consistently high finishes. He has not finished out of the top five in seven events this year. Further, he has completed 2,684 of a possible 2,687 laps.

Following Earnhardt, Rudd, Bodine, Waltrip and Ruttman was Allison in sixth place, with Harry Gant in seventh in the Skoal Bandit Chevrolet, Kyle Petty in eighth in the Wood Brothers/7-Eleven Ford and Elliott, ninth in the Coors/Melling Ford. Elliott was the last driver to complete all 400 laps. Rusty Wallace finished 10th, one lap back in the Blue Max/Alugard Pontiac Grand Prix 2+2.

Willy T. Ribbs, the first black driver to compete in a Winston Cup event since Randy Bethea in 1975, finished 22nd, 13

laps down, despite two spinouts.

Richard Petty, the 15-time North Wilkesboro winner who had stirred the allegiance of fans by qualifying in the No. 2 position, led 11 laps before faltering with a cut tire and then retired with engine failure after completing 131 laps. He finished 29th in the 30-car field in his STP Pontiac.

The attrition rate was low. Only six of the 30 drivers fell out. They were Petty, Trevor Boys (wreck), J.D. McDuffie (wreck), Terry Labonte (engine failure), Mike Waltrip (transmission) and Marcis.

The race took two hours, 49 minutes and 40 seconds to complete. The day's eight caution periods took up 70 laps, with two created when brief showers pelted the track. Earnhardt's winning average speed was 88.408 mph and he earned his victory in front of a record North Wilkesboro crowd announced at 29,500. ∎

IT WAS ANOTHER RUNAWAY EFFORT FOR THE NO. 3 WRANGLER CHEVROLET.
DAVID CHOBAT PHOTO

TERESA, DALE JR. AND ELDEST DAUGHTER KELLY DON'T MIND HANDLING THE DAY'S SPOILS.
DAVID CHOBAT PHOTO

dale earnhardt

SECOND PLACE FINISHER AND REGULAR TRACK RIVAL TIM RICHMOND CONGRATULATES EARNHARDT ON HIS THIRD WINSTON CUP WIN OF THE SEASON.
DAVID CHOBAT PHOTO

No. 3 Wins

Earnhardt Toughest
When It Counted

No. 3 Of The Season

By STEVE WAID

Dale Earnhardt usually wins races by attacking a speedway like a bull. But, in the Coca-Cola 600 at Charlotte Motor Speedway, he was more like a crafty fox.

Playing a sly waiting game with Coors/Melling Ford Thunderbird driver Bill Elliott, Earnhardt took the lead when Elliott had to pit for needed gasoline just 16 laps from the finish and then brought his Childress/Wrangler Chevrolet Monte Carlo SS home 1.59 seconds ahead of Tim Richmond in the Hendrick/Folgers Chevrolet.

It was the first Coca-Cola 600 victory of Earnhardt's career and his third of the season, as the Doolie, N.C., resident also won at Darlington, S.C., and North Wilkesboro, N.C., in April. He is the winningest NASCAR Winston Cup driver of the season to date.

But, it did not come easily on the 1.5-mile CMS track, Earnhardt's "home" speedway. Although he was one of a record 15 drivers to swap the lead 38 times, his presence wasn't felt until after his final pit stop on lap 336, when the leaders began a series of green-flag stops.

When they were completed, Earnhardt was 1.96 seconds behind Elliott – but there were a couple of significant differences. Earnhardt's Chevrolet had finally attained the balance of wedge and tire stagger his team had been seeking all day to improve its handling and everyone present knew that Elliott would have to stop for fuel one more time.

Because Elliott's Ford simply could not achieve the gas mileage afforded Earnhardt's Chevrolet, a final pit stop was inevitable. Elliott's only hope was that he could do it under caution.

But that was not to be. Therefore, all Earnhardt had to do was pace himself behind his rival and move into the lead when the opportunity arose.

"We made a good stop the last time," said Earnhardt, who earned $98,150 for his victory. "We filled the car up with gas and we knew that Bill had to make one more stop. Still, I kept the car loaded and ready. I wasn't playing with Bill, but I was content to run behind him.

"I didn't pressure the car. I was saving it and the tires and I felt I had enough left to get by Bill at the end if I had to."

By lap 349, Earnhardt had caught Elliott and rode his bumper until lap 384, when Elliott made the pit stop he had to make. He spent just 4.15 seconds off the track for a splash of fuel, but it sent him into fifth place, some 18 seconds behind Earnhardt.

"We just had to stop for fuel," said Elliott, who was seeking his first Winston Cup win of the season. "If we hadn't we would have been out of gas and we ran out twice in the

"Now that I have won,
it is my dream come true."
—Earnhardt
on winning the 600

race as it was. Our problem was that we kept the burned piston from the Talladega race (the May 4 Winston 500) in our mind and we jetted the engine a little richer than we usually would for here. We sacrificed a little horsepower for a little more conservative engine, which we hoped would run all the way.

"We needed a yellow flag there in the last 30 laps or so and I think we would have made life VERY interesting for those who finished the race ahead of us at the end."

After taking the lead from Elliott, Earnhardt's only task was to be wary of Richmond, who lurked less than two seconds behind. But Richmond, who started from the No. 2 position, couldn't make up any ground and ended up holding off Cale Yarborough in the Ranier/Hardee's Ford in a furious battle for the runner-up position, which Richmond won by a hood length.

"I knew he was there," said Earnhardt of Richmond. "I kept radioing back to the pits to find out his position. I felt I had enough to put the pressure on if he hooked up with someone and caught up with me."

"The track came to Dale at the end and I had to keep the rear end of my car hung out," said Richmond. "It wasn't the first time I've had one taken away from me here. I would have liked to have won."

Despite not winning, Richmond was one of the day's dominant drivers. He joined Harry Gant in the Skoal Bandit Chevrolet, Yarborough and Elliott as a potent front-runner. Each sped away from the remainder of the field during intervals of the race and, combined, they led 340 of 400 laps.

Earnhardt was not among them, leading just twice for 26 laps, including the all-important final 16.

"It was so important to get the right tire combinations and stagger here," he said. "The wedge (weight on either side of the car) and tires have to work together.

"I didn't feel at the start of the race that we had a shot at winning. We were running a higher gear than anyone else and I wasn't sure that's what we should have done. It was a decision between me and Richard (Childress, team owner).

"Halfway through the race, I still wasn't happy. But Kirk (Shelmerdine, crew chief) and Richard kept working with the stagger

and wedge and, with about 100 laps to go, I found the groove I needed.

"The track came to me, so to speak. The higher gear went to work. I could run high on the track and get the RPMs I needed. That's where I beat the others. They got loose in the corners and while I didn't beat them going in, by the time I got to the middle I got the power I needed."

Rainfall in the first and second turns brought out the day's sixth and final caution period on laps 267 to 276. Before the yellow flag, leader Yarborough and runner-up Richmond had built a commanding 10-second lead on the field and were in a position to put Earnhardt a lap down, since the eventual winner was no more than a half-straightaway ahead.

But the caution changed things. Elliott pitted early while Yarborough and Richmond opted for a four-tire change just two laps before the green flag flew. As a result, Elliott was in command for the next 54 laps. When he pitted on lap 327, Earnhardt took over for 10 laps, then pitted, giving Richmond the lead for two laps. Then Darrell Waltrip in the Johnson/Budweiser Chevrolet, led for one lap. The lead passed to Gant for a lap before Elliott took over for 44 more laps, giving the lead – and the win – to Earnhardt with 16 laps remaining.

The win was especially pleasing to Earnhardt, the son of former dirt-track and Late Model Sportsman great Ralph Earnhardt, who passed away in 1974.

"I can remember standing on a flatbed truck in the infield watching this race with my daddy," said Earnhardt, the 1979 NASCAR rookie of the year and 1980 Winston Cup champion. "I told him, 'Maybe someday you will win here,' and I always have

EARNHARDT IS ALL SMILES AFTER WINNING HIS FIRST COCA-COLA 600 ON HIS HOME TURF IN CHARLOTTE. DAVID CHOBAT PHOTO

CAR OWNER RICHARD CHILDRESS AND EARNHARDT SHARE THE SPOTLIGHT AND THE SUCCESS.
DAVID CHOBAT PHOTO

wished that he could have raced here with a competitive car because I think he could have won.

"But it was my dream to win here. I won the National 500 in 1980, and that was good but it wasn't the 600. Now that I have won, it is my dream come true."

Earnhardt, who now has 18 career victories and whose previous high finish in the Coca-Cola 600 was second to Bobby Allison in 1984, padded his Winston Cup points lead over Waltrip. He now has 1,767 points, 144 more than Waltrip, who has 1,623.

"It is a long way to the end of the season," said the 35-year-old Earnhardt. "Every race counts. We're fortunate in that we've been able to pick up bonus points for leading in every race and we've had good finishes. It's our goal to win races and win the championship for Richard Childress and his team."

Going into the Coca-Cola 600, two drivers, Allison and Geoff Bodine, were looking for victory and a $100,000 bonus from

R.J.R. Nabisco in its Winston Million program. The program awards the cash to any driver who can win two of the four selected events and $1 million to the competitor who wins three of them. The events are the Daytona 500, the Winston 500, the Coca-Cola 600 and the Southern 500. Bodine won the Daytona 500, and Allison the Winston 500. However, Bodine fell out of the Coca-Cola 600 with a broken camshaft after 319 laps to finish 31st and Allison came home 12th, two laps down.

With his win at Charlotte, Earnhardt becomes the third candidate for the $100,000 bonus when the Winston Cup series rolls into Darlington, S.C., for the Aug. 31 Southern 500.

Behind Earnhardt, Richmond and Yarborough came fourth-place Gant. Waltrip finished fifth with Elliott, who was the last driver to complete all 400 laps, sixth. Seventh place went to Sterling Marlin in the Ellington/Bull's Eye Chevrolet. Ricky Rudd took eighth

in the Moore/Motorcraft Ford. Morgan Shepherd was ninth in the Race Hill Farm Buick LeSabre and Rusty Wallace rounded out the top ten in the Blue Max/AluGard Pontiac Grand Prix 2+2.

Thirty-one of the field's 41 starters were running at the finish. Among those who fell out were David Pearson because of overheating and Benny Parsons, a victim of a broken shock mount. Greg Sacks retired after an accident and engine failure eliminated Richard Petty. Petty, whose STP Pontiac was rendered useless after an accident in practice on May 23 that gave him a concussion and kept him in a hospital overnight, drove D.K. Ulrich's Chevrolet and left after 123 laps. He finished 38th.

Next for the Winston Cup competitors is the June 1 Budweiser 400 at the 2.62-mile Riverside, Calif., road course. "We're going out there loaded for bear," said Earnhardt.

He was loaded in the Coca-Cola 600, also – when it counted. ∎

Steve Waid looks back on a special win for Dale Earnhardt in the Coca-Cola 600

There was no doubt that, at this point in time, the victory in the Coca-Cola 600 was the biggest in Earnhardt's career. It was achieved at his hometown track in front of his fans, friends and neighbors. He had already won at Charlotte in the fall of 1980. But the magnitude of the Coca-Cola 600, the longest race on the Winston Cup schedule and one of the circuit's premier events, made the triumph much more special.

Earnhardt would go on to win at Charlotte again in 1986, but six years would pass before he would win on the 1.5-mile track again. The Charlotte victory helped Earnhardt shift from the year's villain to its eventual Winston Cup champion.

In February of '86, Earnhardt found himself in the middle of a firestorm following the Miller High Life 400 at Richmond. With three laps remaining in the race on Richmond's half-mile oval, Darrell Waltrip was leading. Earnhardt, already considered a master on the short tracks, gave chase.

As the two headed into the third turn, Earnhardt clipped the right rear bumper of Waltrip's Chevrolet. That sent Waltrip headfirst into the steel guardrail. The wreck set off a chain reaction that involved four drivers on the lead lap. Only the fifth, Kyle Petty, was spared and he went on to win the race.

Waltrip was furious. "I haven't had a run-in with Earnhardt before," he said. "Everyone else has, so I guess he's not choosy."

> **"I haven't had a run-in with Earnhardt before,"** Waltrip said.

Junior Johnson, Waltrip's team owner, was more blunt. "What Earnhardt did was no different than if he had put a loaded gun to Darrell's head and pulled the trigger," he said.

NASCAR weighed in on Earnhardt, also. It fined him $5,000, put him on a year's probation and ordered him to post a $10,000 bond before he could compete on the Winston Cup circuit again.

The penalties were harsh. Earnhardt and team owner Richard Childress thought they were too harsh and appealed. After a hearing at the Charlotte airport, NASCAR reduced the fine to $3,000 and dropped the probation and bond.

Interestingly, Earnhardt showed up at the meeting with a "state of character" letter signed by at least 20 people in Winston Cup racing. All upheld Earnhardt's integrity.

But a letter wouldn't be enough to shift the perception shared by many that Earnhardt was overly aggressive and a potential on-track danger. It would take a clean slate and some significant achievements.

Four months and three victories later, Earnhardt remained No. 1 in Winston Cup points following the emotional Coca-Cola 600 triumph.

In October, Earnhardt again won at Charlotte, solidifying his hold on the points lead and further putting the Richmond incident into the past.

Earnhardt's fifth and final win of the 1986 campaign came at Atlanta in November. With it, he clinched his first Winston Cup championship with Childress, taking the title by nearly 300 points over archrival Waltrip.

Earnhardt had taken the points lead after the season's ninth race, at Talladega, and never relinquished it. ■

—Steve Waid
VP Editorial Development
NASCAR Scene and Illustrated

dale earnhardt

EARNHARDT PASSED TIM RICHMOND AND HARRY GANT TO ASSUME THE LEAD AT THE HALFWAY POINT (LAP 166), EARNING A $10,000 BONUS.
DAVID CHOBAT PHOTO

Earnhardt Makes It A Sweep
At Charlotte

Earnhardt Rallies For Big Win

By STEVE WAID

It was a championship performance and the ultimate reward may be just that – a championship.

Dale Earnhardt overcame adversity in the form of a two-lap deficit to the leaders in the Oakwood Homes 500's early stages and came back to win the race at Charlotte Motor Speedway. In doing so, Earnhardt tightened his grip on the NASCAR Winston Cup points lead, a grip that isn't likely to be loosened.

By winning his third event at Charlotte this season, and his second in a row following his triumph in the All Pro 300 Busch Series race on Oct. 4, Earnhardt picked up 37 points on Waltrip, the ninth-place finisher and his closest challenger for the championship.

Earnhardt now has 3,953 points to 3,794 for Waltrip, a difference of 159 points with just three races remaining in the 1986 campaign. All Earnhardt has to do is finish 10th in the trio of events and the championship will be his, regardless of what Waltrip does.

The victory gave Earnhardt, driver of the Childress/Wrangler Chevrolet Monte Carlo SS, a sweep of CMS Winston Cup events. He also won the Coca-Cola 600 in May (ironically, his last win prior to the Oakwood Homes 500), and his take from Charlotte events this year totals $255,095, including the $82,050 he won for this 334-lap race. That elevated his season winnings to $1,057,650, and he became only the fourth driver in auto racing to win more than $1 million during a single season.

But such accomplishments did not come easily. By lap 48, Earnhardt had fallen two laps in arrears to leader Tim Richmond after two unscheduled pit stops. The first came on lap 38 when Earnhardt suspected a tire had equalized. Running third at the time, he elected to pit and the first lap was lost. The equalized left-side tire was replaced, but Earnhardt still felt a vibration in his car. On lap 48, he pitted again and this time a cut right-rear tire was replaced, costing him a second lap.

"We had a left-front tire going down at first so I had to pit to get a tire," said Earnhardt. "Then we went back out and had a right-rear to go down. I think we cut down both tires at separate times.

"Concerned isn't the word. Worried is the word. That's what I was. Any time you fall behind so early in the race with so many cars out there, it's tough. It knocked the wind out of my sails.

"I was really discouraged.

"But what really discouraged me was that we've got a lot of great race fans who come to the races to enjoy what is going on. But there

"We need to weed out those fans

who choose to throw things on the track." —Earnhardt on can- and bottle-throwing fans.

are one or two who throw beer cans and bottles on the track. I saw more cans and bottles in the first turn today and that might have been a factor for me. I thought I was racing in the parking lot.

"We need to weed out those fans who choose to throw things on the track," said Earnhardt.

Fate has a way of being kind to those who are determined, which is exactly what Earnhardt and crew were.

On lap 84, on the restart from the day's third caution period, Earnhardt slipped around Benny Parsons' Jackson/Copenhagen Oldsmobile Delta 88 to make up one lap. His timing was perfect as a multi-car incident was triggered behind him, immediately bringing out the race's fourth caution flag.

"The circumstances were right," said Earnhardt, who now has won four times this year. "I had to be in the right position when I came out of the pits. I had to get out front and in the left lane. I was able to do that. Benny hadn't pitted and I could blow right by him.

"I didn't really want to see anything bad happen to the cars behind me, but when I saw the wreck, I knew I could beat Benny to the caution and get a lap back. That put a fire under me and the team."

Then, on lap 101, on a restart from that fourth caution, Earnhardt went past leader Geoff Bodine in the Hendrick/Levi Garrett Chevrolet to make up the last of his lost laps. He was still nearly a lap in arrears, however, and his chances at victory, while improved, didn't seem good.

"I had to work to get into position again but, this time, Geoff was much tougher to get by," said Earnhardt. "I had to work hard to get in front of him and get the second lap back."

Again, a caution period came to Earnhardt's rescue. On lap 119, Bobby Hillin and Bill Elliott got together at the fourth turn exit. The result was a battered Coors/Melling Ford Thunderbird for Elliott while Hillin's Stavola/Miller American Buick LaSabre slid down the frontstretch wall. The fifth caution flag of the day flew and Earnhardt was right back in the lead pack as he stayed ahead of

Bodine in the dash to the yellow flag.

By lap 166, Earnhardt got past Richmond to take the lead and was the leader at the halfway point of the 334-lap race, thereby earning one of four $10,000-lap bonuses available. He and Richmond began battling for the lead in earnest, swapping the lead three times until lap 191, when Earnhardt slipped and nearly clobbered the second-turn wall. Richmond, in the lead at the time, was able to greatly improve on it.

"Tim and I are competitive racers," said Earnhardt. "He is about as strong as I am when we are both in cars that can handle and run. What we were racing for at the start was the halfway bonus. Then he got under me and we started some really competitive racing.

"It was fun, and I got too involved in it. I got high in turns one and two and I thought I was in the wall. I don't know how I stayed out of it, but I did.

"When I did that, it brought me to my senses. He got ahead of me by eight car lengths and I thought to myself, 'Boy, you had better calm down and start thinking about the end of this race.'"

At first, that didn't seem to help. On lap 214, both Earnhardt and Richmond pitted under green, with Richmond taking on left-side tires and Earnhardt right-side rubber. That put Harry Gant, driver of the Skoal Bandit Chevrolet, into the lead for the first time in the race. He surrendered that to Bodine when he pitted on lap 221, and when Bodine pitted on lap 225, Richmond again assumed control.

Richmond held a comfortable lead and seemed well on his way to a seventh win this season. But it all ended abruptly on lap 266, when his Hendrick/Folgers Coffee Chevrolet slowed drastically on the backstretch and was retired.

"Basically, what happened was the car started losing power in turns one and two and finally it just let go," said Richmond. "At first, we thought it might have been the ignition."

Richmond, who led seven times for 123 laps, wound up in 27th place and, thus, his hopes for a first championship have been all but dashed. He remains in third place in the point standings, but he lost 88 points to Earnhardt and is 232 behind with 3,721 points.

After Richmond fell out, Gant took over. Looking for his first win of the '86 season, Gant held a healthy advantage of 6.23 seconds over Earnhardt. On lap 277, Gant was the last of the leaders to make a green-flag pit stop and, at that time, his lead was nearly a lap.

On lap 281, Bodine, who assumed the lead when Gant pitted, was cut off from his pits by the exiting Ford of Connie Saylor. He had to make another lap before pitting for

CHARLOTTE HAS BEEN GOOD TO ITS NATIVE SON IN '86. EARNHARDT TOOK BOTH EVENTS AT HOME THIS YEAR.
DAVID CHOBAT PHOTO

longest time ever before the race got over."

Earnhardt beat Gant by 1.9 seconds at the finish.

"We ran the same kind of laps Earnhardt did," said Gant, who finished a runner-up for the 27th time in his career. "But he was a little better than we were. The tires were the big thing, though. The car ran good today and everything was perfect. It sure feels good to finally be back up there. The team worked hard on the car but we just go beat."

Twenty-six of the race's 42 starters were running at the finish. Neil Bonnett, in one his strongest runs this season in the Johnson/Budweiser Chevrolet, finished third, one lap down to Earnhardt and Gant. Ricky Rudd finished fourth in the Moore/Motorcraft Ford, while Buddy Baker rounded out the top five in the Baker/Crisco Oldsmobile. Both were a lap down, too.

Bodine, Elliott, Rusty Wallace, Waltrip and Phil Parsons rounded out the top ten.

Among those eliminated from the field through mechanical failures and wrecks were Bobby Allison, A.J. Foyt, Cale Yarborough, Richard Petty, David Sosebee, Sterling Marlin, Morgan Shepherd, Tommy Ellis, Benny Parsons, Ken Schrader and Richmond.

Now, it appears, the championship race is down to two men – Earnhardt and Waltrip – and it is clear Earnhardt has the upper hand.

"To be honest, the odds might be on my side but it is fun racing against someone with the competitive spirit that Darrell has," said Earnhardt, who won with an average speed of 132.403 mph. "I don't think this is going to silence the man as far as the 'psych' game goes. But, it's not a matter of what you say, it's a matter of what happens on the race track.

"He had a good day at North Wilkesboro (N.C., where Waltrip won the Sept. 28 Holly Farms 400), where I had a bad day. I had a good day here and he had a bad day. He said I was talking to myself after the North Wilkesboro race, but I imagine he was talking to a lot of people after today.

"Our odds at winning the championship are better now, but we haven't clinched it," said Earnhardt. "We are working hard for Rockingham (N.C., site of the Oct 19 Nationwise 500). We are going to test down there. We ran well there earlier this year, but we seemed to fall off in the middle of the race and, now, we're going to see if we can't run all day long down there.

"When I won my first championship in 1980, I won at Charlotte. Now, I've won here again, twice, and maybe I can match that championship."

There's no denying he seems to be in the perfect place to do just that. ∎

four fresh tires and the result was more than a lap lost.

Afterward, Gant was again the leader and he was 4.23 seconds ahead of Earnhardt. But, this time, he would not hold his advantage.

Earnhardt steadily gained ground, running a very high groove around the 1.5-mile Charlotte track that allowed him to make up nearly three-tenths of a second per lap.

By lap 296, he had caught Gant and passed him on lap 297 to take the lead. He led the final 38 laps and for the race, led four times for 80 laps.

"I had waited until late in the race in May to run the high groove to catch (Bill) Elliott," said Earnhardt. "And when I saw Harry running up there, I figured I had to run up there too and see what I could do. I was close enough to him to see him slipping and sliding up there and I was able to get by him. After that, I thought it was the

DALE SHARES HIS SECOND POINTS CHAMPIONSHIP WITH HIS MOTHER, MARTHA.
DAVID CHOBAT PHOTO

The Year Belongs
To Earnhardt

Earnhardt Romp$ And A eaon I$ Won

By STEVE WAID

It was there for Dale Earnhardt's taking and take it he did – by the bushel.

Just about every major post-season award available in NASCAR Winston Cup racing fell into Earnhardt's hands after his imposing victory in the Atlanta Journal 500 at Atlanta International Raceway.

Unquestionably, the most significant of these was the 1986 Winston Cup championship, which Earnhardt officially clinched on lap 303 of the 328-lap race on the 1.522-mile AIR track. Entering the race with a lead of 144 points over rival Darrell Waltrip, Earnhardt was presented a golden opportunity to end the title war when the engine in Waltrip's Johnson/Budweiser Chevrolet Monte Carlo SS expired after just 83 laps.

Earnhardt seized his chance with a vengeance. In his typical style, which has been called everything from "aggressive" to "crazy," Earnhardt put his Childress/Wrangler Chevrolet at the point four times for 162 laps and mauled the field, finishing one lap and three seconds ahead of Richard Petty in the STP Pontiac Grand Prix 2+2. In doing so, Earnhardt established a track record average speed for a 500-mile race at AIR, coming home at 152.523 mph and bettering the old mark of 144.925 mph set by Benny Parsons in March of 1984.

With the convincing victory, Earnhardt became the first driver to clinch a Winston Cup championship before the last race of the season, the Winston Western 500 at Riverside, Calif., since 1978. In October of that year, Cale Yarborough won the Nationwise 500 at North Carolina Motor Speedway and thereby locked up the title by 424 points over Bobby Allison with two races remaining.

Earnhardt now goes to Riverside with an unbeatable 278-point pad over Waltrip (4,293-4,015). The margin is so great Earnhardt could choose not to enter that West Coast race and still retain the championship.

But, there's more.

Including the $67,000 he earned for winning the race, the bonus money from clinching both the Stewart Warner miles leader and True Value Hardware lap leader awards and the $716,000 in various contingency awards he will be presented for his championship, Earnhardt had an astonishing payday of $833,950.

It was Earnhardt's second championship and the first for his Winston-Salem, N.C., team owned by former "independent" driver Richard Childress. In 1980, while driving for Rod Osterlund in only his second full year on the Winston Cup circuit, Earnhardt won his first title.

"How could it have been more perfect?" said Earnhardt of his day. "Maybe if I had won the pole (taken by Dawsonville, Ga.'s Bill Elliott at a track record 172.905 mph), but then the Georgia fans wouldn't have liked it.

"Yes, it was bittersweet to see Darrell go out. It is always better, always more exciting to race for the championship. Darrell and Junior Johnson have been strong for several years, but Richard Childress and his team worked hard all year long. This year, I think they did the better job. Me, I just tried to do my part and it is the team that deserves all the praise for this championship.

"It was Richard's effort that built the team and put it in the position it is in today. Anytime you run an entire season without a lot of loose ends to tie, you have confidence and you know you are going to do well."

No one thought Earnhardt would not do well at Atlanta, but there was some question about a victory, particularly as the early stages of the race developed.

At that time, the race belonged to Harry Gant. Driving the Skoal Bandit Chevrolet and looking for his first win of the 1986 season, Gant took the lead on lap 67 when Waltrip pitted under the green. Gant was not obliged to follow since he had made a stop under the day's first caution period on lap 18. That proved to be beneficial because it put

EARNHARDT EMERGED FROM HIS WRANGLER CHEVROLET THE RACE WINNER IN ATLANTA, A TWO-TIME WINSTON CUP CHAMPION AND $833,950 RICHER.
DAVID CHOBAT PHOTO

him out of synch with the remainder of the field, which was constantly having to make green-flag stops since the race experienced only two caution flags for seven laps.

By the halfway point of the race, Gant had pushed his margin to nearly six seconds over second-place Tim Richmond in the Hendrick/Folgers Chevrolet, while Earnhardt ran third.

But Gant lost his advantage on lap 189, when Alan Kulwicki spun his Quincy's Ford Thunderbird in the fourth turn to bring out the second caution. Gant was forced to pit with the other leaders but came out in second place behind Earnhardt when the race resumed on lap 194.

"When you go out to kick ass... kick ass!"
—Earnhardt on being relentless.

From that point until the checkered flag, it was all Earnhardt. He continuously expanded his lead over Gant and third-place runner Morgan Shepherd in the Rahmoc/Nationwise Pontiac. Then the end came prematurely for both of his rivals.

Gant had begun backing up with a dropped cylinder and was forced to retire with engine failure on lap 285. Shepherd followed two laps later with the same malady. Therefore, the question was not would Earnhardt win but, rather, by how much. It was answered quickly. He led 135 of the final 138 laps.

"We were really whistlin' there for a while," said Gant. "We lost a cylinder and finally it blew. I actually warped a valve and she just blew."

"At the first of the race, Tim and Harry were running better than I was," said Earnhardt, a 35-year-old resident of Doolie, N.C. "On those green-flag stops we all had to make, Harry had us beat, but then things turned around when we got that second caution. It enabled us to change tires and get the right stagger on our car, which then became the car to beat."

It was on the 303rd lap that Earnhardt became the champion because, at that point, the worst disaster would have relegated him to 26th place – still good enough to beat Waltrip, who finished 39th, for the title.

"No, they didn't tell me on the radio that I had won the title," said Earnhardt, who won for the fifth time this season. "We just kept racing, trying to win the race. We didn't talk about being careful before the race, either. We just wanted to go out and do a good job. We knew we had to work hard and

be competitive in the pits and on the track. We had 500 miles of racing to think about.

"I didn't even see Darrell fall out. They did tell me on the radio that he had gone behind the wall. I said, 'Are you sure?' Then later, under a caution, I said, 'Is that No. 11 car still behind the wall?' They said, 'Yeah, he's even gone home.'

"I never backed off," he added. "I knew we couldn't break our stride. If you pull up on a horse, it wouldn't ride as good. If the car couldn't run the pace I wanted, I would have run its pace. But that wasn't necessary.

"When you go out to kick ass...kick ass."

After the demise of Gant and Shepherd, Neil Bonnett put his Johnson/Budweiser Chevrolet into second place. But he was in the midst of a gamble, attempting to complete the last 69 laps of the race without making a pit stop for gas.

He came up short as his fuel supply ran out with one lap remaining. That dropped him to sixth place, a lap down, and allowed Petty, who made a quick stop on lap 311 for fuel, to move into second place and thereby record his best finish since his triumph in the 1984 Firecracker 400 at Daytona Beach, Fla.

Petty, however, was a lap in arrears and so was Bill Elliott, who finished third in the Coors/Melling Ford. Richmond took fourth, while Buddy Baker put his Crisco Oldsmobile Delta 88 in fifth place. Both, too, were a lap down.

Rounding out the top 10 were Bonnett, Kyle Petty in the CITGO/7-Eleven Ford; Terry Labonte in the Hagan/Piedmont Airlines Oldsmobile; Joe Ruttman in the Bernstein/Quaker State Buick LaSabre; and Phil Parsons in the Jackson/Skoal Oldsmobile.

Other than Gant and Shepherd, drivers retiring with mechanical problems included Ron Bouchard, Geoff Bodine, Cale Yarborough, Dave Marcis, Sterling Marlin and Mark Martin.

For Earnhardt, the race victory and the championship culminated a season in which he had experienced great success, few failures and a measure of controversy. Accomplishing what he did before the last race of the season removed some pressure, to be sure, but it did not provide an immediate sense of relief.

"Relief?" said Earnhardt. "No, I don't feel relief. I feel excitement. Anytime you win anything you feel excitement."

And that leads to celebration.

"I imagine the team will do some celebrating later," Earnhardt said with a grin. "We had planned to go to Riverside to test. We won't now. So that means I'll celebrate by going deer hunting until the end of the week."

And then he will go to Riverside, where he will race simply to have fun. ∎

Atlanta Journal 500
ATLANTA RACEWAY

A First
For Earnhardt

Earnhardt A Model Of Perfection In Victory

By STEVE WAID

Going into the Goodwrench 500, Dale Earnhardt, surprisingly enough, had never won a NASCAR Winston Cup race at North Carolina Motor Speedway.

But when the checkered flag fell, that changed.

Oh, boy, did that change.

With his Childress/Wrangler Chevrolet Monte Carlo SS operating at peak efficiency, Earnhardt easily subdued his rivals and won the race by a dominating 11 seconds, or nearly a half-lap, over Ricky Rudd in the Moore/Motorcraft Ford Thunderbird.

In gaining his first NCMS Winston Cup win in 17 career starts, Earnhardt put on a characteristic display of consistency and power. He led 11 times for 319 of the event's 492 laps, including 155 of the last 165.

After starting 14th, he was in the lead by the 30th lap. Only during a series of green-flag pit stops between laps 216 and 221 did he fall out of the top five afterward. Earnhardt took the lead for the final time on lap 419, again following a series of green-flag stops, and was 7.16 seconds ahead of Rudd. He simply ran away from that point until the end of the four-hour, 15-minute and 23-second race.

Earnhardt's first Winston Cup triumph at NCMS was long overdue, but it seemed imminent given his and his team's record at other events on the 1.017-mile speedway. Earnhardt won the last two consecutive 200-mile Busch Series races at the track while his Kirk Shelmerdine-led crew captured the last two straight Unocal Pit Crew Championships.

"We were fortunate because we came down here to test last week," said the 35-year-old Earnhardt. "We were really pleased with the way we tested (he had posted the fastest unofficial speed) and we were pleased with the car when we practiced Thursday (Feb. 26), until I messed up in qualifying. I tried to go about five car lengths too deep in the first turn before I turned the car. The brain gears locked and the foot wouldn't come up.

"We had two days of rain to think about how I messed up. Kirk, Richard Childress (team owner) and I talked about what we needed in the chassis and we thought we were pretty close.

"Everything worked. It showed that the car was capable of running up front even though I screwed up in qualifying," he said.

Because his car was far stronger that its 14th-place time trial effort, Earnhardt decided to move to the front quickly.

"At the start of the race, the

ABOVE: EARNHARDT CAN NOW CROSS ANOTHER ITEM FROM HIS 'TO-DO' LIST. HE HAS NOW WON A WINSTON CUP RACE AT EACH OF THE TRACKS IN THE CAROLINAS.
DAVID CHOBAT PHOTO

LEFT: EARNHARDT BEAT HIS NEAREST COMPETITOR, RICKY RUDD, BY 11 SECONDS TO WIN THE GOODWRENCH 500.
DAVID CHOBAT PHOTO

track was green and my car seemed stronger than anyone else's, so I decided to run up front. I would impress my sponsors. Besides, you never know what can happen at this track and you need to get Winston Cup points any way you can."

Earnhardt dodged the many accidents – there were 10 caution flags for 55 laps – and began putting competitor after competitor a lap down.

But Neil Bonnett, driver of the Rahmoc/Valvoline Pontiac Grand Prix 2+2, showed some strength of his own and challenged Earnhardt for the lead by lap 146. He finally moved ahead on lap 191 and was to hold his edge until he pitted under green on lap 224.

That pit stop was costly. Out of gas, he overshot his pit area, stopping instead in the Childress team area.

The Childress/Wrangler crew, showing the consideration characteristic of the racing fraternity, dumped fuel into Bonnett's car, but he returned to the track a lap down. Later, he had to stop under green on lap 271 to replace two right-side tires, which cost him another lap.

But Bonnett made up both laps and came home in third place, one of only four drivers to complete all 492 laps. He passed Earnhardt on lap 338 to finally make up the lost distance.

"Boy, all I needed was another caution, but we never got it," said Bonnett. "Even when we lost the laps, I told the crew that we could still win the race, the car was that good. If we had any luck getting a last yellow flag, I think we could have."

Earnhardt wasn't so sure.

"Neil ran really strong," he said. "We were putting on the show there for a while. But I think that even with a late caution, I could've beaten them all. I had been running hard all day, but I wasn't driving the car as hard as it could run. I was just trying to be consistent. When Neil went by me, I didn't cut him off or run him into the infield.

"He was driving harder than I wanted and I thought I would let him go in case Rudd moved up and I had to race with him."

Rudd was unable to move up at all. In a final series of green-flag stops that began on lap 403, he was the first to pit and was running second at the time. His stop took 16.2 seconds. Three laps later, Earnhardt pitted – for right-side tires and gas, same as Rudd – and spent 15.5 seconds off the track. That gave him that much more of an edge over his challenger and the result was no challenge at all.

"I can't say enough about the team," said Earnhardt, who now has 21 career Winston

Cup wins. "They were the guys who got me out of the pits ahead of Rudd and that helped. It was one of the keys to winning."

Finishing behind Rudd and Bonnett in fourth place was Bill Elliott in the Coors/Melling Ford. Morgan Shepherd, making an outstanding run in the Bernstein/Quaker State Buick LaSabre, finished fifth, one lap down, while Rusty Wallace finished sixth, also one lap down, in the Blue Max/Kodiak Pontiac. Darrell Waltrip took seventh, two laps back, in the Hendrick/Tide Chevrolet.

> "To win on all the Carolinas tracks is something I've always wanted because they are my
> # home tracks."
> —Earnhardt

Finishing eighth was Terry Labonte in an ill-handling Johnson/Budweiser Chevrolet, ninth place went to Davey Allison in the Ranier-Lundy Ford and Ken Schrader rounded out the top 10 in the Donlavey/Red Baron Pizza Ford.

the same multi-car mishap on lap 81.

Engine failure put the Hendrick Motorsports cars of Benny Parsons and Geoff Bodine out of the race, which was the same fate for Harry Gant and Buddy Baker. Transmission problems eventually sidelined Cale Yarborough.

With his victory at NCMS, Earnhardt, a resident of Doolie, N.C., has now won Winston Cup events on all the Carolina tracks – North Wilkesboro and Charlotte, N.C., and Darlington, S.C. He joins racing legends Richard Petty, Yarborough, David Pearson, Bobby Allison, Waltrip, Bonnett and Fred Lorenzen as the only drivers to accomplish that feat.

"I knew with our team we could win anywhere," said Earnhardt, who won the Goodwrench 500 with an average speed of 117.556 mph. "But Rockingham was always one of the toughest places for us. We kept working and working at it, though.

"Today, I tried to ignore all the noises I heard in the car with 50-100 laps to go. I tried to watch for all the debris on the track. I tried to pass the lapped cars carefully.

"To win on all the Carolina tracks is something I've always wanted because they are my home tracks," he added. "And, I always wanted to win here because of its toughness. I remember coming here in 1979

AFTER A FAIRLY EASY DAY AT THE OFFICE, EARNHARDT CLOWNS AROUND DURING THE TROPHY PRESENTATION. DAVID CHOBAT PHOTO

A rash of accidents sidelined several cars. Among the victims were newcomers Jesse Samples Jr., Patrick Latimer and David Sosebee. Tommy Ellis, James Hylton and Ron Bouchard were also put out by wrecks, as was Dave Marcis. All were involved in

(his rookie season) with team owner Rod Osterlund and having all kinds of trouble. So, today means something special to me."

And it should because, in this year's Goodwrench 500, Dale Earnhardt was, indeed, something special. ∎

JUST A DAY EARLIER, EARNHARDT'S CHILDRESS/WRANGLER CHEVY WAS BADLY DAMAGED IN PRACTICE. THE TEAM WORKED THROUGH THE NIGHT AT A RICHMOND, VA., BODY SHOP TO GET THE CAR BACK TO THE TRACK.
DAVID CHOBAT PHOTO

Earnhardt Makes It
Two In A Row

Earnhardt Beats the Track That Nearly Beat Him

By GARY McCREDIE

In what may someday be labeled the "comeback" of the 1987 NASCAR Winston Cup season, the defending series champion took a Childress/Wrangler Chevrolet Monte Carlo SS that a day earlier had been badly mangled and destroyed the opposition to win the Miller High Life 400 at Richmond Fairgrounds Raceway.

Apparently, the Doolie, N.C., driver also struck back at a race track that had bitten him badly twice in the space of a year. In this race last year, Earnhardt tangled with Darrell Waltrip with three laps remaining while racing for the lead and both drivers crashed out of the event.

A day before this year's race, Earnhardt, who had qualified third, blasted the first-turn guard rail in a practice session accident that almost destroyed the Chevrolet. Instead of

going to a backup car, his team, under the direction of its owner, Richard Childress, and crew chief Kirk Shelmerdine, chose to repair it and took it to a race car shop in Richmond.

Aside from sheet metal damage and the destruction of suspension parts, the car's frame was also badly bent. But, somehow, the car was restored and returned to the speedway. The Childress crew had worked until 8 p.m. the day before the race getting the car ready.

Earnhardt then wasted little time in proving his machine's worth. First, while challenging Alan Kulwicki for the lead, he made contact with Kulwicki's Zerex Ford Thunderbird in turn four on lap eight and spun. Although no caution was displayed while Earnhardt straightened out, he lost the better part of a lap and spent much of the first 100 laps trying to make it up.

Then, in about the same spot on the 127th lap, Earnhardt made contact with

Harry Gant's Skoal Bandit Chevrolet. Gant was running second and Earnhardt again was challenging for position. That incident brought out the race's second caution flag and ended Gant's victory hopes.

Earnhardt then assumed the lead for the first time on lap 133, taking the No. 1 spot from Bobby Allison. He led through lap 145 and then four times more for 235 of 400 laps.

At the finish, Earnhardt was 0.57 second in front of Geoff Bodine's Hendrick/Levi Garrett Chevrolet. Rusty Wallace finished third in his Blue Max/Kodiak Pontiac Grand Prix 2+2, fourth was taken by Bill Elliott in the Coors/Melling Ford, and Terry Labonte, driving the Johnson/Budweiser Chevrolet, was fifth.

The victory was Earnhardt's 22nd in Winston Cup competition and the second this year. He won a week earlier at Rockingham, N.C.

"The guys on the crew worked awfully hard putting this car back together. It could have been a little better, but it was still better than everybody else's," said Earnhardt.

"Richard (Childress) said, 'I think we can fix this car and make it more competitive.' So I just kept working, but that's what racing's all about – making up ground. And I made up a lot of ground.

"Today is Kirk's (Shelmerdine) birthday so I thought I'd have to give him a little something. I didn't have any doubts the car was fixed. I was just wondering how it would do."

The event ran caution-free for the first 114 laps with the first 65 being led by pole winner Kulwicki. But, by the end of the afternoon, the yellow flag had been displayed a half-dozen times for 35 laps. Those incidents helped increase Earnhardt's chances of winning but, by the time he had taken the lead for the final time, it was clear his was the dominant car.

While Earnhardt denied the incident with Gant was entirely his fault, he did take the responsibility for the run-in with Kulwicki.

"I made a mistake there at first, racing with Alan, and then I spun the car out," he said. "Then I got to racing with Harry and I thought he knew I was there.

"I clipped him and I hate that it happened."

Gant countered, "Earnhardt is as blind as a bat. He ran all over me. I saw him in my rear view mirror, but I saw he was below me so I turned down low.

"I was in the dirt and he also went down there through the dirt and bam! He ran right across the dirt and into me."

"Maybe I was (blind)," said Earnhardt. "We did bump when I hit that dirt."

After Gant dropped out with a broken rear end on his Chevrolet, Earnhardt went nearly unchallenged. However, two drivers, Darrell Waltrip and Elliott, did each mount short challenges.

After the third caution came out on lap 145 – the result of a 10 car crash on the front straightaway – Waltrip put the Hendrick/Tide Chevrolet into the lead on the next lap. He led through lap 168 but was passed by Earnhardt as they came out of turn four.

But Waltrip's car befell the same fate as Gant's. Its rear end began smoking and throwing oil and Waltrip pitted the car on lap 340. After being black-flagged once and then pitting three more times, he went behind the wall for good on lap 351 and finished 20th.

"I hate he had trouble, and I looked forward to giving the fans what they missed last year," said Earnhardt of Waltrip's demise. "They're (Waltrip's team) having problems, but they'll get it together."

Elliott's challenge to Earnhardt came on lap 224 when he took the lead from the Wrangler driver on the backstretch. That lasted through lap 231 and then Earnhardt resumed the lead.

"Earnhardt is as
blind as a bat.
He ran all over me."
—Harry Gant

"Ol' Bill got in there and raced and rubbed," said Earnhardt. "But I thought my car would work better (than Elliott's) on hot tires – and sure enough, it did."

While Bodine was not one of the race's seven lap leaders, he said he was somewhat pleased with the way the event went for him. He noted that his engine worked well, he managed to stay away from the accidents, and the car performed well, even though its chassis setup was off.

the caution flag came out the next time on lap 209 when Davey Allison spun between turns three and four. A two-car accident involving Neil Bonnett and Jerry Crammer slowed things for a fifth time on lap 326, while the last caution occurred on the 357th lap because of a spin by Eddie Bierschwale in turn three.

And, just as Earnhardt was heading toward the start-finish line on the last lap, Ken Schrader looped his car, also in turn three, causing Bobby Hillin Jr., to spin, and the event ended under the yellow and checkered flags.

"I haven't seen anybody lately who could total out of a car and get it fixed at the track," said Earnhardt, who won a Richmond record of $49,150 and also assumed the lead in the Winston Cup points. "It's hard to do without all your tools.

"They did a heck of a job, though. I just didn't think they could fix a car at a track and it would be competitive.

"I was going to get in there and dig, but I wasn't 100 percent sure until I got in, sat down in that car and ran a lap."

Kulwicki finished sixth, the last car on the lead lap. Following him in, seventh through ninth, respectively, and all a lap down were:

EARNHARDT IS HAPPY TO HAVE WON, BUT GIVES THE CREDIT FOR THIS ONE TO HIS TEAM AND OFFERS THE WIN UP AS A BIRTHDAY PRESENT FOR CREW CHIEF KIRK SHELMERDINE.
DAVID CHOBAT PHOTO

"We got behind for a while at the start because the car was tight, but in the middle of the race we made some adjustments and it ran much better," he said. "This was a different car than we have run here in the past and we are happy with it.

"We thought it would be hot, but it was cool and that meant our setup was a bit off. That hurt us, especially on the restarts.

"All in all, it was a very good day."

Following the multicar melee on lap 145,

Kyle Petty, Wood Brothers/Citgo Ford (the race's defending champion); David Marcis, Helen Rae/Lifebuoy Chevrolet; and Bobby Allison, Stavola/Miller American Buick LaSabre. Benny Parsons, in a badly mangled Hendrick/Folgers Chevrolet, was 10th, two laps off the pace.

Earnhardt completed the race in two hours, 39 minutes and 34 seconds at an average speed of 81.520 mph in front of a reported record Richmond crowd of 30,000. ∎

Mark Up No. 3
Of Year For No. 3

Last Gas(p) Means Victory For Earnhardt

By STEVE WAID

Although he had the dominant car in the race, it was a failed gamble on the part of Bill Elliott that allowed Dale Earnhardt to take home the chips in the TranSouth 500 NASCAR Winston Cup race at Darlington International Raceway.

Taking what they felt was their only chance at victory, Elliott and his Coors/Melling team stretched the limits of their Ford Thunderbird's fuel capacity in hopes of holding off a charging Earnhardt.

But on the 367th, and last, lap their hopes were dashed. Elliott ran out of fuel in the third turn, about

> **EARNHARDT HAD THE DOMINANT CAR IN THE TRANSOUTH 500, BUT NEEDED BILL ELLIOTT TO RUN OUT OF GAS IN THE THIRD TURN OF THE FINAL LAP TO TAKE THE CHECKERED FLAG.**
> DAVID CHOBAT PHOTO

a quarter-mile from the checkered flag, and Earnhardt sped by between turns three and four to take his second consecutive TranSouth 500 victory. That tied him with David Pearson (1972-73) and Richard Petty (1966-67) as the only drivers to win the event in successive years.

It was Earnhardt's third victory of the season and it solidified his No. 1 spot in the Winston Cup point standings. The defending Winston Cup champion became only the third man to win a Darlington race with a last-lap pass, as was done by Lee Roy Yarbrough over Pearson in the 1969 Southern 500 and by Darrell Waltrip over Petty in the 1979 TranSouth 500.

"It turned out the way I wanted, but the circumstances…well, we were just lucky, fortunate, whatever," said the 35-year-old Earnhardt. "Bill ran out of gas, we dodged all those wrecks. I wrecked myself and I still won the race. Man, that is tough to do."

But Earnhardt, the driver of the Childress/Wrangler Chevrolet, has proven equally tough this season. Once again, he dominated the event by leading eight times for 238 laps. In four of the last seven races contested on superspeedway ovals, dating back to 1986, Earnhardt has emerged the winner. Five times in the last seven races, he has led more laps than any other competitor.

But, even with his power, it seemed he was doomed to a runner-up finish. The day's final caution period created the scenario. Bobby Hillin Jr., spun his Stavola/Miller

EARNHARDT WAS ALONE UP FRONT FOR 238 OF 367 LAPS.
DAVID CHOBAT PHOTO

American Buick LaSabre into the second turn wall and was then clipped by Cale Yarborough's Hardee's Oldsmobile Delta 88 to bring out the 10th yellow flag of the day.

Leading at the time, Earnhardt and the remainder of the frontrunners pitted for tires and gasoline. Elliott made his stop with 73 laps remaining and, according to his brother and crew chief Ernie Elliott, the Ford could go 71.8 miles on a tank of gas. Others would be cutting it equally close on fuel consumption.

Earnhardt whisked by Ken Schrader's Donlavey/Red Baron Pizza Ford to retake the lead on lap 299 and steadily increased his margin from there. He built up a 12-second lead over Elliott, who took second place from Schrader on lap 355, when he suddenly dove into the pits for what everyone knew would be a stop for a splash of fuel. He made the move on lap 357, just 10 laps from the finish, and the stop took 3.69 seconds.

"I was going down the backstretch and saw the fuel gauge bobble," said Earnhardt. "I radioed, 'Boys, I'm coming in.'"

"We knew that if we went on, we would run out of gas, probably on the last lap," said Richard Childress, Earnhardt's team owner. "We almost knew exactly where we'd run out of gas, either on the backstretch or the frontstretch. We knew Elliott was going to make the gamble and it would be close if we stopped.

"But we learned a real expensive lesson at Daytona a year ago (when Earnhardt ran short of fuel chasing eventual winner Geoff Bodine)."

Given the precious drops of gas, Earnhardt began the chase of Schrader and leader Elliott, who was nearly four seconds ahead. On lap 362, he passed Schrader to move into second place. Then, one lap later, disaster struck.

Elliott got bogged down in between the first and second turns by slower cars and it appeared Earnhardt had a golden opportunity to catch and pass his rival. But as he drove into the first turn, his Chevrolet slid into the wall. Earnhardt did not spin out and managed to keep going, but it seemed his chances at victory were as severely damaged as his car.

"I saw Bill get slowed down and in my exuberance I forgot to slow down in the turn," said Earnhardt. "I hit the hell out of the wall. It messed up the toe-in and it got the fenders to rubbing against the tires.

"I wrecked myself and

I still won the race.

Man, that is tough to do."
—Earnhardt

"Drive your passenger car as fast as you can backwards and you get the feeling of what it's like driving with the toe-in knocked out.

"My heart fell to my shoes. But I knew I still had a chance to win because Elliott might run out of gas. I climbed back on the steering wheel and drove it as hard as I could."

Earnhardt's effort was rewarded on the last lap. Elliott slowed down going into the third turn, obviously out of gas. Then, midway between turns three and four, Earnhardt flew by and took the victory by three seconds.

"The sun came back out when he ran out of gas," said Earnhardt, whose victory was worth $52,985. "I knew there was that

chance so I was still after it even though the car was bent up. If I had given up and just run around, I probably would have lost.

"When I went by Bill, I thought, 'I wonder what he might do?' Who knows? He might have pinched me into the wall. All I know is it is a strange feeling to be out there knowing some guy is going to pass you and there isn't a thing you can do about it. Or is there? Whatever happened, I was ready. I would have dodged up or down."

Elliott, winner of this year's Daytona 500, said that he took the only possible course of action.

"We did the only thing we could do," said the driver from Dawsonville, Ga. "With the way Earnhardt was running, that's the only way you could have beaten him. He was just playing with us. We ran out of gas on the last lap and I don't even know where he passed us."

"Bill was in turn three and said over the radio, 'That's it, I'm out of gas,'" said Coors/Melling chassis specialist Ivan Baldwin. "He drove a helluva race – smart race."

The race was marred by a series of multi-car accidents that took out several of the competitors. The most serious occurred on lap 145 and involved six cars. It was created when Benny Parsons' Hendrick/Folgers Chevrolet broke loose in the third turn and slammed into the wall, sending cars spinning behind it.

Involved were the cars of Morgan Shepherd, Lake Speed, Greg Sacks, Ricky Rudd and Terry Labonte. Labonte suffered a broken right scapula in the incident and was kept overnight at McLeod Medical Center in Florence, S.C. It is expected to take as long as six weeks for him to recover, which means that his Johnson/Budweiser team will most

EARNHARDT STAYED OUT OF TROUBLE AND RAN IN THE LEAD TO WIN HIS THIRD OF THE SEASON.
DAVID CHOBAT PHOTO

likely have to find a substitute driver for the next few events.

On lap 216, Davey Allison's Ranier/Havoline Ford hit the wall between turns three and four and collected his father Bobby's Stavola/Miller American Buick in the process. When Davey Allison's car cut through the infield guardrail, its fuel cell erupted and a frightening fire ensued. Both Allisons escaped injury, however. The resulting caution period was lengthy due to repairs on the rail.

Perhaps no one offered a stronger challenge to Earnhardt than Buddy Baker, driver of the Crisco Oldsmobile. For much of the race, he was the only driver who could keep pace with Earnhardt and, in fact, led three times for 51 laps. But on lap 250, while lead-

ing, Baker lost control of his car in the fourth turn and slammed into the wall, which eventually put him out of the race.

"Buddy was tough," admitted Earnhardt. "If he had been around at the end of the race, he would have been the one to beat. But, even though they have repaved this track, it is still Darlington. You have to concentrate all the time.

"The track rose up and bit Buddy and when I let my guard down, it bit me, too."

Finishing third behind Earnhardt and Elliott with a strong performance was Richard Petty in the STP Pontiac Grand Prix 2+2. Sterling Marlin turned his best finish in '87 by finishing fourth in the Hagan/Piedmont Airlines Oldsmobile. Schrader came home fifth while Neil Bonnett was the last driver to

complete all 367 laps and finished sixth in the Rahmoc/Valvoline Pontiac.

Rounding out the top 10 were Harry Gant, Ron Bouchard, Phil Parsons and Darrell Waltrip. All were a lap in arrears.

Earnhardt, who won with an average speed of 122.540 mph, credited his crew for his strong performances in 1987, which have put him atop the Winston Cup point standings by 71 points (840-769) over Elliott.

"For the last several races, Kirk Shelmerdine (crew chief) and the guys have got this car working for Dale Earnhardt," he said. "They have done the work and right now, man, I'm telling you they are pumped up. They are ready to race again right now."

And don't bet that, if they did, they wouldn't win. ∎

Earnhardt Is Now
Earnhardt Makes Fourth Win Look Easy

Four-For-Six
in '87

By STEVE WAID

EARNHARDT TAKES THE TROPHY FOR THE FOURTH TIME IN SIX EVENTS THIS SEASON. DAVID CHOBAT PHOTO

In another display of power and finesse, Dale Earnhardt humbled the field in winning the First Union 400 NASCAR Winston Cup race at North Wilkesboro Speedway.

In what has become commonplace this season, Earnhardt led more laps than any of his rivals to win – get this – for the fourth time in six races.

Seemingly unbeatable, the driver from Doolie, N.C., led 319 of the 400 laps on the 0.625-mile track and crossed the finish line a comfortable 1.72 seconds ahead of Kyle Petty's Wood Brothers/Citgo Ford Thunderbird.

In the Childress/Wrangler Chevrolet Monte Carlo SS that has led 60.45 percent of the laps run in '87 (1,322 of 2,187), Earnhardt won the First Union 400 for the second straight time. The defending Winston Cup champion became the first man to do that since Darrell Waltrip accomplished that feat in 1982-83. For his career, Earnhardt has earned $213,265 in 17 starts at North Wilkesboro.

"This is the same car we ran at Richmond (Va., site of his victory in the Miller High Life 400), and it just repeated itself," said the 35-year-old Earnhardt. "Now, I know I have confidence in it and the guys on the team. But it amazes me how good and consistent our cars run.

"If I keep my head on straight and the car does what it is supposed to do, we will have a great season."

It's a great one already. In fact, Earnhardt, with just a tad more luck, could have won all six races staged in '87. A bad pit stop put him out of the hunt in the season-opening Daytona 500 (he finished fifth) and a failed alternator relegated him to 16th place in the Motorcraft 500 at Atlanta.

Unlike his exciting victory in the March 29 TranSouth 500 at Darlington, S.C., where he overwhelmed a helpless Bill Elliott, who had run out of gas on the last lap, this one was easy. Very easy. Only caution flags kept Earnhardt from lapping the entire field.

He snatched the lead away from Elliott's pole-winning Coors/Melling Ford on lap 11 just as Bobby Hillin Jr., brought out the day's first caution when his Stavola/Miller American Buick LeSabre smacked the third-turn wall. He was in command for the rest of the event, giving up his advantage only during pit stops under caution. Earnhardt was never passed under green.

By lap 180, he began to mow down the competition like a thresher. He lapped Morgan Shepherd on lap 180, Ken Schrader on lap 181, Bobby Allison on lap 185 and Elliott on lap 187, leaving just seven cars on the lead lap with less than half the race completed.

On lap 190, Earnhardt held a 9.67-second lead over a strong Petty – and he kept putting the competition a lap down. Rusty Wallace was his victim on lap 196 and by lap 203, he had put Kyle's father, Richard, a lap in arrears. Harry Gant was next on lap 221 and, by then, there were just four cars on the lead lap. At that point, Earnhardt was just 4.11 seconds away from passing them, too.

But, when Geoff Bodine's oil leak brought out the sixth caution on lap 241, his chance was foiled.

On lap 259, a multicar accident brought out the seventh of the race's eight caution flags for 54 laps. Involved in the melee between turns three and four were Buddy Baker, Mike Waltrip, Shepherd and Larry Pearson. Earnhardt took the opportunity to pit for gasoline only, as did the younger Petty.

That put Neil Bonnett, driver of the Rahmoc/Valvoline Pontiac Grand Prix 2+2, into the lead when the green flag flew on lap 267. Alan Kulwicki was running second in the Zerex Ford and Earnhardt emerged in third place, followed by Petty.

On lap 267, Earnhardt passed Kulwicki and then began his chase of Bonnett. By lap 316, after a sometimes spirited battle, he found the inside line out of the fourth turn

and got by, trading some body paint with Bonnett in the process.

"I got to battling with Neil and the car got loose," said Earnhardt. "I passed him and that allowed me to run my pace again. The car then started working again."

That was bad news for everyone else. Earnhardt would not surrender his lead for the remainder of the race, even during pit stops under the eighth caution on laps 367-373.

When the race restarted for the last time, Earnhardt and Petty broke away from third-place Bonnett, who found himself boxed in by lapped cars. Earnhardt's margin over Petty wasn't great, just 0.52 second, but he kept expanding it, which obviously gave Petty little chance to challenge.

> "If I keep my head on straight and the car does what it is supposed to do,
> **we will have a great season."**
> —Earnhardt

"When I was trying to get around Neil, I knew we could go all the way without having to stop," said Earnhardt. "I felt Neil had to stop. But I still wanted to get around him so I could return to my easy pace and I wasn't sure how strong Kyle could be."

"I was pleased," said Petty. "We set the stagger and adjusted the wedge as the race went on and I thought we had a real good shot at it. But Dale was just a little bit more than we could handle."

"I was ticked with the way we ran," said Bonnett, who had to hold off a charging Kulwicki for third place. "But the last set of tires, well, I could hardly steer the car. But I'm not complaining. Yeah, me and Earnhardt scrapped a little bit and if I'd been just a bit faster, I might have been able to put a little blue stuff (paint) on him."

Kulwicki's fourth-place finish matched his best in Winston Cup competition, having done the same at Martinsville, Va., last year. During the race's first caution period, John Junk, his crew chief, was struck by a tire reportedly flung from Elliott's car and was taken by ambulance to Wilkes General Hospital, where he was treated for abrasions and released.

Fifth place went to Ricky Rudd, one lap back in the Moore/Motorcraft Ford.

Richard Petty was sixth, also a lap down, in the STP Pontiac, while Phil Parsons took seventh in the Jackson/Copenhagen Oldsmobile Delta 88.

The record shows that Terry Labonte finished eighth in the Johnson/Budweiser Chevrolet, but it was a young Brett Bodine who did the driving as a replacement for Labonte, who has been sidelined by a broken right shoulder blade. Labonte took the parade lap in the car before giving it to Bodine, who had to start at the rear of the field. In an impressive performance, Bodine brought the car home only two laps down – and in one piece.

Ninth place went to Rusty Wallace in the Blue Max/Kodiak Pontiac, while Elliott rounded out the top 10.

The attrition rate was low, as 25 of the 32 cars which started the race were running at the finish.

Earnhardt, who won $44,675 (and has now earned $298,155 for the season), has led the most laps in the last five consecutive Winston Cup events and in six of the last eight, dating back to 1986.

"The confidence level I have in the team has as much to do with that as anything," he said. "Nothing slows us down. We work hard every week. I try to be consistent on the track and we try to keep the car consistent. We work hard. There's no lollygagging.

"We fixed up the car from Darlington and went to test at Bristol (Tenn., site of the April 12 Valleydale 500).

"The way we feel right now, we always look forward to the next race. We wish Bristol was tomorrow."

Earnhardt's torrid victory pace is ahead of Elliott's in 1985, when the Dawsonville, Ga., driver set a modern-day record of 11 superspeedway victories. Through the first six events of that year, Elliott won three times.

"It is going to be tough to win 11 times," said Earnhardt. "It would be tough for anyone to do. There's a lot of competition out there and it is going to get stronger as the year goes on. Neil and his team are going to get better. So are Darrell and his team. And there are a lot of others who are going to get their act together.

"I think we'll be stronger, too. We would like to win 12 to 15 times. That's what we are going to try to do. Our philosophy is to win, not to finish.

"Me? I enjoy myself when I'm in a race car."

That seems obvious. Earnhardt, incidentally, wears a special cap which bears the words, "Top Gun."

Right now, that is exactly what he is. ∎

dale earnhardt

ON LAP 388, EARNHARDT TAKES THE LEAD FROM MORGAN SHEPHERD AS THE TWO CARS EXIT TURN FOUR. DAVID CHOBAT PHOTO

Red-Hot
Earnhardt Scorches 'Em Again

For Earnhardt, It's Five And Counting

By GARY McCREDIE

The Valleydale Meats 500 NASCAR Winston Cup event at Bristol International Raceway was named appropriately – almost.

Considering what Dale Earnhardt did to the rest of the 30-car field – and what he and many fellow competitors inflicted upon one another – the "Mincemeat 500" might have been a better designation.

Earnhardt, driver of the Childress/Wrangler Chevrolet Monte Carlo SS, led the event three times for 134 laps, including the last 115 and cruised to a 0.78 second victory over Richard Petty's second-place STP Pontiac Grand Prix 2+2.

One of the "hottest" drivers to emerge in Winston Cup racing in recent years, Earnhardt now has won five of this season's seven races. That statistic breaks the old record for single-season consecutive victories – four of the year's first seven – set by Petty in 1975.

Races at this 0.533-mile short track with 33-degree banking in the corners are usually rough on drivers and equipment. This event was especially so, as there were 125 yellow-flag laps, a record for Bristol, eclipsing the old mark of 105 set in the 1974 July event.

But on to Earnhardt, who now has been victorious in seven of his last 11 races. He was one of 11 drivers who shared the lead 19 times. He led for the first time on laps 59-70 and again on lap 253, just before a caution. Then on the 377th lap he overcame Geoff Bodine's Hendrick/Levi Garrett Chevrolet for second place coming out of the second turn and a lap later took the lead from Morgan Shepherd, in the Bernstein/Quaker Stake Buick LeSabre, as they exited turn four.

Just after the day's 11th yellow-flag (laps 385-388), with Earnhardt still in the lead, the event's complexion had seen one of its many changes. Bill Elliott, in the Coors/Melling Ford Thunderbird (in one of his best-ever short-track efforts), was second but was losing ground to Earnhardt.

On lap 410, there was a 1.79-second gap between the two cars. Two laps later it was 2.04 seconds, it stretched to 2.73 seconds by lap 422 and on lap 426, Earnhardt had a 3.5-second lead.

Two more yellow flags again mixed up the order behind Earnhardt and, when the checkered flag finally fell on the decimated field, the defending Winston Cup champion had another win to his credit. Ricky Rudd finished third in the Moore/Motorcraft Ford, Elliott was fourth and last year's rookie of the year, Alan Kulwicki, was fifth in the Zerex Ford.

Pole winner Harry Gant was sixth in the Skoal Bandit Chevrolet and Kyle Petty, driving the Wood Brothers/Citgo Ford, finished seventh, the last driver to complete all 500 laps.

During the race, there was a chain of events that involved Earnhardt and created a bit of controversy – controversy that had almost 90 minutes to germinate.

In his first season, driving the Piedmont Airlines Oldsmobile Delta 88 for owner Billy Hagan, Sterling Marlin "came alive" in this event. He took the lead on lap 198 while the race was under another caution flag (starting on lap 196), held it through a subsequent yellow-flag period (commencing on lap 214), and by the 250th lap was just inches in front of Earnhardt.

On lap 253, as Marlin charged down the frontstretch and dove into the first corner, Earnhardt touched Marlin's left-rear corner, sending the blue Oldsmobile spinning and crashing. Also involved were Ken Schrader's Donlavey/Red Baron Frozen Pizza Ford and Bodine.

The incident brought out the day's 10th yellow flag and knocked Marlin out of the event. Then, on lap 265 at 3:13 p.m., the race was stopped because of rain and did not resume until more than one hour and 28 minutes had elapsed.

"I was racing behind Sterling for several laps before Geoff caught up," said Earnhardt. "I got under Sterling several times before he chopped me off.

"We just sort of closed up and went sideways, or whatever, there. Geoff hit me; it was an accident."

Marlin and his teammates were irate and blamed Earnhardt for the wreck. Bodine, on the other hand, said he was the cause.

"First of all, there was a lapped car up there," said Marlin. "If he (Earnhardt) had been up beside me it might have been different, but he hit me from behind and spun me.

"I'm the leader of the race and it's my track. He has to pass me, not spin me out."

"If that's what it takes to be the national champion, they can have it," said Wayne King, Marlin's team co-owner. "Sure, that's what I want to say and you can use it, too, or I wouldn't be saying it. I'd like to see a little stronger language. That's at least three cars I know today he has run all over."

"I guess I caused that wreck," added Bodine. "I had pulled up behind the No. 3 (Earnhardt) and was doing my best to get around him. He knew that and just threw his hands up in the air, indicating there was no place for him to go or there was nothing he could do.

"I guess he (Earnhardt) just got frustrated. He knew I was about to pass him, so I guess he just got a little impatient."

The race was a difficult one for many drivers, including Earnhardt. He took the lead away from Dave Marcis on lap 59 but on the 70th circuit slowed noticeably. He made an unscheduled pit stop on lap 71 and after 11.9 seconds emerged one lap down.

The culprit was a flat right-side tire.

> "I'm the leader of the race and **it's my track.** He has to pass me, not spin me out."
> —Sterling Marlin on Earnhardt's nudge that forced him from the lead and race.

"We ran a comfortable race as long as we had an open race track," said Earnhardt. "Richard (Petty) would run a little bit and catch up with us, but it tickled me to see him behind me. He's had his troubles in the past.

"We cut a tire down but, once we got our lap back, we ran a good pace. It was a pretty tough pace all day but, once I got back out front, I could run the car where I wanted to.

"Kirk (Shelmerdine, crew chief) and the boys in the pits did a good job. They made it look easy for me," he said.

It was the high number of caution flags that came to Earnhardt's aid. The field went under the yellow on lap 75 and back to green on lap 82. Three laps later, the race was slowed again and, when that caution period ended on lap 88, Earnhardt was back on the lead lap.

Although he was at the end of the field, he was in front of race leader Elliott, and it was there that the strength of his Wrangler

TERESA HELPS DALE CELEBRATE HIS FIFTH WIN IN JUST SEVEN EVENTS. DAVID CHOBAT PHOTO

Chevrolet became evident. Earnhardt increased the distance between himself and Elliott by more than a second in less than eight laps.

Following the lengthy rain delay, it looked as though Earnhardt was pacing both himself and his machine. He made no immediate move toward the front and seemed content to slowly edge his way forward.

Kyle Petty led laps 256-306, Elliott led the next 38 times around the speedway and Shepherd became the leader on lap 345.

"I was running my own pace," said Earnhardt once again. "One thing, after it rains, it washes the rubber off the track and you've got a green track.

"So, I started to run a higher groove."

Earnhardt has been praised by some for his hard-charging style, while others have criticized him for being too "enthusiastic." For whatever reason, it was announced in the press box during the rain delay by a NASCAR official that, if the driver exhibited "any more overly aggressive driving," it would result in a black flag and a "visit" from Winston Cup Director Dick Beaty to account for this "wayward ways."

Earnhardt denied knowing he might be faced with such a chat and said he took a nap during the stop-race period.

"As far as NASCAR coming to my team, you'll have to ask (car owner) Richard Childress about that," he said. "This is Bristol and you've got to be aggressive. You've got to be ready for contact.

"Bad things can happen to you here and God forbid something should happen to anybody. We've been lucky fixing things and getting back in it. If that race car is around at the end, I think it will win.

"I got into that deal with Sterling and that was no fun – sitting in seventh place. But our team just got stronger all the time. Several things happened to our advantage.

"It's not always going to be easy," said Earnhardt. "It was not easy today."

Thirty drivers began the race and, while 19 finished, many of their cars were dented and banged up. Filling in spots eight through 10 were Shepherd and Brett Bodine (driving relief for Terry Labonte) in the Johnson/Budweiser Chevrolet, both a lap down, and Dale Jarrett in the Freelander Chevrolet, three laps back.

Earnhardt completed the race in three hours and 31 minutes at an average speed of 75.621 mph and won $43,850. The 185 Winston Cup points he earned increased his lead in the chase toward another championship to 127 over Elliott, who now has 1,078 to Earnhardt's 1,205. ∎

SOVRAN BANK 500

EARNHARDT TAKES THE CHECKERED FLAG, WINNING HIS SIXTH WINSTON CUP EVENT OF THE SEASON IN A RACE THAT WAS IN THE HANDS OF GEOFF BODINE UNTIL A LATE-RACE SPIN.
DAVID CHOBAT PHOTO

Earnhardt–And Lady Luck –Do it Again

A 'Lucky' Day For
Dale At Martinsville

By GARY McCREDIE

Not too many people can define the word luck, but everybody in NASCAR Winston Cup racing certainly knows what it is – especially Dale Earnhardt and Geoff Bodine.

With victory in the Sovran Bank 500 NASCAR Winston Cup race at the 0.526-mile Martinsville Speedway firmly in his grasp, Bodine, in the Hendrick/Levi Garrett Chevrolet Monte Carlo SS, continued to put distance between himself and Earnhardt's Childress/Wrangler Chevrolet as the event wound to an end.

Bodine, winless since last May at Dover, Del., took the lead on lap 368 while the field was under the last of 11 caution flags for 65 laps. Once back on the track, he found it relatively free of traffic because of the attrition rate and this made pulling away from Earnhardt a bit easier. On lap 441, Bodine had a 4.5-second lead on Earnhardt; it was 4.9 seconds on the 450th lap and 20 circuits later, he was almost five full seconds – a full straightaway – ahead of his rival.

Then, on lap 484, Bodine came up on the Wood Brothers/Citgo Ford Thunderbird of Kyle Petty in the first corner. Petty was hugging the inside apron and Bodine attempted to move around him.

The two cars made contact. Petty got squirrely but managed to keep control. But Bodine spun around and ended up backing onto the infield grass. No caution flag was thrown, but the incident paved the way for Earnhardt's 26th career victory, his third at Martinsville, and a record sixth in the year's first eight races.

Reportedly, no one, at least in the modern-day history of Winston Cup racing, has won even six of a year's first 10 events.

"If you can't have a little luck, you can't win and maybe luck smiled on us," said Earnhardt. "I think that was all luck right there.

"I didn't want to wish anyone back luck, but...I couldn't believe what happened."

Neither could Bodine. It was the second time in two races at the picturesque southern Virginia short track that he had been deprived of an almost certain win. In last fall's Goody's 500, he exited the pits late on the last stop due to a miscue and lost the race to Rusty Wallace.

"I don't know what to tell you. What happened really hasn't sunk in," said Bodine. "You're leading the race with 20 laps to go and spin out down there.

"I try to tell myself it's all right, but I'm still hurting. I don't know what happened down there and I kind of wish they had thrown a caution so we could catch back up."

Earnhardt was one of seven drivers who

led the 500-lap race, pacing the field five times for 156 laps, more than anyone. He took control for the first time on lap 55, again on lap 127, a third time on the 256th lap, for a fourth occasion on lap 353 and for the last time on that critical 484th circuit.

However, following the last restart on lap 470, Earnhardt's car was by no means as strong as it had been. He attributed that to hard racing with Wallace, the two cars were so close that Earnhardt's bumped the track's inside curbing, thus disturbing its toe-in (front end alignment).

"For a little while it helped the car, but then it got loose," said Earnhardt. "But, if we had new tires on it, I think I could have done something with him. Bodine was leading and I couldn't do anything with him. He had us beat and I couldn't just drive off and beat him.

"They said a car had spun in (turns) one and two and when I got there I saw it was Bodine. I thought there would be a caution, but Richard (Childress, team owner) got on the radio and said, 'C'mon, let's go. There's no caution.'"

Earnhardt was a comfortable 2.73 seconds ahead of Wallace's Blue Max/Kodiak Pontiac Grand Prix 2+2 at the finish. Then came Bodine, followed by Phil Parsons in the Jackson/Copenhagen Oldsmobile Delta 88 (his best career finish in 81 races), while Terry Labonte was fifth, two laps down in the Johnson/Budweiser Chevrolet.

It had rained the two days before the race and practice time was all but eliminated. So, as a safety precaution, 10 "pre-race" laps were run before the green flag was waved. The first caution came out on the seventh lap, not because of an accident or debris on the track, but so the field could slow and the drivers could check the condition of their cars' brakes.

The second caution, however, was something of a prelude to the Bodine-Petty incident. Morgan Shepherd, who had won the pole in the Bernstein/Quaker State Buick LaSabre, led from the first lap and was in command on the 34th.

He then came upon Jimmy Means' Pontiac in about the same spot that saw Bodine and Petty later collide. His car and Means' came together. At the time, Means was racing the Pontiac of Steve Christman for position.

The yellow flag was displayed several times more for a series of spins (two separate flags came out because of Bodine and Phil Parsons). But the dozen drivers who failed to finish were actually the victims of mechanical malfunctions.

Bodine led once for 116 straight laps, Bill Elliott, seemingly getting stronger on the circuit's short tracks, paced things three times for 66 laps, and Wallace also led three times for three laps less than Elliott. Also going to the front were Harry Gant, once for 20 laps and Darrell Waltrip (one time for 45 laps), in his best showing yet in the Hendrick/Tide Chevrolet.

> Earnhardt, the circuit's defending champion and a **hero to his fans,** has been criticized by others for supposed "overly aggressive" driving.

In the end, though, it was Earnhardt again.

"Ain't none of them easy and you have to work hard and do the best you can," said the winner. "I felt that Darrell, Geoff, Rusty and some of the others would be the ones to beat because of their experience here."

Earnhardt had said a bit earlier in the year that, once certain teams began to "gel," it would make it harder for him to continue his current dominance.

For Wallace, it was a matter of tire wear. He said that the pace set by Earnhardt late in the event was almost too torrid for his Pontiac and, once his tires began to heat up, he would lose ground.

"We needed a caution," said Wallace. "I would run hard to catch Earnhardt, but I'd run so hard I'd wear the tires out.

"I would have to back off to cool them down and then try again."

Earnhardt said again that circumstances did play a major role in his win. Had Bodine not run into trouble, he most likely would have been in victory lane and not the Wrangler team driver.

"I don't think I could have caught him. I was running the car as hard as I could and he was running a comfortable pace," said Earnhardt.

"But we still gave it all we could."

That was not the case earlier in the event, though. Although Earnhardt led twice in the first half, he seemed to be in no rush to charge to the front, as he's done in several other events this year.

"All through the race I ran a smooth, conservative pace," he said. "I didn't have to run hard.

"Rusty wanted to lead one time, so I let him lead. Darrell wanted to lead and I let

MISS WINSTON IS GETTING USED TO MEETING EARNHARDT IN VICTORY LANE THIS SEASON. DAVID CHOBAT PHOTO

him. I was going to run as hard as I could the last 50 or 100 laps, but I was running my own race and saving my brakes."

Earnhardt, the circuit's defending champion and a hero to his fans, has been criticized by others for supposed "overly aggressive" driving. After he was involved in a couple of on-track incidents at Bristol, Tenn., on April 12, he was warned by NASCAR that its officials would be eyeing his tactics a bit closer than they had been.

"What NASCAR said, I took to heart," he said. "They sit down and talk to you when they get 215 letters from people who don't like how you race.

"But, I didn't have any problems with anybody and I feel like a winner.

"I guess we're having one of them Junior Johnson-Waltrip seasons. Waltrip could be a lap down and still come back to win a race."

Waltrip, in six seasons with Johnson, won 43 races and three championships. Today, however, he dropped out with engine failure after running 360 laps.

Elliott finished sixth, two laps down, as was seventh-place finisher Ken Schrader in the Donlavey/Red Baron Frozen Pizza Ford. Bobby Allison was eighth, three laps back, in the Stavola/Miller American Buick, ninth-place finisher Neil Bonnett completed 496 claps in the Rahmoc/Valvoline Pontiac, and 10th went to Mike Waltrip in the Sadler-Bahre Racing Pontiac. He completed 495 laps.

Earnhardt continued to pad his Winston Cup points lead and now has 157 more than runner up Elliott – 1,390 to 1,233. Bonnett moved into third place, while Richard Petty dropped to fourth.

Earnhardt won in front of a packed house. An estimated 40,000 spectators watched him win in three hours, 36 minutes and 44 seconds at an average speed of 72.808 mph. ■

AFTER A WILD DAY ON AND OFF THE TRACK, EARNHARDT BECAME THE THIRD DIFFERENT WINNER IN THE THREE-YEAR HISTORY OF THE WINSTON.
DAVID CHOBAT PHOTO

It's Earnhardt In The Wild Winston

Earnhardt Wins Amid Controversial Finish

By STEVE WAID

They wanted a shootout in the third annual running of The Winston. They got it. And an argument or two. And some blown tempers. And a fistfight. And a lot more.

In a wham, bam, controversial 10-lap dash finish, Dale Earnhardt spectacularly avoided disaster and withstood the rage of his rivals to record the victory worth $200,000 at the 1.5 mile Charlotte Motor Speedway. In doing so, Earnhardt became the third different winner in the three-year history of the event and spoiled what had been the perfect dominance of Bill Elliott, who humbled the field in the first two segments of the special race by leading 121 of the 125 laps therein.

So, it came as no surprise that Elliott was frustrated after his loss but, beyond that, he was furious with what he felt were Earnhardt's unsportsmanlike, and dangerous, tactics en route to the victory.

The scenario:

The first segment of the event, which ran 75 laps, ended with just three men, Elliott in the Coors/Melling Ford Thunderbird, Geoff Bodine in the Hendrick/Levi Garrett Chevrolet Monte Carlo SS, and Kyle Petty in the Wood Brothers/Citgo Ford, sharing the lead. Elliott led 71 of those 75 laps.

Segment Two: It began after a 10-minute delay during which time all 20 teams in the event made NASCAR-legal alterations to their cars. Nearly all did while Elliott took on four tires and patiently awaited the green flag. No other work was done to his car.

The race resumed and, again, Elliott dominated, if that is a strong enough word. He led all 50 laps of the segment and, when it ended, Earnhardt was running second.

Then came the ten-lap trophy dash. Under the new format of The Winston, these ten laps must be run under green. Cautions do not count. It's what everyone had been waiting for.

Elliott started on the pole, with Bodine second and Petty third – they are the only race leaders, hence they received the top three starting spots. Earnhardt is in fourth. On the start of the first lap, Bodine jumped to a quick start and nudged ahead of Elliott. But, going into the second turn, Bodine's Chevrolet turned sideways after contact with Elliott's Ford. Bodine looped his car and, remarkably, no one made contact.

But, as that happened, Earnhardt, who had moved into third, shot to the inside and found himself all alone in the lead. The complexion of the race changed dramatically.

Even so, it marks the first episode that Elliott will later recall as another disreputable Earnhardt driving tactic.

The caution was displayed and Bodine made a pit stop to change tires. Elliott recovered from the mishap suitably enough to run second to Earnhardt and give chase. There's no doubt he has enough strength in his car, but Earnhardt's team has made enough adjustments to his during the two ten-minute stops to ensure that it, too, is stout.

Elliott immediately rode Earnhardt's rear bumper. Just seven laps from the finish, it becomes clear the war is for real. Coming out of the fourth turn, their cars make contact and Earnhardt is sent into the infield grass at the front trioval. In a remarkable display of driving talent, Earnhardt keeps the car on a straight line through a 150-foot plowing job and roars back onto the asphalt, holding his advantage. But, as he later explained, his hackles were up.

One lap later. As the duo raced into the third turn, Elliott came to the outside of Earnhardt. Clearly displeased with what transpired earlier, Earnhardt squeezed Elliott to the wall. He claimed he never made contact. Elliott said otherwise and allowed that it was at this point Earnhardt's maneuver crumpled the left-rear fender onto the tire. The damage was sufficient to cut the tire, resulting in its demise just a lap later.

While the two drivers indulged in this episode, Terry Labonte snaked into the lead in his Johnson/Budweiser Chevrolet. But his advantage did not last long. Earnhardt roared past by the time the field raced into the first turn. He went on to win by 0.74 second. Elliott, after a pit stop to change tires, came home 14th.

But that was far from the end of it. On the final lap, Elliott's Ford limped around the track like a crippled soldier. As Earnhardt raced toward the checkered flag, an obvious winner over Labonte, he closed in on the Coors/Melling Ford. Suddenly, on the backstretch, Elliott's car found life and sped toward the finish line.

Then, on the "cool-down" lap, Elliott's displeasure became obvious. He blocked Earnhardt coming out of the first turn. On the backstretch, he turned toward Earnhardt, on the outside, and forced him to hit the brakes so hard smoke billowed from the tires. He cut his rival off at the entrance to pit road and then, at the entrance to the garage area, he once again turned toward Earnhardt and forced him to move to the outside of pit road.

This was done in the presence of the Wrangler crew, who, ironically, pitted just one space away from Elliott's team. Words

were exchanged; fists shook.

It wasn't over. In the garage area, Kyle Petty and Rusty Wallace, driver of the Blue Max/Kodiak Grand Prix 2+2, exchanged blows and were separated by Richard Petty, Kyle's father.

The final rundown showed that behind Earnhardt and Labonte, Tim Richmond finished third in his first race in the Hendrick/Folgers Chevrolet since being felled by double pneumonia in December. Bodine wound up fourth, with Wallace fifth, Kyle Petty sixth, Morgan Shepherd seventh in the Bernstein/Quaker State Buick LaSabre, Bobby Allison eighth in the Stavola/Miller American Buick, Darrell Waltrip ninth in the Hendrick/Tide Chevrolet and Benny Parsons tenth in the Jackson/Copenhagen Oldsmobile Delta 88.

Elliott earned $110,150 for his day's work, $100,000 of which came in leader bonuses through the race's first two segments. He stood to pocket $300,000 with a victory.

> "The aggressiveness has gotten out of hand. This is not Saturday night wrestling. I've been to Talladega, Daytona and everywhere else and I'm beat up by the same guy."
> —Bill Elliott

His side of the tale:
"It really got started (on the final 10 laps) at the start. The pace car didn't get out of the way quickly enough. Geoff got a good start but the pace car was in my way and I couldn't keep up. When we got to the corner, Earnhardt got in front of me and he turned left on me. He hit me. I don't know what happened with Bodine, whether he cut down on me or what, but the next thing I know we are both spinning all of a sudden.

"A lot of things are going on when the green flag drops. I don't know exactly what happened, but it was a situation that never should have happened.

"Then we went into the fourth turn and Earnhardt turned left on me and tried to run me through the grass. I did what I could to keep us both off the grass and wrecking. Then the next thing, well, when a man pulls alongside you and tries to run you into the wall, that's pretty obvious. I had the position. He let me get alongside him and then turned

into me. That's when the tire was cut. It crumpled the left fender onto the tire and a couple of laps later it blew. You look at the tape. He hit me several times. The fans saw it. You saw it.

"Yes, when the race was over, I was still ticked off. I admit it. If a man has to run over you to beat you, it's time to stop. I'm sick of it. Everyone knows his style. I am sick and tired of it. If that is what it takes to be the Winston Cup champion, I don't want it.

"The aggressiveness has gotten out of hand. This is not Saturday night wrestling. I've been to Talladega, Daytona and everywhere else and I'm beat up by the same guy.

"Yes, I'm frustrated. My car worked good here. It ran good. I think that was obvious. If you had a car that ran that good only to have it all taken away from you the way it was, how would you feel?

"I think that more than racing, he discredits his sponsor and himself. But I have nothing to say to him. If that is the way he wants to win races, then I hope he wins 1,000 of them. He'll be doing it all on Saturday nights."

With his victory, Earnhardt laid claim to wins in the last four Charlotte events. He swept both the Coca-Cola and the Oakwood Homes 500 in Winston Cup competition last year and won the fall All-Pro 300 Busch Series race. For his career, he has won $709,748 in Winston Cup competition at CMS and $885,673 overall. In the last 12 months, the total is $380,200 for Winston Cup racing, $455,095 overall.

His comments after The Winston:
"Bodine and Elliott wrecked in the first turn. I guess Bodine chopped down on him and turned him around, but all I know is that I didn't touch anybody. I guess it was reflexes. I checked up and I started to move where I thought they wouldn't be. I decided to go to the bottom of the track and I was by myself. I don't know why they threw the caution flag. No one was stopped.

"Then, as we came into the trioval two laps later, Elliott got under me and clipped me sideways. I almost got the car started the other way before I went into the grass and then I was able to get it right while I was in it. If I hadn't, I might have gone right up into the flagstand right there with Harold Kinder (flagman). I can guarantee you that, if I had turned someone side-ways like that, I would be hanging from the flagpole right now.

"I wasn't upset earlier, but that got me upset.

"On the next lap, he got alongside me on the outside and I took him up the track, but I never touched him. That's when Labonte got by and I knew then I had to race him.

"Bill got frustrated. Look, if I had done

DESPITE ALMOST COMING TO POST-RACE BLOWS WITH BILL ELLIOTT'S CREW, TEAM CHILDRESS IS ALL SMILES IN VICTORY LANE. DAVID CHOBAT PHOTO

what he had through the first two segments of the race only to lose in the last 10 laps, I would be frustrated, too. He waited on me after the checkered flag and then tried to run me into the wall. That was very unsportsmanlike. After that, I tried to stay away from him. I motioned my crew to stay away from his. This between me and Bill. Not between Ernie (Elliott's brother and crew chief) or anyone else. No one else was on the track.

"I'm not mad at Elliott. I know he was frustrated. If he wants to carry this on, then we will. I will stand flatfooted against him."

Said Cecil Gordon, the former driver who serves as the shop foreman for the Wrangler team owned by Richard Childress: "All you have to do is print what you saw. We've taken the heat from NASCAR at Bristol (Tenn.) and Richmond (Va.) and to have what happened after the race was over, well

NASCAR has to do something about it."

Elliott agreed, but in a different way: "I think the only way to stop this is to start fining points. Take them away in cases like this."

NASCAR officials, who stated in the pre-race drivers' meeting that no protests would be allowed since The Winston was a special event that awarded no points, said that they would study videotapes of the final 10 laps and, if needed, make a determination of disciplinary action within a few days.

Elliott won the pole for the event with a track record of 170.827 mph, posted in time trials on May 16. That bettered the one-lap mark of 169.252 mph set by Richmond last October. Richmond was second in qualifying with a

lap of 170.23 mph in the Hendrick/Folgers Chevrolet, while Davey Allison was the third man to beat the record with a lap of 169.274 mph in the Ranier/Havoline Ford.

For the record, Earnhardt now has won seven of the 10 events staged this season, although The Winston has no part in the Winston Cup championship and is not listed as an official event as such. He won with an average speed of 153.023 mph. The race had only one official caution flag, thrown when Neil Bonnett and Richard Petty collided in the fourth turn on lap 64. Bonnett, taken to Cabarrus Memorial Hospital for treatment, was released with water on his elbow and right knee. His arm was placed in a sling. ∎

Earnhardt Powers Way To Seventh

By STEVE WAID

Earnhardt Has Old Form And A New Deal

It seemed only fitting that Dale Earnhardt once again displayed the form which has made him the most dominant driver of the 1987 NASCAR Winston Cup season. Perhaps there couldn't have been a better time.

After all, two nights before he won the Miller American 400 at Michigan International Speedway for his seventh victory in 14 races this season, Earnhardt and his Richard Childress Racing team signed a two-year sponsorship contract, with a year's option, with Mr. Goodwrench. A division of General Motors, Mr. Goodwrench will replace Wrangler as the team's sponsor. Wrangler has been with Earnhardt since the inception of the 1980 season, during which he won his first Winston Cup title.

The contract, worth a reported $2.2 million, means the formidable Earnhardt-Childress combination will be intact for at least the next two years. And, judging from how well things have gone for it in the Winston Cup championship in 1986 and now in '87, that can't be good news for the opposition.

On the two-mile Michigan track, Earnhardt was definitely bad news for his rivals. He led 152 of the race's 200 laps but, more important, he kept his sputtering Chevrolet Monte Carlo SS ahead of Davey Allison's charging Ranier/Havoline Ford Thunderbird in the closing laps to earn his first MIS and 27th career victory.

Only by caution periods and pit stops did the field manage to catch Earnhardt, who built a huge lead early in the race and seemed to hold it at will. However, when the day's fifth and final yellow flag came out on lap 185, things changed dramatically. Earnhardt remained on the track while his challengers pitted. Among them were Allison, Kyle Petty, Bobby Hillin Jr., Rusty Wallace and Tim Richmond.

When the green flag restarted the race on lap 189, Petty ran second to Earnhardt with Allison third. One lap later, Allison passed Petty for second and began chasing Earnhardt.

In three laps, Allison's deficit to Earnhardt went from 0.62 second to 0.28 second. While the Ranier/Havoline Ford was strong, Earnhardt's Chevrolet began experiencing a fuel system problem that caused the engine to "flutter" down the straights.

"I really started to pick up the pace with about 15 laps to go," said Earnhardt, whose victory was worth $60,250. "I started to push the car harder than I had earlier in the race. But then it developed a fuel problem of some sort. About halfway down the straights, I saw the fuel pressure fluctuate.

Earnhardt has an insurmountable 304-point lead over Elliott in the point standings (2,314-2,010).

"I wondered if there was a problem in the fuel pickup so I would run low on the track to keep the fuel on the right side. That helped some, but it was obvious that things were getting worse.

"Davey was strong. He was catching me. I was running smooth, but I started going into the corners harder. But, the car was getting worse every lap. Yes, if there had been another lap or two left in the race, he would have passed me. But it was the end of the race," he said.

And, so it was. When Earnhardt took the checkered flag, he was just one second ahead of Allison, who, in turn, was just a few car lengths ahead of Petty's Wood Brothers/Citgo Ford.

"I'm happy with second," said rookie Allison, who already has won twice this year and seems destined for the '87 Champion/Sears rookie title. "We thought we were catching up all day after we got behind on a couple of pit stops.

"The car worked best at the end and I thought I had the fastest car on the track."

Allison made a last-ditch attempt to get by Earnhardt on the final lap. He took the high route into the fourth turn and actually pulled alongside Earnhardt, but had to let up to avoid trouble.

"I got alongside Dale at the end, but I had gone into the corner too hard and I couldn't steer out of it," Allison said. "I had to back off a bit. I did that because I knew Dale would never give up the inside. I got where I wanted to be on the outside, but the car pushed, and he beat me to the line."

Few observers could have thought the race would end the way it did. Earnhardt was poised for a rout.

It began after his first pit stop under caution on lap 34, brought on when H.B. Bailey spun in turn two. After a change of tires, Earnhardt, who had been running third, wasted little time in taking the lead. On lap 38, when the green flag flew, he shot by Ken Schrader's Donlavey/Red Baron Frozen Pizza Ford to move into the lead for the first time.

"We had to start the race on the tires we qualified on," explained Earnhardt, who started from the No. 5 spot. "Those were very loose. We had planned all along to get them off and, when we did, we had a different combination on the car and we knew it would pick us up.

"The stagger stayed very consistent all day. When we changed left-side tires, it got a bit looser than I wanted and that's about the time I was racing with Richmond out there, even though I thought I had a little more than he had.

"We had been working hard on getting better tire combinations up here and it paid off."

Bill Elliott, driver of the Coors/Melling Ford, who had won the last four straight events at MIS, passed Rick Wilson's Kodiak Oldsmobile Delta 88 to take second on lap 49. The man many considered to be the odds-on favorite to win for a fifth straight time could do nothing to catch Earnhardt, however.

In fact, he lost distance lap by lap. By the time Earnhardt had pitted on lap 79, he had an 11-second pad over Elliott. By lap 84, when all the leaders had completed routine

dale

HAVING WON
SEVEN RACES
THIS YEAR,
EARNHARDT
NEEDS A NEW
'TROPHY POSE'.
DAVID CHOBAT
PHOTO

EARNHARDT, JUST A DAY REMOVED FROM SIGNING A NEW SPONSORSHIP AGREEMENT WITH MR. GOODWRENCH, WINS ONE MORE FOR WRANGLER.
DAVID CHOBAT PHOTO

stops, Earnhardt was again the leader and this time he was 12.3 seconds ahead of Elliott.

Elliott's bid for No. 5 at MIS failed on lap 105, when he began slowing because of a dropped valve. He was forced to retire from the race after completing 126 laps. He finished 34th.

"The car felt good and I thought I had a chance to win this race until the valve problem," said Elliott, who showed early strength by leading 19 laps. "It's going to be hard for us to win the championship dropping out of races."

Pole position winner Rusty Wallace, who led 15 laps, was second late in the race when a black flag from NASCAR took him out of contention.

His Blue Max/Kodiak Pontiac Grand Prix 2+2 smoked throughout a large portion of the race and on lap 181, NASCAR ordered him into the pits because it suspected he was putting oil on the track.

There was some question about that but, nevertheless, Wallace complied with NASCAR's order and returned to the race in sixth place. He had moved into fifth by the race's end.

Wallace was one of six drivers to complete all 200 laps. Richmond finished fourth in his Hendrick/Folgers Coffee Chevrolet behind

Earnhardt, Allison and Petty. Then came Wallace and Hillin in the Stavola/Miller American Buick LeSabre. Taking seventh, one lap down, was Darrell Waltrip in the Hendrick/Tide Chevrolet, Schrader was eighth, Lake Speed ninth in the Wynn's/Kmart Oldsmobile and Benny Parsons tenth in a Hendrick/Folgers Coffee Chevrolet.

With his victory, Earnhardt locked away the $150,000 bonus from Winston to the driver leading the season's mid-point. With only the July 4 Pepsi Firecracker 400 at Daytona International Speedway left before the season is half over, Earnhardt has an insurmountable 304-point lead over Elliott in the point standings (2,314-2,010). That is a bigger margin than he enjoyed at the same time last year when he won his second Winston Cup title.

"It's an instant replay," he said with a grin.

The Miller American 400 win was the first official Winston Cup triumph for Earnhardt since he won the April 26 Sovran Bank 500 at Martinsville, Va., which capped a string of four straight victories. Although there were none in the month of May and most of June, he did win the May 17 The Winston at Charlotte, N.C.

"We've just had some small problems," Earnhardt explained. "All year, the guys on

the crew have been mentally pumped up and as serious as they can be. They've worked hard. In our last start at Riverside (Calif.), we were way off and had more problems with a couple of flat tires. That made it worse.

"But before the Pocono (Pa.) race (on June 14) we came up here and ran. We brought the same car we won at Atlanta with to clinch the championship and it's the same car that won The Winston.

"It was especially good to win here for Chevrolet. It hasn't won here in a long, long time and it has really wanted to. It was nice to turn things around a bit."

The day's biggest disappointment belonged to Derrike Cope. The driver from Spanaway, Wash., who now works with Fred Stoke's Hendersonville, N.C.-based team, surprised everyone by qualifying second fastest. However, just before the race started, he suffered a broken camshaft in his Alugard Ford when he fired up the engine in the garage area. He was unable to start the race.

Others who left the event because of mechanical problems included Mike Waltrip, Buddy Arrington, Cale Yarborough, Alan Kulwicki and Wilson.

Earnhardt's winning average speed in the two-hour, 41-minute, 40-second race was 148.454 mph. ■

SUMMER 500

Earnhardt Rolls On; Wins No. 8 Of Year

Earnhardt Victorious In Battle of Pocono

By STEVE WAID

DALE JR. JOINS IN THE CELEBRATION FOLLOWING DADDY DALE'S EIGHTH WIN OF THE SEASON.
DAVID CHOBAT PHOTO

Dale Earnhardt won a furious race-closing battle with Alan Kulwicki to claim the Summer 500 NASCAR Winston Cup race at Pocono International Raceway and thereby earn his first career victory on the 2.5-mile track.

In a dramatic finish to what otherwise had been a war of attrition, Earnhardt won for the eighth time in 16 races this season, continuing his domination and tightening his hold on the Winston Cup points lead.

Where contender after contender fell by the wayside, Earnhardt, in the Childress/Wrangler Chevrolet Monte Carlo SS, and Kulwicki, in his Zerex Ford Thunderbird, remained competitive all day.

Their scrap for victory began just after Kulwicki passed Buddy Baker's Crisco Oldsmobile Delta 88 on lap 191 to take second. One lap later, Steve Christman wrecked in the second turn – called the "tunnel turn" – to bring out the day's ninth and final caution.

When the green flag flew on lap 194, Earnhardt got off to a quick start and pulled away from Kulwicki. But Kulwicki, perhaps surprisingly to some observers, made up the distance and rode Earnhardt's bumper until lap 198.

That was the time Kulwicki made a move to the inside of the triangular track's third turn and pushed ahead of Earnhardt. By his own admission, Kulwicki thought he had the race won. He believed he would have a time getting around his rival but, if he could, he would win.

It didn't work that way. On lap 199, Earnhardt regained the lead when he pulled alongside in the second turn and eased ahead in the third. On the final lap, Kulwicki came back, exciting the crowd even more.

He was on the inside of Earnhardt in the second turn and charged ahead when, suddenly, he drifted a bit higher on the track than he would have liked. Seeing the opening, Earnhardt shot to the inside and left Kulwicki several car lengths behind in his

wake. He went on to win by one second.

"It was close racing," said the 36-year-old Earnhardt, the defending Winston Cup champion. "Alan was awful tough. It was fender to fender over those last three laps when we pulled away from the crowd and it was just a matter of who got to the finish line first. If I finished second, I finished second. But I was going to try to win.

"On the last lap, we went into the tunnel turn and I got on the brakes hard to get behind Alan so I could get to the inside. We scuffed bumpers and that forced Alan to go higher than he wanted. I knew I could get by."

Kulwicki, the 1986 Champion/Sears Rookie of the Year, who was bidding for his first Winston Cup victory, never had finished higher than third prior to the Pocono event.

"It's a tossup right now," he answered when asked how he felt to finish second in the agonizingly close race.

"With 50 laps to go, I would have been happy with fourth or third and at one point I would have been very happy with second. But to come this close and not win is very disappointing.

"I really did think we were a little bit faster than Dale. I thought it would be tough to get by him but, once we did, I thought we had it made.

"But he got inside me there in that corner and, if he hadn't done that, I think I would have gone on. I was right where I wanted to be in that corner but, all of a sudden, one way or another, he got me out of shape.

"But it was a good race. I'm not going to complain. I haven't been around here all that long so it's good to learn something else, although I couldn't tell you exactly what that is. I'll just rub a little harder next time."

To be in a position to win, Kulwicki had to overcome two equalized tires, which he said was accomplished by the work of his crew.

"We just had to come from back to front

all day," Kulwicki said. "And even when I was behind, they told me I was running just as fast as the leaders."

Earnhardt's victory put him 409 points ahead of Neil Bonnett, who now occupies second in the Winston Cup points standings. His lead is one of the largest in NASCAR's modern era, dating back to 1972.

He started in the 16th position but it didn't take him long – 22 laps, to be exact – to move into the lead. From there, he was in contention all day and was one of a record 15 drivers to swap the lead 35 times.

Such notables as Bill Elliott, Geoff Bodine, Harry Gant, Tim Richmond (who was bidding to tie Elliott's mark of four straight wins on superspeedways), Bobby Allison, Ricky Rudd, Sterling Marlin and Kyle Petty either retired from the race or were mechanically crippled before the event reached lap 150. Several had led the event.

On lap 107, Rusty Wallace's Blue Max/Kodiak Pontiac Grand Prix 2+2 inherited the lead following the sixth caution. He led until Earnhardt passed him on lap 109, but that was just the beginning of the fight.

Earnhardt gave up his lead under the seventh caution, but was back in control on lap 130, with Wallace fighting all the way.

Green-flag pit stops – the only ones of the day for the leaders – began on lap 166 and, again, Earnhardt relinquished his advantage, as Benny Parsons in the Hendrick/Folgers

But it wasn't to be. On lap 178, Wallace's car began smoking badly, the victim of an oil pan leak. It had been struck by a flying rock.

Rocks played havoc with the teams all day. As cars cut into the dirt in the second turn, the debris flew, cutting tires and cracking windshields.

Earnhardt assumed the lead, but Wallace continued to give chase. On lap 181, he was black-flagged by NASCAR and just one lap later, the eighth yellow flag flew due to the oil he deposited on the track. A series of pit stops put him out of contention, but he pressed on to a 14th-place finish.

"I'll just rub a little harder next time."

—Alan Kulwicki on what he learned tangling with Earnhardt and taking second place.

That seemingly gave Earnhardt an unchallenged path to the win. Until Kulwicki's presence, that is.

"Me and Rusty ran hard all day," said Earnhardt, who now has 28 career victories.

hadn't won previously. His other win came in the June 28 Miller American 400 at Michigan International Speedway.

"Every race driver yearns to win everywhere he goes," said Earnhardt. "I guess I have set a personal goal to win where I've never won.

"Here at Pocono, it's been hard to win. I know I've come here with a good car but it's been tough. I've hurt myself twice here. I nearly killed myself in 1979, my rookie year, when I cut a tire and hit the wall hard. It cut me up and bruised my heart. I missed four races and I was lucky to win the rookie-of-the-year title that year.

"It feels great to finally win here. It's a big boost particularly in the points. That's what we want to do. We want to win but, if we can't, we want to get the points, as many as we can."

Baker finished third, while Benny Parsons came home fourth. Fifth went to Davey Allison in the Ranier/Havoline Ford, sixth to Terry Labonte in the Johnson/Budweiser Chevrolet, seventh to Bonnett, eighth to Richard Petty in the STP Pontiac, ninth to Dave Marcis in the Helen Rae/Lifebuoy Chevrolet and 10th to Ken Schrader in the Donlavey/Red Baron Frozen Pizza Ford.

Earnhardt, who led seven times for 84 laps, won with a record average speed of 122.471 mph, which bettered the old mark

AT TIMES THIS YEAR, AS WAS THE CASE IN THE SUMMER 500 AT POCONO, EARNHARDT SEEMS TO BE RUNNING ALONE, WITHOUT COMPETITION OR PEER.
DAVID CHOBAT PHOTO

Chevrolet led lap 166 and Bonnett, in the Rahmoc/Valvoline Pontiac, led lap 167. Wallace led laps 168-171 and over the next seven circuits swapped the lead with Earnhardt two more times. It seemed the two were destined to fight to the finish.

"It was close racing, just like it was later with Alan. We never pushed each other to the wall or nothing like that."

Earnhardt, who won a Pocono record $55,875, has claimed two of the last three races, and both have come on tracks where he

of 122.166 mph set in the Miller 500 in June. By winning from the 16th starting position, Earnhardt again entered the record book. Previously, Cale Yarborough held the distinction of winning from the lowest qualifying position, 12th, in 1984. ∎

Earnhardt **Puts Crush** On Bristol Field

Earnhardt Still Perfect On Short Tracks

By STEVE WAID

Dale Earnhardt remains unbeaten. On the short tracks, that is.

As if he hasn't long proven his domination of the 1987 NASCAR Winston Cup season, the driver from Doolie, N.C., made it five for five on the short tracks with his drubbing of the field in the Busch 500 at Bristol International Raceway.

Earnhardt, winner of nine of the 20 Winston Cup events run to date, has won every short-track race this year. He is rapidly approaching the modern-era record of seven short-track wins in a season, shared by Cale Yarborough (1976) and Darrell Waltrip (1982). There are three events remaining on those tracks this year, beginning with the Sept. 13 Wrangler Indigo 400 at Richmond, Va., and Earnhardt will be the heavy favorite at each.

At Bristol, where he also won the Valleydale Meats 500 in April, Earnhardt once again was a picture of perfection. In his Childress/Wrangler Chevrolet Monte Carlo SS, he led 415 of the 500 laps on the 0.533-mile track and withstood a couple of spirited challenges from Rusty Wallace in the Blue Max/Kodiak Pontiac Grand Prix 2+2. Other

AFTER A TYPICALLY HEATED NIGHT ON THE BANKS OF BRISTOL, EARNHARDT IS HAPPY TO WRAP HIS HANDS AROUND A COLD ONE.
DAVID CHOBAT PHOTO

than Earnhardt, Wallace has been the hottest driver in the second half of the '87 campaign.

"The driver just gave out a bit there at the end," a weary Earnhardt said of his race-ending chase with Wallace. "My neck is still bothering me after that IROC race in Michigan (where he tangled with Michael Andretti) and I thought I might not be tough enough. But Richard (Childress) and the crew just keep making the car better for me, and I could keep up the pace."

Earnhardt is also setting the pace in the Winston Cup point standings. The defending Winston Cup champion has been entrenched in first place since the third race this season and, with his victory at Bristol, he extended his lead over runner-up Bill Elliott.

Earnhardt gained 47 points with the win and now leads Elliott by 545 points (3,336-2,791). That is the largest lead after 20 races since Richard Petty had a 573-point pad over Dave Marcis in 1975.

"Naw, the points thing ain't over," said Earnhardt. "I could catch double pneumonia like Tim Richmond and be out for the rest of the season. You can't call it over until you've clinched it.

"The tracks that are left are strong ones for us. Really, we haven't had a bad race since the first Riverside (Calif.) race. I would like to win the title at Martinsville (Va., on Sept. 27) so I could go deer hunting and not worry about this point thing."

As far as the Winston Cup title goes, Earnhardt might get his wish if he keeps going like he has. But he'll be the first to say nothing comes that easily and that includes this Bristol triumph, which was the

WINNING AT BRISTOL IS BECOMING COMMONPLACE FOR NASCAR'S TOP DRIVER. DAVID CHOBAT PHOTO

Moore/Motorcraft Ford Thunderbird, Terry Labonte, who won the pole position with a track-record lap of 115.758 mph in the Johnson Budweiser Chevrolet, was fourth, and Richard Petty took fifth in the STP Pontiac. They were the only drivers to complete all 500 laps.

Geoff Bodine was sixth in the Hendrick/Levi Garrett Chevrolet, three laps down. In seventh was Rick Wilson in the Kodak Oldsmobile Delta 88, four laps down. Harry Gant was eighth, five laps down, in the Skoal Bandit Chevrolet, while Elliott was ninth, six laps down in the Coors/Melling Ford. Neil Bonnett, with relief from Ken Schrader, was 10th in the Rahmoc/Valvoline Pontiac, also six laps down.

"I admit I was giggling
a little bit." —Earnhardt on pulling away from Rusty Wallace

Schrader was sidelined after 179 laps when his Donlavey/Red Baron Frozen Pizza Ford crashed on the backstretch. Kyle Petty lasted 158 laps before engine failure put his Wood Brothers/Citgo Ford on the sidelines. Bobby Hillin Jr., retired his Stavola/Miller American Buick LaSabre after a wreck on lap 118. Teammate Bobby Allison's Buick suffered a blown engine after 344 laps, while Benny Parsons retired his Hendrick/Folgers Chevrolet with the same problem after 200 laps.

Those are the kind of problems Earnhardt has avoided all season, while it appears Wallace has recovered from the mechanical bugaboos that plagued him and his team during the first half this season.

"Rusty and I are great competitors. We enjoy mixing it up," said Earnhardt, who won with an average speed of 90.373 mph in the two-hour, 56-minute, 56-second race. "It's fun for us. We enjoy it. I know it was frustrating for him to see me get away and I admit I was giggling a little bit. Then he'd get on my bumper and I'd say, 'C'mon, c'mon.' He's going to be a great one. I think if his car had held together like ours has, he'd be the one to race for the points lead.

"I enjoy racing at Bristol. I've driven it without power steering. It's just the kind of tough track I like, but there are others who like it, too – guys like Rusty, Terry and Darrell. They are great competition."

But, not this time. ■

fourth of his career at the track.

Bothered by a severe headache over the last two days, Earnhardt got no relief from powders, tablets or Wallace. Over the last 153 laps, Wallace pressured Earnhardt constantly, although he never managed to snatch the lead away from him.

Wallace lost a lap on lap 118 when he made an unscheduled pit stop to change right-side tires. But, on lap 213, he regained his lost distance and then got a break on lap 251, when the race's fifth caution period began. That allowed him to move to the front of the pack when the race restarted on lap 256. He was in fifth place and had moved into third by lap 280. At the end of the sixth caution period on lap 292, he was in second place and remained there for the rest of the race.

Wallace, winner of the Aug. 10 Budweiser At The Glen in Watkins Glen, N.Y., was on

Earnhardt's bumper by lap 400 and again shortly after the race's eighth and final caution period ended on lap 417.

But Wallace, as physically beaten as Earnhardt, began to fade in the closing laps.

"Rusty ran me hard," admitted Earnhardt, whose winnings totaled $47,175 and who now has earned $1,122,320 for the season. "Rusty caught up with me toward the end but I was pretty beaten down. It was hard to hold my head up.

"I tried to work the traffic as best I could and then I decided to change the groove. I went up into the top lane because it allowed me to get on the throttle faster out of the corners.

"I decided to bear down for the last 15-20 laps and then breathe on it for the final five laps."

Earnhardt beat Wallace to the finish by 5.50 seconds. Ricky Rudd was third in the

dale

EARNHARDT CELEBRATES WINNING THE SHORTEST-EVER SOUTHERN 500 AFTER HE WAS CROWNED THE VICTOR IN THE RAIN-SHORTENED EVENT.
DAVID CHOBAT PHOTO

Earnhardt Logs
10th
Victory
Of The Season

It's Short, But It's Sweet For Earnhardt

By **STEVE WAID**

Dale Earnhardt's already-spectacular 1987 NASCAR Winston Cup season continued to roll on with a victory in the shortest Southern 500 in history at Darlington International Raceway.

For only the second time in 38 years, all 500 miles of the Southern 500 were not completed. A thunderstorm struck the speedway at 3:44 p.m. and the race was red-flagged on lap 202, after 275.9 miles. Just 11 laps earlier, Earnhardt had snatched the lead from a determined Richard Petty and was in command when the cars stopped on the frontstretch.

At 5:11 p.m., NASCAR officials made the announcement the race would not resume and, since more than half its distance was completed, it went into the record books as complete – with Earnhardt a winner for the 10th time in 21 races this season.

The only other time the Southern 500 was shortened by rain was in 1969, when 230 laps, or 314.18 miles, were completed with the late Lee Roy Yarbrough the winner.

Earnhardt, driving the Childress/Wrangler Chevrolet Monte Carlo SS, led seven times for 109 laps and was the leader when the rain first slowed the race on lap 184. The third caution period lasted five laps and when racing resumed on lap 189, Petty's STP Pontiac Grand Prix 2+2 surged past Earnhardt going into the 1.366-mile track's third turn.

The estimated crowd of 75,000 cheered mightily as Petty put himself in a position to win his first race since July 4, 1984, and his first Southern 500 in 20 years. With more rain rapidly approaching, signaling a sure premature end to the race, he was in command.

But not for long. On lap 191, Earnhardt passed Petty in the third turn and began pulling away. Rusty Wallace, in the Blue Max/Kodiak Pontiac, gave chase as he passed Petty between turns three and four to move into second place.

However, he was 10 car-lengths behind Earnhardt when rain pelted the track again, bringing out the fifth, and final, caution flag. The race was halted just four laps later.

With his victory, Earnhardt became the first driver to sweep both Darlington events since Bill Elliott did so in 1985. Further, he padded his lead over Elliott in the Winston Cup point standings. He has a 583-point margin with eight races remaining in the season – which means, barring any catastrophic incidents, the 1987 Winston Cup championship will be his.

"Yes, winning the Southern 500 is something special," said Earnhardt, who added that to capture a rain-shortened one made no difference in its significance. "It always seemed in the past that something would happen to me and I couldn't put it all together. I would be running good and then the driver would put it into the wall or something would happen to the car.

"It's special because this race is close to home (Earnhardt is a Kannapolis, N.C., native), and it is the granddaddy of 'em all. It's a race David Pearson has won, Cale Yarborough has won it and you are a part of history if you can do it, too."

Earnhardt dominated the event, giving only Davey Allison in the Ranier/Havoline Ford Thunderbird the opportunity to be a serious challenger. Allison led three times for 86 laps, which meant he and Earnhardt combined to lead 195 of the event's 202 laps.

Allison was trailing Earnhardt on lap 164 when he found out how quickly and severely mean ol' Darlington can slap a competitor. Going into the fourth turn, his Ford broke loose and slid into the outside wall. It cut across the track in front of Mike Potter's spinning Ford, which drifted upward and collected Lake Speed's Wynn's/Kmart Oldsmobile Delta 88 and Benny Parsons' Hendrick/Folgers Chevrolet. Allison was through for the day.

Afterward, only Elliott and Petty could take the lead from Earnhardt, the former for a single lap and the latter for two.

"Richard (Childress, team owner) told me on the radio that Richard (Petty) was running strong," said Earnhardt. "I could see him in my rearview mirror passing the guys behind me. And, yes, I could see the crowd. There were people climbing the fences over there and I wondered what the hell was going on. I knew, though, and I was sorta getting excited myself."

> "Winston told me that the champagne bill in New York (for the NASCAR Awards Banquet) would be unlimited if I saved them the $100,000. In New York, **I would like to invite all of you to the Dale and Teresa Earnhardt suite at the hotel."**
> —Earnhardt

Earnhardt, though, added he chose not to race Petty when the STP Pontiac driver shot around him on lap 188.

"I think I was still racing the track even though we knew the rain was coming," said Earnhardt, whose winnings of $64,650 pushed his season total to $1,186,190. "You can get into trouble so easily here, like I did in

AFTER JUST 202 LAPS OF WORK, EARNHARDT WAS ABLE TO WIN AND RELAX UNDER DARKENING SKIES.
DAVID CHOBAT PHOTO

the spring race when I was racing Bill (Elliott) and I hit the wall in turns one and two.

"When Richard got by me I didn't want to race that hard. I thought it would be better to let off and get myself settled for a lap before I tried to pass him. Yes, when the rain came, I did want to be in first place but Richard was going just a little bit harder than I wanted to go.

"I don't know what would have happened if the race had continued because I didn't know how much more Richard had left. We could see the black clouds coming, but you just can't forget where you are racing. I'm telling you, this track will get you. It rose up and bit Davey today," he said.

Wallace's runner-up finish was another in what has been a strong second half of the season for him.

"We had changed our tire stagger on the last stop and it really helped," he said. "The car felt really good. I would have liked to restart the race, but I'll take second place."

Earnhardt is the first driver to post double-digit victories in a season since Elliott won 11 events in '85. He is closing in on the modern-era record of 13 established by Petty in 1975.

"You always think your team is capable," Earnhardt explained. "We won five races last year and the championship and the way the team works and works me, well, it all comes together. We really compliment each other.

"And this car is the same car we won with twice at Bristol, once at Pocono (Pa.), once at Rockingham (N.C.) and now twice at Darlington. This car has won six races for us."

Earnhardt's victory meant the $100,000 bonus paid by Winston would not be presented. Only three drivers – Allison, Elliott and Kyle Petty – had a shot at the money, which goes to any driver who wins two of four selected events in the Winston Million program if no one claims the $1 million prize for winning three of the four. Elliott won the Daytona 500, Allison the Winston 500 at Talladega, Ala., and Petty the Coco-Cola 600 at Charlotte, N.C.

At Darlington, Elliott wound up eighth, Petty 14th, two laps down, and Allison finished 29th after his wreck.

"Winston told me that the champagne bill in New York (for the NASCAR Awards Banquet) would be unlimited if I saved them the $100,000. In New York, I would like to invite all of you to the Dale and Teresa Earnhardt suite at the hotel," Earnhardt said.

Earnhardt's winning average speed was 115.520 mph in a race that took two hours, 23 minutes and 19 seconds to complete. ∎

Earnhardt Wins
The Battle
Of Richmond

By GARY McCREDIE

Earnhardt Works Hard
For Richmond Win

In an amazingly close contest pitting raw power and unabashed driving talent against one another for almost 90 laps, the finale of the Wrangler Indigo 400 NASCAR Winston Cup race came down to a fight between one driver who has, so far this year, dominated the circuit and another who has struggled all season to regain his championship form.

In the end, however, Dale Earnhardt, driving the Childress/Wrangler Chevrolet Monte Carlo SS, got the better of Darrell Waltrip and crossed the finish line 2.5 seconds – under caution – in front of his archrival's Hendrick/Tide Chevrolet.

For Waltrip, it was his best finish this season since he signed with Hendrick last year and helped form a new team. For Earnhardt, that victory bolstered an already impressive statistical list. To wit:

He has won every short-track race run this year – six. In doing so, he's tied a record set by Waltrip in 1983 and is one short of equaling Waltrip's record of seven out of 10 short-track victories set in 1982.

Twenty-two races have been contested this year. Earnhardt has won 11.

Of his 31 career victories in 267 starts, 16 have come on tracks less than a mile in length. Since 1971, the year Winston began sponsoring the series, only Waltrip (40), Richard Petty (37) and Cale Yarborough (29) have won more.

There were 12 caution flags for 82 laps with 12 of the 30 starters falling by the wayside. And most of those completing the race had cars ready for extensive work in the body shop. Earnhardt and Waltrip, though, survived it all, thus setting up the scenario for their dramatic duel to the finish.

On lap 295, pole position winner Alan Kulwicki, Sterling Marlin and Phil Parsons crashed in the first corner and Kulwicki hit the guardrail so hard that the event had to be stopped for repairs to the barrier.

After a 20-minute delay, the field began moving again at 4:04 p.m. and the green flag was displayed on lap 313 with Earnhardt in the lead, Rusty Wallace's Blue Max/Kodiak Pontiac Grand Prix 2+2 in second, Waltrip in third and the Fords of Ricky Rudd and Bill Elliott in fourth and fifth, respectively.

A lap later, Wallace began slipping and Waltrip took second. On lap 317, Earnhardt and Waltrip began a nose-to-tail and side-by-side run that brought them even on the tight 0.542-mile Richmond track on several occasions.

This two-car battle continued uninterrupted even when Wallace pasted the turn-two guardrail on lap 373 and no caution was thrown. Waltrip and Earnhardt continuously traded a bit of paint here and there, but three circuits from the finish, Earnhardt started pulling away.

Then, on the next-to-last lap, while

IN HIS LAST YEAR PILOTING THE WRANGLER CHEVROLET, IT IS FITTING THAT EARNHARDT CAPTURE THE WRANGLER INDIGO 400.
DAVID CHOBAT PHOTO

Earnhardt and Waltrip were on the back straightaway, Neil Bonnett looped his Rahmoc/Valvoline Pontiac coming down the frontstretch and hit the wall. That brought out the yellow and white flags as the leaders exited turn four, and the race was over.

Rudd was third in the Moore/Motorcraft Ford, Elliott was fourth in the Coors/Melling Ford and fifth, a lap down, was Richard Petty in the STP Pontiac.

"That was probably the toughest short-track race I ran this year," said Earnhardt, who appeared far from fatigued during his post-race interview. "Bristol (Valleydale 500 last month) was tough on me physically; here, I feel fine, but Darrell put some pressure on me.

"We bumped and rubbed; it was nothing serious and I held my groove. Then we got the yellow and white and he passed me, but when we got the yellow, that was it."

EARNHARDT'S WRANGLER CHEVY BEARS THE DONUT SCAR OF A LITTLE RUBBING WITH RIVAL DARRELL WALTRIP.
DAVID CHOBAT PHOTO

"Darrell and I were racing as clean as anybody those last 50 laps and we still scuffed fenders. You just can't get away from that here," he said.

"We didn't have a big game plan here. I was just running my line and I didn't let him get me excited. I was just running my best line as consistently as I could and I feel like, if Darrell could have gotten by me, he would have.

"He tried several times. I knew that and I think he knew that," said Earnhardt.

Earnhardt called the event "the best racing" he'd been involved with in quite some time and credited Waltrip for "putting on a good show." He said he knew the outcome would be decided during the final 10 laps but because he could run at the top of the track – while Waltrip couldn't – the advantage was his.

"I couldn't run on the bottom and win, slipping and sliding down there," said Earnhardt. "But I could run more consistently up top and that's the reason I beat him off the corners.

"He was stronger than me several times during the race and, like I said, if he could have gotten by me, I don't think I could have gotten it back."

In an action-packed event that saw its fair share of short-track "framin' and bammin'" featuring spinouts and accidents, Earnhardt led the most – four times – for 219 laps. Waltrip led twice for 86 laps, Wallace went to the front one time for 57 laps, Phil Parsons paced the field once for 15 laps, Terry Labonte and Kulwicki each led a lap, and the surprise of the day, Jimmy Means, led four times for 21 laps.

During the pre-race drivers' meeting, NASCAR Winston Cup Director Dick Beaty was adamant in explaining that anyone engaging in rough driving or other unnecessary behavior on the track would be penalized. Hotheaded behavior would not be tolerated and any offender would be called into the garage for a "cooling off" period.

And, sure enough, two drivers, Bobby Hillin Jr., and Geoff Bodine, were brought briefly in. The ruling also affected Earnhardt and Waltrip.

> "He (Waltrip) was in the wrong for being where he was," said Earnhardt.
> **"I don't care what that SOB said.**
> He ought not to have been up under me on pit road."

The day's seventh yellow flag came out on lap 181. A crewman on Buddy Arrington's team, Roger West, had been injured in the pits and, since there's no tunnel at Richmond, the race was slowed so West could be removed in an ambulance.

The field began pitting, Earnhardt and Waltrip included, and the two cars banged together as they headed toward their respective pits, both at the end of the lane. A lap

later, they returned to the track but were held by race officials at the start/finish line.

Each driver was disciplined for the incident by being placed at the rear of the field.

While Earnhardt was credited with leading lap 182, both he and Waltrip had to work their way back to the front. Earnhardt took the lead for good on lap 245.

"NASCAR black-flagged us and said we weren't supposed to pass on pit road, but he (Waltrip) was in the wrong," said Earnhardt, who also noted he was "pleased that NASCAR has begun taking action against someone they should have (disciplined) all along."

"As for the thing on pit road, Earnhardt tried to pinch me against the No. 8 car (Bobby Hillin Jr.), so I couldn't get into the pits," explained Waltrip. "I saw what he was going to do and I got alongside him. Everything else from that point on was his doing.

"No, I wasn't too concerned too much about the penalty. They put him back there, too, so I accepted that."

Earnhardt disagreed – vehemently – and said his car owner, Richard Childress, had filed a protest with NASCAR. Les Richter, NASCAR competition vice president, said the protest was disallowed because, when a penalty is levied during a race, it is not "appealable."

"He (Waltrip) was in the wrong for being where he was," said Earnhardt. "I don't care what that SOB said. He ought not to have been up under me on pit road.

"I started down pit road and he was under me. I was going to my pits."

Accidents removed the cars of Morgan Shepherd, Doug French, Dale Jarrett, Kulwicki, Sterling Martin, Phil Parsons and Michael Waltrip, while mechanical failures sidelined Kyle Petty, Trevor Boys, D.K. Ulrich and Ernie Irvan.

Completing the top-10 finishers were Bodine, Dave Marcis, Labonte, Means and Bonnett. Earnhardt completed the race in three hours, three minutes and 56 seconds at an average speed of 67.074 mph and won $44,950.

That purse increased his winnings this year to $1,231,920 versus $1,000,535 for Elliott. And, as far as Winston Cup points are concerned, Earnhardt is 608 points in front of runner-up Elliott. The tally now stands at 3,706 for Earnhardt to 3,098 for Elliott.

"I think it's the team more than the driver," said Earnhardt of his success this year. "It's a good combination.

"That's the way our team is. They go to each race and try to be No. 1. That's the season." ■

Earnhardt Roars
To Busch Clash

'Same Ol' Dale' Holds
Off Allisons For Win

By STEVE WAID

It's a new year and the colors on his car and uniform are new. But, he's the same old Dale Earnhardt.

It took little more than 15 minutes to prove that fact as Earnhardt sped to victory in the Busch Clash at the 2.5-mile Daytona International Speedway.

Driving the gleaming silver and black Childress/GM Goodwrench Chevrolet Monte Carlo SS, Earnhardt, the "tough guy" defending NASCAR Winston Cup champion, held off a challenge from the father-son team of Bobby and Davey Allison to record the third Busch Clash victory of his career.

Daytona "slingshot" pass on the last lap. With father Bobby in the Stavola/Miller American Buick Regal running in third, Davey had the momentum in the high-speed draft to snatch the win from Earnhardt's grasp.

But it wasn't to be. Earnhardt used up as much of the track as possible and managed to keep young Allison at bay, earning a record-tying $75,000 in the process. Earnhardt's winnings included $15,000 in bonus lap-leader money.

"I'm real happy to win the Busch Clash because I believe it is one of the most prestigious races we run, maybe next to the Daytona 500," said Earnhardt. "It's

behind Bodine until the end," he noted. "Rusty Wallace was right behind me and I figured we could have waited to pass on the last lap."

But, on the sixth lap, Bodine surrendered the lead to Earnhardt, who passed high in the fourth turn with Wallace in tow.

"Bodine kept moving around and that was causing all of us to move around behind him," said Earnhardt. "So we drafted by him and that put me up front quicker than I wanted.

"Still, I was content to be there with Rusty behind me, but all of a sudden it was Davey. I had been

"I got a cramp in my foot from holding it wide open."
—Earnhardt

EARNHARDT SHOWS OFF HIS NEW-LOOK BLACK AND SILVER CAR...
DAVID CHOBAT PHOTO

In winning the inaugural event in the stock car portion of Daytona's SpeedWeek, Earnhardt took the lead from Geoff Bodine in the Hendrick/Levi Garrett Chevrolet on the sixth lap and held it until the race concluded 14 laps later.

But it wasn't as simple as it sounds. Earnhardt had to rely on his driving savvy to keep Davey Allison, in the Ranier/Havoline Road Thunderbird, from making the classic

prestigious because of the way we have to qualify for it. It's all the pole winners.

"Davey ran strong. But what really got me worried was when I saw his dad behind him. I figured they were going to put the 'Alabama Shuffle' on me."

Earnhardt drew the second starting position, behind Bodine, and said he would have been content to stay there until the last lap.

"Yeah, I would have been happy to stay

watching him move up through the pack and I knew he would be strong."

On lap 12, Allison moved around Wallace to take second place. As Wallace faded back to sixth, Bill Elliott occupied third in his Coors/Motorcraft Ford and Bobby Allison moved into fourth.

That was the running order until lap 18, when the elder Allison passed Elliott for third place. Elliott then engaged in a battle for posi-

tion with Bodine and, as a result, Earnhardt and the Allisons began to pull away.

"I had my hands full, but I wasn't worried about Davey when it was one-on-one," said Earnhardt, who won the Busch Clash in 1980 and again in 1986. "But, when that No. 12 of Bobby's came in there, it was the Alabama Gang behind me."

Going down the backstretch, Earnhardt moved high and low, keeping the Allisons behind him.

"Davey and I stayed in line, but Bobby pulled down once and it looked like he was going to try to get around Davey," Earnhardt said. "When Bobby got out of line, it took Davey a little longer to get up some momentum to get by me.

"I was using up as much of the track as I could and Davey was trying hard to get around me. He scraped my rear bumper once.

"When we came off the fourth turn, I was in the right line. I was low and that was the right place to be to keep him behind me."

"I just ran out of room with Dale, that's all I can say," said Davey Allison. "But it was fun out there racing with my dad. I knew he'd be tough at the end, but I knew I couldn't get out of the draft with Dale. If I had pulled out, I couldn't do anything with him. So I had to stay behind him and I couldn't get out and race with my dad."

Earnhardt's margin of victory over Davey Allison was one car length. Bobby Allison was third while Bodine finished fourth. Elliott came home in fifth place, Wallace was sixth, Ken Schrader seventh in the Hendrick/Folgers Chevrolet, Morgan Shepherd eighth in the Winkle/AC Spark Plugs Buick, Terry Labonte ninth in the Johnson/Budweiser Chevrolet, Harry Gant tenth in the Skoal Bandit Chevrolet, Alan Kulwicki 11th in the Zerex Ford and Benny Parsons finished last in the 12-car

race in the Donlavey/Bull's Eye Barbecue Sauce Ford.

Earnhardt, who now has won seven races at Daytona, but has yet to claim a Daytona 500 victory, said he would use his Busch Clash winning car in the 500 on Feb. 14.

"We were going to run a different car in the Busch Clash to start with but, after

...HIS COMPETITION GOT A GOOD LOOK AT IT FROM BEHIND.
DAVID CHOBAT PHOTO

qualifying yesterday, all we did was change the spoiler – we used the same engine and setup," he said. "And I got a cramp in my foot from holding it wide open."

Earnhardt's winning average speed was 191.489 mph in the 15-minute, 40-second race – long enough to prove the Doolie, N.C., resident still has the championship form. ■

EARNHARDT CAPTURED HIS THIRD CAREER BUSCH CLASH WIN.
DAVID CHOBAT PHOTO

EARNHARDT FLEW BY THE COMPETITION TO RECORD HIS FIRST WINSTON CUP VICTORY AS 'THE MAN IN BLACK.' DAVID CHOBAT PHOTO

Earnhardt
Back In Form With
AIR Win

Earnhardt Is The Dominator Once Again

By STEVE WAID

They can't say he didn't warn 'em.

Dale Earnhardt, never one to mince words, came right to the point following qualifying for the Motorcraft 500 NASCAR Winston Cup race on March 19. Taking the No. 2 starting position and eclipsing the old track record in the process, Earnhardt grinned and said, "They better get ready. I'm gonna unload on all of 'em tomorrow."

He did just that. Boy, did he ever.

In the swashbuckling style that has characterized his career, Earnhardt routed the field on the way to victory in the Motorcraft 500. It was the first victory in 1988 for the defending Winston Cup champion and his first since he won the Wrangler Indigo 400 at Richmond (Va.) Fairgrounds Raceway on Sept. 13, 1987. He thus ended a 10-race losing streak.

day. As he had done throughout the entire event, Earnhardt blasted away from his rivals on the restart and went on to win the 32nd race of his career.

"I said we would be tough because we tested good down here and had a good qualifying run," said the 36-year-old Earnhardt. "I really thought we would win the pole and we missed it by a tick. That was the driver or maybe the tire stagger.

"Once I passed (Geoff) Bodine on the first lap, I felt I had the car to beat all day long. We stayed with our game plan all day. We wanted to put the pressure on everyone else. We came in a couple of times and put four tires on the car during the green and that enabled us to put a couple of cars a lap down. We went out and lapped everybody but Rusty."

"They better get ready.

I'm gonna unload on all of 'em tomorrow."

—Earnhardt's pre-race prediction.

Earnhardt's only serious challenge came from Benny Parsons, driver of Junie Donlavey's Bull's Eye Barbecue Sauce Ford. Parsons started eighth, charged through the field and by lap 69 had snatched the lead away from Earnhardt. He held it for one lap, then retook it on lap 87. He held it during the day's fourth caution, created by A.J. Foyt's blown engine because he did not pit.

Earnhardt, however, did. And, when the race resumed on lap 91, he was in 17th place.

Earnhardt's car began to show its power. By lap 96, Earnhardt was fifth. He was fourth on lap 98 and third on lap 101. By lap 105, he had passed Kyle Petty's Wood Brothers/Citgo Ford to take second place.

On lap 114, Earnhardt snatched the lead from Parsons and was in control again. It would stay that way as he led 190 of the remaining 214 laps.

On lap 200, Earnhardt pitted under green and had four tires changed in 22.2 seconds by his crew, three times the Rockingham/Unocal pit crew champions. By lap 213, after the other leaders had pitted for just two tires each, Earnhardt was in front again, tops among the eight cars on the lead lap.

Twenty-five laps later, there were just five cars on the lead lap. Then, Earnhardt did it again. He dashed into the pits on lap 254 and made another four-tire change, this one

accomplished in 22.9 seconds. At the time, he held an 11.30-second lead over Parsons.

"We kept getting a larger lead with four fresh tires and we had the cushion we needed to make the stops, so why not use it? Those two stops were the best I had ever seen," Earnhardt said. "We changed four tires in about the same times it takes a lot of teams to change two.

"No, I didn't worry about blistering new tires. We were on Goodyears, and Goodyear has worked hard over the last five days to get us a good tire for here and Darlington (S.C.). They are working as hard as we are to win races."

Parsons moved to the front and held a 22.9-second pad – nearly three-quarters of a lap. Earnhardt moved back into second place by lap 264, but he was still well behind. Parsons, whose pit stops were out of synch with the other leaders, had only to stop for two tires to maintain a still-strong lead.

But disaster struck. Parsons' Ford slowed dramatically in the first turn on lap 206 and it was clear he had run out of gas. He had gone 60 laps, or 90 miles, since his last stop and it was just too much.

As Parsons limped into the pits for a stop, which would cost him the lead, Earnhardt retook the lead. He never surrendered it, pacing the field for the final 63 circuits.

Meanwhile, Parsons was reduced to making a Sunday drive. His engine suffered a burnt piston and the Ellerbe, N.C., driver who has not won a race since the Motorcraft 500 of 1984 – 76 events ago – came home in 13th place, six laps down.

But, it was the best performance of the year for his team.

"I hope the team gets a lift out of this one, because it's only the fourth race we've ever been together," said Parsons. "When my car ran out of gas, it felt like my dog died. But today, we got it all together."

Earnhardt agreed. "Benny ran about as consistent as I did," he said. "He didn't surprise me because he ran good in practice. This is one of his good tracks. So is Darlington (site of the March 27 TranSouth 500)."

When Parsons was forced to leave the track after running out of fuel, Darrell Waltrip moved into second place in his Hendrick Tide Chevrolet. But on lap 270, he was forced to pit and lost a lap to Earnhardt.

That put Kyle Petty in second place, but his pit stop on lap 276 put him a lap down also. That left only Earnhardt and Wallace on the lead lap.

Richard Petty's STP Pontiac dropped a cylinder on lap 297 and that brought out the day's sixth caution period. This allowed Wallace, who was 20.67 seconds behind

It was also the first Winston Cup triumph for Earnhardt wearing the black and silver colors of his new sponsor, GM Goodwrench. With the combination of skill, excellent pit work by his Kirk Shelmerdine-led pit crew and a flawless Childress/GM Goodwrench Chevrolet Monte Carlo SS, Earnhardt led 270 of the race's 328 laps and finished 1.5 seconds ahead of Rusty Wallace in the Blue Max/Kodiak Pontiac Grand Prix SE.

Wallace was that close only because of a late caution. When Bill Elliott's Melling/Coors Ford Thunderbird crashed into the second-turn wall on lap 318, it brought out the day's seventh and final caution period. Cleanup crews moved Elliott's battered car to the infield in time for just three more laps of racing.

While Wallace was poised to make a last-ditch effort, he never mounted an attack; it was something he had been unable to do all

dale

Earnhardt, to move in behind his old rival on the restart, which came on lap 302.

Wallace couldn't mount a charge and Earnhardt was ahead by 3.2 seconds when Elliott brought out the final caution, which offered Wallace a second chance, one he could not utilize.

"Dale was just too tough," said Wallace. "We definitely had the second-toughest car and I ran my butt off. But Dale was just too tough."

"I really didn't know what would happen and I was concerned there at the end," said Earnhardt. "What if Rusty didn't pit during the caution and we never got back to green? It looked like they were taking a lot of time to get Bill's car off the track. And I could have gotten a set of tires that were too tight or loose and his could have been perfect."

Neither scenario developed, however.

Elliott, a favorite at AIR, started third but was out of contention early. He lost six laps

in the pits when a faulty distributor was replaced, beginning on lap 31. Then came his race-closing accident.

Terry Labonte came home in fourth in the Johnson/Budweiser Chevrolet while Kyle Petty rounded out the top five. Taking sixth place was Bobby Hillin in the Stavola/Miller High Life Buick Regal; Buddy Baker was seventh in the Red Baron Pizza Oldsmobile Cutlass; Ken Schrader took eighth in the Hendrick/Folgers Chevrolet; Brett Bodine was ninth in the Moore/Crisco Ford and Rick Wilson rounded out the top 10 in the Kodak Oldsmobile.

Earnhardt's victory quelled the talk that the two-time champion was in a slump.

"I'm asked that all the time, 'What's wrong?'" said Earnhardt, who dominated last year's Motorcraft 500 until a broken alternator ruined his victory chances with just 14 laps to go. "We have worked very hard to repeat as champions. But we've had a prob-

lem here and a flat tire there, things like that.

"We tried to figure out what was wrong and all it was is that you make your own luck and to do that you just work harder. That's what I think we did and I think we've proven we can dominate again and win races again."

Perhaps he and his team can do more. The victory moved Earnhardt into second place in the Winston Cup point standings with 628 points, just four fewer than leader Neil Bonnett. Bonnett suffered engine problems in his Rahmoc/Valvoline Pontiac and had to coast to a 22nd place finish, 39 laps down.

"Boy it's time to put pressure on Neil now," said Earnhardt, who won with an average speed of 137.588 mph in the three-hour, 37-minute, 42-second race.

"He'd better get going."

After Earnhardt's prediction for the Motorcraft 500, Bonnett might do well to listen. ∎

HE WARNED 'EM. EARNHARDT PREDICTED A DOMINATING VICTORY AND HE GOT IT IN THE MOTORCRAFT 500.
DAVID CHOBAT PHOTO

Earnhardt Prevails At Martinsville

Consistency And 'Bandit's' Poor Luck Spell Victory For Earnhardt

By GARY McCREDIE

A lthough the Pannill Sweatshirts 500 was a typical Martinsville Speedway race with its fair share of fender-to-fender contact, the track's 33rd annual spring NASCAR Winston Cup race undoubtedly will never be forgotten by Dale Earnhardt or Harry Gant.

For Gant, who has been contending with an over-two-year-old string of incredibly foul luck, it appeared his first victory since 1985 was finally within his grasp. He took the lead from pole winner Ricky Rudd on lap 38 of the 500-lap event on the 0.526-mile short-track and led for 29 circuits. And, with his Skoal Bandit Chevrolet Monte Carlo SS riding on Hoosier tires, he went to the front again on the 68th lap and had a firm grasp on the race until he pitted for tires and fuel on lap 205.

A 14.4-second pit stop put Gant back into the fray but, on the 209th lap, his green

> **EARNHARDT IS JOINED IN VICTORY LANE BY WIFE TERESA, DAUGHTER KELLY, DALE JR. AND MISS WINSTON.**
> DAVID CHOBAT PHOTO

PANNILL SWEATSHIRTS

and white car was back in the pits with its hood up. The Taylorsville, N.C., resident was the victim of still more ill fortune – a blown engine.

The lead then went to Sterling Marlin, in the Hagan/Piedmont Airlines Oldsmobile Cutlass (41 laps), Buddy Baker, in the Red Baron Frozen Pizza Oldsmobile (one lap) and back to Marlin, who led through lap 286.

Following pit stops while the race was under caution, Bobby Hillin Jr., became the race leader (laps 287-291), but he was overtaken by the more potent car of Marlin, who seemed to be on his way toward his first-ever Winston Cup victory. Marlin stayed out front until the day's fifth of seven caution flags was displayed on the 312th lap because of a blown engine in Mark Martin's Roush/Stroh Light Ford Thunderbird.

When the event went back to green on lap 319, Hillin was the leader, but his ascendancy was all too brief. As he entered the second corner, Hillin fell victim to Earnhardt's experience – and a well-prepared Childress/Goodwrench Chevrolet. Earnhardt passed the Stavola/Miller High Life Buick Regal on the outside in turn two and shot down the back straightaway.

Even two more interruptions could not hold Earnhardt back. He was never passed and ended up beating Marlin to the checkered flag by 1.99 seconds at the end. Hillin finished third, one lap down, while Terry Labonte, in the Johnson/Budweiser Chevrolet, and Darrell Waltrip, driving the Hendrick/Tide Chevrolet, were fourth and fifth, respectively, both two laps in arrears.

The victory, worth $53,550, was Earnhardt's 33rd win in Winston Cup competition. And, as this event's defending champion, it was his fourth No. 1 finish at Martinsville.

It also may have been one of his most difficult. Earnhardt readily admitted that Gant would most likely have been the race winner had not engine failure knocked him out and he said the only possible way he could have gotten the best of the "Skoal Bandit" would be to run the car easily early on and then press harder toward the race's end.

And, too, Earnhardt acknowledged that Gant might have had the edge by running Hoosier tires while he did not. Of the 32 starters, 10, including Marlin and Hillin, chose Hoosier.

Earnhardt's team, however, is remaining loyal to industry giant Goodyear.

"We just had a good day and dodged all bullets. We stayed in good shape," said Earnhardt. "Harry Gant had us beat.

"What it was, we ran a little tight at the beginning of the race. We kept working on the stagger with the tires to see what we could do.

"We tried to run as hard as we could without pressing the car," he added. "It was unfortunate he (Gant) had trouble, but we were running a consistent pace because we knew we couldn't beat Harry."

In the early stages, it was evident that Gant and his team had found the quick way around the speedway, and a check of the stopwatch verified the fact. On lap 108, he was 2.5 seconds in front of Earnhardt, six laps later he'd stretched the margin to 3.94 seconds, and by the 133rd lap, Gant was over five seconds in front of the Goodwrench Chevrolet.

"We just had a good day and **dodged all bullets."**
—Earnhardt

The same held true when Marlin was second to Gant. Earnhardt had dropped to third and the deficit between Gant and Marlin was, for example on lap 165, 8.13 seconds. It was only later that Earnhardt, who regained the lead, began to pull away from any of his rivals. And toward the finish Marlin began to close in, but ran out of time.

Marlin was over five seconds behind Earnhardt on lap 370, but he had chopped that advantage to about 3.3 seconds eight laps later.

In the waning laps, though, Earnhardt began to increase the distance between him and Marlin but, once he seemed assured of victory, either he backed off just a tad, or Marlin began to pick up speed. Marlin had whittled the spread to a little over four seconds 30 laps from the finish and he was about six car lengths – or two seconds – behind at race's end.

Both Earnhardt and Marlin avoided most of the day's troubles and, except for an incident with Rudd's Bernstein/Quaker State Buick following the final caution, Earnhardt's race was free of incident. When the green flag came out on lap 411, Rudd, who had earlier gone a lap down, passed Earnhardt to get back on the lead lap.

Earnhardt rode Rudd's rear bumper in an attempt to get by and on lap 419, he shot by Rudd going into the first corner. Contact was made and Marlin, who was running a close second at the time, also got involved and hit the inside track apron in the second corner.

"I hadn't really run the car hard all day, but I really punished it getting away from Sterling and Ricky," said Earnhardt. "The only contact I made was with Rudd. I knew

I was better on fresh tires, but I knew the tires would go away. So I wanted to put some distance on Sterling.

"It looked like a normal Martinsville race to me. Our car looks pretty good and we didn't bump it up.

"We felt like Gant and the Hoosier tires were going to beat us, so we ran at a good, consistent pace," he said. "We kept working on the car and beat the rest of the Hoosier cars, but I don't think we would have beat Gant."

Marlin's second-place finish was his best showing of the year, as well as his fourth in the top five. He expressed pleasure at the feat but said the incident with Rudd and Earnhardt had knocked his car's front end out of kilter and had affected the toe-in.

"I almost had one," he said. "Our Olds

EARNHARDT TAKES THE CHECKERED FLAG IN THE PANNILL SWEATSHIRTS 500 AT MARTINSVILLE SPEEDWAY.
DAVID CHOBAT PHOTO

worked super all day long and I thought I had a chance.

"But we'll get it right before the season is over."

While there were two yellow-flag periods within the first 100 laps, the event went caution-free from lap 95 to 245. There were no overtly serious accidents, though, and the cautions were caused by spinouts, engine failure and debris on the track.

The attrition rate was high, however, and engine failure claimed all but two of the dropouts. Among the less than fortunate were Richard Petty, Neil Bonnett, Lake Speed, Gant and Martin. Michael Waltrip was knocked out by a faulty fuel pump, and broken timing chains claimed both the Ford of Brett Bodine and Rudd's Buick.

Earnhardt said a combination of good tires, proper tire stagger and a well-trained pit crew all figured into his victory — and it was his Richard Childress-Kirk Shelmerdine-led crew which was responsible for his overall success and two straight Winston Cup championships.

"They just don't give up and work at it all the time. Consistency is the reason we won the championship last year — and it makes a difference here when you get out in front and save your brakes.

"Richard has fine-tuned the team. They work on consistency and, when they get to working good, it just sort of snowballs. It gets better all the time.

"We had good brakes from start to finish and we had a full pedal at the end," he noted. "It was hard on my leg, but I'd rather wear my leg out than the brakes.

"I don't want to sound cocky, but I think consistency is what beat them."

Completing the top-10 finishers were Davey Allison, in the Ranier/Havoline Ford; Baker, the Stavola/Miller High Life Buick of Bobby Allison; Phil Parsons, in the Crown/Skoal Classic Oldsmobile; and Ken Schrader, in the Hendrick/Folgers Coffee Chevrolet.

In all, there were 10 lead changes among seven drivers. Earnhardt led the most laps — 182 — and completed the event in three hours, 31 minutes and eight seconds at an average speed of 74.740 mph.

Earnhardt also padded his early-season lead in the Winston Cup points and, with 1,244, has 77 more points than runner-up Marlin. Prior to this event, Marlin was fourth in points, while Rusty Wallace was second. ■

dale **earnhardt**

NASCAR'S OWN ROYAL FAMILY, THE EARNHARDT'S: KELLY, TERESA, DALE AND DALE JR.
DAVID CHOBAT PHOTO

Earnhardt Wins
At Bristol
For No. 3 Of Year

Earnhardt Rebounds With Victory At BIR

By STEVE WAID

Dale Earnhardt rebounded from a disappointing finish one week earlier to win the Busch 500 NASCAR Winston Cup race at Bristol International Raceway and help tighten the 1988 point standings.

Snatching the lead from Alan Kulwicki on lap 391 of the 500-lap race on the 0.533-mile track, Earnhardt held off a strong challenge from Bill Elliott in the closing laps to win by one car length. In so doing, the driver of the Childress/GM Goodwrench Chevrolet Monte Carlo SS picked up 31 points in the standings and presently resides in third place with 2,901 points.

Elliott's runner-up finish in the Melling/Coors Ford Thunderbird moved him into first place in the standings for the first time this season. He passed Rusty Wallace for the lead spot and has 3,027 points, 16 more than Wallace, who has 3,011 points. Wallace

gamely started the race after being involved in a spectacular one-car accident during practice Aug. 26. Wallace was uninjured and started the event in the Blue Max/Kodiak Pontiac Grand Prix SE, but was relieved on lap 211 by Busch Series driver Larry Pearson. Pearson drove to a ninth-place finish.

"There was a lot of racing through the pack," said Earnhardt, who won for the third time this season. "I lost a lap early, made it up and that was tough. It was tough for everyone out there tonight.

"At the end, my car seemed to push in the middle of the turns and that bothered me, because I didn't know if I was having a tire problem or not. Bill began to run me down. But I started to take it a bit easy and that seemed to help. I think I had just enough to survive."

Earnhardt led five times for 220 laps but, in the early going, he lost a lap when he was forced to pit on the 99th circuit after experiencing a flat right-rear tire. Two laps later, the fourth of 14 caution flags was flown when Butch Miller spun down the frontstretch in the Clark/Slender You Oldsmobile Cutlass. On the restart, Earnhardt was one of a trio of drivers who quickly managed to regain their lost distance and then move up when the fifth caution flew on lap 123 after Bobby Hillin Jr., spun in the fourth turn.

Earnhardt ran among the top ten until lap 167, when he pitted under green for left-side tires. Again, he lost a lap. But, on lap 244, he regained it when he passed leader Lake Speed's Wynn's/Kmart Oldsmobile. Just as he did so, he got a break when the ninth caution period began on the next circuit when Ken Schrader looped his Hendrick/Folgers Coffee Chevrolet into the wall in the second turn.

Earnhardt continued to pursue the leaders throughout the race and by lap 268, when the 12th caution period ended, he was in fourth place behind leader Speed, Kyle Petty and Ricky Rudd.

He moved into third on lap 273 and, on lap 277, he took over second. On lap 281, he passed Speed to take the lead for the third time in the race.

Meanwhile, Alan Kulwicki, driver of the Zerex Ford, followed Earnhardt into second. On lap 371, nine laps after the end of the 13th caution period, Kulwicki passed Earnhardt on the front-stretch to assume the No. 1 position, but it didn't last. Earnhardt retook control on lap 391.

But, he wasn't home free. By lap 411, Elliott passed Kulwicki to assume second. Then, on lap 418, Phil Parsons spun in the third turn to bring out the 14th caution flag, just one short of the record set in 1985. Earnhardt, Elliott and Kulwicki, running first through third, respectively, pitted and each took on four fresh tires.

On the restart on lap 423, Earnhardt and Elliott began pulling away, with Earnhardt getting the measure of his rival. But, on lap 482, Earnhardt ran up on the rear bumper of Darrell Waltrip's Hendrick/Tide Chevrolet, which was two laps down, and had to back off. That allowed Elliott to close in and set up the final scenario.

"Darrell was a couple of laps down and I don't know why he didn't get out of the way," said Earnhardt. "I thought he should have moved over, but I guess he thought he was racing for position."

Elliott remained close, but could not pass.

"I thought the right-front tire was pushing because I would skate up high in the turns," said Earnhardt. "I didn't know if I could hold off Elliott much longer. If the race had gone

10 more laps, I don't think I could have."

"We did everything we needed to do tonight to win this race, but we came up just a little short," said Elliott. "We lost two laps and made them up. I just wish a few more breaks would've gone our way at the end. Earnhardt

> "Darrell was a couple of laps down and I don't know why
> **he didn't get out of the way."**
> —Earnhardt

could pull off the corners, no matter how high he drifted, and that's what killed us."

Earnhardt's victory, his fifth in the last eight BIR races, was worth $48,500. And it could not have come at a better time.

"Damn right," responded Earnhardt, when asked if the win was the tonic he needed after a broken valve relegated him to also-ran status

started to drive aggressive against the track. I put the car where I wouldn't have had I been leading the race by a comfortable margin.

"It was a rough track and I'm surprised we finished without a bunch of broken A-frames and ball joints on the car. It's a tough SOB but I get around it good. We have a consistent combination on short tracks – our car works on every lap around the track. If we don't win the points championship, I would like to have about eight or nine in the win column."

Geoff Bodine finished third in the Hendrick/Levi Garrett Chevrolet, one lap down. Davey Allison took fourth in the Ranier/Havoline Ford, also one lap down, while Kulwicki limped home fifth with a dropped cylinder, also one lap down.

Among the retirees through accidents were Dave Marcis, Mark Martin, Dale Jarrett and Brett Bodine. Mechanical problems took out Derrike Cope, Rick Mast (in his first run in Buddy Baker's Red Baron Frozen Pizza Oldsmobile), Terry Labonte and Mike Alexander.

BY WINNING THE BUSCH 500, EARNHARDT TIGHTENED THE RACE FOR THE CHAMPIONSHIP.
DAVID CHOBAT PHOTO

in the Aug. 21 Champion Spark Plug 400 at Michigan International Speedway.

"We broke that valve in the engine up there, but here we ran consistent in qualifying and in practice runs. I ran more conservatively early but, after I got the second lap back, I

There were 23 lead changes among 13 drivers, a track record, which happened before Earnhardt took command for good on lap 391. Earnhardt, who ultimately led five times for 220 laps, won with an average speed of 78.775 mph. ∎

Earnhardt Wins
First In '89

Earnhardt And Radials Team Up For Victory

By STEVE WAID

Armed with the Goodyear radial tires which exceeded the most optimistic performance predictions, Dale Earnhardt swept to his first victory of the year in the First Union 400 NASCAR Winston Cup race at North Wilkesboro Speedway.

In what evolved into a rout for Goodyear's newest product over Hoosier's bias-ply tire, Earnhardt won for the first time since the Busch 500 at Bristol, Tenn., last August. He ended his 15-race losing streak when he crossed the finish line three seconds ahead of a determined Alan Kulwicki.

In his GM Goodwrench Chevrolet, Earnhardt was dominant, leading 296 of the race's 400 laps on the 0.625-mile track. The victory vaulted him back into first place in the Winston Cup point standings with 1,054, just three more than Geoff Bodine.

Earnhardt paced a field of cars that ran Goodyears exclusively by lap 110, or just 69 miles into the race. The evidence that the radials would win the day came quickly. Rusty Wallace started on the pole with Hoosiers and intended to change under the first caution period, a strategy several other Hoosier drivers — there were 15 of them among the 32 in the field when the green flag fell — also planned to implement.

However, before that caution finally began on lap 117, the superiority of the radial tires had forced them to change under green. No better proof could be provided after Wallace was lapped by leader Darrell Waltrip on lap 77, just 48 miles into the race.

"Goodyear did a good job with the radials," said Earnhardt. "Everyone questioned the radials before the race, but in my case, the more I ran them the better I liked them.

"I didn't have a set all day that was all that much different. I think the radial will be a good tire at certain tracks and I would like to see 'em tested. I'm behind Goodyear all the way. I hope they get the best out of all this, because they have worked very hard. They have stood behind it and have proven themselves."

Earnhardt started third and was confident he would be able to take the lead early. He did, grabbing it for the first time when he passed Bodine's Levi Garrett Chevrolet on lap 26.

"I knew once the race started I would be in fat city," said Earnhardt, whose victory was worth $51,225. "We had tested the radials up here and made 30-40 lap runs on them. Based on that, we knew the consistency was there.

"Hey, I was glad all those guys qualified on Hoosiers. I knew that, before long, they would have to change 'em. If they were all on Goodyears, it might have been a lot rougher

EARNHARDT BOUNDS PAST A LAPPED RUSTY WALLACE, WHO HAD STARTED ON THE POLE, BUT SUFFERED ON HOOSIER TIRES BEFORE CHANGING TO GOODYEARS LATE IN THE RACE.
DAVID CHOBAT PHOTO

out there racing guys like Rusty."

After Earnhardt took the lead for the first time, he was seldom out of it. He gave way to Waltrip on lap 66 and the driver of the Tide Chevrolet was in charge through lap 128, just three laps after he tapped the rear end of Wallace's Kodiak Pontiac and sent it spinning in the first turn.

Earnhardt retook the lead at that point and gave it up for only 16 of the remaining 272 circuits.

He wasn't without his challengers. Waltrip gave him a tussle and might have fared better if his engine had not lost a cylinder. By lap 275, Earnhardt was in a war with Wallace, who was trying to regain his lost lap. The two bumped and thumped – not unexpected given their aggressive styles – and were warned by NASCAR to "calm down."

"Hell if I know," replied Earnhardt when asked why he was warned. "NASCAR gets all excited when I go bumping with someone who has bumped me. There were a couple of guys who bumped me at the end of the race and I'm sure NASCAR didn't say anything to them."

The confrontation with Kulwicki's Zerex Ford came after the restart from the 10th and final caution period on lap 358. Earnhardt had a sizable lead, but Kulwicki kept closing the gap. By lap 393, he had caught Earnhardt and made his first attempt to pass, which came up short.

Then, on lap 395, Kulwicki darted underneath Earnhardt in the first turn. But he was unable to hold his car down and it slid precariously close to the wall. His last chance had failed.

"I did think I had more car than Alan after the restart," said Earnhardt. "The car was consistent and I could pull away. But I got to racing a bit with Rusty again and I was punishing the tires trying to get by him before he finally let me by.

"I think Alan had to do the same thing and he punished his tires, too. So he got a bit loose there in the first turn and I took it easier after that."

Kulwicki said that brake problems hampered him.

"I ran out of brakes or I would have had him," he said.

Mark Martin put the Stroh's Light Ford in third place behind Kulwicki while Dick Trickle turned in another good performance in the Miller High Life Buick with a fourth-place finish. Terry Labonte took fifth in the Budweiser Ford, while Ricky

KELLY, TERESA, DALE AND DALE JR. LOVE WINNING, ESPECIALLY WHEN IT'S CLOSE TO HOME.
DAVID CHOBAT PHOTO

Rudd finished sixth in the Quaker State Buick.

Bodine finished seventh, while Waltrip took eighth and was the last driver to complete all 400 laps. Wallace was ninth, a lap in arrears, while Ernie Irvan took 10th in the Kroger Pontiac, four laps down.

"There were a couple of guys who bumped me at the end of the race and I'm sure
NASCAR didn't say anything to them."
—Earnhardt

Twenty-four of the 32 starters were running at the finish. Engine failure sidelined Rick Mast and Sterling Marlin, while failed brakes put Jim Sauter out of the competition. Jimmy Means was eliminated with a broken rear-end gearing.

The day's only multicar accident – there were several single-car spins – occurred on lap 275 and brought out the fifth caution period. It was triggered when Brett Bodine's Motorcraft Ford made contact with Marlin's Sunoco Oldsmobile and spun in the fourth turn amid a pack of cars.

Involved were Bodine, Michael Waltrip – whose car was slammed by Rick Wilson's Kodak Oldsmobile – Lake Speed and Greg

Sacks. Bodine, Waltrip and Wilson were eliminated from the race.

The victory was the 35th of Earnhardt's career and it put him in sole possession of 12th place in the all-time standings, breaking a tie with the late Fireball Roberts.

It wasn't expected, given Earnhardt's consistency this year. Prior to North Wilkesboro, he had scored a second-place finish and three thirds in six events. A crash relegated him to 33rd place at Darlington, S.C., and a bent tie rod put him back in 16th at Bristol.

"Last year, we did have tire problems," said the 37-year-old Kannapolis, N.C., native. "The problem was trying to figure out which was the better tire. This year, we didn't have that.

"What happened was, a cut tire and a crash put us out at Darlington and then I hit a tire that had been left on pit road at Bristol and that bent the tie rod. Those were two competitive races for us, races we felt we could have won.

"But we've been competitive all year. We've got second- and third-place finishes and, today, we started up front and stayed there all day. The season is young, but it's still the same – it's consistency that wins the Winston Cup.

"Sure, I was frustrated that we hadn't been winning. But the guys on the team always worked hard. It wasn't them, it was just a little bad luck."

Earnhardt didn't need luck at North Wilkesboro. He was equipped with the unbeatable combination of a good car and a revolutionary new tire that might well be the staple of NASCAR in the future. ∎

BUDWEISER 500

dale earnhardt

EARNHARDT BLOWS PAST POLESITTER MARK MARTIN AFTER THE FINAL CAUTION FLAG OF THE RACE. EARNHARDT WOUND UP BEATING MARTIN BY .5-SECOND AT THE FINISH.
DAVID CHOBAT PHOTO

Earnhardt
Earnhardt Nabs First Dover Win

Tames
The 'Monster Mile'

By DEB WILLIAMS

For 10 years, Dale Earnhardt attempted to conquer Dover Downs International Speedway and, when he finally accomplished the objective in the Budweiser 500, he did it with style.

Earnhardt tamed the "Monster Mile" by dominating the track and his competitors in a fashion rarely seen at the one-mile oval. En route to his second Winston Cup victory this season and the 36th of his career, Earnhardt broke track records for the 50-, 100-, 250-, 300- and 350-mile marks.

The three-time Winston Cup champion led eight times for 456 of the 500 laps, including the final 63, and he was passed only once on the track for the lead. Only Richard Petty, who led 491 laps en route to victory in 1974, has been more dominant.

Earnhardt said the last race he remembered when everything was perfect like at Dover was at Darlington, S.C., in 1986 when he led more than 300 of the 367 lap TranSouth 500.

"When the race started we did what we wanted to do," said Earnhardt, who won

$59,350. "We kept our stagger the same and the car was consistent all day.

"We didn't have any problems all day and that's a rare thing at Dover. Usually, even the winner has a problem.

"I'd run my pace and when the guys would want to come and run hard I'd bear down a little bit, but I really didn't get after the car all day except when Kenny (Schrader) and me were running."

It was evident from the race's beginning that Earnhardt's Chevrolet was the dominant car. Starting from the outside of the front row, Earnhardt assumed the lead on lap two and led 79 laps before pitting for right-side tires and gas.

When the Kannapolis, N.C., native resumed the lead on lap 89, he built up what appeared to be an insurmountable lead. By lap 132, Earnhardt was only ten seconds away from lapping the field when he pitted for a four-tire change. However, because of the large lead he possessed when he stopped, he didn't lose a lap.

Earnhardt managed to stay in front of leader Schrader until Morgan Shepherd caused the first caution period when the engine blew in his Pontiac and he smacked the wall in turn three. A fire erupted under the car, but was quickly extinguished by firefighters. That caution allowed Earnhardt to come around the track and when everyone pitted for tires and fuel, Earnhardt received only fuel. That got him off pit road first and into the lead on lap 145.

The only time Earnhardt was passed on the track for the lead during the race was when Schrader sideswiped him in turn two to assume the top spot at the halfway point and collect $10,000. The two had raced side by side for several laps before Schrader finally bumped Earnhardt.

"He got a little rough so I got out of the way," said Earnhardt, who noted the only change his team made to his car during the final practice session involved raising the sway bar.

"He was racing for that halfway money and I didn't want to hit that wall when he got into me, so I let him go.

"He (Schrader) got a little rough
so I got out of the way."
—Earnhardt

"It was one of those deals where I'd like to have gotten the halfway money, but I didn't want to get out of the groove. The groove is not wide up here and I wanted to take care of the car. After he got that money, he eased up a little bit and we went back around him at our consistent pace."

Schrader said he wanted the halfway money and he knew Earnhardt did, too.

"I got underneath him and I thought, 'Heck, what would Dale do?' So I just glanced at him."

In his post-race interview, Earnhardt noted he was like an elephant and didn't forget such things.

It appeared pole position winner Mark Martin might be able to challenge Earnhardt for victory, but even he was unable to capitalize on a caution that occurred with 15 laps remaining when Michael Waltrip hit the wall in turns three and four. When the race restarted with eight remaining, Earnhardt quickly jumped out ahead of the pack and Martin couldn't catch him.

"I could actually run faster than Dale after about 30 laps, gaining a 10th, to two 10ths a lap," Martin said. "But he was so far gone, there wasn't anything I could really do to catch him."

Earnhardt, who finished half a second ahead of Martin's Ford, averaged 121.702 mph in the race, slowed by six caution flags

for 36 laps. There were 19 lead changes among seven drivers in the four-hour, six-minute, 29-second raced before an estimated record crowd of 66,000.

The win was the first for Chevrolet at Dover since the 1986 Budweiser 500, which was won by Geoff Bodine. Until race time, Earnhardt had heard Dover was a Ford track but he didn't believe it.

"I don't believe in a Ford or a Chevrolet track," Earnhardt said. "A race track is a race track and a race car is a race car. If you get the four springs, the tires and everything going the right way, and a good motor and a good driver, you're going to win."

In addition to the win being the second in three races for the new Chevrolet Lumina, it also moved Earnhardt to within two points of Darrell Waltrip in the battle for the Winston Cup championship.

"It's going to be a tough championship between me and Darrell," Earnhardt said. "There's going to be name calling and it's going to be one of those good ol' days like we've had before and he's had with some other people. It'll be a classic championship, and who can handle the pressure will decide it." ∎

EARNHARDT BRINGS A LITTLE COMIC RELIEF TO THE POST-RACE 'HAT DANCE'.
DAVID CHOBAT PHOTO

TIRED OF JUST HOLDING THE PLASTI-KOTE SPRAY CAN FOR PICTURES, EARNHARDT DECIDED TO DO A LITTLE PRODUCT TESTING BY 'TAGGING' VICTORY LANE WITH GRAFFITI.
DAVID CHOBAT PHOTO

Victory Caps
Special
Weekend
For Earnhardt

Third Win Of Season Highlights Memorable Darlington

By STEVE WAID

For Dale Earnhardt, it could not have been a better setting.

It was mean ol' Darlington International Raceway; it was the venerated Heinz Southern 500, the oldest NASCAR Winston Cup superspeedway race of them all.

Two nights before, Earnhardt was formally inducted as a member of the prestigious Unocal-Darlington Record Club and elected its president. The night before the race, he had felt pride as his late father, Ralph, one of the greatest drivers of the past, was inducted into the National Motorsport Press Association's Hall of Fame.

The time was right. It was time to win. What better way to end a weekend at Darlington?

That is exactly what happened. With his GM Goodwrench Chevrolet prepared diligently by the Richard Childress-owned team, Earnhardt led 153 of 367 laps to win the Heinz Southern 500 by 1.5 seconds over Mark Martin.

It was Earnhardt's third victory of the 1989 season and his first since June, when he took the checkered flag in the Budweiser 500 at Dover, Del. He has now won 37 times in his career, including five times at Darlington, and twice in the Heinz Southern 500.

But statistics didn't mean much to him when the race was over. That he had won capped one of the most fulfilling weekends of his life.

"They inducted me into the record club and then on Saturday night (Sept. 2) they inducted my father into the Hall of Fame," said Earnhardt. "My mom and my family came down and it was a super night. It got to me. I had a lot to say when I went up to speak, but I couldn't say anything but 'Thank you.'

"There were a lot of people Dad raced for and against there and it was just a great night. I kept thinking when we got back to the motel, 'Wouldn't it be great if I could win this race tomorrow?'"

In achieving the victory, Earnhardt did not have the fastest car, by his own admission. But he ran consistently – which has been his pattern all season long.

"I felt confident. I felt good before the race," said the 38-year-old driver from Kannapolis, N.C. "But I didn't want to get my hopes up too high. This GM Goodwrench team has been running good for the last several races, but we've just had problems.

"I think, today, we finally dodged all them bullets that have been hitting us."

Earnhardt, who qualified 10th, vaulted into the lead early, by the 54th lap. He was to remain a contender with the likes of Rusty Wallace and Harry Gant until the first "bullet" was fired at him. It came on lap 166, when he scraped the wall between the first and second turns of the 1.366-mile Darlington track.

That forced him into the pits for a right-side tire change and he dropped 25 seconds behind leader Gant, driver of the Skoal Bandit Oldsmobile. Fortunately, he remained on the lead lap.

It was for that reason he was able to recapture the lead on lap 270 when leader Ken Schrader pitted during a series of green-flag stops. Earnhardt was forced to come in a lap later, but regained good track position when the third caution period began on lap 227 for debris in the second turn.

On the restart on lap 235, he was in fifth place as Wallace held sway. He moved by Bill Elliott on lap 238 to take fourth place and then got by Geoff Bodine on lap 239 to take third. Two laps later, he passed Gant for second.

He passed Wallace high in the third turn to retake the lead on lap 268. He and his Kodiak Pontiac rival then staged a show for the crowd, doing some close racing that saw Wallace resume the point on lap 282 for 10 circuits.

Except for a single lap, when Ken Schrader took the lead, Earnhardt and Wallace were to swap the lead two more times and dominate the field.

But the situation changed on lap 305, during the fourth and final caution period, which began on lap 300 following Dave Marcis' collision with the back pit wall.

Wallace pitted twice during the yellow-flag session and, as a result, was caught well back in the pack when the race restarted on lap 307. Earnhardt, meanwhile, pulled away from second-place Bodine who was soon eliminated from contention on lap 316 when a valve dropped in his Levi Garrett Chevrolet.

That put Martin, driver of the Stroh's Light Ford, in second place, 1.2 seconds behind. But, for the final 63 laps of the race, Martin could do nothing to challenge Earnhardt who, at one point during the closing laps, built up a margin of 2.5 seconds.

"The car was mediocre but we did run that consistent pace," said Earnhardt, whose victory was worth $71,150. "After about 35-40 laps, the car would get so loose I would have to be very careful with it. That's when Rusty and Harry could beat me early in the race.

"But, as the track got greasier, it seemed they got worse. I stayed about the same. We had made some adjustments on the car and they helped.

"Rusty must have gotten a mismatched set of tires on that last stop because he couldn't do

much. After our last stop, I asked if we had enough gas and I was told we did. I never said another word. I kept going until the finish. I wanted to watch the gas gauge, but I didn't."

The victory tightened, however slightly, Earnhardt's hold on first place in the point standings as he bids for a fourth career title.

> "I think, today, we
> # finally dodged
> # all them bullets
> that have been hitting us."
> —Earnhardt

He now has 3,037 points, 73 more than Wallace, who finished fourth and has 2,964 points. That was a gain of 20 points for Earnhardt. Martin is in third place in the standings with 2,904 points, 103 behind Earnhardt.

Darrell Waltrip came into the Heinz Southern 500 looking for the victory that would earn him a $1 million bonus in the Winston Million program. But the driver of the Tide Chevrolet had a tough day. He rapped the fourth-turn wall twice and that caused his rear-end suspension to go away.

HAVING MUSCLED PAST, AROUND AND THROUGH HIS COMPETITION, EARNHARDT FLEXES ONE LAST TIME.
DAVID CHOBAT PHOTO

As a result, he finished 22nd, eight laps down.

Additionally, Waltrip lost points to Earnhardt. He is in fourth place in the standings with 2,813 points, 224 in arrears.

"This (the championship race) is a long way from being over," said Earnhardt, who won titles in 1980, 1986 and 1987. "Each race will make a difference. Rusty is running real consistent and he's a tough competitor. I was happy to see Mark beat him today and then I beat them both. That

means I gained on both of them.

"There are eight races to go. Rusty has to play 'catch-up' and I'm leading. I'm not worried."

Wallace, Schrader and Gant, who lost his chance at victory when he damaged the toe-in on his car after whacking the wall between turns one and two five times, finished fourth through sixth, respectively. Elliott took seventh in the Coors Ford while Bobby Hillin Jr., was eighth in the Miller High Life Buick, the last driver to complete all 367 laps.

Morgan Shepherd was ninth in the Valvoline Pontiac, one lap down, while Sterling Marlin rounded out the top ten in the Sunoco Oldsmobile, also one lap down.

The four caution flags for 27 laps – the fewest ever for a Heinz Southern 500 – helped

EARNHARDT SHARED SOME OF THE POST-RACE SPOTLIGHT WITH HIS SISTER CATHY.
DAVID CHOBAT PHOTO

Earnhardt win with a race-record speed of 135.462 mph. That bettered the mark of 134.033 mph set by Cale Yarborough in 1973. Ironically, that was the same year Ralph Earnhardt died of a heart attack.

Victims of the 13-car attrition rate included pole winner Alan Kulwicki, Terry Labonte and Jimmy Means, who fell prey to engine problems. Greg Sacks, Jimmy Spencer, Richard Petty and Marcis were put out due to accidents.

Asked if he would have swapped $1 million – the money on the line for Waltrip – for his father's Hall of Fame induction on Sept. 2, Earnhardt replied, "Definitely not.

"My dad raced hard. He won a lot of races and he was almost forgotten – but not by my family and friends," Earnhardt said. "When he was nominated, it was a big thrill for everyone.

"I've won three Winston Cup championships. Maybe someday I'll be elected and I'll be there with him."

There seems to be little doubt about that. ■

September 17, 1989

PEAK PERFORMANCE 500

dale earnhardt

EARNHARDT LOOKS CALM, EVEN SMUG BEFORE THE START OF THE PEAK PERFORMANCE 500. COULD HE HAVE KNOWN THE OUTCOME?
DAVID CHOBAT PHOTO

Earnhardt Outduels Martin For Fourth Win Of '89

Sidesteps Three Encounters With Possible Disaster For Triumph At Dover

By DEB WILLIAMS

Prior to 1989, Dale Earnhardt never had won at Dover Downs International Speedway. But this year the three-time NASCAR Winston Cup champion has led a charmed life at the one-mile track.

In June, Earnhardt demolished his competition by leading 454 of the 500 laps en route to victory in the Budweiser 500.

This month, he easily controlled the first half of the Peak Performance 500, set six track records during the race, sidestepped three incidents that could easily have ended his day, regained a lap he lost to Mark Martin on lap 416 when he pitted for four tires and fuel, and then emerged victorious from a torrid 10-lap duel with Martin to claim his fourth win of this season.

By finishing a 0.28 second ahead of Martin's Stroh's Light Ford, Earnhardt earned his 38th Winston Cup career win. The track records he broke occurred at the 150-, 200-, 250-, 310-, 350- and 400-lap marks. The record of 125.775 mph at the 310-lap mark broke the old record of 124.693 mph set by Earnhardt in June, while the record of 129.590 mph at 150 laps broke the one of 125.494 mph set by Geoff Bodine in 1985.

With his win, Earnhardt also gained 39 points on Rusty Wallace in the Winston Cup title battle, increasing his lead to 102 points with six races remaining.

The heated duel between Martin and Earnhardt occurred after the event's final caution period, which lasted through lap 466 of the 500-lap race.

On lap 469, Earnhardt possessed about a three-car length lead over Martin but by lap 473, Martin was hanging on to Earnhardt's rear bumper. The Arkansas native's first attempt at passing Earnhardt came on lap 484. Martin took the low groove while Earnhardt went high and, on lap 485, they scrubbed sheet metal as they raced side by side down the frontstretch. They continued their torrid battle for another lap before Martin fell back in line.

On lap 492, Martin shot below Earnhardt on the backstretch and stayed beside him for two laps before he bobbled, nearly losing control of his Ford, on the frontstretch as they exited turn four. Martin returned to the follow-the-leader position with Earnhardt, falling to a two-car length deficit on lap 495, and never challenged for the lead again.

"Mark gave me a tough run," said GM Goodwrench Chevrolet driver Earnhardt, who noted track position played an important role in the race's outcome. "It was a good battle. He raced hard and he raced clean. I've got to hand it to him, he ran a hard second. He raced me good. He's a good racer. He's going to win in his time.

"He would get under me and I would give him room on the bottom because I didn't want to pinch him off. I didn't want him to knock me loose. I was ready for anything.

> "NASCAR tried to give me a hard time about that.
> ## What are they going to do, spank me
> or fine me? It was just a half a lane."
> —Earnhardt

"I could cool my tires a little better up a groove or two and then I could run on the bottom the next lap and seem to gain some ground. After we ran a while the last 30 laps, he didn't seem like he could do much with me on the bottom; only hold me at bay on the outside. I could get back by them, then his tires seemed to be hot and I could put some ground on him. That worked to my advantage, and we were lucky to win. The last 10 or 20 laps were a lot of fun racing Mark, but I would rather have had a little edge on him."

Martin had nothing but compliments for Earnhardt after the race.

"Dale Earnhardt gave me all the room that I needed to win that race," Martin said. "I just didn't quite have the car to do it. I slid up into him and got sideways a couple of times. We took our shot. We burned up our tires trying. I tip my hat to him."

It was evident from the race's beginning that Earnhardt's Chevrolet definitely was one of the cars to beat. The Kannapolis, N.C., native started 15th in the 40-car field and charged through, passing Wallace for fourth on lap 26. He grabbed the lead for the first time on lap 63 when he blew past Dick Trickle in turn two.

"I wanted to run my pace and try to get to the front," said Earnhardt, who now has won two of the last three races. "I was worried about the leaders getting away in a long green and we might not have the track position we needed. I wanted to get up front as quick as I could. I wasn't punishing it when I was running it at the front. I was just running a good pace."

Earnhardt led 94 laps after passing Trickle and, at one point, held a straightaway advantage over Davey Allison. He turned the top spot over to Allison on lap 157 when he pitted for four tires, but later led on five more occasions for a total of 375 laps, including 35 of the final 57.

During those laps, Earnhardt once led by a half lap. By lap 410, everyone but Earnhardt, Martin, Ken Schrader and Davey Allison were at least one lap down.

"We just seemed to hit on a good setup," said Earnhardt, 38. "It was the same car we ran here in the spring. I wrecked it at Bristol (Tenn., Aug. 26), we fixed it back and it's just as good."

During the race, three incidents occurred directly in front of Earnhardt that could have cost him the win. The first was on lap 249 when Rob Moroso's Preston Oldsmobile spun in turn two after colliding with Dale Jarrett's Hardee's Pontiac.

Then, on lap 276, Alan Kulwicki's Zerex Ford blew its engine as he entered turn one and, on lap 454, a multicar crash that hospitalized Neil Bonnett, blocked the track briefly

dale earnhardt

in front of the eventual winner.

"Fortunately, everything cleared just as I got there," said Earnhardt, who collected $59,950. "We weren't just exactly on top of it, but we were close enough."

In the race's early stages, it appeared Kulwicki and pole position winner Allison might provide Earnhardt with a challenge. But that wasn't the case after the 200-lap mark.

"I was surprised that Davey and Kulwicki didn't run any better chassis-wise than they did, and Rusty, too, because of how they practiced and how they've raced here before," Earnhardt said.

At the race's midpoint, Schrader and Earnhardt dueled fender to fender and, on lap 336, found themselves in a tight situation with Wallace's lapped car. Entering turn three, Earnhardt went high, Schrader dove low and Wallace was in the middle with Jimmy Spencer in front of him. Schrader stole the lead as Wallace went high with Earnhardt. But Schrader held the lead only briefly, as Earnhardt regained it before the lap was completed.

"We got in there and Kenny and I were going faster than they were," Earnhardt explained. "We got to racing with them and Rusty got into me there in (turns) three and four and carried me up the race track."

While Earnhardt sometimes gambled on the track, team owner Richard Childress was doing the same thing in the pits. He just didn't bother to tell his driver. On lap 362, Childress ordered only one can of fuel into Earnhardt's Chevrolet.

"We knew we had to get in one full can to make up the distance to get back in the lead where we could control the race at that point," Childress said. "We knew if we put on four tires, that anybody who wanted to win would have to follow suit. We knew we could stop again within 45 or 50 laps and that would give us enough to go the distance. We knew we'd have to put four tires on at that point and fill the car completely with fuel.

"It was just a gamble. It would have cost us if a caution had come out when Mark had us a lap down. We might not should have gambled that early in the race, but we knew to win that's what we had to do. Everything went just like we planned it. Usually the leader dictates what everybody else has to do. We were trying to pull everybody into a

four-tire stop."

Earnhardt averaged 122.909 mph in the race, slowed by five caution flags for 31 laps. It was stopped for 11 minutes, 41 seconds while workers cleared the track following the Bonnett incident. During the red flag, Phil Parsons climbed from his Oldsmobile and inspected his car's right-side until a NASCAR official made him get back into his car. Earnhardt parked up on the banking in turns one and two and NASCAR officials weren't pleased with that action either.

"I parked up on the bank so if the starter wouldn't work or something, when we got ready to go again, I could roll it off," Earnhardt said. "I don't like to cut it off for a red flag.

"NASCAR tried to give me a hard time about that. What are they going to do, spank me or fine me? It was just a half a lane."

There were 18 lead changes among seven drivers in the race that occurred before an estimated crowd of 64,000 and took four hours, four minutes and five seconds to complete. ∎

Deb Williams looks back on
Dale Earnhardt's fourth win of 1989

There was never any doubt that Dale Earnhardt possessed a velvet touch when it came to driving a race car. Many would have described it as golden, but no matter the adjective, it all boiled down to his special, almost uncanny, ability with a race car.

A race car wasn't a mechanical object to him; it was his dancing partner. And the September Dover race in 1989 was one of those events where that fact was clearly evident.

In the Peak Performance 500, Earnhardt set six track records, sidestepped three incidents that could have ended his day and regained a lap he lost to Mark Martin before emerging victorious from a torrid 10-lap dual with the Arkansas driver. However, it was the manner in which he raced Martin that day that made it memorable.

Earnhardt's respect wasn't given. It had to be earned, and it was clear in that event that Martin was one of only a select few who enjoyed a special type of respect from the tough competitor. Earnhardt didn't invent the bump-and-run tactic, but he made it famous, and no driver

appeared to be immune from his front bumper. No one, that is, except Martin.

Earnhardt was notorious for laying a bumper to someone to obtain the position he wanted, but that didn't happen on this day when he battled Martin, recognized as one of the circuit's cleanest drivers.

> A race car wasn't a mechanical object to him; it was his dancing partner. And the September Dover race in 1989 was one of those events where that fact was clearly evident.

"Dale Earnhardt gave me all the room that I needed to win that race," Martin said after the event. "I just didn't quite have the car to do it. I slid up into him and got sideways a couple of times."

Earnhardt, however, always knew the difference between a "just-racing" hit and a deliberate one, and with Martin it was always the former. Earnhardt and

Martin raced by different codes, but they respected the one each had chosen.

"It was a good battle. He raced hard, and he raced clean," Earnhardt said after his fourth victory of the season.

"He would get under me, and I would give him room on the bottom because I didn't want to pinch him off. I didn't want him to knock me loose. I was ready for anything."

And that included knowing what his car needed during a red flag.

When the race was stopped to clear the track following Neil Bonnett's accident, Earnhardt parked up on the banking in turns one and two, so if he had trouble starting his car when the race restarted, he could roll it off. His actions displeased NASCAR officials, but that didn't bother him.

"NASCAR tried to give me a hard time about that. What are they going to do, spank me or fine me? It was just a half a lane," he said.

But that was Earnhardt, prepared for anything and determined to handle it his way.

—Deb Williams
Editor
NASCAR Scene

DESPITE FLYING AROUND THE ATLANTA TRACK AT DIZZYING SPEEDS AND LEADING THE RACE FOR 269 OF 328 LAPS, EARNHARDT COULD ONLY WIN THE DAY, NOT THE CHAMPIONSHIP, WHICH WAS WON BY RUSTY WALLACE, DESPITE A 15TH-PLACE FINISH.
DAVID CHOBAT PHOTO

dale earnhardt

Earnhardt Romps To Victory

Wallace Sweats Out A Title

Winston Cup Championship Battle
Ends As Second-Closest Ever

By STEVE WAID

True to his reputation, Dale Earnhardt ran like a bat out of Hades. Rusty Wallace, considered his match in aggressiveness, was never afforded that luxury.

However, both emerged winners in the Atlanta Journal 500 NASCAR Winston Cup race – a contest that was darkened by the death of part-time driver Grant Adcox.

In an awesome display of muscle, Earnhardt led seven times for 269 of the 328 laps on the 1.522-mile Atlanta track to record his fifth win of the season. He made the ultimate effort to wrest the Winston Cup title from Wallace's hands, but to no avail.

Instead, Wallace encountered a myriad number of problems and proved no factor in the outcome. However, his 15th-place finish, three laps down, was good enough to win the coveted championship by 12 points (4,176-4,164), the second-closest margin in NASCAR's modern era. Only Richard Petty's 11-point win over Darrell Waltrip in 1979 was closer.

It was an ironic turn of events, one that was so similar to last year's scenario at Atlanta when Wallace lost the championship to Bill Elliott by 24 points. In that race, Wallace powered his way to a dominant victory, yet Elliott's 11th-place finish was sufficient enough to gain the championship, as he needed only an 18th-place run to do so.

Earnhardt came to Atlanta in third place in the point standings, 79 behind Wallace and one behind Mark Martin. This time, it was Wallace who could win the title with an 18th-place finish. By his own admission, Earnhardt had no recourse but to run as hard as possible, piling up laps led and, hopefully, emerge victorious.

He followed his strategy to the letter. His GM Goodwrench Chevrolet, prepared under the guidance of team owner Richard Childress and crew chief Kirk Shelmerdine, never skipped a beat. At the finish, Earnhardt was an astonishing 25.71 seconds, nearly a full lap, ahead of second-place Geoff Bodine.

"No, I don't think we've run a better race," said Earnhardt, three times a Winston Cup champion. "We had a good race at Dover (Del., in June) and a couple of other places, but here we came down and just did everything we could do. The only thing we didn't do was win the pole and we had a shot at that.

"All we asked is that things go as smooth as they could in the race and they did. We just came up short, that's all there is to it."

Adcox died as the result of a crash in the second turn on lap 202, when his Chevrolet slammed into the wall and caught fire. The 39-year-old driver from Chattanooga, Tenn., who had established a reputation as one of the best drivers on the Automobile Racing Club of America (ARCA) Permatex Supercar Series, was pronounced dead at Georgia Baptist Hospital in Atlanta at 4:15 p.m. due to massive head and chest injuries.

Earnhardt, who has now won 39 times in his career, showed his strength early. Starting from the third position, he blew past pole winner Alan Kulwicki and second-place starter Ken Schrader on the second lap and went on to lead 51 circuits before pitting under green on lap 52.

Eight laps later, he was in front again and this time led 25 laps, surrendering his advantage while making a pit stop under caution. By lap 89, he set sail for 52 more laps, once again giving up first place for a pit stop under green.

"Rusty will be a good champion,"

said Earnhardt. "He's got good people on his team and I wish all of them the best."

That was the pattern all day. Earnhardt was never beaten on the track. The last time he relinquished first place was on lap 283. He took it back on lap 293 and led the remaining 36 circuits, pulling away easily.

"We came here with a good car and we knew what we could do after testing here earlier," said Earnhardt, who resides in Doolie, N.C., on the shores of Lake Norman. "We felt we would be able to run hard but, in practice here, Rusty was beating me a couple of times. That bothered me.

"So, we made a few changes in the car; did a few things and the car responded. It just never quit. I stayed after that car all day. I really rode it hard and I never gave it a break. It just did the job it was supposed to."

That was more than enough to win the race – but not the championship.

"The crew didn't keep me posted on Rusty and it really didn't matter," said Earnhardt. "The deal was we were going to run to win and then see where we stood.

"Circumstances did get Rusty today. He had a lot of problems. But I reckon he just didn't have enough of 'em. He kept getting a lap down here and there but it just wasn't enough. I never wished him any bad luck but I didn't wish him any good luck either."

Wallace's problems? Well, in brief, they were: A missed chassis setup, a fuel mixture that was too rich in the carburetor, a flat tire that wasn't there, loose lug nuts, and unfortunate timing during pit stops.

Wallace started fourth in the Kodiak Pontiac, but it was quickly evident he would be no challenger for Earnhardt. Drifting back into the pack, he lost a lap when he pitted for right-side tires on lap 50. Any chance he might have had to recapture it was lost when the second caution period of the day came out on lap 59 for Greg Sacks' spin in the second turn, which triggered a wreck involving Richard Petty and Jimmy Spencer.

Then, on lap 91, Wallace made an unscheduled stop under green because he thought his right-front tire was going flat. It evolved he was wrong; the vibration he felt was being caused by rubber buildup on the tire. A second lap was lost and, more disturbing for Wallace, he fell to 33rd place.

Wallace pressed on and, helped by a high attrition rate, moved as high as 14th place by lap 256.

On lap 281, he pitted under green again but lost no distance because Earnhardt did the same thing a lap later. But, on lap 286, Wallace was forced into the pits for a final time because of loose lug nuts. The left-side tires on his car were changed, but another lap was lost in the process.

Remarkably, even though Wallace was three laps down, he was in 13th place. He wound down to 15th by the race's end.

"I don't care how sloppy this looked, this is the highlight of my career," said Wallace, winner of six races and four pole positions in 1989. "We lost a lap when we were out of synch on pit stops, another when I thought we had a flat and then another with loose lug nuts. On top of that, we had too high a gear in the car, too much fuel in the carburetor and I can't believe we missed on the setup.

"I told Dale before the race that he had to do the same thing I did last year and that's what he did. I think if he couldn't win the championship, he would want to see me win it and I think he would tell you that.

"No matter where I was on the track, I ran the car hard. I wish I could have run it hard to win, but it's a championship and I won it. That's all I could do."

Wallace became the first driver to win a championship in a Pontiac since 1962 when Joe Weatherly claimed the title with team owner Bud Moore. Wallace is only the second Pontiac driver to win the title.

For his own part, Earnhardt was forced to play the hunter over the last four races of the season. The leader in points going into the Oct. 8 All Pro 800 at Charlotte Motor Speedway, Earnhardt suffered a disastrous stroke of bad luck in that race as a broken camshaft led him to a last-place finish.

Wallace assumed the points lead and held it thereafter.

EARNHARDT KNEW WHEN HE JUMPED FROM HIS CAR THAT HE'D WON THE BATTLE, BUT NOT THE WAR.
DAVID CHOBAT PHOTO

"The only thing I really fault in all of this is the broken camshaft at Charlotte," said Earnhardt. "That really put us behind and I've wished 100 times we could have done something about it. For the rest of the year, there was a lot of pressure and a lot of situations. I thought we got things turned around a bit at Phoenix (in the Nov. 5 Autoworks 500) and we put ourselves in a position to win the title.

"I took a vacation in Hawaii, did some deer hunting in Canada and then came to test here. We knew after that we were good enough to beat anyone here in long runs.

"We did just that, but it wasn't good enough. It's over and Rusty is the champion and we're second," said Earnhardt. "I congratulate Rusty and his team on winning the championship. We did all we could do and we ended up on a winning note. Maybe we can keep this up in 1990."

Bodine, in his Levi Garrett Chevrolet, slipped past Schrader to take second place on the last lap as Schrader ran out of fuel. Sterling Marlin, with an excellent run in the Sunoco Oldsmobile, also got around Schrader to take third. Schrader came home fourth in the Folgers Chevrolet, while Darrell Waltrip rounded out the top five, one lap down, in the Tide Chevrolet.

Kyle Petty in the Peak Pontiac, Bobby Hillin Jr., in the Miller High Life Buick, Morgan Shepherd in the Valvoline Pontiac, Neil Bonnett in the Citgo Ford and Lake Speed in the Bull's Eye Barbecue Sauce Oldsmobile rounded out the top 10.

Sixteen of the 42 starters failed to finish the race. Engine failure claimed Phil Parsons, Terry Labonte, A.J. Foyt, Dick Trickle, Dave Marcis, Rick Mast and Martin.

Martin's engine blew in flames on lap 226, and the Arkansas driver, who had settled comfortably among the top 10 the time, saw his hopes for a title go up in the blaze. He finished 30th in the race and third in the final standings with 4,053 points, 123 behind Wallace and 111 behind Earnhardt.

Alan Kulwicki, who could have pocketed $410,400 if he could have paired a race win with his pole victory, lost a lap early with a pit miscue and finished 13th, three laps down, in his Zerex Ford.

With six caution periods in the three-hour, 33-minute, 36-second race, Earnhardt won with an average speed of 140.229 mph. With bonuses totaling $19,100 for laps led, he earned $81,700.

"Rusty will be a good champion," said Earnhardt. "He's got good people on his team and I wish all of them the best. But, look out for 1990.

"Hell, right now I'm ready to go deer hunting."

Which is what he did. ∎

EARNHARDT

EARNHARDT

EARNHARDT

NASCAR WINSTON CUP SCENE

EARNHARDT

EARNHARDT

EARNHARDT

EARNHARDT

EARNHARDT

EARNHARDT

Earnhardt Displays Strength In 125-Mile Win

Trickle Victory Bid Foiled By Empty Gas Tank

By DEB WILLIAMS

With 11 laps remaining in the second of two 125-mile qualifying races for the Daytona 500, Dale Earnhardt stormed through the field – much as Union Civil War Gen. William T. Sherman stormed through Georgia – to claim his first victory in 1990.

Sherman's famous "March to the Sea" wreaked havoc on the Peach State. And, in the second twin, a Georgia resident was also the primary victim.

Try as he might, Bill Elliott just couldn't overtake Earnhardt and had to settle for the runner-up slot, 0.47 second behind the three-time NASCAR Winston Cup champion.

For Earnhardt, who started from the pole position, a yellow flag in the event's later stages at the 2.5-mile track was the key to the Kannapolis, N.C., native's third career win in the twin qualifying races. Earnhardt was fourth when Mark Stahl and Mickey Gibbs spun off turn two on lap 36. Elliott and Earnhardt were among 10 drivers who elected to pit, taking on four fresh tires and fuel. Dick Trickle and Jimmy Spencer, who were first and second respectively, remained on the track.

"I was a little looser than I wanted to be at the start of the race," said Earnhardt, who averaged 157.123 mph. "I thought Elliott and I could run together but after eight or 10 laps we got shuffled back and the Pontiacs started filtering to the front. It seemed the Pontiacs were handling a lot better than the rest of us.

"We were really lucky to get the caution. I'm not really sure we could have beaten those guys. We put four tires on and it worked. Elliott took four tires, too, and he ended up being the car I had to race to win."

The race restarted with 11 laps remaining and with 10 laps to go Earnhardt was 12th. Elliott latched onto Earnhardt's bumper and the two began breezing past the cars in front of them. With eight laps remaining, Earnhardt was eighth and a lap later he was sixth.

Earnhardt claimed third and Elliott fourth with five laps remaining as they raced through turn four.

With four laps to go, Earnhardt was second and the following lap he dove low on Trickle as they sped down the backstretch. Trickle moved low and then Earnhardt went high to snatch the lead as they entered turn three.

"Tried to help him (Elliott) all I could when we were drafting up toward the front, and then when we got to Trickle I had my hands full get-ting around Trickle, so I had to forget about Elliott," Earnhardt said. "I sort of let him (Trickle) have a little bit of room going through one and two.

"When we came off the corner he falls to the inside and just about the time he was going back to the right, I go to the left. When I go to the left, he comes back to the left," he said.

"We go down to the grass just about all the way to the third turn. It was just one of them deals. I was going to go by him, or I was going to make a shot at him. He must have thought he was at Milwaukee or something on a short track. I'm not sure what he thought."

Elliott remained third, behind Trickle, with 1½ laps to go but the Georgia driver's Ford tapped Trickle's Pontiac as they exited turn two when Trickle's car ran out of gas. That tap sent the Wisconsin native spinning. The incident relegated Trickle to a 22nd-place finish, while Elliott captured second.

"At first, it looked like he (Trickle) was going to get loose and I waited a second to check up because I had everybody above me and it looked like someone was going to go below me," Elliott said. "Man, you're racing them, you're trying to look all around to see what's going on in front of you and the next thing I knew he had checked up and I had tagged him."

"There wasn't a thing in the world I could do. I truly hate it."

Elliott said his Ford was extremely loose in the first part of the race.

"When somebody got up under me I was so loose I couldn't do anything," the Dawsonville, Ga., resident continued. "I decided I'd lay back, ride my own race and, if something happened, I'd go from there.

"When the caution came out, we decided to come in for four tires, Earnhardt did, too, and that's really what got us back to the front," said Elliott, who noted he also had some wedge jacked into his car.

"We got to Spencer and we got a little out of shape coming out of turn four. I was trying to get by him and Dick came down in front of me."

Elliott said the speedway was the slickest he'd ever seen it.

"I had a handful in traffic. It's going to be a situation (in the Daytona 500) of whoever has the best handling car," he said. "I'm still not perfect but I was able to run wide open the last session. I just ran out of laps to catch Earnhardt.

"I think I could have passed him (Earnhardt) if I could have gotten a slingshot on him, like going down the back straightaway where he wouldn't have had enough time to catch me back. But he was strong."

Trickle, who completed 48 laps, said his team believed it could go the distance without a fuel stop. But, when he came off the second corner, he "lost the throttle" on his Pontiac. He waved to Elliott to let him know his car was out of gas, but he said there was nothing Elliott could do.

"You can't come off the throttle in the corner and not have someone hit you. It wasn't his (Elliott's) fault. There wasn't anything he could do," Trickle said.

"Evidently, we should have stopped when everyone else did. If we had put on tires and taken on gas, I think we could have run with anybody."

Like Trickle, Spencer didn't stop for fuel or tires in the 50-lap race. But, unlike Trickle, he completed the distance and finished third.

"If that last caution hadn't come out, I think I would have been a factor," Spencer said. "The 66 (Trickle) ran out of gas but I think I had him covered."

Spencer said his crew decided not to pit for fuel because it knew the team's qualifying speed was good enough to get them into the race and everyone wanted to go for the win.

"But we got third and that gives us a top-10 starting position in the Daytona 500. That's a dream come true for this team," said Spencer.

Spencer denied he was protecting his spot with various maneuvers on the track.

"You're just staying in the draft out there," he said. "You're not doing any cutting off of people. You can't cut anybody off at Daytona. You would kill somebody.

"You're in the draft and you need to see everything in front of you. If a bird flies in front of you, as Buddy Baker says, follow that bird. You need everything that breaks your air."

Earnhardt led twice for 24 laps, while Trickle paced the field for 26 laps. There were two lead drivers and two caution flags for six laps.

Defending Winston Cup champion Rusty Wallace never was a factor in the race and finished 16th in the 31-car field. He had to get into the Daytona 500 field via his qualifying speed of 190.267 mph. That left him starting near the rear of the field. ∎

BABY TAYLOR EARNHARDT TAKES HOLD OF HER FATHER DALE'S TROPHY. HE'S GOT TWO OTHERS. THIS ONE BELONGS TO HER. DAVID CHOBAT PHOTO

dale earnhardt

AFTER A TOUGH DAY ON THE TRACK, EARNHARDT SETTLES IN FOR SOME CELEBRATING.
NWCS ARCHIVE PHOTO

Earnhardt's
Dominance
Pays Off In First Win Of Year

After Flogging The Field, He Guns Down
Shepherd In Wild Finish

By STEVE WAID

For those watching the Motorcraft Quality Parts 500, the NASCAR Winston Cup race presented a familiar sight.

There was Dale Earnhardt, driver of the GM Goodwrench Chevrolet, humbling his rivals. Lap after lap, he led them around the 1.522-mile Atlanta International Raceway, staying comfortably ahead in a display of power.

But, in the end, Earnhardt had to use all that power in a stirring comeback, which won the event.

The victory was Earnhardt's first of the

1990 season and the sixth of his career at AIR. To get it, he had to best Morgan Shepherd in his Motorcraft Ford in a two-lap duel to the checkered flag.

"This was a much tougher race than in November," said Earnhardt, who won last year's season-ending Atlanta Journal 500 with ease, leading 294 of 328 laps. "About halfway into the race, I started feeling sick to my stomach and I thought about calling the guys and getting a relief driver. But I just put it out of my mind."

Earnhardt had other things on his mind. After leading 214 laps – and by as much as 16

seconds – Earnhardt pitted under green on lap 276 to change left-side tires, surrendering his lead to Budweiser Ford-driving Geoff Bodine.

Trouble struck. The stop took 19.9 seconds, unusually long for the GM Goodwrench team, four-time world champions of the Unocal-Rockingham Pit Crew Competition.

"We came in for left-side tires and I think the air wrench messed up," said Earnhardt, who ultimately led 216 laps.

"Then, when I went back out, the left rear tire spun and a ratchet locked up. That heated up the tires and it took a couple of laps for it to straighten out. I was really nervous then, but I was finally able to start catching Bodine."

The pit stop allowed Bodine to put a lap on Earnhardt, who was in a very vulnerable position. If a caution period began before he could make up his lost distance, his chances for victory would be doomed.

But the race proceeded under the green flag. In fact, at the time of Earnhardt's pit stop, only one yellow flag had flown – on lap six for three circuits – because of Terry Labonte's engine failure.

Bodine pitted on lap 291 for right-side tires. He spent 13.2 seconds off the track and returned still in the lead. Earnhardt had regained his lost lap but was 6.8 seconds behind.

However, the Kannapolis, N.C., native

came charging forward. He was 4.60 seconds behind by lap 300, then 2.45 seconds behind by lap 310. Finally, he was nipping at Bodine's heels on lap 315, just 13 laps from the end of the race.

"Bodine had taken just one can of gas on his stop, which is one reason why he was able to stay in front of me," said Earnhardt, who now has won 40 times in his career and is tied with Tim Flock in 11th place on NASCAR's all-time list. "I had to concentrate. I didn't even think about being sick. I was able to catch Bodine and I wanted to work on him a bit before passing him."

Before Earnhardt could make a move, the scenario changed dramatically. On lap 318, the engine in Rusty Wallace's Miller Genuine Draft Pontiac blew as Wallace exited the fourth turn. Behind him, the cars of Earnhardt and Bodine were shrouded in smoke.

> "About halfway into the race, I started **feeling sick to my stomach** and I thought about calling the guys and getting a relief driver. But I just put it out of my mind."
> —Earnhardt

"I didn't want any cautions," Earnhardt said. "I was worried about them because it would allow other cars to jumble up with me on the restarts and I'd have to race them."

On lap 320, Bodine and Earnhardt pitted for tires, along with several other members of the front pack. The exception was Shepherd, who opted to stay on the track and assumed the lead when the race restarted on lap 322. Mark Martin, driver of the Folgers Coffee Ford, beat Earnhardt out of the pits to take second. Earnhardt restarted in third and Bodine was fourth.

Two laps later, the scene changed again. Bodine and Bobby Hillin Jr.'s, Snickers Buick collided in the fourth turn and, as a result, Hillin's car was sent into a smoking spin and Bodine lost valuable distance. With Shepherd in the lead, Earnhardt and Martin raced back to the yellow flag, with Earnhardt winning the dash and second place in the process.

The estimated crowd of 45,000 eagerly awaited what it knew would be an exciting, dramatic finish. With two laps left, the green flag flew. Shepherd's hope was that he had enough left in his tires to hold off Earnhardt.

But, on lap 327, Shepherd was shifted to the outside going into the first turn as the

lapped Zerex Ford of Alan Kulwicki took the middle groove.

Seeing the hole created inside, Earnhardt blasted through to take the lead.

"I didn't have time to look at what might have been going on between Morgan and Alan," said Earnhardt. "The groove is wide over in that turn and I saw a hole open up on the inside. I think I went lower than I usually do but there was plenty of room."

As Earnhardt sped ahead, a furious battle for position was waged behind him. When it was over, Shepherd was second, six car lengths behind Earnhardt. Ernie Irvan completed a brilliant run as the new driver of the Kodak Films Oldsmobile by finishing third and Ken Schrader's Kodiak Chevrolet nosed out Martin's for fourth.

"When I got by Morgan, he had to start racing with those guys behind him and that gave us a clean shot for the last two laps," said Earnhardt.

Shepherd maintained Kulwicki interfered with him on the last restart.

"He slowed me up and let Earnhardt go under me," Shepherd said. "He should have let me have the hole since I was the leader and he was lapped."

"I don't think I cost him the race," Kulwicki replied. "I don't think I did anything wrong. If Earnhardt got tires and Shepherd didn't, I don't see how Shepherd thought he could have won the race."

Kyle Petty finished sixth in the Peak Antifreeze Pontiac, while Bodine wound up seventh. Kulwicki was eighth, one lap down, while Harry Gant took ninth in the Skoal Oldsmobile, and Sterling Marlin rounded out the top 10 in the Sunoco Oldsmobile. Each was a lap in arrears.

Earnhardt won the race with an average speed of 156.849 mph, a track record that eclipsed that of 152.523 mph he set in the 1986 Atlanta Journal 500. The race's three caution periods lasted only 10 laps, which contributed to a stretch of 310 laps under the green flag.

The victory was a tonic for Earnhardt, who started with a similarly dominant performance in the Daytona 500, only to lose the race when a cut tire from a piece of bell housing forced him to give way to eventual winner Derrike Cope on the last lap.

"You don't ever get over Daytona," said Richard Childress, Earnhardt's car owner. "Nothing makes up for it. But this helps. We're not looking back, we're looking ahead."

Earnhardt started on the pole by virtue of car owner points, which were utilized after qualifying was rained out March 16 and 17. Because of that, he was ineligible for the

$7,600 bonus offered in the Unocal 76 Challenge to the driver who wins the pole and the race.

Earnhardt thus earned $85,000 for his victory.

"All we did on our car was a couple of plug checks and a wax job," said Earnhardt, the three-time Winston Cup champion and current points leader. "We scuffed a couple of sets of tires, too. We didn't change anything from last November. Everything worked great. Atlanta is a handling track and I like a car to be loose and wide open. If you can get a car to handle like that here, you are going to be all right."

In the Motorcraft 500, Earnhardt was more than "all right." He was the picture of perfection and, this time, nothing kept him from his goal. ■

DAUGHTER TAYLOR SEEMS TO ENJOY 'TROPHY-TRAINING.'
DAVID CHOBAT PHOTO

TRANSOUTH 500

TEAM GOODWRENCH IS ON A ROLL AND READY FOR MORE. NWCS ARCHIVE PHOTO

Earnhardt Prevails Over Challenges At Darlington

Earns Second Straight Win At Track And Second Straight Of Year

By STEVE WAID

Certainly Geoff Bodine or Morgan Shepherd could have won the TranSouth 500 NASCAR Winston Cup race. Perhaps one of them should have.

But, in racing, "coulds" and "shoulds" don't count. And, so it was that Dale Earnhardt, driver of the GM Goodwrench Chevrolet owned by Richard Childress, did win.

In a tense finish, which saw the Kannapolis, N.C., driver square off with his rivals on restarts from two caution periods in the last 18 laps, Earnhardt finally crossed the finish line two car lengths ahead of the Folgers Ford of Mark Martin to win for the second time in the first five races of the 1990 season. Earnhardt also won the fourth race,

the March 18 Motorcraft 500 at Atlanta International Raceway.

It was also Earnhardt's second consecutive win on the 1.366-mile Darlington track, as he took the victory in the Heinz Southern 500 last September. His latest triumph pushed his career earnings to over $10 million - $10,060,638 – and he thus joins Darrell Waltrip as the only drivers to reach that financial plateau.

"We stayed out of trouble today and tried to get the car to do what we wanted it to," said Earnhardt, who now has 41 career Winston Cup victories, 11th on the all-time list. "The car was loose at one time and it pushed at another time. Then there was the big wreck in the fourth turn that I was lucky to get through.

"I tried to pace myself, run a consistent race, and it paid off."

Earnhardt admitted he was worried before the race began and his mood during the week's preparation reflected it. His concern involved the radial tires, used at Darlington for the first time.

"I was concerned about them all week," Earnhardt said. "That's why I wasn't a good interview the entire week. We only qualified 15th and I wasn't happy with the way the radials fell off after 40 laps.

"That was our problem during the long runs under green. The tires would go away; you couldn't push them or barrel into the turns and cut left like you could with the bias-ply tires."

Despite his fears about the radial tires, Earnhardt ran well enough to take the lead for the first time on lap 54 when he passed Bodine's pole-winning Budweiser Ford, which had led 50 laps to that point.

Earnhardt would lead until lap 100, when Bodine again took command during the fourth caution period caused by Dick Johnson, who hit the wall in the second turn. Bodine's Junior Johnson-owned Ford would remain the leader for 71 laps before giving way to Bill Elliott's Coors Ford during a pit stop. Bodine then retook the lead for 32 more circuits on lap 174.

The sixth caution period began on lap 205 following Rick Wilson's spin in the second turn and when the restart came on lap 210, Bodine was in second place behind Ken Schrader. On lap 211, trouble struck.

Ernie Irvan, who had lost 10 laps due to a spin and mechanical problems in his Kodak Film Oldsmobile, was attempting to regain one of them when he made contact with Schrader's Kodiak Chevrolet in the fourth turn. Both cars slid and caused a melee behind them. Bodine was involved, as his car was popped in the rear end, which bent sheet metal and affected its handling capabilities.

Also caught up were the cars of Sterling Marlin, Neil Bonnett, Ricky Rudd, Michael Waltrip, Derrike Cope, Richard Petty, Mark Martin, Rob Moroso, Jimmy Means and Wilson. Of the group, Means, Irvan, Bonnett and Wilson were eliminated.

Bonnett, knocked unconscious briefly, was taken to McLeod Regional Medical Center in Florence, S.C., where tests, including a CAT scan, proved negative. However, he was kept overnight for observation.

"Bodine was getting away from us because we had adjusted the chassis and it didn't work," Earnhardt said. "Then we adjusted it again and it got better. Then came that wreck and, when I saw it, I just jumped off the banking, found a hole and got through it."

Morgan Shepherd, driver of the Motorcraft Ford, got through it as well and it was his turn to hold sway after Bodine had led 154 laps. He led the 11 laps of caution until Earnhardt took over on the restart and led 24 laps. Then, on lap 248, Shepherd passed Earnhardt in the first turn to retake the point.

Shepherd kept building his advantage, increasing it to 9.4 seconds over Earnhardt by lap 274. He gave up the lead on lap 275 when he pitted during a series of green-flag stops, but then retook it on lap 281 when the field completed its pit road runs. He was now 7.66 seconds ahead of Earnhardt.

Earnhardt caught a break with the eighth caution period, created by a wreck between Alan Kulwicki and Dick Trickle in the first turn. When it happened, he was a whopping 11 seconds behind Shepherd.

"Morgan ran strong, but then again when we could make adjustments on the car and get new tires, we could race with him," said Earnhardt.

Earnhardt got his chance to do just that when the green flag flew on lap 306. On that lap, Shepherd clipped the wall between turns one and two and, as a result, Earnhardt was able to slip past him in turns three and four. Shepherd gave chase, but hit the second-turn wall on lap 324. He recovered from that to move within a car length of Earnhardt when the ninth caution period began on lap 349.

Jack Pennington spun in the fourth turn

in front of the leaders. Earnhardt went to the outside, while Shepherd and Harry Gant, who was running third in the Skoal Bandit Oldsmobile, went to the inside.

"When Pennington spun, everything in front of me went up in smoke," said Earnhardt. "Richard Petty was in front of me and he put on the binders and I put on the binders and I hit him, but it didn't do any damage. Morgan and Harry got by me then."

> "I tried to pace myself, run a consistent race, and
> ## it paid off."
> —Earnhardt

But, not for long. On the resulting pit stops, Earnhardt's GM Goodwrench crew got him out first.

"That's what made the difference," Earnhardt said. "We adjusted the car one more time, got new tires and got out first. We beat them in the pits and the crew did the job."

Earnhardt was the leader until the finish, 18 laps later. But not without some tension. With seven laps remaining, Mike Alexander wrecked down the frontstretch to bring out

Twenty-one of the 40 cars that started the race were running at the finish. Completing positions seven through 10 were Elliott, Brett Bodine in the Quaker State Buick, Michael Waltrip in the Country Time/Maxwell House Pontiac and Schrader.

"We kept adjusting things today," said Childress. "We went the wrong way and adjusted back and got it right the last time. I didn't want that last caution but, by that time, we felt we could handle anybody on the last restart if nothing went wrong.

"We were just loose on a long run. We haven't learned everything about the radial tires we need to know, but we got it better because, near the end, Dale was able to hold off Morgan and then Mark at the very end."

Earnhardt, bidding for a fourth Winston Cup championship, remains in first place in the point standings by 78 points (839-761) over Shepherd. Neither driver has finished out of the top 10 this season, but Earnhardt can count two victories in his tally.

"We're in pretty good shape right now," said Childress. "We've got the Chevrolet working and the attitude of the team is real good. We've just got to stay on top of it. We're working on our front-steer chassis now and, if we get it right, I think we're going to be really tough."

A FAMILIAR SCENE: EARNHARDT RACING TO THE FLAG A WINNER AT DARLINGTON
DAVID CHOBAT PHOTO

the 10th and final caution period. That bunched up the field for the final three circuits. On the restart, Earnhardt was ahead of Martin, Shepherd, Davey Allison and Gant.

Allison, who had made up two lost laps and recovered from three scrapes with the wall, passed Shepherd on lap 365 to claim third place. Bodine, remarkably, recovered from his involvement in the multicar accident that took the lead away from him, and finished fourth. Shepherd was fifth with Gant sixth.

"Today, I had to drive the car very consistently," said Earnhardt, who won with an average speed of 124.073 mph, led 129 laps, and earned $61,985. "We didn't get into trouble, which you can't afford to do at Darlington, because it's a tough old race track to get through. To run 367 laps here and win a race, you've got to come home with all your wheels going straight.

"Consistency won it for us today, that, and the guys' work in the pits." ■

EARNHARDT SHOWERS SOME OF HIS FELLOW REVELERS AFTER NOTCHING HIS THIRD WIN OF THE SEASON.
NWCS ARCHIVE PHOTO

dale earnhardt

Earnhardt Lives Up To Nickname The Dominator

Sacks Falls Short Of Upset

By GARY McCREDIE

D ale Earnhardt added more credence to one of his nicknames, "The Dominator" at the 2.66-mile Talladega Superspeedway, while Greg Sacks, doing his best to add another winner to Rick Hendrick's NASCAR Winston Cup stable, came just two car lengths short of accomplishing his goal.

In simple terms, Earnhardt, driving the Childress/GM Goodwrench Chevrolet Lumina, led eight times for 107 of 188 laps to win the Winston 500. Although it was the first time he had won the event, it was his third win at Talladega, third of the season and 42nd in a career that began in earnest in 1979.

Although Sacks had rides in so-called "movie cars" this year and drove this Lumina in the Busch Clash at Daytona Beach, Fla., his appearance at Talladega marked the debut of a "research and development" team owned by Hendrick and actor Paul Newman and backed by Ultra Slim-Fast.

While it was clear early in the event that Earnhardt and Sacks were two of perhaps four dominant cars, the two drivers began showing their combined hand following the sixth of seven caution flags for 28 laps. The yellow was thrown on lap 164 for debris in the first corner and most of the field pitted for fresh tires.

When the race went green on lap 166, the running order was Michael Waltrip, Earnhardt, Mark Martin, Sacks, Ernie Irvan and Terry Labonte, the only cars on the lead lap. Two laps later, Earnhardt and Sacks had left the other four well behind.

The caution flag was thrown for the last time on lap 169, this time for debris in the second corner and, when it went green for the final time on the 172nd circuit, Earnhardt and Sacks were still running one-two. With 10 laps to go, Earnhardt and Sacks were almost 3.5 seconds in front of Martin's third-running Folgers Coffee Ford and at the finish that margin had increased to about six seconds.

Martin finished third; Irvan was fourth in the Kodak Film Oldsmobile, Waltrip fifth in the Country Time/Maxwell House Coffee Pontiac, and Labonte sixth in the Skoal Classic Oldsmobile.

"We were racing with Greg. He was pretty strong," said Earnhardt. "We worked well today, but he was the one I was worried about.

"When we were racing, I was watching him in the mirror. When he started falling off in the corners, I knew he was testing me, so I started to fall off, too.

"It's hard to know what a guy will do, but it worked to my advantage," added Earnhardt. "I think he was surprised. It worked to my advantage this time but, when he reads this in

DALE JR. CAN'T MASK HIS EXCITEMENT AS DALE GETS READY TO LET LOOSE AND SOAK THE CREW.
DAVID CHOBAT PHOTO

the press, he'll know about it."

With Sacks glued to his rear bumper for the final 28 laps, Earnhardt – toward the very end – noticed Sacks was slowing just a wee bit. With the two Chevrolets about equal in horsepower and handling, Earnhardt also backed off and the race became something of a guessing game.

It was a game Earnhardt won.

"The last caution was just what I wanted," said Sacks. "I wanted to be one-two with Dale and just let the two of us race for the win.

"It was great. I wasn't wide open all the way. There was a little cat and mouse going on.

"Dale was real strong and we just came up a lap short," he said. "I think if it wasn't for the traffic on that last lap that I would have had a better shot at the win.

"I wish I had made my move a lap earlier."

While there were 25 lead changes among 12 drivers, Earnhardt led the lion's share of the race. Sacks led four times for 41 laps, while Ken Schrader put his Hendrick/Kodiak Lumina up front on three occasions for 20 laps.

Schrader was the other car that worried Earnhardt. It was strong, too, and it was owned by Hendrick.

Would Schrader and Sacks have "teamed up" to possibly thwart Earnhardt? Because Schrader dropped out with distributor problems on the 155th lap, Earnhardt found the question hard to answer.

"That (Schrader's demise) helped us," said Earnhardt. "Greg's car was a little looser than my car and in working with him I got away.

Kenny didn't make it to the end, so I didn't know what they'd do. I felt like Greg would wait until the last lap or two to make his move."

"Working together" meant just that. During the last caution period, the two teams agreed their drivers should link up, put some distance on the rest of the field and then race for the win at the end.

"Greg and I worked together and got away from the rest of the guys," said Earnhardt. "On that last caution, we went down to his pit and said, 'Let's work together.'

"Let's get away and then race."

At the very start, pole position winner Bill Elliott fell back to eighth, allowing Schrader to lead for one lap. Earnhardt then took over, leading laps two through 19 and then it was Sacks' turn to go to the front.

He led laps 20-25 and Earnhardt took over again, leading laps 26-40. In all, the two drivers swapped the lead between themselves five times.

The first caution came out early – on lap four, when the engine in Derrike Cope's

Chevrolet let go in the second corner. That was followed by the second yellow on lap 11, which came out so safety crews could mop up oil from the blown engine in Rick Wilson's Oldsmobile.

When Bill Elliott and Dick Trickle crashed coming out of the second turn off lap 77, the third yellow went into effect, with subsequent cautions coming on laps 105 for a nine-car accident, 122 when Phil Barkdoll hit the wall, and 163 and 169, both for debris.

It was a good day for Earnhardt in many respects. First, he won $98,985, and that made him the all-time money winner in American motorsports. With a total of $10,213,278 in 341 starts, he surpassed Darrell Waltrip, who, in 494 races, has collected $10,201,565.

Earnhardt also has a shot at the "Winston Million." If he can win the Coca-Cola 600 at Charlotte, he's guaranteed a $100,000 bonus and, if he can also win the Heinz Southern 500, he'll be $1 million richer.

Next, he padded his lead over Morgan Shepherd in Winston Cup points and, with 1,460 markers to his credit, he now leads second-place Shepherd by 90 points. Shepherd, by the way, finished eighth and continued his streak of nine top-10 finishes in as many races.

Finally, Earnhardt won five additional contingency awards that totaled $22,500.

"It's never an ordinary day, but it was a smooth day for us," said Earnhardt. "The guys in the pits didn't miss a beat and everything worked to our advantage.

"I was on the defensive all the time (during the closing laps). That's when it's time to watch your Ps and Qs.

"I didn't back off on the last lap. I came out of (turn) two leading by several more car lengths than the last several laps. Then he (Sacks) had a longer run to make up.

"The last caution was just what I wanted. I wanted

to be one-two with Dale

and just let the two of us race for the win."—Greg Sacks on his bid for the upset.

"I had already beat him down the backstretch and that's where I worried about him. But I made a good run on him coming out of the (second) turn," he said.

Earnhardt was fast and was clocked at speeds just under 200 mph on several occasions. He noted that, "it says we're just learning to work with the cars and that every time you put a restrictor plate on it (engine) you work hard to get around it."

NASCAR, of course, is trying to discourage high speeds at Talladega and Daytona Beach, Fla., by making a 15/16-inch restrictor plate mandatory at the two tracks. It didn't seem to deter Earnhardt, who was clocked at 200.587 mph on the 159th lap.

"No, don't write that! You all got that wrong," said Earnhardt. "It was 199.999.

"If Bill France (Jr., NASCAR president) reads this, we're going to be running with smaller restrictor plates."

Completing the top 10, all a lap down, were Kyle Petty, Shepherd, Hut Stricklin and Darrell Waltrip. Earnhardt ran the event in three hours, eight minutes and two seconds at an average speed of 159.571 mph.

Forty cars started the race and 27 completed it. ∎

EARNHARDT PACED THE PACK AND NEVER GAVE UP THE LEAD.
DAVID CHOBAT PHOTO

dale earnhardt

It's No Sweat

Leads All 70 Laps En Route To Second Career Win In 'All-Star' Event

Earnhardt Takes Dominating Victory

By STEVE WAID

It surprised no one, yet it was still an awesome thing to see.

Dale Earnhardt, who had been heralded as the man to beat in The Winston, proved that no one could do so, as he led all 70 laps around the 1.5-mile Charlotte Motor Speedway to become the first driver in the six-year history of the special event to win it twice. Earnhardt first won it in 1987.

With his pole position, which he and his GM Goodwrench team earned on May 18, and his victory, Earnhardt grabbed a record payout of $325,000 – which included bonuses for leading both the first 50-lap segment of the race and the final 20-lap segment.

"There was no question who beat who today," said Earnhardt. "I don't mean for that to sound like bragging but, today, the race was won without controversy.

"There aren't many mad fans. Oh, maybe some are because their man didn't win, but not because someone knocked anyone else out."

The 39-year-old Earnhardt, a native of Kannapolis, N.C., did what everyone thought he would do – broke away in his GM Goodwrench Chevrolet at the start of the first 50-lap segment. Darrell Waltrip, who started third in the Tide Chevrolet, immediately moved into second place past Havoline Ford-driving Davey Allison.

Earnhardt, however, remained uncontested. But, behind him, a challenge began to mount. Bill Elliott, who started sixth in the Coors Ford, passed Mark Martin's Folgers Ford on lap 23 to take over second place, 1.18 seconds behind Earnhardt.

As the laps passed, Elliott began to close. On lap 30, he was 0.59 second in arrears. Twenty laps later, Elliott was a half-second behind as the race stopped for the mandatory 10-minute intermission.

During the intermission, teams were allowed to make routine pit-stop changes to their cars – procedures such as replacing springs and sway bars were not permitted.

Earnhardt's only complaint about the first segment was that his car was a bit tight.

"We worked on changing that but, other than that, the first 50 laps were good," he said. "There was some good racing. Guys got to race a few other people out there.

The lineup at the start of the final 20-lap segment was Earnhardt, Elliott, Martin, Ken Schrader in the Kodiak Chevrolet and Alan Kulwicki in the Zerex Ford.

It was up to Earnhardt to make the first move, the first in what many thought would be a race-closing duel between him and Elliott.

But Earnhardt pulled a "tricky" maneuver.

He maintained a low pace; forcing Elliott to do likewise, and then quickly sped away as the green flag fell, leaving Elliott in his wake.

"Actually, he was leading me a little bit," said Earnhardt. "I thought he would wait on me. When I got to where I wanted to start, I just did. It caught him."

Elliott fell back as far as seventh place, as Martin, Kulwicki and Schrader fell in behind Earnhardt.

But, on the fourth lap, a caution flag was thrown when debris was spotted between the first and second turns. Caution laps did not count in the final segment so, when the race's fifth official lap began with the restart, Earnhardt was bunched up with Martin, Schrader and Kulwicki.

On the sixth lap, Schrader began racing for position with Martin while Elliott, who had moved back up to fifth place, had to contend with Winston Open winner Dick Trickle. This permitted Earnhardt to open up breathing room over his opponents. Schrader then got around Martin and trailed Earnhardt by a half-second.

Once again, it seemed Earnhardt would be challenged. By the 10th lap, Schrader closed to 0.35 second, or about two car lengths, behind Earnhardt. By the 15th lap, he was nearly hooked onto the rear bumper of Earnhardt's Chevrolet.

But that would be as close as Schrader would get. There would be no duel, no metal-tapping, no controversial spins, wrecks, or other assorted incidents. Instead, Earnhardt took the checkered flag 0.34 second ahead of Schrader.

Schrader's second-place finish earned him $82,500, while Martin picked up $62,500 for third place. Elliott ended up fourth, worth $57,500, while fifth place and $42,500 went to Allison.

"No we didn't know we could lead this race flag to flag," said Earnhardt. "But I need to tell you something about our Chevrolet. It's a 1987 Monte Carlo and we put on a front-steer snout and added the Lumina sheet metal.

"It's the same car we pulled off the track at Richmond (Va.) earlier this year to use as a spare (he finished second) and we won with it at Darlington (S.C.). It also ran well at Bristol (Tenn.) until I messed up and spun.

"When we brought it here, I was a bit puzzled because I thought we would use more of a superspeedway car. When we tested, we didn't test all that well so we took the car back to the shop and found out what was wrong and made adjustments.

"When we brought it back, it ran a lot better. I was impressed when we won the pole – the guys did a great job in the pits – and to lead the first 50 laps from flag to flag was impressive, too. Whenever anyone would close on me, I could change my line on the track and the car would respond really well," he said.

> "He told me after the race that, if he had caught me, he would have clipped me. Well, I've got a steering wheel, too. I'm glad it didn't come to that." —Earnhardt

"The only problem was the car was a bit tight, especially through the third and fourth turns. During the intermission, we made some changes and that's just what we needed."

Earnhardt said he tried to run consistent laps throughout the final segment.

"I was running hard, but I was watching my rearview mirror, too. I wanted to stay consistent in case anyone did catch me. Then I could have something for them," he said.

NO, YOU CAN'T TAKE THAT AWAY FROM HIM. EARNHARDT NOW HAS MATCHING BOOKENDS, TAKING HOME HIS SECOND TROPHY IN THE WINSTON. DAVID CHOBAT PHOTO

Earnhardt admitted he was concerned about Schrader.

"He seemed to be really strong," he said. "He told me after the race that, if he had caught me, he would have clipped me. Well, I've got a steering wheel, too. I'm glad it didn't come to that.

"This is an even year, and there's not supposed to be any controversy in The Winston."

True enough. In 1987, Earnhardt was involved in a scrap with Elliott and last year, Rusty Wallace and Waltrip engaged in a controversial incident in the fourth turn that saw leader Waltrip slide through the grass and pave the way for Wallace's victory with just one lap remaining.

Two years ago, though, the event was non-controversial.

Ironically, neither Wallace nor Waltrip figured in the sixth edition of The Winston. Wallace left the race after just eight laps and finished 20th, the victim of a blown engine in his Miller Genuine Draft Pontiac. Waltrip experienced problems with his carburetor – which NASCAR said could not be changed during the intermission – and finished 13th.

Other casualties were Brett Bodine, who fell victim to a throttle linkage problem in his Quaker State Buick and completed just 55 laps to finish 19th. Derrike Cope finished 18th in the Purolator Chevrolet, two laps down due to an early pit stop to change a flat tire.

Rounding out positions six through 10 were Trickle, who fashioned an excellent run after starting 20th due to his victory in the Winston Open; Harry Gant, seventh in the Skoal Oldsmobile; Kulwicki, eighth; Morgan Shepherd, ninth in the Motorcraft Ford; and Bobby Hillin, 10th in the Snickers Buick.

Positions 11-17 were taken by Lake Speed in the Prestone Oldsmobile; Ricky Rudd in the Levi Garrett Chevrolet; Waltrip; Terry Labonte in the Skoal Classic Oldsmobile; Kyle Petty in the Peak Pontiac; Geoff Bodine in the Budweiser Ford; and Phil Parsons in the Mack Tools Oldsmobile.

Earnhardt's performance was characteristic of his season. He leads the Winston Cup point standings in his bid for a fourth career title and has won three Winston Cup races this year – at Richmond, Darlington and Talladega, Ala. He also won the first round of International Race of Champions competition at Talladega and now adds The Winston to his list.

"If you work hard, you can dominate and sometimes you make your luck," said Earnhardt. "Winning like we have puts pressure on people and that's what you have to do. If you are a consistent competitor, you make the others work hard and sometimes they work themselves right into the wrong position. Of course, it can turn on you and that's happened to us before.

"But, we intend to keep going like we are. We are going to carry the momentum from this victory right on to the end of the season in Atlanta (in November)."

Earnhardt's average speed in the 38-minute, 39-second race was 163.001 mph, which stands as the fastest The Winston on record. ■

Earnhardt Breaks String Of Bad Luck

Wins First Race At MIS Since 1987

By DEB WILLIAMS

Ford drivers Bill Elliott and Mark Martin dominated the Miller Genuine Draft 400 but, when the checkered flag dropped, it was General Motors' competitors Dale Earnhardt and Ernie Irvan who wore the smiles.

Earnhardt had clinched his fourth victory this season and had broken a four-race string of bad luck that sent him from first to fifth in the Winston Cup point standings.

Irvan had produced the best finish of his young Winston Cup career, placing a slim 0.22 second behind Earnhardt's Chevrolet in an Oldsmobile.

Elliott, who led four times for 102 laps in the 200-lap race, was sitting in the garage with an ailing engine. It faltered with 15 laps remaining while the Dawsonville, Ga., driver was leading.

Martin, who led twice for 59 laps, couldn't get past fellow Ford driver Geoff Bodine in the closing laps and had to settle for fourth.

"I had my favorite underwear on today.

Did that have anything to do with it?" —Earnhardt

"Damn it was fun!" a smiling Earnhardt said after his 43rd Winston Cup career victory and second at the two-mile track. "When I got through turns one and two OK and I didn't have any trouble down the backstretch, I knew I could get through the bottom of (turns) three and four and I could beat him (Irvan) back to the flagstand. It worked perfect.

"That last lap or two, Rusty (Wallace) was in front helping with the draft. I didn't want to catch him but, yet, I was hoping he

wouldn't get too far away. That was working for us. The 11 (Geoff Bodine) and the 6 (Martin) got to racing each other, and that didn't help the 4 car (Irvan). It worked perfect. But it worked because Rusty was running in front and the 11 and 6 cars were running side by side. It was just a combination that sort of fell into place."

That wasn't the case for Earnhardt in the early going. The three-time Winston Cup champion had to start fifth because the starting lineup was determined by car owner points since qualifying was rained out. With car owner Jack Roush leading those standings, that gave Martin the pole position.

The drama then unfolded some 65 to 70 miles from the Motor City where a victory means bragging rights until the next Winston Cup event in Motown's backyard.

In the early going, Martin ran away from the field.

After only 10 laps, Martin had built a three-second lead over Earnhardt. A mandatory caution for the teams to check their cars' tires and setups after 20 laps closed the field, but it was the same story after the restart on lap 24. By lap 38, Martin again had constructed a three-second lead over Earnhardt.

Earnhardt led for the first time during the second caution flag when he beat Martin off pit road. Martin was pitting nine stalls closer to turn one than Earnhardt. However, as Martin prepared to exit pit road, Earnhardt quickly ducked to the inside of Martin and passed him for the lead. The Kannapolis, N.C., native led nine laps before Elliott sailed past him on lap 71 and immediately took up where Martin left off.

Within seven laps in the lead, Elliott had assumed a three-second advantage over Earnhardt. At the halfway mark, Earnhardt had dropped to fourth and Elliott led Ken Schrader by slightly more than five seconds.

"The car started out a little tight and we worked with the chassis all day long," Earnhardt said.

"The car I have here is my Atlanta car which has now won three out of four races. It's won the last two Atlanta races as a rear-steer car. It's a front-steer car now. We came here basically with an untested car because we hadn't tested it with the front-steer chassis. When it rained we were

EARNHARDT NAVIGATES HIS WAY TO THE FRONT IN THE MILLER GENUINE DRAFT 400.
DAVID CHOBAT PHOTO

TEAM GOODWRENCH WORKED ON THE CAR ALL DAY. THEIR EXPERTISE IN THE PITS CONTRIBUTED TO THE WIN.
DAVID CHOBAT PHOTO

a little bit puzzled as to whether we had the right setup.

"On the green flag stop (lap 105), the ratchet didn't lock in until I got to the back straightaway, so we were a little slow exiting the pits. But it still didn't hurt us all that much."

Elliott, the race's defending champion, appeared to be on his way to his eighth victory at the two-mile track on lap 117 as he possessed nearly a straightaway advantage over the second-place Harry Gant.

On the restart following the fourth and final caution period – laps 172-176 – Elliott found himself fifth behind Schrader, Terry Labonte, Earnhardt and Irvan.

Schrader's Chevrolet faltered first, blowing an engine after completing 179 laps.

Elliott regained the lead on lap 182, going low to make it three abreast with Irvan and Earnhardt. He only held it for four laps, however, as his engine expired going into turn one. An oil fitting had broken off the motor.

"It's sad to see a guy (Elliott) have problems when he's been so dominant all day," Earnhardt said. "But it opened the doors for us, so it's good and bad. I didn't cheer or anything, but it was a sigh of relief, and then there was the 4 car (Irvan) I had to race. I knew it wasn't over."

Elliott's exit turned the event into a four-way battle between Irvan, Earnhardt, Martin and Bodine.

Earnhardt inherited the lead from Elliott but could hold on for only two laps before Irvan passed him.

"We were racing Ernie for second, and then Elliott's engine blew up," Earnhardt said. "Mark and the 11 car (Bodine) helped Ernie draft by me that one time. He got enough momentum to get by me down the straightaway. Lucky enough, I hung on for second, and Ernie was trying to get up and lap Rusty."

Irvan kept the top spot for seven laps before Earnhardt pulled to the inside as they entered the third turn. The two raced side by side for a lap before Earnhardt inched ahead in turns three and four and took the lead for good with six laps remaining.

"I kept playing Ernie and watching him, working with my car," Earnhardt said. "I saw I could beat him through the middle of the corner if I just did everything right. I knew I couldn't run the car too hard in, get it turned quick enough, and get it off the corner good. I finally got under him and got by him.

"He (Irvan) raced good and he raced hard and he tried to win without getting into me hard or anything like that," continued Earnhardt, who won $72,950 in the race he led five times for 22 laps. "He's a good racer. He's taken everything he's learned and everything he's seen and he tries to learn from it. He's got some good equipment there and he is capable of driving. I think he's gonna go far if he keeps his head clean and keeps going like he's going."

After the race, Irvan noted he could have taken Earnhardt out but he didn't.

"It was good, clean racing," Irvan said. "As long as we keep going like this and (crew chief) Tony Glover keeps giving me some good, clean pit stops, we are going to win some races.

"We had a good, close run, but Dale had a good car."

Earnhardt, who gained 15 points on point leader Martin, but remained fifth in the standings, averaged 150.219 mph in the race that was slowed by four caution flags for 16 laps.

There were 16 lead changes among seven drivers.

Richard Childress, Earnhardt's team owner, said he didn't believe his driver could have beaten Elliott if he'd still been in it at the finish.

"We'd been improving our car all day long and we got it a little better there at the end," Childress said. "It was my decision to change this car from a rear-steer to a front-steer, and some people didn't agree with that decision, but I feel real good about it now. The heat's off me now.

"We couldn't get the horsepower with the rear-steer that we get with the front-steer. I thought we had a good chance to win, but I don't ever predict anything in racing until that checkered flag falls."

Earnhardt couldn't pinpoint the reason for his turnaround after four discouraging weeks, but he did offer some humorous possibilities.

"The day after The Winston, Neil Bonnett and I went fishing and we caught a lot of bass," Earnhardt said. "After that, I didn't have good luck, for some reason. I don't know if Neil did it, the fish did it, or I should have been doing something else that day instead of fishing.

"The Monday after Pocono we went fishing again and caught a lot of bass. My luck changed. Does that have anything to do with it?

"(Atlanta Braves catcher) Jody Davis hadn't been here for four weeks either and he was here today. Does that have anything to do with it?

"I had my favorite underwear on today. Did that have anything to do with it?

"I think you make your own luck a lot of times.

"It was his (Irvan's) race to win today. It was ours, too," Earnhardt continued. "He bumped me a couple of times and I scuffed fenders with him a bit earlier with about 10 laps to go. I watched him push up and I could beat him through the middle and I was running lower. I felt that was the best way and that's where we beat him. As equal as I felt we were, he was a little stronger down the straightaway and I was a little stronger in the corner.

"It was just good racing and I didn't see a problem with it either way. We beat him, luckily." ∎

EARNHARDT GOES HIGH ON THE COMPETITION. MOST OF THE DAY, HE JUST WENT BY THEM.
JIM FLUHARTY PHOTO

At Last, Daytona Is A **Breeze** For Earnhardt

Scores First Winston Cup Win At Track With Dominating Form

By STEVE WAID

At last, Lady Luck embraced Dale Earnhardt at Daytona International Speedway.

Her favor and the undeniable competitiveness of his Richard Childress Chevrolet combined to help give the Kannapolis, N.C., native the victory in the Pepsi 400 and the first NASCAR Winston Cup win of his career on the 2.5-mile speedway.

Although Earnhardt had won 10 times in 56 starts on NASCAR's premier track, not once before had he claimed a Winston Cup victory. He almost had it in February when a cut tire on the last lap forced him to give way to Derrike Cope.

That was undoubtedly one of the most disappointing moments in Earnhardt's career, in which he has now fashioned 44 victories.

Earnhardt dominated again, just as he had in February. This time, however, he avoided misfortune – not once, but twice.

"It's not the Daytona 500, but it's one I've never won," said Earnhardt, who had his 13th career start in the Pepsi 400. "Daytona is one of my favorite places. This is the same car we ran at Daytona earlier this year and at Talladega (Ala.).

"We felt if we got it close, we would be all right."

Earnhardt started third but snatched the lead away from pole winner Greg Sacks as the field entered the first and second turns on the first lap. It was good that he did because, just as the lap was completed, one of the most spectacular wrecks in recent years was triggered.

Sacks was caught between the cars of Richard Petty, on the inside, and Cope, on the outside, as the three jockeyed for position behind Earnhardt. A little jostling was all it took. Cope and Sacks made contact on the frontstretch and Sacks' Chevrolet clipped the right-rear of Petty's Pontiac, which was turned sideways.

With the track effectively blocked, the field of cars turned into a spinning, smoking mass. By the time the melee had ended, 23 cars had become involved in one way or another.

Many of the drivers figured to challenge for the victory – Petty, Sacks, Ernie Irvan, Morgan Shepherd, Mark Martin, Cope and others – were either eliminated from the race or so severely crippled they could only limp home after repairs.

"I hate to see things like that happen," said Earnhardt. "I'm a competitive driver and the others are competitive drivers. You don't want things like wrecks and injury to happen.

"I wish all of them had stayed in the race. I think our Chevrolet was strong enough to handle them."

There was plenty of evidence. Earnhardt led the first 31 laps, giving way to Jimmy Spencer during the second caution period, brought out after the right-rear tire in Elliott's Ford gave out and forced him to clip the second-turn wall.

Earnhardt retook the lead by lap 35 and held it for 27 circuits. He then made an unscheduled pit stop on lap 62 for right-side tires.

"The car had picked up a push," Earnhardt explained. "I had seen what happened to Bill when he crashed after having a flat right-rear tire. I told Richard on the radio I didn't want to take any chances and that I wanted to pit to get tires. I didn't want a right-front going flat.

"That put us out of sync with the others, as far as pit stops were concerned, but then we got another caution and that put us back."

Before that, however, Earnhardt had reassumed the lead after his rivals made their scheduled pit stops under the green flag. On lap 80, Rob Moroso pitted to allow Earnhardt's Chevrolet to once again take the point. It had a whopping 13.1-second margin over Harry Gant's Oldsmobile.

The third caution came on lap 91 when Martin spun his Ford out of the second turn. Now back in sync, as far as pit stops were concerned, Earnhardt remained in front when green-flag racing resumed on lap 96.

But where he once held sway with conviction, he now had to contend with the surprisingly strong Bobby Hillin. Although Earnhardt kept Hillin's Buick at bay easily for several laps, by lap 128 of the 160-lap race, Hillin had taken advantage of Earnhardt's handling problems to close on his rear bumper and threaten to pass.

"The car was a little tight in the corners and that's why Hillin could catch up," Earnhardt explained. "It would push more as the gas was used up.

"One time, Bobby tried to race me but I slowed both of us up. So I waved to him to stay in line and that sped us up."

There was one final scheduled pit stop to be made and Earnhardt made his on lap 134.

"We didn't change any tires," he said. "We knocked the spoiler down a bit, took out a round of wedge and the car was perfect after that."

Then Hillin, the new leader, pitted on lap 139. It would be his downfall.

He charged into the pits too hard and looped his car at his pit area, nearly taking out front-tire changer Tim Petty in the process. His crew refilled his gas tank and

pushed him away, the stop having taken 24 seconds and dropping him well back in the lead pack.

"If he would have made a clean pit stop, he would have been the one I was racing at the end," Earnhardt said.

Gant, Ken Schrader, Kulwicki and Moroso each led the race – giving way for pit stops – until Earnhardt took over on lap 144 when Moroso pitted. He was in front of Kulwicki by 7.5 seconds.

By lap 150, Earnhardt had expanded that lead to 10.3 seconds, but he was denied a stroll to the finish. On lap 154, J.D. McDuffie, driving his Pontiac, which had started with Dave Marcis behind the wheel, spun in the first turn – in front of Earnhardt.

"I saw it happen and it was very close," said Earnhardt, who earned $72,850 for his victory. "I locked the car down and dodged the right way.

"I just did the best I could under the circumstances and I got out of the way."

Earnhardt's luck was holding out. But the fourth and final caution period allowed Kulwicki, making his best run of the season, to close on Earnhardt's bumper at the restart, which came on lap 158. There were three laps left.

Earnhardt got a tremendous jump as the green flag fell. Kulwicki could not challenge. All that remained for Earnhardt was to hope that the same, last-lap misfortune, which cost him the Daytona 500 victory, would not happen again.

"Alan was laying off me pretty good as we got into the third turn," said Earnhardt. "So I slowed down to back up to him. Then, when we got to the grass at the fourth turn, where we're supposed to start, I did.

"We've been working on our engines to help us get off the corners and that's helped us with restarts. That's how I got by Sacks and Elliott at the start of the race, too.

"On the last lap, I drove in the middle groove. I didn't want to drive on the edges and take the chance of getting into some debris. I wanted to run it smooth. I had gotten away from Alan and just wanted to get back to the line.

"That's when I would win the race and I didn't think about winning until I got there."

The three-time Winston Cup champion got there 1.47 seconds ahead of Kulwicki, with Schrader third, Terry Labonte fourth and Sterling Marlin fifth. Rounding out the top 10 were Hillin, Gant, Dale Jarrett, Moroso and Kyle Petty.

Earnhardt's finish catapulted him back

into second place in the Winston Cup point standings. Martin, despite his problems, retains the lead with 2,221 points but Earnhardt is just 63 points behind with 2,158. The big loser was Shepherd. Hobbled by the race-opening crash, he finished 34th and fell from second to fifth in the standings after losing 69 points.

Not only did the Pepsi 400 win change Earnhardt's fortunes at Daytona, it also enhanced his performance record of late. It was his second straight win and his fifth of the season, coming after a four-race dry spell that dropped him from No. 1 in the point standings.

"It's not the Daytona 500,
but it's one I've
never won."
—Earnhardt

IT'S GOOD WORK, IF YOU CAN GET IT.
NWCS ARCHIVE PHOTO

Prior to Michigan, mechanical problems and accidents had sent Earnhardt spiraling to finishes of 30th, 31st, and 34th in the three consecutive events before he struggled to a 13th-place at Pocono, Pa., on June 17, one week before Michigan.

"You go through your spells of bad luck," said Earnhardt, who averaged 160.894 mph in his victory. You just have to work hard and things will come back to you.

"Now we've won the Pepsi 400 and who knows? It's a lot different than the Daytona 500. There are 100 more miles in that race. We'll just have to race here in 1991 and see what happens.

"We've been getting right back to where we need to be. We want to be as competitive as we can. We want to keep the consistency we've found in the last two races for the rest of the season." ■

EARNHARDT STARTED IN THE TOP SPOT AND RARELY LOST HIS GRIP ON IT IN CRUISING TO THE WIN. DAVID CHOBAT PHOTO

Earnhardt Dominates
DieHard 500

Leads Record Number of Laps

By DEB WILLIAMS

Dale Earnhardt crowned himself the 1990 king of the Winston Cup circuit's superspeedways, claiming three of the four major races this season with his victory in the DieHard 500, a race that had two dramatic accidents.

The first incident occurred on pit road, while the other was on the backstretch on the final lap.

The frightening pit road incident occurred on lap 56 during the second yellow flag period. Tracy Leslie's crew was servicing his Oldsmobile when Stanley Smith's Pontiac slid sideways into the unsuspecting crewmen. Five men were affected – four were taken to the infield hospital and three later were transported to the hospital in Anniston, Ala., where they were treated and released.

The other accident occurred on the final lap while Earnhardt and Bill Elliott were battling for the victory and involved Ken Schrader and Jimmy Spencer.

"When Michael (Waltrip) ran out of gas, Kenny Schrader hit him in the right rear quarter panel and that put Schrader in the

wall," Spencer said. "When Schrader hit the wall he hit it hard, and then he came back and got me. He caught me in the right rear quarter panel and turned the car sideways."

That's when Spencer's Pontiac began rolling. It rolled three times before stopping upright.

"I'm just glad the car started again, and that I didn't land on my roof," Spencer said. "At the time, all I wanted to do was get out of the middle of the race track. I was in the middle with the left side looking at traffic coming and I just stepped on the gas as hard as I could and the car took off. After the car took off, I hit the apron, made sure I had steering, shifted it into third gear and then down into second and went around real slow."

Spencer, amazingly, took the checkered flag on the track.

For Earnhardt, however, the day was one of celebration. The Kannapolis, N.C., native became only the second driver to win three of the four major Winston Cup superspeedway races in a single season. The only other driver to accomplish the feat was Pete Hamilton in 1970 when he drove for Petty Engineering. That year, Hamilton

won the Daytona 500 at the 2.5-mile Daytona International Speedway, and the Alabama 500 and the Talladega 500 at the 2.66-mile track then known as Alabama International Motor Speedway.

In addition to the DieHard 500, Earnhardt, 39, won the Winston 500 at Talladega and the Pepsi 400 at Daytona this year. He came within approximately a mile of winning the Daytona 500. A cut tire on the final lap as he entered the third turn kept him from sweeping on ovals measuring more than two miles in length. In those four races, Earnhardt led 522 of 736 laps, for a 0.709 lap-leading percentage.

Earnhardt dedicated his sixth victory this season and the 45th of his career to his public relations manager Benny Ertel and his wife, Cheryl, whose six-week-old son died unexpectedly July 27 of heart failure connected to sudden infant death syndrome.

Although Earnhardt's average speed of 174.430 mph wasn't a record, the number of laps he led – 134 – was, breaking the old mark of 123 set by Darrell Waltrip in 1988.

By winning the 188-lap event, Earnhardt became the third driver this season to claim the Unocal 76 Challenge bonus, which goes to the competitor who earns the pole position for the event and then wins the race. Kyle Petty accomplished the feat in March at Rockingham, N.C., and Geoff Bodine repeated it at Martinsville, Va., in April. For Earnhardt, the bonus was worth $68,400.

Driving a Chevrolet, Earnhardt led six times in the race that had 23 lead changes among 13 drivers. The majority of those lead changes, however, were the result of green flag pit stops. Only twice was Earnhardt passed under racing conditions – on the first lap when Davey Allison took the lead and on lap 151 by Elliott.

Even Elliott, whose Ford finished less than a second behind Earnhardt, couldn't do anything with the dominating driver in the final stages.

"If I had had somebody with me out there, we might have done something," Elliott said. "I could lead, but I couldn't do it alone. I needed someone pushing me. If I'd had Mark Martin or another of the frontrunners, then we might have done something."

Elliott was the only one in position to challenge Earnhardt in the last five laps after Martin pitted for fuel with eight laps remaining.

> "I'm just glad
> **the car
> started again,**
> and that I didn't land on my
> roof." —Jimmy Spencer

Fuel also was a question mark for Earnhardt, but not Elliott. Earnhardt last pitted on lap 141, while Elliott stopped on lap 146.

"They were telling me, now these are (team owner) Richard Childress' words, 'You can make it. Don't worry. Maybe you ought to draft all you can,'" a smiling Earnhardt said after the event.

and maybe get away from everybody," said Earnhardt, who won $152,975. "Then the pit stops proved that, so we sort of shook the crowd."

However, just when Earnhardt believed Martin was his only concern, Elliott appeared.

Elliott led laps 144-145 and, after his green flag stop, returned to the track on Martin and Earnhardt's bumpers.

"There at the end, we're stretching our gas mileage, and there is Bill Elliott," said Earnhardt, who has won three of the last four Winston Cup races. "I don't know where in the heck he came from or how he got in sync enough to be in that position and have the gas (to go the distance).

"If it had been Mark and Bill against me, it might have shook out different. But they were telling me Mark was going to run out of gas."

Elliott followed Earnhardt until lap 141 when he took the lead after Earnhardt motioned him by so he could draft in an effort to conserve fuel.

"I fell back and got in behind Bill and drafted Bill," said Earnhardt, who moved to within one point of Winston Cup points leader Martin.

"When we got through that last bunch of

TERESA TRIES TO KEEP DAUGHTER TAYLOR AND DALE COOL IN THE HOT ALABAMA SUN.
DAVID CHOBAT PHOTO

spot in turn four with 20 laps remaining.

"After I made my move, when I was in front of Elliott the last 10 or 15 laps, I could part throttle it a little bit when he would fall off of me and save the gas," said Earnhardt, who admitted he was worried about possibly running out of fuel. "The last five laps I just ran it pretty hard and didn't worry too much because I felt like I had enough to beat him. I think it was wise to fall back and draft Bill for 10 or 12 laps. I think we had a lap left on fuel. That was a cushion and that was all we needed."

Earnhardt's Chevrolet, which he described as the best superspeedway car he's had in his Winston Cup career, ran out of fuel when it reached victory lane.

Early in the race, Earnhardt said several competitors were running lower on the track than he wanted.

"Mark's and those guys' cars kept getting loose," Earnhardt said. "What they were doing was heating the tires on the bottom. I wanted to run a little more sweep through the corners to cool the tires, save the tires. They kept running around the bottom and when they would do that they would run up under me a little bit. Then I would get them back down the straightaways. If they had just run that bigger sweep, they would have kept their tires cooler, had a little bit better handling and we would have all drafted faster."

DALE JR. LOOKS ON IN AMAZEMENT, BUT KNOWING HE LIKES THE LOOK OF WINNING.
DAVID CHOBAT PHOTO

Only 12 laps of the event were run under the caution flag with the last yellow flag being lap 61. Earnhardt said he was pleased with the long run under the green flag.

"The way Mark Martin and I were running I felt like we could run good together

traffic, I told Richard to just tell me when he thought he was sure (we could make it). I wanted to go ahead and make my move. I didn't want to wait until the last lap."

The Dawsonville, Ga., driver led 18 laps before Earnhardt charged back into the No. 1

Earnhardt Takes
Measure Of Darlington

Earnhardt Rules At
Darlington Again

By STEVE WAID

The speedway that is recognized as the toughest and most unforgiving on the NASCAR Winston Cup circuit was once again Dale Earnhardt's playground.

Recovering from an encounter with the second-turn wall of the 1.366-mile Darlington track in a car that later vibrated badly over the final 30 laps, Earnhardt went on to win the Heinz Southern 500 by 4.19 seconds over Ernie Irvan.

In his Richard Childress Chevrolet, Earnhardt won for the seventh time this season and for the seventh time at Darlington in his career. He now has won six of the last 10 events at NASCAR's oldest superspeedway, including the two conducted this season and the last three in a row. The driver from Kannapolis, N.C., also swept Darlington races in a single season in 1987.

It was a lucrative victory, to say the least. By winning from the pole position, Earnhardt claimed the Unocal 76 Challenge Bonus ($30,400) for the second time this season. That drove his earnings to $110,350.

There's more. Earnhardt also claimed a $100,000 bonus from the R.J. Reynolds Tobacco Co. as he won two of the four selected events that make up the "Winston Million." The three-time Winston Cup champion also won the Winston 500 at Talladega, Ala., this year.

Earnhardt's total take of $205,150 made him the first man in motorsports to top $11 million in career earnings, listed at $11,190,358.

"It was a rougher race than I would have wanted," said the 39-year-old driver. "But all I can say is we surprised ourselves by winning the pole and we worked on the car all during practice and got it to where it was just about the same as last year.

"Then we put on a set of tires that made the car really loose and I overdrove it trying to make up the lost distance. I got into the wall and we were fortunate it didn't damage the car much.

"Then we came back, got track position and passed Ernie after the last pit stop. Ernie must have burned up his tires trying to catch us and that hurt him.

"Then came the vibration, but the car held up to the end."

Earnhardt, who won three of the last four Heinz Southern 500s, also benefited nicely in his quest for a fourth Winston Cup title. Mark Martin, the current points leader, finished sixth and lost 35 points to Earnhardt. He has 3,169 points to 3,143 for his challenger, a difference of just 26 points with eight races remaining in 1990.

Earnhardt took advantage of his No. 1 starting position to lead the first 42 laps of the 367-lap race. He was behind Geoff Bodine on the restart from the third caution period on lap 46.

By lap 49, Earnhardt fell to fourth place as Bill Elliott, winner of the 1988 Southern 500, put his Harry Melling Ford in front for 32 laps.

Earnhardt came back as high as second place, trailing Bodine, and was running third when he smacked the wall in between turns one and two on lap 133.

"You saw the old girl slap me when I got fresh with her, didn't you?" asked Earnhardt. "You try to run consistent laps here by racing the track.

"But we had lost ground with the loose tires we had put on during the pit stop (under caution from laps 42-45) and I just ran too hard. We were very fortunate because there wasn't any damage to the chassis. The body got bumped up a bit."

And Earnhardt got bumped back to fifth place after the mishap. But he once again moved as high as second place before falling back to seventh when Irvan, in the Morgan-McClure Chevrolet, swept into the lead past

Bodine on lap 161 and held sway for 52 laps.

Through caution-period and green-flag pit stops, several drivers gained the lead but it was Elliott who showed the muscle again as he moved to the front on lap 231 and remained there for 65 laps.

Finally, on lap 296, Earnhardt regained the lead when Elliott pitted under green in what was to be the last series of stops. Irvan passed Earnhardt on lap 298 and Earnhardt subsequently pitted on lap 300 for four tires and fuel.

The stop was critical. Earnhardt returned to the track and quickly made up his lost lap by passing Irvan on lap 302 in the third turn. Irvan pitted on lap 306 and was in fourth place when all stops were completed. By lap 314, Earnhardt was the leader, followed by Elliott, Alan Kulwicki, Irvan and Harry Gant.

"I was lucky to get my lap back as soon as I got onto the track," said Earnhardt. "We were on new tires, so we caught and passed Ernie really early. That's a credit to the crew. They gave me track position.

"Then, when Ernie pitted, he was well behind me. I knew he'd have to work hard to catch up."

Irvan, indeed, was labor intensive. He and Kulwicki passed Elliott on lap 316 to occupy third and second place, respectively. Then, four laps later, Irvan took the measure of Kulwicki in the third turn to assume the runner-up position. He was 4.5 seconds behind Earnhardt.

By lap 330, he was 3.38 seconds behind. And, two laps later, the margin was just 3.2 seconds.

Earnhardt was suffering. He thought he had an equalized tire and informed Childress by radio.

"The car was vibrating really, really bad," Earnhardt said. "It was just terrible. Richard came back to me on the radio and told me that the lap times were fine and that I should go ahead and ride it out and see what happens.

"Richard was also timing the distance between me and Ernie and he was telling me that Ernie wasn't getting any closer. All I could do was hold on and hope to make it to the finish without blowing a tire or something. I was just trying to run consistent laps. That probably helped me, because I didn't jam the car into the corners and then jump on the throttle.

"But I tell you, it made my hands and fingers numb."

When the final 10 laps began, Irvan still trailed by 3.2 seconds. With each completed lap, it became more obvious he wasn't going to catch Earnhardt and earn his second career Winston Cup victory in as many weeks.

"I was running as hard as I could without hitting something," said Irvan, winner of the Aug. 25 Busch 500 at Bristol, Tenn., who led four times for 70 laps and, ironically, finished second to Earnhardt in the Aug. 19 Champion Spark Plug 400 at Michigan. "Dale had a little trouble early, then he got his problems straightened out and he was tough at the end.

"And he gained about four or five seconds on us because we waited to pit on that last series of stops."

"For the last 10 laps, I was stroking," said Earnhardt, who paced all competitors by leading three times for 99 laps. "I was just trying to make it to the end. Even if I had a tire problem, I believe I could have made it to the checkered flag."

Kulwicki, in his Ford, finished third while Elliott fell back to fourth. Gant wound up fifth in Leo Jackson's Oldsmobile while Martin, in Jack Roush's Ford, finished sixth.

Seventh went to Ricky Rudd in a Hendrick Motorsports Chevrolet, eighth to Bodine whose Ford sagged in performance after leading six times for 89 laps, ninth to Derrike Cope in the Bob Whitcomb Chevrolet and 10th to Brett Bodine in the King Racing Buick.

Rusty Wallace's bid for a second-straight championship is in jeopardy after he finished 40th – dead last – when the engine in his Blue Max Racing Pontiac blew after just 14 laps. Wallace lost 107 points with the finish and is in fourth place in the standings, 334 points behind Martin.

"You saw the
old girl slap me
when I got fresh with her, didn't you?" —Earnhardt

There were 10 caution periods for 51 laps, which helped slow Earnhardt's winning average speed to 123.141 mph. Most were caused by accidents, which eliminated Ken Schrader, H.B. Bailey, Jimmy Means, Chad Little, Butch Miller, Greg Sacks and Bobby Hillin.

Victims of mechanical failures included Philip Duffie, Richard Petty, Mark Stahl, Lake Speed, Sterling Marlin and Michael Waltrip.

Earnhardt was involved in a mishap with Waltrip on lap 245 that ultimately put Waltrip out of the race and effectively ended the day for the strong-running Sabco Racing Pontiac of Kyle Petty.

Petty had been a consistent top-five runner when Earnhardt brushed Waltrip's rear end as the two ran through the third turn. Waltrip slid into the wall where his car was pounded by Petty's. The two were running fourth and fifth, respectively, when the accident happened.

"I was running loose through the third turn and I had my eyes on Mike," said Earnhardt. "I was low and just got into him and he jammed the brakes and went into the wall.

"When we touched, I got straight, but then Kyle hit Mike and bumped him out."

Waltrip came back to complete 272 laps and finish 26th while Petty had extensive repairs to his car and limped to a 25th-place finish.

Earnhardt's seven wins are second to David Pearson's 10 as the all-time Darlington record. "I think if I stay healthy and the team stays healthy, we have a chance to catch him," Earnhardt said. "I have all the respect for him and for what he's done here with the Wood Brothers and other teams.

"Naturally, I am proud and thankful for what I've been able to accomplish here and elsewhere because I come from a racing family. I grew up watching guys race with my dad (Ralph), then I worked on race cars after he passed away and I raced part time.

"Since then, all of my accomplishments have made me proud. And to be the leading money winner, well, I never thought anyone would pass Darrell Waltrip after all he did.

"It's all because of the Richard Childress team. I am lucky to be a part of it. It is because of what the team has done that I have what I do." ■

EARNHARDT BLOWS PAST ALAN KULWICKI, WHO FINISHED THIRD.
DAVID CHOBAT PHOTO

MILLER GENUINE DRAFT 400

ACTION IN THE PITS AND DECISIONS MADE BY EARNHARDT'S CREW BECAME THE DECIDING FACTOR IN THE CLOSING LAPS OF THE MILLER HIGH LIFE 400.
DAVID CHOBAT PHOTO

Richmond:
Earnhardt Takes Eighth Victory of Season

Closes On Points Leader Martin

By DEB WILLIAMS

A gamble on fuel mileage by Dale Earnhardt and the Richard Childress crew paid big dividends in the Miller Genuine Draft 400, as the team came away with its eighth victory this season.

Earnhardt's fifth win in the last nine events also allowed him to close within 16 points of Winston Cup point standings leader Mark Martin in the battle for the series championship.

"I think it's more of a pressure situation for me with me being behind Mark than it would if Mark was behind me," Earnhardt said after his fourth victory at Richmond. It was, however, his first triumph there since the track was redesigned following the February 1988 race.

"If I was leading, I'd be relaxed because I would have the points lead. Right now, I have a point deficit that I have to make up. It's tough because you have to make everything count."

Earnhardt, who led the final 25 laps, said Martin carried him high once.

"Martin cut me off into the wall one time and about wrecked us both," Earnhardt said. "Mark got to beating on me, knocked me up into the wall coming off (turn) four and I had to let him go, hit the wall or crash both of us

and I didn't think that would look good."

Earnhardt, however, praised Martin as a driver.

"He has paid his dues and he has come a long way," Earnhardt said. "In the past two years, he has made himself a great race car driver and he's going to be one of the great ones."

The win was Earnhardt's 47th of his NASCAR Winston Cup career. That places him in 10th on the all-time victory list.

The Kannapolis, N.C., native's winnings of $59,225 pushed his season total to $1,510,005 – the seventh highest single season winnings in Winston Cup history. Bill Elliott holds the motorsports record of $2,383,187, which was set in 1985.

Fuel mileage became the issue in the final 100 laps, which were caution free until the last four circuits when Ernie Irvan spun his Chevrolet in the fourth turn.

On the green flag stops, Rusty Wallace was the first frontrunner to pit. While leading, he stopped on lap 347 for right-side tires and fuel in 11.2 seconds. At the time, he held a 2.22-second advantage over Martin.

Martin constructed a 4.9-second lead over Earnhardt before having to pit for fuel on lap 376. It took only 2.9 seconds, but two laps later he trailed Earnhardt by 9.35 seconds and Ricky Rudd was second.

The issue then became whether leaders Earnhardt and Rudd could go the distance without stopping. Both decided to gamble. Earnhardt rolled a lucky seven, while Rudd "crapped out."

Rudd's Chevrolet ran out of gas on the restart on lap 398 and was pushed around the 0.750- mile track by Jimmy Spencer for the final 1 1/2 laps. However, Rudd wasn't officially scored on the final lap because NASCAR rules prohibit a car receiving help after it takes the white flag.

Earnhardt began working to conserve fuel near the end.

"With about 20 laps to go, I was backing off on the straightaway and not getting on it as hard off the corner, trying to save all I could," Earnhardt said. "That's hard to do on a short track because you don't save that much. But you do save a little and a little was enough.

"It was sputtering at the end. I ran out after the (checkered) flag and I coasted back to victory lane. We were lucky Mark wasn't on our bumper on the restart.

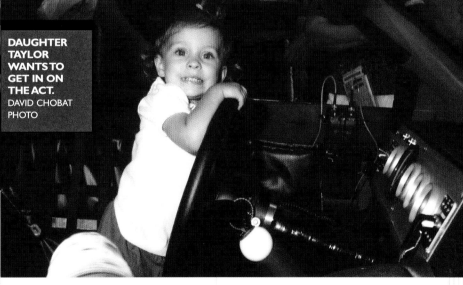

IT'S ANOTHER "THUMBS UP" FOR EARNHARDT, HIS EIGHTH OF THE SEASON. DAVID CHOBAT PHOTO

DAUGHTER TAYLOR WANTS TO GET IN ON THE ACT. DAVID CHOBAT PHOTO

"We were lucky to win this race."

Earnhardt completed slightly more than 90 miles without stopping for fuel and held more than a seven-second advantage when the final caution appeared for Irvan's spin.

Even though the three-time Winston Cup champion led the most laps – six times for 173 of the 400-lap race – he didn't believe he had the best car. In fact, early in the race, he dropped back through the field.

"The car was a little on the tight side all day," said Earnhardt, 39. "I don't think we were the fastest car at the end. I think Mark and Rusty were a little stronger than I was.

"It was just a little bit off today. I think we had the car geared a little bit high," continued Earnhardt, who dedicated the win to his gasman, Danny "Chocolate" Myers, who wasn't at the race because of his grandmother's death.

"The sun came out and we got pretty good and then the sun went in, then we had the red-flag situation and the track cooled off some. The car was tighter after that.

"I think, if the race had stayed green and we hadn't had the red flag, we would have been better off.

"But we are in victory lane and that is all that matters. I think the best race team won the race. Our car was a little off and we worked to make it win," he said.

Martin, in a Ford, finished second, about four car lengths behind Earnhardt, but only after battling Harry Gant, who was a lap down in Hut Stricklin's Buick. Gant attempted to move into the frontrunning line on the restart, but was shoved down into the lapped cars by Rudd in turn two as they prepared for the double-file restart. When the race restarted, NASCAR said Gant passed illegally and was black-flagged. He ignored the flag and raced Martin, for what he believed was second.

By the time Martin passed Gant, only one lap remained. Because Gant disregarded the black flag, NASCAR put him at the end of those cars which were on the same lap with him. He finished 13th, one lap down.

3:35 p.m. on lap 281.

During that time, Earnhardt remained behind the wheel, but several drivers awaited the restart outside their cars.

Darrell Waltrip, who competed in his first race since suffering a leg injury July 6, finished third and crew chief Jeff Hammond said he was grateful for the interruption.

"...We are in victory lane and that is all that matters. I think the **best race team** won the race. Our car was a little off and we worked to make it win."—Earnhardt

"It's the biggest plus he could get," Hammond said. "I hate it happened to the 21 car (Jarrett), but it allowed him (Waltrip) to get his second and third wind."

Waltrip's third-place finish was his second best this season.

Fourth went to Bill Elliott in a Ford, while Wallace claimed fifth in a Pontiac.

Earnhardt averaged 95.567 mph in the race slowed by nine caution flags for 55 laps. The event also was stopped for 31 minutes 42 seconds while the inside guardrail was repaired in turn three. The guardrail was damaged when Dale Jarrett's Ford hit it following a collision with Rob Moroso's Oldsmobile on the backstretch.

The rail had to be spot-welded to the three I-beams that had to be replaced into the ground. The red flag was thrown at

In the eight accidents, only one driver was injured. Chad Little suffered a concussion and a sprained left ankle in a multicar crash in turn three.

Also involved in the accident were Brett Bodine, Alan Kulwicki, Martin and Ken Schrader. Little was transported to the infield care center, and then transferred to St. Mary's Hospital in west Richmond where he underwent a CAT scan. The tests were negative and he was released. ■

EARNHARDT MOTORED THROUGH THE DESERT, AND HIS COMPETITION EN ROUTE TO VICTORY LANE IN THE CHECKER 500.
DAVID CHOBAT PHOTO

Earnhardt Takes
Victory
Earnhardt Cruises To Ninth Win This Season
At Phoenix

By DEB WILLIAMS

Dale Earnhardt strode into the Old West brimming with confidence, sporting that sly grin that always means trouble for his competitors. And when the green flag dropped on the Checker 500, everyone knew why.

Earnhardt made a mockery of the word "race" in the 312-lap event at the one-mile track, leading all but the first 50 laps.

"It couldn't have gone any better for us," said Earnhardt, who shook numerous fans' hands as he briskly walked through the grandstand to the press box for his post-race interview. "It went the way you would have

wanted to plan it, except for those last cautions (three in the final 24 laps).

"My car was perfect today. I was running Rusty (Wallace) and I was running consistently with him. I didn't see any reason to push the car at that time even though I would like to have led a lap or so at first just to get the insurance."

The three-time Winston Cup champion started third and, on lap 14, Wallace had a 1.08-second advantage over Earnhardt. That had increased to 1.71 seconds within another 16 laps.

On lap 49, a multicar crash in turns three and four brought out the first caution flag

and the leaders ducked into the pits. Earnhardt's crew quickly changed four tires and he returned to the track in the lead, which he possessed for the rest of the event.

"Rusty would have been the one to beat but he had problems," Earnhardt said. "When we got the tires and beat him out of the pits, we just sort of had it to ourselves the rest of the day.

"There were a lot of cars who could run with me on a restart on fresh tires but, after our tires would come in and their tires would sort of give up or something, we could start pulling off from them. I kept wanting to see a long run."

Although Earnhardt was the top lap leader, his largest advantage over the second-place car was 2.72 seconds on lap 155 when Darrell Waltrip was attempting to catch him.

"The cautions at the end worried me as to whether some of the guys would pit and get back up to me." Earnhardt said. "Fortunately, that didn't happen. We sort of set the pace by not pitting. We got a couple of more cautions and it narrowed it down to the seven-lap run there."

Earnhardt's victory gave Chevrolet a three-point lead in the struggle for the manufacturers' championship – 188 to 185 – and allowed the Kannapolis, N.C., native to take a six-point advantage over Mark Martin

– 4,260 to 4,254 – in the battle for the Winston Cup title with one race remaining. It's the first time Earnhardt has led the point standings since June when he exited the May 27 Coca-Cola 600 at Charlotte Motor Speedway with a 20-point advantage. He lost the point lead to Morgan Shepherd June 3 at Dover, Del., falling 59 behind, when a camshaft broke in his Chevrolet and he helped his crew repair the engine so he could return to the event.

Martin had possessed the point lead since the June 10 race at Sonoma, Calif., when Shepherd's Ford had problems. But his 10th-place finish in the Checker 500 gave Earnhardt, who trailed by 45 points going into the event, a 51-point gain.

Earnhardt's biggest point lead this year was 90 after the May 6 Winston 500 at Talladega, Ala. The closest he had been to Martin was when he trailed by one point after the July 29 DieHard 500 at Talladega.

Entering the Nov. 18 finale at Atlanta, Earnhardt's six-point lead over Martin makes the battle the second closest since the current point system was instituted in 1975. The closest was in 1979 when Darrell Waltrip went into the final race at Ontario, Calif., leading Richard Petty by two. Petty ended up winning his seventh championship by 11 points. It is the first time, however, that this close of a championship battle will be decided in the sport's birthplace – the Southeast.

"Now, Mark and I will have to go out and run the battle," Earnhardt said. "It's going to be a good match-up down there because the track has been real good to me, but still Mark has run good there. I think it will be an ideal place to end the championship and it will be a good race.

"Mark and Jack Roush are not going to go down there (Atlanta) and hope for us to have bad luck. I think they're going to go down there and try to race like we did today, force the issue.

"The key to winning this championship is to run competitively, and be around at the end to try to win," Earnhardt continued. "You do that and you've got a shot at winning this championship. When we go to Atlanta, you're not going to be able to run in the top 10 and win it. You're going to have to run in the top two or three to win it."

Earnhardt said the car he would use in Atlanta was the same one with which he was victorious in March, except then it was a rear-steer Chevrolet and now it had been converted to front-steer.

In the Checker 500, Earnhardt finished 0.53 second ahead of Ken Schrader's

IT'S A HUG FOR TERESA AND A "THUMBS-UP" TO THE CROWD.
DAVID CHOBAT PHOTO

Chevrolet. Placing third was Morgan Shepherd in a Ford. Darrell Waltrip finished fourth in a Chevrolet, and Bill Elliott was fifth in a Ford.

"Today, I ran seemingly hard to a lot of people but still I was pretty comfortable all day," Earnhardt said after Chevrolet's first win at Phoenix since the Winston Cup circuit began visiting the track in 1988.

"I wasn't running out of control. When you can do that and run like we did today – that's how I'd like to run in Atlanta – comfortably fast. We've done it there in the past and I think if we can go down and get a good test in Wednesday and Thursday (Nov. 7 – at Atlanta) we can go back and have a good shot at doing the same thing."

> "I wasn't running
> ## out of control.
> When you can do that and run like we did today – that's how I'd like to run in Atlanta – comfortably fast." —Earnhardt

The drivers used bias-ply tires at Phoenix instead of radials, as had been the case in recent races in the series. That made Earnhardt happy, and he's also pleased that bias-ply tires will be used at Atlanta.

"We felt more comfortable on the bias tires," he admitted. "You can work with the stagger and you need a little stagger here. We scuffed some sets and worked on the tires

before the race and I think that was the key to running as good as we did and as consistent as we did. The last set was a little tighter than I would like for them to have been but still they worked out good.

"There's more danger of puncture (with the bias-ply) but it seems you can get the stagger right and work with the stagger and chassis in conjunction and get the car more consistent."

Earnhardt averaged 96.786 mph in the race that was slowed by nine caution flags for 48 laps.

The six-car crash that caused the first caution flag sent Bobby Hillin and Michael Waltrip to Good Samaritan Hospital in Phoenix. The accident occurred on lap 48 when Shepherd attempted to pass Hillin on the inside, tapped the Texas native's Buick and Hillin went sailing into the outside wall. Hillin spun across the track and then was broadsided by Waltrip's Pontiac. Also involved in the incident were Sterling Marlin, Kyle Petty, Dave Marcis and Derrike Cope. In addition to Hillin and Waltrip, Petty was the only other driver eliminated from the race by the accident.

Hillin and Waltrip were taken to the infield care center before being transported to the Phoenix Hospital. It was reported initially that Waltrip might have a concussion. A team spokesman said Waltrip was released from the hospital the night of Nov. 4 with a bruised upper chest area and soreness in his upper back.

Hillin remained at the hospital after some trouble spots were discovered in his neck area after X-rays were taken. Doctors wanted to check for a possible cracked vertebra, a track spokesman said. ∎

Earnhardt Turns Clash Into Rout At Daytona

Shades Of 1990: Earnhardt Shows His Muscle In 13th Clash

By BEN WHITE

It has often been said that the cream always rises to the top.

That age-old phrase could easily be compared to Dale Earnhardt's efforts in the 20-lap Busch Clash of 1991. His unquestionable abundance of horsepower over the race's front-row starters and one "wildcard" entrant invited into the race created an early feeling of helplessness among fellow competitors.

Earnhardt simply pushed the Richard Childress Chevrolet to the front in intimidating fashion. But that rise to the top was never more evident than when he moved from last in the 14-car field to the lead in only two laps.

This version of the event features a twist of sorts. In an attempt to bring forth more competition in the 13th running of the annual event, a revision of the race format was used which called for two 10-lap segments. After completion of the first half, the field was inverted in hopes of curtailing a runaway by one driver.

But the organizers of the shortest race of the NASCAR season didn't count on the patented strength that Earnhardt appears to marshal at Daytona each February. It was his first appearance in the race since 1988.

EARNHARDT PACES THE FIELD, AND THEN WHIPS 'EM IN THE BUSCH CLASH.
NWCS ARCHIVE PHOTO

"Getting back to the Busch Clash was one of our goals this year," Earnhardt said, "I was really having a good time out there.

"Everybody did a great job racing. The car just worked really well down on the bottom (of the race track) and really worked well with air around it.

"It's the combination that's working, Richard Childress and the guys working on the car. It all works together and comes together on race day."

The starting order by drawing was: Derrike Cope; Kyle Petty; Alan Kulwicki; Geoff Bodine; Brett Bodine; Earnhardt; Dick Trickle; Greg Sacks; Ernie Irvan; Rusty Wallace, Ken Schrader; Mark Martin; Bill Elliott and Ricky Rudd. For Cope, Petty, Brett Bodine and Trickle, it was their first time in the race.

Before the first lap could be completed, the field shuffled dramatically and, by the second lap of the first segment, Earnhardt took the lead from Geoff Bodine. From there, he led the remaining nine laps to complete the segment.

As the white flag waved to signal the final lap, however, Geoff Bodine spun on his own in the fourth turn. The spin, which he said was unintentional, placed his Junior Johnson Ford on the pole for the second segment.

After a brief caution period to invert the running order, Earnhardt found himself at the tail end of the pack.

Once the green flag fell to begin the second segment, his poor starting spot proved academic. Bodine held the lead for only one lap until Earnhardt shot through the field like a missile. In the distance of five miles, he had successfully picked off 13 cars to retake the lead.

"Geoff saw me coming, I reckon, or the spotter told him I was coming," Earnhardt said. "I just drafted up behind him and moved under him going into (turn) three.

"To come back leading the race after two laps was amazing to me. I didn't believe we could do it. I thought it would take King Kong to come from 14th in 10 laps, and I sure didn't think we could do it in two.

"All week long we've thought about this thing and thought about the strategy we were going to use," Earnhardt added. "We kept thinking that maybe we shouldn't try to win the first segment, that maybe we should just sit back and not try to win.

"We're a go-for-it team. We go try to win races."

Martin emerged as Earnhardt's closest rival but he, too, was unable to deal with Earnhardt's unmatched supremacy.

"I had him caught," Martin said. "I only had one chance to pass him and he blocked it (coming out of turn four). After that, the best I could do was second.

"I had one run at him and he did what he was supposed to do. He did what I would have done had I been the one leading."

The strong run by Earnhardt was no surprise to his competitors and gave them a preview of what might come in the 500 a week later. When asked what he thought of when he saw Earnhardt's strength, third-place finisher Elliott said, "Me in 1985! That's all there is to it. There's not going to be any way of beating him (in the 500) unless he has troubles.

"All you've got to do is look at the (lap) times. In the first race, he just messed around. The second race was about a half-second faster than the first race. That's the only difference.

"We didn't run that bad," Elliott said. "This is a 10- and 10-lap race. We'll know more when we go through the twin-125 qualifying races. But I guarantee you he'll win the race."

Irvan looked to be Earnhardt's strongest competition early on, but was forced to settle for fourth.

"We started it (the Morgan McClure Chevrolet) too tight and, on the restarts, I just didn't get quite the jump that I needed," Irvan said. "If you didn't have a car with you, you couldn't run with them."

Fifth-place finisher Wallace blamed track position for his not being able to make a bid for the win.

"At the start of the race, I took off, but the 18 (Sacks) was in front of me and was slowing me up and I couldn't get around him," Wallace said, "If I could have popped in front of the 18, I might have won the thing."

It was possibly Kyle Petty who summed up Earnhardt's domination of the field best by saying, "What's new? Earnhardt is always tough when it comes to Daytona.

"If we could have gotten the right position at the end, maybe we could have made a run on him. As far as pulling away, that's a whole different story (referring to carburetor restrictor plate requirement).

"But I just got messed up on restarts and got behind."

Finishing sixth through 14th were: Schrader; Petty; Rudd; G. Bodine; B. Bodine; Kulwicki; Cope; Sacks and Trickle.

The only accident of the day came on the second lap of the second segment involving Schrader, Rudd and Cope. As the three exited the fourth turn, Cope found himself squeezed between the Hendrick Motorsports drivers while exiting turn four.

"I hate that it took three Chevrolets out of the race," Cope said. "That's irritating, and I feel bad about it." ∎

DALE EARNHARDT AND RICHARD CHILDRESS MAKE THE 125S LOOK EASY, BUT HAVE STRUGGLED IN DAYTONA'S PREMIER EVENT.
DAVID CHOBAT PHOTO

Earnhardt Sets Pace
In Second 125-Mile Qualifier

Darkness Settles In As Race Ends

By BEN WHITE

UNCERTAINTY.

That could be the best way to describe the 1991 edition of the Gatorade Twin 125-mile qualifying races at the 2.5-mile Daytona International Speedway – but with one exception. It would not be an appropriate word for describing Dale Earnhardt's desire to win the second qualifying race, which he did easily by leading all 50 laps.

Earnhardt's obvious plan was to put the Richard Childress Chevrolet up front and leave it there. And he did just that.

From his third starting position, Earnhardt made his presence known early, as he did in the Busch Clash just days before. He quickly passed No. 1 starter Ernie Irvan – who gained that spot by posting the second best one-lap qualifying run of 195.639 mph behind Davey Allison – and took the lead halfway down the backstretch. Once in front, he held off Irvan, in the Morgan-McClure Chevrolet, to take the win.

"Ernie didn't bother me there (when running second) but bothered me pretty hard when he ran into the back of me and knocked me sideways," Earnhardt said. "It was pretty out of control there for a little bit, but he was trying to do all he could do to get by me."

On second thought, maybe there was one part of Earnhardt's plan that was uncertain. There was no question that he would try to go to the front. But he was forced to use a measure of fuel conservation once he did arrive at the head of the field.

"Our gas mileage was questionable," Earnhardt said. "We worked the drafting with Ernie. I didn't use the throttle real hard at times. I sort of feathered it, but not much.

"We drove up high and conserved all we could. I drove to victory lane, and the engine still had some fuel pressure so we must have had enough to go another lap or so."

Not only did Earnhardt have a handful with Irvan, but Kyle Petty was a bit aggravating to him as well. Petty finished a strong third in the Sabco Pontiac.

"I felt like Kyle was going to run strong because his car was handling pretty good," Earnhardt said. "In the Busch Clash, he got together with Rusty (Wallace) and ran pretty good."

With Earnhardt clearly in command of the event, it was a chase for second. The runner-up spot looked to be Darrell Waltrip's in the opening laps, but a chassis problem forced his Chevrolet to drift back through the pack.

"We were pushing too much," Waltrip said. "I thought I could catch back up, but I couldn't. Once I got in fifth all by myself, I saw I couldn't catch back up so I was happy to stay right there.

"We just need to do a little more work for the 500. We've got a fast car. We've just got to get a wee bit better.

"This wasn't our best engine," Waltrip added. "We saved our best engine for the 500, so we're going to have a little more horsepower. We'll work on the car just a little bit more."

Once Waltrip was out of the picture, Irvan and Petty seemed to be the only other cars with a remote chance of catching Earnhardt, or at least could inherit the lead in the event that Earnhardt experienced problems.

"I thought I had a good chance at getting Dale on the last lap," Irvan said. "I got a good run on him on the back straightaway, but he slid the car up and blocked the line. That's racing."

Had Irvan not encountered a pushing problem in his Morgan-McClure

Chevrolet, he felt that the outcome may have been different.

"We had a faster car than Dale," Irvan continued. "But we had a push in the front all day and as long as the car was pushing we couldn't really make a move (or) get a run on Dale.

"This one (engine) ran awful good, but I think this other one will accelerate a little better."

When asked why his car did not get up to speed on the first lap when Earnhardt grabbed the lead away on the backstretch, Irvan said, "The motor wouldn't accelerate with the gear we had it in. Once we were up to speed, the car went right to the front.

"I felt I could pass anybody I wanted to - except Dale.

He was running awful good."
—Ernie Irvan

"I felt I could pass anybody I wanted to – except Dale. He was running awful good."

Before the race, however, NASCAR officials questioned a technical point on Irvan's engine. But, after a discussion with crew chief Tony Glover, the part in question was brought up to legal standards.

"Two years ago, NASCAR said that the inserts in the intake could not float or come up," Irvan said. "What happened was the welds keeping the inserts down broke on the intake and they had slid up on us. We had to slide it back down, set-screw it and weld it.

"That's about all there was to that."

As for Petty, his strong performance was somewhat of a surprise, as his Sabco Pontiac moved forward in the field until the closing laps. Both he and his father, Richard, were impressive in each of their respective races.

"We just didn't have quite enough muscle to get past them at the end," Petty said. "We'll just have to wait and see about the 500. I still don't know how we stack up. That's what kept us in the race and made us run good.

"To come down to Daytona and run like that right out of the box and qualify so well for the Daytona 500, we're really pleased."

Richard Petty had a strong run in the first qualifier with a second-place finish. To that, the younger Petty said, "He beat me again. Every time I come down here and run well, he beats me.

"I guess I should expect that."

Again, the word was uncertainty.

For NASCAR, it was a race within a race. The sanctioning body had to make fast time in its decision whether the races would be held as scheduled or set back a day on a schedule already busy with events.

Heavy morning rains postponed the start of the twins for four hours while wet conditions and darkness threatened to halt the day's activities entirely.

The storms then passed, leaving a window of about one hour for NASCAR to make preparations to race. Finally, after a hurried pre-race schedule, cars assigned to the first twin 125 rolled off pit road at approximately 4:30 p.m.

To ensure that the second race could be completed, since long late-afternoon shadows had begun to appear, NASCAR called drivers in the second race to their cars before the first race was completed.

The second race came to a finish just before dusk, as lights were turned on down the front trioval in the closing laps just past 6 p.m.

There were two accidents but only one caution-flag period. The yellow was displayed when Brett Bodine slammed his King Racing Buick hard against the inside wall after belting the outside in the fourth turn.

After the car's top was removed using heavy-duty rescue equipment, Bodine walked on his own with the help of brother Geoff Bodine to the awaiting ambulance and was transported to Halifax Hospital for further tests. After a CAT scan, he was released but complained of severe dizziness and loss of memory after having suffered a concussion.

The other incident involved Dave Marcis, who had a tire on his car explode in the pits with such impact that the hood hinges broke free at the windshield.

"I smelled smoke at about the same time NASCAR said they saw smoke coming from my car," Marcis said. "I pulled down on the apron and told my guys I did have a flat, but I didn't know which tire it was.

"As I was coming down pit road, the tire blew."

Rusty Wallace and Waltrip finished fourth and fifth, while spots six through 15 went to: Sterling Marlin; Joe Ruttman; Buddy Baker, Mark Martin; Bobby Hamilton; Jeff Purvis; Ken Schrader; Rick Wilson; Dick Trickle and Chad Little. ■

EARNHARDT'S CREW AVOIDED PENALTIES THAT HURT KEN SCHRADER AND ALAN KULWICKI'S TEAMS FOR HAVING TOO MANY CREW MEMBERS OVER THE WALL.
DAVID CHOBAT PHOTO

Earnhardt Takes
First Win of '91
Earnhardt Edges Rudd
At Richmond
By DEB WILLIAMS

Dale Earnhardt held off a determined Ricky Rudd on the final lap of the Pontiac Excitement 400 to claim a 1½ car length victory, but the event's final lap didn't accurately portray the rest of the 400-lap NASCAR Winston Cup race at the 0.75-mile track.

After the first round of green-flag pit stops, there was very little racing for the lead and with 20 laps remaining Earnhardt possessed a four-second advantage over Rudd.

The race's complexion changed with seven laps to go when Hutt Stricklin and Brett Bodine collided in turn two. Stricklin

managed to nurse his Buick back to his pit but Bodine's slammed into the wall and stayed there. During the four-lap caution period, Darrell Waltrip, who was the last car on the lead lap in seventh, pitted and Stricklin's scorecard was taken. A NASCAR spokesman said the action was taken because Stricklin ignored instructions to stop and then disobeyed the inspector who was attempting to hold him in his pit.

When the race returned to green on lap 398, Earnhardt's Chevrolet jumped ahead on the restart, but Rudd cut the margin. When Earnhardt bobbled off turn four, Rudd dove low to pull alongside Earnhardt. The two

dueled side by side through turns one and two before Earnhardt edged ahead of his fellow Chevrolet driver as they exited turn two.

Rudd never regained the lost ground and Earnhardt had his first win in 1991 and the 49th of his Winston Cup career. That moved him into sole possession of ninth place on the all-time victory list.

"The tires were a little bit on the hot side and we couldn't punish them too much. I broke it loose coming off of four on the white flag and Ricky got under me," Earnhardt said. "I just had to race him high, and he raced me clean that lap."

Rudd agreed with Earnhardt that the two

raced each other clean on the final lap.

"I got under Dale going into turn one, and I tried to get by him, but I couldn't," Rudd said. "I went down into turn three and I had to go low. My car wouldn't turn because I had such a tight inside line. Just that least little bit is what caused us to push and we couldn't get by him at the finish."

In recent years, Rudd and Earnhardt have been involved in a few incidents that have resulted in fines and hard feelings. Two of them occurred at North Wilkesboro, N.C., when they were racing for the win.

"It sort of set a precedent after all the bumps and run-ins we've had the last couple of years," Earnhardt said about the final lap that occurred before an estimated attendance of 51,000. "I think that set a precedent that we can race clean from here on. I'm sure I will if I'm on the inside of him. I'll give him all the room he needs. It was a good race."

Earnhardt and Rudd dominated the event, leading all but 96 laps. Rudd possessed the top spot on five occasions for 154 laps, while Earnhardt held the advantage five times for 150 laps, including the final 76.

In the event's first 100 laps, there were often three drivers – Alan Kulwicki, Rudd and Harry Gant – racing for the lead. That all changed, however, after the first set of green-flag pit stops. That's when Rudd took over and held the lead, once by 7.71 seconds, for 99 laps.

Rudd again assumed the top spot following the second round of green-flag stops but this time the race's second caution occurred and that allowed Earnhardt to close on Rudd's bumper. The two raced side by side and bumper to bumper, exchanging the lead at least three times, with about 150 laps remaining before Earnhardt took over on lap 255 for a 67-lap stretch.

Earnhardt lost the lead when he made his final stop for tires and fuel on lap 322, but regained it when Waltrip pitted on lap 325. Rudd and Rusty Wallace closed on Earnhardt when Sterling Marlin, who was two laps down, passed the leader, and remained in front of him.

"He got by me and he never did go on. He was stopping in the middle of the corner," Earnhardt said about Marlin. "Ricky got in on me pretty hard and I bumped him (Marlin). I got him a little loose and I got by him and I just went on.

"I really didn't mean to get into him but when I did, it broke him loose. He was a lap down, and we were racing for the lead, so it really didn't bother me."

With only six caution flags for 23 laps, Earnhardt set a track record average speed of 105.397 mph. The old record was 95.770

mph, set by Davey Allison in September 1988 in the first race on the remodeled speedway. There were 25 lead changes among seven drivers, but the majority of those occurred during green-flag pit stops.

> "I really didn't mean to get into him but **when I did, it broke him loose.** He was a lap down, and we were racing for the lead, so it really didn't bother me."
> —Earnhardt

EARNHARDT TAKES THE INSIDE ON MICHAEL WALTRIP. DAVID CHOBAT PHOTO

Gant, driving an Oldsmobile, edged Wallace, in a Pontiac, for third at the finish and Kulwicki placed fifth in a Ford.

At one point, the race went 229 laps without a caution flag but Earnhardt said that didn't bother him.

"I was glad to see it go green that long with the strategy we were using in the pits," Earnhardt said. "We wanted to run all the green-flag stops we could. We were just running gas stops and changing tires. I think that's about what everybody did."

The four-time Winston Cup champion said the only drivers who concerned him at the end were Rudd, Gant, Wallace and Kulwicki.

Earnhardt, who was sick with the flu on

pole day, qualified 19th. However, when the race began, he didn't let an ill-handling race car thwart his efforts. After 127 laps, he was in 10th, and he took the lead for the first time on lap 105 during the initial series of green-flag pit stops. He led through lap 107 when he pitted for four tires. The Kannapolis, N.C., native led again for two laps during the second round of green-flag stops. On the early stops, his crew made adjustments that proved extremely beneficial in the event's second half.

"The car was a little bit pushy in the middle (of the turn) but it was loose at the end," said Earnhardt, who won $67,950 and took a 22-point lead over Rudd in the Winston Cup standings.

"We put some wedge in it and I just had to work the car a little different getting it into the corners to keep it from being tight in the middle. What I tried to do was get the car turned early and then work it off the corner off the bottom and it worked well for us. You would think tightening it up would make it push more but it didn't. It helped it get in and off the corner and the push stayed the same."

The car was the same one Earnhardt used at Phoenix, Ariz., last November, when he won and snatched the point lead from Mark Martin with one race remaining in the season.

The pit road rules were altered slightly from the opening race at Daytona Beach, Fla., with the competitors allowed to change tires under caution if they were flatspotted or going flat. However, if a tire change was made, the driver had to return to his pit on

EARNHARDT GOES WIDE IN RICHMOND.
NWCS ARCHIVE PHOTO

his odd or even lap number and change the same number of tires he changed under caution. Also, a 15-second penalty was assessed to a team for each man too many over the wall on a pit stop.

Kulwicki was the first to receive the penalty when he had too many crewmen over the wall during his green-flag stop on lap 180. He was running third when he pitted for four tires.

Ken Schrader was assessed the same penalty on lap 225 while also in third place.

Jimmy Spencer and Kyle Petty received time penalties after they were involved in a brush with the wall and a spin, respectively, and then began heading towards their pit after the caution flag was waived.

The altered pit rule that allows tire changes under caution doesn't apply in the final 25 laps. At that time, the rule reverts to its original form of a one-lap penalty, which became a two-lap penalty at the season's first short-track race, for any driver changing tires under caution.

"Our strategy worked out good with pit position and the way the car worked all day, so we had a pretty good race," Earnhardt said. "All we did was just throw the caution flags out, as far as our strategy goes. You can change four tires while you're filling the car up with gas. So, our strategy was to change four tires each time we pitted.

"You lose a lap when you change two, so why not lose a lap and a half and get four

fresh tires? I think that was pretty much everyone's strategy. It worked well here and I think you'll see a lot of it next week at Rockingham (N.C.). I feel like tires will go away in 60 to 80 laps there.

"You had a lot to take into consideration (at Richmond), such as where everybody was on the race track and where you were, and how good you were running against each of them and go from there."

"In the driver's meeting, NASCAR told the competitors they might as well get used to the pit road rules because, even though they might be refined, they were here to stay. That, however, didn't keep some of the drivers from again commenting on their negative points.

"It's hard to adjust anything during a race with the rules the way they are," Stricklin said. "You almost have to go overboard at the start of a race and hope you've done the right thing."

Seven-time Winston Cup champion Richard Petty, who finished 11th two laps down, said the rule worked better than in the Daytona 500 because there weren't as many cautions as there were in the opening event.

"They probably wouldn't have played into the outcome anyway," Petty said. "Overall, they didn't play an important deal, so they got by with it again."

Dick Trickle said he, too, was waiting for changes.

"The way it is now, it's hard to keep many

cars on the lead lap," said Trickle, who finished 15th, four laps down. "It's going to hurt the show as time goes on."

After the first round of green-flag pit stops, 13 of the 35 cars that started the race were on the lead lap. That dropped to seven after the second round and remained at that number. Only three cars failed to finish the race, an extremely low attrition rate for Richmond.

Earnhardt said it would be interesting to see how the pit road rules work at Rockingham since that will be their first test at a track where there are two pit roads.

"We're just going to have to work with it and get used to it," he commented. "NASCAR seems pretty set on doing what they're going to do.

"The main thing we started all this for was for safety on pit road. As long as they don't lose sight of that, it'll be fine. They still don't caution you during drivers' meetings on how important it is for drivers to keep their cars under control on green-flag stops.

"I think they need to keep stressing the pit rules are there for the safety of the crew on pit road. It's more dangerous pitting under green than pitting under caution, so everybody needs to keep in mind to be as safe as you can. There's some good points about it and there's some bad points about it. The main thing is we want to try to keep pit road safe and work with NASCAR trying to refine the rules." ■

Earnhardt Gets
Birthday Present

By DEB WILLIAMS

Earnhardt Gets Early
39th...40th?...Birthday Present
With Win At Martinsville

DALE NEEDS A HAND
HANDLING ALL THAT
HARDWARE.
NWCS ARCHIVE PHOTO

Dale Earnhardt celebrated his birthday one day early by dominating the Hanes 500 for his second NASCAR Winston Cup victory this year.

He also continued to close on Ricky Rudd in the battle for the series championship.

Earnhardt, who led five times for 251 laps, became the first repeat winner in 1991. His other win came at Richmond, Va., in February. Prior to the Martinsville event, the circuit had experienced a different winner in each of the first seven races.

"It's a great birthday present," said Earnhardt, who claims he turns 39 April 29, but whose mother maintains he will be 40.

The victory was Earnhardt's fifth at the 0.526-mile track, his third in the spring race in his last five starts, and his 50th Winston Cup career win. That ties him for seventh on the all-time victory list with Junior Johnson and Ned Jarrett.

"Those guys raced my dad and I can pick at them now," Earnhardt said with a grin.

"All the accomplishments you have, you to have to earn in Winston Cup racing," Earnhardt said seriously. "To tie or to get even with those guys I looked up to and admired, it's pretty impressive. It's an honor.

"Who knows, maybe one day I can win seven championships. I wish Richard (Petty) would retire so I could have a better chance at it. That rascal might mess up and win another one."

Petty is the all-time leader with seven division titles.

Kyle Petty, Richard's son, driving a Pontiac, finished 3.34 seconds behind Earnhardt for his second top-five finish this year. Darrell Waltrip placed third in a Chevrolet, while Brett Bodine took fourth in a Buick.

Harry Gant claimed fifth in an Oldsmobile, one lap down.

"We were pitting on the backstretch and that kept us behind all day long," said Petty, who led twice for 10 laps. "Dale ran a whole lot better than I did on fresh tires. I was better on tires with 25, 30, 40 laps on them.

"We just came up a little short today."

In the race's closing stages, Earnhardt received the break he needed to make one more adjustment on his Chevrolet when leader Davey Allison cut a right-front tire. Allison had built a 4.35-second lead over Petty with 59 laps remaining when he experienced the bad luck. Earnhardt was fifth at the time behind Rusty Wallace and Rudd, respectively. Waltrip was sixth and Geoff Bodine was seventh, the last car on the lead lap.

Allison's Ford slowed drastically on lap 457 as he entered turn three. He limped around on the flat tire to the backstretch and then collided with Alan Kulwicki at the pit road entrance.

The incident removed Allison, who led three times for 110 laps, from contention.

Wallace, who pitted on the frontstretch with Earnhardt during the caution period, stalled his Pontiac when he attempted to leave his pit and his crew had to push him behind the wall. The problem: the transmission had lost all of its gears.

Even though Petty pitted on the backstretch, he managed to return to the track ahead of Earnhardt, who had received a chassis adjustment and four fresh tires on his Chevrolet. When the race restarted on lap 463, Petty was leading, Earnhardt was second, Rudd third, Waltrip fourth and G. Bodine fifth.

Before the race ended, however, Rudd and G. Bodine also dropped from the top five. Rudd's Chevrolet lost its left-rear brake and G. Bodine's Ford had transmission problems. Rudd placed 11th and G. Bodine 20th.

Earnhardt overtook Petty on the outside and moved into the lead for good on lap 464. Within eight laps, Earnhardt had stretched his advantage to 1.32 seconds and he was never challenged.

"I needed the caution. We took a lot of wedge out the last time we pitted, put the tires on and it came back to where it was," said Earnhardt, who won $63,600 before an estimated record crowd of 44,000.

Had the race's 11th caution period not occurred, Earnhardt said the race would have boiled down to fuel mileage. He said he knew he and Waltrip didn't have to stop again, but his crew figured Allison would have to pit for gas.

Earnhardt started the 500-lap race in 10th but didn't challenge for the lead until after the second caution period, which consumed laps 84-90. For about three laps, Gant and Earnhardt battled side by side with Gant leading lap 93, Earnhardt nosing ahead on lap 94, and Gant moving back ahead on lap

96. The Taylorsville, N.C., driver then maintained the lead for the next 38 laps.

Earnhardt, meanwhile remained second.

"We were using different brake pads; they faded and it spooked me," Earnhardt said. "They came back and from then on, we just sort of adjusted the car.

"It's a great birthday present,"

said Earnhardt (40), who claims he turns 39 April 29, but whose mother maintains he will be 40.

"We got real good at one point and I raced Harry so I could lead a lap. We got five points and then we just sort of settled back behind him."

From lap 134, when Earnhardt took the lead for the second time, until Allison's problem in the race's later stages, the event became a duel between those two drivers. But it was also during this time that Earnhardt's crew overadjusted his Chevrolet.

"It was loose going in, tight in the middle, and loose coming off (the turns)," said Earnhardt, who averaged 75.139 mph in the race slowed by 11 caution flags for 53 laps.

"Each time we adjusted it, it got a little worse. We took a lot of wedge out of it when we pitted that last time.

"If we hadn't got that last caution, I don't think we'd have won the race."

The victory allowed Earnhardt to close within 42 points of Rudd in the battle for the series championship. That means Earnhardt, who trailed Rudd by 142 points after the April 14 Valleydale Meats 500 at Bristol, Tenn., has made up 100 points in the last two events.

"It's early in the year, but I believe that's when you've got to win the championship," Earnhardt said. "You've got to get all you can every race.

EARNHARDT TAKES THE CHECKERED FLAG AT MARTINSVILLE.
DAVID CHOBAT PHOTO

Gant, who led three times for 129 laps, relinquished the lead to Earnhardt on lap 134. Two laps later, Gant spun in turn two while running second.

Martin, who was third, went high to avoid Gant but then spun down and into Ken Schrader. Martin continued but later retired his Ford with a blown head gasket. He finished 29th. Schrader's crew repaired his Chevrolet and returned him to the race for a 23rd-place finish.

"We had a couple of bad races at Darlington and Bristol and got behind in the points. We felt we were inconsistent but I think the guys got that consistency back at North Wilkesboro. We need to be consistent and run smooth.

"I'm not comfortable because we're not leading the points, but we are working on it."

The Hanes 500 took three hours, 26 minutes and 41 seconds to complete and had 13 lead changes among five drivers. ■

DAUGHTER TAYLOR LOVES A WINNER.
NWCS ARCHIVE PHOTO

Earnhardt
Masters
Talladega Again

Earnhardt Becomes Talladega 'Chess Master'

By DEB WILLIAMS

For NASCAR's Winston Cup drivers, the DieHard 500 was a 188-lap chess game with each competitor a pawn but, when the final move was made, it was Dale Earnhardt who got to proclaim, "Checkmate."

Earnhardt edged Bill Elliott by 1½ car lengths to claim his third win this season and the 51st of his Winston Cup career. That moved him into sole possession of seventh on the all-time victory list.

The four-time Winston Cup champion now has won three of the last four races at the 2.66-mile track and, with five victories at the speedway during this Winston Cup career, he becomes the facility's all-time winner.

"It feels great," Earnhardt said when asked to comment about becoming the leading winner at Talladega. "Anytime you set a record it's another piece of history in your career.

"Winning a race at Talladega is pretty special. It's one of my favorite race tracks."

Earnhardt's 1991 Die Hard 500 win may be remembered as one of his toughest, even though he led seven times for 101 laps, including the final 28. At no point during the race did the leader ever have more than a two-car-length advantage. Also, there were 32 lead changes among 13 drivers with the seven caution flags for 43 laps slowing the average speed to 147.383 mph.

Throughout the race, there was continuous shuffling in the lead pack with the competitors often racing three abreast.

"It was a real strategy race," a tired but happy Earnhardt said. "You had to look behind you as much as you did in front of you. There were a lot of cars moving around. The draft worked well and we tried to stay in the top three or four.

"One time the car got loose and I fell back several positions. But I got to draft in the end and we were able to draft real well."

Earnhardt had his hands full in the race's closing stages because of a yellow flag that appeared on lap 180 for an air cleaner on the backstretch, which came off Ernie Irvan's car. When the race restarted, six laps remained and there were 15 cars on the lead lap.

Earnhardt was leading, Ricky Rudd was second, Michael Waltrip third, Rusty Wallace fourth, Sterling Marlin fifth, Davey Allison sixth, then Elliott and Darrell Waltrip.

On the restart – lap 183 – Marlin moved to the inside to pass Wallace with Allison and Elliott in tow. The following lap, Marlin stole second from Rudd by going low through turns three and four, but then Allison moved to the inside of Marlin as they raced through the trioval, taking second from him.

Throughout it all, Earnhardt remained the leader.

"I don't know if you have a buddy out there," Earnhardt said. "Our teams (his and Rudd's) talked during the caution about working together."

Rudd said he and Earnhardt worked together as long as they could.

"We basically came to an agreement that we'd work together as best we could until the last lap," Rudd said. "Then, we were going to have at each other."

On lap 186, Allison pulled low alongside Earnhardt as they entered turn one but Earnhardt got the momentum he needed coming off turn two and moved back ahead of Allison with Elliott, Martin and Rudd on his bumper.

"All we needed were four more inches and we could have moved up in front of Earnhardt and we would have had him," Allison said. "If you trust another Ford driver and he's the only one you can really work with or you're the only one that can work with him, and then they leave you hung out to dry, then that's pitiful.

"We were fighting with each other instead of working together."

Martin called it the "most frustrating day I've had on a race track."

Earnhardt knew he had to pull in front of the Fords or they would pass him.

"I was not going to run second so Ricky could run third," he commented.

No one made a move on lap 187 but chose, instead, to wait until the final lap to implement their strategy. Earnhardt moved low and Elliott went high as they raced off turn four. Earnhardt then drifted up the track. Elliott dove low as they came through the trioval but came up a car-length short at the checkered flag.

"There was just nothing I could do," Elliott said. "The problems was, if I could

ever get a run at Earnhardt and, if I ever backed off, I had the No. 6 (Martin) and the No. 5 (Rudd) behind me. I was hoping that the No. 6 would help me get on up there beside Earnhardt, but the problem is, if I made my move too early, then those two were going to pass me.

"I was just in a bad situation."

Earnhardt, who won $88,670, said he was more comfortable racing Elliott and Martin than he was Allison and Marlin.

"Bill is sharp on the speedways," he said. "I saw him and I knew he was going to make a run at me off four. Coming through the trioval, I moved around to mess up the air, but I didn't cut him off. We were lucky to beat him."

> "I'm OK, except that I
> might need a new
> # pair of britches
> after getting upside down like
> that." – Rick Mast on his scary
> trip down the track upside down.

Finishing behind Elliott's Ford in third was Martin, also in a Ford. Rudd placed fourth in a Ford in the race that took three hours, 23 minutes and 35 seconds to complete.

"You could see them all (Fords) coming and it's pretty hard to do anything when you've got that many of them against you," said Richard Childress, Earnhardt's team owner. "When you've got Dale Earnhardt in the car you've got a little advantage too – anytime you're in a race.

"We went to the wind tunnel after we got beat so bad at Daytona, and Terry Laise (Chevrolet Raceshop engineer) showed us where we had made some mistakes on the car. We corrected the mistakes, and I think it helped us."

In the battle for the Winston Cup championship, Earnhardt's win allowed him to gain 20 points on the second-place Rudd, who now trails by 160 with 12 races remaining. Earnhardt gained 42 points on the third-place Allison, who finished ninth, and 15 on Martin.

Irvan, who was involved in a 10-car accident in turn two on lap 105, lost 121 points

to Earnhardt and dropped from third to fourth in the standings. Ken Schrader, who completed 77 laps before the engine blew in his Chevrolet, lost 142 points to Earnhardt and dropped from fifth to sixth in the points. Darrell Waltrip, with his 15th place finish, remained seventh but lost 63 points to Earnhardt.

"We're taking them one on one," Earnhardt said about the upcoming races. "We go to Watkins Glen (N.Y.) next and we know Ricky will be strong, so we need to go in there and be as tough as we can."

Five of the race's seven caution flags were caused by accidents that involved Wally Dallenbach Jr., Harry Gant, Buddy Baker, Irvan, Jimmy Spencer, Ted Musgrave, Stanley Smith, Richard Petty, Lake Speed, Terry Labonte, Rick Wilson, Bobby Hamilton, Hut Stricklin, Geoff Bodine and Rick Mast.

The scariest incident occurred on lap 166 in the trioval and involved Mast and Baker. The two were racing for position when the left rear of Mast's Oldsmobile barely clipped Baker's right front.

Mast turned sideways and, when his car's front hit the track's flat portion it became airborne. The car overturned, landed on its roof and then slid at least 100 yards, hitting the outside wall, before stopping on the grassy apron near the start-finish line.

"I'm OK, except that I might need a new

AS HE GETS READY TO HIT THE TRACK, IT'S EASY TO SEE THAT EARNHARDT LOVES HIS JOB. DAVID CHOBAT PHOTO

pair of britches after getting upside down like that," said Mast, who crawled from his upside-down Oldsmobile and walked away.

"The first thing you think is, 'Please stop,' and then you think, 'Please don't anybody hit me while I'm sitting here,' and then you think, 'Please don't catch fire while I'm trying to get out of here.' I'll tell you, my heart was beating about 300 times a minute." ■

THE CHILDRESS AND EARNHARDT FAMILIES ARE GETTING USED TO THIS POSE. NWCS ARCHIVE PHOTO

Earnhardt!
Puts End To Gant's Hot Streak With Victory At N. Wilkesboro

Earnhardt Plays Spoiler's Role And Gets Rewards

By STEVE WAID

It came with nine laps remaining in the race.

Dale Earnhardt snaked his RCR Enterprises Chevrolet around Harry Gant's Leo Jackson Motorsports Oldsmobile on the outside in the third turn and went on to win the Tyson Holly Farms 400 NASCAR Winston Cup race.

With the victory, his fourth of the 1991 season, Earnhardt brought to an abrupt halt Gant's hopes of becoming the only driver in the modern NASCAR era to win five consecutive Winston Cup races.

Gant came to North Wilkesboro as "Mr. September," a driver who had won four straight races dating back to the Sept. 1 Heinz Southern 500 at Darlington, S.C. With thousands of friends and neighbors looking on, Gant, from nearby Taylorsville, N.C., pursued victory with a vengeance, leading 340 of the race's 400 laps.

Finally, though, Gant's luck ran out.

With Earnhardt in relentless pursuit over the event's final circuits, Gant radioed back to his pits that he had lost his brakes. Although he hoped he could hold on until the checkered flag, he simply could not do so as Earnhardt emerged victorious for the 52nd time in his career by 1.47 seconds.

"Harry looked unstoppable," admitted Earnhardt, who was not aware immediately after the race that his rival had lost his brakes. "At the end, I just wanted to stay in range and hope that maybe I could do something with Harry over the final 15 laps. I was close enough that he could see me in his rear view mirror and maybe that made him anxious.

"I couldn't get around him on the inside. Harry protected his groove. He races hard and clean.

"I could see I wasn't going to make it on the inside, so I moved to the outside. When I got by him, I thought Harry was trying to save his tires and be more consistent so he could race with me, but he never did."

Earnhardt did much more than end Gant's winning streak. His victory ended what had been a summer of mediocrity for him and the RCR Enterprises team. Beset by nagging problems and ill luck, they last won at Talladega, Ala., on July 28, and spent the next eight races doing little more than surviving.

"I've been on vacation since Talladega," said Earnhardt with a grin. "It's a relief to finally win again. After Talladega, it seemed like every time we turned around, some aggravating little problems happened to us.

"We had bad luck, but the important thing is we came on to finish races anyway. And, where we finished bad, it seemed like Ricky Rudd finished bad, too."

That leads to the second benefit Earnhardt received from his victory. He picked up 53 points on Rudd, his rival for the 1991 Winston Cup championship, who finished 12th, one lap down.

Earnhardt now leads by 112 points with only four races remaining. Clearly, he has the upper hand.

"I feel it's definitely a two-man race now," said Earnhardt, who earned $69,350 for his victory on the 0.625-mile North Wilkesboro track. "I hope with three races to go, it's a one-man race.

"But there are still four races to go. Our next race is a Charlotte and, while that's been a good track for me, you can have bad luck and end up in 44th place. All we want to do is try to be consistent and win. If we can't do that, we want at least a top-five finish.

"This win takes the pressure off us a bit and puts a bit more on Ricky. But, as I said, anything can happen in four races."

By virtue of his pole victory on Sept. 27, Gant was afforded the opportunity to win the $144,400 Unocal Challenge Bonus if he could also win the race.

It appeared that he would do just that – easily. Running

EARNHARDT PASSES HARRY GANT IN TURN THREE ON THE FINAL LAP TO ICE HIS COME-FROM-BEHIND VICTORY IN THE HOLLY FARMS 400.
DAVID CHOBAT PHOTO

smoothly and unchallenged, he lapped 21 cars by the 93rd lap and sped on to lead the first 252 laps. As he pitted under caution with the other cars on the lead lap, he always returned to the point, thanks to the efficient work by his Leo Jackson Motorsports team.

Morgan Shepherd inherited the lead on lap 253, during the race's sixth caution period, when he elected not to pit his Bud Moore Engineering Ford. Shepherd, having one of his better runs of the season, managed to hold Gant off until lap 294 when the Oldsmobile driver retook the No. 1 spot with

a pass coming out of the fourth turn.

Gant once again showed his muscle and got a break to replace his tires when Sterling Marlin's spin brought out the seventh caution period on lap 360.

Earnhardt got a break, too. He had been in third place, chasing Shepherd, when the yellow-flag came out. His crew was able to put him back on the track in second place, giving him the opportunity to make a run at Gant.

"The guys in the pits did as much to win this race as I did," said Earnhardt. "I was behind Morgan at the start of that caution and I came out ahead of him and behind Harry. I figured then if I could run consistent, I could get a shot at him.

"But I was worried about Morgan. I had to keep him at bay, too."

The eighth and final caution period began on lap 367 after Geoff Bodine spun in the first turn. It was the start of the scenario change, which would ultimately mean Gant's defeat.

The restart came only one lap later and, while Gant retained his lead, Earnhardt began to make up ground. By lap 388, he had caught the leader.

"I felt the brakes go away and I think, with 10 taps remaining, I didn't have any brakes at all," said Gant. "I tried to make it to the end, but I think Dale sensed I had a problem.

"When he passed me, I had no choice but to let up because otherwise I would have gotten into him."

"I wanted to know how many laps were left in the race because I wanted to do what I could with maybe 10 or 15 laps left," said Earnhardt. "I radioed to Richard (Childress, team owner) and asked him how many were left. He said 25. Then Kirk (Shelmerdine, crew chief) came back and said, 'No, no! There are 15 laps left!'

"I began to notice that I was getting into the corners better than Harry. I reckon then he was having the brake problem, but I didn't know about it until I was told long after the race was over.

"There was no way I was going to pass on the inside. Finally, I moved to the outside and, when I hit the throttle, I was able to pull Harry."

Even in victory, Earnhardt remained respectful of Gant's accomplishments.

"I'm glad I beat him, but I sorta hate to see the end of his streak," said Earnhardt, who shares the modern-day record of four wins in a row with Gant, Darrell Waltrip, and Cale Yarborough. "Harry is such a good competitor.

"Just last week at Martinsville (Va.), he crashed and tore up the front end of his car and he still came back to win. I needed a handicap to beat him today and I got it. If he didn't have his problem, he would have won today hands down."

Shepherd finished third while Davey Allison, who spent much of the early part of the race running behind Gant, ended up fourth in the Robert Yates Racing Ford. Fifth place went to Mark Martin in the Roush Racing Ford.

"I've been on vacation since Talladega," said Earnhardt with a grin. "It's a relief to finally **win again.**"

Rounding out the top 10, in order, were: Rusty Wallace, Brett Bodine, Ken Schrader, Dale Jarrett and Alan Kulwicki. All completed 400 laps.

The attrition rate was low as only Rick Wilson and Ernie Irvan – victims of accidents – and Dave Marcis failed to finish the 33-car event.

"At first the car was a little tight but then the track came to us," said Earnhardt, who won the two-hour, 39-minute, 23-second race with an average speed of 94.113 mph. "Once the track got rubber back on it, we were all right.

"We were able to put together a consistent run and that's all we wanted. My qualifying bug flew out the window. I didn't do a good job there and we ended up starting 16th and had to come through the field from there – but we've done that before.

"Now that we've won again and have a bigger lead in points, we just want to take it one race at a time from here on out and have a shot a winning. We still haven't won a pole and we'd like to do that.

"Maybe we can do that and win a race and get that Unocal money. I saved them some money today."

The fact that a fifth career championship looms large for Earnhardt wasn't lost on the native of Kannapolis, N.C. He knows where the titlist receives his $1 million reward.

The last thing he said as he left the post-race interview was, "New York, New York." ∎

Earnhardt Prevails One More Time

Takes Third Straight 125-Mile Victory; Crashes Decimate Field

By STEVE WAID

dale

D ale Earnhardt's prowess in the Gatorade Twin 125-Mile Qualifying Races for the Daytona 500 was fortified by yet another victory, this time by slightly more than a car length over Mark Martin in an event marred by crashes.

Driving the RCR Enterprises Chevrolet, Earnhardt won his third-straight 125-miler and matched the record set by Fireball Roberts in 1960-62.

That he did so was a testament to his driving skill and his car's preparation. Handling well in a race where poor handling could prove disastrous, Earnhardt slipped by Martin on lap 41 of the 50-lap race to take the lead and hold on until the checkered flag.

But, by his own admission, Earnhardt would not have won without the cooperation of fellow Chevrolet driver Ernie Irvan, who finished third. On the last lap, Martin pulled alongside Earnhardt on the outside as they sped through turns three and four. Irvan pulled in behind Earnhardt, giving him a shove through the draft, which would enable Earnhardt to keep Martin at bay.

"I was racing with Mark and I was able to hold him off on the inside," said Earnhardt, who earned $35,400. "Ernie came up to help me and, I think with him being there, I was able to beat Mark. I think Mark would have beat me to the line otherwise.

"It's a really big relief to win a 125. It gets you pumped up for the Daytona 500. We're handling good and running good."

Earnhardt was in a position to win because his car handled well and he avoided the problems shared by many others. Crashes, which reduced the 29-car starting field to 18 by race's end, created three caution periods for 20 laps.

In each case, the cause was blamed on a loose car which was sent sideways while contending with traffic – or receiving a rear-end nudge.

On lap five, the day's most serious incident occurred. Coming out of turn four, Alan Kulwicki was on the high side of Irvan with Martin directly on his rear. Kulwicki's Ford broke loose – he later said he thought he had been bumped – and got sideways in front of a large pack of cars. He bounced off Irvan and was tagged by Terry Labonte's Chevrolet. That created a melee which involved eight cars.

Eliminated from the race were Ben Hess, Dave Mader III, Rick Wilson, A.J. Foyt, Labonte, Kulwicki and Richard Petty. After

repairs, Hut Stricklin's Chevrolet was able to stay in the event.

Foyt, who had to borrow an Oldsmobile from Precision Products after his was demolished in a crash during practice on Feb. 12, again took a loaner in order to compete in the Daytona 500. It came from Eddie Bierschwale, whose 20th place finish wasn't good enough to make the main event.

Kulwicki was taken from his car by stretcher and transported to the infield medical center, where X-rays on his left leg and foot revealed no broken bones. He left sore and with a crutch.

On lap 20, Sterling Marlin, the pole winner for the Daytona 500, was eliminated after his Ford broke loose directly in front of Earnhardt – again while exiting the fourth turn. After viewing a videotape replay, Marlin maintained Earnhardt caused the mishap.

> "You'd think a guy like that who had won a lot of **championships** would race a little cleaner…but, whatever." —Sterling Marlin

"He hung me in the rear quarter panel down the short chute," he said. "You'd think a guy like that who had won a lot of championships would race a little cleaner… but, whatever.

"I was just minding my own business and he turned me around over there. It was a real quick turnaround. Usually, you can feel it when you get loose."

"I got up there under Sterling and he got loose and got off the gas and I tapped him. Then I just tried to clear him," said Earnhardt. "He got into the brakes as I tapped him and then he spun. It wasn't my fault or his fault.

"If your car is loose, it's tough coming off the turn anyway. It's one of them deals where you've got to have your car right and have a little extra spoiler."

On lap 36, Dale Jarrett and Kyle Petty were taken out of the race in a similar incident, again coming out of turn four.

Jarrett, making a strong run in his first outing in the Joe Gibbs Racing Chevrolet, put the blame on himself.

"I just got myself in a bad position," said Jarrett, who was on the low side of the track amid a pack. "I was trying to get myself out of it but there really wasn't anywhere to go with-

out putting on the brakes and going to the back of the pack. Race drivers have too much pride, or not enough sense, to do something like that.

"When I turned the car, I was going through a bump at the same time and it just lifted the back end up and there I sat. It was all Dale Jarrett's fault."

Jarrett, both Pettys, Kulwicki, Labonte, Stricklin and Wilson all went to backup cars for the Daytona 500.

Earnhardt shot low by Marlin in the third turn on lap No. 1 to take the lead for the first time. He would hold it for 13 laps until Marlin retook it on the 14th circuit.

Martin took the lead on lap 20, after Marlin's spin, and held it through lap 40, when the green flag was displayed following the caution caused by the Jarrett-K. Petty incident.

Then Earnhardt took over.

"I felt I had to get by Mark quickly and take command in order to have a shot at winning, so I went around him as soon as I had a chance," said Earnhardt. "I jumped around him on the restart and I was lucky to be able to do that.

"Mark was strong enough to come up beside me on the last lap and, luckily, Ernie followed me and helped me stay ahead of Mark."

"I was real disappointed Dale got by me on the restart," said Martin. "I thought I could hold him back. He did a real good job of getting a good run. He had enough to get by on the outside. And the pass stuck.

"I was optimistic there on the last lap. I dropped back and managed to get a good run and was real surprised to get up beside him, but I couldn't buck that wind. Dale had a partner and I didn't and without somebody to help me, I couldn't stay ahead of him at the line."

Greg Sacks, in the Larry Hedrick Chevrolet, finished fourth to give Chevy three of the top four finishing positions. Harry Gant finished fifth in the Leo Jackson Motorsports Oldsmobile while Rick Mast, in the Precision Products Oldsmobile, took sixth. Ken Schrader was seventh in the Hendrick Motorsports Chevrolet, Rusty Wallace was eighth in the Penske Racing South Pontiac, Phil Parsons was ninth in the Melling Racing Ford and Kerry Teague rounded the top 10 in the Team USA Oldsmobile.

All were admitted into the Daytona 500 field, along with Dave Marcis, Phil Barkdoll, Delma Cowart and Mike Potter, who finished 11th to 14th. Making the race through qualifying speeds were the Pettys, Labonte, Jarrett, Wilson and Foyt. Kulwicki and Stricklin were given the two provisional starts. ∎

LEFT: EARNHARDT ENJOYS ANOTHER TRIP TO VICTORY LANE IN THE GATORADE 125-MILE QUALIFIER.
DAVID CHOBAT PHOTO

Earnhardt: Back In Form
With Victory in Coca-Cola 600

Earnhardt Makes It All Happen

By STEVE WAID

It took a while, but Dale Earnhardt and General Motors have found their way back into victory lane.

Earnhardt, the defending NASCAR Winston Cup champion, held off Ernie Ivan in a nail-biter of a finish to win the Coca-Cola 600 and thus record his first victory of the season and allow GM to snap Ford's 13-race victory streak.

For the 41-year-old Earnhardt, the victory was his first since he won in North Wilkesboro, N.C., in October of 1991, 13 races ago. Ironically, Ford's streak began a week later when Geoff Bodine took the checkered flag in the Mello Yello 500 at CMS.

But upon the return visit to the 1.5-mile Charlotte track, it was not to be Ford's day as the race boiled down to a scrap among a trio of GM cars – and ultimately hinged on the outcome of the final pit stops.

When the checkered flag fell, Earnhardt had successfully kept Irvan at bay by 0.39 second, or about three car lengths. For the native of Kannapolis, N.C., it was his 53rd career victory – and certainly one of his most satisfying, since he became the man who put GM back in the spotlight.

"It feels great," said Earnhardt of the win, which earned him $125,100. "It feels great to be the one to stop Ford's streak and it feels especially good to win in my 400th career start.

"I said before the race it was time for something big to happen. That's why I picked Richard Petty to win the race. But he didn't and I did. And, to me, that's big – believe me."

Earnhardt was in position to win as the laps wound down. But he was in an even better position to finish third, behind Kyle Petty in the Sabco Pontiac and Irvan, driver of the

Morgan-McClure Chevy. Petty, in fact, led the most laps in the race (141) and was in front of Irvan when the two pitted for the final time on lap 346 of the 400-lap race.

Petty's stop took 19.72 seconds for four new tires while Irvan spent 21.19 seconds on

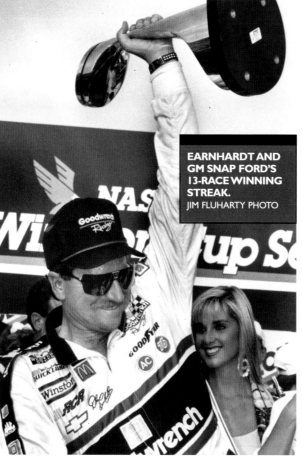

EARNHARDT AND GM SNAP FORD'S 13-RACE WINNING STREAK.
JIM FLUHARTY PHOTO

pit road for the same service. By leaving the track, they elevated Earnhardt – who had been a distant third – into the lead for the first time in the race.

Earnhardt took over on lap 347. On lap 348, he darted into the pits for his final stop. It would be a real test for his pit crew, four-

time winners of the world championship pit crew competition.

Earnhardt came down pit road as quickly as he could within NASCAR rules, which dictate a specific, slow entrance. His crew then performed a four-tire change in 19.40 seconds, 0.32 second quicker than Petty's team. Earnhardt left the pits, sped around the return lane low around turns one and two and came back onto the track still in first place.

That made all the difference.

"That pit stop was the key," said Earnhardt. "The guys did a great job and I probably fudged as much as I could coming down pit road. When we tested the tachometer coming down pit road on the pace lap (required by NASCAR), mine read 4,000 rpms in second gear. When I came down pit road the last time, I kept it at 4,050 rpms.

"Then I got out of the pits as quick as I could and came through the lane there in one and two pretty quick, too."

Although Earnhardt's stop befuddled a few observers and fellow competitors – particularly Petty, who felt there was no way his rival could emerge in first place by one second – the fact remained Earnhardt had gained the advantage.

"By being in front, it meant the others behind me would have to run their tires harder to catch up while I could work on saving mine," he said. "That was the key to beating Ernie because, even though he was strong, I had the edge. I couldn't get him when he was in front of me."

Over the last 53 laps, Irvan gave a strong effort. At times, Earnhardt would pull out to a three- or four-car length advantage. But then, Irvan would make up the distance, usually in turn three, and close on his opponent's rear bumper.

EARNHARDT TAKES THE LEAD ON DEFENDING COCA-COLA 600 WINNER DAVEY ALLISON, WHO FINISHED FOURTH.
DAVID CHOBAT PHOTO

But he never had the chance to pass.

"I ran my line, " said Earnhardt. "In turns three and four, the car would push a little in the middle and I had to be careful because then the car would push out and I didn't want Ernie to get under me.

"I was extra cautious and I wanted him to make a move on me or take another line. I was a bit surprised at Ernie there, but I have to admit he raced me clean and hard and he's really coming around as a race driver."

Irvan made an attempt to take the high route on the last lap, but it was to no avail.

"He did try the outside, but his car wouldn't hold," Earnhardt said.

Most of the race belonged to Petty, who was bidding to win his first race of the season as well. He had led 102 of 104 laps from cir- cuits 243-346 before the final pit stops began. But the handling characteristics of his Pontiac changed at the finish and he couldn't keep up. He finished third, about three sec- onds in arrears.

Meanwhile, Davey Allison, driver of the Robert Yates Racing Ford and defending winner of the Coca-Cola 600 who was bid- ding to win his fourth race of the season and a $1 million bonus in the Winston Million program, fell short. He finished fourth after leading 33 laps. He can still claim the bonus with a victory in the Mountain Dew Southern 500 at Darlington (S.C.) Raceway on September 6.

The first half of the race was characterized by "stop-and-go" racing due to a rash of cau- tion periods. There were 10 by the time the event was 204 laps old, eight of which fell between laps 101 and 185. Nearly all were caused by crashes, which Earnhardt avoided.

"Boy, there were some close calls," he said.

"One time I went down pit road at full speed to avoid one and another time I went through the grass on the frontstretch. I was lucky not to get caught up in any of them and wreck the car or knock the front end out or anything, but it was close."

Earnhardt wasn't a factor for most of the race. That was due to the fact his car wasn't

> "Charlotte had been
> **a great track**
> for me; a lot of great things have
> happened to me (here)."
> —Earnhardt

handling properly. But, all things considered, he was lucky to have the car at all. He uti- lized the one which was wrecked on the last lap of The Winston on May 16 in an alterca- tion with Petty.

Hasty repairs were made to restore the car for the Coca-Cola 600. Among the repairs were replacement of the rear frame, rear quar- ter panel, trunk deck, left front fender, A-frame. The chassis was taken out and a new engine put in.

"The repairs should have taken over a week but the guys worked all day Sunday and Monday and the body guys worked overnight," said Earnhardt. "The car was primed and painted in one night. Everything worked out and we had the car here Wednesday (May 20).

"But it was very loose at the start. We took the pan out from the front end but then that's when it picked up the little push later in the race. It was really good through turns

one and two but the push came between three and four. We were sacrificing there but we held 'em off."

Harry Gant, in the Leo Jackson Oldsmobile, followed Allison in fifth place while Terry Labonte took sixth in the Hagan Racing Oldsmobile. Seventh place went to Alan Kulwicki in the Kulwicki Racing Ford while Ted Musgrave posted an eighth-place finish in the RaDiUs Racing Chevrolet, Ricky Rudd was ninth, in the Hendrick Motorsports Chevrolet, and Dick Trickle, in the Stavola Brothers Ford, was 10th.

The rash of accidents proved fatal to Richard Petty, driver of the Petty Enterprises Pontiac, who was involved in three incidents. Early in the race, Petty ran as high as eighth place before being eliminated and relegated to a 41st-place finish.

Engine failure or accidents claimed or hampered Mark Martin, Hut Stricklin, Geoff Bodine, Morgan Shepherd, Jimmy Spencer, Ken Schrader, Michael Waltrip, Sterling Marlin, Brett Bodine and Bobby Hamilton. Earnhardt's victory was his first in the Coca-Cola 600 since 1986. Until this race, his best finish had been a pair of thirds at Talladega, Ala., and Atlanta.

"Charlotte had been a great track for me; a lot of great things have happened to me," said Earnhardt, who now has four career victories at the track. "But a lot bad has happened to me, too. Even though I've won a couple of The Winstons since 1986, I hadn't won the 600 or the 500 in the fall. It was good for me and the team to get back into victory lane."

Earnhardt's victory also propelled him into fifth place in the Winston Cup championship point standings, 144 points behind leader Allison with 19 races remaining in the season.

"We still feel good about the champi- onship," Earnhardt said. "We look at the points situation at every race. We want to run good and consistent and be there at the end of each race and, today, we were first at the finish.

"But the main goal is to keep the car con- sistent because that is what is going to win the championship."

Earnhardt didn't hesitate to say he felt pleased to be the man to end Ford's streak.

"I feel great to be the one to stop it," he said. "I'm just sorry it took so long.

"But I don't like to run second to anyone. When we're not in victory lane and Fords are, it's not good. Hey, when I was following Kyle and Ernie, I wasn't happy to see them in front of me.

"But the pressure is on the corporate side. It's not on me or the team. This is definitely a turnaround for us and all the GM teams."

Perhaps those words will prove prophetic, indeed. ∎

Earnhardt's Back!

Veteran Claims Fifth Busch Clash Victory In Car Tested By Bonnett

By DEB WILLIAMS

Twice Dale Earnhardt had to come from the rear before he could win his fifth Busch Clash, but the ease with which he accomplished the task served notice to his peers that he's rebounded from his dismal 1992 Winston Cup season.

"I reckon the black's back!" a happy Earnhardt said, referring to his ebony RCR Enterprises Chevrolet Lumina while displaying his familiar mischievous grin. "We're at Daytona, we're in victory lane, and we're happy."

"He tested my Busch car for four days."

Bonnett, a close friend and hunting buddy of Earnhardt, hasn't competed in a Winston Cup race since April 1990 when he suffered a head injury and temporarily lost his memory in a multicar crash at Darlington (S.C.) Raceway. He had, however, tested one of Earnhardt's cars last fall at Charlotte Motor Speedway.

"Neil's test session was pretty close to what we needed for the race season. The car was perfect. We didn't change anything on the pit stop except four tires and clean the windshield."

Petty, driving a Pontiac, finished seventh and noted it helped to have a decent running partner.

"Sometimes I had someone like that behind me and sometimes I didn't," Petty said. "We tried a different transmission in this car and, when I shifted into second, I didn't go anywhere and Brett (Bodine) hit me from behind. I mean, it wasn't his fault. I just about stopped in front of him. I couldn't get it into second on that restart."

Earnhardt, a five-time Winston Cup champion, completed the Busch Clash in

EARNHARDT RAN WITH THE PACK, BUT NOT FOR LONG, BEFORE ELIMINATING THE FIELD IN THE BUSCH CLASH AT DAYTONA.
NWCS ARCHIVE PHOTO

How about this: Earnhardt made it to victory lane in an RCR Chevrolet tested at Daytona and Talladega, Ala., solely by former Winston Cup driver Neil Bonnett. Earnhardt never tested his Busch Clash car, concentrating instead on his Daytona 500 Chevrolet, and hadn't driven the car with the new body on it until he reported to the 2.5-mile track for Speed Weeks.

"I'd call Susan (Bonnett's wife) and say, 'Send Neil over,'" Earnhardt said with a smile.

Earnhardt said his Busch Clash car was about two- to three-10ths of a second slower in testing than the car he selected to run in the Feb. 14 Daytona 500.

Finishing second, two car lengths behind Earnhardt, was Ken Schrader and directly behind Schrader was Ernie Irvan, both in Chevrolets. Fourth went to Mark Martin in a Ford and Ricky Rudd finished fifth in a Chevrolet.

Daytona 500 pole position winner Kyle

16 minutes, three seconds, and averaged 186.916 mph. There were six lead changes among five drivers.

Earnhardt won $60,000 for his efforts, while Schrader pocketed $29,000 and Irvan $37,500. The Kannapolis, N.C., driver's other Busch Clash wins came in 1980, '86, '88 and '91. After three of those wins, Earnhardt went on to win the Winston Cup championship for that season.

"They worked hard all winter and changed bodies on the cars two or three different times," Earnhardt said about his crew.

"We had to fit the new templates and everybody had to get within thousandths instead of a quarter of an inch. We just had to redo the whole car and fine-tune the bodies.

"Down here testing, every time we would make changes and go out and run, we'd come back in and go through the measurements again to make sure we weren't getting the car off the measurements and getting false readings. It was real meticulous down here testing this year. Preparation is the key to what won that race today."

With the larger spoiler this year, Earnhardt said the cars were a little slower in coming up to speed.

"Richard (Childress, team owner), Andy (Petree, crew chief) and myself have worked on several things to make the car run free, to run in the draft or in the air (by itself)," Earnhardt said. "I think the homework paid off, being able to run in the draft and to draft by cars better."

Earnhardt, who believes he has one of his better chances to win this year's Daytona 500, drew the 13th starting position in the 15-car field and won the first 10-lap segment. That meant he had to start last for the final 10 laps on the 2.5-mile track.

"I'd rather move around and get to the front," Earnhardt said. "The longer you stay in 15th, you've got 14 chances of something bad happening in front of you.

"When I come to Daytona, if I'm entered in a race, I'm entered to win."

The race's beginning was delayed about 12 minutes because of oil spilling from Bill Elliott's Ford. All of the cars involved in the 20-lap, 50-mile event were brought onto pit road while oil dry was applied to the track and the crews cleaned the windshields.

When the race for last year's pole position winners and one "wildcard" finally began, Ernie Irvan jumped into the lead from the top starting spot and held it through the first five laps. By that time, Earnhardt had picked his way to the front.

On lap six, Earnhardt dove to the inside of Irvan as they exited turn two and snatched the lead away from his fellow Chevrolet driver. For the rest of the way in the 10-lap segment, Earnhardt was never challenged.

Elliott was black-flagged for his oil problem on lap four and again on lap five. He pitted on lap six and returned to the race on lap seven.

Ricky Rudd dropped off the pace on lap nine and Darrell Waltrip slowed to allow Rudd to pass him on lap 10.

"We were overheating there a little bit toward the end of the first segment and we had to drop back and cool off a little bit,"

Rudd said. "It was pretty hot. We had to take some tape off the grille."

During the two-lap caution at the halfway mark, all of the cars pitted for fresh tires. Davey Allison reported a little vibration in his Ford before the green flag reappeared and he made a second pit stop for four tires.

By winning the first segment, Earnhardt collected $25,000 but had to start last for the second 10 laps. Finishing second was Irvan, Rusty Wallace was third, Allison fourth and Bodine fifth. Rounding out the field, in order, was: Alan Kulwicki, Petty, Rick Mast, Sterling Marlin, Schrader, Jimmy Means, Martin, Rudd, Waltrip and Elliott.

"We can take 'The Intimidator' any time."—Darrell Waltrip

"I felt like I could handle three-quarters of the field but I was pretty concerned about two or three of those cars," Earnhardt said. "You really didn't know what everybody had until the race started, and then you really didn't know until the second half started."

When the race restarted for the final 10 laps, the field was inverted, thus giving Elliott and Waltrip the front row positions.

Elliott led lap 11, but then Waltrip pulled ahead for the next two laps.

"We got our car a little bit too tight and made some changes on that first pit stop," said Waltrip, who finished 11th. "It helped a little bit but, if we'd been able to make another stop, we would have been a lot better.

"We're happy because this car was dog meat yesterday. I'd blow the horn and it would bark.

"This race got the edge off the driver, so now we'll just have to wait and see what happens Thursday. I think we'll be real tough in the Daytona 500. We can take 'The Intimidator' anytime."

Elliott returned to the front on lap 14 but, when Marlin took the low groove through turn one on lap 15, that was the maneuver Earnhardt needed. Elliott lost at least five positions when Marlin shot into the lead and Earnhardt went with him with Schrader in tow.

On lap 16, as the field raced through turn three, Earnhardt moved low on Marlin and, with the help of the draft from Schrader's Chevrolet, he moved around him and into the lead for good.

Earnhardt admitted he became a "little impatient" during the last 10 laps.

"I was wanting to go quicker (to the front) than I was going," said Earnhardt, who flew to Nashville, Tenn., after the race to sign autographs at a Mac Tools convention. "I got caught up on the outside.

"When everybody started here on the short chute they fell to the inside; I thought there was an opening on the outside. It seemed like the outer line was trying to go faster and bottom line was getting jockeyed around and nobody could muster anything.

"I started passing one car at a time and getting up on that inside groove. I kept getting closer to that front line. When I finally got to the (No.) 8 car (Marlin), I could draft on him and push him on out front. Then, I drafted by him and brought Schrader with me. Schrader helped me to get that point.

"I was pretty concerned Schrader and the No. 4 car (Irvan) would get to pulling together and try to draft by me. I kept working them around and working the throttle into the corner and off the corner to try and see where they were pulling me and maybe where I could pull them.

"It seemed to be better for me coming off the corner. I got that little edge and they couldn't do anything on the back straightaway on the last lap, so I knew if I just held my line, I'd be OK."

Shortly after the win, Childress said he felt good about his team.

"We've got a few hurdles we've got to cross yet, but I feel pretty good about it," Childress said. "Dale said the car would drive just about wherever he wanted it to. The engine ran perfect all day, and Dale did his job.

"Andy (Petree, crew chief) has a lot of talent, and we were lucky to get someone of his caliber to replace Kirk (Shelmerdine, former crew chief). He's a very detailed person and he fits in with our group right now like he's been working with us the past 10 years."

Petree, who became Earnhardt's crew chief after the 1992 season ended, said he was "a little surprised that Earnhardt was able to come from the back to the front twice.

"I'm still shaking over that, "Petree said. "The guy's awesome. I can't say enough about him.

"We're in the transition stage, still, but this is a good way to get over the hump and get going. We know Dale can get the job done and we've got a proven pit crew. We knew we weren't going to qualify that well (for the Daytona 500), but we felt like our cars were going to be competitive. That's really all Dale needs. If the car is competitive, Dale can do the rest." ∎

Earnhardt Holds Off
Surprising Bodine

Registers Fourth Consecutive Qualifying Race Win

By DAVID GREEN

The Speed Weeks rampage of "The Man in Black" continued into the Gatorade 125s, where Busch Clash winner Dale Earnhardt made it two for two with a victory in the second qualifying race.

"We're going to try and make it three for three on Saturday (in the Goody's 300 NASCAR Busch Series race), but we're looking at the one on Sunday," said Earnhardt, referring to the Daytona 500. "That's the one we're really worried about."

Earnhardt, winner of the Feb. 7 Busch Clash, reaffirmed his role as the favorite in the 500 and secured the fourth-place starting spot in the 41 car lineup when he edged Geoff Bodine by $1^1/_2$ lengths to win a Daytona qualifying race for the fourth year in a row.

Dale Jarrett and Ernie Irvan were third and fourth, giving Chevrolet three of the top four spots, and last year's Winston Cup champion, Alan Kulwicki, was fifth. He and Bodine both drove Fords.

Earnhardt, the 41-year-old, five-time Winston Cup champion, has never won the 500, but was confident about his chances after the qualifier.

"I think it's as good a chance and as good a year as ever for us to win the Daytona 500," he said, reflecting on an apparent turnaround for the Richard Childress Racing team after a sub-par 1992.

Longtime crew chief Kirk Shelmerdine resigned at the end of last season and was replaced by Andy Petree.

"When Kirk resigned, that sort of shook the team up a little bit and made us take notice," said Earnhardt. "Everybody has been just so positive in testing and everything, and when you go out and win races, it's just proof of the hard work we've been doing. We're positive and confident that we can win the race Sunday."

DALE EARNHARDT CELEBRATES HIS SECOND WIN OF THE WEEK IN DAYTONA. MAYBE SUNDAY HE'LL MAKE IT THREE FOR THREE FOR 3.
NWCS ARCHIVE PHOTO

But Earnhardt said the 125 was no cake-walk, despite the strength his black No. 3 Chevrolet showed. He denied a suggestion that he toyed with challengers in an attempt to cool controversy between Ford and Chevrolet teams.

"I tell you, that was a tough race today," he said. "It (the car's handling) was a little neutral there. We had it set up for a push, but it never pushed. It started getting loose. I just had to run a little higher and just fight 'em off."

Earnhardt led 34 of the 50 laps. He moved from his outside front row starting spot to command the first two circuits, then saw Ricky Rudd's Chevrolet assume the top spot. Rudd led until lap 18, when Earnhardt went back in front, and except for one lap when Ernie Irvan nosed ahead at the start/finish line, Earnhardt was in front the rest of the way.

> "When Kirk resigned,
> **that sort of
> shook the
> team up a
> little bit**
> and made us take notice."
> —Earnhardt.

He held off repeated challenges from Irvan, who was able to pull alongside, and Bodine, who could close on the leader's rear bumper but never could attempt a pass.

Bodine outdueled Irvan in a two-wide battle over the last few laps, working a high groove while Irvan tried to pass on the inside. Jarrett got past Irvan for third by following Bodine's lead.

Earnhardt, too, went up the racetrack when Bodine challenged.

"My car would feel a little better when Bodine was up behind me," he said. "That's the reason I was running up high in front of him. I would've liked to have gone down and helped Ernie, but I was too loose on the bottom."

Bodine, 31st fastest in first-round qualifying and only sixth-best in the second round, showed surprising strength, but credited handling, not horsepower.

"When you drive within two inches of the wall, that's not power, that's handling," he said. "The Chevrolets are still quicker than we are. We just had better handling than some of those other guys."

Earnhardt gave the runner-up credit.

"He was capable of being in front of me, he just never got the help to get there," Earnhardt said of Bodine.

"That's a good effort," said Bodine, who clinched the outside spot in the third row for the 500. "It means a lot to be up front on Sunday. We were concerned before this race with our starting spot because we didn't qualify that well. This really puts us in a good position."

The first of two caution flags flew on lap five, for Wally Dallenbach's spin in turns three and four. Dallenbach, making a bid for second place, was tapped from behind by Irvan and turned sideways.

Dallenbach recovered, and drove to an 11th-place finish.

The race's only other incident took out Indianapolis 500 champion Al Unser Jr., whose Chevrolet blew a right-rear tire in turn two of lap 11. Jimmy Hensley, driving in place of the injured Jimmy Means, clipped Unser's spinning car and both were eliminated.

Hensley was one of four drivers in the 27-car field who resorted to backup cars after a crash in practice on Feb. 10, and moved to the rear of the field at the start.

The other three all made the 500 lineup by finishing in the top 15. Darrell Waltrip was 13th, Michael Waltrip 14th and Jimmy Spencer 15th. ■

HOPEFULLY, THIS IS GOOD POST-RACE PRACTICE FOR DALE JR.'S CAREER. DAVID CHOBAT PHOTO

READY TO RUMBLE
NWCS ARCHIVE PHOTO

Earnhardt Ends Victory
Drought

Claims First Win Since May '92,
Ties Lee Petty In Career Victories

By DEB WILLIAMS

The clouds that kept the sun from beaming down on Darlington Raceway during the second half of the TranSouth Financial 500 might have saddened some, but for Dale Earnhardt and his crew, it meant nothing but smiles at the finish.

Earnhardt's Chevrolet performed flawlessly in the race's second half when many cast a wary eye toward the darkening skies. But the veteran driver pointed more towards the set of tires he received on his fifth pit stop and the difference with which he drove the car in the race's second half as being more instrumental to his win than the weather.

"The track changed a little but I think it stayed fairly consistent," said Earnhardt, who noted he changed the car's chassis setup a

"considerable amount" after competing in the March 27 IROC race at the 1.366-mile track.

"If it did anything, it got a little tighter along the middle of the race. Towards the end, it was about the same. It didn't change a drastic amount because the sun never came out and got real hot.

"When I went to the back of the field after we caught up on that pit stop, I started running the car in a different groove," said Earnhardt, who led four times for 212 laps, including the final 46, in the 367-lap race.

"I started running pretty high getting in (the corner) to try and make the car come off the corner without pushing, and it worked. I came back to second place and the car was driving better and better. Then, we got another set of tires, we took the lead, and we started

pulling away from Mark (Martin). I think that was a better set of tires than we got the last time.

"The key to the car coming back was changing the line on the race track. I tried to run the car so it wouldn't be so tight off (turn) two and off (turn) four. That was the biggest change of the day as far as changing the way my car ran. It was a good race car. When the driver got his attitude right, the car showed what it could do.

"Andy (Petree crew chief) and Richard (Childress, car owner) adjusted a little bit, and Will (Lind) and the guys adjusted on the air pressure some. We didn't change a whole lot. We pulled half a rubber out of the right front, but that was about the only change.

"This car was the car we ran second with at Rockingham (N.C.) and too fast on pit road at Richmond (Va.), so you know it was a good car."

The win was Earnhardt's first win since May 1992 at Charlotte Motor Speedway in the Coca-Cola 600, and Earnhardt summed up his feelings about the drought very simply, "It's been too damn long."

Earnhardt, who felt ill when he arrived in Darlington, averaged a record 139.947 mph, which broke the 500-mile mark at Darlington of 139.364 mph, set last year by Bill Elliot in a Ford. For Earnhardt, 41, it was his eighth Darlington victory, making him second on the all-time win list behind David Pearson, who was considered the master of the track. His fifth TranSouth 500 victory also tied him with Lee Petty for sixth on the all-time NASCAR Winston Cup win list with 54.

Ironically, it was the same race at Darlington when in 1967, Richard Petty broke his father's career victory mark by claiming his 55th win.

"It's pretty neat to catch or get close," Earnhardt said about approaching Pearson's record.

"I'm two championships behind (R.) Petty and I'm two races behind David here and those are two drivers who I admired and looked up to all my career. David drove a car for (Rod) Osterlund here when I was hurt (1979 Southern 500) and won the race. His input from the little bit he drove it and I dealt with him have been a big plus.

"It's pretty gratifying. I don't know if I will ever catch him or Richard, but hopefully, we've got a few more years of racing and we can win a few more."

Earnhardt also considered it "pretty neat" that his win tied him with L. Petty.

"I don't pay much attention to records and things, or analyze things that much," Earnhardt said. "It's pretty neat though to look and see what you've accomplished.

"But then, you turn around and look and there's a guy like Jeff Gordon who's coming back and set those same records again and got a chance to do better. There's always somebody behind you. You're always chasing somebody or they're always chasing you. It's pretty exciting. I just enjoy it and enjoy being a part of it."

Earnhardt's victory bode well for the Kannapolis, N.C., native's bid for his sixth Winston Cup title. Each year that Earnhardt has claimed the series championship, he's always scored his first victory of the season by that year's sixth race. The TranSouth 500 was the season's fifth event.

Since qualifying was rained out, the starting lineup was determined by point standings and that gave Earnhardt the No. 1 spot. Geoff Bodine, who started second, hung with Earnhardt and, in fact, the two collided as they exited turn two side by side on lap 10.

"I was coming off (turn) two and I was right against the wall and I couldn't go any further," said Earnhardt, who led the first 49 laps.

"He just used me sort of as a bumper. No problem. We raced on. I've got no problem with that."

After Bodine faded, Martin became Earnhardt's top challenger and finally wrestled the lead from him on lap 50. Shortly thereafter, the first round of green-flag pit stops began and once they were completed, Earnhardt was back in the lead on lap 61. This time, Earnhardt led 14 laps before

Martin took his Ford low through turns one and two to regain the lead. For 27 laps, Martin set the pace, once stretching it to 2.06 seconds over Earnhardt.

Earnhardt was second when he elected to make his next green-flag pit stop on lap 99 and his crew completed the four-tire change and refueling in 22.9 seconds. He lost a lap and then, on lap 100, Gordon's Chevrolet smacked the first-turn wall after being tagged by Michael Waltrip's Pontiac and the first of three caution flags had appeared.

That yellow allowed all of the lead cars who hadn't pitted to stop and left Earnhardt and Rusty Wallace on the tail end of the lead lap when the race restarted on lap 106.

"When the driver got his **attitude right,** the car showed what it could do." —Earnhardt

With Earnhardt and Wallace playing catchup, Martin became the event's dominator, leading the next 51 laps. On lap 144, Martin possessed a 3.05-second advantage over Dale Jarrett's third-place Chevrolet, and on lap 156, he unsuccessfully attempted to put Earnhardt a lap down.

"It looked pretty grim then because I couldn't make the car do what I wanted it to do. I was trying too hard, I reckon," Earnhardt said.

There was another round of green-flag stops before the day's second caution – when the engine blew in Jimmy Means' Ford on lap 178 - which allowed Earnhardt to drive around the track and catch up to the lead cars. This time, on the restart on lap 184, Martin was leading, but Earnhardt was 10th and he immediately began maneuvering towards the front.

About the same time, clouds began rolling in across the track, blocking the sun and the race turned from Martin, who paced the field six times for 124 laps in his Ford, to Earnhardt.

On lap 202, Earnhardt passed Ken Schrader for fifth, and two laps later he and Jarrett zipped past Kyle Petty to move into second and third. Then, on lap 206, Earnhardt claimed second. At that time, Martin held a 6.01-second advantage, but that was erased on lap 215, when Bobby Labonte spun in turn two and Jimmy

Spencer hit the wall.

The leaders pitted and Earnhardt's crew returned him to the track first. After that, the only time Earnhardt lost the lead during the final 150 laps was

EIGHT TIMES, EARNHARDT HAS WON AT DARLINGTON, SECOND ONLY TO DAVID PEARSON ON THE ALL-TIME TRACK WINNER'S LIST.
NWCS ARCHIVE PHOTO

when he made his last pit stop. He relinquished the No. 1 spot to Martin on lap 321, and then when Martin pitted on lap 322, Earnhardt inherited the lead for good.

"We were on the money and as good as anybody should ever ask. Dale was just exceptional during the second half of the race," Martin said. "The first half, I think we could do something with him. But they got better and better and we couldn't do anything with them at the end."

With 11 laps remaining, Earnhardt possessed a 5.19-second advantage over Martin, but by the race's end, the deficit had narrowed to 1.63 seconds.

"I ran hard until about 20 laps to go when I saw Mark better than a half straightaway behind me," Earnhardt said. "Then, I ran a consistent pace. I didn't try to spin the tires or get too rough on them. That way, I thought if he did catch me, I would have a little left."

The race consumed 3 hours, 34 minutes and 56 seconds, and had 17 lead changes among 10 drivers. There were three caution flags for 15 laps, the fewest ever in Darlington's spring race.

Earnhardt's winnings totaled $64,815. ∎

Three For 3

Earnhardt Takes Third Winston

By STEVE WAID

EARNHARDT DOUSES THE CROWD IN CELEBRATION OF HIS THIRD VICTORY IN THE WINSTON.
NWCS ARCHIVE PHOTO

dale earnhardt

Dale Earnhardt's reputation as one of NASCAR Winston Cup racing's most aggressive competitors was enhanced nicely as he passed Mark Martin with just over a lap to go and scored the victory in the 1993 version of The Winston.

Driving the RCR Enterprises Chevrolet, Earnhardt shot to the outside of Martin's Roush Racing Ford as the ninth of the race's 10 "Shootout" laps began and then passed his rival as they sped out of the first turn to begin the final circuit.

After that, Earnhardt completed the last 1.5 miles around the CMS trioval 0.16-second ahead of Martin to earn his third career victory in The Winston. The Mooresville, N.C., resident also won in 1987 and 1990. No other driver has claimed more than two victories.

"When you have a situation like that, he's the guy you want driving your car," said Richard Childress, Earnhardt's team owner.

But as befits The Winston, the finish was not without controversy. It was set up after the 70-lap race's first two 30-lap segments. Ernie Irvan, who started on the pole in the Morgan-McClure Chevrolet, easily won the first segment and picked up a $50,000 bonus. Martin was second ($15,000 bonus) and Rusty Wallace, in the Penske South Pontiac, was third ($7,500 bonus). Earnhardt finished fifth, behind Ford-driving Bill Elliott.

The second segment began with an inverted start as voted by the fans, with a count of 17,485 for such a start and 4,255 against.

That put Earnhardt 15th on the restart. On the 10th of the segment's 30 laps, Rick Mast put his Ford into the lead with Earnhardt trailing. Surprisingly, try as he might, Earnhardt could do nothing with Mast, who won the segment and the $50,000 bonus. The finish was: Mast, Earnhardt, Martin, Bodine, Ken Schrader and Irvan.

Then came the 10-lap "Shootout." On the first circuit, Mast was victimized as Martin blew by on the low side and Earnhardt passed on the high side. Irvan followed with Bodine and Schrader in tow.

It appeared to be Martin's race – something even Earnhardt admitted. But fate stepped in. With just two laps left, Terry Labonte's Chevrolet spun and crashed between turns three and four, bringing out the caution flag. Caution laps during "The Shootout" don't count, so when the race restarted it would revert to the last complete green-flag lap. That meant there would be two laps left when the green flag flew.

Then came the controversy.

When the green came out, Earnhardt was well in front – he had jumped the restart. He pled guilty.

"My spotter came on the radio and said, 'NASCAR is putting the yellow flag out again and you know why,'" said Earnhardt. "How about that restart? I tried it, I didn't think I would get away with it and I didn't. I got my hands spanked; I got called down for it. It's lucky I wasn't put at the rear of the field."

Some, particularly Irvan and Jack Roush, Martin's team owner, thought Earnhardt should have been punished.

But NASCAR said the yellow flag was redisplayed to ensure a fair start. The explanation was that under normal circumstances, a car on the outside in a double-file restart – where Earnhardt was – would have been on the lead lap and thus allowed to restart the race.

But since all the restarts in The Winston were double-file, that was no longer the case and the restart belonged to the car on the inside – Martin's Ford.

Additionally, it was explained that NASCAR could have displayed either the yellow flag or the black flag for Earnhardt. If it had displayed the black flag, it would have to do so for three laps before scoring for Earnhardt would have ceased. That meant with just two laps remaining, Earnhardt could have won with his jump.

Hence, the caution flag flew to arrange another restart.

Told of the complaints from other competitors, Earnhardt said, "Well…I'm sorry."

"If you go back to the original rules for The Winston, NASCAR said anytime anyone jumped the restart, there would be a yellow flag," he continued.

As the field lined up for the second restart, Earnhardt said he pulled alongside Martin going down the backstretch and tried to attract his attention.

"I was looking over at him and waving, but he didn't look back at me," said Earnhardt. "I just wanted to see what he was thinking. Maybe I'd rattle him."

When the race restarted in earnest, Earnhardt adopted the outside line going into turn one, where he pulled alongside Martin.

"No doubts at all about going to the outside," said Earnhardt. "No second thoughts at all. It's time to go. You're going for the win. If I had backed off trying to get

behind him so I could move to the inside, Ernie would have been there. So my only opportunity was to the outside. I took my opportunity and it worked."

Earnhardt stayed alongside Martin down the backstretch and then nosed

"It's The Winston. You **race like hell** over the last 10 laps until you cross the finish line or you turn over somewhere." —Earnhardt

ahead in the third turn before clearing his rival in the fourth.

"I drove deeper in the third turn than I thought I could but the car stuck," Earnhardt said. "I looked up in four and saw he was behind me and I knew all I had to do was keep going and I had it won.

"I can't believe I won. Mark was so strong. For the first seven or eight laps of the final segment, I think I could have caught him but I never could have passed him. I was trying hard…the car was pushing and skating…but I never could have won it without that last caution."

Irvan was third and Schrader nipped Bodine for fourth.

Earnhardt said the key to winning The Winston is "to get in the best shape you can for the last 10 laps." In the first segment, he finished fifth but said the car wasn't as good as it needed to be.

"During the break (the 10-minute pause between the first and second segments which permits routine work on the cars), we made some adjustments and the car was better," Earnhardt said.

It must have been, because Earnhardt moved from 15th place (on the inverted start) to second.

"When they started the final segment, I don't know if Mark pushed Rick (Mast) up or what, but it all pushed me up and when I came off the corner, there was Mark. We were one-two," Earnhardt said.

And then came the finish.

"It's The Winston," said Earnhardt, who

received $222,500 and has now earned $977,500 in nine The Winstons. "You race like hell over the last 10 laps until you cross the finish line or you turn over somewhere."

The final rundown of the 45-minute, 6-second race saw Darrell Waltrip, Sterling Marlin, Wallace, Davey Allison and Brett Bodine complete the top 10.

The race's only other caution came on the second lap of the second segment. It was caused by a crash in the second turn involving four cars. Michael Waltrip's Pontiac was nudged in the rear by Harry Gant's Chevrolet and hit the wall. Before it did, it was hit by Jimmy Hensley's Ford and that brought Dale Jarrett's Chevrolet and Marlin's Ford into the fray.

Waltrip, Hensley and Jarrett were forced to retire from the race. Kyle Petty was out at the end of 30 laps with a blown engine.

"I figured that because he was so strong, Mark would get back on my rear bumper in turn one on the last lap," said Earnhardt. "I

EARNHARDT LOVES HOISTING THE TROPHIES BUT MUST BE RUNNING OUT OF PLACES TO PUT THEM.
DAVID CHOBAT PHOTO

don't know if Ernie was so close to him it was messing up the air on his rear or what, but he couldn't get to me. I gained about a car length down the backstretch and I knew then he was going to have to go over my hood to get by me in three and four.

"That was all there was to it." ∎

Penalties Don't **Stop** Earnhardt

Veteran Is First To Reach $17 Million In Career Winnings

By DEB WILLIAMS

Dale Earnhardt shook off two penalties and came from a lap down on two occasions to win his second straight Coca-Cola 600 and the third of his NASCAR Winston Cup career.

With the victory, Earnhardt became the first driver to win the circuit's longest race at night when he celebrated by taking a Polish victory lap around the 1.5-mile speedway in honor of the late Alan Kulwicki.

"With this being Charlotte and being so close to Alan's shop and CMS paying tribute to Alan before the race, it seemed only fitting that we do that and the team was really behind it," Earnhardt said, who was the top lap-leader, setting the pace four times for 152 laps in the 400-lap event.

"The team was really behind it, and it felt good to do it. I had a lot of respect for Alan and he was a good champion."

A happy Earnhardt said he "drove hard all day and half the night" to claim the win that made him the first driver to earn consecutive Coca-Cola 600 victories since Darrell Waltrip in 1988-89. And Earnhardt did it with an event record of 145.504 mph. The old record was 145.327 mph set May 25, 1975, by Richard Petty in a Dodge.

"I drove hard all day and it seemed like I was behind after I was ahead," Earnhardt said.

The Kannapolis, N.C., native now has 55 Winston Cup career wins, giving him sole possession of sixth on the series' all-time victory list. Prior to the event, he shared the position with Lee Petty at 54.

With his third win this year in a Winston Cup points race, Earnhardt increased his lead in the quest for his sixth title to 129 points over Rusty Wallace. When they entered the event, Earnhardt possessed a 20-point advantage over Wallace.

With this 29th-place finish, Wallace also lost ground to the third-place Dale Jarrett. With his best finish ever in the Coca-Cola 600, Jarrett jumped from sixth to third in the Winston Cup points and found himself just 79 points behind Wallace.

Jarrett, driving a Chevrolet, finished third behind rookie Jeff Gordon. Ken Schrader and Ernie Irvan placed fourth and fifth respectively, both in Chevrolets.

There were 29 lead changes among 10

drivers in the race that took 4 hours 7 minutes and 25 seconds to complete. It was slowed by seven caution flags for 32 laps before an estimated crowd of 162,000.

"The car got better and better as the night got cooler," Earnhardt said. "The car, at the end of the race, was running more like last Saturday night (when Earnhardt won The Winston).

"Andy (Petree, crew chief), (Richard) Childress (car owner) and I ran the same setup that we did last Saturday night. We suffered some at the start.

> "I'm glad Gordon didn't catch me,
> ## He is a tough little driver
> and he is going to be hard to handle." —Earnhardt on rookie driver Jeff Gordon

"We changed a pound of air pressure here and there. We did that for the temperature of the track. Not the chassis, but for the grip."

When the race began at 4:30 p.m., the track's temperature was 120 degrees. At the halfway mark, after 200 laps, it had dropped to 82 degrees, and when the race ended, it was 77 degrees.

Earnhardt also said a chassis adjustment was made with "one turn of wedge."

Earnhardt, 42, won a Coca-Cola 600 record $156,650, thus giving him $905,245 for the season. For his career, Earnhardt became the first driver in motorsports history to reach the $17 million mark with $17,000,027. And in three races during the last week at CMS, Earnhardt collected $380,545. That's $222,500 in The Winston, $1,395 in the Champion Spark Plug 300 Busch Series race, and the rest in the Coca-Cola 600.

For Earnhardt, this year's win in the 600-mile race was probably one of his more difficult ones as he had to overcome two penalties and come from one lap down on two separate occasions. Also, during his first pit stop, one of his tire carriers slipped and was tagged by Gordon's Chevrolet, which was

pitting directly behind Earnhardt.

"It's really satisfying to win after getting penalized," Earnhardt said. "To get a lap penalty, as competitive as everybody is, you would think you might have a bad time making it up. To make it up early as easy as we did, we caught a caution and we were lucky there. Then we got back to the lead pretty good. That says something for the race car and the team."

NASCAR assessed Earnhardt a 15-second penalty on lap 221 for entering pit road too fast.

"Was I going too fast on pit road?" Earnhardt asked the media in his post-race interview. "I don't know how fast I was going on pit road but the 28 (Davey Allison) was catching me."

During that green-flag pit stop, Earnhardt lost a lap and when Wallace spun off turn two and his Pontiac hit the inside wall, that left only Jarrett and Bobby Labonte on the lead lap when the fifth-caution flag appeared. It also allowed Jarrett and Labonte to pit under yellow.

Earnhardt passed the two leaders on the restart, thus putting him on the tail end of the lead lap. With 100 laps remaining, Earnhardt had made his way into second but he was a half lap behind leader Jarrett.

Then, on lap 327, Greg Sacks' Ford spun off turn four and NASCAR ruled, after watching a video replay and talking with Sacks' crew chief Dave Fuge, that Earnhardt would be penalized one lap for rough driving.

"We looked at the replays of the incident five or six times and there was absolutely no question in our minds of what happened in turn four and why it happened." NASCAR spokesman Chip Williams said in a prepared statement distributed to the media.

"We also checked with the driver of the 68 car (Sacks) and he confirmed what we had seen.

"The incident was uncalled for. We instituted the penalty and that made up for any advantage the 3 car might have gained."

After the race, Sacks statement didn't match what NASCAR said he told the sanctioning body earlier. Sacks said, "If Dale touched me, it was just because we were racing hard. He took the air off my car and I got loose. If Dale touched me, it didn't matter."

"I didn't hit him, per se, hit him,"

EARNHARDT HELD OFF CHARGING ROOKIE JEFF GORDON TO WIN THE COCA-COLA 600 AND BECOME THE FIRST DRIVER TO TOP $17 MILLION IN CAREER EARNINGS.
DAVID CHOBAT PHOTO

earnhardt dale

EARNHARDT WAS ABLE TO KEEP GORDON IN HIS REARVIEW MIRROR MOST OF THE DAY.
DAVID CHOBAT PHOTO

Earnhardt said. "I caught a lap penalty for it, so undoubtedly, they (NASCAR) think I hit him. He says I hit him. We got the lap back and won the race, so it's neither here nor there, is it?

"I still won't say I hit him. If we rubbed or the bumpers touched a bit, it wasn't like I just went up there and knocked the crap out of him and turned him over or around or whatever. I don't think I nudged him. I still don't think I hit him."

Since Earnhardt didn't believe he hit Sacks, he was surprised when NASCAR penalized him. He said he came in for a routine pit stop and when he prepared to leave, the NASCAR official assigned to his pit stopped him. Earnhardt thought he was being held on pit road for speeding again.

"Richard asked him and he said, 'No, they penalized you a lap for rough driving.' I didn't hit him. All I was thinking about was getting back on the track and trying to make my lap up." Earnhardt said.

On the restart, Earnhardt and Jimmy Spencer immediately passed leader Labonte to get back on the tail end of the lead lap. That maneuver put Earnhardt seventh and Spencer eighth . When Wallace hit the third-turn wall on lap 350, that resulted in the seventh and final caution flag and enabled Earnhardt, Spencer, and Gordon, who lost a lap on a stop-and-go penalty for jumping the previous restart, to come around the track

and catch up to the rest of the field. Irvan was the only driver on the lead lap who didn't pit under the final caution, so when the race restarted, he was leading. Mark Martin was second, Schrader was third, Labonte fourth, Jarrett fifth, Gordon sixth, Spencer seventh, Earnhardt eighth, and Bill Elliott ninth.

Martin's Ford blew its engine on lap 355 when the race restarted and Earnhardt quickly clicked off the cars in front of him. On lap 362, Earnhardt went under Irvan for the lead as they raced through turn two and Schrader went with him to take over second. Schrader remained on Earnhardt's bumper for a few laps but then Earnhardt began pulling away. With 11 laps remaining, he held a 2.52-second advantage over Schrader.

With five laps to go, Gordon had taken over second and he trailed Earnhardt by 3.52 seconds.

"I'm glad Gordon didn't catch me," said Earnhardt, who finished 4.1 seconds ahead of Gordon. "He is a tough little driver and he is going to be hard to handle."

Earnhardt qualified 14th for the event and had moved to seventh by lap 20. He was never out of the top 10 the rest of the day, even on the two occasions when he was a lap down.

Earnhardt took the lead for the first time on a daring move on lap 98. Entering turn three, Martin was the leader, but Earnhardt chose the outside while Irvan moved to the

inside. With Martin in the center, instead of making it three abreast through turn four, Martin backed off and Earnhardt swept into the lead with Irvan on his bumper.

Earnhardt held the No. 1 spot for the next 38 laps until Joe Ruttman's Ford spun off turn two, causing the third caution flag. Earnhardt pitted, turning the lead over to rookie Rich Bickle who held it for one lap before returning it to Earnhardt when he pitted.

For the next 11 laps, Earnhardt was the person on the point, but then Irvan decided he wanted the position and he grabbed the lead as they entered turn one.

Earnhardt led two other occasions before the event ended. One was for 64 laps – 157-220 and the other was the final 39 laps – 362-400.

With his success this season, Earnhardt said his team's confidence is high.

"You think Andy came in and it made a big difference, well it did," said Earnhardt, who noted Neil Bonnett would test his car this week at Michigan International Speedway.

"But the team had a big rethinking last October, November when Kirk (Shelmerdine, former crew chief) announced he was leaving. So, even before Andy came on board we had a big rethinking. We started working hard at reorganizing at that point. Andy added to that part of the team. And it shows they are getting it done." ∎

Jeff Owens remembers the 1993 Coca-Cola 600 as a bright spot in an otherwise dark year for NASCAR

It had already been a tough year. There was really no other way you could sum up things in the spring of 1993.

The season had already gone south, with 1992 Winston Cup champion Alan Kulwicki losing his life in a plane crash on April 1. And the worst was yet to come. Three months later, in July, Davey Allison would lose his life after crashing his helicopter.

It was shaping up to be a miserable year, and not much could brighten the mood.

Except maybe another thrilling performance and a light-hearted moment courtesy of the great Dale Earnhardt.

It was my first season covering NASCAR full time, and it was shaping up to be a daunting task, to say the least.

How many other sports require you to switch from sportswriter to obit clerk at a moment's notice? You know that about racing going in. And it doesn't help any when brave drivers get killed off the track, in accidents normally reserved for normal, everyday people.

Kulwicki's death put an early damper on 1993, one that dampened with Allison's accident and never lifted, casting a dark cloud over the whole season.

Though no one really got over that dreadful season, Earnhardt's charge to his sixth championship and his week-to-week duels with friend and rival Rusty Wallace at least brought some excitement and made things interesting toward the end.

Earnhardt, of course, always had a way of lightening the mood when he entered a room. He could charm people almost the way he handled a race car — effortlessly.

One of his magical moments came on that May night in the Coca-Cola 600. As usual, Earnhardt had the fastest car at Charlotte. But, as usual, there were times when he drove it a bit too fast — like on pit road — and a bit too roughly — like into Greg Sacks' rear bumper.

> As usual, Earnhardt had the fastest car at Charlotte.

Perhaps Earnhardt knew what he was doing. NASCAR's longest race, as usual, was turning into a dud, lulling the crowd to sleep. When Earnhardt got caught for speeding on pit road, sending him to the rear of the field, he revved things up, charging through the pack as only Earnhardt could do.

Then, when things got boring again, Earnhardt provided even more drama, tapping Sacks' rear bumper just enough to send him spinning, bringing out the caution flag that he needed and that everyone watching was desperately hoping for.

Sacks' spin allowed Earnhardt to get back on the lead lap and, eventually, take the lead en route to his second straight Coca-Cola 600 victory.

Never mind that he was penalized a lap for rough driving. He got that lap back in no time.

The move was vintage Earnhardt. He needed a caution in order to win, and he knew just how to get it.

Though everyone watching, including NASCAR officials, knew what Earnhardt did, he was so good at it that he left everybody wondering. As usual, he left just enough doubt to make you believe his shenanigans might have been an accident, or at least unintentional.

Even Sacks, angry at first, wasn't sure if he'd been hit or not after watching the replays.

"He took the air off my car, and I got loose," he said, offering Earnhardt an out. "If Dale touched me, it didn't matter."

After the race, during his winner's interview, Earnhardt, with one of his famous sly grins, offered a classic, unforgettable line.

"I didn't hit him, per se, hit him," he said. "But I might have been agin' him."

That was Earnhardt, always on the edge of right or wrong, good or bad. That's why people loved and hated him. He was the ultimate good-guy outlaw.

And he always knew exactly what it took to win. And how to do it with flair and style. ■

—Jeff Owens
Executive Editor
NASCAR Scene

Earnhardt Claims
Third Dover Win

Loses Lap Twice, Overcomes Setbacks To Score Narrow Victory

By DEB WILLIAMS

Twice during the Budweiser 500 Dale Earnhardt lost a lap because of a cut tire, but each time the five-time NASCAR Winston Cup champion regained the deficit and eventually claimed his third series win this season.

With his second straight points victory, Earnhardt extended his lead in his quest for a sixth championship to 209 points over Rusty Wallace. That's a 310-point swing in the last four races. After the April 25 race at Martinsville, Va., Wallace possessed a 101-point lead and three straight wins.

"We're going to pack in all those points we can while we can," said Earnhardt, who won $68,030 in claiming his 56th Winston Cup career win.

"You might have a streak of bad luck and need that cushion, so I'm tickled to death to have it."

Earnhardt, driving a Chevrolet, led six times for 226 laps in the 500-lap race, to gain his third win at the demanding one-mile track and second in the Budweiser 500.

"The car was consistently strong all day," Earnhardt said. "I drove the heck out of this thing today.

"It's a long day at Dover. To run consistent and run strong all day is really rare. We were in that mode today. We just needed to keep it up front.

"You can't keep a good team down. Every time they got down today, they just kept coming back. I'm really proud of them.

"The crew has worked hard and it shows on race day. That's a testimony to how the car is prepared and how consistent it is. Making the lap up is tough, but you've got to have a good car to do it and that kind of shows itself."

Earnhardt, who finished 0.22 second ahead of Dale Jarrett's Chevrolet, had cut tires cost him a lap early in the race then again after the halfway point.

"We were working on them (tires) hard and we ran over some stuff after about 70 laps each time," Earnhardt said after the race that took 4 hours, 44 minutes and 6 seconds to complete.

"They were getting thin. That was the biggest problem we had all day.

"I dodged some wrecks, but they weren't that close. That was the problem today. A lot of guys were spinning and clipping each other. I think they were a little anxious at times."

A track record-tying 14 caution flags for 78 laps were instrumental in Earnhardt regaining his lost laps.

Earnhardt's first cut tire came on lap 69 while he was leading. He slowed in turn two, relinquishing the No. 1 spot to Mark Martin and then Brett Bodine passed him on the backstretch for second. The eventual victor pitted for four tires and his crew completed the task, including refueling, in 19.6 seconds.

On lap 120, Earnhardt passed Martin in turn four, one lap after the restart from the fourth caution period. Two laps later, the third-place Chevrolet driven by Ricky Rudd slammed into the first-turn wall to bring out the event's fifth yellow flag. That allowed Earnhardt to come around the track and catch up to the rest of the leaders.

Then on lap 280 while running second, Earnhardt's Chevrolet suffered another cut tire. This time, his crew changed four tires and refueled the car in 19.2 seconds, but he still lost a lap.

A sequence of green flag pit stops enabled Earnhardt to regain his lost lap and gave him a 10-second advantage over Wallace on lap 317 once the pit stops were completed. However, when Hut Stricklin's Ford spun on the backstretch on lap 320 for the 10th caution period, Earnhardt's large lead was erased.

Earnhardt relinquished the lead only once in the final 100 laps, that being on lap 437 when Martin passed him in turn three. But Earnhardt regained the top spot the following lap down the backstretch and held onto it the rest of the way.

"Mark got up under me pretty tight and got me just a little loose," Earnhardt said about the pass that occurred before an estimated crowd of 86,000.

"Then I got air under him and it made him loose and I got back around him. As it went on, his car got a little looser all the time, I pulled away from him and in the last 15 or so laps, I started cruising. I was sort of taking it easy on my tires and hoping I wouldn't have any problems."

Of the last 154 laps, Earnhardt led 153 of them, including the final 63.

Jarrett took second from Martin on lap 479, and with 19 laps remaining, he trailed by 1.48 seconds. Each lap, Jarrett cut away a little from Earnhardt's lead and with two laps to go, he was less than a second behind the veteran North Carolina driver.

"I was just biding my time and watching Jarrett," Earnhardt noted. "If he had caught us, I think I could have outrun him pretty easy."

Davey Allison claimed third for his best finish since Martinsville and Martin finished fourth for his first top-five since March 28 at Darlington, S.C. Both drove Fords.

Fifth went to Ken Schrader in a Chevrolet, giving him three straight top-five finishes.

While it was Jarrett whom Earnhardt had to be concerned about in the closing laps, he cited Wallace, Allison, Martin, Kyle Petty and Bodine as being strong at various times during the event.

Bodine led twice for 51 laps and Petty once for five laps before they were involved in an accident in turns three and four. The incident was triggered on lap 113, when Sterling Marlin dove under Bodine in turn three and Bodine's Ford spun into the wall. Petty slowed his Pontiac and shot to the inside in an attempt to avoid Bodine's car but was hit in the rear by Dave Marcis' Chevrolet.

Bodine returned to finish 16th, but Petty had to retire his Pontiac with handling problems after completing 243 laps. He placed 29th and dropped from fifth to seventh in the point standings. Marcis, who led once for eight laps, was unable to return to the event and had to settle for 36th.

"When I let off when the guys let off in front of me, some of them behind us let off and some of them didn't," Petty said. "We just all got together. It's one of those things and you can't do a lot about it."

After leading twice for 82 laps, Wallace was eliminated on lap 426, when his Pontiac slammed into the fourth-turn wall, shot across the frontstretch and smacked the inside wall before being T-boned in the driver's door by the rear of Jimmy Hensley's Ford. Geoff Bodine was also eliminated in the accident.

Wallace was racing Martin side by side for second when the accident occurred. Martin's Ford got into the side of Wallace's Pontiac and that sent him careening into the wall.

"I hated to see Rusty have that problem," Earnhardt said. "Rusty had been racing awfully hard and he's had a lot of hard luck since Talladega. I hope he can rebound from

that. I thought we were really going to have a good race between me and him today. We had one really good strong run with each other. I thought it was going to be between me and him there at the end."

The car Earnhardt used to obtain the victory was an old short-track car he drove at Dover last September that had received new sheet metal. Only 1½ turns of wedge were needed for a chassis adjustment during the race.

"When you win races, that's what it's all about," said Earnhardt, who averaged 105.97 mph in the race that had 23 lead changes among 12 drivers, a track record for the number of drivers.

"We worked hard last year, but it seemed like the harder we worked the further we got behind. There's a new air about the team. You can go in the shop and see it. The guys have a lot of focus, new-found energy or whatever you want to call it." ∎

EARNHARDT TAKES THE CHECKERED FLAG IN DOVER, DEL., AFTER HOLDING OFF A SURPRISING LATE-RACE CHARGE BY DALE JARRETT. NWCS ARCHIVE PHOTO

The Intimidating

Earnhardt Continues
Hot Year With Pepsi
400 Win

Game

By TOM STINSON

dale

D ale Earnhardt, "The Man" at Daytona International Speedway in everything except "The Race," kept that claim by dominating the Pepsi 400, extending his Winston Cup points lead at the season's mid point.

Earnhardt led 110 of the race's 160 laps and held off Sterling Marlin and Ken Schrader in a wild last lap for the victory, his second in the 400 and 20th overall at Daytona despite never winning the Daytona 500. Earnhardt increased his points lead to 251 over second-place Dale Jarrett (2,342-2,091), with Rusty Wallace a distant third, 345 points back.

And it all came under stifling conditions. The kind of heat that bears down on a person, rides one all day and never lets go. No sympathy from such heat.

The weather was hot, too.

Despite the summer Daytona sun putting temperatures near 100 degrees during the race, which Earnhardt said meant near 140 degrees in the race cars, the most heat Earnhardt felt all day came from a dicing pack of cars that chased him throughout the event.

"Racing with a lot of guys behind you who are wanting to pass you and pass everybody else, you're sort of like playing a high-speed game of chess," said Earnhardt, who collected $75,940 for his 57th Winston Cup career victory. "You see who moves with who and who does what to know that the last move will be yours. Fortunately, it worked out for us.

"It's really a mental game as much as anything else and, with the heat and the driving too, it's a tough game…It's a tough game to play."

But Earnhardt's the master.

The five-time Winston Cup champion continually drove to the front, taking the lead 11 different times, the longest stretch being for the race's final 29 laps.

Earnhardt hovered around the lead all day after moving from his fifth starting spot to first by lap five. Only once, a 28-lap stretch after being passed by Martin on lap 100 and then going through a series of green-flag pit stops, did Earnhardt stay out of the lead for more than four laps.

He just dominated, and it all came from passing cars on the track. After each pit stop, the last coming on lap 123 during the fourth caution period, Earnhardt exited back in the field.

But each time, he charged to the front within a couple of laps.

"When you can take the lead, that's the time to do it," Earnhardt said about running up front so often.

"Any time you can pass with a carburetor restrictor plate, that's the time to do it.

"If I could lead 'em all, I'm going to lead 'em all. You've got less worry. The worry is behind you, instead of in front of you."

Earnhardt's worry was all around him on the last lap.

Earnhardt's Chevrolet had been getting tight during the closing laps, but he was able to lead a single-file pack of cars to the white flag lap. On that lap, while trying to hold off Schrader, Earnhardt's car nearly pushed into the wall as he exited turn two. That forced him off the gas, which gave Schrader a shot on the outside.

But Earnhardt closed that opening, and it was the last one he showed all day.

"I about got into the wall," Earnhardt said. "Or I thought I was going to get into the wall. The car sort of swayed out sideways. I cracked the throttle a bit. I swayed back over and Schrader tried to go on the outside, so I swerved back and got him pinched between the wall.

"He bumped me a bit and had to crack the throttle, and (Marlin) came up beside him. That's what put them side by side."

And that gave Earnhardt the buffer he needed to take the checkered flag. Schrader had a little more condensed version of the last lap.

"There are a lot of guys who haven't won a race at Daytona.

I just haven't won the Daytona 500."

"I got my nose in there and he kind of wiped it for me," he said.

After Marlin challenged Schrader, the two raced side by side to the flag, with Marlin nosing ahead for second. Schrader was third, followed by Ricky Rudd and rookie Jeff Gordon, who now has notched two top-five finishes in two Daytona starts. Also, the threesome of Schrader, Rudd and Gordon gave car owner Rick Hendrick three top-five finishes.

Rounding out the top 10 were: Mark Martin; pole position winner Ernie Irvan; Daytona 500 winner Dale Jarrett; Terry Labonte and Ted Musgrave. Nineteen cars finished on the lead lap.

Only two, though, had a shot for the victory against Earnhardt.

For Marlin, the second-place finish marked the ninth runner-up finish of his

career in 263 Winston Cup starts. And, for a moment, he thought his first victory was in sight.

"I got under Schrader, and I 'bout had enough to get up under Earnhardt," Marlin said. "But I'd have been out there in the pond somewhere, so I checked up a little bit."

Ironically, Schrader said he was hoping Marlin would find a place to pass, despite Earnhardt being a fellow Chevy driver and Marlin being in a Ford.

"I was hoping Sterling could pull it off," Schrader said. "Nothing against Dale. I'm glad to see a Chevy win, but if you're talking about a guy who's past due, Sterling's the guy."

The third-place finish could be Schrader's last Winston Cup appearance for a while. An illegal carburetor was found on his car during July 1 qualifying, and the National Stock Car Commission was scheduled to meet July 6 to determine if he should serve a four-race suspension.

Schrader says he knew nothing of the illegal part and hopes to keep racing in what has become one of his most successful seasons. He's currently fifth in the points battle, just 20 points out of third, and he has seven top-five finishes in the season's first 15 races.

Whatever the verdict, Earnhardt said he was happy to see Schrader overcome the controversy, as well as his 41st starting spot.

"I was really happy to see him run up front because you need to get all you can when you're fixin' to go on vacation," Earnhardt said jokingly of Schrader's potential suspension.

"I think he'll probably get that thing turned around to where he can be able to drive. Yeah, I was glad to see him run good. He about ran too good, though."

Not good enough, though, as NASCAR's "Intimidator" remained "The Dominator" in 1993.

Still, as usual for Earnhardt, at Daytona, some of the first answers he had to give concerned not his win in the Pepsi 400 but his lack of a win in the Daytona 500.

"I've won more races at Daytona than a

AFTER FIGHTING TEMPERATURES TOPPING OUT AT 140 DEGREES INSIDE HIS CAR, EARNHARDT MIGHT SPEND THE REST OF THIS FOURTH OF JULY WEEKEND SITTING ON THAT COOLER. NWCS ARCHIVE PHOTO

lot of guys," Earnhardt said in response to the usual question. "There are a lot of guys who haven't won a race at Daytona. I just haven't won the Daytona 500. Like any racetrack, you just go and try to do the best you can. I've never won on a road course either, but it's not going to dampen my career.

"We've had good success here at Daytona as a team, and me as a driver. I feel good about Daytona. I don't have any regrets about not winning the 500. Maybe when I retire, I might have some (regrets), but right now, I feel great about it."

Earnhardt's just feeling great all around lately. With the 400, he already has four wins this season, as well as victories in the Busch Clash and The Winston. He also has a dominating lead in his quest for a sixth series championship.

Life is fun again. And he plans on keeping it that way for a while.

"It's pretty neat to be chased," he said. "At my stage in my career and feeling as good as I do, it's still neat to be the guy to beat…The fire is still as hot as ever." ∎

MILLER GENUINE DRAFT 500

Dale Earnhardt and Team Memorialize
Allison After Pocono Victory

By STEVE WAID

Dale Earnhardt stopped at the Pocono finish line to remember a friend, then took off on the most appropriate victory lap ever turned. No champion could have done it better.

Earnhardt had just won his fifth race of the season - taking the Miller Genuine Draft 500 – and he further increased his Winston Cup point lead. It mattered little, though, following the death of Davey Allison earlier in the week, and the death of Alan Kulwicki earlier in the season.

So Earnhardt stopped his Chevrolet at the start/finish line and joined his kneeling teammates for a prayer, an emotional end to yet another tragic time for both racing and the Allison family.

Following the prayer, Earnhardt took off on one of Kulwicki's patented Polish victory laps, all while holding a No. 28 flag out his window in honor of Allison.

"I think it all came to heart right there,"

Earnhardt said of the prayer, led by David Smith, the jackman on the RCR Enterprises team.

"We came in and said a prayer for Davey and Liz and the kids, then took a victory lap in remembrance of Davey and Alan. It's been a tough year, losing two friends.

"I wish I could bring 'em back. We are going to miss 'em."

That moment ended a somber week for the Winston Cup circuit. Allison's death on July 13 marked the second tragedy in four months, and left most emotionally spent after the Pocono race.

"It's really a dark year for racing," Earnhardt's crew chief, Andy Petree, said. "We are really going to miss those guys, Davey and Alan. We're happy, but we've got sadness in our hearts."

That sadness was universal at Pocono. In honor of Davey Allison, all the teams carried a No. 28 on their cars and uniforms. Also, shortly before the race, a lone trumpeter

played "Taps" while the flag was lowered to half staff and a crowd of about 100,000 remembered Allison.

"I'd have been glad to run second to him today to have him back," Earnhardt said. "Davey was a heck of a good friend. We didn't hang out all the time, but I hunted and fished with him over the years.

"It's pretty emotional, and tough to describe. There's nothing anybody can say or do – just honor and remember him the best way we can."

Earnhardt did that by winning his second race of the month, leading seven times for 71 laps and holding off Rusty Wallace for the final 17.

The victory also regained some of the points Earnhardt lost after a dismal New Hampshire debut, giving him a 209-point lead over Dale Jarrett (2,612-2,403). Wallace still sits third, 260 back with 2,352.

Ironically, losing 95 points to Wallace the week before primed Earnhardt for Pocono.

A FITTING TRIBUTE. EARNHARDT HEADS OUT FOR ONE OF ALAN KULWICKI'S POLISH VICTORY LAPS WHILE ALSO HONORING DAVEY ALLISON.
NWCS ARCHIVE PHOTO

"I race better under pressure," he said. "I'm not good at stroking or just being consistent or anything. To have Rusty back in form the last two races and to be a contender is pretty neat."

Neat, when Earnhardt's beating him, that is.

Earnhardt hovered around the lead most of the day. He charged from his 11th-place starting spot to the front by lap 13, and he never fell out of the top five except for green-flag pit stop sequences.

"I'd have been glad to run second to him today to have him back. **Davey was a heck of a good friend."**
—Earnhardt

Earnhardt took the lead for good on lap 183 of the 200-lap event, driving by Wallace out of turn one and holding the line into the second turn of the flat, triangular track. He held off Wallace from there, which included a restart on lap 190 after a spin by Jimmy Horton brought out the eighth and final caution.

Wallace chased Earnhardt late, but he never got close enough to challenge for the lead.

"I couldn't catch him, and he couldn't pull away," Wallace said. "We stayed three car lengths apart for 30 laps."

That separation helped the two pull away from a pack that battled hard for the third spot. Bill Elliot led that group, ahead of Morgan Shepherd, Brett Bodine and pole winner Ken Schrader.

Those four diced throughout the closing laps. Elliot diced the best and, in the process, notched his first top-five finish of an otherwise frustrating season.

"I could see the leaders from there," Elliott said. "Well, at least we could see an improvement.

"It just looked like Rusty and Dale outpowered me. Traffic hurt, but I really think Dale was playing with Rusty. Rusty and I ran together earlier in the day, but Dale could just go on."

Earnhardt said he neither toyed with Wallace nor relaxed much during the race. He did say he raced hard, all the while biding his time for a late sprint.

"I wanted to save my tires there at the end, but those guys behind me started racing

hard and we had to go," he said, "I was just going to bide my time. I raced hard all day long and stayed up front most of the day."

Biding his time may have helped Kyle Petty. Petty, who dominated the Pocono race in June, once again drove to the front. He even led twice for 26 laps, and raced Earnhardt and Jarrett hard for the lead several times during the middle stages of the race.

Trying to race out of the pits, though, cost Petty.

After pitting on lap 129 – and while running second to Jarrett, who also pitted on 129 – Petty tore out of his pits in pursuit of Jarrett. Unfortunately for the Sabco Racing team, he tore out the clutch in his Pontiac at the same time.

"We could race with Earnhardt and those guys up front," Petty said. "It was driver error. I just tore the clutch up leaving the pits… I don't know if I could have beaten Earnhardt or not."

Jarrett and Bodine appeared strong enough at times to beat Earnhardt. Jarrett led four times for 48 laps, Bodine once for 14. And both led during the race's second half.

Bodine's laps at the point came as late as 163-176, after he and Wallace didn't pit during the caution that was triggered by Geoff Bodine's spin down the frontstretch. But another caution, this one for oil on the track on 176 brought all the leaders to the pits.

This time, Bodine exited third, behind Wallace and Earnhardt. Four laps after going green on 180, Bodine sat sixth, his chances for an upset victory pushed aside, much like he was in the third turn.

"We had a shot at winning it," said Bodine, who still recorded his first top-five finish since September and only his second since 1990. "But, we got shuffled out of the deal there in three."

After the victory and his tribute to Allison, Earnhardt began looking toward the DieHard 500 at Talladega, Ala.

EARNHARDT CELEBRATES FOR THE FANS AFTER A TOUGH WEEK IN THE MOTORSPORTS' FAMILY. NWCS ARCHIVE PHOTO

The race will be bittersweet for Earnhardt – and everyone in racing. Longtime friend Neil Bonnett is set to return to racing in Earnhardt's backup car after three years off because of a head injury.

But overshadowing the week, will be the return to Allison's home track, also the sight of his fatal helicopter crash.

"It's going to be tough next week," Earnhardt said. "The 28 car will probably be back, and seeing it without Davey will be tough.

"Some of the family will probably be there. You can't help but respect the Allisons. It's sad to see a family go through so much, but I think Bobby will bounce back.

"…This is tough for everybody. Anybody involved in racing knows how these teams feel today." ∎

DIEHARD 500

EARNHARDT REFINED HIS FOCUS BEFORE HE TOOK TO THE TRACK AND EDGED ERNIE IRVAN BY INCHES. NWCS ARCHIVE PHOTO

Earnhardt By A Nose
Over Irvan

Race Punctuated By Two Terrifying Crashes

By DEB WILLIAMS

After more than an hour delay to repair a damaged catch fence, Dale Earnhardt edged Ernie Irvan by inches to claim his fifth DieHard 500 in a high-speed chess game that had two horrifying crashes in which one driver was critically injured.

Stanley Smith, 43, was flown by helicopter from the 2.66-mile track to Carraway Methodist Medical Center in Birmingham, Ala., after receiving emergency treatment at his race car on the turn two apron.

Also involved in the accident were Kenny Wallace, Rick Mast, Ritchie Petty and Jimmy Horton, whose Chevrolet became airborne in turn one and rolled over the concrete retaining wall. It came to rest on its wheels, outside the track.

It was the first time a car has landed outside the track in an accident since last year at Watkins Glen (N.Y.) International when Greg Sacks' car rolled outside the road course. It was the first time a driver's car has flown over a retaining wall at an oval since June 1979, when Blackie Wangerin sailed out of Michigan International Speedway.

Horton, who walked away from his battered car, said he was "bruised up a little bit." He said he remembered seeing Wallace get sideways, tried to avoid him and then someone hit his Chevrolet in the right rear quarter panel. That's when his car sailed over the wall.

Petty said he believed his Ford ran into Smith's Chevrolet. Petty said when he attempted to move up the track, Smith's car shot up the speedway in front of him.

The other terrible crash occurred on lap 132 when Neil Bonnett's Chevrolet became airborne in the trioval, rolled over and then slammed into the catch fence on the frontstretch. He was thrown back on the grassy apron and stopped right side up.

While Bonnett's Chevrolet was ripping away about 25 feet of catch fence, Ted Musgrave's Ford slammed backwards into the outside wall and the car caught fire as it slid beneath the flagstand.

The race was stopped for 1 hour, 10 minutes and 8 seconds while the fence was repaired. No spectators were injured in the incident.

When the race returned to green flag conditions on lap 140, Earnhardt was third behind Irvan and Ricky Rudd, respectively, and there were 25 cars on the lead lap. For the rest of the way, the leaders were engaged in a high-speed chess game that saw Rudd, Ken Schrader and Jeff Gordon, all key players through most of the event, fall by the wayside with engine problems.

With about 40 laps remaining, rookie Bobby Labonte's Ford latched onto Kyle Petty's Pontiac's rear bumper and for at least three laps, they raced side by side with Irvan and Rudd, who was on Irvan's Chevrolet's rear bumper. Irvan was credited with leading laps 131-146, while Petty set the pace for laps 147-155.

> "I still
> # shake my head
> sometimes when I see what Dale Earnhardt does in a race car," said Andy Petree, Earnhardt's crew chief.

On lap 154, pole position winner Bill Elliott, who had run among the leaders throughout the day, got squeezed into the backstretch wall and the toe-in on his Ford was knocked out, causing him to fall out of the lead draft.

Irvan regained the lead from Petty on lap 156 and held the point in the 13-car lead draft for the next eight laps.

Then, on lap 164, Petty moved high to snatch the lead from Irvan. With 20 laps remaining, Petty was still leading, Earnhardt was second, Irvan third, Labonte fourth and Bobby Hillin fifth. Five laps later, the lead draft contained only eight cars with Dale Jarrett trailing Hillin. Then came Mark Martin and Brett Bodine.

On lap 176, Jarrett moved to the outside of Labonte and Martin followed Jarrett. With 12 laps remaining, Martin was notified via his radio that Jarrett wanted to go with him when he pulled out to pass.

Petty still had the lead with five laps remaining, but then Earnhardt made his move. On lap 185, Earnhardt dropped to the inside of Petty as they raced into turn three and Irvan followed Earnhardt. Jarrett followed and they shuffled Petty back to fourth with Martin fifth and Labonte sixth.

Earnhardt, 42, led the final four laps, but it was no easy task for the North Carolina driver who now has 59 career Winston Cup wins. On lap 187, Earnhardt moved ahead by about five car lengths when the cars behind him began racing side by side. But that quickly changed on the white-flag lap as Earnhardt remained high and Irvan moved to the inside.

"I don't know how we all mixed up and got to where we were, but we (Irvan and Earnhardt) were side by side going into three," said a happy Earnhardt, who won $87,315.

"I figured somebody would come down and make it three wide coming off (turn) four and then we'd be racing three and four wide and maybe I could sneak on the outside and still beat them. I figured I was going to run second or third.

"Then, Kyle stayed behind me and Mark was behind Ernie, Ernie beat me a little through the trioval and then I stuck it right against him and beat him back by inches.

"We were lucky, just really lucky. All of them were players and all of them were important. You didn't know who was going to push who, or who was going to hurt who. They moved, we moved. It was just an all day game. I just had to play the game until the last move. We got the last move and it worked."

Earnhardt claimed his victory by a mere six inches.

"Dale and I had a heck of a drag race to the finish," Irvan said. "I didn't have anybody on my bumper. That was the problem, but everybody chooses where they want to go and you have to live with it."

Martin finished third, Petty fourth, and Jarrett fifth. Labonte's Ford ran out of gas on the final lap and he had to settle for 15th.

The win was Earnhardt's eighth at Talladega, tying him with the late Davey Allison for the most victories at the circuit's largest speedway. Earnhardt now has six Winston Cup, one Busch Series, and one IROC win at the track. Allison won three Winston Cup, four ARCA and one IROC race at the speedway.

"You can't say enough about Davey and the Allison family," said Earnhardt, who had won five of the last eight Winston Cup races.

"We've mourned Davey for two weeks now. It's been a real tragic thing for the Allison family, but it's like Bobby Allison told Neil a couple nights after that accident, 'You've got to go on and you can't blame yourself for what happened.' Neil tried to do all he could in getting Davey out of that heli-

copter. You just do what you can and get through what you can get through.

"I think the racing community has pulled together and helped each other get through this trauma with Davey. But you have to go on."

Earnhardt averaged 153.857 mph in the race slowed by five caution flags for 27 laps. There were 26 lead changes among 10 drivers in the race that took 3 hours 15 minutes and 1 second to complete. And Earnhardt said the final 50 laps were tougher than the first 138.

"I knew it was going to be a closer and hotter race (than the first half)," said Earnhardt, who has an average finish of eighth in restrictor plate races, making him the only driver with a top 10 average finish in the restrictor plate events.

"I was more tense right there at the end than I was the whole time,"

Earnhardt led five times for 59 laps, while Irvan held the No. 1 spot on six occasions for 56 laps. Petty was the third highest lap leader, setting the pace five times for 39 laps.

TAYLOR KNOWS WHOSE DAD IS NO. 1 DAVID CHOBAT PHOTO

"I still shake my head sometimes when I see what Dale Earnhardt does in a race car," said Andy Petree, Earnhardt's crew chief. "It looked like we were going to get beat today, and then the next thing I know, he's out front again. I don't know how he does it, but he seems to always get the job done."

Team owner Richard Childress said he knew Earnhardt's plan when he saw how we was racing on the last lap.

"I've seen him do it before," Childress said. "I had confidence in him. You never know exactly what's going to happen once they go out of sight, but I never lose confidence in Dale." ∎

Nothing New Here

Earnhardt Takes Fifth Straight Win In Second Qualifier

By STEVE WAID

Really, you had to expect the outcome.

After all, it was a Gatorade 125-Mile Qualifying Race for the Daytona 500 and Dale Earnhardt was entered. Even Las Vegas – which has become tuned in to NASCAR Winston Cup racing in recent years – had a feeling what might happen and listed the driver of the RCR Enterprises Chevrolet as a 7-5 favorite to win.

And win he did, for the fifth straight year. As it has been in the past, it was a matter of routine. The defending Winston Cup champion started first in the second of the 125-milers by virtue of earning the No. 2 starting position for the Daytona 500 on Feb. 12. He led 34 of the 50 laps around the 2.5-mile Daytona track, roared back from the middle of the pack after a restart from the second and final caution period and went on to beat Sterling Marlin by two car lengths.

It was the seventh career 125-mile qualifying race victory for Earnhardt, which puts him No. 1 on Daytona's all-time list as he broke out of a tie with Hall of Fame driver Cale Yarborough. Earnhardt routinely romps through the Daytona 500's preliminary events only to see victory in the big race slip through his grasp.

This time, even though routine, the victory was nonetheless special. Earnhardt was able to offer the win as a memorial to his departed friend Neil Bonnett, who was killed in a crash during Daytona 500 practice Feb. 11.

"It is an emotional time for us and everybody knows why," Earnhardt said. "Neil had a tremendous input into RCR Enterprises and into my life, especially over the last two or three years. He helped develop this car for restrictor plate racing.

"I think everyone remembers Neil had a lot of input with this car. He did a lot of testing for us. He put in 1,200 miles of testing for us at Talladega. He was definitely with us today, and he is in our hearts all the time."

Earnhardt wasted little time establishing his superiority.

He led the first 19 laps, all with Marlin in tow, until Marlin was able to shove his Morgan-McClure Motorsports Chevrolet under Earnhardt between turns three and four and lead lap 20. Marlin led the next lap before Earnhardt went back out in front for laps 22-24. It was Marlin's turn again on lap 25, Earnhardt's on laps 26-27 and then, on lap 28, Marlin again shot by and was able to pull away over the next nine circuits.

But his reign would end there. The race's second caution period, caused by Chuck Brown's spin out of the fourth turn, began on lap 36.

All but five cars opted to pit for fresh tires and chassis adjustments, among them those of Earnhardt and Marlin. Morgan Shepherd, in the Wood Brothers Ford, did not pit and inherited the lead.

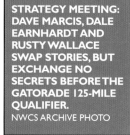

STRATEGY MEETING: DAVE MARCIS, DALE EARNHARDT AND RUSTY WALLACE SWAP STORIES, BUT EXCHANGE NO SECRETS BEFORE THE GATORADE 125-MILE QUALIFIER.
NWCS ARCHIVE PHOTO

When the race restarted on lap 40, with 10 laps remaining, Earnhardt was ninth and Marlin 10th. No one figured they would have any trouble moving through the pack, particularly since the front five cars – Shepherd, Ted Musgrave, Ricky Rudd, Derrike Cope and Jimmy Horton – had not pitted.

"Our car was a little loose at the start and then it got a bit looser," said Earnhardt, who received $35,200 for winning the race with an average speed of 146.772 mph.

"When we had that second caution, we had the opportunity to change all four tires and make adjustments to our car. I don't really understand why anyone wouldn't pit to take on tires and make adjustments."

Earnhardt thought he would have no problem going to the front.

"I felt confident because I had done it in the Busch Clash," he said. "Why not? There were 10 laps to go and that was plenty of time."

Earnhardt moved into the lead on the 41st lap, taking Marlin with him. They were able to break away easily as a group consisting of Jeff Gordon, Bill Elliott, Brett Bodine and Shepherd fought for position behind them.

Without much of a problem, Earnhardt led the final 10 circuits.

"Sterling ran good, but the problem was it was hard for him to keep the draft on me without help and he didn't have any,"

Earnhardt said. "And he wasn't going to get around me without help. We were pretty equal in that sense. If he had been in front, I don't think I could have gotten around him."

"I needed someone to push me," admitted Marlin, who led 12 laps. "I couldn't get one.

> "I think everyone
> **remembers Neil**
> had a lot of input with this car
> ...He was definitely with us
> today, and he is in our hearts
> all the time."

Our car ran great on the long runs, and I wish that last caution hadn't come out. We were going to stay out, but we saw all the leaders pit so we had to pit, too.

"We came in and got four tires to stay in sync. We did what we had to do, but just came up one spot short."

Prior to the race, NASCAR announced that teams would be allowed to switch tire brands within the first 20 laps of the race, a change from the earlier edict which said teams must run the brand of tire with which they qualified.

That never came into play in the second

qualifier, as the top 15 finishers started and finished on Goodyear tires.

The race hardly got started before the only multicar wreck in both qualifying races brought out the first caution. As the field wound its way into turn one on the first lap, Dale Jarrett's Chevrolet slowed dramatically due to a failed cylinder. That caused a group of cars to swerve behind him, creating contact and then spins.

Involved in the mishap were the cars of Jeremy Mayfield, Rich Bickle, Buddy Baker, Steve Grissom, Ward Burton, Bobby Hillin, Cope and Nemechek. Mayfield, Nemechek and Cope were able to continue. Although Jarrett was sidelined with a 25th-place finish, the defending Daytona 500 champion was awarded a provisional starting position for the race. He was scheduled to start 41st.

Finishing third, about 15 car lengths behind Marlin, was Gordon in a Hendrick Motorsports Chevrolet. He was followed by Elliott in the Junior Johnson & Associates Ford, Bodine in the King Racing Ford, Shepherd, Michael Waltrip in the Bahari Pontiac, Cope in the Cale Yarborough Motorsports Ford, Wally Dallenbach in the Petty Enterprises Pontiac and Ricky Rudd in his Ford.

Next in positions 11-15, all of whom made the Daytona 500 field, were Lake Speed, Musgrave, Kyle Petty and Rick Mast. ∎

EARNHARDT FIRES THE ENGINE AND LETS OUT A SCREAM HEADING INTO THE RACE.
NWCS ARCHIVE PHOTO

Earnhardt Masters Darlington
Again

He Earns Ninth Career Win At
Track, First Of The Season   **By STEVE WAID**

If indeed rugged old Darlington Raceway is to have a new master, Dale Earnhardt seems poised to be that person.

He indicated so in his convincing victory in the TranSouth Financial 400 NASCAR Winston Cup race. It was Earnhardt's 60th career victory and his ninth on the 1.366-mile track

he won the DieHard 500 at Talladega, Ala., last July, 16 races ago. "But whatever name you use, she deserves respect. She demands it. And if you give it to her and run a consistent race, you will have a good day.

"I don't care if the race is 300 or 400 laps or miles. The key is having respect for the track. I don't know if it was experience or maturity that gave it to us, but we had it

But now we have and this is a good turning point for us."

Earnhardt quickly admitted his RCR Enterprises team geared up to make the most of the circumstances at Darlington. Before the race started, everyone knew perhaps the deciding factor in its outcome would be the tire wear – and that wasn't going to be anything spectacular.

EARNHARDT WAS SUCH A BLUR IN THE TRANSOUTH 400 THAT...
DAVID CHOBAT PHOTO

that has been called "The Lady in Black," "Too Tough To Tame" and several other things not so complimentary.

Only David Pearson, the retired Hall of Fame driver, has produced a better Darlington record. His shows 10 victories.

But even Pearson would admit Earnhardt has found the proper Darlington technique, which combines patience, a bit of daring and a healthy amount of respect for an old track that will deposit a driver into its walls should he make the slightest mistake.

"This old race track has been called all kinds of things over the years," said Earnhardt, who earned his first victory since

today. We didn't get into trouble or make any trouble for ourselves."

Earnhardt's victory was his sixth in the TranSouth Financial 400 and, for the fifth time, it served as his first win of the season. Four previous times, he went on to win the Winston Cup championship.

"The first win of the season is always the toughest to get under your belt," said the 42-year old Earnhardt. "I think when you get it at a place like Darlington, it makes a statement. It sets the trend.

"But I felt good about our efforts in the first four races of the season. Because of circumstances and our mistakes, we didn't win.

Because of softer compounds offered by both Goodyear and Hoosier Tire and a gritty surface, tires were simply not going to last as long as they should, or at least as long as they once did at Darlington.

NASCAR realized the potential problems and made two rulings. The first came before the race, when it announced that if a caution period hadn't been created before 25 of the race's 293 laps had been completed, it would mandate a yellow flag so teams could check tire wear.

Then the extensive use of tires began to affect the supply, particularly of Goodyear tires, used by all but five of the teams in competition. The tire company brought 1,850 Winston Cup tires to Darlington, 912 for the left side and 940 for the right.

But the window for tire wear was so small, the supply began to deplete. On lap 163, NASCAR waived the rule which forbade teams to switch tire brands during the race. Any team that switched was required to use all four new-brand tires. Obviously, it cleared the way for Goodyear teams to acquire tires if Goodyear's supply ran out.

None of this seemed to affect Earnhardt, although he wasn't pleased with it.

"We knew we could run 36 laps before we had to make a tire change and that is fewer than before," Earnhardt said. "We could run more laps than that, but we figured out where our speed would fall off and worked with that.

"What helped us was our car's setup. We made a camber adjustment and changed a spring and sway bar this morning and that helped the car run consistent. It handled more neutral toward the end but by that time, I was pacing myself.

"When you make a camber adjustment, you give up on the chassis and you have to contend with that. But we had to compensate for the tire wear and not abuse it, so we ran at a slower speed."

Despite the RCR Enterprises team's ability to deal with the tire problems, Earnhardt said, in effect, they should have not existed.

"The tire situation is not good," he said. "The tire companies are having a race and the team owners, drivers, engine builders and everyone else are swept up in it. We have to go along with it. I know Goodyear has done a good job and will do a good job. I have all the confidence in them. I just hope the durability improves along with the speed of the tires.

"We are behind Goodyear 100 percent and hopefully they can stay dominant, wear out the other tire company and they will go away."

Earnhardt led 166 laps, including the final 33, and beat Mark Martin to the finish line by 7.4 seconds. So the dominance of his Chevrolet was obvious.

But it wasn't without its challengers. Rusty Wallace seemed poised to take the victory in his Ford, but a couple incidents rendered him helpless. He led 56 laps, but during a pit stop under green on lap 104, he started out of his pits with the left-rear lug nuts loosened. The intent had been to change just two tires, but his crew had begun procedures for a four-tire change, hence the loose lug nuts. As a result, Wallace fell from the lead to 10th place.

He was making his way back into contention and was in fourth place when he

...EVEN THIS GUY COULDN'T STOP HIM FROM CRUSHING THE FIELD AND WINNING HIS NINTH RACE AT DARLINGTON
NWCS ARCHIVE PHOTO

suddenly slid into the third-turn wall as a tire was going flat. Wallace, who thought he had run over some debris, was forced to go to the garage area to repair the damage, but the worst damage had been done. He finished 33rd, 75 laps off the pace.

> "...whatever name you use,
> ## she deserves respect."
> —Earnhardt on the legend of Darlington Raceway.

Ernie Irvan led 24 laps in his Ford, but was forced to take a stop-and-go penalty when NASCAR discovered his Robert Yates team had eight men over the wall, one more than allowed, during a pit stop on lap 221. He bounced back to finish sixth on the lead lap, but he could never press Earnhardt.

Earnhardt was in the lead when he pitted for the last time on lap 259, giving the lead over to Chevrolet-driving Ken Schrader. Two laps later, Schrader pitted and Earnhardt again was at the point – where he would remain for the rest of the race.

On lap 268, Martin, who had swept the IROC and Mark III Cans 200 Busch Series races on March 26, passed Bill Elliott's Ford to take second place. He was 6.97 seconds behind Earnhardt.

By lap 282, Earnhardt was 8.15 seconds ahead. By lap 290, he was 8.28 seconds in front and it was obvious he was merely pacing himself to the 53rd super-

speedway victory of his career.

Elliott finished third behind Martin while Dale Jarrett took fourth in a Chevrolet. Lake Speed wound up fifth in a Ford, followed by Irvan, Schrader, Harry Gant in a Chevrolet, Ricky Rudd in a Ford and Ted Musgrave in a Ford. Gant, Rudd and Musgrave were one lap down.

Of the five caution periods for 26 laps, only one was caused by an accident. It occurred on lap 62, when Bobby Labonte's Pontiac smacked the fourth-turn wall in an incident that saw Morgan Shepard's Ford clip the wall, also.

With the victory, Earnhardt moved into a tie for second place in the Winston Cup point standings with Mark Martin. Each has 779 points, 81 behind Irvan, who has 860.

Earnhardt's winning average speed was 132.432 mph, just a shade off Darlington's 400-mile race record of 132.703 mph, set May 11, 1968 by David Pearson – of course. The last 500-mile race held at Darlington before the format was reduced for the 1994 Rebel 400 on April 16, 1972 was won by Pearson – of course.

"David gave me a lot of crap when I was a rookie (in 1979)," Earnhardt said. "His advice to me usually was, 'Get out of my way.'

"But he would talk about the cars and how to drive them. He even drove my car for me when I was injured (in 1979) and won here (in the Mountain Dew 500). He taught me a lot and treated me as a friend over the years. Any time you can come close to accomplishing the kind of things a guy you respect, think a lot of and watched closely as you grew up has to mean a lot."

Undoubtedly, Pearson would be proud. ∎

EARNHARDT'S CREW, ARGUABLY THE BEST IN RACING, KNOWS THAT SPEED IN THE PITS CAN MAKE THE DIFFERENCE AT BRISTOL.
DAVID CHOBAT PHOTO

Earnhardt Claims Second
Straight Win

Victory Is Veteran's First On Short Tracks Since '91

By DEB WILLIAMS

Dale Earnhardt isn't known for his patience, but that was a virtue he employed in the Food City 500, and coupled with quick pit work, the RCR Enterprises team walked away from the 0.533-mile track with its second straight win this season.

The victory was Earnhardt's first on a short track since October 1991 when he broke Harry Gant's four-race win streak at North Wilkesboro, N.C.

"We really didn't have 'em covered today. We just caught the cautions right. I guess you could say we were in the right place at the right time," Earnhardt said after winning his 61st Winston Cup race.

Even though it was Earnhardt's first short-track win since '91, he said he thought the drought was just bad luck, that nothing was wrong with the team's short track program.

Earnhardt now has eight victories at BIR, the site of his first Winston Cup career win in April 1979. Five of those wins have come in the spring race, tying him with Darrell Waltrip for the most in that event.

The six-time Winston Cup champion finished 7.6 seconds ahead of Ken Schrader's Chevrolet, leading once for the final 183 laps. He also took the Winston Cup points lead for the first time this year, moving to a 40-point advantage over Ernie Irvan, whose Ford had timing chain problems on lap 111. Irvan eventually finished 33rd in the 37-car field.

"That's what it's all about in the points race, to be consistent and work hard," said Earnhardt, 42. "You've got to get all you can get all year. You've got to take one race at a time from the start and that's what we do and that's what we've done all along.

"We've been pumped up from the first of the year. But we equalized a tire at Daytona and left some lug nuts loose at Rockingham. We had a jackscrew back at Atlanta, so we've had some problems. But now it's turned around for us. Maybe now we can put this thing together and really do some damage in the points."

By coming from the 24th starting position, Earnhardt became the first driver in the track's history to come from that far back for a win.

"I was disappointed in qualifying with the car, but Andy (Petree, crew chief) said we made the choice and we qualified and we had to work on it so we could get it to go," Earnhardt said about the car that was purchased two years ago from the Martin Birrane's team but never raced by Richard Childress' organization until the Bristol event.

"It had a push in the middle of the corner and it was loose off the corners. We worked with that the first of the race and got it consistent."

Earnhardt said his team had tested the car a lot and it had been raced once by Dave Marcis at Rockingham, N.C.

The Kannapolis, N.C., native admitted it was difficult to have patience at Bristol when starting back in the field, but it was crucial. After 24 laps, Earnhardt had gained only three positions and was only up to 20th after the second caution period that covered laps 34-37.

In addition to patience, Earnhardt cited his crew's work as being key to giving him good track position. The first break in that category occurred during the third caution period – laps 69-74 – when Dale Jarrett's Chevrolet hit the fourth-turn wall. The lead lap cars pitted and Earnhardt returned to the track 12th.

> "I know it looked like
> **I tapped him,**
> but I never touched him."
> —Earnhardt

Derrike Cope brought out the fourth caution flag on lap 134 when his Ford hit the first-turn wall, and on the restart Earnhardt was seventh. He moved into the top five with his crew's help during the fifth yellow flag – laps 169-77 – after Dick Trickle's Chevrolet blew an engine and spun in turns three and four. The leaders stopped for four tires and fuel but Geoff Bodine who was pitting on the backstretch, received only left-side tires. When the race restarted Bodine was leading, followed by Rusty Wallace, Earnhardt, Jeff Gordon and Mark Martin. It was during this stretch that Bodine led 148 of the 160 laps that he held the No. 1 spot.

Bodine relinquished the lead to Earnhardt on lap 318 when he made a scheduled green-flag stop for four tires and fuel. Before Earnhardt, Schrader and Lake Speed could pit, the ninth caution flag came out for Rick Mast's crash in turn four. That resulted in those three drivers being able to pit under caution and emerge from their final stop as the only ones on the lead lap.

"That (caution flag) was the key to the track position we got," Earnhardt said. "When everybody pitted under green and me, the 15 (Speed) and the 25 (Schrader) stopped under the caution."

Even though there were 10 caution flags for 75 laps, Earnhardt said he was close to only one incident. That was the one that brought out the eighth caution flag on lap 210 of the 500-lap race.

Earnhardt was behind pole position winner Chuck Brown as they exited turn two. Brown's Ford turned sideways, spun into the backstretch's outside wall and then seven other cars, four of them on the lead lap were collected behind Brown, who was several laps down. Those who were on the lead lap were Ted Musgrave, Rick Mast, Terry Labonte and Todd Bodine. Also involved were Kyle Petty, Brett Bodine and Steve Grissom.

"He (Brown) broke loose. I know it looked like I tapped him, but I never touched him," Earnhardt said. "We were close, but his car jumped out from under him and caused that wreck on the back straightaway.

"That was the biggest thing I was close to as far as anybody spinning in front of us."

The most serious accident was a single-car incident involving Ricky Rudd. On lap 188, Rudd's Ford spun on the frontstretch and slammed head-on into the inside retaining wall. After a trip to the infield care center, he was transported to Bristol Regional Medical Center for additional examination of his shoulder. He was released after no broken bones were found. Rudd's accident gave him a 32nd finish and dropped him from fifth to eighth in the point standings.

Only two of the top 10 qualifiers finished in the top 15. Wallace qualified second and finished seventh, while Bobby Labonte started ninth and placed sixth.

Martin led once for eight laps before two cut tires and possible problems with his car's suspension ended his day on lap 428 when he spun in turn three and collected Gordon, who set the pace on three occasions for 68 laps.

KEEPING IT STEADY ON BRISTOL'S BANKS HAS BECOME AN EARNHARDT SPECIALTY. DAVID CHOBAT PHOTO

"I believe if we hadn't had any problems, we had the car to beat," Martin said.

"We had a flat, rebounded from that, made both laps up, and then we had another one. I pretty much decided just to take my fifth-place finish, ride around and take it. And then, I don't know what happened.

"I can't do any more than what I did here. And if I can't race on tires that I can't drive hard on, then I may as well just spend the day hitting the wall, because I can't drive like my grandmother. I'm a racer. I can't just ride around. But this is exactly what you get when you have a tire war."

In a prepared statement, Leo Mehl, head of Goodyear Tire and Rubber Co's motorsports operations, said, "The tire situation (at Bristol) was caused by low air pressure failures, which caused deflection, resulting in loss of air in the shoulder.

"That did require tire changes. Goodyear was not happy with the tire construction, nor pleased with our performance."

Goodyear's test session at Bristol was rained out. Mehl's statement was made through spokeswoman Mai Lindstrom after he discussed the situation with his engineers and staff at BIR.

Wallace led four times for 81 laps, but like Martin, he had tire problems. The Missouri native cut one tire and blistered three others.

"Rusty and Mark were really strong," Earnhardt said. "Their trouble enabled me to get laps on 'em. I didn't outrun those guys. We just worked track position and got the luck of the cautions."

Earnhardt averaged 89.647 mph in the race that took 2 hours, 58 minutes and 22 seconds to complete before an estimated crowd of 73,000. There were 11 lead changes among six drivers. ∎

IT'S ALWAYS A TEAM EFFORT WHEN EARNHARDT AND THE BOYS TAKE TO THE TRACK.
NWCS ARCHIVE PHOTO

dale earnhardt

Earnhardt Stays Cool
Under Pressure

Veteran Claims Ninth Talladega Victory

By DEB WILLIAMS

Dale Earnhardt doesn't like restrictor plate races, but his disdain for them hasn't kept him from becoming the most successful driver at the Winston Cup circuit's longest track.

With his narrow victory in the Winston Select 500, Earnhardt now has won seven 500-mile races at the 2.66-mile track – five of them since restrictor plates were instituted at the speedway – one Busch Series event and one IROC race. That gives him nine wins overall, breaking a tie with the late Davey Allison.

"It's an honor to have known and raced Davey," an exhausted Earnhardt said. "To set a record or break a record is an honor, too. He (Allison) was a great racer, but I was glad to beat Ernie (Irvan)."

It was Allison's former team, with Irvan now the driver, who Earnhardt beat by 0.067 second for his 62nd Winston Cup career win and his third victory this year.

"The whole deal this year is to accumulate points," said Irvan, who led seven times for 78 laps. "We want to win races, but I think we got the same points as Earnhardt today because we led the most laps."

Irvan leads Earnhardt by 25 points, 1,454 to 1,429.

With the win, Earnhardt joins Sterling Marlin as having a chance at a $1 million bonus paid by R.J. Reynolds Tobacco Co. to the driver who wins three of four selected races. Marlin earned his chance at the bonus by winning the Daytona 500. The next race in the Winston Million Select is the May 29 Coca-Cola 600 at Charlotte Motor Speedway.

Earnhardt always has been known for his blocking technique at the super speedways but in this particular event he couldn't rely solely on that ability. Instead, he had to maneuver his way from 11th to the front in 21 laps, pass leader Jimmy Spencer and then hold off 10 other lead lap cars for the victory.

"I had to get around a couple people to get where I was at, but it's hard to explain the last lap at Talladega," said Earnhardt, who led 10 times for 64 laps.

"I can't remember where I was with five to go or with three to go. I know I wanted to be in a position where I could drive by the leader. I don't know why with two or three to go I passed the leaders."

Green-flag pit stops on laps 155 and 159 of the 188-lap race split the lead cars into two separate packs. On lap 155, Earnhardt, who was the leader peeled off onto pit road with Spencer, Michael Waltrip, Gregg Sacks, Ted Musgrave and Marlin in tow. All received fuel only.

That turned the lead over to Morgan Shepherd for one lap and then Irvan took over on lap 156. He led until lap 159 when he stopped for fuel only and Shepherd, Lake Speed, Kyle Petty and Brett Bodine followed him onto pit road. That group didn't get back up to speed fast enough to stay ahead of Earnhardt but some of them, including Irvan, were able to mesh back in the first group of cars that pitted. At this time, Dave Marcis and Bobby Hamilton were the leaders but they still had to pit.

Then, on lap 161, Kirk Shelmerdine's Ford cut a tire and he hit the third-turn wall. That incident brought out the fourth yellow flag.

Irvan's crew used the event's final caution

period to repair his spoiler, which had come loose on the car's right side, and changed right side tires. Irvan pitted twice.

Unlike many of the other leaders who received fuel only during the caution period, Earnhardt and his crew changed all four tires on his Chevrolet.

"Our car just didn't feel right. I was worried about a tire equalizing or one going flat," said Earnhardt just two days after his 43rd birthday. "That was a call I more or less asked to do. Andy (Petree, crew chief) and Richard (Childress, car owner) did it. They had faith in me to do the job I did and come back to the front."

When the race restarted on lap 167, Marlin was leading, Spencer was second, Steve Grissom third and Marcis was forth. Earnhardt was 11th and Irvan 17th, the last car on the lead lap.

While Earnhardt and Irvan worked their way back toward the front, Marlin and Spencer diced for the lead.

On lap 170, Spencer dove to the inside of Marlin. Speed elected to draft with Spencer and that gave Spencer's Ford the momentum it needed to take the lead as they sped into turn three. Seven laps later, Spencer was still leading Marlin in second; Earnhardt had moved to third and Irvan rode fourth. On lap 178, Earnhardt dispensed with Marlin, making it Spencer in the lead, then Earnhardt, Irvan, Shepherd and Waltrip.

That running order remained unchanged until 184 when Earnhardt moved to the inside of Spencer as they entered turn one. Irvan elected to go with Earnhardt but Spencer moved between them in turn two.

"He (Spencer) just sort of drove up the track and I had the momentum," Earnhardt said. "I just ran around the bottom and figured Ernie would come with me. He did and Spencer got between us.

"You just use the opportunities as they come up. You don't say, 'I'm going to wait until he goes high or I'm going to wait until he does this.' You're just there and you're watching the moves and you use your experience and make the best of the opportunity. Opportunity came knocking and we answered the door."

Spencer attempted to regain the lead on lap 186, splitting the lapped car of Todd Bodine with Earnhardt at the start-finish line. Earnhardt went to the outside of Bodine and Spencer squeezed between them.

"I didn't think it was too smart on Spencer's part, but he made it," Earnhardt commented about his rival's maneuver.

Earnhardt maintained the lead, but by now Waltrip had joined the jockeying cars

and he went low as they entered turn three to take the lead on lap 186. However, by the time they reached the scoring stand, Earnhardt had regained the No. 1 spot.

Entering the final lap, it was Earnhardt, Waltrip, Schrader, Irvan and Spencer. Waltrip attempted to make his move on the backstretch, shooting to the inside of Earnhardt. Schrader took the outside lane, while Irvan managed to slide in behind Earnhardt, while Waltrip tucked in on Irvan's bumper and Spencer moved to fourth dropping Schrader back to fifth.

> "I'm real concerned when people are pushing fenders in
> ## on 2½-mile race tracks."
> —Earnhardt, on Jimmy Spencer's aggressive driving

"I was concerned the 30 car (Waltrip) was going to get real racy and they did," said Earnhardt, who averaged 157.477 mph in the race that had 30 lead changes among 11 drivers and was slowed by four caution flags for 23 laps.

"That's what happens when they go to racing each other and forget about the guy leading the race. At that time of the race, everybody is trying to go for what they can get and go for the win."

"I took the lead when I could. It wasn't a point of when I wanted to. I didn't have the car to do what I wanted it to. It was one of them deals when the opportunity was there, I took advantage."

"I was pretty surprised when Ernie didn't have enough to come back up there on the last straightaway through the trioval. We were just really fortunate."

Even though 17 cars finished on the lead lap, several drivers who were contenders early in the event were eliminated in two multicar crashes.

The first occurred on lap 103 when Jeff Gordon was attempting to pass Gregg Sacks on the inside in the trioval and Sacks got into the left rear quarter panel of Bodine's Ford, which turned sideways. Involved in that accident were Ricky Rudd, Jeff Burton, Mark Martin, Gordon, Chuck Brown and Loy Allen. Martin took the scariest ride in the incident as his Ford plowed the guardrail at the track's road course entrance and slammed head-on into another guardrail separating the road course from the infield.

"It scared me a little bit there," Martin said. "I thought that could be a bad one. Thank goodness for the roof flaps. The car didn't get upside down when it got sideways at full speed. Thank goodness for NASCAR and its rules."

Burton and Bodine had lost a lap because of a stop-and-go penalty for excessive speed on pit road and were running with the leaders in an effort to get their lap back when the accident occurred.

That caution period covered laps 104-111.

The other major crash occurred on lap 113 when Spencer's Ford tagged Terry Labonte's Chevrolet in the rear near the start-finish line. Labonte spun, slammed the outside wall on the driver's side, then slid across the track and into Rusty Wallace. Also involved were Dick Trickle, Derrike Cope, Brown, Jeremy Mayfield, Jeff Purvis, Wally Dallenbach, Dale Jarrett, Harry Gant, Hut Stricklin, and Jimmy Hensley.

"It was a shame," an angry Labonte said. "The 27 (Spencer) likes to take people out every week and I guess it was just our turn. He's still out there running like nothing happened."

When Earnhardt was asked about Spencer's driving in his post-race interview, he replied, "I better not dig my hole, but I'm real concerned when people are pushing fenders in on 2-1/2-mile race tracks."

In victory lane, however, Earnhardt said, "It was a little rough out there. The 27 car, he thought he was still at Martinsville or Richmond or North Wilkesboro. He was into the side of just about everybody, I think."

Prior to the two multi-car crashes there had been only one caution flag. That occurred on lap 21 when Geoff Bodine's Ford smacked the fourth-turn wall.

Earnhardt's closest call came in an incident with Sacks early in the event.

"We had been running real close and Sacks got into the back end of me too hard and turned me sideways," the six time Winston Cup champion said. "I don't think he did it intentionally. It's just one of them deals when you're not paying close enough attention. I was fortunate to get out of it."

At one early point in the event, when Earnhardt and Irvan were leading, a few spectators in the short chute area, near the flagstand, were throwing beer cans onto the track.

"At one time there were about six or eight," Earnhardt noted. "They would hit the track and bounce up into the cars. People who would do that have no respect for the drivers or the other fans."

A track spokesman said those people were escorted from the speedway. ∎

Earnhardt Victorious At
The Rock

63rd Career Win Wraps Up Seventh Winston Cup Title

By DEB WILLIAMS

Dale Earnhardt conquered "The Rock" and NASCAR's Winston Cup circuit all in the same day, winning the AC-Delco 500 by a car length and his record-tying seventh series championship.

The only other driver with seven Winston Cup titles is Richard Petty.

"It's great to be No. 1 all the way around on race day," said an emotional Earnhardt, who dedicated the championship to his best friend, Neil Bonnett, who died in a crash during practice in February at Daytona International Speedway.

"Winston Cup racing is my kind of racing. I wouldn't change a thing."

Earnhardt, who dedicated his race victory to Frank Wilson, the track's president who died in August, now has 63 Winston Cup career victories. The win was his fourth this year and his first since the May 1 Winston Select 500 at Talladega, Ala. It was his second victory at the 1.017-mile track and his first in the fall race.

In the last eight races, Earnhardt has produced one win, three seconds, three thirds and a seventh.

Six of his Winston Cup championships have come with car owner Richard Childress, while his first, in 1980, was with Rod Osterlund.

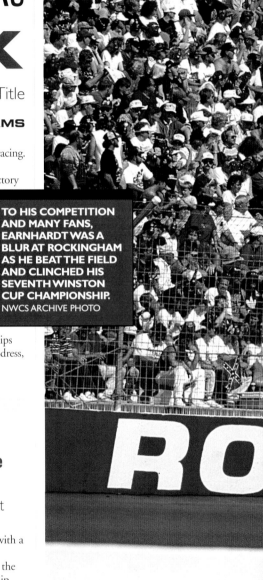

TO HIS COMPETITION AND MANY FANS, EARNHARDT WAS A BLUR AT ROCKINGHAM AS HE BEAT THE FIELD AND CLINCHED HIS SEVENTH WINSTON CUP CHAMPIONSHIP.
NWCS ARCHIVE PHOTO

"It's great to be
No. 1 all the
way around
on race day." —Earnhardt

Earnhardt entered the 492-lap race with a 321-point lead over Rusty Wallace and needed to gain only 50 points to clinch the title. On lap 303, Wallace's championship hopes ended when the engine expired in his Ford and he made that sickening left-hand turn into the garage.

"Well, the championship is over – no doubt about that," said Wallace, who finished 35th and trailed Earnhardt by 448 points with only two races remaining.

"I congratulate Dale Earnhardt on a great job. We just blew too many engines this year. I've got a good engine department and I'm behind 'em. Now it's time to get back and see what's going on."

Earnhardt said he was told Wallace had taken his car behind the wall, but nothing else was said until he won the championship.

"I was just racing like I was before," Earnhardt said. "That's a tough way to go out. I know he's a racer and he's a tough racer and he doesn't want to go out because of broken pieces. There's always next year. That's what you look forward to when the season's over or you end up second. I'm sure it's going to make him more determined."

Even though Earnhardt was the top lap leader, setting the pace on four occasions for 108 laps, he didn't dominate the event and he

IT'S GO TIME.
NWCS ARCHIVE PHOTO

fought off a strong challenge from Rick Mast in the closing laps.

Earnhardt qualified 20th and didn't take the lead for the first time until lap 173. And even then he led for only one lap, giving himself five bonus points. On lap 173, Earnhardt dove to the inside of leader Ken Schrader, inched ahead of him at the scorer's stand located at the fourth turn exit, but Schrader moved back into the No. 1 spot on lap 174 for 21 laps.

Earnhardt didn't lead again until well after the halfway mark. He inherited the top spot

from Terry Labonte on lap 297 when the Hendrick Motorsports driver made a scheduled green-flag pit stop. Earnhardt led only four laps before he made his green-flag stop.

It took Earnhardt 26 laps to move back to the front, but this time it was his crew who put him into the lead. When Hut Stricklin, Dave Marcis and Mark Martin crashed on the backstretch, the leaders pitted during the five-lap caution period. Earnhardt's crew completed its work first and the No. 3 Chevrolet returned to the track in the lead.

This time, Earnhardt led 26 laps, and he only had to deal with Morgan Shepherd and Mast in the final 141 laps. Shepherd set the pace for 33 laps while Mast led 31, but it was all Earnhardt in the final 77.

"I drive a race car 100 percent-plus every race and that's what I intend to do until I retire," Earnhardt said.

With 56 laps remaining, Earnhardt possessed a 2.14-second advantage over Mast, who's still searching for his first career Winston Cup victory. Gradually, Mast began cutting the

dale earnhardt

next 58 laps. The only driver who could stay with Bodine was Mast and, on lap 46, the two had a 3.34-second advantage over third-place Ward Burton.

WHEN YOU'RE GOOD, YOU'RE GOOD.
NWCS ARCHIVE PHOTO

Mast finally snatched the lead from Bodine on lap 61. He led for 25 laps and was in the top spot when he became squirrelly in turns one and two, slipped into the side of Sacks' Ford and carried the two cars up the track and into the wall. The wreck on lap 86 eliminated Sacks, but Mast's crew worked throughout the race on his damaged Ford.

After Mast's crash, the Hendrick Motorsports stable took command of the event for 209 of the next 211 laps. During that span, Labonte led on four occasions for 67 laps, Gordon three times for 101 laps and Ken Schrader three times for 41 laps. The only two drivers to lead a lap each during the Hendrick

deficit. On lap 463, when Earnhardt got held up behind the lapped cars of Dale Jarrett and Darrell Waltrip, Mast pulled to within a fraction of a second of Earnhardt.

With 21 laps remaining, Mast closed in on Earnhardt's bumper as they came upon Lake Speed's Ford. On lap 473, Mast stuck the nose of his car to the inside of Earnhardt's Chevrolet but couldn't complete the pass.

Then, on lap 477, Darrell Waltrip's Chevrolet spun and smacked the fourth-turn wall, bringing out the 10th and final caution period. The leaders pitted, but the fresh tires they received helped Earnhardt more than Mast.

"Rick Mast was catching me and he was going to be a factor. I don't know if I could've held him off," Earnhardt said. "My tires were getting loose going into the third turn and I was not able to negotiate that corner as well as I needed to.

"The fresh tires definitely helped us and getting out of the pits first definitely helped us, too."

Mast said it took him 10 to 15 laps after each restart to get his Ford going.

"I caught Earnhardt and I really thought I might have had a shot at passing him, but you know, his bumper gets mighty wide there at the end," Mast said. "Anyhow, when that caution came out there at the

end I kind of figured it was over then because I wasn't strong enough for the first five or 10 laps to beat him."

When the race restarted with nine laps remaining, Earnhardt was leading, followed by Mast, Shepherd, Labonte and Ricky Rudd. Earnhardt jumped out to about a 10-car length lead, while Rudd quickly dispensed with Labonte to move into fourth.

On the final lap, Mast went high as they exited turn four and attempted to slingshot low on Earnhardt, but came up a car-length short.

"I eased up on that last corner so I wouldn't make a mistake and Rick almost caught me and got by me," Earnhardt said. "I knew he wanted to win. It would have been his first. I wanted to win, too, and win that championship."

Earnhardt's closest call came on lap 86 during a series of green-flag pit stops. The 43-year-old driver had just ducked onto pit road when Mast and Greg Sacks crashed in turn one. He immediately returned to the track, even though he thought he had a tire going down, so he could remain on the lead lap.

While Earnhardt showed his strength in the race's latter stages, the first half belonged to Geoff Bodine, Mast and Jeff Gordon.

Pole position winner Rudd led the first two laps before Bodine shot underneath him on the backstretch and into the lead for the

domination were Dick Trickle on lap 163 and Earnhardt 10 laps later.

Schrader's chance at victory ended on lap 221 when the drive shaft came out of his Chevrolet in turns one and two. That piece of debris resulted in Sterling Marlin, Dave Marcis, Ted Musgrave and Jeremy Mayfield crashing as they exited turn two after one of them ran over the drive shaft.

The incident relegated Schrader to a 32nd-place finish.

Gordon's Chevrolet encountered engine problems on lap 226 while running second. On lap 274, he took it to the garage for repairs and returned to the race on lap 307. Gordon salvaged a 29th-place finish.

Even though there were 10 caution flags for 52 laps, there were two incidents that didn't require a yellow flag. One occurred on lap 69 when Steve Grissom's Chevrolet slid off turn four and onto the grassy frontstretch. Grissom kept the car off the track until the traffic had passed and then returned to the race.

The other occurred on lap 121 when Randy MacDonald spun off turn four after being tagged by John Andretti.

Earnhardt averaged 126.407 mph in the final 500-mile race to be held in October at the track. Next year's event will be 400 miles. The race took 3 hours, 57 minutes and 30 seconds to complete. ∎

Deb Williams looks back on Dale Earnhardt's inspired Rockingham win

For the motorsports community, the 1993 season had been a devastating year with the loss of 1992 Winston Cup champion Alan Kulwicki and young superstar Davey Allison, both in aircraft crashes. But it was the beginning of the 1994 season that sent Dale Earnhardt's heart into a tailspin.

Practice for the season-opening Daytona 500 was less than 30 minutes old when Earnhardt's best friend, Neil Bonnett, was killed in a single-car crash in turns three and four at the 2.5-mile track. Bonnett's death was so devastating to Earnhardt that the Kannapolis, N.C., native never again visited one of the ponds on his Mooresville, N.C., farm where he and Bonnett used to fish.

When Earnhardt captured his sixth NASCAR Winston Cup championship in 1993, talk began immediately about when - not if - he would tie Richard Petty's record of seven championships. Earnhardt wasted little time in answering that question, reeling in his seventh the following year and dedicating the title to Bonnett.

However, Bonnett wasn't the only person remembered on the day Earnhardt claimed his record-tying championship. He dedicated his Rockingham victory - his fourth of the season - to track President Frank Wilson, who had died in August.

> "I drive a race car 100 percent plus every race, and that's what I intend to do until I retire."
> —Earnhardt

All but one of Earnhardt's coveted championships came with team owner Richard Childress, and the second-generation driver claimed his final driving title in typical Earnhardt fashion. He latched on to it before the season ended, taking a 448-point lead over Rusty Wallace with two races remaining.

"Winston Cup racing is my kind of racing. I wouldn't change a thing," Earnhardt said that day.

And Rockingham was Earnhardt's kind of track. Opened in 1965, the 1.017-mile facility boasted a surface that was rough on tires because of the sand in the region, and one's ability to succeed on it rested squarely on the driver's shoulders, not aerodynamics. To reach victory lane at the track, it meant one didn't flinch at close-quarter racing, often going two wide on worn, slick tires. It was the type of racing where Earnhardt excelled and where he could often be intimidating to his fellow competitors.

Throughout his racing career, Earnhardt never lost his burning desire to win. He always remained "hungry" no matter the amount of his monetary wealth, and it was that hunger to excel, to be the best at whatever he did that made him such an exciting racer.

"I drive a race car 100 percent-plus every race, and that's what I intend to do until I retire," Earnhardt said after collecting his seventh championship in the track's final 500-mile October race.

And he remained true to his word. ■

—Deb Williams
Editor
NASCAR Scene

Same Story, Different Year

Earnhardt Goes From Back To Front To Claim Clash Win No. 6

By STEVE WAID

I t's an all-too-familiar scenario. But obviously, it hasn't played itself out just yet.

Yep, Dale Earnhardt won the Busch Clash. Yep, he did it by blasting his way from the rear of the field to the front of the race's second 10-lap segment. Then, on the last lap, he seemed to cast a spell over challengers Sterling Marlin, Bill Elliott and Jeff Gordon, none of whom made a move and simply followed him across the finish line.

It was the sixth career Busch Clash win for Earnhardt in only nine starts, making him easily the winningest driver in the special race for Busch Pole winners. Earnhardt's other victories came in 1980, 1986, 1988, 1991 and 1993.

In '91 and '93, Earnhardt swept both segments of the Clash, each time coming from the back of an inverted start for the final 10 circuits to win. In his RCR Enterprises Chevrolet, he almost did the same thing in the 17th edition of the race.

He started ninth after the inverted start, took the lead after just a lap and a quarter and was in control thereafter. Sterling Marlin came home second in the Morgan-McClure Chevrolet, followed by Bill Elliott in the Elliot-Hardy Ford, Jeff Gordon in the Hendrick Motorsports Chevrolet and Todd Bodine in the Butch Mock Motorsports Ford.

Earnhardt was the star of a particularly strong showing by Chevrolet's new Monte Carlo, which took the top three positions after the first segment – with Gordon the winner – and three of the top four in the second.

"It was a great day for us," Earnhardt said, "The Monte Carlo did a super job. This is the result of all the hard work that Neil (Bonnett) and all the others did on the car a year and a half, two years ago. Neil's legacy lives on.

TAYLOR EARNHARDT KNOWS HER DADDY'S #1. NWCS ARCHIVE PHOTO

"All the hard work and testing we did during the winter paid off. We won the outside pole for the Daytona 500 and now we've won the Busch Clash. It's a great introduction for the new Chevrolet."

For Earnhardt, it was very nearly a bust. Starting second in the first segment by virtue of the draw, he wasted no time taking first place away from polesitter Geoff Bodine, whom he passed in the first turn on the first lap.

By the third lap, Gordon and Marlin were on Earnhardt's rear bumper and would remain there at the start of the 10th lap, the last before the race would be stopped to invert the field.

Earnhardt got loose in the second turn and that allowed Gordon and Marlin to pull by, clearing Earnhardt in the third turn.

"Whoever got up front was going to **win the race** and it looked like 94 (Elliott) wasn't handling," Marlin said.

"I wrecked but didn't crash over there in the second turn," said Earnhardt, who earned $57,000 for his victory. "I was lucky to make it back to the finish line alive.

"Jeff and Sterling got under me and did a good job of getting by me."

"I didn't want to win the first segment but Dale got real loose off turn two and I had to go by him," Gordon said. "He tried to keep me from going by and we bumped. I think he wanted to win 'em both.

"I wanted to start ahead of him in the second segment and hope he'd push me to the front. Nobody was going to pass him. I was surprised I got by in the first half."

Gordon held off Marlin to win the first segment and earn $25,000. Earnhardt held on for third, followed by Elliott and Ford-driving Ted Musgrave.

The only accident of the race occurred on the first lap of the first segment. Apparently nudged in the rear by Loy Allen's Ford, the Pontiac of Greg Sacks was shoved into Mark Martin's Ford and then slammed into the wall in the third turn. Martin could not regain control of his car and spun in the fourth turn.

Sacks and Martin retired from the race, while Allen, after several pit stops, lost two laps and finished 14th in the first segment.

On the fourth lap, Todd Bodine made a great save of his Ford after it was nudged to the inside of the front trioval after contact with Jimmy Spencer. He, Spencer and Geoff Bodine were running three abreast at the time.

Allen was placed at the rear of the field for the start of the second segment, as was Busch Series champion David Green, who was experiencing engine problems in his

STERLING MARLIN AND BILL ELLIOTT CHASE EARNHARDT ACROSS THE FINISH LINE. NWCS ARCHIVE PHOTO

Ken Schrader-owned Chevrolet Lumina.

Earnhardt started ninth, Elliott 10th, Gordon 11th and Marlin 12th.

"We changed four tires and worked on the rear spoiler during our pit stop," said Earnhardt of the allowed pit stop between segments. "We thought that would make the car good for the second segment. We also put some cool water in the radiator so we could tape up the car some more and gain a tick of speed."

Nearly everyone figured Earnhardt, Marlin and Gordon would hook up in an all-Chevrolet draft and try to work their way to the front quickly. Earnhardt and Marlin locked up almost immediately, but Elliott tagged along and kept Gordon behind him.

"I knew that drafting with Sterling would help me go to the front," Earnhardt said. "I felt being at the front at the end of the segment was where I wanted to be. I didn't want

to have to try to draft around someone on the last lap."

With Marlin in tow, Earnhardt snatched the lead away from Ricky Rudd going into the first turn on the second lap. Then the race settled into an Earnhardt-Marlin-Elliott-Gordon train and remained that way until the checkered flag.

"Whoever got up front was going to win the race and it looked like 94 (Elliott) wasn't handling," Marlin said. "He couldn't help me down the back straight and that's where I wanted to pass Dale on the last lap. He just couldn't get up to me to give me the push in the draft." Marlin earned $42,500.

"I got on it when I thought I should at the start of the second segment but it wasn't soon enough," Gordon said. "Those other guys got between me and Earnhardt. I don't know. It might have ended up the same way if I'd been right there. It's just one of those deals."

Earnhardt, who averaged 188.482 mph in a race he led for 18 of 20 laps, has now earned $445,500 in his nine Busch Clash starts.

"The race just suits us," he said. "It suits me, the team and Richard Childress. I told Richard it was going to be tough to draft back through that pack but he said, 'Try to lead every lap if you can.' So that's what I did."

Nope. Nothing new here. ■

No. 3 Makes It
Six Straight

Earnhardt, New Monte Carlo Impressive In Qualifier

By TOM STINSON

Chevy wanted to test its new Monte Carlo in Daytona's Twin 125-mile qualifying races but, unfortunately, Dale Earnhardt was in one of 'em. Not that Earnhardt can't tell anybody about anything when it comes to a stock car, it's just that he sort of spoils the bell curve when it comes to Twin 125-mile qualifying races.

You see, Earnhardt won Twin 125s in the old Monte Carlo, he won 'em in the Lumina and, now, he's winning 'em in the new Monte Carlo. The guy just wins Twin 125s period, no matter what car he's driving.

Earnhardt won his sixth straight Daytona qualifier, a streak that spans the five-year life of the Chevrolet Lumina and now the debut of the new Monte Carlo. Earnhardt also has eight career Twin 125 wins, from the original Monte Carlo in 1986 to a Ford in 1983.

The true test seems to be what Earnhardt can't use to win a Twin 125. A Cadillac? Pacer? Fisher-Price Big Wheel?

OK, actually Chevrolet learned loads about its new choice of race car, particularly with Earnhardt and Jeff Gordon seemingly putting their Monte Carlos wherever they darned well pleased during the second Daytona 500 qualifying race. Gordon chased Earnhardt for the final nine laps before finishing second by 0.28 second.

Ford's Mark Martin, Todd Bodine, Bill Elliott and Ted Musgrave followed Chevy's lead pair across the line, with Ricky Craven, Lake Speed Ricky Rudd and Bobby Labonte rounding out the top 10.

None of those, though, appeared to have much for Earnhardt and his new Monte Carlo, at least not in the 125-mile tune up. So, after Earnhardt dominated yet another qualifier in yet another type of car, what could anybody really learn from the second Twin 125?

"It tells you I know how to set up a car for the 125," Earnhardt said with a smile, the same kind of smile he sports every Thursday during Daytona's Speedweeks – or at least the last six Thursdays during Daytona's Speedweeks.

Earnhardt started from the pole and, after Robert Pressley, Speed, Morgan Shepherd and Martin all swapped the lead in the race's first 20 laps, he dipped past Martin on lap 21 and controlled the race from there. Jim Sauter led a couple laps (34-35) after the leaders pitted under caution, but Earnhardt moved right back to the point once the green flag flew. In all, he led 28 of the race's 50 laps, including all but the caution-flag two of the final 30.

> "I hope Earnhardt graduates soon, because **he's taken Jeff to school** enough here at Daytona." —Ray Evernham

It was just a typical Twin 125, really, or just a typical one with Earnhardt.

"I've been real fortunate to be with good race teams," Earnhardt said in explaining his streak, which has come solely with the RCR Enterprises team. "The work they put into the cars and the focus they put into the races is the difference. I feel like they do a good job, and I can go out there and drive the car."

Earnhardt did have to charge from sixth following the pit stops on lap 34 – it took him three-quarters of a lap – and then had to hold off several challenges by first Martin and then Gordon.

"It wasn't that easy of a drive," Earnhardt said, almost sounding convincing. "It was a competitive race, and we had to come back by several cars there and Jeff was drafting us. It wasn't that easy of a race. Having Jeff behind and not knowing where he might try to draft by you, it's competitive out there."

Earnhardt's bumper – a rear end that, when viewed from behind, rivals that of Rush Limbaugh – kept Gordon at bay, the 23-year-old said.

"If we wanted to wreck, we could have wrecked very easily," Gordon said. "Earnhardt would wreck himself to keep you from going by him. He'll squeeze you anyway he can to get it out of you. You don't want Earnhardt to be leading with five laps to go."

Gordon's crew chief, Ray Evernham, added: "I hope Earnhardt graduates soon, because he's taken Jeff to school enough here at Daytona."

Martin, who clearly had the strongest Ford in the 32-car field, said lack of drafting partners kept him from staying at the front.

"We just couldn't get a lot of help with the draft," said Martin, who led 13 laps. "I can drive just about anywhere I need to go on the race track, but it's going to take more than one car to be a winner on this track."

The top 15 finishers advanced to the 500, with Derrike Cope, Randy LaJoie, Ben Hess, Jeff Burton and Shepherd rounding out the transfer spots.

Three of the race's four cautions knocked Winston Cup regulars from the 500 field.

Jimmy Spencer and Billy Standridge got together on lap 15, collecting Loy Allen. That knocked both Spencer and Standridge from the big race. Chad Little's single-car crash on lap 32 bumped him from the 500 field, and Phil Barkdoll's crash on lap 42 collected Sauter, Phil Parsons and Greg Sacks. Of that bunch, only Parsons was able to make the 500 field.

Which, once the 500 lineup was filled, left only one question – that one about the return of the Monte Carlo and, although Earnhardt won the qualifier like he always does, how it performs in race conditions.

"The car worked just great," Earnhardt said. "Chevrolet, with this aerodynamic package they've got on this Monte Carlo, they've done a great job. The car's balanced and really felt good today.

"We sort of fine-tuned it this morning and did a few little changes on it, and the car handled great. It didn't give a bit there when Gordon was trying to make me loose."

Like any part Earnhardt ever gives in the Twin 125s. ∎

EARNHARDT HOISTS HIS SIXTH-STRAIGHT GATORADE 125-MILE QUALIFIER TROPHY.
NWCS ARCHIVE PHOTO

THE FIRST WIN OF THE YEAR FEELS GOOD IN EARNHARDT'S HANDS.
NWCS ARCHIVE PHOTO

Finally,
It's Earnhardt's Turn

Consistency Pays Off With First Victory Of Season

By STEVE WAID

It was something of a time bomb – you heard it ticking and you knew sooner or later it was going to explode. The only question was when?

For Dale Earnhardt, the time came in the First Union 400. After a series of consistently high finishes that indicated a victory was easily within his grasp, the driver of the RCR Enterprises Chevrolet exploded with a runaway win over Jeff Gordon.

Earnhardt led 227 of the race's 400 laps around the 0.625-mile North Wilkesboro layout and beat Gordon to the checkered flag by 13.48 seconds, or nearly two-thirds of a lap. The victory was the 64th of Earnhardt's career and it gave Chevrolet its seventh consecutive win of the 1995 campaign.

"I know people are getting sick of seeing Chevys win, but these are good race cars," Earnhardt said of the Monte Carlo, which returned to Winston Cup racing this year. "For us, we've been right there every race and we got it all right today. Everything went right for us. Consistency counts. We knew if we kept at it, we'd get our win and those (Winston Cup) points one by one."

Consistency has been the pattern for Earnhardt this year, with only one finish out of the top four in seven races. Coming into North Wilkesboro, he had finished second three times, third once and fourth once before being involved in a crash in the April 2 Food City 500 at Bristol, Tenn., and falling to a 25th-place finish.

Despite not showing a victory until the First Union 400, Earnhardt's record was good enough to keep him at No. 1 in the Winston Cup point standings. He held a 17-point lead over Sterling Marlin when the race started and expanded that to 56 (1,113-1,077) when it was finished. Marlin finished seventh, one lap down in the Morgan-McClure Motorsports Chevrolet.

"We have been close all year long and after today, it really looks good for now and for the future," Earnhardt said. "We need to keep taking 'em one by one, race by race."

Because of the rough track surface at North Wilkesboro, tire wear figured to play a prominent part in the race. On fresh rubber, drivers were fast – and then speeds dropped drastically as the gritty asphalt did its work.

Earnhardt seemed relatively unaffected by all that. Where green-flag pit stops were usually conducted after 50-55 laps, he made his last one on lap 314, retook the lead on lap 317 and led the rest of the way.

Prior to the series of pit stops, Earnhardt snatched the lead from Gordon, already a winner of three races this season, on lap 290.

EARNHARDT
NOT ONLY WINS,
BUT INTERVIEWS
HIMSELF.
NWCS ARCHIVE PHOTO

On lap 297, Mark Martin moved ahead of Gordon into second place.

On lap 314, Gordon and Earnhardt pitted. Martin followed one lap later, elevating Kyle Petty into the lead.

But on worn tires, Petty – who was ill and would later retire from the race – was no match for the others. Earnhardt breezed by on lap 317 with Gordon and Martin in tow.

Earnhardt began to pull away. By lap 340, his lead over Gordon was 7.78 seconds. Thirty laps later, it was up to 10.25 seconds.

"Today, the car was good, the driver used his head and the tires worked in our favor," Earnhardt said. "We had to save the tires. You couldn't punish 'em. Say you had to race lapped cars or you raced another lead car for position. That would cost you.

Asked how it felt to finally get the better of Gordon, Earnhardt said with a chuckle:
"Amazing! We beat Wonder Boy!"

"I raced Rusty (Wallace) hard one time there and I punished the tires. They went away. After that, we put fresh tires on and I took care of 'em. You have to make them work for you."

Asked how it felt to finally get the better of Gordon, Earnhardt said with a chuckle: "Amazing! We beat Wonder Boy! Really, he's just another driver…there's no problem.

"Racing the track, saving the tires and judging the pit periods – that was what won me the race. Other drivers were in the equation, but they weren't the factors why I won the race."

Even Gordon, who knows what it is like to dominate a race, admitted there was nothing he could do with Earnhardt. In fact, during the closing laps he found himself scrapping with Martin to preserve second place.

"This was something we just did not anticipate," said Gordon, who started from the pole and led five times for 95 laps. "We never thought we could start from the pole and finish second. We had a great battle with Mark there at the end, but I'm sorry we couldn't make a race out of it with Dale. He just had us covered."

Wallace finished fourth behind the trio of Earnhardt, Gordon and Martin. Steve Grissom recorded a career-high fifth, followed by Ted Musgrave, Marlin, Rick Mast, Brett Bodine and Darrell Waltrip in the top 10. ■

THERE AREN'T MANY 'FIRSTS' LEFT FOR EARNHARDT, BUT WINNING HIS FIRST-EVER ROAD COURSE EVENT IS ONE WORTH CELEBRATING.
NWCS ARCHIVE PHOTO

Earnhardt
Snatches A Career First

Defending Winston Cup Champion Passes Dominant Martin To Earn Road-Course Win

By **STEVE WAID**

Everybody thought this one belonged to Mark Martin, and rightly so.

After all, the driver of the Roush Racing Ford had taken the lead on lap six of the 74-lap Save Mart Supermarkets 300 and was hardly challenged as the event wound to its conclusion.

But instead of a ho-hum tour around the 2.52-mile, 11-turn road course for Martin, the race evolved into something decidedly more dramatic. On lap 73, after several laps of dogged pursuit, Dale Earnhardt took advantage of Martin's slip in a patch of grease in the sweeping sixth turn to take the lead.

From there, Earnhardt powered his RCR Enterprises Chevrolet to the checkered flag to earn his first victory on a road course in his 16-year career, which now spans 490 starts.

"Mark just got into some oil over there in the turn and I got past him," said an elated Earnhardt. "After that, I just wanted to be very careful and not get into trouble, because it was a greasy race track out there.

"We had a car that was very consistent here and that is what we wanted. I could use what I wanted from the car when I wanted it and I can't thank the guys on the crew enough for giving me what I needed."

The victory was the second of the season for Earnhardt, who also won at North Wilkesboro, N.C., in April - the 65th of his career. It was also his 36th career start on a road course with his previous best finish being second, three times.

Earnhardt maintained his lead in the Winston Cup point standings, breaking out of a tie with Jeff Gordon. Earnhardt has 1,494 points, just nine more than Martin, who moved into second place. Gordon, who finished third in the Save Mart Supermarkets 300, fell to third in the points, 15 behind Earnhardt.

Oddly enough, Richard Childress, Earnhardt's team owner, was not around to see his driver score the victory. Seems he was in Africa on a safari.

"Richard told me that I would probably win my first road course race since he was in Africa and wouldn't be around to see it," said Earnhardt, who received $74,860 for the victory. "Well, I got news for him. He's going to Africa instead of the Daytona 500."

Earnhardt has never won the Winston Cup circuit's premier event.

"It's been a goal for me to win on a road course and the Daytona 500," Earnhardt said. "Some things never come to you. But now we've got the road-course win, so we've got that out of the way."

But it didn't come easy. In fact, after pole winner Ricky Rudd gave up his lead after five laps – allowing Martin to whip by him after Rudd missed a shift coming out of turn 11 – the race quickly settled into a Sunday drive for Martin.

The only times Martin surrendered his advantage came when he pitted under green. Following his last pit stop on lap 51, Martin led a trio of himself, Earnhardt and Gordon, all of whom had a comfortable cushion over fourth-place runner Rusty Wallace.

A full-course yellow came out on lap 57 after Hut Stricklin blew an engine in his King Racing Ford. The running order didn't change, it merely tightened when the green flag few on lap 61.

It took less than a lap for another yellow flag to be thrown, and it was for a doozy of a wreck among Wallace, Dale Jarrett and Davy Jones. The three spun in the seventh turn and

as a result, Jarrett's Ford came to rest on its right side, eventually to be put back on all four wheels through the efforts of track workers.

Wallace went back to the pits to have sheet metal pulled away from his tires and then returned to the race.

Through all of this, Earnhardt kept his runner-up position, although most of the time, it seemed he was no match for Martin.

"I was just trying to run smooth and consistent," he said. "There were times when the 2 (Wallace) and the 24 (Gordon) would pressure me and that's when I would lose some of what I had. And when I tried to pressure Mark, I would lose it, too.

"We had worked on the shocks and the carburetor before the race, and when it started we seemed to have enough for everybody but Mark. We changed the air pressure a few times and it got better and better. My job was to take the right lines and make sure I stayed on the asphalt."

The race restarted on lap 66 with 29 cars on the lead lap. However, this time Martin could not find the dominance he had held earlier. Earnhardt maintained the pressure, keeping it up for several laps while third-place Gordon began to fall off the pace.

Then, on lap 73, it happened. In the sixth turn of the track area called "The Carousel," Martin slipped high and Earnhardt dove low, taking the lead.

"I smelled rear end grease around turns three, four or five – I don't know which – and I saw a streak of it in turn six when I was on the crest of the hill," Earnhardt said. "My spotter said he thought he saw oil in the turn and there was a car smoking up ahead.

"I moved to the outside and crossed the streak rather than run through it. Mark ran through it and that caused him to slide out. I got inside him and got past him."

After that, Earnhardt's only goal was not to make a mistake and return the lead to Martin.

"I was thinking I had to make a good line and stay on the racing surface and stay out of any oil," Earnhardt said. "I was extra careful in a couple of places and Mark came back on me, but I was able to put a few yards on him."

Asked if he felt he could have caught Martin without the presence of grease on the track, Earnhardt said he would have done all he could to win.

"I was going to be on his back bumper and alongside him if I could," Earnhardt said. Then he added with a smile:

"I was going to race him hard and clean. And by clean, I mean I wasn't going to knock him off the race track…Now why did I say that?

"Mark ran with me at Talladega (on April 30) and he deserved to win that race. He

deserved to win this one, too, but we were there when he made the mistake."

Rudd followed the trio of Earnhardt, Martin and Gordon in fourth, suitably recovered from transmission problems in his Ford. Fifth went to Terry Labonte in a Hendrick Chevrolet while Ted Musgrave finished sixth in a Roush Racing Ford. Sterling Marlin took seventh in the Morgan-McClure Chevrolet while Todd Bodine was eighth in the Butch Mock Motorsports Ford, Ken Schrader was ninth in the Hendrick Chevrolet and Michael Waltrip completed the top 10 in the Bahari Racing Pontiac.

"I think **I enjoy wins more now** in my career than I did earlier."
—Earnhardt

While Wallace ran as high as third, he pitted under the race's fourth caution period – caused by Stricklin's engine problems – along with Jarrett, and thus was put in the wrong place at the wrong time. His crash with Jarrett and Jones in the seventh turn helped relegate him to 20th place.

It was a circumstance similar to Earnhardt's a week ago at Talladega, where he was in the wrong place at the wrong time. A last-lap altercation with Morgan Shepherd sent him from a possible third-place finish to 21st. That resulted in the tie with Gordon for first place in the point standings coming into Sears Point.

"What happened last week just happened last week," answered Earnhardt when asked if his Sonoma victory made up for the disappointing Talladega finish. "It is over and done with. That is the way this team treats it. We race one week and go on to the next race."

As for road racing, Earnhardt admits he feels somewhat vindicated.

"I have always thought I was a good road racer," he said. "I've won poles here and at Watkins Glen (the other road course on the Winston Cup circuit). I've had good cars here, too. But I never seemed to be around at the finish. I would tear up transmissions or rear ends or something.

"But I don't really think this win is any more special than any other. They are all special. I think I enjoy wins more now in my career than I did earlier. They just don't seem to come quick enough for me. But I consider myself fortunate to be able to have some wins after all these years in racing."

And with this one, perhaps all that is left is the big one in Daytona. ■

dale earnhardt

EARNHART
LIKES
HOLDING
THE BIG
CHECKS.
NWCS ARCHIVE
PHOTO

No. 000001

NET AMOUNT

$200,000.00

Dale Takes Second-Ever
Brickyard

Earnhardt Beats Old Rival To Gain Indy Glory

By STEVE WAID

The Brickyard 400 is a new race on the Winston Cup circuit, but its exciting finish had an old, familiar ring to it.

Dale Earnhardt, the defending Winston Cup champion whose name has recently dropped out of the headlines as Jeff Gordon has become the darling of the stock car world, held off old rival Rusty Wallace – another whose fortunes have not been good lately – and a charging Dale Jarrett to win the second running of the Brickyard 400.

In a thrilling conclusion to what was an extraordinarily long day at the 2.5-mile Indianapolis oval, Earnhardt beat Wallace to the checkered flag by 0.426 second to win his third race of the season and his first since he won on the road course at Sears Point Raceway in early May.

Since then, Earnhardt's best run had been a third in the Pepsi 400 at Daytona Beach, Fla. He had suffered three finishes of 20th or worse and drifted as far back as fourth in the Winston Cup point standings, which he led through much of the first six months of the season. After the Dover, Del., race in June, he was atop the standings by 100 points, but he was in third place, 146 points behind Gordon, when the Indy race began.

The Brickyard 400 was one race Earnhardt desperately wanted to win, especially after he whacked the first-turn wall on the first lap of last year's race and ultimately had to settle for a fifth-place finish.

The only other race as coveted by Earnhardt is the Daytona 500, which he has never won.

"This is a neat deal," an excited Earnhardt said from victory lane. "I've never won the Daytona 500, but the Brickyard 400 is a special race. It's right next to Daytona, so I'll take it. Hey, only two of us have won this race."

Earnhardt was referring to Gordon, the winner of the inaugural Indy race who has gone on to win five times this year and take the lead in the point standings – and be something of a thorn in Earnhardt's side.

"I can't thank (team owner) Richard Childress and all the guys back in the shop enough," said Earnhardt, who now has 66 career victories. "We put a new Chevrolet together for this race and got in only about 40 laps of practice, and then we go out and win.

"We made changes to the car all week and we made changes to it this morning, to tell the truth. But our car and crew are hard to beat when they're on, and they were on today."

> "Well, it's not as much (money) as Jeff (Gordon) won last year, so **I guess I can't afford to go to Disneyland,"** Earnhardt said. "I guess I'll have to go to Opryland."

When the day began, it appeared the race was certain to be rained out. The residue of Hurricane Erin enveloped Indianapolis and the race's planned starting time of 1:15 p.m. EDT came and went with fans, officials, crewmen and drivers seeking shelter from the weather.

As bleak as the prospects were, by 4:25 p.m. the green flag fell, with many fans who had departed speedway grounds scrambling to return to their seats. The last time a race was delayed at Indianapolis came in 1991, when the Indianapolis 500 started 55 minutes late.

Pole winner Gordon, who took qualifying honors on Aug. 3 before the second round of time trials was rained out, quickly pulled away. In his bid to win a second straight Brickyard 400, he led until lap 31, when he pitted. He obviously didn't know it at the time, but he would lead only four more laps.

The race was then dominated by some of NASCAR's top veterans. Bill Elliott, another driver whose fortunes haven't been the best lately, led the majority of laps as the first 100 circuits of the 160-lapper were completed.

On lap 109, Wallace took the lead when he passed Gordon's Hendrick Chevrolet in the first turn. Wallace would lead through lap 128, when he pitted under green. Earnhardt had pitted a lap earlier. He was thus able to take track position ahead of Wallace, whose cause was not helped when he was forced to check up on pit road after Joe Nemechek cut in front of Rich Bickle and clipped Bickle's Pontiac.

During a series of green-flag stops, John Andretti inherited the lead on lap 130.

Then, on lap 132, the first caution period of the race was created when Jeff Burton spun coming out of the second turn in front of Earnhardt, who escaped. Burton's car then crossed Wallace's path and nearly hit him.

Andretti pitted and the quick work done earlier by Earnhardt's RCR Enterprises put the seven-time Winston Cup champion in front when the green flag fell on lap 137. Wallace was second, followed by Elliott, Jarrett and Gordon.

"That last stop was the key," Earnhardt said. "We got out in front of Rusty and that was the key to the win. When the race restarted, I had all the clean air out front."

Earnhardt would not give up his lead throughout the final 27 laps. Wallace tried hard to overtake him – and on occasion seemed to be in position to do so – but could not.

"At the end, I put pressure on myself to drive hard, be consistent and not make a mistake," Earnhardt said. "I was out front with the clean air and that worked well for me. I wasn't worried about Rusty, although if he got under me he would be trouble. But he had to be the one to make a move and do whatever he could do. I just had to stay consistent. I was going to drive my line and keep my line and not worry about it."

Meanwhile, Jarrett, who had started 26th, used the handling and power of his Ford to its best advantage. He chased Elliott down and then passed him on lap 149 in the third turn to take third place.

The finish evolved into an Earnhardt-Wallace-Jarrett chase. By lap 154, they had built a substantial lead over fourth-place Elliott, who was having to lift a sticking brake pedal with his foot.

Earnhardt withstood the challenge.

"I was better out front than I was behind," Earnhardt said. "When I got behind, it pushed. It just wouldn't go as good. When I got out front, it was real good. That's where I

TERESA TAKES A MOMENT TO CONGRATULATE DALE.
NWCS ARCHIVE PHOTO

wanted to be.

"We beat 'em out on that last green-flag stop, so we had track position when that caution period started. The 8 car (Burton) wrecked in front of us. He clipped me a little bit and sort of spun me a little bit and got me real loose, but we recovered from that. And so, we were out front. We had the track position."

Wallace, who has won only once this year – after compiling 18 victories in 1993-94 – scored his best finish since his victory at Martinsville, Va., in April.

Jarrett, another driver whose fortunes were sour until he won at Pocono three races ago, kept his streak going. He now has a victory, a runner-up finish and a third-place run in the last three events. And Elliott's fourth-place finish was his best of the season.

Martin finished fifth, followed by Gordon, Sterling Marlin, Rick Mast, Bobby Labonte and Morgan Shepherd.

Gordon held on to first place in the point standings. He has 2,860 points, 82 more than Marlin. Earnhardt remained third, now 121 points behind.

By being the points leader after the Indy race, Gordon collected a $100,000 bonus for the second time this year. The first came after

the Winston Select 500 at Talladega, Ala., in April. His earnings for the race totaled $299,200.

For winning, Earnhardt took home $565,600, just a little less than Gordon received last year.

"Well, it's not as much as Jeff won last year, so I guess I can't afford to go to Disneyland," Earnhardt said. "I guess I'll have to go to Opryland."

Earnhardt put much more emphasis on the victory than could be provided by money alone.

First, he won at Indy.

"To come here and to race here is a big honor and experience," he said. "And to finish fifth in the first race was a great accomplishment as far as I was concerned.

"But to win at the same track where a Rick Mears, or the Unsers or all those other great names have won, to have your name in the same group of names of drivers who have won an Indy 500 or a Brickyard 400, that is pretty impressive."

And to once again have your name on everyone's lips has its merits, too, although Earnhardt is not about to criticize Gordon – the driver who has clearly stolen the Winston Cup thunder in 1995.

"Do you think I need to reestablish myself?" he responded when asked if his Indy victory did just that. "Do you think people have forgotten me? I don't think I need to reestablish myself. I just needed to win again.

"I'm not going to take anything away from Jeff, his talents or his team. His future is bright. He's a great racer who is due all the press and the reputation he's got. But there have been a lot of others who have come along before him."

The victory also provided Earnhardt with a forum to declare that he and his team are not ready to be counted out, despite the downward shift in the point standings or attention given anyone else.

"I've overheard comments that the 3 team is under pressure and is pulling at each other while the 24 team (Gordon's) is laid back," Earnhardt said. "Our guys are confident and hard-working. As a team they pull together and don't give up. They don't feel under pressure even when we're behind Gordon and Marlin in points.

"You're not going to beat us by talking about us. You've got to beat us on the track."

And on a long day at Indianapolis, no one could do that. ■

Steve Waid remembers Dale Earnhardt's victory in the 1995 Brickyard 400

Dale Earnhardt's victory in the Brickyard 400 culminated, for him, a dream that began two years earlier.

No one had to tell Earnhardt, nor any other Winston Cup driver, about the mystique of Indianapolis Motor Speedway. When it came to motor racing, it was hallowed ground. But for years, it was ground on which NASCAR could not trod. Despite efforts by the sanctioning body to open the grip the open-wheel cars had at Indy in the form of the Indianapolis 500, they always failed.

In 1992, rumblings began that NASCAR had come to an agreement with Indy's leader, Tony George, to stage a race. That year, tire tests were conducted, and once they were completed, it was announced that the inaugural Brickyard 400 Winston Cup race would be held in August of 1994.

Earnhardt joined several other drivers at the test. They were welcomed with open arms by fans eager to see the stock cars take on the 2.5-mile Indy track.

No one was more excited than Earnhardt. As the time came for the tests to begin, he was the first driver on pit road. He had made it clear he was going to be the first Winston Cup driver to hit the track - and he was. "I've never seen him so excited," said team owner Richard Childress.

Naturally, Earnhardt was pegged as a pre-race favorite when the first Brickyard 400 rolled around in '94. Although he ran well, the victory was claimed by Jeff Gordon, who was raised in Pittsboro, Ind., located not far from Indy.

> "I've never seen him so excited,"
> —Richard Childress

In 1995, Earnhardt found himself in a battle for the Winston Cup championship with - you guessed it - Gordon.

Certainly his victory in the Brickyard 400 helped Earnhardt's cause. He left Indy in third place in the point standings, 121 points behind Gordon.

Earnhardt then made a strong season-closing effort to wrest the title from Gordon's hands. He piled up 10 consecutive top-nine finishes, including seven top-three finishes in the string. He won at Martinsville in August and domi-nated the season finale at Atlanta.

At Atlanta, Earnhardt not only won, but he led the most laps. It wasn't enough. Even though Gordon ran poorly and wound up in 32nd place, 14 laps behind Earnhardt, it was good enough to give Gordon his first Winston Cup title.

Earnhardt had done all he could from Indy to the end of the season.

Interestingly, a couple of poor finishes at Michigan Speedway were acknowledged to be the reasons why he couldn't claim a record eighth title. In June and again in August at Michigan, Earnhardt finished 35th. Gordon, meanwhile, finished second and third. That was a swing of 234 points in Gordon's favor.

When the season ended, Earnhardt lost the title to Gordon by a mere 34 points.

As disappointing as that was for Earnhardt, he was buoyed by his Indy victory. For years afterward, when he spoke of the loss of the '95 championship, he always added that he had won at Indianapolis that year. He won on hallowed ground, and no one could take that away from him. ■

—Steve Waid
VP Editorial Development
NASCAR Scene and Illustrated

EARNHARDT CELEBRATES THE WIN WITH MARTINSVILLE TRACK PRESIDENT, CLAY CAMPBELL. NWCS ARCHIVE PHOTO

Earnhardt Earns
Relaxing
Martinsville Win

Gordon Maintains Large Lead In Point Standings

By DEB WILLIAMS

For much of the Goody's 500, Dale Earnhardt appeared to make a mockery of the competition.

The seven-time Winston Cup champion often used just his left hand while resting his right on the roll cage to maneuver his Chevrolet through the field. He dominated the 500-lap race on the 0.526-mile Martinsville Speedway, leading six times for 251 laps, including the final nine.

And when asked why he often drove with just one hand during the race, he simply grinned and remarked, "I was just relaxing.

"I had the CD on and my foot propped up on the dash," he joked after claiming his fourth win this season and the 67th of his Winston Cup career. "Brooks and Dunn was on the CD player. I played a little Alabama, too. I'm in a hurry and I don't know why."

On a more serious note, Earnhardt said his car was simply really good and he was relaxed.

With the victory that netted him $78,150, Earnhardt gained 34 points on leader Jeff Gordon in the Winston Cup title battle with five races remaining. Gordon, who fought an ill-handling race car throughout the event and was never in contention for the win, finished seventh and holds a 275-point lead.

"Our car had no forward bite at all, but it was looking a lot worse there a couple of times than it actually ended up," Gordon said about his new car. "We feel fortunate to finish seventh. As bad of a day as we had, we can't complain too much.

"We just couldn't dial it in no matter what we did. I was bouncing going in and spinning coming out. Ray Evernham (crew chief) did everything he could do, but we just couldn't hit it."

Evernham described his team's performance as "embarrassing."

"We were saved by cautions and guys were taken out in front of us. We were just junk, so I feel pretty embarrassed," Evernham said. "We'd planned to run the same car next week at North Wilkesboro, but we're not going to now. We're going back to the car that finished second at North Wilkesboro in the spring. We won't run any new cars now for the rest of the year. Our new cars will be parked."

Even though there were 16 lead changes among eight drivers, the race was basically a three-way battle among Earnhardt, Rusty Wallace and Terry Labonte.

Wallace gambled during the ninth caution period and didn't pit on lap 464 with the rest of the lead-lap cars. Earnhardt pitted, as did Labonte, and took on right-side tires. When the race restarted, Wallace was leading, followed by Earnhardt, Bobby Hamilton, Labonte and Derrike Cope in the top five.

"We took on two tires on that last stop and Rusty didn't take on any," Earnhardt said after his sixth Martinsville victory and his fourth in the fall event. "It took a couple of laps for me to get my tires worked in and once I did, I was able to come on to him."

The final caution period began on lap 475 after Cope and Dale Jarrett spun in turns three and four while battling for fifth position. No one pitted and when the race restarted on lap 480 Wallace was still leading, Earnhardt was second and Labonte was fourth. It took Earnhardt until lap 492 to finally slip to the inside of Wallace in turn three and then move into the lead when Wallace slid high as they exited turn four.

"He started slipping and it was just a matter of time until I could get by him," Earnhardt said. "I just waited until he slipped, I got under him and eased on by him. I just kept the car smooth from there on in. I saved my brakes; saved my car pretty much all day. It worked out. If Terry had gotten by Rusty and come up there to race us, I would have been ready for him. I don't know if I could have held him off."

While Earnhardt coasted the final nine laps, Labonte and Wallace fought for second, a battle Labonte barely won at the checkered flag.

"We had problems with the ratchet," said Labonte, who drifted high in turn one on lap 412 when the race restarted after the eighth of 10 caution periods ended. "On that one restart there when I was behind Dale and I went way back, I thought I had a broken axle or drive-plate."

Despite Labonte's problems, Earnhardt cited the Hendrick Motorsports Chevrolet as the strongest car at the race's end.

"I had the CD on and
my foot propped up on the dash."
—Earnhardt on his one-handed driving technique.

"Our car worked good pretty much through the race," said Earnhardt, who finished 1.3 seconds ahead of Labonte. "It got a little loose there in the middle of the race. We worked on it and got it better toward the end, but still, I think the 5 car (Labonte) was the strongest car at the end. He just had some trouble and got behind."

Earnhardt, who started on the outside of the front row, led the first 61 laps, possessing as much as a 2.82-second advantage.

"The trucks (team haulers for the SuperTrucks) came in last night and laid a nice coat of mud and dirt down on the inside, and since I didn't have any dirt tires up here, I figured I'd better stay up high on some asphalt and cement," Earnhardt said after the race that took 3 hours, 33 minutes and 21 seconds to complete.

"Our car worked really good, we just sort of used the high lane until the groove wore in down on the bottom,"

On lap 62, Wallace scooted under Earnhardt as they entered turn three to take the lead and finally cleared him on lap 63 as they raced through turns one and two.

Wallace possessed the No. 1 spot for the next 86 laps before an encounter with Ward Burton relegated him to the back of the field. The former Winston Cup champion was lapping Burton in turn four when the incident occurred. Wallace passed Burton and then Burton clipped him on the left rear, spinning him.

"He just ran into me, spun me out and that was about it," Wallace said. "I was lapping him, he was trying to hold me down a lap real bad, and as I got past him, he got into the back of me and spun me."

Burton said Wallace caught him in the door on the backstretch.

"I guess he was wanting me to leave him alone and back off," Burton said. "I thought that was uncalled for. He moved up the track and I might have gone in a little too deep. I didn't mean to spin him."

Wallace had to pit several times during the second caution period so his crew could pull the crushed right rear fender away from the tire. On the restart, Steve Grissom was leading, with Earnhardt second, Labonte fourth and Wallace 25th.

Grissom managed to hold off Earnhardt for 11 laps before Earnhardt dove under him in turn three. This time, Earnhardt set the pace for 29 laps, stretching his advantage to 4.68 seconds over Sterling Marlin on lap 122.

The third caution, which was for debris in turn one, gave the lead to Jarrett for a dozen laps. Most of the lead-lap cars elected to pit during the yellow, but Jarrett, John Andretti, Mark Martin and Bill Elliott chose to remain on the track. Therefore, when the race restarted, Earnhardt was fifth, Labonte seventh and Wallace ninth.

Earnhardt resumed the lead on lap 140 and held it for the next 93 circuits until pit stops occurred on lap 233 when the fifth caution began. Rookie Ricky Craven led only one lap before pitting.

Labonte won the race off pit road and kept Earnhardt and Wallace at bay for the next 86 laps.

In the race's second half, the only time someone other than those three drivers led was during pit stops. Michael Waltrip led two laps – 324-325 – and Gordon four – 403-406.

"We just tried to get a rhythm and stay consistent for the end," Earnhardt said. "Lapped traffic was a little bit of a problem today. There's one special guy who's been a problem a couple of times before.

"This is a tough race track, and the points battle is a tough deal right now being so far behind. We hope this will turn it around for us. We've got to do what we've done here in the last couple of races. We've got to lead the races and get top-five finishes. I don't wish (Gordon) any bad luck, but I hope the good luck stays with us." ∎

Earnhardt Runs
Rampant At Atlanta

Seven-Time Champ Buries Field, But Title Goes To Gordon

By STEVE WAID

J eff Gordon may have reaped the glory in the NAPA 500, but Dale Earnhardt stole all the thunder.

Earnhardt, showing the dominating form that has helped him earn seven career Winston Cup championships, humbled the field en route to a runaway victory that very nearly brought him an eighth title.

The Kannapolis, N.C., native led six times for 268 of 328 laps. He built up such huge margins over his rivals that all he had to do at the finish was preserve fuel. He crossed the finish line 3.74 seconds ahead of Sterling Marlin.

> "I love kickin' ass.
> **And I'll tell ya, that black SOB car kicked ass today."**
> —Earnhardt

But it wasn't enough. Earnhardt came into the race 147 points behind Jeff Gordon in the quest for the 1995 Winston Cup championship. Gordon was in the enviable position of having to finish only 41st or better, or lead a single lap, to keep the title out of Earnhardt's hands.

That was almost not safe enough. Gordon did lead a lap to clinch the championship, but he had a wealth of problems and finished 32nd, 14 laps down. By winning and leading the most laps, Earnhardt sliced away 113 points and lost the title by 34 points (4,614-4,580).

The victory was the fifth of 1995 for Earnhardt and the 68th of his career. It was also his seventh at the 1.522-mile Atlanta track, which tied him with Cale Yarborough for the all-time speedway record.

"I want to congratulate Rick Hendrick (Gordon's team owner) on winning the championship," said Earnhardt, driver of the RCR Enterprises Chevrolet. "His team did a great job. He's due a championship, Rick is. He's been in racing a long time. So I sort of feel good for him.

"But our team's the best. The car was real loose getting in but it was good getting off the turns. I could drive the car pretty hard. This is a good win for us because ol' Andy Petree (crew chief) is leaving us. I wanted to go to victory lane one last time with him."

By the 18th lap, the race was in Earnhardt's pocket, although no one knew it at the time. He pulled alongside leader Ricky Rudd down the backstretch and then passed him for the lead going into turn three. He would lead 37 laps.

Earnhardt then pitted on lap 55 under the green flag as part of the scenario that would give Gordon the title. On lap 61, Marlin, the leader, made the pit stop that elevated Gordon into the lead. After Gordon led lap 61 – the only lap he led – he was officially crowned the 1995 champion.

That came as no surprise to Earnhardt, who simply continued to dominate. He retook the lead on lap 82 when he passed Bill Elliott and Rudd and this time he would lead 47 circuits before pitting under green on lap 129. Again, it was amid a string of green-flag stops and by lap 138, Earnhardt was in front once more.

He led 48 laps, often by huge margins. By lap 180, he was 8.72 seconds ahead of Marlin. His explanation was simple.

"I told the guys after qualifying that we

THAT 'OLD BLACK MAGIC' HELPED EARNHARDT DESTROY THE FIELD AND TAKE THE WIN IN ATLANTA, BUT JEFF GORDON EDGED 'THE INTIMIDATOR' BY 34 POINTS TO WIN THE CHAMPIONSHIP. NWCS ARCHIVE PHOTO

had a real good car," Earnhardt said. "We made a few changes in it this morning to soften up the front end and I kinda drove in a hung-out state all day. I was on the throttle all day until at the end, when they started telling me to save gas. I didn't want to.

"I gave some guys an interview the other

day and I said I had mellowed out in my old age. But when I got up this morning, I was feeling pretty cocky.

"You don't have a race car like I had every race. You don't have it a lot of times, and when you do have it, it's pretty neat. I really enjoy it. I love kickin' ass. And I'll tell ya, that black SOB car kicked ass today."

On lap 185, Earnhardt again pitted under green and his rivals followed suit. When Bobby Labonte went down pit road on lap 201, the fanny-pounding began again.

Earnhardt was back in the lead and would be there for 67 more laps. During this stretch, Ernie Irvan captured attention when he moved into second place in a second Robert Yates Racing Ford, clearly indicating his return to competition from life-threatening injuries. But he was nearly six seconds behind Earnhardt.

The final push to the finish came after

Earnhardt pitted under green for the last time on lap 267. His stop for four tires and fuel took 21.45 seconds and he regained the lead on lap 270 after Elliott pitted. He was now in the lead by 11.25 seconds over Marlin.

It was no contest over the final 59 laps.

"I had an awesome car today," Earnhardt said. "I've got to give it to Andy and the team. They put a great car under me. I just went out and did my job."

Marlin wound up second to take third place in the final point standings away from Mark Martin, who experienced handling problems and finished 17th. Rusty Wallace took third place, with Elliott in fourth and Ward Burton in fifth. Jimmy Spencer, Irvan, Bobby Labonte, Bobby Hillin and Rudd rounded out the top 10.

Ricky Craven finished 30th, but that was enough to earn him the 1995 Maxx Race Cards Rookie of the Year title. His points total was 255, 13 more than Robert Pressley, who dropped out of the NAPA 500 with engine failure after 40 laps. He finished 41st and was one of only six drivers not running at the finish.

The race was slowed only twice for 11 laps by caution flags, which allowed Earnhardt to win with a track-record speed of 163.632 mph. That broke the old mark of 156.849 Earnhardt set in the fall of 1990.

Gordon, meanwhile, had little explanation for his woes, which were clearly noticeable by lap 107. By then he had fallen from third place to 14th in the space of 35 laps.

"I have no idea what happened today," Gordon said. "It was just one of those days. We weren't that great in practice yesterday and we tried some things and I honestly felt like something broke."

> ## "RJR is going to serve milk at the banquet this year instead of champagne."
> —Earnhardt giving another good-natured jab to Gordon

Gordon made numerous and costly pit stops so his Hendrick crew could make as many changes as possible, but nothing worked. Thereafter, all he wanted to do was get to the finish.

Earnhardt said he got no satisfaction by constantly lapping his rival.

"I mean, I could have passed him 50 times out there and wouldn't have made a bit of difference," he added. "He wasn't worried. He knew he had the championship locked up and it's a real good feeling to know that."

Earnhardt got a measure of satisfaction from his victory, too, even though it wasn't enough to earn him the championship.

"Well, it's OK, but you know how I feel about second place," he said. "But we had a good year. We had a shot at the championship. I wish I had Michigan back (Earnhardt had consecutive 35th-place finishes at Michigan International Speedway), because that hurt us. But we were a great team this year. We lost the championship because we had problems. We didn't get beat on the race track.

"I finally won a road course race for the first time in my career. And I won at Indy – I'm the first man to win at Indy."

The latter comment was another good-natured jab at Gordon that Earnhardt has made his specialty this season.

"RJR is going to serve milk at the banquet this year instead of champagne," Earnhardt continued.

But then he added:

"All kidding aside, he's going to be the one sitting at the head table drinking that milk, not me."

Earnhardt expects to be equally competitive in 1996, a year in which he will again race for team owner Richard Childress and try to win his eighth career championship.

"I look forward to 1996," Earnhardt said. "Winning makes you feel real good for next year. There's been a lot of questions asked about contracts and where we're going. Richard has pretty much finalized a deal with GM Goodwrench to extend the sponsorship, but I haven't finalized my deal with Richard yet. I've got until May to do that and that's what I am working toward. We've negotiated in good faith and that's where we're headed. That's all there is to that.

"We're looking toward February of 1996, when we're going to try again to win the Daytona 500, and who knows, I might do it. That's where we're headed. I tested there this week trying to get ahead for next year.

"That's what we want to do, focus on winning races and another championship. Going out on a winning note makes you feel good about the upcoming year.

"So yes, it is satisfying to win this race. It sank in after Phoenix that the championship was pretty much over. That put us in a bad mood and this has helped us change that mood a little bit.

"Now, I'm going to Texas to do a little hunting, relax and forget about racing – maybe for a day." ∎

EARNHARDT DOESN'T WIN TOO MANY POLES, BUT WAS FASTEST IN ATLANTA. NWCS ARCHIVE PHOTO

Rollin' A Lucky Seven

Earnhardt Prevails Again For Seventh Straight Time

By STEVE WAID

It has become an oft-told tale, but be prepared. It is going to be told again.

Dale Earnhardt, whose mastery of Daytona International Speedway ends only with his failure to win a Daytona 500 – so far – continued his dominance with his seventh-straight victory in a Gatorade Twin 125-Mile Qualifying race.

Earnhardt's uncanny ability to win a 125-miler has now accounted for nine such victories in his career and 27 overall at the 2.5-mile Daytona track, more than any other competitor.

This time, it seemed almost routine as Earnhardt put his RCR Enterprises Chevrolet past the strong Chevy of Sterling Marlin in the first turn with 21 laps to go. Thereafter, he remained out front as his challengers fought for position behind him, failing to link up in a draft that conceivably could have powered them into the lead.

> "This is just **one more step** toward winning the Daytona 500 and that is what we want to do."
> —Earnhardt

"I'm happy to keep the streak going," said Earnhardt, who claimed his first-ever Daytona 500 pole on Feb. 11. "It's pretty impressive. It's even impressive to me. I feel really good about it."

Earnhardt, whose streak of seven consecutive wins in a 125-miler began in 1990, started the first of the day's two races from the pole position. But before the first lap was completed, Marlin snatched the lead away with help in the draft from Chevy-driving Terry Labonte.

Marlin, winner of the last two Daytona 500s, held the lead for 29 of the race's 50 laps while Earnhardt fell as far back as third place. On lap 17, Earnhardt shot by Labonte between turns one and two to take second place, where he remained for the next 12 laps.

On lap 20, the first caution period started when light rain pelted the second turn. The race restarted three laps later.

Then, on lap 30, Earnhardt made his move. He cut to the inside of Marlin in the first turn, getting help in the draft from the Ford of Dale Jarrett, winner of the Busch Clash. Earnhardt and Jarrett broke away as Marlin and Labonte scrapped for position behind them, and then fell back in line two laps later with Marlin third and Labonte fourth. On lap 32, Marlin passed Jarrett to assume second place.

On lap 36, rain again fell, this time in the third and fourth turns. The race was slowed under caution until lap 39, when the restart came with Earnhardt first followed by Marlin, Jarrett, Labonte, Ward Burton, Michael Waltrip, Wally Dallenbach, Mark Martin and Jimmy Spencer.

Without incident, the race would have become a real test of draft strategy, as Earnhardt's challengers would have to figure when to attempt a move and with whom to draft.

But there was an incident. On lap 45, the third and final caution period began when a multicar accident occurred on the backstretch. It was triggered after Bobby Hillin's Ford clipped the front of Brett Bodine's Ford and sent both into the backstretch wall. As they bounced off, the cars of Geoff Bodine, Kenny Wallace and Bobby Labonte scattered.

Labonte's Chevrolet unavoidably hit Brett Bodine's crippled Ford and flipped over on its roof, skidding down the backstretch until it finally righted itself. None of the drivers involved were injured.

The race restarted with three laps to go. Immediately, with Earnhardt leading, Marlin moved high in the fourth turn. Earnhardt went with him and left the low side open for Jarrett, who moved into second place. Marlin was left fighting Labonte for third.

On lap 48, Marlin retook third place and the trio of Earnhardt, Jarrett and Marlin held position until the start of the last lap. Marlin moved to the outside of Jarrett and Labonte joined him, locking up in a draft that put them past Jarrett's Ford.

But time ran out and they could do nothing to catch Earnhardt. Marlin finished 0.16-second behind, with Labonte third, Jarrett fourth, Dallenbach fifth, Waltrip sixth, Burton seventh, Martin eighth, Mike Wallace ninth and Jimmy Spencer 10th.

While Earnhardt held off Marlin and Labonte at the finish, a scramble for the 15th and cutoff position for a starting spot in the Daytona 500 ended with Kyle Petty in the payoff slot.

Earnhardt said he won the race by following a basic strategy.

"Our focus was to sit in line until we had a chance to get the lead," he said. "We waited and then when the opportunity came, we took it. Then the shuffle came behind us and it worked to our advantage.

"I kept in front with Sterling and when we were drafting, the 88 (Jarrett) got under us there at the end. Then he and Sterling both got to racing with the 5 (Labonte). By the time they got it sorted out and Sterling came back up there, the deal had already worked out for me.

"HEY DALE, HOW MANY GATORADE 125-MILE QUALIFIERS HAVE YOU WON?" NWCS ARCHIVE PHOTO

"It's different now. It takes two cars to make a pass. Everyone is talking teammate now; that you have to have another car out there to race with you. It's a different trend and we're just one team, so we have to go it alone. It's just getting harder and harder to win.

"But our car felt good out in front. It was comfortable there. I would rather stay in the lead draft and lead or push another car up there and then wait for the end, where you might be racing a couple of other cars for the win and then do what you can.

"This is just one more step toward winning the Daytona 500 and that is what we want to do."

That, too, is an oft-told tale. ∎

Dale Beats Dale **Again**

But This Time, It's Earnhardt Who Prevails

By STEVE WAID

EARNHARDT STAYED JUST AHEAD OF DALE JARRETT, TAKING THE FLAG UNDER CAUTION.
NWCS ARCHIVE PHOTO

Dale Earnhardt won for the first time in 1996, took a big step toward earning his eighth career Winston Cup championship and gained a measure of revenge over Dale Jarrett with his victory in the Goodwrench Service 400.

But it wasn't pretty.

A rash of wrecks and a controversial incident between Earnhardt and Bobby Hamilton played major roles in the 69th victory of Earnhardt's career. It was his third at the 1.017-mile NCMS layout.

Earnhardt, driving the RCR Enterprises Chevrolet, took the lead for good on the 379th of the race's 393 laps when he passed Jarrett's Robert Yates Racing Ford on the inside in turns one and two. He began to expand his lead and then coasted to the checkered flag when the race ended under caution.

With two laps to go, the 10th and final caution period began after Bobby Hillin hit the wall in the second turn. Earnhardt took the white and yellow flags ahead of Jarrett, Ricky Craven, Ricky Rudd and Steve Grissom, sealing the victory.

However, it was not a vastly popular one.

Bobby Hamilton led three times for 36 laps in the Petty Enterprises Pontiac, bringing both the Petty organization and Pontiac back into the limelight. He put a Petty car into the lead for the first time at NCMS since October 1986.

After the sixth caution period ended on lap 338, Earnhardt was in the lead with Hamilton second.

The two staged a terrific battle. On lap 342, Hamilton went low in turns three and four to take the lead. On the next lap, Earnhardt pulled alongside Hamilton and then shot back to the front out of the second turn. One lap later, it was Hamilton's turn again, passing Earnhardt out of turn two.

But on lap 345, Hamilton was on the high side of Earnhardt going into the fourth turn. The front end of Earnhardt's Chevy clipped the left rear of Hamilton's Pontiac, causing the car to scrub the wall and slide dangerously out of the turn.

Hamilton collected the car and continued to race but dropped from first to fifth place.

Many fans' reaction to the incident was decidedly anti-Earnhardt and the question was raised if the seven-time Winston Cup champion might be sent to the "penalty box" by NASCAR for unsportsmanlike driving.

"The penalty box has been used when we have no doubt the incident was intentional," said Kevin Triplett, NASCAR's Winston Cup media coordinator. "We did not get that in this situation. We saw a lot of hard racing today, but in that situation, we didn't see anything intentional."

For his part, Earnhardt considered it nothing more than a bumping incident and clearly said so.

"You'll have to watch the replay because I am not sure what happened," he said. "We just got together and bumped a bit. It was a bumping incident. There are bumps over there in turn four and when we got there,

I didn't turn the steering wheel into him at all. We were lucky that he was able to gather up his car and save it because it could have been a bad crash.

"Something happened and he recovered from it. That ain't what put him out of the race."

Hamilton made it clear Earnhardt was to blame, concluding his assessment by saying, "I'm real disappointed Earnhardt didn't race me clean."

On lap 347, the seventh caution period began when debris from Hamilton's car was spotted in the fourth turn. Then, on lap 366, Hamilton's run was finished when he spun in the second turn and clobbered the wall. He limped to a 24th-place finish.

Hamilton made it clear Earnhardt was to blame, concluding his assessment by saying, "I'm real disappointed

Earnhardt didn't race me clean."

The Hamilton incident aside, Earnhardt's Chevy was one of a handful of cars capable of winning the race. But he was not a factor during the early stages as he was busy steadily making his way to the front from his 18th-place start. He did so in tandem with Ford-driving Jimmy Spencer, who started 28th.

"Spencer and I started way back," Earnhardt said, "and I was really busy at the start of the race, working to see which way my car would work – low or high.

"We sorta worked together, because he was running good and I was running good and we came on up. I think he might have been the one to beat, but he had problems."

While Earnhardt and Spencer were doing their thing, pole winner Terry Labonte blasted out front and held the lead for 88 laps. Spencer took over when Labonte took his turn in a series of green-flag pit stops on lap 89, but Labonte was back in front by lap 90 and led 48 more laps.

Again, it was Spencer's turn to lead when he passed Labonte high in turns one and two on lap 138. He led for 33 laps until Labonte passed him on lap 171 and stayed in front for 11 laps, surrendering the point on lap 193 when Earnhardt led for the first time.

EARNHARDT SHARES THE SPOTLIGHT, AND THE HOOD OF HIS RIDE, WITH MISS WINSTON.
NWCS ARCHIVE PHOTO

THE ROCK

It was on lap 173 that the fourth caution period began when Loy Allen slammed into the second-turn wall, followed by Bobby Labonte's collision with the first-turn wall.

Allen's Ford came to rest at the entrance to the back pit road, effectively blocking it and forcing NASCAR to throw the red flag because cars needed to pit for fuel. The field was parked along the backstretch for nine minutes, 15 seconds.

During that time, safety crews removed the front windshield of Allen's car and took him out. When the crews arrived, Allen was unconscious, but he was conscious and alert when he was taken from the infield medical center to the helicopter that transported him to Carolinas Medical Center in Charlotte. It was later reported he had suffered a fractured right shoulder blade.

By 235, Terry Labonte had led six times for 198 laps. But his bid for victory came to an end one lap later. He pitted after his car began to overheat, throwing water out of the headers. It was discovered it had sustained a cracked cylinder head and the Hendrick Motorsports driver retired to a 34th-place finish.

It was not a good day for the Hendrick organization altogether. Defending Winston Cup champion Jeff Gordon suffered engine failure in his Chevrolet and finished 40th. Ken Schrader recovered from brake fires and pressed on as best he could. He wound up 29th.

After Labonte's demise, Earnhardt led for 37 laps, giving way to Jarrett for the first time on lap 273. Rudd then led a couple of laps before Spencer was back out in front on lap 277.

Hamilton then took the lead on lap 296 when he passed Spencer high in turns one and two. It was at this point Spencer began to experience problems in his Ford. It developed a miss in the engine and he began to lose positions. On lap 326, he clipped the wall between turns three and four and the oil he left on the track caused the ninth caution period to begin three laps later.

During the caution, Spencer retired from the race with engine failure.

"Labonte was the strongest all day and then he had his problems, and the 23 (Spencer) was strong, too," Earnhardt said. "But then he had problems. There were several guys who had a shot at this and some of them could run away from us.

"It all depended on tires. Different cars were stronger on different runs. In our case, we ran our fastest laps at the end of the race. In those last couple of runs, I may

have been the strongest. I may have been the strongest at the end, but then those other guys were not around."

After Hamilton's crash created the eighth caution period and ended his run, Earnhardt had led 28 laps. But he was behind Jarrett when the green flag flew on lap 372. On lap 379, Earnhardt retook the lead he would hold until the end of the race.

That he was able to pass and then hold off Jarrett was a pleasant turnaround for Earnhardt, who lost his bid for a career-first Daytona 500 win to the Ford driver just seven days earlier.

"Hey, we finished second at Daytona and that felt good and this time we beat Jarrett, so it feels good again," Earnhardt said. "We were racing pretty good, and he was really good on new tires. But they seemed to go away after a couple of laps and so I was patient, got by him and just went on.

"Jarrett's team looks to be the strongest at this point. It's working well now but maybe we'll have to see who is next and then we'll have to race them."

The duo of one-two finishes between Earnhardt and Jarrett has created a tie atop the Winston Cup point standings. Each has 355 points, 52 more than Rudd, who stands third.

Following the top five cars of Earnhardt, Jarrett, Craven, Rudd and Grissom came the Chevrolet of Sterling Marlin, which took sixth place. Seventh went to Kenny Wallace – the last driver on the lead lap – and eighth to Derrike Cope, both in Fords, while Joe Nemechek finished ninth in a Chevrolet and Rick Mast was 10th in a Pontiac.

Earnhardt's victory brought him $83,840 and continued the momentum he and his team gained with their runaway victory at Atlanta last November. In his last three Winston Cup races, Earnhardt has finished first, second and first.

"We've still got that momentum from last year and we're keeping it going," said Earnhardt, who has made it clear his eyes are on that eighth title. "Everyone on the team has a great attitude. They are winners even when we lose.

"I've had my problems early in a season and I've had them late in a season. Our focus is not to miss a beat. It's a new season with new teams and we'll have to race whoever is out there racing.

"If we keep doing this and keep our focus, we'll be all right." ■

TAYLOR EARNHARDT ALWAYS HAS TIME FOR ANOTHER HUG FROM DAD IN VICTORY LANE. NWCS ARCHIVE PHOTO

dale earnhardt

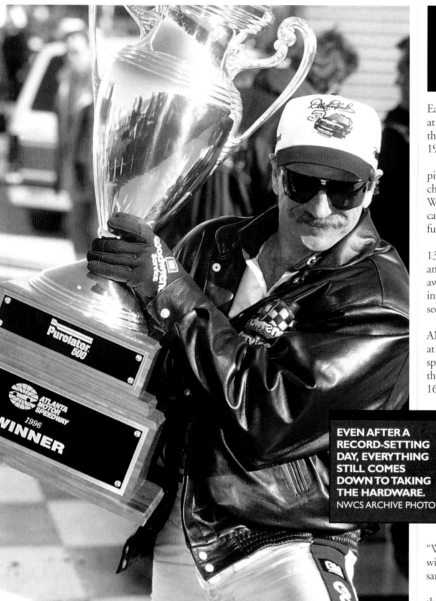

EVEN AFTER A RECORD-SETTING DAY, EVERYTHING STILL COMES DOWN TO TAKING THE HARDWARE.
NWCS ARCHIVE PHOTO

Once Again
Earnhardt Dominates

Seven-Time Champion Sets Record With
Runaway Atlanta Win

By STEVE WAID

In case anyone forgot the image of Dale Earnhardt storming to victory in the last NASCAR Winston Cup race of the 1995 season, he brought it back vividly in the Purolator 500.

It was last November that Earnhardt rocked the field in the NAPA 500 at Atlanta, dominating the race and earning the victory as Jeff Gordon cruised to the 1995 Winston Cup championship.

Many took it as a sign Earnhardt had picked up enough momentum to strongly challenge for a career, and record, eighth Winston Cup title in 1996. If that is the case, consider the momentum to now be at full steam.

Earnhardt started 18th, led seven times for 136 laps, more than any other competitor, and, propelled by a fast final pit stop, ran away from the field to win for the 70th time in his career. He took the checkered flag 4.17 seconds ahead of Terry Labonte.

With the victory, Earnhardt set numerous AMS records. It was his eighth career victory at the 1.522-mile track, making him the speedway's all-time winner with one more than Cale Yarborough. His average speed of 161.298 mph was a Purolator 500 record, beating the mark of 156.849 mph he set in 1990. Earnhardt holds the track record of 163.633 mph, which he set with his fiery performance last November.

The victory was worth $91,050 to Earnhardt, raising his career AMS winnings to $1,335,670 – again, a record.

"This was the same car we raced here last November," said Earnhardt, who has now won twice this season. "We adjusted her a little bit here and there with the chassis, but not much. She was the same car."

Earnhardt was one of 12 drivers to lead the race – you guessed it, a record – but lost the No. 1 spot to Ernie Irvan on lap 265 when Irvan slung his Ford low around Earnhardt's Chevrolet in the third turn. On lap 266, Labonte, in a Chevrolet, shot to second ahead of Earnhardt.

Labonte retook the lead on lap 268 – he would lead five times for 100 laps – putting Irvan back to second with Earnhardt holding on to third.

The restart from the third, and ultimately final, caution period began on lap 246, 82 laps from the end of the 328-lap race. Barring another caution, the field would have to make a last stop under the green flag since the cars were averaging about 55 laps between stops.

On lap 290, Labonte had built a lead of 1.47 seconds over Earnhardt, who had taken second away from Irvan. Then, one lap later, Earnhardt was the first of the leaders to dart down pit road.

"David Smith (crew chief) and Richard Childress (team owner) made the call," Earnhardt said. "There was no strategy about it. I was running out of gas and it was time to pit."

Earnhardt's crew changed four tires and filled the fuel tank in 19.72 seconds.

On lap 292, Labonte made his stop and his Hendrick Motorsports crew performed the same services in 21.81 seconds, more than two seconds slower. The difference played a critical role as the race wound down.

"I've got to hand it to the guys, they did a super job," Earnhardt said. "I could tell it was a fast stop because after they changed the right-side tires and dropped the jack, I spilled the Coke I was drinking all over me. I knew I had to throw it out, because it was time to go.

"When I was going down the front straightaway after the pit stop and I saw Terry just rolling out of his pits, I knew we were in great shape."

By lap 300, the series of pit stops had ended. Earnhardt was the leader, with Labonte second, Irvan third, Gordon fourth and Jeremy Mayfield fifth in his Ford. Earnhardt had a lead of more than three seconds.

By lap 308, the lead had expanded to 3.7 seconds. Ten laps later, it was 5.13 seconds. It was clear Labonte would have no chance.

"I wasn't cruising," Earnhardt said. "I was bearing down as hard as I could go, trying to put distance on Terry. He was stronger on long runs and I wanted to keep all the distance I could on him. I was probably running harder then than at any other point in the race. My car was running great.

"Yes, Terry was faster – to a point. If he was in front, I was the one who had to run hard behind him and cars get pushier for the guy who is running behind. And like I said, Terry was faster on long runs. At one time, he passed both me and Rusty (Wallace)."

The runner-up finish was the season's best for Labonte, who has two pole positions in '96. Gordon, Labonte's Hendrick teammate, finished third while Irvan wound up fourth, his best of the season.

Mayfield took fifth and that constituted the best finish of his career.

Ken Schrader finished sixth in a Chevrolet, followed by Jimmy Spencer, seventh; Ricky Rudd, eighth; Michael Waltrip, ninth; and Bill Elliott, 10th, all in Fords.

> "I think they
> ## sucked the guts
> out of their engines trying
> to keep up with Rusty, Terry
> and Dale Earnhardt."
> —Earnhardt

Of the 11 cars that failed to finish the race, 10 were sidelined because of engine problems. Among them were the cars of Wallace, Steve Grissom, Johnny Benson, Rick Mast, Mike Wallace, Bobby Hillin and Robert Pressley.

"I think they sucked the guts out of their engines trying to keep up with Rusty, Terry and Dale Earnhardt," Earnhardt said.

Dale Jarrett, who had posted a win and two runner-up finishes through the season's first three races, did not have a good day at Atlanta with an 11th-place finish in an ill-handling Ford. However, he held on to first in the Winston Cup point standings, with 660 points.

Earnhardt vaulted to second place from fourth, largely because of his second victory in four races and the fact Jeff Burton, who had been second in the points prior to Atlanta, failed to qualify for the Purolator 500 and plummeted to 14th place. With 610 points, Earnhardt is now 50 behind Jarrett in his quest for an unprecedented eighth title.

"It's just hard work and determination that is going to make the difference this year," Earnhardt said. "We've got a great team. We've worked hard over the winter trying to be a better team and today, I think we worked together more than ever before.

"Who knows? Maybe it is our year to win the eighth championship. But the other guys out there are trying just as hard as we are. It's tough racing today."

With 70 wins, Earnhardt has scored a victory on all of NASCAR's current Winston Cup tracks except Watkins Glen and Loudon, N.H. He is now the winningest driver at Atlanta and can tie David Pearson's mark of 10 career wins at Darlington Raceway with a victory in the March 24 TranSouth Financial 400.

"It's pretty impressive to come to Atlanta and run as well as we do," Earnhardt said. "I hope Cale is not mad at me for breaking his record. It's a great honor to be mentioned in the same sentence with him. It's neat to win eight races here and others at a lot of tracks – even though we haven't won the Daytona 500 yet.

"Could I have a 10-win season? It could be. I am that confident with the team. But 40-some odd guys are betting against it. It is tough to win another race or another championship. It is not as easy to win as in the past. To win five races is a pretty good feat. Gordon won seven last year and I think that is an all-time high for this kind of competition."

It may be. But Earnhardt is on a pace to do at least as well, or better, in 1996.

"Well, we'll see," he said. ■

EARNHARDT'S RICHARD CHILDRESS RACING PIT CREW PULLING OFF YET ANOTHER SUB-20-SECOND PIT STOP.
NWCS ARCHIVE PHOTO

Death, Taxes And

Seven-Time Champ Rolls To Eighth
Straight Qualifying Race Victory

Earnhardt

By TOM STINSON

Death, taxes and Dale Earnhardt in the Gatorade 125s. Not a questionable one in the bunch.

In what's become one of those sure things in life, Earnhardt cruised to victory in his Gatorade 125-mile qualifying race, giving him the fourth starting spot in the Daytona 500 and extending his unbeaten streak to eight straight years on the Thursday before the 500.

"Well, did you expect someone else?" Earnhardt asked afterward.

Umm ... actually, no.

With the streak, Earnhardt has never lost a Daytona qualifier in the '90s, and he's won 10 of them overall, counting victories in 1983 and '86. No other driver has won the race more than six times.

"It is a race I have fun with," Earnhardt said, stating the obvious, since he wins the thing all the time. "It's an important race. You get a streak going like this that's history; history that I don't think anybody else has matched or will match. It's a great race. It's a race that you can really let your car out."

Earnhardt let his Richard Childress Racing Chevrolet out early in the 50-lapper, moving up from his fifth-place starting position and driving past John Andretti on lap 19 for the lead, getting help from Jeff Gordon, Rusty Wallace and Darrell Waltrip in the difficult Daytona draft.

"The key, I think, was to be out front," Earnhardt said. "It seemed to me that the guy out front could sorta predict what would happen behind him, if you could just keep the guys in line.

"I was worried about Terry Labonte and those guys getting hooked up with Jeff and making a run on me, but they never could. It worked to my advantage being in front. I don't think we could have won it from second."

Gordon – and the rest of the 26-car field, for that matter – chased Earnhardt for the final 30 laps, but Gordon never could challenge for the lead. He trailed Earnhardt by 0.182-second at the checkered flag, giving Chevrolet a one-two sweep.

"I waited until 10 (laps) to go to try to make some moves and see if we could get some momentum, but I just couldn't get anybody to really give me a big enough boost," said Gordon, who took second from Wallace on lap 20 and followed Earnhardt the rest of the way. "Once Dale got out front, there was nothing we could do with him."

Bill Elliott, Ken Schrader and Michael Waltrip rounded out the top five, followed by Wallace, Johnny Benson, Terry Labonte, Robby Gordon and Darrell Waltrip in the

second 10. Just as important, though, Dave Marcis, Wally Dallenbach, Hut Stricklin and Kyle Petty secured the final transfer positions, 11th through 14th.

Only the top 14 from the qualifier automatically moved into the 500 since front-row starter Steve Grissom failed to finish the 125. Grissom parked his Larry Hedrick Motorsports Chevrolet after only 17 laps, saying a chassis gamble wasn't working and the team decided not to jeopardize its car for the 500.

For the 55-year-old Marcis, it extended

his streak of Daytona 500 starts to 30 straight years, dating to 1968.

"We did a great job today, and now we're in our 30th consecutive Daytona 500," said Marcis, who started 22nd and used Mike Skinner's pole-winning RCR engine to get into the big race.

"Richard (Childress) put a fresh engine in our car yesterday. Where can you find somebody to do that for you? I knew I could finish where I needed to today as long as I could get someone to run up high with me."

In Petty's debut with his new pe2 team, and therefore with no provisional starting spot to rely on, his weekend looked about finished while running 15th late in the race – or outside of the transfer spots. But luck – or at least luck for Petty – came when Andretti scrubbed the fourth-turn wall on lap 45, dropping him off the pace and allowing Petty to advance into the 500.

EARNHARDT WINS HIS EIGHTH STRAIGHT 125-MILE QUALIFYING RACE, HIS 29TH VICTORY AT THE TRACK.
NWCS ARCHIVE PHOTO

"Eight in a row,"

Earnhardt reiterated, seemingly amazed himself. "That's a good omen for eight championships."

"I've prayed for six months now to get this thing in the Daytona 500," said Petty, whose car suffered slight damage in an early accident and appeared a long shot to make the cut. "That was the one I was worried about.

"Now I get to stay through Sunday. I guess that seven-night minimum on the hotel room paid off."

The race's only incident came on lap 10, when Ricky Craven tried to squeeze in front of Chad Little coming out of turn four. Contact between the two sent Craven spinning, collecting Lake Speed and Loy Allen, as well as causing minor damage to the cars of Little, Petty and Morgan Shepherd.

"I just screwed up," said Craven, who finished 26th – and last – in his debut with the No. 25 Hendrick Motorsports team. "I had a hole to jump into and the guy behind me didn't give me a break. ... But I'm not going to push anything. I'm going to take responsibility. I tried to squeeze in there and I couldn't do it."

Earnhardt's streak, of course, came in his first race weekend with crew chief Larry McReynolds, further proof of what he says will be a championship turnaround in 1997.

"Eight in a row," Earnhardt reiterated, seemingly amazed himself. "That's a good omen for eight championships." ∎

Back In Black

Earnhardt Wins For First Time In A Year, Takes Ninth Straight 125

By JEFF OWENS

You've read this story before.

Eight times, in fact.

Dale Earnhardt proved once again that he is the best Thursday race car driver in America.

Earnhardt, who enters the Daytona 500 0-for-19, won his ninth consecutive Gatorade 125-Mile Qualifying Race for the Daytona 500. It was his 11th qualifying race victory and his 30th win overall at Daytona International Speedway.

A victory in one of the Thursday qualifiers at Daytona has become almost automatic for Earnhardt. The only thing more commonplace is the disappointment he usually feels at the same track on Sunday.

"I guess it's just a heckuva lucky race for me," he said. "I don't know why, I really don't. I sat there leading it, thinking about who was going to get hooked up and who was going to draft by me and what was going to happen, and nothing happens.

"I don't know why I've won nine of these things, and I don't know why I lost (the last time) in 1989. I can't remember back that far."

After failing to win a points race for the first time since 1981 last season, Earnhardt was determined to win an event he almost never loses. In fact, his last victory came in this race last year.

"It's been a long, long year," he said. "It's about time we got in the winner's circle again. We ended up here last year, and didn't win after that, so we're going to start our winning streak with this race and go from there."

Not even a stomach virus that nearly made him throw up in his car could stop him on this day. He charged past pole-winner Terry Labonte in the fourth turn of the first lap and never looked back.

His car nearly got away from him on the daring pass, but he reeled it in and led all 50 laps. It was a sign of how determined he is to snap his surprising 0-for-59 slump.

"It just makes you more determined when somebody says, 'Well, has he still got it?'" he said. "When I drove off into (turn) three over there on the first lap outside of Terry, my car felt sideways. Instead of checking way up, I drove the car on through the corner and came out with the lead.

> ## "I don't know if that's craziness or stubbornness,
> but I'm still determined to do it."
> —Earnhardt

"I don't know if that's craziness or stubbornness, but I'm still determined to do it."

Once Earnhardt got the lead, the race for the win was over. The only question was who would finish second.

Michael Waltrip, Mike Skinner, Ernie Irvan and Rusty Wallace all jockeyed for the spot, and they wound up finishing in that order.

At times it seemed as if they were more concerned with finishing second than trying to draft by Earnhardt.

"If I could have put myself in the right spot, I could have won instead of Earnhardt winning nine in a row," Irvan said. "He's never won the Daytona 500 if I recall, and he keeps winning this race. Maybe that's an omen."

Wallace, who won the Feb. 8 Bud Shootout, stayed glued to Earnhardt's bumper the first half of the race, but Waltrip blew past him on lap 33 and held on to finish second.

"I'd have won for sure if we would have had 10 more laps," Waltrip said with a laugh, knowing he had no shot at Earnhardt.

While Waltrip and the rest played follow-the-leader, the best race was between Kenny Wallace and Robert Pressley for the last transfer spot into the Daytona 500.

Both drivers lost the draft, but raced hard about a mile behind the lead pack. They raced side-by-side for several laps until Pressley finally gained the advantage on lap 33.

With two laps remaining, Wallace tried to use the draft of Loy Allen to power past Pressley. Instead, he took the air off Allen's spoiler and sent him spinning through the trioval grass.

The spin halted the race and caused it to end under caution. It gave Earnhardt the victory, Pressley a spot in the Daytona 500 and Wallace a sick feeling in the pit of his stomach.

"My car just didn't have the speed it needed to run and pass in the draft," said Wallace, who finished second in the Bud Shootout.

"I ran up on the (No.) 14 car hoping I could draft him. Instead, I got into him. I can't believe I missed the Daytona 500. It's pretty tough to take."

Pressley, one of only a few drivers to race the '97 Thunderbird, knew he was lucky. His engine soured on the first restart, forcing him to battle Wallace's slow Taurus the whole race.

When Allen wrecked, it put him safely in the 500.

"That was the only thing that really saved us right there," Pressley said. "We're just happy to be in the Daytona 500."

While the rest of the field raced and wrecked behind him, Earnhardt kept his black Chevy aimed like an arrow toward victory lane. After leading just 10 races all last year, he was enjoying himself.

"It felt good," he said. "You sit out front and watch the race track in front of you and you watch in the mirror what is going on behind you. When you've got a good race car like we had today, it's very comfortable and very satisfying to run like that. That's the place to be."

His only worry was his stomach. And that really wasn't a big concern.

"I knew I could make it to the end, I just didn't know if I could keep from throwing up 'til the end," he said. "But I was going to drive whether I was throwing up or not." ∎

dale earnhardt

At Last

Earnhardt Finally Bags The Big One

By STEVE WAID

I t evolved into a cloudy, gray day. But for Dale Earnhardt, it was the brightest of his career. Who needed the sun?

At last ... at last.

In one of the most emotion-charged finishes in the history of Daytona, Earnhardt, a seven-time Winston Cup champion whose racing achievements are the stuff of dreams, did something he hadn't been able to do for 20 years.

He won the Daytona 500 – finally.

Now, as Earnhardt put it, "The monkey is off my back!" And he so exuberantly illustrated that fact by hurling a stuffed monkey across the press box.

With the victory, Earnhardt removed the one stigma of his celebrated career. No longer can it be said that Earnhardt, one of the greatest drivers in NASCAR history, can't win the Daytona 500.

And no longer will he be bothered by the question, "When will you win the Daytona 500?"

"Yes! Yes! Yes!" said an excited Earnhardt in victory lane. "Twenty years! Can you believe it!"

Believe it. After years in which Earnhardt lost the Daytona 500 in just about every way imaginable – out of gas here, a cut tire there, a missing lug nut over there – this time fate would not deny him.

Earnhardt, who has now won 31 races at Daytona including this first Daytona 500, also ended a 59-race losing streak and effectively hushed the talk that he could no longer drive 500 hard, competitive miles – talk that intensified after he mysteriously blacked out on the first lap of the Southern 500 at Darlington last year.

He was clearly the sentimental favorite in Daytona. Even those who do not count themselves among his fans said that if their chosen driver could not win, they wanted Earnhardt to win to end his years of futility.

And wouldn't victory for the long-suffering Earnhardt be a perfect fit for NASCAR's year-long 50th Anniversary celebration?

"This win is for all our fans and all the people who told me, 'Dale, this is your year,'" Earnhardt said. "I mean, you can't believe all the people who told me that, from the top to the bottom in the garage area. Team owners

> **ELATION ERUPTS IN VICTORY LANE AS EARNHARDT TAKES TO THE ROOF OF HIS GM GOODWRENCH CHEVROLET TO CELEBRATE HIS CAPTURE OF THE ONE TITLE THAT HAS ELUDED HIM – THE DAYTONA 500.**
> NWCS ARCHIVE PHOTO

to crewmen. Bill France. Todd Parrott (Dale Jarrett's crew chief).

"There was a lot of hard work that went into this and I have to thank every member of the Richard Childress Racing team. I have had a lot of great fans and people behind me all through the years and I just can't thank them enough.

"The Daytona 500 is over. And we won it! We won it!"

But he very easily could have lost it – again – and if he had, it would have gone down as one of the most disappointing episodes of his career.

As it turned out, Earnhardt held off a furious attack from the likes of Jeremy Mayfield, Rusty Wallace and Bobby Labonte as the 200-lap race around the 2.5-mile Daytona track sped to its conclusion.

Earnhardt, in a Chevrolet, was the race's dominant figure. But as he himself will tell you, that's never been enough in itself for him to win the Daytona 500. This time, it was.

Earnhardt, who led five times for 107

later, Earnhardt led the parade of leaders down pit road.

It was obvious that this would be the final stop and the leaders opted to make it as

Now, as Earnhardt put it, "The monkey is off my back!" And he so exuberantly illustrated that fact by hurling a stuffed monkey across the press box.

quick as possible. With the exception of Ernie Irvan, all took on right side tires only.

"We had learned from the 125-mile qualifying race that track position was very important," said Larry McReynolds, Earnhardt's crew chief who had won Daytona 500s in 1992 with Davey Allison and in 1996 with Jarrett. "We knew what all the

"On the last stop, I was focused," Earnhardt said. "I wanted to make sure I didn't do anything wrong and that we got out quick. And we did."

Earnhardt was followed by Skinner, Mayfield, Wallace and Jeff Gordon, the winner of the 1997 Daytona 500.

When the race restarted, there were just 12 laps to go. Earnhardt was in front with teammate Skinner behind him. That gave Earnhardt the ideal drafting partner and he would need it, because in third and fourth were Mayfield and Wallace, who became teammates in the Penske organization this season when Roger Penske became a partner with Michael Kranefuss on Mayfield's team.

It was clear Earnhardt and Skinner would combine their forces to escape Mayfield and Wallace, if they could.

"Mike did help a tremendous amount on that last restart," Earnhardt said. "I know he would have liked to have won this race as much as me."

EARNHARDT GLUED A LUCKY PENNY TO HIS DASH BEFORE THE 500.
NWCS ARCHIVE PHOTO

laps, more than any other driver, made a pass around teammate Mike Skinner on lap 140 to take the lead he would hold for the remainder of the race, although he certainly didn't know it at the time.

On lap 174, the race's second caution period began after Robert Pressley and John Andretti spun down the backstretch. One lap

other teams were thinking and to us, there was no question to go for just two tires. In fact, Goodyear brought such a good tire here we might have been OK if we just took gas.

"We knew it would take five or six seconds to take fuel and the guys made about an 8.5-second stop for tires and that let us get back out on the track first."

But the strategy was doomed. On lap 179, Skinner was pushed high out of the draft in turn one and that allowed Mayfield and Wallace, in Fords, to close on Earnhardt's rear bumper. Gordon moved to fourth place and Skinner fought Labonte for fifth.

Five laps passed as Earnhardt, now on his own, eyed his rearview mirror and kept his foot in the throttle as the Penske Fords lurked just behind.

"I felt like I could do pretty good, but Jeremy and Rusty were hooked up good," Earnhardt said. "I don't know, but I just felt like this was it."

On lap 184, Gordon shot to the low side of Wallace in the first turn, but Wallace made a blocking move that broke his effort with Mayfield and allowed Earnhardt some precious space.

On lap 194, Gordon made another move. This time he went to the high side of the Fords ahead of him and split them, moving into third place behind Mayfield.

The running order stayed that way until lap 197, when Wallace shot by Gordon on the backstretch and once again united with his teammate.

Then, one lap later, pole-winner Labonte pushed his Pontiac to the high side and managed to clear Mayfield coming out of the fourth turn to move into second place. As he did so, Gordon drifted back out of the melee, the victim of a dropped cylinder.

There were two laps remaining.

On lap 199, the race's third and final caution period began when Andretti, Lake Speed and Jimmy Spencer tangled on the backstretch. When the leaders got back to the line, they would see the yellow and white flags fly simultaneously.

The first one to the flags would win the race.

Earnhardt gave it all he had. He was able to utilize the lapped Ford of Rick Mast as a pick and got a bit of a break as Labonte and Mayfield jostled each other for position.

He crossed the line ahead of them. And the grandstands erupted.

One last, comfortable, tension-free lap was all Earnhardt had left to make. With the checkered flag came the end of 19 years of frustration.

"We worked awful hard and just kept playing our cards," said Earnhardt, 46. "They'd go this way and I'd go with them or do what I thought was best. The years of experience helped me out there.

"I was hoping they would stay in line with about 10 to go or eight to go. It got down to five and they got to racing. They started dicing and that made me feel better. I could pick who I wanted to dice with as they were passing each other.

"When Bobby got in behind me, he was pretty much by himself. He didn't have any help. And we had Rick's lapped car there. I felt like I could hold him off."

Earnhardt admitted he got emotional as

he sped past the yellow and white flags.

"My eyes watered up in the race car," he said. "I don't think I really cried. My eyes just watered up on that lap to take the checkered. I knew I was going to win it then, no matter what. I knew I was going to win unless something happened to the car.

"I was driving slow down the backstretch and I said, 'I want to go fast. I don't want to go slow. I want to get back around there.' I

EARNHARDT'S SATISFACTION SHINES BRIGHTER THAN ANY TROPHY. NWCS ARCHIVE PHOTO

took off, came back around, took the checkered and really got excited."

By his own admission, what happened next will be forever etched in Earnhardt's memory. As he made his way down pit road toward victory lane, he was met by crew members from virtually every team in the Daytona 500, all of whom wanted to congratulate him for his victory.

"I sorta expected a few of them to come out there, but not as many as there were," Earnhardt said. "All the guys came up congratulating me, all of them wanting to shake my hand or give me high-fives, thumbs-up. There was Michael Waltrip, Rusty ... I had to go real slow or my arm would've gotten torn off."

As if to display his excitement to the fans, Earnhardt sped off pit road, into the grass

and cut doughnuts with his spinning tires. Later, fans would retrieve chunks of the torn-up sod for souvenirs.

The victory was worth $1,059,105 to Earnhardt and marked the first time in Winston Cup racing the winner's share of the purse was over $1 million. He won with an average speed of 172.712 mph, the third-fastest race in Daytona 500 history.

"I had confidence in myself, the team and everybody," Earnhardt said. "People say, 'Did you hear things? Did you wonder who was going to pass?' I was working to keep the race car out in front. I was working to do that until somebody turned me over or we got to the finish.

"I wasn't thinking about what could happen. I was thinking about what I was doing and focused on what I had to do."

Labonte wound up second, Mayfield third and Ken Schrader, broken sternum and all, came home fourth. Wallace was fifth, with Ernie Irvan sixth, Chad Little seventh, Skinner eighth, Michael Waltrip ninth and Bill Elliott 10th.

Earnhardt now is eligible for a $1 million bonus from Winston in the No Bull 5 program. He joined the other top-five finishers, Labonte, Mayfield, Schrader and Wallace, as candidates for the reward if any one of them can win the Coca-Cola 600 at Charlotte on May 24.

While Earnhardt would be the first to tell you he wouldn't turn down a $1 million bonus, he's out for greater rewards.

"Another championship is going to make it complete," he said. "Honestly, I'm telling you this and not because we won the race, but because we've got a race team. We have guys who are ready to win races. We are going to concentrate on winning the eighth championship."

And now, there is no longer any need to concentrate on that first Daytona 500 win after coming so excruciatingly close over the years. Earnhardt ran out of gas to lose to Geoff Bodine in 1986. Then there was the now-famous cut tire on the last lap in 1990 that passed the win to Derrike Cope. Three times in the last five years he has finished second.

Today, he was second to no one.

"It was my time," Earnhardt said. "That's all I can say. I've been passed here. I've run out of gas. I've been cut down with a tire. I've done it all.

"I wrote the book and this is the last chapter in this book. I'm going to start a new book next year. It's over with.

"Every which way you can lose it, I've lost it. Now I've won it and I don't care how I won it. We won it."

At last. ∎

Clean Sweep

Earnhardt Completes Amazing 10-For-10 Twin 125 Run During The '90s

By TOM JENSEN

EARNHARDT MAKES IT 10-FOR-10 IN THE GATORADE 125. NWCS ARCHIVE PHOTO

Well, what did you expect to happen? Dale Earnhardt has won a Gatorade 125-Mile Qualifying Race during every Speedweeks since 1990. Why would anyone think 1999 would be any different?

Why indeed?

And it wasn't. Not even close, as a matter of fact.

Earnhardt completed his amazing, decade-long domination of the Twin 125s, driving his black Richard Childress Racing Chevrolet to a deceptively easy 0.251-second victory over Jeremy Mayfield's Penske-Kranefuss Racing Ford. Third was Dale Jarrett in his Robert Yates Racing Ford, followed by Mayfield's teammate, Rusty Wallace, and his Penske Racing South Ford and Mike Skinner in the second RCR Chevrolet.

In claiming victory for the 10th year in a row, Earnhardt led the final 43 laps and averaged 155.280 mph. There were two cautions for six laps during the race.

"Well that's pretty awesome in itself," said Earnhardt after the race, his 12th career victory and 10th in a row in a Twin 125. "Twelve races you've won and ... you don't know really why you do. All I can say is I love Daytona, I've got a great race team, it worked out. I come back every year thinking, 'Well, this will be the year I lose the qualifying race.' And we win again. It just makes you feel great, makes you feel proud of the team. I don't know how to explain it, other than it's a great race team."

Third-place finisher Jarrett agreed that Earnhardt's streak bordered on miraculous. Asked to put it into context, Jarrett said, "I've never won 10 in a row of anything, hardly, so I don't know what that would be like, exactly. It's pretty phenomenal to think somebody could come here and win it 10 times in a row."

Earnhardt, who had qualified fifth in the second of the day's Twin 125s, put the hammer down from the minute the green flag fell, diving down to the apron and going all the way into second place on the first of the race's 50 laps, taking teammate Skinner with him into third place.

Pole-winner Tony Stewart had jumped into the lead at the start and looked stout early on in his Joe Gibbs Racing Pontiac. But the young rookie got a hard lesson in super-speedway drafting around the high banks of Daytona.

Earnhardt bumped Stewart in turn three on lap seven, but Stewart held sway until the following lap, when the seven-time Winston Cup champion blew by the rookie's Pontiac on the high side, taking Jarrett with him. By the end of the lap, Stewart was all the way back to fifth. A lap after that, he was back in 10th and out of contention for the day, though he would finish a respectable sixth.

> "It just makes you feel great, makes you feel proud of the team. I don't know how to explain it, other than **it's a great race team.**"
> —Earnhardt

"At first, he got me down in the grass on the back straightaway. I checked up on him just a bit. To get back in line, we bumped a bit," said Earnhardt. "Then I got by him on the front straightaway."

"I learned a lot today," said Stewart. "If I told you what I learned, I'd be telling everybody else what I learned, and I'm not going to help them any."

And once Earnhardt was out front, nobody was going to get by. Nobody ever does that in a Twin 125.

About the only real excitement came further back in the pack where drivers sometimes went three-deep and three-wide jockeying to crack the top 15 and lock in a spot in the Daytona 500.

The event's one and only moment of drama came when Mayfield ran down Jarrett on the final lap to take second place. Other than that, it was simply business as usual for Earnhardt.

"I felt like they were going to make a run on me," Earnhardt said of the second- and third-place finishers. "I think if Mayfield would have helped Jarrett more than trying to beat him, Jarrett would have probably won the race or maybe Mayfield. But Mayfield kept getting greedy and trying to pass Jarrett and that didn't give Jarrett the opportunity to push by me.

"They were in the position to try and make something happen and I was in the position to try to keep it from happening and I just kept driving my race," Earnhardt said.

As for the runner-up, Mayfield felt good about his race and confident about his chances in the Daytona 500.

"We had a great car today, we've had a great car ever since we've been down here," said Mayfield. "This is probably the best car we've ever had here and it showed today. We didn't win the race, but we finished second. We fell back in the middle of the pack and came back. ... This thing's ready for the 500." ∎

DIEHARD 500

Still The Man

Earnhardt Flashes Championship Form In Dominating Victory

By TOM JENSEN

The night before the DieHard 500, when Dale Earnhardt unveiled his new car for next month's The Winston all-star race, a crowd of about 100 rabid fans flocked to the International Motorsports Hall of Fame to see their hero in person.

As Earnhardt and car owner Richard Childress took the stage and took the wraps off their special Wrangler-sponsored car, the noise was deafening as the fans whooped, hooted and hollered, undaunted by the fact that Earnhardt had visited victory lane in Winston Cup just once since the spring of 1996 and hadn't led a single lap so far in 1999.

"You're still the man, Dale!" they yelled, over and over and over again, with a fervor that bordered on evangelism.

In the DieHard 500, the seven-time NASCAR Winston Cup champion proved those fans right, at least for one day.

For on this muggy Alabama afternoon, Earnhardt was indeed still the man – "The Intimidator," "The Dominator," "The Man In Black," all rolled into one. Maybe he won't flash this form at the next race, or the race after that, but today he looked like a man with 72 career Winston Cup wins, seven titles and eight career victories at the circuit's fastest and most dangerous track.

This wasn't the Earnhardt who was hurt here in 1996 and '98 when he ended up on his roof in two horrifying wrecks. Instead, this was the man who left the rest of the field fighting for second place, the man who inspired such phenomenal fan loyalty and passion.

This was the Earnhardt people remembered and he made one thing absolutely certain: No one is tougher to pass at the end of a restrictor-plate race.

"I want to tell you guys something," car owner Richard Childress would say after the DieHard 500. "People came up and asked if Dale Earnhardt was too busy to win races. I had a couple of different reporters ask me if I thought Dale was past his prime. I think today should answer a lot of those questions."

Talladega Superspeedway is a track where you can always count on something happening, typically a 200-mph wreck that takes out half the field.

Earnhardt had been in two of them in the last three years, in fact.

> "I had a couple of different reporters ask me if I thought Dale was
> ## past his prime.
> I think today should answer a lot of those questions."
> —Richard Childress

"(The crash) in '96 broke me up pretty good and '98 burned me up pretty good," Earnhardt said. "It's a tough track to race on. Crashes happen and it gets serious. A lot of metal is coming at you."

And so the day began with a mixture of dread and anticipation, waiting to see what would occur in 188 laps of high-speed restrictor-plate racing.

The weirdness began early. Real early, in fact.

On the very first warm-up lap, Winston Cup points leader Jeff Burton's Roush Racing Ford began blowing huge plumes of thick white smoke out of its headers and he was forced into the pits. He went back out and rejoined the field at the tail of the pack, his car still smoking heavily, though it mysteriously stopped and he was able to continue.

When the green flag fell to start the race, Bobby Labonte muscled by pole-sitter Ken Schrader to assume the lead on the first lap, a spot he held until Wally Dallenbach went high in turn two to take the lead on lap six.

By this time, Earnhardt already had moved from his 17th starting spot all the way to third, and from there he would pass both Jeff Gordon and Dallenbach on lap 11 to move into the lead, the first of seven times he would hold the top spot.

Already, the madness was starting, with clusters of drivers running three- and four-wide, jockeying for position and looking for all the world like the only question would be when the 20-car pile-up would happen, not if it would happen.

Over the first 49 laps, the lead changed hands seven times among Earnhardt, Bobby Labonte, Dallenbach, Mike Skinner, Tony Stewart and John Andretti.

Predictably, whenever the cars went three-wide, someone would lose the lead draft and fall far back into the pack. It happened to Skinner once, dropping him from fourth to 15th in a single lap. It would later happen to Andretti and Labonte as well, and even once or twice to Earnhardt.

With all the dicing for position, sooner or later somebody was going to make a mistake. A big one.

This year's edition of the big crash occurred on lap 49, when Skinner led Stewart as both dove down near the grass on the backstretch. Stewart's Pontiac tapped the rear of Skinner's Chevrolet, sending it spinning into the middle of the pack, where it was struck by Jeff Gordon's Chevrolet. As Gordon's Chevrolet careened helplessly toward the top of the backstretch, it was nailed by Rusty Wallace's Ford and Ernie Irvan's Pontiac.

Also caught up in the melee were Chad Little, Kenny Irwin and Dallenbach.

On the ensuing pit stops on lap 54, Ward Burton and Johnny Benson collided on pit road. Burton got the worst of it, his right front heavily damaged, though both stayed in the race.

It could have been a lot worse. This time,

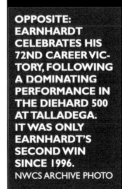

only eight cars were involved and no one was hurt, though there was plenty of bad tempers and finger-pointing afterward, as there always is.

When the clean up was completed and the track went green again on lap 58, Earnhardt was fourth, trailing leader Andretti and Bobby and Terry Labonte.

It only took one lap for Earnhardt to put his familiar black No. 3 Chevrolet back in front, going three-wide with Andretti and Michael Waltrip, who would run near the front all day before fading late to finish 18th.

Waltrip, in fact, assumed the lead on lap 68, going high on the backstretch to take the lead, a lead he would hold until near the race's midpoint. On lap 92, Jarrett took the lead for the first time, though only for one lap until Earnhardt sailed past him on the backstretch. They swapped places again on lap 101, with Jarrett taking the lead in turn three.

The leaders all pitted under green on lap 109, with first Schrader and then Jeremy Mayfield taking the lead, while Earnhardt dropped briefly to eighth as he opted for four fresh tires while Schrader and a couple of other drivers only took two.

Earnhardt was back in front on lap 120, a position he would hold for 15 laps until the day's second caution for Terry Labonte's spin in turn four.

When the leaders pitted on lap 135, Earnhardt's day took what looked like an irreversible turn for the worse. His crew changed four tires and inspected the right front for a suspected vibration.

"We took a little extra time," Earnhardt explained. "Everything looked good, so we came out a little further back than we wanted to, but we had the race car to come back to the front."

Boy did he ever.

When Earnhardt rejoined the race, he was all the way back in 16th place, with barely 50 laps to go. But he made up ground in a hurry. The green flag flew on lap 140, and Earnhardt charged to sixth by lap 145, and third behind Andretti and Waltrip just one lap later. On lap 147 he eased into second and on 148, he went high into turn three as leader Andretti lost the draft and dropped from first to seventh in the blink of an eye.

Just like that, the black Chevrolet with the No. 3 on the side was out front.

"Everybody was pretty racy," Earnhardt said. "I wanted to get to the second or third position so I could work my way to the front or have the opportunity to race for the win."

That he did, but not without a fight.

On lap 151, Waltrip took the lead, only to be overtaken the very next time around by Bobby Labonte.

Then it started getting wild again. Jarrett went high in turn two on lap 163, taking Earnhardt with him into second past Labonte, who promptly repassed Earnhardt the next lap.

As the laps dwindled down, three-wide running became the norm, with drivers sometimes going even four- and five-wide in a restrictor-plate free-for-all.

For a time, it looked as though Jarrett's Robert Yates Racing Ford, the car which had won here last October, might have the measure of Earnhardt. But the last of the race's three cautions flew on lap 170 when Bobby Hamilton and Robert Pressley wrecked in turn one.

"Trying to pass Dale Earnhardt at one of these restrictor-plate tracks with two or three laps to go is a pretty tall order," said Jarrett.

"He makes the No. 3 car pretty wide."

Earnhardt, who had been strong on restarts all day, wasted no time. The green flew on lap 174, and the leaders went three-wide on the backstretch, with Earnhardt going under Andretti to take second in turn three.

Then he and Andretti passed Jarrett on the backstretch on lap 175.

And once Earnhardt is out front on a restrictor-plate track with only 13 laps to go, he is not an easy man to pass, though everyone tried. Labonte and Stewart worked with Mark Martin, who hadn't been much of a factor all day. Jarrett gave it all he had, too.

With nine laps to go it was Earnhardt ahead of Andretti, Mayfield, Jarrett, Schrader and Martin. With six to go, Jarrett was back up to third and two laps later, the luckless Andretti was hung out and headed for a ninth-place finish.

"I knew something was going to happen," Earnhardt said. "The 88 (Jarrett) got a run on the 43 (Andretti) and he wasn't going to sit there. He wanted to be behind me or in front of me. When he made that move, I countered, and that made the decision that the 88 was going to be the better car. It worked out for us. It was a game of chess, knowing when to move and where to move

to, and I can't play chess."

Oh, yes he could. And he did.

Earnhardt and Jarrett began to pull away, with Martin joining the fray two laps from the end.

"They got to racing so much there behind us, it allowed Jarrett and I to run our laps," Earnhardt said. "I didn't know if it would last until the end or they would mount a charge and a string would come back. Mark did break away and Mark came to the back of Jarrett in the last lap.

"It was a little too late and Jarrett couldn't make a move to run on me. It was fortunate it worked out that way and there wasn't any more laps left. They would have probably got to me and got by me."

But at the end of the day, the only thing the two Ford drivers had for Earnhardt was praise.

"Trying to pass Dale Earnhardt at one of these restrictor-plate tracks with two or three laps to go is a pretty tall order," said Jarrett. "He makes the No. 3 car pretty wide."

"He's sort of the master of restrictor-plate racing," agreed Martin. "He's the best I've ever come up against."

And that's how the DieHard 500 ended: Earnhardt winning by 0.137 second over Jarrett and Martin, after leading a race-high 70 of 188 laps.

The Joe Gibbs Racing Pontiac teammates Labonte and Stewart were fourth and fifth, respectively, followed by another pair of teammates, the Andy Petree Racing duo of Schrader and Kenny Wallace. Rounding out the top 10 were Jerry Nadeau in the Melling Racing Ford, Andretti and Bill Elliott.

Needless to say, it was a big day for Earnhardt, Childress and Kevin Hamlin, who earned his first Winston Cup win as a crew chief, after plenty of frustrations and a couple of near-misses.

"We've been real close, but in this sport, you can't just be close, you've got to be right on," Hamlin said. "We're really working hard with the cars and the pit crews, the whole package. Hopefully we can carry some of this momentum forward."

Earnhardt is sure the team can and he's looking ahead to the May 2 California 500.

"We've got a brand-new car for California and if it doesn't go fast it'll be my fault because the car is really good," he said. "We've had a real crappy year so far, but I think it's going to turn around for us. We've got some good race cars coming out now. We've got a lot of things going on that are going to get better as we go."

Although it's hard to image how they could get much better than they were at Talladega. ∎

LEST YOU FORGET WHY HE'S 'THE INTIMIDATOR'...
NWCS ARCHIVE PHOTO

'Ironhead' By TOM JENSEN

vs. 'Iron Man'

Earnhardt Pushes Way To
Controversial Last-Lap Win At Bristol

"It wasn't right.
It wasn't right,"

second-place finisher Jimmy Spencer
said of Earnhardt's roughhouse tactics.

Surreal. Absolutely surreal. Wrecked race cars littered across the track as the checkered flag flies, outrageous controversy, screaming and finger-flipping fans teetering on the edge of delirium, angry race teams and a race no one will soon forget.

In other words, just another typical August Saturday night at Bristol Motor Speedway, deja vu all over again.

Tempers run hot and out of control at the high-banked 0.533-mile Bristol pressure cooker, a place where you damn well better be ready to fight if you come.

And in the entire half century history of NASCAR, you can make a pretty compelling case that no one's ever spoiled for a fight more than seven-time champion Dale Earnhardt.

Call him "The Man In Black," "The Intimidator," "Ironhead" or what you choose, no one has a stronger will to win than Earnhardt. And while some were ready to dismiss the 48-year-old, Kannapolis, N.C., native as being over the hill after a winless 1997 season and just one victory last year, Earnhardt proved he's far from finished at this year's running of the Goody's Headache Powder 500 in Bristol.

In fact, Earnhardt laid waste to the old adage about not teaching old dogs new tricks, 'cause he sure learned an important one here: You can't win wrecking Terry Labonte in the last turn of the last lap, as he did in 1995. To win, you've got to wreck him in the first turn of the last lap.

Four years ago at Bristol, Earnhardt rammed the back of Labonte coming out of turn four, but the Texan's mangled Hendrick Motorsports Chevrolet still managed to slide across the finish line first with Earnhardt second.

This time was different. Tonight, before God, country, a full moon and 141,000 fired up race fans, Earnhardt again popped Labonte, this time between turns one and two of lap 500, igniting a firestorm of rage among rivals and race fans alike and relegating Labonte to eighth, after he had made a miraculous late charge and seemed certain of victory.

Finishing between the victorious Earnhardt and the vanquished Labonte were Jimmy Spencer, Ricky Rudd, Jeff Gordon, Tony Stewart, Mark Martin and Sterling Marlin in seventh. Rounding out the top 10 were Ward Burton and Ken Schrader.

It was Earnhardt's second win of the season, ninth at Bristol and 73rd overall of his illustrious career. And while Earnhardt and the Richard Childress Racing team were happy, few others were. The fans roared their collective discontent, ringing the track with obscenities, upraised middle fingers and choruses of boos. Many competitors were angry afterward as well.

"It wasn't right. It wasn't right," second-place finisher Jimmy Spencer said of Earnhardt's roughhouse tactics. Spencer, himself no stranger to aggressive driving, said, "I used to fight for stuff worse than that on Saturday nights."

"To tell you the truth, I knew there was going to be a wreck," added Rudd. " ... In that situation, you've got to look at who you're dealing with."

Earnhardt, as you might expect, was unapologetic.

"If it comes down to the last lap and you're going for it and you get into somebody, you get into them. You don't mean to, but you mean to race them."

The chaotic finish led NASCAR officials to huddle for more than hour before letting the victory stand.

Well after midnight, NASCAR Chief Operating Officer Mike Helton stood outside the NASCAR trailer trying to explain why Earnhardt's victory was allowed to stand despite the hard contact that sent Labonte into the wall.

"After seeing the end of the race and reviewing all of the tapes, NASCAR is going to let the finish order stand as it completed," Helton said.

"Naturally it would have been better had the race finished under different circumstances, but inasmuch as in having to make a decision whether or not you take a race away from someone for something that happens on the race track, the information that you have or the result is, you have to be very inconclusive and be certain about that. And in this case it's not inconclusive that it was a racing accident on the way back to the checkered flag. And therefore we're going to leave the standings the way they were at the finish of the race.

"If there were going to be any actions taken, they would have been taken tonight. Whether or not NASCAR takes a look at future steps to avoid these types of incidents in the past that are not clearly handled, we may take a look at that, but tonight's results will stand the way they are."

Earnhardt, who has seen both sides of bump-and-run moves over the years, shrugged off the criticism.

"I've always just took my medicine, took what happened and just sucked it up and just go to the next race. You can't change or do anything about it," he said.

Labonte, naturally was unimpressed.

"I won't even waste my time to go to the (NASCAR) trailer and talk to them about it. I've been there before."

And he was none too subtle about giving Earnhardt a payback.

"He better tighten his belts," warned Labonte.

It didn't take long for the action to heat up. Second-qualifier Rusty Wallace grabbed the lead from pole sitter Stewart at the start, powering around the outside of the Joe Gibbs Racing Pontiac when the green flag dropped.

Hapless Robert Pressley was the first casualty of the Saturday night bullring madness, wrecking his Jasper Motorsports Ford

EARNHARDT SLIPS PAST A SPINNING AND FUMING TERRY LABONTE AFTER 'BUMPING' HIM ON THE FINAL LAP. LABONTE CRASHED INTO THE INSIDE WALL WHILE EARNHARDT TOOK THE CHECKERED FLAG.
NWCS ARCHIVE PHOTO

between turns one and two on lap three to bring out the first caution of the night.

Although he lost the lead at the start, Stewart hounded Wallace and on lap 22 popped him in the rear bumper between turns three and four just to let him know he was still there.

On lap 27, Stewart finally made it by Wallace, taking over the point off of turn two, a move Gordon would repeat a lap later to drop Wallace to third place.

Up front, Stewart held on comfortably, with the order of the top three staying the same for the next 50 laps.

Then came the first key moment of the race.

On lap 78 points leader Dale Jarrett got squirrelly off of turn two, and as the parade of Cup cars made their way to three, all hell broke loose as Jarrett spun and collected John Andretti, Hut Stricklin, Michael Waltrip, Bill Elliott, Jeremy Mayfield and Bobby Hamilton.

Although Jarrett suffered only right side damage, the worst was yet to come.

Jerry Nadeau, who was subbing for the injured Ernie Irvan in the MB2 Motorsports Pontiac, tagged the back of Jarrett's Ford on the frontstretch, bringing out another yellow flag and sending the Robert Yates Racing Ford into the pits for lengthy repairs that would take 155 laps.

Jarrett, who began the night with a seemingly unassailable 300-point lead over Mark Martin in the Winston Cup championship, saw his margin dwindle to a still-comfortable 213 points by the end of the race.

To his credit, Jarrett took responsibility for the first wreck.

"I created the problem for some other people and myself," Jarrett said. "It was my fault."

NASCAR, however, penalized Nadeau two laps for rough driving, which did not go over well with his team and crew chief Ryan Pemberton.

"Where's the justice at?" Pemberton asked after the race. "What the 3 car did, that was blatant. I don't know, that was at least two laps, I think."

As the night wore on, rookie Stewart set the pace, leading a race-high 225 laps. But before long, the usual Bristol hijinxs started to play out.

David Green hit the turn-three wall midway through the race to bring out the yellow flag again. When the leaders all pitted on lap 252, it was Gordon out first, then Martin, Stewart, Marlin and Bobby Labonte.

Ten laps later, Kyle Petty tapped Stricklin coming out of turn four, an accident that also snared Johnny Benson.

EARNHARDT POPS THE CORK ON HIS SECOND WIN OF THE SEASON.
NWCS ARCHIVE PHOTO

The track went green on lap 269, and five laps later Earnhardt and Rusty Wallace had contact, causing Wallace's left rear to go down. Wallace pitted for fresh rubber on lap 278, but he was two laps down and effectively out of contention for a win.

It got worse. Chad Little spun Mayfield and collected Kenny Irwin and Wally Dallenbach in turn two on lap 290.

The green flew again on lap 296, and on the restart Stewart almost lost it in turn one as he went high, allowing Martin to retake second place.

Then Irwin brought out yet another yellow flag, getting loose into Nadeau in turn four, and wrecking half a dozen other cars in the process.

With the yellow out, the complexion of the race changed.

About half of the lead-lap car pitted on lap 300, but when the green flag came back out on lap 305, the order was jumbled by the cars that stayed out: Terry Labonte ahead of Earnhardt, Spencer, Geoffrey Bodine, Rudd, Gordon, Bobby Labonte, Stewart Martin and Marlin.

Stewart's decision to pit proved to be a good one: His right rear tire was going flat.

Then the race settled down, with veterans Labonte and Earnhardt in command out front, which is how it stayed for the final 200 laps, as they swapped the lead seven more times.

Dave Marcis slowed high on the track on lap 411, after he couldn't get an opening

down low to pit. The track went yellow and NASCAR assessed Marcis a one-lap penalty for intentionally bringing out a caution.

The leaders all pitted on lap 412, with Labonte emerging ahead of teammate Gordon, Earnhardt, Stewart, Bobby Labonte, Martin, Rudd, Spencer, Little and Brett Bodine.

Labonte remained in the lead until lap 435, when Earnhardt passed him and stayed in front for four laps, before Labonte went back into the lead, a position he would hold onto until the 490th of 500 laps.

The final 10 laps were pure bedlam. Mayfield and Wally Dallenbach collided on the backstretch on lap 490, as the leaders rushed by. Labonte made it safely into turn three when he was spun by Darrell Waltrip.

"I don't know what he was thinking," a peeved Labonte said afterward.

Labonte ducked into the pits for fresh tires and seemed out of it. But with few cars left on the lead lap, he emerged from the pits fifth behind Earnhardt, Stewart, Gordon – none of whom had pitted – and Martin.

When the green flag came out again on lap 496, Labonte took off like a shot on his fresh tires, quickly passing the three cars ahead of him, Martin first, then on lap 498 getting by Gordon and Stewart, respectively.

On lap 499 he muscled past Earnhardt, bumping him a little in turns three and four. It appeared certain he was headed for victory lane. At least until Earnhardt nailed him on the last lap, that is.

"I don't think I spun Terry intentionally," Earnhardt said. "You'll have to go to NASCAR about all that. I've got big shoulders and I can take the pressure or the blame or whatever. It was not an intentional bump, but it happened.

"I'm sure we'll hear about the race for awhile, and we'll just have to take it like it is. Like I said, I have broad shoulders. I have to take what comes and race from here on.

"If it would have been on the other foot and I'd been the one turned around, I would think about it pretty hard and know he was going to race me hard to win.

John Hendrick argued driver Labonte's case afterward in the NASCAR trailer, but to no avail.

"They made their ruling, they're not going to change anything," said Hendrick. "It stands. We're not happy with it at all. Everybody saw what happened. It's a shame for Terry 'cause he fought back so hard."

Runner-up Spencer, however, may have had the definitive word on the last-lap melee.

"I went into the final turn, and wow, Ironman and Ironhead got together," he said.

And that was that. ∎

Jeff Owens looks back on
a wild night at Bristol

The grin said it all. It always said it all when it came to Dale Earnhardt.

Earnhardt developed many trademarks throughout his illustrious career. There was the black No. 3 that he drove with reckless abandon. There was the outlaw mustache, the one that made him look like a character out of the old West. And there was the confident, tough-guy swagger, the one that said, "Don't mess with me."

Then there was the mischievous grin, the one that made you think he was holding the winning hand, or, perhaps more accurately, had pulled a fast one on somebody.

Even when the heat was on, when heavy pressure was being heaped on his broad shoulders, Earnhardt almost always flashed that sly grin.

Though it wasn't evident to most, he carried it with him that infamous August night at Bristol, the night he wrecked Terry Labonte on the backstretch, stealing a win in a devious case of grand larceny.

It was a race few will ever forget, Earnhardt roaring through the field, pushing and shoving his way to the front, leaving plenty of carnage in his wake.

With one lap to go, Labonte was on his way to another smooth win at Bristol. But as he took the white flag, Earnhardt came charging into the first turn. As he came flying out of turn two, he plowed right into the back of Labonte, spinning him out of the lead and leaving cars wrecking behind them.

As Labonte fumed and drivers all around him tried to restart their cars and creep across the finish line, Earnhardt took the most questionable checkered flag of his career.

> Earnhardt was booed loudly, a sound rarely heard during his heyday.

Afterward, he was booed like a masked man dragging a steel chair into the ring.

Earnhardt was booed loudly, a sound rarely heard during his heyday.

Though many hated him, no one had a legion of fans like Earnhardt. His faithful following was so loud you could barely hear the boos. Even fans who professed to hate him could be seen at times cheering him. A genuine folk hero, he was just too good — or too cool — to really hate.

But on this night, after the treachery he was clearly guilty of, Earnhardt was booed and cussed as never before.

Fans who spent a fortune pledging their allegiance to "The Man in Black" ripped off their No. 3 T-shirts and threw them on the track. Others threw their black and white coolers over the fence, some of them half full of beer.

Their disdain poured down on Earnhardt like summer rain, showering him with discontent. Suddenly, for the first time in years, Earnhardt was the villain, many of his own fans turning on him and siding with Labonte, who had clearly been wronged.

Even Earnhardt seemed a bit stunned, declaring: "I didn't mean to wreck him. I was just trying to rattle his cage." Later, he admitted he understood the ramifications of his actions, saying: "I've got broad shoulders. I can handle it."

But that was publicly. That was his message to the media and to his fans.

Privately, Earnhardt was flashing that sly, mischievous grin, knowing he had gotten away with another one.

As he headed to the press box elevator for the customary winner's interview, he was met by a throng of angry fans, many shouting insults, flashing obscene gestures and throwing things.

It was a tense moment for Earnhardt, suddenly the hated man.

But when the elevator doors closed, Earnhardt breathed a sigh and grinned.

"Man, I love this [stuff]," he said, a broad smile stretching across his face.

To Earnhardt, it was another pressure-packed victory, one filled with controversy, intensity and drama.

All Earnhardt trademarks.

Just like his grin. ■

—Jeff Owens
Executive Editor
NASCAR Scene

EARNHARDT STILL SAVORS THESE MOMENTS, EVEN THOUGH THERE HAVE BEEN 73 OTHERS.
NWCS ARCHIVE PHOTO

Basic Black Still In Fashion

Earnhardt Again Proves He's Master Of The Wind In Talladega Shootout

By TOM JENSEN

Dale Earnhardt set the record straight at Talladega: His fans are going to have to wait for his retirement tour. And the wait could be a lengthy one.

The seven-time Winston Cup champion is close to finalizing a new contract with car owner Richard Childress, and of course is actively involved with son Dale Jr.'s upcoming Winston Cup rookie season in 2000.

More significantly, perhaps, Earnhardt is seriously stoked about his prospects for the future, despite being 48 years old and being written off after winning just one Winston Cup race between March 1996 and the end of last season.

Reports of Earnhardt's demise, though, have proven greatly exaggerated.

This year "The Intimidator" has flashed his championship form of yesteryear, winning a bump-and-grind bash at Bristol and on this Indian Summer Alabama afternoon, he completed a Talladega sweep with a stunning victory in the Winston 500.

The Talladega victory was the 74th of Earnhardt's storied Winston Cup career, including 45 on superspeedways. In addition to sweeping both races at Talladega this year, he finished second in both Daytona races, the Daytona 500 and Pepsi 400, the only other track on which Winston Cup cars use restrictor plates.

And if you listen to Earnhardt, there's a whole lot of winning still left to be done before he even thinks about hanging up his helmet.

In the post-race interview at Talladega, he flashed as much form as he did on the track, mixing the trademark bravado with a few semi-sarcastic one-liners.

In other words, it was vintage Earnhardt.

"I'm not thinking about retirement by any means," said Earnhardt in the press box. "It's real funny to me that all of a sudden I became Dale Sr. I mean, Darrell Waltrip's the guy who's talking about retirement, not Dale Earnhardt. And I'm still winning races and running in the top 10 in points all the time and have for the last several years.

"And I don't see where I should be getting older just because Darrell is or anybody else, or I've got a son in racing now and he's Dale Jr. I shouldn't be Dale Sr. I should just be Dale Earnhardt."

Bold words, perhaps, but if Earnhardt's proven anything over his career, it's that he doesn't just talk the talk, he walks the walk, too.

"We're going to win that eighth championship, that's our No. 1 goal right now," said car owner Childress. "Dale Earnhardt can still do it, and anyone that's ever doubted it made a big mistake."

It sure seemed that way in Talladega.

A blown engine in first-day qualifying meant Earnhardt started the Winston 500 way back in 27th place. But he wasted absolutely no time going to the front.

Astonishingly, he moved all the way up to third place by lap eight and remained in contention the rest of the day.

It has been said of Earnhardt that he can see the air in the draft, and the way he drove early in this affair did little to dispel the myth.

"We started off at a deficit there at 27th, but we were rolling along there and it got sort of two-wide and then sort of opened up in the middle. I was sort of seeing some things that I thought would work. I went for it and went through the middle."

And so he did, blowing by the competition as if his black Chevrolet was the only car out there without one of those damnable restrictor plates choking back the horsepower of his engine.

But it would take awhile for Earnhardt to get all the way to the front – lap 106 of 188, to be exact – while all around chaos reigned.

From the get-go, drivers ran three-, four- and even five-wide around the giant 2.66-mile Talladega track, trading positions with wild abandon.

It looked like a 15-lap feature at some half-mile dirt track, or maybe a 200 mph rugby scrum. That the high-speed anarchy resulted in only one crash, a five-car affair midway, rather than the 20- or 30-car pileup that's come to be the norm at restrictor-plate tracks was nothing short of miraculous.

In the first 20 laps alone, eight different drivers led, as drivers repeatedly got shuffled in and out of the draft, as is the custom at Talladega.

One lap, a guy would be in the lead, the next lap he'd be hung out to dry and end up eighth or 10th or even 20th.

It happened to Earnhardt. It also happened to Dale Jarrett, Bobby Labonte, Jeff Gordon and Tony Stewart, Joe Nemechek and Sterling Marlin, all of whom at one time or another seemed to have cars capable of winning.

Gordon, in particular, looked stout, as if he could win for the third time in a row with new crew chief Brian Whitesell. He led four times for 71 laps, by far the most of any driver.

Jarrett, too, looked strong, running the car that had won this race a year earlier and the Pepsi 400 at Daytona in July.

But the only one who seemed capable of muscling his way back up front, especially late in the race, was Earnhardt.

Of course, so much depended on teamwork and temporary alliances. If drivers worked together, they could move up. Drift out of line and you went straight back.

"It's tough to pick your partner at any point of that race," Earnhardt said. "I would see guys that would be sitting in line racing and guys would pull out on you and run along on the bottom and you'd draft by 'em.

"Guys would line up and you'd get back by 'em, and you'd look in your mirror and they'd be back about 15th place. It was just a tough day. I did that one time and slipped back to about 12th. You just had to be careful on what moves you made and when you made 'em and who was around when you made 'em."

And what set the stage for Earnhardt's final moves occurred

when most of the leaders pitted for their final stops of the race. At the same time Terry Labonte suffered a punctured oil cooler in the trioval, bringing out a caution on lap 140.

"And I don't see where I should be getting older just because Darrell is or anybody else, or I've got a son in racing now and he's Dale Jr. I shouldn't be Dale Sr.

I should just be Dale Earnhardt."

Of the cars that were coming down pit road when Labonte's oil cooler blew, only Bobby Labonte, Earnhardt and Ward Burton completed their service.

The rest of the leaders pitted again on lap 142, and when the track went green on lap 146, the order was Bobby Labonte, Burton,

USED TO 'CLEANING UP' AT TALLADEGA, EARNHARDT SWEEPS UP THE FUNNY MONEY IN VICTORY LANE.
NWCS ARCHIVE PHOTO

Earnhardt, Bobby Hamilton, Michael Waltrip, Jarrett, Steve Park, Kenny Irwin, Elliott Sadler and Gordon.

Earnhardt reassumed the lead on lap 147, only to be passed by the surprising Waltrip after just three laps. Unfortunately for Waltrip, his stay up front was short, as he blew an engine on lap 155, one lap after Jarrett passed him to take the lead.

During the last 35 laps, Jarrett led twice for 20 laps and appeared ready to back up last year's victory here.

By his own admission, Earnhardt didn't have the best car, but he again proved he is the master of the draft.

"As far as seeing air, I know it's there," he said. "I've just got to play the hunches right and hope it's there when I need it."

And that he did.

As the laps wound down, RCR teammate Mike Skinner and Labonte hooked up with Earnhardt to get up front. And on lap 185, the black No. 3 made the decisive pass of Jarrett for the win.

"Jarrett was hanging tough on the bottom. I knew it was going to be tough to get by him," Earnhardt said. "Skinner and the 18 car (Labonte) worked hard and helped me get up there. Once I cleared the 88 (Jarrett), I tried to pull Skinner with me and he got hung up with the 88. The 18 got to racing and got by him.

"Then, they got to going three-wide. It was getting down to the last two laps and everybody was panicking. They were making all the moves they could."

But as he so often does, Earnhardt had the last word about holding off the competition from up front.

"You can play defense better than you can play offense from the back," he said.

As the checkered flag fell, Earnhardt scored his third win this season and ninth of his career at Talladega, giving him a sweep of both 1999 Winston Cup races at the Alabama superspeedway.

Earnhardt set a blistering pace all afternoon, averaging 166.632 mph in the 188-lap race, which saw a whopping 32 lead changes among 16 drivers, and only three cautions for 17 laps.

Finishing second just 0.114 second behind Earnhardt was Jarrett, who took a giant step toward clinching his first Winston Cup championship, leaving with a 246-point lead over Bobby Labonte.

Ricky Rudd came home third, followed by Ward Burton, Kenny Wallace, Stewart and Labonte. Rounding out the top 10 were Jeff Burton in the Roush Racing Ford, the Morgan McClure Motorsports Chevrolet of Hamilton and Kenny Irwin in the Robert Yates Racing Ford. ■

dale earnhardt

Earnhardt Rules

Veteran Beats Labonte By Inches In A Classic Finish

By DEB WILLIAMS

For a few seconds after the checkered flag fell on the Cracker Barrel Old Country Store 500, no one was quite sure who had won.

Dale Earnhardt's Richard Childress Racing crew stood along pit road with bewildered looks on their faces.

Bobby Labonte's Joe Gibbs Racing team wasn't too sure, either.

There was no roar from the fans, and the media in the press box looked at each other and asked, "Who won?"

Finally, the RCR crewmen released shouts of joy. Earnhardt had been declared the winner in what can be defined as a classic stock car race; the kind of race that rocketed NASCAR Winston Cup racing to national popularity.

And the type of race NASCAR needed after the reaction it had received from many fans and media members who had called the first three events of the season boring.

For the cool, sunny day, Hollywood

EARNHARDT HELD BOBBY LABONTE AT BAY BY MERE INCHES AT THE FINISH.
NWCS ARCHIVE PHOTO

couldn't have written a better script as the maturing youngster battled the seasoned veteran for the victory. Side by side they raced off turn four for the checkered flag with the fans cheering wildly. For NASCAR's camera located at the finish line, it became a victory frozen in time.

Labonte had no idea who had won.

"I couldn't tell," he said in his post-race interview.

Earnhardt, however, felt he was the winner.

"When we were getting close to the line, I looked over and his car wasn't really side by side with me as far as looking into the driver's door … so I felt pretty good about what our chances were that we beat him out by a nose," Earnhardt said.

He was correct. He had collected his 75th career win by inches, and some might argue by the two inches NASCAR allowed the Chevrolet teams to extend their front air dam.

"I just came up about a valence too short, two inches too short, whatever you want to call it," a disappointed Labonte said. "It's just one of those deals. I haven't seen the replay and don't really care to. It doesn't really matter to me. I just ended up a little short."

> "I haven't seen the replay and don't really care to.
> ## It doesn't really matter to me.
> I just ended up a little short."
> —Bobby Labonte

Since the fall of 1996, the track had belonged to the 35-year-old Labonte, who had celebrated victory in four of the last seven races. The 48-year-old Earnhardt, meanwhile, hadn't won at the speedway since the spring of '96 and not since it had been reconfigured into a 1.54-mile track for the 1997 season.

In this 325-lap event, Earnhardt was better on the short runs and Labonte held the advantage on the long ones.

With 13 laps remaining, the race restarted from its final caution flag, and it was clear it would be a two-car battle.

On lap 316, Labonte challenged Earnhardt on the outside on the backstretch, and they raced side by side through turns three and four. Earnhardt pulled back ahead as they began lap 317.

Labonte elected to follow Earnhardt until he saw the white flag. It was now or never, and this time Labonte elected to try the low groove, inching ahead of Earnhardt, who went high in turns three and four. They never touched as each driver held his line through the dogleg and to the checkered flag.

"I was just running the outside in (turns) one and two better than I was running the outside in (turns) three and four," Labonte said. "I could get up off of two better than I could get up off of four. So I was running through one and two high.

"On the last lap, Dale moved up a little bit. I still had a good run off the corner. It really bit on the rear, and I had a run on him. I got right on his back bumper down the back straightaway. I knew he was going to go high because I had been running up there, and it was just kind of how the trend had been going all day. I had no option but to go low.

"You really don't stick that good down low. But I guess I had run high long enough that my tires stuck a little bit better than I anticipated. I didn't even figure I'd get close to his rear bumper to be honest with you. When it stuck, I got back on the gas as hard as I could and just used up all the race track I could to get down to the start/finish line as fast as I could."

Earnhardt, who noted he and Labonte almost wrecked when Skinner's engine blew and left oil in turns one and two, described the last lap as "good racin'."

"I got after it as hard as I could there at the end and ran hard," he said. "I found a pretty good line through (turns) three and four. In (turns) one and two, I was on the bottom. In three and four, I was up a little bit. I held him off.

"It sort of seemed he was waiting, biding his time. Sure enough, he made his run there on the last lap and got close to beating us. It definitely wasn't a boring race."

It wasn't until the race's second half that Labonte and Earnhardt became factors in the event. Skinner, Earnhardt's teammate, had

EARNHARDT CELEBRATES HIS 75TH CAREER VICTORY WITH RETIRED GEN. COLIN POWELL. EARNHARDT LISTS POWELL AS ONE OF HIS HEROES. NWCS ARCHIVE PHOTO

"I think we've got a better race car (now) to race with, and our balance is better than what we had. We just need to keep tuning on it."

One thing that possibly helped Earnhardt in the race was crew chief Kevin Hamlin's planning ahead. Hamlin was aware activities at the track might get rained out the day before the event. He called Earnhardt and asked if he had any problem with them practicing some race runs on pole day rather than just concentrating on qualifying. Earnhardt had no objections.

"Our plan was to get a little bit of race practice in and have an idea of what this new valence change was going to do for us, especially here at Atlanta," Hamlin said. "I think it was a good thing for our whole team to do that, and it paid off for us today."

Still, when they began the race they were quite loose.

"We put a rubber in on the right front on the first pit stop that we had taken out and adjusted it a little bit with wedge and track bar," Earnhardt said. "We adjusted a little bit, as we went, really not a lot after that.

"We were really afraid to do too much one way or the other because we were worried about one set of tires being too tight or loose. We just sort of stayed there and it worked out for us. We had a consistent race car once we got all the fenders knocked back out straight and quit running over things."

Earnhardt also noted speedway officials "messed up a good race track when they put this dogleg in it."

"But that's their choice. They bought the race track, they can do what they want to with it," he said. "It's a good race track, but it was a great race track before. It's an OK race track now. It's a lot different than it was. That dogleg is not a favorite of mine, neither here nor Texas nor Charlotte."

For the owner of seven Winston Cup championships, the win was special. Not just because it was his ninth one at Atlanta, but because retired Gen. Colin Powell was in attendance.

"I've always been a big fan of his and how he worked hard for the American way and for the dream that we have," Earnhardt said. "To get to meet him today at the drivers meeting and then to get to receive the trophy from him was a great honor. That's going to be something that will go down in my scrapbook. Maybe I can get him to autograph a picture for me. That was neat because he was here today." ∎

dominated and appeared headed for his first-ever Winston Cup win before his car's engine blew with 20 laps remaining. He led eight times for 191 laps and at one point drew the ire of his teammate.

On lap 207, Earnhardt moved to the inside of Skinner as they headed for turn three. Skinner cut him off, clipping Earnhardt's left front. Earnhardt later said it was too early to be using those tactics; Skinner felt he was justified with the maneuver.

"I'd wreck my mom to win my first race," Skinner said. "Dale did what he had to do, and I did what I had to do. He's my teammate and I wouldn't wreck him, and it was too early in the race to be wrecking anybody, but I blocked him. He probably was further alongside me than I thought."

Earnhardt said he was angry with Skinner

for bending his right front fender.

"It was too early to be racing like that," he said. "I was under him coming off the corner, and as I was coming off the corner, he kept coming down and kept coming down, and I just kept going and going. We finally got together, and I was past the stripe on the inside. It just didn't need to happen at that stage of the race. We had two good race cars, and we could have torn them up right there."

While Skinner and Earnhardt fans will argue over who was right and who was wrong, it was the finish that probably will cause intense arguments to erupt among Ford and General Motors fans. Even Earnhardt admitted he couldn't have won with the Monte Carlo he raced the previous week.

"I think it would have pushed too much through the center and off the corner," he said.

Kenny Bruce recalls just how close Dale Earnhardt came to a record-setting eighth championship.

Heading into the 2000 NASCAR Winston Cup season, Dale Earnhardt was tabbed a longshot to capture the championship.

A seven-time champion, a winner of three races the year before and 74 during his career, a longshot? A master at restrictor-plate races and a force for years on the series' short tracks, a darkhorse?

Hard to believe, perhaps, but that was indeed the case.

Earnhardt, who would turn 49 on April 29, had finished seventh in the points in 1999. In 1998, he had wound up eighth. And although he hadn't been shut out - winning four times during that two-year span — the consistency that had made him one of the favorites each week for nearly two decades could no longer be counted on. Time, it seemed, had finally begun to catch up to the driver many considered to be the best ever.

At least, that's what most folks thought.

Earnhardt, though, knew better.

Team owner Richard Childress, who had seen his driver pull off near miracles behind the wheel of the daunting black No. 3 Chevrolet, knew better. And soon, the competition would know better, too.

Off-season surgery had eased more than a year's worth of back pain and numbness in Earnhardt's hands. Chevrolet teams, in the meantime, had rolled out a new version of the Monte Carlo. The only thing left to do, it seemed, was for Earnhardt to prove to others what he himself had always known - that he was still a force to be reckoned with on the race track.

That proof came on a sunny March afternoon in Atlanta.

Earnhardt, though, didn't come away empty-handed. Far from it.

Back-to-back top-10s in the two races leading up to the Cracker Barrel Old Country Store 500 had thrust Earnhardt into the top 10 in the points battle. But it was at Atlanta Motor Speedway, a track where he had eight previous wins, that Earnhardt took a major step in reasserting himself as a legitimate threat to win an unprecedented eighth championship.

Although he qualified a woeful 35th, Earnhardt wasted little time in racing his way towards the front. By the end of the day, the list of contenders had dwindled to include only two drivers - himself and Bobby Labonte. The two combined to lead on six different occasions, so it was fitting that they were side by side as they came off the fourth turn for a final time.

At the line, the pair seemed locked together, one driver striving to take his place among those who would be champion and another fighting to keep his rightful place in the sport. In the end, video of the finish told the tale: Earnhardt had nipped his Joe Gibbs Racing rival by a mere 0.010 second.

But there would be no eighth title that year for Earnhardt.

Labonte, who had been creeping closer and closer each year to the top, finally reached the summit, beating Earnhardt for the title by 265 points.

Earnhardt, though, didn't come away empty-handed. Far from it. His efforts proved beyond a doubt that at 49, he was just as competitive, just as hungry as ever.

A darkhorse? That's what most folks thought.

Earnhardt, though, knew better. ∎

—Kenny Bruce
Associate Editor
NASCAR Scene

earnhardt · dale

Crowd Pleaser

Earnhardt Puts On A Show In Yet Another Talladega Triumph

By MARK ASHENFELTER

Dale Earnhardt hates restrictor-plate racing. Always has. Always will. And that's not going to change no matter how many times he wins at NASCAR's biggest track.

The day before the Winston 500, he said they'd taken racing out of the drivers' hands here years ago when they first bolted carburetor plates on the cars. So the fact that NASCAR changed the size of the plate less than 24 hours before the race was something he could shrug off as just another reason to hate plate racing.

Yet the more he gripes about it, the more determined he seems to go out and prove himself wrong. In another trademark performance, Earnhardt maneuvered from 22nd to the lead in the final, frantic 10 laps on the way to his 10th career win at Talladega Superspeedway. If that's not the mark of a great driver, nothing is.

Earnhardt may not truly see the air as has long been discussed, but he sure can see the way to the front when it matters most.

Just don't ask how he got there. Or what he thinks of restrictor plates. Not even winning Winston's No Bull 5 $1 million bonus could change his opinion.

"I still don't like restrictor-plate racing," he said. "I'm not that good at it."

Well, if he ever gets to the level he considers proficient, the other 42 drivers ought to take the afternoon off. But if that happened, fans wouldn't know what to do at Daytona and Talladega. If Earnhardt's not leading, the most fun is watching his black Chevrolet to see how he gets to the front.

You pretty much have to watch for yourself. And you should probably take notes – or have the VCR running at home – because even Earnhardt had a hard time explaining exactly how he won for the 76th time in a legendary career. It was simply that spectacular.

One minute he was nowhere to be seen, up to just 16th with six laps left, then he was blowing by Richard Childress Racing teammate Mike Skinner with two laps remaining for the lead. He then outran drafting partners Kenny Wallace and Joe Nemechek to the stripe, while Skinner was shuffled to sixth behind Jeff Gordon and Terry Labonte.

> "I hit Earnhardt once square and I knocked the hell out of him three or four times and **I personally won the race for him.**"
> —Kenny Wallace

"I don't know how I won it, honestly," Earnhardt said. "We had moved up and got pushed back again. I was up and down there between 10 and 15 (laps) to go. To be 18th or wherever we were with five to go is pretty impressive and says a lot for the rules and spotters and everything to make the racing more competitive. The problem is, it's hard to move through these cars. You've got to work your way around and by them.

"We just were fortunate to get hooked up with Kenny and Joe Nemechek there and work our way to the front. Basically, that's how I won the race, because Kenny and Joe got in there and all three Chevrolets got together and worked their way to the front."

Childress, Earnhardt and Andy Petree, who owns the cars of Wallace and Nemechek, have an engineering alliance to help the cars aerodynamically. But thoughts of being teammates in some broad sense played no role in the outcome. Wallace sim-

ply knew the best chance for his first Winston Cup win would come by working with Earnhardt on the way to the front.

That's why he kept bump-drafting with the seven-time champion.

"I had no choice but to hit him and keep pushing him into the lead," Wallace said. "... I was doing everything but hitting him through the trioval. I realized once I hit him I wasn't going to lift him. Sometimes you hit these guys and it lifts them up. I hit Earnhardt

THE TALLADEGA STRAIGHTAWAY LOOKS LIKE RUSH HOUR ON THE FREEWAY AS DALE EARNHARDT AND HIS SON, DALE JR., LEAD THE PACK.

NWCS ARCHIVE PHOTO

once square and I knocked the hell out of him three or four times and I personally won the race for him."

Earnhardt had help beyond that provided by Wallace and Nemechek, including some from his son. On a day when NASCAR's new aerodynamic rules helped produce 49 lead changes among 21 drivers, it appeared Earnhardt Jr. might post his third career win until John Andretti got by on lap 185. Skinner led the next circuit

before things got even crazier than normal.

Earnhardt Jr. tried getting a run on Skinner and got down on the apron alongside him before thinking better of the maneuver, which might have triggered a huge wreck had he forced the issue. Still, Skinner had to check up for an instant, which is when Earnhardt got back in front.

"Dad just got a great run on the outside," Earnhardt Jr. said. "Skinner was not going to win the race in the position he was

in, so I either had to get by him or finish behind him."

Master that he is, Wallace and Nemechek simply couldn't make a move on Earnhardt, whose win was greeted with a rousing ovation from the faithful, many of whom rarely sat the entire day.

And while many were fans of the racing brought on by the new aero package, not all were smiling.

"It's 43 cars that look like they're in a

parking lot," groused Frankie Stoddard, Jeff Burton's crew chief. "You could take a picture of the road that goes to Oxford, Ala. that's four lanes wide, and that would look exactly what it was like watching this race. Boring. Boring. Boring."

Considering Chevrolets swept the top six spots and Burton's Ford finished 29th after losing a lap to a cut tire, Stoddard's sentiments are understandable. But it wasn't just the Ford contingent griping.

Jimmy Makar, crew chief for points leader Labonte, was rather displeased after his driver got shuffled back to 12th during the furious finish.

"It was exactly what we expected," Makar said. "(NASCAR) got what they wanted, a bunch of junk. We'd accomplish the same thing in a 10-lap or a 25-lap race here. It's all the same. It ain't about good race cars, it's about a chess match: who makes the right move, who makes the wrong move; who slips, who doesn't. That's what happened there at the end. Little E got down on the bottom, slipped, about wrecked, caused one line to slow up and the other line went, and that's all it took.

"It's not about racing to me here. It never has been since they've gone to this kind of restrictor plate racing. It's great for the fans, I know. It's a great show. But it's not much fun racing."

It was certainly harrowing at times, not

Or as Wallace said of his run to the front with Earnhardt:

"That was Earnhardt and Talladega."

to mention nostalgic. Dave Marcis led the second lap after starting ninth, Bill Elliott ran like it was 1988 and Ken Schrader had moments where it looked like he might earn his first Cup win since 1991. Cars were running three- and sometimes four-wide with abandon and you just kept waiting for the huge crash that usually punctuates affairs at Daytona and Talladega.

Instead, the race was slowed by just three cautions as Earnhardt averaged 165.681 mph. And the biggest wreck, involving five cars, came after those on the lead lap had taken the checkered flag. By then, Earnhardt's crew was celebrating, though it was a mild-mannered affair for crew chief Kevin Hamlin, who injured his back a night earlier while driving a Monster Truck.

With many drivers privately predicting a wreckfest prior to the event, Earnhardt and Wallace were among

those pleasantly surprised.

"I can't say enough about the way they worked together," Earnhardt said. "I've got to hand it to the drivers. ... I know there at the end they got a little antsy, a little bumping and a little bit of rubbing. I know they wrecked there at the start-finish line. They were going for it, but it was a pretty good day seeing that kind of racing."

"It was a deal where we said, if anybody goes underneath the yellow line all day long, we're going to name them idiots," Wallace said. "Then, with five to go, we said, if you want to be an idiot, it's OK."

For the most part, though, everyone kept their heads. A number of drivers complained of being worn out physically and mentally afterwards, but Earnhardt, not surprisingly, had a spring in his step. In fact, he even did a little jig for fans gathered outside the press box, where Earnhardt traveled for his post-race interview.

"They need to work out, don't they?" he asked. "I'm pretty relaxed. It was a good race for me, my car drove good all day. It just worked well. I didn't get tired or burned out during the day. I really felt great after the race. I was excited about the win. I seemed to be more relaxed than usual. And I still am. I'm not a bit tired. I don't feel like I raced at all today from the way I feel."

Earnhardt was even charitable enough to commend NASCAR for taking chances by changing the aero rules in an attempt to create better racing at Daytona in 2001. Still, he wasn't about to let them completely off the hook.

"It was a good race," he said. "But I think you'd have seen just as good a race with the other (bigger) plate, too. ... They made a change, it worked. ... It's not easy for anybody to make a call like that. It's a big responsibility. I think they did a good job with it. I don't like restrictor-plate racing. But they made a call and stuck by their guns. You have to support them for that."

If the cars are equipped with parachutes next year, it probably won't slow Earnhardt. But whatever he does here next, he'll have a hard time topping this performance.

"Coming from the back to (win), I can't compare this one with any race I've won on that kind of scale," he said. "To come back and pass on the white-flag lap, take the lead and win the race is pretty awesome. It's one of the great, if not the greatest, Talladega races I've probably ever run."

Or as Wallace said of his run to the front with Earnhardt: "That was Earnhardt and Talladega." ∎

SUCCESS IS A DRINK BEST SERVED COLD; AND IN AN OVERSIZED CHAMPAGNE BOTTLE.
NWCS ARCHIVE PHOTO

Mark Ashenfelter reflects on
Dale Earnhardt's Talladega mastery

OK, so maybe Dale Earnhardt really couldn't see the air. But the mere suggestion that he could sure added to his legend.

Not that that legend needed any embellishment after races such as the Winston 500, mind you. No, Earnhardt built his legend one race at a time. And while no one knew it, one of his most dramatic victories would prove to be his last.

But the 76th win was certainly one to remember him by. Nothing against the previous 75 - many of them were spectacular in their own right – but the Winston 500 looked like something possible only on a video screen.

Instead, the typical Talladega throng witnessed it one scintillat-inglap at a time. And over the final 10 laps, it's likely they couldn't quite fathom what they were seeing.

Earnhardt had made more than his share of amazing moves over the years, but this one left fans with wide eyes and jaws dropped into their laps. Except for the moments when those jaws were helping to cheer on that black GM Goodwrench Chevrolet as it maneuvered from 22nd to the lead in less than 10 laps.

Imagine how quickly he'd have gotten to the front if he actually enjoyed what he was doing. Sure Earnhardt loved racing, but he hated doing so at Daytona and Talladega.

The tracks weren't the problem by any means, but the power-sapping restrictor plate that limited his Monte Carlo's horsepower was a different story.

"I still don't like restrictor-plate racing," Earnhardt said afterwards. "I'm not that good at it."

> **He didn't decide how the game was to be played. He just went out there and played it to the best of his ability no matter the circumstances.**

Yes, Earnhardt was the master of the understatement, just as he was the master of restrictor-plate racing.

To understand his take on it, think back to your days in school. Whether a straight-A student or one just passing through on the way to the next phase of your life, there was undoubtedly a class you didn't like. That said, you knew it wasn't going to go away, so you did your best. Sometimes the results even left you surprised.

That's sort of how it worked for Earnhardt at Talladega or Daytona. He didn't like the rules - but it was his job to win the race whether he liked the rules or not. He didn't decide how the game was to be played. He just went out there and played it to the best of his ability no matter the circumstances.

More often than not, he seemed to do so better than anyone else strapped into a car at those two tracks. Sure he didn't win every race at Daytona or Talladega. His epic struggle to finally win the Daytona 500 proved that being the best didn't always translate to a trip to victory lane.

But when everything worked perfectly, Earnhardt left them spellbound.

Now, that legacy is being carried on by his son, as Dale Earnhardt Jr. is the latest to dominate at Talladega. The one certainty, though, is that he'll have a hard time ever topping the show his father put on at the end of the Winston 500. ∎

—Mark Ashenfelter
Associate Editor
NASCAR Scene

dale earnhardt

LAST AMERICAN

By JEFF OWENS

HERO

Earnhardt's skill, toughness made him a champion's champion

H is race car was a mangled mess, so crumpled that his fans couldn't believe he had just climbed out of it.

They were even more shocked when he climbed back in.

Jeff Gordon, his newest rival, was in victory lane, having just slipped by him to win the Daytona 500, denying him a victory in NASCAR's biggest race for the 19th straight year.

Yet there was Dale Earnhardt, standing on a tool box in the middle of the garage area at Daytona International Speedway, flashing his trademark grin, charming the media and holding court as only he could.

DALE EARNHARDT

Born: April 29, 1951
Parents: Ralph and Martha Earnhardt
Hometown: Kannapolis, N.C.
Marital Status: Wife, Teresa
Children: Kerry, Kelly King, Ralph, Dale Jr.,
  Taylor Nicole
Team: Richard Childress Racing
Team Owner: Richard Childress
Crew Chief: Kevin Hamlin
Car: No. 3 Chevrolet Monte Carlo
Primary Sponsor: GM Goodwrench
  Service Plus

Earnhardt was by far NASCAR's biggest star, had been for years. Yet his myth and his legend had just taken another giant leap. Just when you figured he couldn't possibly do anything to expand the mystique and aura that surrounded him, he does the unthinkable, walking away from an ambulance ready to take him to a hospital and back to a race car that seemed battered beyond repair.

"We went bouncing off the walls and off the track, and we bounced right back," a smiling Earnhardt said.

A few feet away, his car owner, Richard

Childress, was in tears. He was happy Earnhardt was alive, but stunned that yet another attempt to win NASCAR's biggest race had gotten away.

"That's the toughest man alive right there," Childress said, looking up at Earnhardt. "He deserves to win this race more than anybody ever has."

For the umpteenth time, Earnhardt had come close, challenging for the win in the closing laps of the 1997 Daytona 500 when all hell broke loose. He was in a fierce battle with young Gordon when he lost control of his famous black Chevy, tagged the outside wall and went tumbling down the frontstretch, flipping end over end in a crash frighteningly reminiscent of one that injured him just seven months earlier.

After climbing from his car and waving to the crowd, Earnhardt was taking the mandatory walk to the ambulance when he noticed his car was sitting upright, on all four wheels and with most of its parts and pieces still intact.

What he did next will go down as one of the most dramatic moments in NASCAR history.

Instead of climbing into the back of the ambulance and riding to the infield care center, Earnhardt walked over to his battered race car, fired it up and climbed back in, completing the final six laps in a car that would barely run.

"I looked back over and said, 'Man, the wheels ain't knocked off the car yet.' So I went back over and told the guy in the car to fire it up,'" Earnhardt recalled. "He hit the switch and it fired, and I said, 'Give me my car back.'

"I just wanted to get back in the race and try to make laps. We were running for a championship."

It was vintage Earnhardt, never giving up and doing things with a stock car most race car drivers never dreamed of. And he did it with a flare for the dramatic that attracted a legion of fans and helped NASCAR become one of the most popular sports in the world.

A year later, Earnhardt would finally capture NASCAR's crown jewel, winning the

1998 Daytona 500 in his 20th try and cementing his legacy as arguably the greatest NASCAR driver ever. It was his greatest triumph, but certainly not his last. He won five more races over the next two years and once again emerged as a championship contender, finishing second to Bobby Labonte in 2000 and establishing himself as a favorite to win a record eighth title in 2001.

"He was the last cowboy."
—Kyle Petty

Sadly, he never got the chance to fulfill his dream, losing his life in a crash on the final lap of the Feb. 18 Daytona 500.

Perhaps fittingly, he died doing what he loved best, racing for the lead at Daytona, where he had won more races (34) than any other driver, and the site of some of his greatest triumphs.

"I loved racing at Daytona," he said often. "There's just something about that track and that race that suits my style."

Fast, fearless and a ferocious competitor. That was Earnhardt, the man known by his fans and peers simply as "The Man in Black."

His death stunned a NASCAR community that was still reeling from three on-track deaths in the last nine months. It was the seventh on-track death in the past 10 years. None, however, has ever been more shocking than the death of NASCAR's biggest star and a cultural icon.

"Dale Earnhardt was the greatest race car driver who ever lived," said two-time Grand National (now Winston Cup) champion Ned Jarrett. "He could do things with a race car that no one else could. You never think anyone will get killed, but he was the last one you'd think that would happen to."

"Dale was the Michael Jordan of our sport," said Lowe's Motor Speedway President H.A. "Humpy" Wheeler, a close friend of

EARNHARDT HUGS CAR OWNER RICHARD CHILDRESS WHILE THE TWO CELEBRATE THEIR GREATEST TRIUMPH, WINNING THE 1998 DAYTONA 500.
PHIL CAVALI PHOTO

Earnhardt's. "We always thought of Dale as being invincible, so when he didn't climb out of that car after the wreck, I knew it was bad."

Even after the shocking news had spread throughout the NASCAR community, Earnhardt's peers and rivals found it hard to believe.

"After the race was over, I heard things didn't look very good," driver Jeremy Mayfield said. "But, man, Earnhardt? You figure he'll bounce right back. Your first thought is, 'Hey, he'll probably come back next week at Rockingham and beat us all.'"

For many, Earnhardt, 49, was the epitome of stock car racing, slinging his ominous black Chevrolet around the track, bumping and banging his way to the front no matter where he raced or who he faced. His aggres-

sive style not only won him 76 races and seven Winston Cup titles, but earned him the nickname, "The Intimidator," a moniker he rode to much fame and glory.

"He was 'The Man,'" said Winston Cup driver Mike Wallace. "That sounds kind of silly to say, and a lot of people use it superficially, but it just fits him. He was 'The Man.'"

Kyle Petty, who grew up as the son of NASCAR's "King," summed up the Earnhardt legacy this way: "For a lot of fans, Dale Earnhardt was what they thought about when they thought about NASCAR racing. He could do so much and was so talented. He knew it, and he knew you knew it. That grin of his, a lot of times you wouldn't know what he was thinking, but you thought you did. And it might not mean a thing in the world,

but he knew you were trying to figure it out.

"He was the last cowboy."

Earnhardt's Winston Cup career began in 1979, when he won his first race at Bristol Motor Speedway and finished seventh in points to capture rookie of the year honors. Until the arrival of young stars like Davey Allison (1987), Gordon (1993), Tony Stewart (2000) and his own son, Dale Earnhardt Jr. (2001), no one had a bigger impact on the sport as a rookie.

The following year, he stunned the NASCAR world by winning five races and beating Cale Yarborough for the Winston Cup championship, becoming the only driver ever to win the title in his second season.

A year later, his championship team fell apart, forcing Earnhardt to drive for three dif-

HIGHLIGHTS

1975: Earnhardt makes his Winston Cup debut in the World 600 at Charlotte Motor Speedway. He started 33rd and finished 22nd in a Dodge owned by Ed Negre. He earned $2,245 and finished one spot ahead of his future team owner, Richard Childress.

1979: Earnhardt wins the Winston Cup Rookie of the Year title while driving for Rod Osterlund. The season includes his first career victory at Bristol. He wins his first career pole at Riverside in his 24th attempt.

1980: Earnhardt wins five races en route to his first Winston Cup championship. He's the only driver to win a series championship after being rookie of the year. His first superspeedway victory comes at Atlanta in his 41st start.

1981: Earnhardt struggles, failing to win a race or a pole. Osterlund sells the team in mid-season and Earnhardt quits. He drives for Childress the rest of the season. Wins his first $1 million with a 25th-place finish at Martinsville in his 76th start.

1982: Earnhardt joins Bud Moore's team. He wins at Darlington in April – his only victory of the year – but fractures a knee in a crash at Talladega. He doesn't miss a race.

1983: Earnhardt wins two races with Moore before bolting back to a car owned by Childress, with whom he'd spend the rest of his racing career.

1986: Earnhardt wins six races in two years while driving for Childress, then hits the pinnacle again with his second Winston Cup title with five victories. It is his first championship while driving for Childress.

1987: Earnhardt wins a third Winston Cup title with 11 victories. He also wins The Winston and is named American Driver of the Year and National Motorsports Press Association Driver of the Year.

1989: Earnhardt finishes second in the final Winston Cup point standings, losing to Rusty Wallace by 12 points. He wins five races.

1990: Earnhardt earns a then-record $3 million in prize money while winning a fourth Winston Cup title, 26 points ahead of Mark Martin. He wins nine races and The Winston. He is voted NMPA Driver of the Year.

1991: Earnhardt wins his fifth Winston Cup championship and second in a row. He wins four races.

1992: Earnhardt finishes 12th in the season's points race, tying his worst showing of his Winston Cup career. He wins just one race, his poorest performance since 1982.

1993: Earnhardt wins a sixth Winston Cup championship. He wins six races, The Winston, the Budweiser Shootout and a Twin 125. He earns $3,353,789, breaking his old record set in 1990.

1994: Earnhardt ties Richard Petty's mark of seven Winston Cup titles with four victories. He tops the $3 million mark in earnings for the third time in five years. Voted NMPA Driver of the Year and American Driver of the Year.

1995: Earnhardt wins the Budweiser Shootout for the sixth time and an eighth Twin 125. He wins five races and three poles and finishes second in the final Winston Cup point standings, 36 points behind Jeff Gordon.

1996: Earnhardt wins the pole for the Daytona 500 and a record ninth Twin 125 and the team's seventh straight at Daytona. He wins a second pole at Watkins Glen two weeks after breaking his collarbone and sternum. Finishes fourth in the final Winston Cup point standings.

1997: Earnhardt goes winless for the first time since 1981. He is the first driver to reach $30 million in all-time American motorsports earnings. He is the first race driver to appear on a box of Wheaties cereal.

1998: Earnhardt claims his only Daytona 500 victory, in his 20th attempt, which breaks a 59-race winless streak. He is the first race driver to address the National Press Club in Washington, D.C. He makes his 600th career start at Dover on Sept. 20.

1999: Earnhardt wins his 10th consecutive 125-Mile qualifier at Daytona. He wins his 73rd career Winston Cup race at Bristol and his 74th at Talladega, sweeping both events at Talladega for the season.

2000: Earnhardt finishes second to Bobby Labonte in the final Winston Cup point standings. He wins his 75th career race at Atlanta in March, edging out Labonte in a thrilling finish. He wins his last career race in October at Talladega, giving him 76 career victories. His career earnings rise to $41,918,886.

2001: Earnhardt is killed in a crash during the last lap of the Daytona 500, while a car he owns, driven by Michael Waltrip, wins the race. His son, Dale Jr. finishes second, also in a car he owns.

ferent teams. After a winless season in 1981, he joined Bud Moore's Ford team in '82 and won three races over the next two years.

In 1984, Earnhardt hooked up with former driver Richard Childress, beginning a relationship that would shape the future of the sport and form one of the most dominant teams in Winston Cup history.

Over the next three years, Earnhardt and Childress won 11 races and captured the 1986 title. In 1987, they had one of the most dominant seasons ever, winning 11 races, finishing second five times and capturing their second straight title.

After coming up short to rivals Bill Elliott and Rusty Wallace in 1988 and '89, Earnhardt returned to dominance in 1990, winning nine races and capturing his fourth series title, his third with Childress. Another titled followed in 1991, giving him more championships than everyone but Richard Petty.

A year later, Earnhardt suffered an uncharacteristic slump, falling out of the top 10 in points for the first time in 10 years following the retirement of crew chief Kirk Shelmerdine. While the late Alan Kulwicki won his only Winston Cup title, Earnhardt won just one race and slipped to 12th.

Not surprisingly, he and Richard Childress Racing returned with a vengeance in 1993. With new crew chief Andy Petree calling the shots, Earnhardt won back-to-back titles again in '93-94, edging Wallace and Mark Martin both years.

The '94 title tied Earnhardt and Petty with seven championships each, putting him one shy of the all-time mark. The '94 season also signaled the arrival, however, of a new challenger to Earnhardt's throne.

A year after winning his first two races, Gordon shocked the NASCAR world by unseating Earnhardt and winning his first title in just his third year. He won a spirited battle despite constant ribbing from the driver 20 years his senior.

As Gordon began to win on a consistent basis, Earnhardt dubbed him "Wonder Boy." And when Gordon wrapped up the title, Earnhardt joked that "the kid" would probably drink milk at the annual Winston Cup Awards Banquet. Indeed, when Gordon accepted his championship trophy, he held up a glass of milk and had a memorable toast with the seven-time champ, a moment many believed signal a passing of the torch.

The arrival of Gordon, who formed his own dominant team with Hendrick Motorsports and crew chief Ray Evernham, seemed to mark the end of Earnhardt's reign. He slipped to fourth in points in 1996, then went winless for the first time

EARNHARDT AND HIS RICHARD CHILDRESS RACING CREW CELEBRATE THEIR SIXTH AND FINAL WINSTON CUP CHAMPIONSHIP TOGETHER AT ROCKINGHAM IN 1994.
PHIL CAVALI PHOTO

EARNHARDT PROUDLY SHOWS OFF HIS BRICKYARD 400 TROPHY AFTER WINNING AT INDIANAPOLIS MOTOR SPEEDWAY IN 1995.
PHIL CAVALI PHOTO

ished sixth in one of the most grueling races of the year.

"I held on. That's about all I can say, I held on," he said as he favored his chest and shoulder after the race. "I felt good after that first little caution. I said, 'Well, heck, I can stand it.'"

"Dale is a determined person," Childress said. "Through pain and everything else, that's the reason he's the seven-time Winston Cup champion. He never gives up."

"Just tell him he can't do something," says his former crew chief Larry McReynolds. "Tell him he can't go to Watkins Glen and qualify with a broken sternum, or tell him he can't outrun you. That's all he needs to hear. All you've got to do is tell him he can't do something, and he will flat prove you wrong."

Six months later, Earnhardt would take his wild ride at Daytona, then get banged up again at Charlotte in May. Less than a year later, he took another wild spin, flipping upside down at Talladega and singeing the hair off his face when Bill Elliott's car burst into flames.

"It singed my hair and burned my mustache up a little bit," he said. "I'll have to grow some new ones ... but I'll be all right."

Childress believes Earnhardt's injuries, beginning with the '96 crash at Talladega, contributed to his winless '97 season and his struggles in '98. He admits that he should have held Earnhardt out of some races, but that's easier said than done, especially when you're dealing with "The Intimidator."

"I've driven race cars hurt, so I can understand," Childress said in June 1998. "You don't want to get out of your race car. I know how they feel inside. That's the reason I'm letting him drive hurt."

After winning the Daytona 500 in '98, Earnhardt fell into another miserable slump, scoring just four more top-five finishes the rest of the season and finishing eighth in points. Though he showed flashes of his former self the following year, winning three races, he finished just seventh in points, leading many to continue writing him off.

His competition knew better.

"He's still strong and his intensity level is there like it always has been," Gordon said prior to the 2000 season. "I won't count him out. I won't ever count Earnhardt out."

"Dale Earnhardt can still do it, and anyone that's ever doubted it made a big mistake," Childress said.

Predictably, Earnhardt came back strong in 2000, silencing his critics with two of the most dramatic victories of the season and finishing second to Labonte in the championship race.

since '81 the following year.

To many, his struggles were the beginning of the end for NASCAR's biggest star. At age 45, Earnhardt began to lose the consistency that won him numerous races on tracks he used to dominate. He was also involved in a string of uncharacteristic wrecks, leading to multiple injuries and causing many to wonder if he'd lost his edge.

While in the midst of another championship race, Earnhardt slammed into the outside wall at Talladega in '96, then tumbled upside-down on the straightaway, breaking his collarbone and cracking his sternum as car after car slammed into his sliding machine.

Beaten and battered, he was not deterred. Two days after being released from a Birmingham hospital, he traveled to Indianapolis Motor Speedway for the Brickyard 400. Despite pain that would have hospitalized most men, he started the race he had won the year before and ran six green-flag laps before turning his car over to teammate Mike Skinner.

As he climbed from his car, he choked back tears during one of the most difficult moments of his career.

"Dadgum, it was hard to get out of that car," he said. "I mean, you know ... it's my life right there. I just hate to get out of that race car."

Though determined to race, Earnhardt gave in to the wisdom of doctors and his teammates, who urged him to give up his ride during one of the season's biggest races.

"My sternum is broke in two," he said. "If I would happen to get in another crash, it would put me even further back in my career as far as this championship run. I don't want to take a chance and do something to injure myself or take a chance and hurt someone else or endanger someone else's life."

A week later, he turned in one of the most courageous performances in recent Winston Cup history, withstanding incredible pain as he muscled his car around the 2.45-mile road course at Watkins Glen to win the pole for the Bud at The Glen.

"It hurts, but it's a good hurt," Earnhardt said to the amazement of his peers.

Two days later, he led 54 laps and fin-

"As millions of race fans mourn the loss of the man they knew as "The Intimidator," the sport and the race that I so truly loved has taken from me one of my best friends. I know I should feel fortunate that I had the opportunity to race with, tangle with, sometimes outrun, and like most, usually finish behind, the greatest driving talent NASCAR racing has ever seen." – Dale Jarrett

"That 3 car scared every driver because they knew what was coming. Dale Earnhardt never gave up. He didn't care if he was five laps down, you were going to have to work to get past him. He would race you just as hard for 20th as he would for the win and us as competitors all realized that and expected that from him." – Jimmy Spencer

"On behalf of everyone at Joe Gibbs Racing, we would like to extend our heartfelt sympathies to Teresa and the entire Earnhardt family, as well as everyone at Dale Earnhardt Inc. and Richard Childress Racing. While Dale was a fierce competitor on and off the track and leader in the community, he was a member of our family and as you can imagine, we are grieving that loss." – Joe Gibbs

"I, like everyone else, am in shock with the passing of Dale Earnhardt. Besides being an incredible driver and spokesman for the sport he so loved, he was a true friend and has been a major influence on my life and career." – Winston Cup champion Bobby Labonte

"Dale Earnhardt made a difference in the world. On the track, he made us all better drivers because he set a standard of excellence we all aspired to achieve. He had a passion and a desire that took the sport of NASCAR to a new level every time he climbed in the car. Off the track he was a kind, giving, loving man who gave his all to his family and friends. He worked tirelessly to make the world a better place for as many people as possible who were less fortunate than he. I did not know him as long as most of the other drivers, but he made a huge impact on my life in the years I have been in NASCAR."
– Tony Stewart

"Brooke and I are deeply saddened by this devastating loss. Not only is it a huge loss for this sport, but a huge loss for me personally. Dale taught me so much and became a great friend. Our thoughts and prayers are with Teresa and the entire Earnhardt family." – Jeff Gordon

"You hate to see anyone get hurt anytime, but it especially cuts deep since it's (Dale) Earnhardt. The guy is a master. He's been doing this for years and he's been doing it better than anybody. ... There's been a Dale Earnhardt as long as I can remember, not just racing, but racing and winning. For the younger guys in the sport, he has been our Richard Petty." – Jeremy Mayfield

"Dale Earnhardt was a winner, through and through. He won when he started on the short tracks, he won in Busch and he won in Winston Cup. I can't remember a Winston Cup race where, when you made a list of who you had to beat to win, that list didn't include Dale Earnhardt." – Joe Nemechek

"He was what NASCAR is. You might look at him and think he was the biggest chauvinist around, but he would always help me if I had a question or a problem. He was not the kind of guy who would cut you one bit of slack on the race track, but he would do whatever he could to help you off of it." – Shawna Robinson

"No matter where it happens or how it happens or even how prepared you think you might be for it, losing somebody close to you hurts. My heart just breaks for Teresa and the family." – Kyle Petty

"I feel like somebody kicked me in the chest. I'm stunned. And I'm really sad. That's about all I can say." – John Andretti

"He was what we were all trying to be on the race track, and he was what we would like to be off the track too. ... This is a big deal. As bad as losing one life is, it's more than just one race car driver losing his life. He impacted a lot of people." – Mike Wallace

My heart goes out to his family, his crew, his friends and his fans. There is no better group of fans in our sport and I feel for them, also. Our sport will go on, but I don't think it will ever be the same. NASCAR is about family, and I can't think of a time in its history when it needs to pull together like a family." – Johnny Benson

"All of us at R.J. Reynolds Tobacco Co. are shocked and deeply saddened by this tragedy. Dale Earnhardt was a fierce competitor and a great champion. More importantly, he was a friend." – Andy Schindler, chairman and chief executive officer, R.J. Reynolds Tobacco Co.

"This is a terrible, terrible loss. For me, it ranks right up there with the death of JFK. ... I knew Dale's father, Ralph, and I've known Dale since he was a little boy. He had things pretty tough when his father passed away when he was young and I was so proud of the way he turned out and the way he represented our sport. Behind that macho facade was a real sensitive individual who did a lot of things for a lot of people ... He was truly an extraordinary human being. To think he is not around anymore is incomprehensible." – H.A. "Humpy" Wheeler, president and general manager of Lowe's Motor Speedway

"He had a tremendous impact on NASCAR racing. He's done so much to help the sport get where it is today. He took the sport to new places. It's going to be hard for anyone else to take it there. He leaves a big, big void here that will be very hard to fill." – Ned Jarrett, former Winston Cup champion and the father of driver Dale Jarrett

"It's always tragic, but he is our main guy. (At Daytona) when they introduced him, he got the biggest applause there. He's the man, he is NASCAR Winston Cup racing." – Ed Clark, president of Atlanta Motor Speedway

"It's hard to put into words what the loss of Dale Earnhardt means. I feel without question he was the greatest driver we have ever had. At a time when the popularity of NASCAR has been rapidly growing across this country, we can thank Dale Earnhardt for a lot of that attention. The fan base he enjoyed is unparalleled in this sport." – Clay Campbell, Martinsville Speedway President

In March, he nipped Labonte by inches in the closest finish of the season at Atlanta. Six months later, he added to his legend by charging from 18th to victory in the final six laps at Talladega. His second-place finish in the season finale vaulted him ahead of Jeff Burton and into second in the final standings.

When the 2000 season ended, Earnhardt was disappointed, but determined – as determined as ever to capture a record eighth title.

"I'm frustrated about letting the eighth championship slip away," he said. "But to think this is the only opportunity I'm going to have to win that eighth championship, I don't. I feel like I've got several opportunities, next year and the year after."

After his dramatic resurgence in 2000, no one doubted him, not anymore.

"When everyone was discussing should he be looking at retiring and he had slipped a little bit, I think most of us on the race track knew that wasn't the case at all," 1999 champion Dale Jarrett said prior to the 2001 season. "I think you have to consider him a major factor in the championship battle."

Though he won seven Winston Cup titles, Earnhardt's most memorable moment came at Daytona in 1998, when he won the coveted race that had eluded him for 20 years. Afterward, he cried tears of joy. ("I don't think I really cried," he said. "My eyes just watered up.") Tears not normally seen from one of the toughest men in sports.

After taking the checkered flag, his peers paid him one of NASCAR's most memorable tributes, lining up one-by-one on pit road to congratulate him on winning the Daytona 500. Earnhardt was moved and taken aback by the emotional response.

"All the guys came up congratulating me, all of them wanting to shake my hand" he said. "There was Michael Waltrip, Rusty ... I had to go real slow or my arm would've gotten torn off.

"This win is for all the fans and all the people who told me, 'Dale, this is your year.' ... It was my time. That's all I can say."

Earnhardt's time ended three years later, seconds before his own driver and teammate, Michael Waltrip, won the 2001 Daytona 500. The legacy he left behind, the one he passed down to his son and drivers like Waltrip and teammate Steve Park, was summed up three days prior to his own Daytona 500 triumph.

"Any time you get the opportunity to win a race, you are going to win the race," he said. "I am never going to back off. I never want to run second. If I'm playing golf or baseball or running a foot race, playing cards or playing checkers, I want to win. I always want to win." ■

EARNHARDT'S CAREER STATS

YEAR	RACES	WINS	TOP FIVE	TOP 10	POLES	MONEY	POINTS
1975	1	0	0	0	0	$1,925	-
1976	2	0	0	0	0	3,085	-
1977	1	0	0	0	0	1,375	-
1978	5	0	1	2	0	20,145	43rd
1979	27	1	11	17	4	264,086	7th
1980	31	5	19	24	0	588,926	1st
1981	31	0	9	17	0	347,113	7th
1982	30	1	7	12	1	375,325	12th
1983	30	2	9	14	1	446,272	8th
1984	30	2	12	22	0	616,788	4th
1985	28	4	10	16	1	546,596	8th
1986	29	5	16	23	1	1,783,880	1st
1987	29	11	21	24	1	2,099,243	1st
1988	29	3	13	19	0	1,214,089	3rd
1989	29	5	14	19	0	1,435,730	2nd
1990	29	9	18	23	4	3,083,056	1st
1991	29	4	14	21	0	2,396,685	1st
1992	29	1	6	15	1	915,463	12th
1993	30	6	17	21	2	3,353,789	1st
1994	31	4	20	25	2	3,300,783	1st
1995	31	5	19	23	3	3,154,241	2nd
1996	31	2	13	17	2	2,285,926	4th
1997	32	0	7	16	0	2,151,909	5th
1998	33	1	5	13	0	2,990,749	8th
1999	34	3	7	21	0	3,048,236	7th
2000	34	2	13	24	0	4,918,886	2nd
2001	1	0	0	0	0	194,111	-
CAREER	676	76	281	428	22	$41,538,362	

EAST EUROPEAN
AIR POWER
No3 IN THE AFM AIRPOWER SERIES

EDITOR:
David Oliver
CONSULTANT:
Hans-Heiri Stapfer
ASSISTANT EDITOR:
Dave Allport

SERIES EDITOR:
Ken Ellis
PHOTOGRAPHY:
Duncan Cubitt
ARTWORK:
Peter West

ADVERTISEMENT MANAGER:
John Barker
MARKETING DIRECTOR:
John Phillips
PUBLISHER:
Frank Ward

Published by Key Publishing Ltd, PO
Box 100, Stamford, Lincs PE9 1XQ.
(0780 55131).
Distributed by IPC Marketforce, Kings
Reach Tower, Stamford Street, London
SE1 9LS. (071 261 5199).

Printed by Southernprint Ltd,
Poole, Dorset.
Typeset by Goodfellow & Egan
(Peterborough) Ltd, Cambs.
Colour process by County
Graphics, Holwell, Herts.

CONTENTS

Norway

Sweden

FINLAND

SOVIET
UNION

EASTERN
GERMANY

POLAND

Western
Germany

CZECHOSLOVAKIA

Austria

HUNGARY

BULGARIA

YUGOSLAVIA

ROMANIA

Italy

ALBANIA

Greece

Turkey

4 **Rolling back the Red Flag.** Personal view of the 'Cold War' and its history from Ken Ellis.

8 **What's in a Name?** Hans-Heiri Stapfer uncovers NATO's reporting names for Soviet aircraft.

15 **Finland.** Small, but potent, the Finnish Air Force flies a mix of Soviet and Western equipment. David Oliver reports.

20 **Swing-wing Solution.** The Sukhoi Su-17, '20 and '22 *Fitter* family described by Paul Rigby.

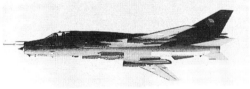

24 **Poland.** Second only to the Soviet Union in terms of the size of its air arm, Jerzy Woda tackles Poland's mighty force.

31 **Eastern Germany.** Now a part of the newly-united Germany, Harry Wisch concludes the East German armed forces and their equipment.

38 **Czechoslovakia.** With an innovative aerospace industry to supply some of its needs, the Czech air arm is a more varied force, Robert Schneider reports.

45 **Water Dipping Sub Hunter.** Piotr Butowski surveys the Mil Mi-14 and its attributes.

50 **Soviet Union.** Clearly a subject in its own right, Josef Djugashvilli takes on the difficult task of summarising the air arms of the USSR.

62 **Hungary.** Istvan Nagy analyses the small Hungarian air arm as it faces a new era.

68 **Flying Tank.** Awesome or overrated? Mike Spick assesses the Mi-24 *Hind*.

73 **Romania.** Recent events have focussed eyes on Romania. Michael Jones outlines its turbulent past and its varied aerial assets.

78 **Bulgaria.** Little detail is known of Bulgaria's armed forces. Pavic Burelov assembles what we have.

80 **Yugoslavia.** Independently socialist, Yugoslavia's air force is also distinctive, Emil Pozar and Steve Bond explain.

86 **Double-Headed Spear.** Two 'noses' and great versitility summarise the MiG-23 and '27 *Floggers*. Leander Rosenfeld outlines their career.

90 **Albania.** The maverick of the Eastern *bloc*.

91 **Index.** Types, units, bases at a glance, courtesy Dave Allport.

Rolling Back the Red Flag

Suddenly the head-on clash of NATO and WarPac has lost its sting. Europe, and more importantly, Germany was at the birth of the era known as the 'Cold War'. This period has shaped the air arms of Eastern Europe - and of most of the western world - Ken Ellis describes the origins and texture of the war that never was.

CIRCULAR arguments tend to have great staying power. Whatever notion may start them off, all information gleaned once they are in motion, all incidents and happenings, tend only to be interpreted as fuelling, or substantiating the argument's existence.

Breaking a circular argument involves the ability to crack through an inertia so well established that it has become self-protecting. The argument is now its own myth, it has its own reality.

Place another circle of thought in opposition to the first. Both rings will close still further to protect themselves

and use the existence of the other to justify the movements within the circle.

Such was the 'Cold War'. A war of nerves and of philosophies and, at times, a war of steel and blood. But no trenches, no declarations, no beginning, no real end.

Post war the World was drawn into a self-fulfilling campaign that moulded the minds and tactics of certainly three, possibly four, decades. Breaking the mould required the will on *both* sides to alter and be prepared to see another way.

While historians will rage forever more about when the so-called 'Cold War'

began, there is at least a general consensus that the events within the Soviet Union and Eastern Europe have proved that it *has* ended, although precisely when remains open to debate.

What is largely accepted as the period of the Cold War is marked by a period of tension between the 'West' – the capitalistic democratic countries, personified by the United States and the 'East' – the socialistic one-party countries orbiting around the Soviet Union. While at the heart of the matter might have been ideology, it was the physical manifestations of this that were to give rise to

aviation enthusiasts and historians having an interest in the Cold War. It was a 'war' in the true sense in that both 'sides' sought to advantage themselves and disadvantage the other – while stopping short of shooting one another in a 'declared' or 'formal' sense.

Thus the post war period found a massive propaganda war developing between the totalitarian, socialistic outlook of the 'East' and the democratic, capitalistic viewpoints of the 'West'. To back up the propaganda, both sides entered into a fierce and wide-ranging arms race.

Iron Curtain

"From Stettin in the Baltic to Trieste in the Adriatic, an Iron Curtain has descended across the Continent . . ." The words of Winston Spencer Churchill in Missouri in March 1946. Churchill had sensed that without the destruction of Nazism as a target, the USA and the USSR were bent on a collision course of their own. His choice of the word 'curtain' indicated that he believed the next era was to be one of subtle antagonism and not of open warfare.

Europe and in particular Germany lay at the roots of the Cold War. Here lay the foundations of the circular argument. Here Soviet troops met Allied troops in the ruins of Berlin – very quickly this meeting was to become a confrontation and then a very real wall. By the time the wall had come down, Europe had evolved almost beyond recognition.

With his troops in Berlin and across Eastern Europe, Stalin appeared to be the new enemy. Western models of his contribution to the circular argument ran like this:

● Under Marxist/Leninist theory the world will ultimately become socialist, either by evolution (Marx) or revolution (Lenin). Stalin was Lenin's man, a revolutionary to the core, his aid to communists in Greece and elsewhere proved this.
● Stalin showed no signs of moving his troops out of Eastern Europe – the areas he had 'liberated' from the Nazis.
● When the Marshall Aid scheme was announced to help the recovery of Europe, the Soviet Union refused to partake and banned the other eastern *bloc* countries and Finland from attending the talks.
● The Berlin blockade of 1948/1949 proved that the Soviet Union wished to force the Western powers out of Germany.
● The Soviets seemed to want to keep Germany flattened and impoverished, thereby keeping central Europe weak and exposed to attack.

Stalin might have seen these actions in a very different way:
● President Truman's Doctrine of "supporting free peoples who are resisting subjugation . . . by outside pressures" could be seen as an organised and possibly hostile attempt to stop the inevitable flow of socialism. The Marshall Plan was

but an economic arm of this strategy and the Mutual Defence Assistance Act a method of arming nations against the Soviet Union.
● Under the terms of the Yalta Accord, the Soviet Union was entitled to reparations including some territorial settlements within Europe and the removal of capital assets. Troops were needed to oversee such changes and to instill order in countries trying to establish themselves again. Besides . . . the Allies were maintaining high levels of troops in their sectors of Germany and beyond. The USSR *had* withdrawn from occupying eastern Austria, as soon as neutrality details were thrashed out.
● Throughout the final phases of World War Two, the Soviet Union had not been privy to the development, and use, of the atomic bomb – this was a threat of the highest order to the Soviet motherland and a destabilizing act from former Allies.
● The blockade of Berlin was brought about through frustration and the unilateral revaluation of the 'west' Mark and the chronic economic pain it put upon shattered eastern German trade.
● Long term peace in Europe relied upon Germany being weak and/or dismem-

■ Left: **Aerial confrontation. Canadian CF-18 from 425 Squadron escorts a Soviet *Bear* off Canada's east coast. (CAF)**

■ Top: **First major 'outbreak' of the 'Cold War' was the Berlin Blockade and subsequent airlift, RAF Dakota at Gatow. (R F Allport)**

■ Above: **Berlin's famous Brandenburg Gate, once a symbol of schism, now a proud portal once more. (David Oliver)**

bered. Twice in the 20th Century a too powerful Germany had caused war, both times wreaking a terrible cost on Russia.

As the C-47s, C-54s, Yorks and Hastings flew in and out of Berlin, the Blockade provided both sides with a physical proof of the Cold War – the circular argument was in motion. Both sides now needed to establish security and to ready themselves for another war – rearmament was the order of the day.

Chronology of Distrust

With the Berlin Airlift supplying on average 4,500 tons of material a day into the City, the Western powers were establishing a counter to the Soviet threat. On April 4, 1949 the North Atlantic Treaty Organisation came into being with Belgium, Canada, Denmark, France, Iceland, Italy, Luxembourg, the Netherlands, Norway, Portugal, the UK and the USA all signing on. Defensive in posture, NATO countries also agreed to regard an act of aggression on any individual member to be an act of aggression against them all. In that year the USSR mastered the atomic bomb.

During 1950 the Korean War broke out, although this was to be an all-too-rare, multi-nation post 1945 'hot' war. An armistice was signed in 1953. Greece and Turkey elected to join NATO in October 1952 and the encirclement of the USSR continued.

Stalin died on March 5, 1953 and the world had hopes that his sort of outlook was also gone. This may have been the case, but the Cold War arguments now had a momentum that did not require a Stalin to fuel them.

In August, a mourning USSR declared its possession of the hydrogen bomb – both sides had the means to 'deliver' such weaponry. The ultimate threat of mutual destruction was beginning to place the world in fear, yet also to stabilize the global relationships of the 'Super-Powers'.

By 1954, recovery of Western Germany was excellent and the country had adopted a federalist, democratic constitution. Military thinking in the West felt that only with an armed West Germany in NATO was Europe truly a powerblock to Soviet expansionism. On May 5, 1955 Federal Germany joined NATO.

Nine days later in Warsaw, the Pact that carries the city's name bound Albania, Bulgaria, Czechoslovakia, East Germany, Hungary, Poland and Romania with the USSR. The two sides in the Cold War cast were complete. The Warsaw Pact showed how seriously the USSR took the joining of West Germany into a

NATO already composed of a powerful array of nations.

Anti-government riots in Poznan, Poland, started on June 28, 1956 and the West began to observe potential cracking of the Eastern *bloc*. This was very short-lived when on November 4, 1956, the Soviet Union intervened in Hungary to suppress a revisionist rebellion. Despite the fine words of the Truman Doctrine, the West decided only to penetrate the Warsaw Pact with words, not tanks, to aid the people of Hungary.

Until then derided, Soviet technology shocked the West on October 4, 1957 when the tiny *Sputnik* went into earth orbit. The age of the Intercontinental Ballistic Missile had dawned. Now both 'Super-Powers' were in a race to complete a nuclear 'umbrella' for themselves and their 'clients'. Coupled with air, land and naval force updates and expansionism, both West and East faced massive costs and debts in an attempt to square up to each other's perceived threat.

As Gary Powers plummeted to earth on May 1, 1960 and his U-2 impacted on Soviet soil, the 1960s opened with a degree of tension not reached in the 1950s. 'The Bomb' and its potential were all-dominating. The U-2 incident was more of a tribute to the tenacity of the Soviet fighter force in their determination to hit one of these high flyers. Both sides saw it as an act of aggression – fuel for the circular argument.

On the Brink

Harsh and ugly though it was, the erection of the Berlin Wall from August 13, 1961 was at least an effective solution to the segmentation of Berlin. Eyes zoomed in on Germany yet again as the source of tension within Europe. To the Soviets, it was intolerable that there should be a capitalistic 'island' within an autonomous, socialistic state, as East Germany had become. The drain on her economy and population had continued ever since the failure of the Allied powers to reorganise the 'occupation' of Germany. The Wall overcame the artificiality of the situation.

Overthrowing the corrupt Batista regime in Cuba on January 1, 1959 the hardline socialist Castro was seen by the USA to be establishing a Soviet satellite 'offshore'. When reconnaissance flights found tactical missiles being shipped into Cuba, a crisis of the highest order was ready to break.

In the form of Khrushchev and Kennedy, both the USSR and the USA had found men of global perceptions and icy resolve. Despite the presence of tactical missiles in Turkey, Kennedy viewed the Soviet equivalents in Cuba as an intolerable threat. Khrushchev saw them as an attempt to redress the balance of power.

As the US Navy enforced a blockade on Cuba on October 16, 1962 the world

held its breath. Khrushchev backed down, but both sides had learnt that such 'brinkmanship' was to be avoided at all costs.

The following year saw the signing of the Test Ban Treaty by the UK, USA and USSR – apart from banning the atmospheric testing of nuclear devices it was a milestone in counter Cold War diplomacy. Much more important was the agreement reached on June 20, 1963 in Geneva. The famous 'Hot Line' was to be created between the two Heads of State of the 'Super-Powers'.

This represented a real 'warming' of the Cold War. Previously, communication between the two major protagonists of the 'war' had been on a formalized and therefore inflexible basis. Both sides had addressed the United Nations (both the USA and the USSR were founder members and held permanent seats on the Security Council) but mostly actions in the 1950s had been followed by silence. The 'Hot-Line' offered a way for leaders to express themselves on a human level – some historians see this very facility as the end of the 'Cold War'.

Tragically, the hope that this new venture gave out was to be relatively short-lived. Kennedy perished at the end of an assassins bullet in Dallas on November 22, 1963 and Khrushchev was ousted by the hardliner Brezhnev on October 15, 1964. Dialogue would have to be rebuilt between the 'Super-Powers'.

■ Above: **Good example of Soviet propoganda – and quite recent. Folk dancers entertain an Army Aviation Unit in the Caucasus, 1985.** (TASS)

■ Right: **Face of repression in Poland, General Wojciech Jaruzelski, inspecting Soviet weaponry.**

■ Far right, top: **Air-to-ground of the famous 'Checkpoint Charlie' – now a museum piece.** (David Oliver)

■ Far right, bottom: **Now a souvenir in the pockets of countless visitors – the Berlin Wall.** (David Oliver)

WarPac's resolve and integrity was exhibited to the full on August 20/21, 1968. In addition to Soviet forces already within the country, Bulgarian, Hungarian, East German and Polish troops entered Czechoslovakia to put down the 'Prague Spring' rebellion. Again, the West was vocal, but made no moves to come to the aid of the rebels. A month later, maverick Albania walked out of WarPac and into the arms of China.

New age

As the early 1960s had been the most terrifying of the Cold War, the early 1970s offered the most hope. The Strategic Arms Limitations Talks (SALT) between the USA and the USSR opened up in Vienna and were to be the first of a wide-ranging series of talks on arms limitation that have continued, with only one major hiccup, to date.

Within Germany itself lay the ultimate solution to Soviet distrust of the country and the East/West split. Willy Brandt was strongly of the belief that the way forward was slow and steady reunification and his *Ostpolitik* bore fruit in the 'Basic Treaty' signed in East Berlin on December 21, 1972 – now at least both Germanies had normalised relations and both could properly join the United Nations. The way forward was established.

Person to person dialogue – the 'summits' that were later to become very fashionable – was re-established in November 1974 when Ford and Brezhnev met in Vladivostok. Here the overall topic was further nuclear arms reductions, but relationships were also being cemented. In 1979 Carter and Brezhnev signed SALT II, but the decade was to end on a sour note. On December 27, 1979 Soviet troops moved into Afghanistan to help the government suppress rebellion.

To the West this was an invasion and the Cold War 'domino theory' was dusted down and brought back to life. The USSR was soon to find herself involved in a costly and bloody conflict – a Russian Vietnam. SALT II was never ratified as the West turned back to colder thoughts.

In Poland, 1980 saw the recognition of the trade union Solidarity – an act that puzzled Eastern *bloc* watchers more than it gave them hope. Martial law cracked down in Poland in December 1981.

Now with Reagan at the helm, the USA turned to a policy of arming the USA with new weapons and systems, while opening talks with the Soviets again. Reagan was engaged upon a path of exhibiting his country's potential to go back to 'brinkmanship'. Thus March 1983 saw the launch of the Strategic Defense Initiative – best known forever more as 'Star Wars' and in November the first cruise missiles arrived in the UK.

While presenting such radical and potentially destabilizing military options,

Reagan was also offering a much more palatable package. In 1981 the Intermediate Range Nuclear Force (INF) and Strategic Arms Reduction Talks (START) commenced. While martial law ended in Poland in July 1983, the shoot down of the Korean Boeing 747 over Sakhalin on September 1 that year brought back much of the Cold War rhetoric. This backlash and the cruise missile deployment brought the USSR out of the INF talks.

Mikhail Gorbachev became the General Secretary of the Communist Party of the Soviet Union on March 11, 1985 and the following day (by long prior arrangement) arms control talks started again in Geneva. Gorbachev was to slowly unleash onto the USSR and the world, the need for his country's socialism to become more pluralistic and for the economy, crippled by mis-management and the forever 'keeping up with the Jones' that the Cold War required to be westernized as soon as possible. Almost overnight his policies seemed so much more like those of any western state.

Geneva in November 1985 saw the first of a series of Reagan-Gorbachev summits. The much-heralded Reykjavik Meeting in October 1986 brought the two to nothing, but the unparalleled unilateral announcement of July 22, 1987 that the USSR was ready to eliminate all INF qualifiable nuclear weapons set the world thinking. The summit that December in Washington produced many initiatives and a closer bond between the 'Super-Powers'. Moscow witnessed another productive meeting in May 1988, days previously the Soviets had started to pull out of Afghanistan.

Within Eastern Europe and indeed within the States of the USSR itself, the new political mood was having a radical effect on the economy and aspirations of their peoples. As the pages within will show, the nations of Eastern Europe all were to evolve in different ways and with different horizons, but the effect has been to create an eastern Europe that no longer gives either side of the circular argument any fuel to perpetuate the notions of 'Cold War'.

No more so than in Germany was this final laying to rest of the 'Cold War' to be so positive. October 3, 1990 saw the joining together of the two Germanies into one, federalist, democratic state. A Germany in which the Soviet Union no longer perceives a major threat. A *united* Germany that can join NATO.

Across Eastern Europe, the Red Flag has been rolled back to reveal a set of nations determined to follow their own paths in their own time. The Soviet Union has shone out as a country of great stature, determined to take the initiative in peace talks and to bring a new realism to global politics.

Whenever and however the 'Cold War' died, nobody can be declared a 'winner'. Both sides recognised the folly of the situation and allowed the circle to be broken with honour.

What's in a Name?

Hans-Heiri Stapfer examines NATO's famous code-name system for Soviet and Eastern bloc aircraft.

■ This page. Top: *Cub-B* – electronic warfare version of the Antonov An-12 transport. (RSwAF via FlygvaapenNytt)

■ Middle: *Flashlight* – Soviet aircrew in a posed shot with a Yak-25. (Novosti)

■ Bottom: *Bear* – the magnificent Tu-20/ Tu-95 series, here escorted by a 111 Squadron Phantom. (via Jelle Sjoerdsma)

■ Opposite page. Top: *Fulcrum* – fine shot of a drop-tanked 'demonstrator' in Alaskan skies during the famous visit to the USA, August 1989. (DoD)

■ Middle: *Helix-B* – Kamov Ka-29B general purpose helicopter, seen here at Hanover's ILA 90. (Dave Allport)

■ Bottom: *Fishbed* – moody sky over Soviet MiG-21s. (Guido Buehlmann)

EVER SINCE the 1917 Revolutions, the Soviets have kept military matters most secret. Their understanding of the word 'secret' is well beyond that of Western understanding. Western countries and the NATO Alliance freely release designations of aircraft, make the public aware of new developments and organise airshows where the public is invited to bases.

It works very differently in the Soviet Union and WarPac countries. News on a particular aircraft can be announced years after it has been flown for the first time. Even material on Soviet-built aircraft withdrawn from operational service is still classified as secret.

Many Soviet aircraft have kept their true designation, the notation of sub-variants and development a mystery to Western eyes. Data released is often not quite accurate or very general. Soviet aviation literature is generally regarded as not very informative and while the West gives accurate information on the manufacturer and the correct designation, the Eastern European press only states phrases like 'Modern Fighter Aircraft', 'New Fast-Flying Bomber' and so on, when captioning a picture in a book or magazine.

With Stalin's attitude of complete secrecy, Western countries were faced with little information other than aircraft occasionally shown on the air displays at Domodedovo and Tushino. In many instances aircraft shown in this manner gave no hint of the manufacturer, let alone a designation. As a result the USAF began to work out its own designations for new aircraft which were reported.

By Number

The number system developed by the US Air Force in 1946 gave each new type reported a continuous number. No difference was made between manufacturer and types (Fighter, Bomber, Cargo). This system came into use for the first time during the Air Parade at Tushino on August 18, 1946, when a number of new aircraft, without any designation or manufacturer were shown to the public and the Western Military Attachés. Type 1 was the Yak-15 and Type 2 was the MiG-9 – the first jet fighters developed by the Soviets.

This numeral code was a little bit difficult to handle, it was not easy to remember the numbers and it showed the Soviets how many new types the Americans had recognised from official and unofficial information. It was also difficult to transmit these numbers during poor radio reception, since some sounded quite similar (fourteen, forty).

In mid-1955 the USAF began to drop this code-system in favour of the more advanced NATO coding system. The numerical code system was only officially used by the USAF. The last aircraft assigned numerical codes were the Tupolev Tu-16 (Type 39) and the Tupolev Tu-95 (Type 40). For a time both systems were used to name new Soviet aircraft. The Ilyushin Il-28 was Type 27 in the USAF and *Beagle* in NATO parlance. Type 28 was named *Fresco* by NATO and MiG-17 in official Soviet designation.

ASCC Codes

ASCC Reporting Names, known as 'NATO codes' or 'NATO-names' by the man in the street were chosen by the Air Standards Co-ordinating Committee (ASCC), a joint committee made up of all member countries. The purpose of these reporting names is to allow rapid radio identification and reporting of Soviet aircraft types. The names are all designed to sound different so that they will not be confused, even under conditions of poor radio reception.

First letter of the name denoted the aircraft type:

■ Below: Initially named *Butcher*, the ASCC name for the Il-28 was quickly changed to *Beagle*. One of the last operational Polish *Beagles* is illustrated.

■ Right, top: Yak-12M *Creek* of the Hungarian Air Force at Budaors.

■ Right, middle: NATO at first thought they should give the *Hind-D* a new reporting name, but settled for a sub-variant.

■ Right, bottom: Remains of an An-26 *Curl* after a guerilla attack in Afghanistan. Far right: Polish SBLim-2A, licence-built version of two-seater MiG-15 with the code name *Midget*. (All via Author).

Bomber
Cargo
Fighter
Helicopter
Miscellaneous (Training aircraft, flying boats, gliders, tankers, etc).

Single-syllable names are used for propeller-driven aircraft, while multiple-syllable names are used for jet powered aircraft. Variants of the basic aircraft are all identified by a suffix letter. The second type would receive the suffix letter -B, the third -C etc. Often this does not follow actual Soviet production, since a type may actually be the third production variant and be identified by NATO before the second production variant came to light.

While the USAF numeral code was only limited to new aircraft observed, the ASCC Reporting Names also included all the aircraft the West thought could be still in service with Soviet Forces at that time. This was why aircraft of World War Two vintage were given ASCC Reporting Names, such as the Petlyakov Pe-2 *Buck,* Yakovlev Yak-9 *Frank,* Polikarpov Po-2 *Mule.*

During World War Two America supplied over 14,000 aircraft to the Soviet Union under Lend-Lease. These aircraft were not returned to the United States and with the thought that some of these aircraft could still be in operational use ASCC Reporting Names were given to the following American manufactured aircraft: Bell P-63 *Fred,* Consolidated PBN-1 and PBY-6A *Mop,* Douglas A-20 *Box,* C-47 *Cab* as well as the North American B-25 *Bank.*

By the time the ASCC Reporting Name system came into use (1955) many of the World War Two types were withdrawn from operational service, as well as the jet-powered MiG-9 *Fargo* and Yak-15 *Feather.* At the time this information was,

of course, not known to NATO.

NATO ASCC Reporting Names are in use with all NATO forces, but in addition neutral countries in Western Europe also use them as identification in exercises, radio transmissions and manuals.

In many cases the ASCC Reporting Name is much more accurate than the Soviet designation. Magazines and books use the system when they are describing Soviet aircraft. For instance the Soviet Union did not release the prefixes for the Sukhoi Su-24 sub-types, so it is much easier to describe the type by using the ASCC Reporting Names *Fencer-B, Fencer-C* etc.

Exceptions

NATO only gave ASCC Reporting Names to Soviet designed and built aircraft. Aircraft types from native production of WarPac countries were not introduced. For instance while the Yak-12 STOL passenger aircraft had the name *Creek,* the Czech built L-60 Brygadyr for the same purpose did not receive an ASCC-name.

Sole exception besides the American Lend-Lease aircraft was the Aero L-29 Delfin, the Czech-developed and built jet trainer. It became the standard jet-trainer of WarPac including the Soviet Union and the name *Maya* was allocated. The *Maya's* successor, the Aero L-39 Albatros did *not* receive an ASCC name. The Mi-2 *Hoplite* was developed in USSR but built only in Poland.

If a Soviet aircraft type is built in variants of very different character, it is possible that a new ASCC Reporting Name can be allocated. The Il-76 cargo version is *Candid,* the Il-76 flying tanker is *Midas* and the Il-76 'AWACS' is *Mainstay.*

Initially the training version of a fighter also had a name beginning with 'M' as part of the 'Miscellaneous' group. The trainer version of the MiG-15 *Fagot* was the MiG-15UTI *Midget,* that of the Su-7 *Fitter,* the Su-7U/UM *Moujik.* As it became apparent that the trainer versions of fighter aircraft were fully combat capable they were integrated into the fighter names and only marked with a suffix

letter. For instance, the MiG-23UM became *Flogger-C.* Only *true* training aircraft still receive the Miscellaneous name.

On some occasions the reporting name has been changed for another for various reasons. The MiG-15 was first named *Falcon* then it was thought that the name was too becoming for a Russian aircraft and it was changed into *Fagot.* For the same reason the name *Beauty* was changed into *Blinder* on the Tu-22.

Variants

At the beginning, ASCC only allocated a new prefix letter when an obvious new change was introduced. For instance, the entire Su-7 family is named *Fitter-A.* But now, ASCC even allocate a new prefix for minor changes. For instance the difference between a Su-17UM *Fitter-E* and a Su-17UM *Fitter-G* is a slightly taller vertical tail on the latter.

The 300lt drop tanks of the Mi-24 *Hind* were initially reported as tanks for chemical agents and *Hind-G* was allocated to all Mi-24s with tanks. Later it turned out that these tanks were in fact fuel tanks and the designation *Hind-G* was given to the electronic warfare variant of the Mi-24.

ASCC names can also work the other way around. Since the official prefix for the Mi-24 *Hind-A* and *Hind-D* are still secret, the two types are designated by aircrew and in the Eastern press as Mi-24A and Mi-24D, simply for lack of the true Soviet designation. A case of WarPac adopting the prefixes of the ASCC names.

Box
to
Mantis

BOMBERS	
Douglas	
A-20	*Box*
Ilyushin	
Il-2	*Bark*
Il-4	*Bob*
Il-10	*Beast*
Il-28	*Butcher* (early)
Il-28	*Beagle*
Il-40	*Brawny*
Il-54	*Blowlamp*
Il-54	*Blowtorch*
Il-54	*Blowpipe*
Myasishchyev	

M-4	*Bison*
M-50	*Bounder*
M-52	*Bounder*
North American	
B-25	*Bank*
Tupolev	
Tu-2	*Bat*
Tu-4	*Bull*
Tu-14	*Bosun*
Tu-16	*Badger*
Tu-20	*Bear*
Tu-22	*Beauty* (early)

Tu-22	*Blinder*
Tu22M/Tu-26	*Backfire*
Tu-85	*Barge*
Tu-91	*Boot*
Tupolev	
Tu-95	*Bear*
Tu-98	*Backfin*
Tu-142	*Bear-F*
Tu-160	*Blackjack*
Petlyakov	
Pe-2	*Buck*
Yakovlev	
Yak-28	*Brassard* (early)
Yak-28	*Brewer*

TRANSPORTS	
Antonov	
An-2	*Colt*
An-8	*Camp*
An-10	*Cat*
An-12	*Cub*

■ Top: *Backfire-B,* carrying an AS-4 *Kitchen* missile. (RSwAF)

Above: *Bison-B,* under escort from RAF Lightnings. (MoD)

■ *Cubs,* wall-to-wall during an exercise. (Novosti)

An-14	Clod	
An-22	Cock	
An-24	Coke	
An-26	Curl	
An-28	Cash	
An-30	Clank	
An-32	Cline	
An-72	Coaler (and Arctic	
	An-74)	
An-124	Condor	
An-225	Cossack	
Beriev		
Be-30	Cuff	
Douglas		
C-47	Cab	
Ilyushin		
Il-12	Coach	
Il-14	Crate	
Il-18	Clam (early)	
Il-18	Coot	
Il-20	Coot-A	
Il-24N	Coot-C	
Il-62	Classic	
Il-76	Candid	
Il-86	Camber	
Lisunov		
Li-2	Cab	
Tupolev		
Tu-70	Cart	
Tu-104	Camel	
Tu-110	Cooker	
Tu-114	Cleat	
Tu-124	Cookpot	
Tu-134	Crusty	
Tu-144	Charger	
Tu-154	Careless	
Yakovlev		
Yak-8	Crib	
Yak-12	Creek	
Yak-14	Crow	
Yak-16	Cork	
Yak-40	Codling	
Yak-42	Clobber	

■ Top: *Clod*, Antonov An-14 in East German Service. *(via Author)* Right: *Foxhound* – MiG-31 based on MiG-25 thinking. (DoD).

FIGHTERS

Bell
P-63	Fred

Ilyushin
Il-40	Frosty

Lavochkin
La-7	Fin
La-9	Fritz
La-11	Fang
La-174	Fantail

MiG
MiG-9	Fargo
MiG-15	Falcon (early)
MiG-15	Fagot
MiG-17	Fresco
MiG-19	Farmer
Ye-2A	Faceplate
Ye-152	Flipper
MiG-21	Fishbed

MiG-23UVP	Faithless
MiG-23	Flogger
MiG-25	Foxbat
MiG-27	Flogger-D/J
MiG-29	Fulcrum
MiG-31	Foxhound

Sukhoi
Su-7	Fitter-A
Su-9	Fishpod-B
Su-11	Fishpod-C
Su-15	Flagon
Su-17	Fitter-C
Su-17M	Fitter-D/H/K
Su-20	Fitter-C
Su-20M	Fitter-F
Su-22M	Fitter-H/J/K

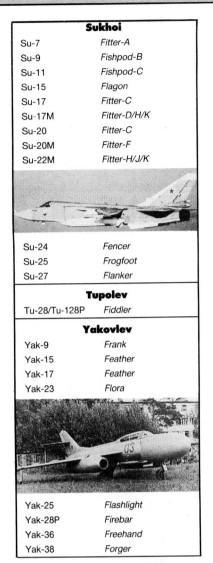

Su-24	Fencer
Su-25	Frogfoot
Su-27	Flanker

Tupolev
Tu-28/Tu-128P	Fiddler

Yakovlev
Yak-9	Frank
Yak-15	Feather
Yak-17	Feather
Yak-23	Flora

Yak-25	Flashlight
Yak-28P	Firebar
Yak-36	Freehand
Yak-38	Forger

■ Above, top to bottom: *Fencer C*, Sukhoi's massive Su-24. (DoD). *Flashlight*, Yak-25 night fighter. *Faithless*, the MiG-23UVP V/STOL experimental. *(Both via Author)*.

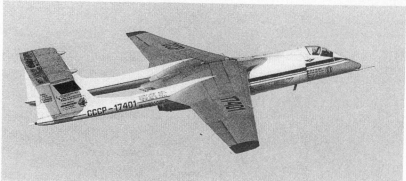

■ Above: *Mystic*, the type that saw the name Myasishchev re-appear. The M-17 *should* have a military as well an environmental use. (TASS)

Ilyushin	
Il-28U	Mascot
Il-38	May
Il-76 AWACS	Mainstay
Il-78T Tanker	Midas

MiG	
MiG-15UTI	Midget
MiG-21U/US/UM	Mongol

Polikarpov	
Po-2	Mule

Sukhoi	

Su-7U	Moujik
Su-9U	Maiden

Taganrog	
GST	Mop

Tsybin	
Ts-25	Mist

Tupolev	
Tu-126	Moss

Yakovlev	
UT-2	Mink
Yak-7UTI	Mark

HELICOPTERS

Kamov	
Ka-8	Hat
Ka-15	Hen
Ka-18	Hog
Ka-20	Harp
Ka-22	Hoop
Ka-25	Hormone
Ka-26	Hoodlum-A

Ka-27, '28, '29, '32	Helix
Ka-126	Hoodlum-B
Ka-136	Hokum

Mil	
Mi-1	Hare
Mi-2	Hoplite
Mi-4	Hound
Mi-6	Hook
Mi-8	Hip
Mi-9	Hip-G
Mi-10	Harke
V-12	Homer
Mi-14	Haze
Mi-17	Hip-H
Mi-24	Hind
Mi-25	Hind-D
Mi-26	Halo
Mi-28	Havoc
Mi-35	Hind-E and F

Yakovlev	
Yak-24	Horse

MISCELLANEOUS

Aero	
L-29	Maya

Antonov	
An-74	Madcap

■ *Moose* of the Czech Air Force – note gun camera fitted on cockpit frame. (via Author)

Beriev	
MBR-2	Mote
MDR-6	Mug
Be-6	Madge
Be-8	Mole
Be-10	Mallow
Be-12	Mail

Consolidated	
PBN-1	Mop
PBY-6A	Mop

Yak-11	Moose
Yak-14	Mare
Yak-17UTI	Magnet
Yak-18	Max
Yak-25RD	Mandrake
Yak-27	Mangrove
Yak-28U	Mascot (early)
Yak-28U	Maestro
Yak-30	Magnum
Yak-32	Mantis

■ Above: *Hoodlum* intended for civilian use, Hungary is the only Eastern European air arm to employ the Ka-26. Above, centre: *Moujik* – Su-7UB landing. (Both via Author).

FINLAND

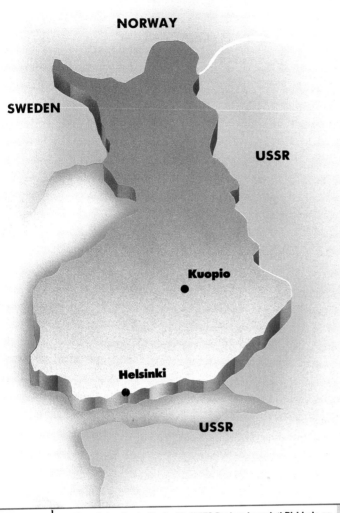

OCCUPYING a unique geographic and political position in Eastern Europe, Finland could rightly appear in *East European Air Power* or *West European Air Power* by virtue of its mid geographic situtaion or its mid Soviet *bloc*/western alliance position.

A young country in terms of independence, Finland was a province of Tsarist Russia until it wrenched itself free during the turmoil of the Communist Revolutions of 1917. Its strategic position on the Baltic made it the focus of Stalin's attentions as Hitler grew more and more expansionist and the Finno-Soviet 'Winter War' of November 1939 to March 1940 saw valiant opposition to the massive tide of Soviet weaponry.

Fortunes flowed the opposite way from 1941 when the Germans moved eastwards during their disastrous invasion of the Soviet Union. From that time onwards, Finland was 'officially' at war with the USSR again, although this time as a vassal of the Nazis. Liberated in 1944 by the Soviets the Treaty of Paris of February 1947 drafted by both the USSR and the United Kingdom, placed severe limitations on the strength of Finland's armed forces.

Finland has since followed a broadly neutral political path, although firmly a democracy along western lines with a complex and expanding free market economy. In 1948, Finland conducted a Mutual Assistance Pact with the USSR, providing for support should either country be invaded.

■ Fine air-to-air of a HavLv 21 J35FS Draken based at Pirkkala as part of the Satakunta Air Defence Wing. (via Hasse Vallas)

■ Above: **Radar equipped Mil Mi-8 in the snow at Rovaniemi, home of the Lapland Air Defence Wing. Mi-8s undertake utility work throughout Finland.** (David Oliver).

■ Below: **MiG-21bis of *HavLv* 13, based at Kuopio – nearest base to the Soviet border. Toned-down markings are being adopted for operational units.** (Jan Jorgensen).

■ Top: **J35FS Draken of the Lapland Air Defence Wing, Rovaniemi, in typically arctic conditions.** (David Oliver).

■ Above: **The attractive and indigenous Valmet L-70 Vinka performs elementary flying training at Kauhava.** (via Hasse Vallas).

■ Left: **Next in the syllabus is the Hawk T.51, also at Kauhava. The Hawks are Valmet-assembled and another order is under consideration.** (via Hasse Vallas).

By treaty neither eastern nor western, Finland's air force has always provided a mixture of Soviet and western types. David Oliver examines a model for post-WarPac nations.

TOGETHER with neutral Sweden, Finland lies directly between NATO and the WarPac countries. There are two strategically important areas in Northern Europe, the Baltic Straits and Baltic area in general, and the North Cap area.

For such a young country, Finland's Air Force (*Ilmavoimat*) has a crowded and proud history having gained a reputation as a formidable fighting force during World War Two. Formed in March 1918 when civil war broke out between 'Red' and 'White' post-Russian Revolution factions that remained in the newly-independent state, *Ilmavoimat*'s first aircraft was a Morane Saulnier Parasol donated by the Swedish Count Eric von Rosen whose personal symbol, a blue swastika, was painted on the wings. Early equipment included a varied collection of ex-World War One types from Germany and France, flown mostly by Swedish volunteer pilots.

In 1924, a British military mission to Finland helped to establish the Air Force Academy at Kauhava and an embryo aircraft industry. This industry was in the forefront of *Ilmavoimat* expansion during the 1930s by producing a number of British and Dutch types under licence.

When Finland was invaded by the Soviet Union in 1939 it possessed 145 combat aircraft, many approaching obsolescence. Nevertheless, it pilots fought with great skill and determination in the harsh conditions to inflict heavy loses on the invading forces. In three seperate conflicts, the 1939/1940 Winter War, the 1941-1944 Continuation War, fought with their German 'allies', and the brief 1944/1945 Lapland War, Finnish pilots destroyed a total of 1,808 Soviet aircraft for the loss of 218.

In 1947 Finland signed the Paris Peace Treaty with Britain and the Soviet Union, as a defeated party. The Treaty imposed severe restrictions on the *Ilmavoimat*'s strength allowing 60 combat aircraft for defensive purposes only, no bombers, and a total strength of 3,000 men. The Treaty also prohibited Finland from possessing, constructing and testing atomic weapons.

Finland also signed a Treaty of Friendship, Co-operation and Mutual Assistance with the Soviet Union in 1948, the essence of which was that if any country should invade the Soviet Union through Finnish territory, the Soviet Union would render Finland military assistance. This treaty also 'encouraged' Finland to remain outside any military pacts with the West.

Immediate post-war equipment included Bf 109G fighters, FW 44 Stieglitz biplanes and Fieseler Storch support aircraft. It was not until 1953 that the Finnish Air Force received its first jet aircraft in the form of six DH Vampire FB.52s. These were supplemented by 10 Folland Gnat F.1s in 1958, but a significant boost to the Air Force's capability came five years later with the delivery of the first of 21 MiG-21F *Fishbed-C* fighters.

Main peacetime tasks of today's *Ilmavoimat* are airspace surveillance, identification and interception, and support of army units. Considering Finland's total area is approximately 130,000 sq miles, the equivalent of Belgium, Denmark and Switzerland combined, with a 758 mile border with the Soviet Union and 445 mile border with Norway, this is no easy task for such a small air arm.

Two factors which help to deter any potential aggressor – the terrain, mainly thick forests or lakes, and the weather. Winter temperature in the north may drop to 35°C below zero with almost total darkness in mid-season.

The Air Force, 75% of which is manned by regular personnel, is divided into three Air Defence Wings each comprising one combat aircraft squadron, long and medium and short-range radar networks and respective ground systems. HavLv (Squadron) 21, part of Satakunta Wing based at Tampere-Pirkkala in Southern Finland, is equipped with Saab J35 Drakens, as is HavLv 11 of the Lapland

Wing at Rovaniemi in the most sensative Northern region of the country. Karelia Wing with MiG-21bis of HavLv 31 at Kuopio-Rissala operates in Central Finland.

Finland's Draken fleet is made up of survivors of 47 aircraft, 24 J35Fs, 12 J35XSs, six J35BSs and five Sk35C trainers delivered between 1972 and 1984. A batch of 30 MiG-21bis *Fishbed-L*s were delivered in the late 1970s to replace the earlier MiG-21Fs that lacked an all-weather capability.

Each combat squadron has one flight of 8-10 Hawk T.51 advanced trainers, 47 of which were assembled in Finland by Valmet. These are used by new pilots before converting to either the Draken or MiG-21. They can also be used as 're-serve' fighters and carry rocket pods for training. The type has proved popular and the Finnish Air Force has a requirement for more – with eight Mk 60s ordered in November 1990. A fourth flight in the squadrons is equipped with a Piper Arrow and Chieftain, and a Valmet Vinka, used for liaison and communications.

It is planned for squadrons to become regiments and flights to become squadrons but exactly how and when this

■ **Left: Finland's Piper Navajo Chieftain fleet is split between support of the combat units and multi-engine training with the Air Academy.**

■ **Above: The Piper Arrows are used in a similar manner, combat squadron 'hacks' and trainers at the Air Academy.** (Both David Oliver)

■ **Right, top to bottom: The MiG-21 force is adopting toned-down markings. F-27 Friendship from the Transport Squadron at Utti, in para-dropping mode.** (Both Hasse Vallas) **Toned-down Hawk in sub-zero conditions, note roundel and serial location.** (David Oliver)

change may be implemented remains uncertain. Other flying units include a Reconnaissance Squadron with MiG-21s and Hawks based at the Air Force Headquarters at Tikkakoski, an Air Force Test Flight at Kuorevesi-Halli, and a Transport Squadron at Utti near Helsinki with Fokker Friendships, Learjets and Mi-8 and Hughes 500 helicopters. A Mi-8 *Hip* fitted with nose-mounted radar also equips an SAR flight at Rovaniemi.

At Kauhava in central Finland is the Air Force Academy with the motto *Skill and Will*. This has an annual intake of 50 students, all destined for combat aircraft, selected from an average of 600-800 applicants. One hundred hours of primary flying training is carried out in the indigenous Valmet Vinka, 30 of which were delivered in the late 1970s. Another 100hr basic course on the Hawk T.51 follows for those selected for further training before successful students are posted to a Fighter Squadron for advanced training and conversion to their respective types.

The Air Academy's Training Squadron has one flight of Hawks, one of Vinkas and a third with the Arrow and Chieftain. The Academy has three Vinka procedural trainers and two Hawk simulators, the latest from Singer-Link includes advanced McDonnell Douglas graphics.

In common with many others, Finland's Air Force has to compete with commercial airlines for pilots. More than half the Academy's 1989 course applied to fill aircrew vacancies advertised by the national airline Finnair, eight succeeded. From 1991 the flying training course will be extended from three to four years.

Despite operating small numbers of two very different combat types, each with different support equipment, armament, even helmets and 'g'-suits, both the Draken and the MiG-21 have proved to be excellent performers. Although rugged and dependable, especially those operating with the Lapland Wing, the cost of maintaining a fleet of four different Draken types is proving a serious drain on both the Air Force's time and resources. A decision on the type's future is already overdue as major and costly rebuilds to take them into the next century, are

looming.

As for the MiG-21 fleet, while the Finnish pilots appreciate the type's 'kick and go' capability – it can be left out in the open overnight in temperature of −30°C and will start on its own power – straight line speed and manoeuvrability, they are less enthusiastic about its limited endurance, avionics, and almost complete lack of forward vision.

With the Air Force activeley considering several combat types from both East and West as potential replacements, several major manufacturers are wooing the *Ilmavoimat* with attractive deals at a time when customers are dwindling.

Of an original short list of four, the F-16 Fighting Falcon, Mirage 2000-5, Saab Gripen and MiG-29, the last two seem to have emerged as the front runners although it has recently been reported that the Soviet Union is now offering Finland the Su-27 *Flanker*.

With rapidly changing relationships between East and West, it is possible that the restrictions imposed on Finland by the Paris Peace Treaty may be relaxed. If this is so it may choose a single combat type, thus saving the cost of duplicating spare parts and ancillary support equipment and spares, although it may be in Finland's own interest to keep a foot in both camps by continuing to operate the latest equipment from East and West if it can be acquired on competitive terms.

Whatever the result, Finland will be a role-model for several countries now considering leaving the confines of WarPac.

■ Two Soviet *Fitters* get airborne. Left is a *Fitter*-H and right a *Fitter*-G. (US Navy).

Faced with the need to create a variable geometry fighter, the Sukhoi Design Bureau took an established design and made its wings swing. Paul Rigby examines the Fitter family.

Swing-wing solution

VARIABLE GEOMETRY (VG) was, until recently, considered to be the answer to many, if not all, of the major problems posed by the increasingly larger and heavier combat aircraft which were being designed and built for the majority of the world's air forces. The option of giving a Mach 2, multi-weapon carrier the flight characteristics of a near STOL aircraft was greeted with cries of joy by many of the long-suffering aircraft designers – not to mention the runway maintenance teams!

Haphazard experiments were initiated during the 1950s but it was not until the 1960s that technology presented the opportunity for VG to be taken seriously. Various studies were carried out in the UK and in the USA which resulted in the publication of several important papers on the subject, which largely hoped to solve any remaining difficulties.

Basically, the theory revolved around the idea of the 'Outboard Hinge'. Later used to the full by the F-111, the whole wing would turn around a hinge set into a 'glove' forward.

Meanwhile, the Soviet Union were being uncharacteristically reticent towards VG. This may have been attributable to the fact that little information of any kind was available on the subject. However, a cautious approach was administered after the publication of the various theories in the West. It was decided to take the safest and cheapest route towards a VG aircraft, that is, to modify an existing type.

After consultations with the various design bureaux (OKBs) it was decided to take the basic Sukhoi Su-7B as the basis on which to build.

Led by Nikolai Zyrin the Sukhoi team began a rather drawn out investigation into VG which involved many tests and studies. This cautious approach resulted in a research and development technolo-

gy demonstrator being built. It was, basically a Su-7, but with swing-wings beginning at the mid-span point and the fitting of large fences, combining with an under-wing stores pylon, to shield the inner wing. It was reasoned that the fences were attached to prevent the separation of airflow from the angle made by the inner and outer wings, at the leading edge. There were no other changes.

In an effort to distinguish this important aircraft it was labelled the S-221 or Su-71G *(Izmenyayema Gayometriya – VG)*. On August 2, 1966 the first example of the S-221 flew. It was shown publicly, at Domodedovo Airport, during the Soviet Aviation Day display, in July 1967, flown by Vladimir Ilyushin. Reports were received in the West, of the formation of two squadrons of, what was to be known as the *Fitter-B*, in the Tactical Air Force with Sirena 2 threat warning radar antenna on the fin tip and a parachute brake. However, no confirmation was received that those squadrons actually existed.

Detailed tests revealed excellent results. The S-221 had improved take-off performance and range over the Su-7 when the wing was in its forward position. With the wing swept back, it was a true fast jet. The Air Force (VVS) decided that full production should proceed, but with a ground attack role rather than the possible air superiority role that was previously envisaged.

Production began with the addition of an improved and more powerful engine. The result was the Su-17. A comparatively simple conversion of an aircraft which held the majority of jigs and tools in store. Thus the whole project was a relatively economical means of upgrading a combat aircraft.

Given the OKB designation S-32 and named *Fitter-C* by NATO the Su-17 entered service with the VVS in 1971 as a ground attack/support aircraft, despite

the fact that it exhibited an odd 'fighter' desgination. Structurally, although the wings had the same profile as the S-221 they were new, being enlarged and with a different internal structure. A new centre section was inserted.

The outer, swing-wing portion is manually operated. The latter having an increased trailing edge sweep. However, the leading edge angle of sweep remains the same as the inner section. Lying parallel to the large fence are two stiffeners, running two-thirds of the chord from the trailing edge, which act as small fences. Along the leading edge of the wing is a slat which almost covers the whole leading edge but tapers before it reaches the wing-tip. On the trailing edge is a slotted flap which is only usable up to 28° sweep, and slotted ailerons.

Semi-monocoque in construction, the fuselage is of a circular section with a ram-air intake in the nose, fitted with a variable shock cone centrebody. Four door-type airbrakes are fitted to each side of the rear fuselage, at the top and base of the tail area. Two assisted take-off (ATO) units can be fitted here. A pitot is fitted to the left side of the nose and a transducer, for fire control information, is attached to the right side.

The cantilever, all-metal tail is swept back on all flying surfaces. The all-moving horizontal tail is fitted with anti-flutter mass balances projecting forwards. The rudder is standard fare with no tabs.

A single wheel is fitted on all units of the tricycle undercarriage. The nosewheel retracts forward, and is covered by a bulged door to accommodate the large wheel, while the main units retract inwards towards the centre section of the wing.

An increasingly distinctive feature of the Su-17 was the spine fairing. It was almost certain that this area was used to accommodate extra fuel, increasing the capacity to 4,550lts. In addition to this, the Su-17 could carry tanks on the outer wing and under fuselage pylons. When the latter are carried only two inboard wing pylons can be used for 1,000kg of ordnance.

Updated avionics included a SRD-5M *High Fix* radar, an I-Band ranging radar in the intake centrebody, ASP-5ND fire control, the 360° Sirena 3 homing and warning system with associated aerials at the base of the rudder and above the brake 'chute container and in each of the leading edges between the fences, SRO-2M IFF, R5B-70 HF and RSIU-5/R-831 VHF/UHF radio.

Weapons include the standard NR-30 cannon with 70 rounds apiece. In addition to the gun, eight pylons are fitted. Two tandem pairs on the under fuselage, one each under the main wing fence and one under the centre section of the wing. The inboard pylons were moved forwards so that they did not interfere with the main wheel wells. Later the VVS could carry the AS-7 *Kerry* air-to-surface missile, rocket pods (UV-16-57 and UV-32-57) with 16 or 32 57mm S-5 or 240 S-24 rockets and 3,200kg of bombs, including nuclear weapons.

New wings and the new Lyulka AL-21F-3 turbojet engine (with a dry thrust of 7,800kg and 11,200kg in afterburner) permitted twice the external load of the Su-7, as well as reducing the take-off run by half and increasing the range by 30%. However, the greater degree of fuel consumption was not totally offsetting the higher fuel content.

In addition to VVS use the new Su-17 was taken by Soviet Naval Aviation as an anti-shipping strike and amphibious support aircraft in the Pacific and the Baltic areas. The Su-17 was, eventually, offered for export under the new designation of Su-20.

Known as the *Fitter-C*, the Su-20 (Su-

■ One of two Su-20 *Fitters* used by the West German *Wehrtechnische Dienststelle* 61 at Manching for trials. This example is due to retire in late 1990. (Gerhard Lang).

17MK) and having an OKB designation of S-32MK, was equipped to a lower standard for export, than the standard VVS aircraft. It was even possible that some of the export models had the older AI-7F-1 engine. Several countries received this variant including Algeria, Czechoslovakia, Egypt, Iraq and Poland. The latter was the first to receive the Su-20, in 1974, with the formation of the first ground attack regiment (*Pulk*).

Two former Egyptian Su-20s reached the news in 1985 when they were acquired by the West German *Luftwaffe* for evaluation at Manching. Numbered 98+61 and 98+62, they came from an original batch of 20 which were delivered, to Egypt, in 1974. Since then the Egyptians had begun an upgrade programme on the Su-20 avionics, from Western sources.

Next variant to appear was the Su-

17M, which was known as *Fitter-D* with an OKB designation of S-32M. Introduced in 1976, it had an improved avionics suite, including a laser rangefinder, and a marked target-seeker in the inlet centrebody.

Terrain avoidance radar was also fitted in front of the new nose pod with Doppler fitted behind. These modifications resulted in a 38cm extension of the nose ahead of the cockpit. With no compensating alteration in the fin area, a certain amount of directional instability was experienced.

Closely following the Su-17M was the two-seat variant, known as the Su-17UM (OKB designation U-32) and *Fitter-E* by NATO. Distinctive feature of the 'UM' was that the whole fuselage forward of the wing, was drooped slightly to give an improved view. Other alterations included the removal of the port gun and the deepening of the dorsal spine fairing, presumably for greater fuel space. A retractable mirror sight was attached to the rear cockpit to increase visibility.

Fitter-H had an enlarged dorsal fin with a square top as well as a ventral strake. It was exported to Algeria, Egypt, Iraq and Vietnam. This variant followed a policy of refinement in the whole Su-17 series. Evidence of this policy was shown with the simplification of the batch of small ram air inlets at the rear of the fuselage around the engine area, to just two inlets. The rear fuselage diameter was increased and an expanded fairing behind the cockpit was fitted to hold more fuel and/or equipment.

The 'H' expanded on its already large weapon-carrying potential by the attachment of two further pylons bringing the grand total to ten. This variant had a deeper nose into which was installed the terrain avoidance radar. While keeping the twin cannon the *Fitter-H* was modified to carry the AS-7 *Kerry* although its primary mission was tactical reconnaissance.

Again, a two-seat model appeared, this time for the *Fitter-H* – the Su-17 *Fitter-G*. While retaining combat capability the fuselage exhibited the deepened dorsal spine and drooped forward fuselage like the *Fitter-E* but with a taller fin and a removable shallow ventral fin. As was the norm with the two-seaters, the

■ Up to October 3, East Germany operated two units of Su-22M-4s, MFG-28 and, below, JBG-77 'Gebhard von Blucher'. (David Oliver).

■ Czech Su-22M-4 *Fitter-G* belonging to the 6th Fighter Bomber Regiment based at Prerov.

left gun was omitted.

In 1984 a new Su-17 model was sighted. It was noted that there was no nose extension, although the laser was retained, and that the left gun was sometimes omitted, yet this was a single-seat aircraft. This was the Su-17 *Fitter-K*. The noticeable feature which readily distinguishes it is the fin root intake which cools internal avionics. The Polish Air Force have examples of it, with full avionics fit, but they sometimes refer to it as the Su-22.

East Germany also received the *Fitter-K* into the *Luftstreitkrafte*, in 1985. Two units were equipped – *Marinefliegergeschwader* 28 based at Lange, with MiG-23BN aircraft, and *Jagdfliegergeschwader* 1 *Fritz Schemenkel* based at Holzdorf, who converted from MiG 21s. A total of 80 were delivered.

Outstanding aspect of the Su-22 *Fitter-F*, apart from its new designation, was the realisation that a Tumansky R-29B-300 engine was fitted, although this is only slightly more powerful than the previous

Lyulka. Speculation as to why there was a sudden change in engine centres around an effort to overcome production problems or possibly a striving for commonality or handling characteristics.

In addition to the two 30mm cannon the Su-22 was fitted with *Atoll* AAMs for self defence. The fin root intake remained. A side effect of this intake may have been to correct the earlier directional instability of the *Fitter-D*. This version was one of the chief export models. Examples are in Czechoslovakia, East Germany, North and South Yemen, Angola, Libya, Peru and North and South Vietnam.

One of those customers, Peru accepted an offer for 36 aircraft (32 *Fitter-Fs*, and four *Fitter-Es*) in 1976. They were purchased because of the US refusal to sell the F-5 Tiger II. Total programme cost, £140.45 million was payable over 10 years.

Assistance over conversion training was given by Cuba's Air Arm, the *Fuerza Aerea Revolucionaria*, at Santa Clara and

Camaguey. In addition Cuba loaned 12 MiG-21s to Peru to help Peruvian pilots and ground crews familiarise themselves with Soviet equipment. 100 Cubans and 75 Soviet technicians assisted with the building of a new air base at La Joya in south Peru.

Initial aircraft were assigned to *Grupo* 12 at BA *Capitan Montes* at Talara on the Pacific coast. First batch equipped two *Escuadrones, Escuadrone de Caze* II *Los Tigres* and 12 *Escuadrone*. The second batch were assigned to *Grupo* II at Ba *Mariano Melgar* at La Joya.

Despite all of the preparations and assistance several problems still occurred. For example, the IFF system on the Su-22 was incompatible with the SA-3 SAMs, which were delivered along with ZSU 23-4 radars and communications centres. From late 1984 the whole fleet was subject to a minor degree of updating of the avionics from Western sources.

Further models were issued with the R-29B-300 engine such as the Su-22 *Fitter-G* export version as used by the East German Air Force and, finally, the Su-22 *Fitter-J* single-seater. (There is a two-seat *Fitter-J* in existence but there is very little information on it.)

Fitter-J is the export version of the 'H', with the Tumansky engine, internal fuel of 6,270lts and a more angular dorsal fin. Supplies have been made to Hungary who received them with the intention of replacing their Su-7Bs in 1981, with the strike and tactical reconnaissance regiment of the *Legiero* based at Kiskunkachaza, south of Budapest. Two squadrons are dedicated to strike missions while a third are dedicated reconnaissance.

Libya also received 'J's, with disastrous consequences. Although purchased as ground attack aircraft they were seen in an air defence mode when the infamous encounter with the US Navy took place on August 19, 1981. Prior to their destruction they were seen to be carrying two *Atolls* on inboard wing pylons and two external tanks on outboard wing pylons.

The encounter between the Su-22s and the F-14s was an important one because it was to be the very first combat between variable geometry aircraft. In some ways the fight was inconclusive. The quality of the pilots and the tactics employed by the two sides do not present a finite set of results and it does not take long for conjecture to appear. The VG possibilities of the Su-22s were never employed to any extent, for example, while the Libyan pilots flew in a 'negative' fashion.

It did prove the manoeuvrability of the large F-14 Tomcat which had also adopted the swing-wing, enabling the classic 'dogfight' to take place, rather than one shot, high speed pass that was only possible with some of the earlier aircraft such as the F-104. Thus showing some of the advantages of VG.

The Su-17 series can be said to have brought the Su-7 into the 1980s. While by no means 'state-of-the-art' the Su-17 series is capable and well-liked by the majority of pilots who fly them. It has its faults and vices, but for an aircraft that was only meant to be a R&D specimen it has proved, along with its Su-7 brethren to be a remarkable aircraft and one of the most cost effective updates, of an original combat aircraft, of all time.

■ Spacious cockpit of the Su22M-4, showing the easy-to-read instrumentation and weapon system switches (at right). (Peter Steinemann)

■ Above: Known locally as the *Humpback*, an Su-22M-4 of *Marinefliegergeschwader* 28 lets down in the twilight to its base at Laage. Apparently, there is no place for the *Fitter* in the 'new' Germany – see page 31. (Duncan Cubitt)

■ Left: Polish Su-22M-4s during a break of formation. As with the East German example above, note the chaff pallets mounted on either side of the fuselage spine.

POLAND

THROUGH the Solidarity movement, Poland is perhaps the first country that comes to mind when the 'new' Eastern Europe is considered. The Polish struggle for democracy has been over a long and hard-fought path.

In September 1939 both Hitler's Germany and Stalin's USSR invaded Poland. Hitler's ignoring of the guarantees made on Poland by the UK and France led to the outbreak of World War Two. Following liberation, a coalition of socialist groups ran the country, until a Communist constitution on Stalinist lines was instigated in 1952. Poland joined WarPac in May 1955 and sent troops into Czechoslovakia in August 1968.

By 1970 the population was exhibiting massive discontent and the long path towards ousting the hard-line government had begun. The strikes of July 1980 were so paralysing that the government made concessions, only to see these taken away by the military when martial law was imposed in February 1981. This was lifted in July 1983 as the economy continued to slide and it was clear that some form of dialogue with the organised opposition, largely centered around the union Solidarity, was unavoidable. More strikes in 1988 led directly to the democratic elections of the summer of 1989. While defence and some internal matters remain with the Communist Party, the coalitions within the new Council of Ministers are setting to a complete restructuring of the country, its outlook and economy.

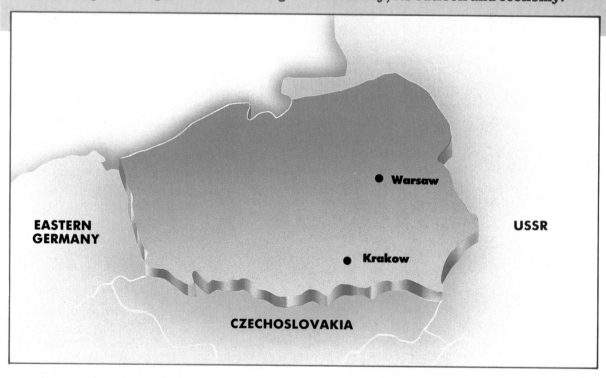

■ Polish MiG-21U *Mongol-B* . (Pete West)

■ Top: **Ground crew hard at work on a 6 Regiment Su-22.** (Wojcieth Luczak).
■ Above: **Tight run-by from a pair of MiG-29s of 1 PLM. With a great air fighting heritage behind them, it is good to see unit markings creeping back onto aircraft** (left). (Both Wojcieth Luczak).

■ Su-7BMs are winding down in Polish service, currently flying in the advanced trainer role. (Wojcieth Luczak).

■ Polish-built An-2, para-dropper and liaison aircraft. (Wojcieth Luczak).

■ MiG-23MFs at Bydgoszcz. (WAF).

Other than the Soviet Union, Poland had the largest air arms within WarPac. Jerzy Woda outlines this force as it goes beyond the zenith.

■ Above: **Podded-up Mi-17 – note unit badge.**
(Roger Gretzyngier)
■ Below: **PZL-130 Orlik, the PWL will use the turbo-prop development as a basic trainer.**
(Wojciech Luczak)

LARGEST of the forces available to WarPac – other than the Soviet Union itself – Poland has always boasted a large and capable air force. The *Polskie Wojska Lotnicze* (Polish Air Force – PWL) was the first Eastern European nation to operate Soviet-built jet fighters. The first Yak-17 *Feather* being shown off to the public on June 20, 1950.

Today, the dominant PWL fighter is the MiG-21 *Fishbed* with up to 350 employed within 11 regiments. First versions in PWL use were 'F-13s, which arrived in 1962 joining the famous 1st Fighter Regiment. Soon after 'PFs and 'PFMs arrived.

Most important version now is the MiG-21MF and MiG-21bis. About 35

MiG-21R are operated in the tactical reconnaisance rôle by the PWL. All three Air Defence Divisions at Warszawa, Wroclaw and Bydgoszcz are equipped with the *Fishbed*. Four Regiments of the Tactical Command also operate the MiG-21.

In the tactical role the *Fishbed* can be loaded with bombs and UB-16/32 rocket pods. Frequent exercises also include take-off and landings from motorways, when prepared, camouflaged (wooded) areas beside the motorways are used. Late variant MiG-21MFs and MiG-21bis should remain in service well into the next century.

Recently, in a search for hard currency, the Government began to sell some of

their MiG-21PFs and MiG-21PFMs via Western dealers to the USA. A number of them were bound for private owners, but some were purchased by the Defense Test and Support Evaluation Agency (DTESA). Their goal is to acquire enough material to form two Frontal-Regiments in the USA for use on exercises.

In 1981 the first MiG-23MF *Flogger-B*s were delivered to the Air Defence Division at Bydgoszcz and the first Regiment was operational in 1986. The PWL operates 45 MiG-23MF *Flogger-B*s and a number of MiG-23UM *Flogger-C* trainers. While all interceptor MiG-23MFs are painted in air superiority grey, a number of the trainer *Flogger-C*s are camouflaged.

First Polish pilots were trained on the Su-7RM in 1964. They took part in an exercise in the Erfurt area of the German Democratic Republic in October 1965.

PWL operates the Su-7BM, Su-7BKL and the Su-7BMK, as well as a number of Su-7UM trainer. Despite their primary role as ground attack aircraft, none of the Su-7s were ever camouflaged. Currently about 15 Su-7BMK are in service as advanced trainers.

Poland became the sole WarPac operator of the *Fitter-C*. The swing-wing attack aircraft is called Su-17 in the USSR, but Poland uses the export designation Su-20. Both types are identical in equipment. The new type was introduced to the public for the first time at the Air Parade on July 22, 1974. Since no Su-17 or '20 trainer was ever built, pupils were trained on the Su-7UB before the new Su-22U *Fitter-G* became available in 1985.

Fitter-C can carry a large variety of armament; UB-16 and UB-32 pods, FAB 100 and FAB 250 bombs as well as GP-9 gun pods on wing pylons. For reconnaissance missions a centreline fuselage ELINT-recce pod can be carried. More than 90 Su-20 *Fitter-C*s are currently in service with the tactical regiments.

In 1985 the first Su-22M-4 *Fitter-K* and Su22U *Fitter-G*s were delivered to Poland to replace the aged Su-7 *Fitter-A*. For the first time, ground attack aircraft in Polish service were camouflaged.

*Fitter-K*s carry the same arsenal of weapons as the *Fitter-C*, but in addition, six pack bomb racks for FAB 100 bombs can be carried. K-60 (AA-8 *Aphid*) short range missiles can be carried for self

defence.

About 100 Su-22M-4 should be in service with the PWL. All *Fitters* are assigned to the three Tactical Divisions based at Malbork, Pila and Smardzko.

In late December 1988 the first MiG-29 *Fulcrum* arrived in Poland. A year prior to this event, the first pilots and ground crews had been sent to the USSR for conversion training, working alongside Czechs doing likewise.

At least one squadron is currently operational on the *Fulcrum*, although future deliveries and the status of the aircraft within the 'new' Poland are still unconfirmed. With the large scale reductions in the Polish armed forces, including the PWL, announced by Tytus Krawczyc in 1989, it is thought the largest cuts would be made in the *Fishbed* force.

Polish soldiers were transported and parachuted for the first time, from a Soviet An-12, in 1963. In 1965 the PWL received its first An-12 transports, they were used in a WarPac exercise in East Germany in October of the same year. These aircraft were also used to transport armament from Poland to Egypt during the Yom Kippur war. About 20 An-12s are in service with the PWL today.

First examples of the twin engined An-26 were acquired in 1972. Like the An-12s they were allocated to the 6th Pomeranian Airborne Division. A year later, a number of them were also used to transport goods to Egypt during the war with Israel. In 1990 about 12 An-26s were in PWL service.

In 1988, the first examples of the Polish built An-28s were assigned to the Transport regiments of the PWL. They are fully camouflaged and have a white four digit tactical number on the rear fuselage.

A fleet of passenger aircraft for VIPs are in use. In 1973 the first Yak-40 arrived with about 15 in current service. Two Tu-134As and a single Il-18 were acquired from LOT to carry large numbers of VIPs inside and outside WarPac countries.

Liaison flying is supplied by the indigenous PZL 104 Wilga 35P, which was introduced in service in 1972. More than 30 Wilgas are currently on PWL strength.

While most WarPac countries use the Czech Zlin Z-42 primary trainer and Aero L-29 and L-39 jet trainer, Poland uses aircraft from its own production lines. The TS-8 Bies flew for the first time on July 23, 1955 and more than 50 are currently in service. This type will be sooner or later replaced by the PZL-130 Turbo Orlik.

The jet trainer TS-11 Iskra flew for the first time in 1960. Poland is the sole operator of this type. 50 each TS-11s are based at Radom and the Air Academy at Deblin. The Iskra will be replaced by another two-seat trainer of Polish origin, the I-22.

First helicopter to enter Polish Air Force service was the SM-1, the WSK Swidnik license-built Mil Mi-I *Hare*, which started operations in 1956. Two years later the Mi-4A *Hound* followed. The

Navy received the Mi-4M anti-submarine warfare helicopter, with the last being withdrawn from operation recently, their duty taken over by the Mi-14 *Haze*.

Although designed in the Soviet Union by the Mil OKB, the Mi-2 *Hoplite* was exclusively produced by WSK at Swidnik. It is the standard liaison/scout helicopter for WarPac. There were a number of armed versions used: an anti-tank Mi-2 with four AT-3 Sagger missiles. One Mi-2 variant carried a flexible 12.7mm machine gun in the passenger compartment. On each side a single MARS-2 pod with unguided missiles can be carried.

Another variant is the smoke-maker Mi-2. With the help of the exhaust blast, chemical is dispensed to produce a smoke-screen, to help camouflage tanks and troops as well as ships in Polish harbours.

Standard transport/assault helicopter is the Mi-8. The first Mi-8TB *Hip-C* arrived in Poland in 1968. A limited number of the passenger variant, Mi-8S, are flown for VIP work. About 50 Mi-8s are in current service with Air Force, Army and Navy.

In 1979 the Mi-24 *Hind-D* gunship had been introduced. They were demonstrated for the first time to the public on June 27 of the same year. In 1985 the improved *Hind-E* entered service and the PWL continues to operate a mixed fleet. At least two regiments with about 60 *Hinds* are in current service.

In 1987 the Polish Air Force put the large Mi-6 *Hook* into service. Three are in

■ Far left: **TS-11 Iskra, long serving basic jet trainer for the PWL.** (Wojciech Luczak)
■ Below: **Locally built Mi-2T *Hoplite*.** (Roger Gretzyngier)
■ Main picture: **Il-14s still give Poland loyal service, seen here at Krakow in October 1990.** (Trevor Hall)

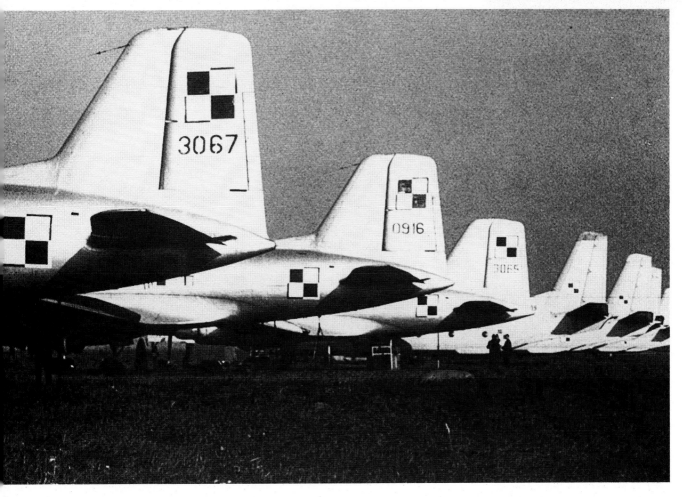

use.

The Mi-14 *Haze* was introduced in Polish Navy service in 1979. The Navy operates three variants of the Haze; the anti-submarine Mi-14PL, the Mi-14BT as sea-mine discovering and destroying variant and the Mi-14PS in the SAR rôle. About 20 *Haze* are based on the Baltic.

The Mi-17 *Hip-H* is the latest acquisition. The first Mi-17s were shipped to Poland in late 1988. Unlike the Mi-8, the *Hip-H* can carry six UB-32 pods on outriggers. While most of the Soviet Mi-17s have a 12.7mm machine gun fitted in the nose, this weapon is omitted on the Polish Mi-17's.

There are ten helicopter regiments operating the Mi-2, Mi-6, Mi-8 and Mi-17. Mi-2s Mi-8s and Mi-14s are also allocated to the Polish Navy.

With new attitudes and directions, the

■ Above: **Lycoming engined prototype PZL M-26 Iskierka basic trainer – hopeful of a PWL order.**
■ Below: **One of the prototype PZL I-22 Iryda, aimed at replacing the TS-11 Iskra.** (Both Wojciech Luczak)

future of the PWL and other armed forces within Poland is wide open to conjecture. With around 350 Soviet combat aircraft based within Poland, it would seem one of the first moves would be their removal.

Economic constraints should continue to put pressure on the PWL inventory with continued cuts in combat types for service, but only through a reliance on exports.

One thing is certain. The second largest air arm in WarPac has reached its zenith. Poland for the remainder of the 1990s will have a much slimmer force.

■ **End of the line. Dismantling 1 PLM MiG-21PFs under the eye of watching journalists.** (Leszek Wroblewski)

EASTERN GERMANY

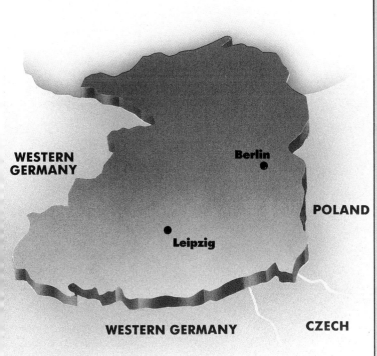

WESTERN GERMANY

Berlin

POLAND

Leipzig

WESTERN GERMANY

CZECH

MIDNIGHT October 2, 1990 saw the culmination of a momentous series of events that less than five years ago would have been considered highly desirable, yet highly improbable. At that moment the Federal Republic of Germany fused with the German Democratic Republic. Germany, split by the occupying Allied forces and then further segregated as those powers turned on one another, was re-united. Accordingly, this section of *East European Air Power* carries no country name, but the banner 'Eastern Germany' which, for the present, is perhaps the most accurate. Changes as the two countries come to grips with the challenges of integration are occurring even as these words are being set and the latest situation appears at the rear of the section. Thus, unlike other chapters, the following words on the air arms of East Germany bask in the luxury of being history – namely a summation of the situation up to the winding down of East Germany.

The East/West split of Germany goes back to the unresolved end of World War Two, with the Eastern area being that occupied by Soviet troops as the last remnants of Hitler's great dream were smashed. Berlin was occupied by the Allies in a similar ratio. In October 1949, with its economy being drained, East Germany enacted its own constitution. In May 1955 it joined WarPac and in October of that year, the USSR recognised the German Democratic Republic as a sovereign state free to conduct its own affairs – prior to this it had no status anywhere as an integral nation. The Berlin Blockade of 1948/1949 was a reaction to the artificial situation of having a capitalist 'plughole' in the middle of a communist state. The ultimate solution to the problem came on Augsut 13, 1961 when construction of the Berlin Wall was initiated. East Germany supported the Warsaw Pact in August 1968 when it sent troops into Czechoslovakia to help suppress the *'Prague Spring'* movement. December 12, 1972 saw the signing of a 'Basic Treaty' with West Germany, paving the way for increasingly better, and more formalised relations with its much bigger and richer neighbour. 1989 witnessed amazing outbreaks of 'people power' all over Eastern Europe and the visions coming out of East Berlin were all the more remarkable considering what the Wall stood for in post-war history. In the wake of this reaction, the currupt Honecker regime fell in October and talks were opened almost immediately to unify the two Germanies.

During November 9/10 1989, the Wall – already hacked to pieces by souvenir collectors – was officially brought down and the borders within the divided city removed. As the unification edict became law in October 1990, so East Germany officially left the Warsaw Pact. A new era had dawned...

■ Below: **Following German reunification, Defence Minister Gerhard Stoltenberg made the surprise announcement that JG3 'Vladimir Kormorov's' MiG-29 *Fulcrum* would be retained in the new air force. It had previously been thought that all Soviet-supplied equipment would be retired or returned.** (David Oliver)

■ Above: **Crew and equipment of a Parow-based *Haze-B* on show, including the dipping sonar for the first time.** (Duncan Cubitt).
■ Right, top row: **One of 12 An-26s operated out of Dresden by *Transportfliegerstaffel* 24.**
Right: **Bautzen-based L.39ZA Albatros.** (Both David Oliver).
■ Right, middle: **Zlin 42 of the Heaquarters Liaison Flight, seen here at Laage.** (Duncan Cubitt).
■ Righ, bottom: **Two Mi-8 units were based at Brandenburg, one for general duties and one for battlefield support. Several are configured for SAR.** (David Oliver).
■ Below: **End of an era. Last MiG-21 flight from Preschen-based JG3, September 27, 1990.** (Lt Col Sauder, CO 3rd Sqn, JG3).

■ Above: **MiG-29UB showing off the two-tone grey scheme that was employed alongside the more traditional scheme (left).** (Jan Jorgensen)
■ Left: **Special colours on Colonel Fichte's** *Fulcrum* **for the final operational flight on September 27, 1990. The** *Fulcrums* **now have** *Luftwaffe* **serials in the batch 29+01 to 29+24.** (Hans Nijhuis)
■ Below: **Flight trials of a former LSK/LV** *Hind* **must be tempting Luftwaffe officials!** (Jan Jorgensen)

Harry Wisch surveys an air arm that is no more. Now a part of the united Germany, East Germany's LSK/LV is consigned to the history books.

LONG BEFORE the creation of the East German Air Force (*Luftstreik-rafte der Nationalen Volksarmee*), the Soviet occupation forces permitted a build-up of aero clubs – mainly equipped with Po-2s and Yak-18s. As a further step towards re-armament the *Volkspolizei Luft* (Air Police) was formed. From these two ventures, the nucleus of the *Luft-streikrafte* was created.

On January 18, 1956, the *Nationale Volksarmee* (People's Army) was formed and in March, work began on a new air force. Inventory of the nascent *Luftstreik-rafte* included Yak-11 and '18 trainers and the Po-2 liaison aircraft. A number of personnel came from aero clubs and the *Volspolizei Luft*.

First action for the very young air arm came in its first year. During 1956, the USA began to launch hundreds of balloons across the Eastern Sector of Germany. They were a threat to the Communist regime in two ways, from the propaganda viewpoint and as a hazard to air traffic. Armed *Luftstreikrafte* Yak-11s were used to intercept and destroy the balloons.

While the Yak-11 was good enough to shoot down balloons, it could not protect the German Democratic Republic from intruding jets. Barely seven months after the *Luftstreikrafte* was established, the first MiG-15s arrived, to become the backbone of the force.

Conversion from the piston-engined Yak-11 was far from easy, but thanks to Soviet instructors the first German pilots received their diplomas on the MiGs in early 1957. About the same time, the *Luftstreikrafte* and the Anti-Aircraft Division were put under a mutual command based at Strausberg-Eggersdorf.

During the summer of 1957 the MiG-17F began to arrive. This type was supplied in large numbers to the *Luftstreik-rafte* and the last examples were not withdrawn until 1986, serving their final years in the ground attack role.

Further modernisation came in 1959 with supplies of the radar-equipped MiG-17PF *Fresco-D* along with the supersonic

MiG-19S *Farmer-D* and the MiG-19PM *Farmer-E*. The *Fresco-D* and the *Farmer-E* could operate under any conditions, day or night, policing violations of East German airspace.

Withdrawal of the *Farmers* started in 1963, shortly after delivery of the first MiG-21 *Fishbeds*. Some MiG-19s were to stay on until the late 1960s.

A *Farmer* was responsible for intercepting a photographic reconnaissance Douglas RB-66 at 30,000ft, some 40 miles inside East German airspace, on March 10, 1964. Having failed to force the USAF RB-66 to land, the MiG-19PM pilot shot it down. Between January 1963 and May 1964 about 50 violations of airspace were recorded.

In 1961 the *Luftstreikrafte* took part in its first joint exercise, becoming fully integrated into WarPac. By the end of the year it had split into two *Luftverteidi-gungs-Divisionen* (Air Defence Divisions).

Fishbed-Es (MiG-21F-13) joined their first *Luftstreikrafte* units in 1962. Up to October 3, 1990 when union with West Germany was achieved, the MiG-21 was still numerically the most important fighter. The last 'F-13s served into the mid-1980s as tactical reconnaissance fighters equipped with a centre-fuselage pod.

The number of MiG-21s in East German service grew steadily and the 'F-13s were followed by MiG-21PF *Fishbed-Ds* and 'Es and MiG-21PFM *Fishbed-Fs*. The *Fishbed-J* (MiG-21MF) was mainly used as an interceptor and the MiG-21UM trainers had a dual role as ECM aircraft. As *East European Air Power* closed for press, it seemed most likely that the surviving MiG-21 fleet would be scrapped and not returned to the USSR.

In about 1978 the *Luftstreikrafte* received its first examples of the MiG-23MF *Flogger-B*, later supplemented with the

■ Above: **LET Turbolet of the Strausberg-based liaison unit.** (Miroslav Sedy)
■ Below: **Immaculate An-2. The type served almost from the beginning of the LSK/LV to the very end.** (Jan Jorgensen)
■ Top right: **The end. Spraying out the nationality markings on a MiG-21 at Preschen, September 27, 1990. It would seem that most of the *Fishbeds* face the axe, some already having gone to a yard at Rothenburg.** (Arnaud Boxman/APT)
■ Bottom right: **Tu-134 from the VIP unit 'Arthur Pieck' at Maxwalde.** (Jan Jorgensen)

MiG-23ML *Flogger-G*. The initial years of operation were marred by a number of accidents and crashes. Up until unity, the *Flogger* had the highest rate of attrition of any other *Luftstreikrafte* type. As with the MiG-21 force, a number of MiG-23UM two-seaters were acquired and used for a combination of training and ECM work.

A change of operational doctrine occurred in 1985. For nearly 30 years, the *Luftstreikrafte's* primary duty was air defence, but the last five years of the force's existence saw more and more *Jagdbombenfliegergeschwader* (Fighter Bomber Regiments) formed. This saw acquisition of the MiG-23BN *Flogger-F* and the Su-22M-4 *Fitter-K*.

About 80 *Fitters* were acquired, along with some Su-22Us. Two units took on the type including MFG28 at Laage.

Last-ever fighter type to be employed by the *Luftstreikrafte* was the MiG-29 *Fulcrum*. First East German air and groundcrews travelled to the USSR in early 1987 to begin conversion flying. Early in 1988 the first aircraft arrived in crates for reassembly under the eye of a Soviet team of technicians. The type took a long time to integrate into *Luftstreikrafte* service as it required an update of landing aids at the airfields that might take it.

Only *Jadgfliegergeschwader* 3 'Wladimir Komarow' at Preschen operated the MiG-29, using 20 of the type and 10 MiG-21s. Upon union with West Germany, there was much media debate as to the fate of these magnificent aircraft. All of the *Fulcrums* have since received *Luftwaffe* four-digit serial numbers and are currenltly being operated "for evaluation", although short span spares and engines have been requested from the Soviet Union.

Luftstreikrafte received its first transport types in 1957. The Il-14 *Crates* originally delivered gave way to An-26 *Curls* but the An-2s from 1957 are still to be found in use, mostly for parachute work. The An-26s were operated by *Transportfliegerstaffel* 24 at Dresden and their aircraft travelled as far as Africa on mercy flights.

At Maxwalde, the VIP unit *Transportfliegergeschwader* 44 'Arthur Pieck' operated a mix of types, from the Mi-8S to Tu-134, Tu-154 and Il-62 airliners. A liaison unit, *Verbindungsfliegerstaffel* 14 at Strausberg used four L.410 Turbolets, six An-2s and several Zlin Z.43 on flights within WarPac until union.

Theoretical lessons towards pilot training started at the Military Academy at Kamenz, before flight training with the *Offiziershochschule* 'Otto Lilienthal' headquartered at Bautzen, with *Fliegerausbildungsgeschwader* 15 'Heinz Kapelle' using 20 MiG-21s (MiG-15UTI previously) and *Fliegerausbildungsgeschwader* 25 'Leander Ratz' with 40 L.39s at Bautzen. Helicopter training was the responsibility of *Hubschrauberausbildungsgeschwader* 35 at Brandenburg, flying Mi-2s and Mi-8Ts. Transport flying training was conducted at Kamenz with *Transportfliegerausbildungsstaffel* 45 using Turbolets and An-2s.

First *Luftstreikrafte* helicopter regiment was *Transporthubschraubergeschwader* 34 'Werner Seelenbinder', using Mi-1s and '4s from 1957. Based at Brandenburg in 1990, the unit was operating 24 Mi-8Ts, having received the first of these in 1968.

First unit to get the Mi-24 *Hind-D* was *Kampfhubschraubergeschwader* 57, showing off their *Hinds* for the first time in public in October 1979. A second unit was also established, both using a mix of *Hinds* with Mi-8TB *Hip-Cs* and Mi-8TBK *Hip-Fs*.

At Parow on the Baltic, *Marinehubschraubergeschwader* 'Kurt Barthel' was established in 1963. Initially with Mi-4Ms, it later took on Mi-8s and was still operating Mi-8TBs in the SAR role in 1990. The unit took on Mi-14 *Hazes* from 1979, operating a mix of Mi-14PLs, 'BTs and 'PSs (see page 45). The 'BTs were being reconfigured for SAR use at this time.

Robert Schneider describes the Czechoslovakian Air Force, which enjoys variety in the form of the products of its own aerospace industry.

RESPONSIBLE for the air defence of the nation and the support of Czech and Allied ground forces, the *Ceskoslovenske Letectvo* (Czechoslovak Air Force) is divided into two Air Armies. The 7th Air Army, headquartered at Stara Boleslav, is independent of Army command and reports directly to the Ministry of Defence. The 10th Air Army carries out tactical support under the direction of the local front commander and has its headquarters at Hradec Kralove.

Under the Warsaw Pact, Czech forces were taken under Soviet command if a collective threat faced members of the Pact. Where Czech commitment to War-Pac currently lies is a matter for her leaders. Should Czechoslovakia work with the Pact, recent planning would have the 10th Air Army attached to the Soviet Central Group forces based in Czechoslovakia at Milovice near Prague and the 7th Air Army would have fallen under Soviet PVO control.

Comprising two Air Divisions (the 2nd Fighter Defence Division with headquarters as Brno and the 3rd Fighter Defence Division at Zatec) the 7th Air Army has three Fighter Regiments (*Stihacich Pluky* – SP) at its disposal. The 3rd Fighter Defence Division hosts the 1st SP with MiG-23MFs at Ceske Budejovice and the 11th SP with a mix of MiG-21MFs and MiG-29s at Zatec. At Brno-Turany, the

■ Above: **Camouflaged Su-7, in use as an instructional airframe.**

■ Below: MiG-21 in natural metal with camouflaged *Fulcrums* behind. (Both Peter Gunti)

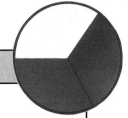

CZECHOSLOVAKIA

AS TANKS rolled into the streets of Prague on August 20, 1968, the reformist aspirations of the people of Czechoslovakia were smartly packed away as the West made loud noises while recognising the impossibility of intervening. The forces that moved in to re-establish more conventinal communist thinking also underlined the strength of the Warsaw Pact. As well as tanks and troops from the Soviet Union — already stationed within the country — contingents from Bulgaria, Hungary, East Germany and Poland were also present.

It is all the more poignant that in the momentous upheavals of the late 1980s, Czechoslovakia was to be proudly resurgent and in the vanguard of the democratisation of East Europe.

Central to the start of World War Two — Czechoslovakia was the "far off place" that Chamberlain would not defend at the Munich Summit — liberation came in 1945 in the form of Stalin's tanks. An in-government *coup* brought in the communists in February 1948 and the joining of the Warsaw Pact in May 1955. A major revision of constitution in 1960 saw the creation of the Czechoslovakian Socialist Republic.

As the state faces a new decade, the exact military and political stance of Czechoslovakia has yet to unfold but should follow the path of both Hungary and Poland towards full independence from the Soviet Union.

■ Putting the weapon pylons on a Mi-24 *Hind-D* to peaceful use at a Czech airshow in August 1990. (Piotr Butowski)

■ Above: **Pleasant aspect of a bombed-up** *Frogfoot*. (Peter Gunti)

■ Right: **Mi-8 taken at Kbely in September 1990. Yellow markings denote a non-combat aircraft, under the terms of the Helsinki Agreement** (David Oliver)

■ Below: **A MiG-29** *Fulcrum* **comes to rest, showing the fin location for the tactical number.** (Peter Gunti)

■ Above: **Test markings on the VZLU's MiG-21UM used for ejector-seat trials.** (Peter Gunti)

■ Left: *Hind* **at rest. Note unit marking under the cockpit.** (Peter Gunti)

■ Below: **Well-known photo-mapping conversion of an Avia 14-40.** (Miroslav Sedy)

■ Few readers will realise that the shapely Aero L.39 Albatros is the largest produced jet trainer currently on the market. Having widely supplied WarPac contries, the new L.39MS is aiming at the wider export market. (David Oliver).

8th SP operates the MiG-21MF.

There are two SP within the 10th Air Army, both part of the 1st Fighter Division, based at Bechyne. These are the 5th SP at Dobrany-Line and the 9th SP at Bechyne, both using the MiG-21MF. Largest division within the 10th Air Army is the 34th Fighter Bomber Division with four Fighter Bomber Regiments (*Stiha-cich-Bombardirovacich Pluky* – SBP) operating a mix of aircraft. Two SBPs use the Su-22M-4, the 6th at Prerov and the 20th at Namest nad Oslavou. At Caslev, the 28th SBP uses the MiG-23BN. Some 75 plus Su-25K *Frogfoots* were received from 1975, replacing Su-7s with the 30th SBP at Pardubice.

There are two regiments devoted to reconnaissance using a mixture of MiG-21RFs, Su-22M-4s and ECM configured Tu-134 transports. Thiry L-39 Albatros

trainers are reported to be camera equipped and employed also within these regiments.

There are two Transport Regiments, the 1st Mixed Transport Regiment at Mosnov and the 3rd Transport Regiment at Kbely-Praha. The former uses a fleet of An-12s, An-26s, L-410M Turbolets and Mil Mi-17s. The An-12 is the largest aircraft on the Czech inventory. The 3rd Regiment uses An-24s, Mi-8s, Tu-134s and Yak-40s. The Avia 14T (Il-14) is reported still to be in use with as many as 20 said to be operational, but it is not known where these fit into the Regiment structure.

Principal training centre is Kosice-Barca, with other training undertaken at Prerov (1st Training Regiment, MiG-21Us), Piestany (3rd Training Regiment, L-39s, Mi-1s and '2s, L-410s), Pardubice,

■ Below: **One of several Il-28R *Beagles* held in store at Kbely.**

■ Above: **L-29 Delfin, also in retirement at Kbely. (**Both Martin E Siegrist**)**

Plzen and Bratislava-Ivanka. At Kosice, the 2nd Training Regiment uses the L-29 Delfin and L-39 Albatros and recently took delivery of an L39MS for evaluation purposes.

Two Helicopter Regiments (11th at Plzen-Bory, the 51st at Prostejov) operate the classic battlefield mix of Mi-24 *Hinds* and Mi-17 *Hip-Hs*. Another Regiment, at Havlickuv Brod, flies Mi-2 *Hoplites* and Mi-8 *Hips*, presumably in the support role.

In its short period between formation as a nation-state and the Nazi invasion, Czechoslovakia made more rapid progress towards industrialisation and self-sufficiency than any other country in Europe. Aircraft production was part of this self-sufficiency and Aero was founded in January 1919 followed by Letov, Avia, CKD-Praga and smaller companies

such as Mraz-Benes and Zlin.

During the occupation, German types were built and after 1945 several designs remained in production. From 1948 when the country became a communist republic, Soviet types such as the Yak-11 and Il-14 were built, leading to the MiG-15 and eventually the MiG-21F.

In 1968 Czechoslovakia became a socialist state and the aircraft industry was accordingly reorganised. The 12 largest factories, Letov, Aero, Avia etc were united into Trust Aero CS with the main office in Praha-Letany.

Following the events of the 'Prague

Spring' in 1968, Czechoslovakia's place within WarPac faded, and Poland became top of the list for modern equipment from the Soviet Union.

Still the largest of the WarPac air arms, it is significant that no fighter has gone into license production since the MiG-21. Today, the only jet built in the country is the L-39 Albatros trainer.

With additional thanks to M van der Wal for his researches on Eastern bloc air arms, particularly Czechoslovakia, Poland and the USSR.

■ Top: **Airshow antics from a pair of L-410M Turbolets.** (Piotr Butowski)

■ Above: **Yak-40, operated by the 3 Regiment for VIP duties.** (David Oliver)

■ Below: **Heavy airlift is provided by the An-12s of the 1st Mixed Transport Regiment based at Mosnov.** (Author)

■ Polish Mi-14PS *Haze*-C search and rescue variant tries its hand at being a motorboat! (Author)

Water-dipping sub-hunter

Piotr Butowski describes the capable Mil Mi-14 *Haze* an adaptable amphibious helicopter

TO BE ABLE to alight on water on the open sea, a lake or a river is a very useful aspect of amphibious helicopters. Also stationary spot-hovering above the water surface is impossible for any other type of aircraft.

After overcoming numerous technical problems, the first amphibious helicopters have been built in the Soviet Union. At the beginning of the 1950s some of the designs of Mikhail Mil and Nikolai Kamov were equipped with floats for alighting on water. These helicopters were not applied for the essential task of sea helicopters – the anti-submarine warfare (ASW). For many years the only Soviet ASW helicopters were ship-based Ka-25 *Hormones* and shore based Mi-4M *Hound-Bs*.

First Soviet ASW amphibious helicopter was the V-14 (prototype Mi-14) designed by Mil, appearing not earlier than 1973. It was similar to the multipurpose Mi-8 *Hip* with a watertight, boat-shaped bottom. This helicopter can operate from land and from water. It can also land, for instance, on a deep snowdrift.

It is worth noting several elements of the V-14 in respect to the later designs.

First of all the Isotov TV2-117, 1,700shp engines were adopted directly from Mi-8 *Hip* (this can be noticed by the lack of a small outlet near the exhaust pipe, which is visible in the TV3-117 engines). Also like the Mi-8, the tail rotor is located to starboard of the tail boom. In the first V-14 the front undercarriage members were retracted into chambers which carefully closed with covers. Later some weight was spared by retracting the front wheels into open niches in the fuselage. (A similar modification was introduced for the Mi-24 *Hind*, where the aeroplane-type landing gear of the first versions was later simplified).

In 1977 the first series production Mi-14 helicopters, code-named *Haze* by NATO, entered service in Soviet Navy aviation. Their performance, equipment and weapon load were much superior to the piston-engined Mi-4Ms of the 1950s. Series production Mi-14s are propelled by TV3-117M turbo-shafts of a maximum rating equal to 2,225hp. (Due to service conditions the power is limited to 1,950hp, full power being used only when flying with one engine). The more powerful TV3-117 is much less heavier and smaller than the TV2-117.

Main rotor of Mi-14 has five articulated blades. The three-bladed tail rotor is of classic design. It has been found during the service, that the tail rotor is not effective enough when turning right and thus the helicopter's manoeuvrability is impaired. Production Mi-14s have the tail rotor rotating in the opposite manner to the V-14. (Formerly the tail rotor blades moved downwards ie according to the main rotor airflow direction – 'push'. With the tail rotor blades moving against the flow – 'pull' – their velocity is added to the flow velocity.)

This has been achieved in the simplest way possible – by moving the tail rotor from the starboard to port side of the tail fin.

The fuselage of the semi-monocoque structure is subdivided into three compartments: cockpit with four crew members; mid section with cargo hold, fuel tanks and weapons bay and the tail boom. Fuel is stored in six tanks of total capacity equal to 3,795 litres, an additional 500 litre tank can be installed inside the cargo hold.

Nose gear retracts into the fuselage, main gear into the side sponsons. The tail rotor is protected against hitting the ground by a tail support with its own float. Two inflatable floats are installed at the sides of the fuselage to keep *Haze* stable when alighting on water. The Mi-14 can float in a sea state up to 2° with side wind up to 10m/s.

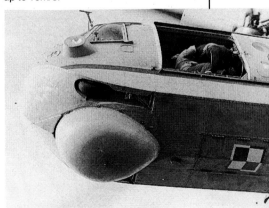

■ Underside view of the Mi-14PS, showing radome and the landing gear stowage. (Author)

Mi-14 HAZE

Haze is well equipped for all-weather conditions. This includes R-842M and R-860 radio stations, ARK-9 and ARK-U2 radio compasses, RV-3 radio altimeter and navigation system with DISS-15 Doppler speed meter and drift indicator. A panoramic 1-2M search radar can detect objects on the sea surface, whereas a Khrom-Nickel system is used for the friend-or-foe identification. An autopilot enables it to perform the flights along a preset course and to spot-hover without the aid of the pilot.

Crew includes four men: two pilots, a navigator and an engineer. They have special waterproof flying suits guaranteeing 24 hour survival in cold water. Internal communication is ensured by SPU-7 intercom system.

Most important application of the Mi-14 is submarine detection and warfare. A helicopter is much better suited for this purpose than an ASW aeroplane. A helicopter, when spot-hovering, can submerge the hydrolocation probe or even float on the surface with engines off, and trace a submarine for a long time. On the other hand, when compared with ASW ships, the helicopter can reach the zone of action much faster than the ship.

There are two variants of the Mi-14PL *Haze-A* (PL for *protivo-lodochnyy*, antisubmarine). The search variant has a hydro-acoustic buoy which, dropped on the water surface, emits signals received by the helicopter detecting system. The onboard computer issues the optimum parameters of attack and sends them to the SAU-14 automatic control system.

Another submarine detecting device on board the Mi-14PL is the Oka-2 hydroacoustic unit. It is lowered into the water via the bottom hatch from the helicopter spot-hovering about 25m above the sea surface. The Oka-2 hydro-acoustic unit can be operated in passive or active mode. Active detection can be carried out by one helicopter, whereas for the passive mode two simultaneously operating helicopters are necessary.

Installed in the rear fuselage is a APM-60 magnetometer or detecting 'bird'. Towed by cable, the APM-60 is used for

■ **V-14 prototype of the Mi-14. Note the covers to the undercarriage, TV2-117 engines and tail rotor on the starboard side.** (via Author)

detecting submarines by means of magnetic field deflections. The hatch with illuminating and signal floats is located near the APM-60 head.

The detected enemy submarine can be attacked by the attack variant of the Mi-14PL. This variant has two electrically powered ASW torpedoes, conventional or nuclear depth charges.

A new variant of the ASW helicopter, the MI-14PLM was presented at the aircraft exposition in Moscow in 1989. This helicopter has more modern equipment and armament. Distinguishing feature externally is the magnetometer 'bird' located lower than in the Mi-14PL.

Another application of the Mi-14 helicopter is the trawling of sea mines. The helicopter can take off from the trawler ship and tow a special raft operating on contact, acoustic or electromagnetic triggering. Due to *Haze's* long flight endurance (up to six hours with the additional tank) and the ability to have the trawl taken over by another helicopter, the trawling can be carried out continually.

Like a ship, this variant can also tow small assault craft or boats. The tow-trawling variant is designated the Mi-14BT *Haze-B* (BT for *buksir-tralshchik*, tug-trawler). The Mi-14BT differs externally from the Mi-14PL by the lack of magnetometer and by the presence of a large 'windmill' in the starboard sponson to drive the winch. Three big trawling cable guide slots are fitted and bulged lookout windows in the rear part of the fuselage.

Third variant of Mi-14 is the search and rescue Mi-14PS *Haze-C* (PS for *poisko-vo-spasatelnyy*, search-rescue). This helicopter has no ASW equipment nor armament, instead it carries ten life-rafts for twenty persons each, which can be dropped for survivors and then towed in a liferaft train. Mi-14PS also has floating containers with clothes, food and medication etc. Via the hatch in the cabin floor, 3,000kg of cargo can be lifted into the cabin.

When compared with the Mi-14PL the Mi-14PS has no magnetometer and has the 'windmill' on the starboard. Two big searchlights are installed on both sides in the front part of the fuselage. The cargo cabin door of the port side is enlarged. The navigator of the crew has been replaced by a winchman.

About 120 Mi-14 *Haze* helicopters are now used by Soviet Naval aviation. The naval forces of Bulgaria, Cuba, East Germany, North Korea, Libya, Poland, Syria, Yugoslavia and Vietnam each have a dozen or so Mi-14s. Poland and East Germany have several Mi-14PSs and four Mi-14BTs have been in East German service from the mid 1980s.

Haze-Bs were used at the beginning of the 1980s for trawling the sealanes of the Red Sea. Most spectacular rescue mission performed to date by Mi-14PSs was in the Baltic near the Latvian town of Yurmala in January 1987. Due to the sudden increase of air temperature a great icefield drifted offshore with some 1,500 people who were walking and fishing on the ice. Quick and efficient action by helicopters mainly Mi-14s and ships, had all those unlucky people rescued with no casualties.

Some Soviet Mi-14s are also used by civil aviation authorities for transport purposes in regions where conventional access is not easy.

■ **Two *Hazes* from the East German *Volksmarine* 'Kurt Barthel' Wing, based at Parow. Above: Mi-14BT in the water.** *(Volksmarine)* Right: **Close-up on a Mi-14PL *Haze-A*.** (Duncan Cubitt)

■ Top left: **Another view of a 'Kurt Barthel' Mi-14PL, showing well the stowed position of the towed 'bird'.** (Duncan Cubitt)
■ Bottom left: **'Kurt Barthel's' trawler 'BTs have been converted to SAR format, including the installation of observation ports in the rear fuselage.** (Duncan Cubitt)
■ Top: **Latest verson of the sub-hunter, Soviet Mi-14PLM at the Moscow aircraft exposition, 1989.** (Author)
■ Above: **Polish Mi-14PS search and rescue variant.** (Author)

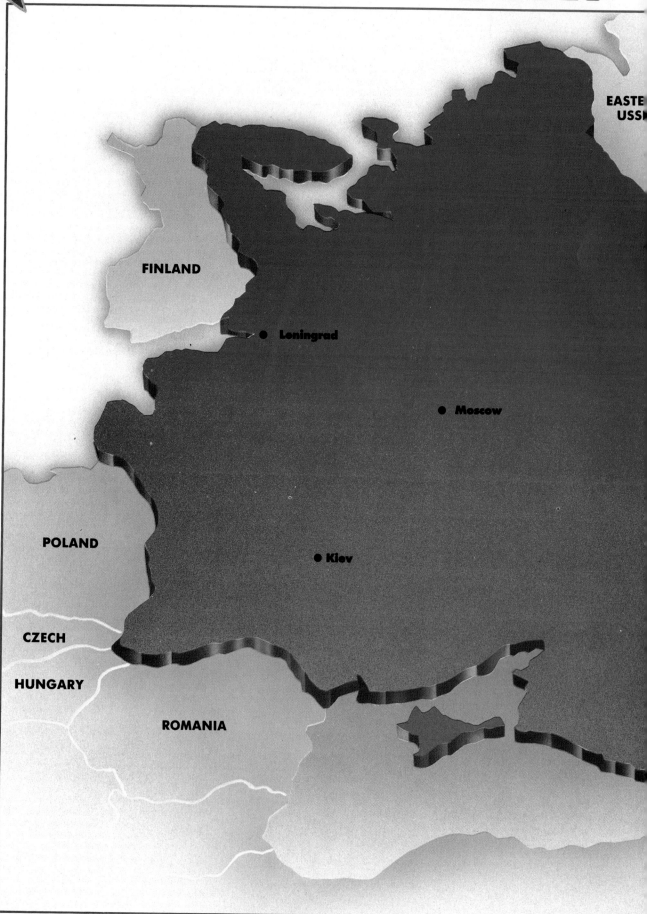

EASTE
USSK

FINLAND

● Loningrad

● Moscow

POLAND

● Kiev

CZECH

HUNGARY

ROMANIA

MIKHAIL SERGEVICH GORBACHEV became General Secretary of the Communist Party of the Soviet Union on March 11, 1985 (and Chairman of the Supreme Soviet on May 25, 1989). In a very short time he was to instigate a brave series of policies that have had a global effect and, if allowed to blossom, will change the face of Eastern Europe more radically than any war.

As Hitler's Germany fell to the Allies, Stalin's forces were to over-run much of Eastern Europe and to a very large extent have remained in place to this day. It was not until Gorbachev's announcement of unilateral withdrawals from Czechoslovakia, East Germany and Hungary that this situation was to see major redress. As a counter to the North Atlantic Treaty Organisation at Warsaw on May 14, 1955 the Treaty of Friendship, Mutual Assistance and Co-operation was signed between Albania, Bulgaria, Czechoslovakia, East Germany, Hungary, Poland, Romania and the USSR — this was the Warsaw Pact. Two years later Soviet Forces within Hungary put down the revisionist uprising there, underlining the requirement to toe the Party line within the Treaty. Erecting the Wall around the Western-occupied sectors of Berlin in August 1961 was another manifestation of the heightening of the so-called 'Cold War' which saw its zenith with the Cuban Missile Crisis of October 1962. The 1970s heralded the age of 'Detente' when weapons limitations talks and summits became more frequent, heralded by the Strategic Arms Limitation Talks which commenced in May 1972. The Soviet invasion of Afghanistan in December 1979 brought a shadow over the end of an otherwise hopeful decade.

Gorbachev's new realism, the need to rebuild the economy, and attitudes of the people of the Soviet Union have dominated the end of the 1980s and look set to do so well into the 1990s if the pace of change can be maintained along with stability within the Soviet Union. The removal of what was previously the German Democratic Republic from the Warsaw Pact coincident with its fusion into the German Federal Republic and the application of several other WarPac nations to leave the Alliance has proved that the defensive "wall of steel" forseen by Stalin (who died before WarPac became a reality) was not necessarily a device to last for ever

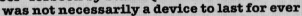

■ Top: Over water shot of the large Su-15 *Flagon*. This is an *'H* variant armed with AA-3 and AA-8 missiles. (RSwAF)
■ Above: Examples of the huge An-124 *Ruslan* transport are now wearing more overt military markings. (Peter J Cooper)
■ Left *Mainstay,* the 'AWACS' version of the Il-76 freighter is rapidly improving IA-PVO's intercept potential. (333 Skv RNorAF)

ITS SHEER vastness means that a true overview of any element of the Soviet Union is difficult to take in. An examination of the USSR's air arms directly affecting Eastern Europe is only possible through a view of the *entire* organisation of military aviation in this massive union of provinces.

It needs also to be stated that the depth with which *East European Air Power* can deal with domestic Soviet military aviation is therefore limited. Soviet air power is a subject in its own right and would take several volumes such as this to adequately outline.

Functional organisation

Soviet military aviation units are based on the hierarchy of the Air Division, Air Regiment and Squadron (respectively *Aviadiviziya*, *Aviapolk* and *Eskadrilya*). This organisation is common to all large air units of the major arms such as the Strategic Air Force, Frontal Air Force etc although it is possible to have Independent Regiments or even Squadrons for specialised roles, eg reconnaissance.

Standard formation is three squadrons per regiment and three regiments per division. For bomber and transport units a squadron can be as small as six to nine aircraft, giving an 18 to 27 aircraft regiment and 54 to 80 plus aircraft per division.

Fighter and fighter-bomber units are normally organised on 13 aircraft squadron sizes to give a 40 plus aircraft sized regiment (including trainers) and 120+ aircraft per division. There are indications that these sizes are being reduced to around ten aircraft per squadron with commensurate reductions for regimental and divisional totals.

The Russian term used to describe the air power of the Soviet Union – *Voenno Vozdushnye Sily* (VVS – Military Air Forces) acts as a convenient reminder of the plural nature of this large organisation. Pronounced *voenno vozdoosh-neeyeh seelee*, VVS comprises two major air arms which are air forces in their own right – the so-called Stategic Aviation (SA – *Strategicheskaya Aviatsiya*) and Frontal Aviation (FA – *Frontovaya Aviatsiya*). Both of these formations have, in varying measures integrated transport, reconnaissance, electronic countermeasures (ECM) and other assets which define their status as an air force.

Falling within the ambit of the VVS, but having separate identity, is Military Transport Aviation (VTA – *Voenno Transportnaya Aviatsiya*) and Army Aviation (AA – *Armejskaya Aviatsiya*) which provide, respectively, the bulk of military air transport needs for the Soviet military and *all* of the Soviet Army's aviation requirements on the battlefield.

Totally separate from all of the above, administratively and organisationally, but looking nevertheless very much like an air force is the interceptor fighter compo-

nent of the Home Air Defence Organisation (IA-PVO *Istrebitel 'Naya Aviatsiya Protivo-Vozdushnoj* or Fighter Aviation of the Air Defence of the Motherland). IA-PVO is charged solely with the responsibility of protecting the national territorial airspace of the USSR, in conjunction with a vast network of early warning radars and surface-to-air (SAM) systems.

Finally, as with most nations possessing the conventional triad of armed forces, the Soviet Union has a large Naval Air Force (*Aviatsiya Voenno – Morskogo Flota* – pronounced *aveeatseeya voenno – morskovo flotta*). Each of these elements will be dealt with in greater depth.

Before proceeding further, it is necessary to define another Russian term commonly encountered in any discussion of the component parts of the VVS as a whole – *Aviatsiya*. To a Russian this means much more than simply 'aviation' in its generally accepted sense. The most useful working definition of this word is

> **An overview of the massive airborne might of the Soviet Union is no easy task. Josef Djugashvilli examines its complex structure, and the changes taking place within.**

'Air Force' and the practicality of this approach will be seen if 'Air Force' is substituted for 'Aviation' in all the previously mentioned titles. Quite simply the word 'aviatsiya' conveys to a Russian the total sense of air power when used in a military context.

These points have been laboured because it is important to remember that Soviet air power resides within groupings which are 'air forces' in their own right even though all VVS personnel wear a common 'Air Force' uniform. Additionally, within the context of the demise of the Warsaw Pact, significant changes have taken place in the Frontal Air Force and Strategic Air Force so it is important to know what we mean when we talk of changes in the Soviet Air Force. Clearly we cannot understand the 'Soviet Air Force' in terms of its being a single entity like, for example, the Royal Air Force, but it is possibly easier to relate some of its component formations to its USAF counterpart: eg Strategic Air Force and Strategic Air Command, Military Transport Service and Military Airlift Command etc.

Strategic Air Force

Most recently established element of the VVS, the Strategic Air Force (SA) combines the old Long Range Air Force with the newer concept of separate Air Armies for the long and medium range bomber forces of *Bears* and *Blackjacks*, and *Badgers*, *Blinders* and *Backfires*. The gestation period for this Force was somewhat protracted throughout the period from the mid 1970s up to the early 1980s, probably reflecting high-level agonising

■ **Mottle-camouflage Su-25 *Frogfoot* showing its weapons-carrying ability.** (Piotr Butowski)

about the best possible structure for these important offensive assets.

Apart from rationalisation of the Command, Control and Communication (C3) aspects for the integration of the heavy and medium bombers in the new organisation, another significant feature of the SA was the introduction of the Su-24 *Fencer* into the two Air Army elements opposing NATO formations in Western and Southern Europe. More recently it is believed that Su-27 *Flankers* have been introduced into the SA Air Armies with headquarters at Legnica and Vinnitsa to provide escort capability compatible with the range performance of the *Fencers*.

It is never possible to be specific about total numbers of Soviet military aircraft, but it is likely that SA operates 80+ *Bear-Hs* equipped with the AS-15 *Kent*, centrally controlled from Moscow, with a smaller but increasing number of Tu-160

Blackjacks armed with both AS-15 and AS-16 *Kickback* air-to-surface (ASM) missiles (perhaps 20-25 aircraft so far). A smaller number of earlier *Bear* variants are probably also used for training but are unlikely to be combat ready.

The medium bomber trio of *Badger*, *Blinder* and *Backfire* are operated by the Air Army headquartered on Smolensk, this being exclusively a medium bomber force. Total numbers are probably of the order of 200 *Badgers*, 90 *Blinders* and 250 *Backfires*. Majority of the *Badgers* are the 'G variant armed with the AS-5 *Kelt* ASM, most of the *Blinders* are AS-4 equipped 'B variants and the *Backfires* are 'B and 'C models armed with AS-4 *Kitchen* and the newer AS-16 *Kickback* missiles.

With headquarters at Legnica in Poland and Vinnitsa in the Ukraine, the two European-based Air Armies have the Su-

24 *Fencer* as their principal offensive aircraft with approximately 200 and 250 aircraft respectively, significant numbers being of the air-to air refuelling (AAR) capable 'D variant. Fighter support for the *Fencer* force is believed to be polarising on the Su-27 *Flanker* which, if true, will provide aircraft with range performance matching that of the escorted frontal bombers. Smaller numbers of MiG-21 *Fishbeds* and MiG-23 *Floggers* are still probably also in service with the units which were absorbed into SA from the Frontal Air Force system when the former was first created.

Sukhoi Su-15 *Flagons* passed from the Home Air Defence organisation to the Frontal Air Force and then back to the Home Air Defence Force during the late 1970s and early 1980s reshuffle. These can no longer be regarded as front-line fighters and probably do not equip any of the SA fighter units.

Final Air Army organisation within SA, with its headquarters at Irkutskin Siberia, is a mixed force of 40 plus *Bear-Gs* (essentially 'Bs and 'Cs converted to carry the AS-4 *Kitchen* as an interim weapon-system pending arrival of the full force of Tu-160 *Blackjack* and a small number – probably 60 each – of *Badgers* and *Backfires*). This force composition reflects a reduced Soviet perception of military threat in the region when one compares it with the other SA components based further West, about 160 aircraft, compared with approximately 550 in the Moscow and Smolensk Air Army areas and a further 450 plus *Fencers* in the Legnica and Vinnitsa units.

Apart from its specific reconnaissance and ECM variants based principally on the *Badger* (ie 'F, 'H, 'J, 'K and 'L variants) and small numbers of *Blinder-C2* reconnaissance and *Blinder-E* ECM aircraft, SA is also the only user to date of the Il-78T *Midas* tanker development of the Il-76 *Candid*. These aircraft, about 30 delivered so far, are used to refuel most of

■ Left: **Early view of the Tu-160 *Blackjack*.** (DoD)

SA's types but particularly the *Bear-H*, *Blackjacks* and *Fencers*, considerably enhancing the combat application of this already very flexible pool of aircraft when they are at full strength.

A small number of *Badger* wing-tip-to-wing-tip tankers are also still in use to refuel other *Badgers* of the medium bomber force and a further smaller number of probe and drogue compatible *Badger* tankers (approx 10-15) are used to refuel *Blinders* and *Backfires*. These *Badger* tankers will probably be replaced by the Il-78T within the next few years to provide a truly comprehensive force-multiplying factor within SA.

Frontal Air Force

A peculiarly Russian concept, gives rise to the term Frontal Air Force (FA). It is based on the notion of the military Front as the focus of all combat activity in a given geographical area. It is, essentially, a Tactical Air Force structure embodying all those types of aircraft which will enable it to carry out the given task with the best possible balance of suitability to the role.

Frontal Air Forces are assigned for the air protection of the various Military Districts (MDs) of the Soviet Union – currently reducing in number from 16 down to probably 10 and are at the disposal of the Army Commander of the MD to be employed as he sees necessary in prevailing circumstances. FA also provides air power to the Groups of Forces in the Warsaw Pact countries.

Individual FA composition varies from less than perfectly balanced aircraft groupings in the Central Asian regions to the almost perfectly balanced force structures of the Far East Frontal Air Force and the Air Force of the Western Group of Forces (AFWGF) in Eastern Germany. Recent events however, compel one to add a rider to the latter statement, particularly with reference to FA in Eastern Germany.

Until the middle of last year the AFWGF could have been regarded as possibly the model example of a perfectly structured Soviet tactical air force, deploying two regiments of long range interdictor *Fencer* (80 aircraft) alongside shorter range but highly capable *Flogger-Ds* and *'Js* (three Regiments – 120 aircraft) and *Fitter-Hs* and *'Ks* (two Regiments – 80 aircraft). Providing integral Air Defence for this offensive force was a mixed batch of *Fulcrums* (two Regiments – 80 plus aircraft) and *Flogger-B, 'G* and *'K* variants (seven Regiments – 280 aircraft). Included in the latter group was a squadron of MiG-25 *Foxbat-Es* probably held to counter the SR-71 threat.

In addition to this offensive and defensive front-line the balance was provided by co-ordinated reconnaissance and transport elements and, reflecting the massive aviation requirements of the five Armies of the Group of Soviet Forces in Germany (now known as the Western

Group of Forces), a large mixed helicopter force. The reconnaissance function was provided by a regiment of Su-17M3R *Fitter-H* dedicated tactical reconnaissance fighter bombers (retaining offensive capability) consisting of about 40 aircraft. More specialised tactical reconnaissance and ECM was performed by a small number of *Foxbat-Bs* and *'Ds* providing photo and radar reconnaissance facilities respectively up to about 65,000 feet and Mach 2 plus. Providing more covert reconnaissance information was one or

■ Fine detail view of the nose of a 'demonstrator' *Frogfoot* that appeared at Paris, 1989. (Duncan Cubitt)

■ Antonov's mighty An-124 *Condor* with both nose and rear doors open. A growing number are moving to military markings in place of the civil 'cover' scheme. (Peter J Cooper)

■ Large numbers of Mil Mi-6 *Hooks* serve in the general purpose assault and transport role. (Hanspeter Abt)

■ Part of the latest production batch of Aero L.39Cs for the Soviet Union, awaiting delivery at Vodochody, September 1990. (David Oliver)

■ **MiG-25** *Foxbat* – 300 plus serve IA-PVO. (Paul Beaver)

two Il-20DSR *Coot-A* electronic surveill-ance aircraft and the possibility exists that the Soviet Army has also operated a number of reconnaissance drones but confirmation of this is still awaited.

It is the provision of integrated trans-port facilities where FA in Eastern Ger-many differs largely from most of the other Air Army formations of this VVS sub-arm. AFWGF has at least one squad-ron of about a dozen An-12 *Cubs* and lesser numbers of An-26 *Curls* for the transport support of short term deploy-ments of its combat aircraft within the European theatre. It also has small num-bers of specialised transport aircraft for such tasks as airborne command post (probably based on the An-26 *Curl* from photography examined to date) and VIP carriage within the Warsaw Pact area. Flagship of this particular fleet is probably a specially equipped Tu-134 *Crusty* and a number of Mi-8S VIP variants of the *Hip* are used to transport military VIPs to exercise locations or to base inspections.

AFWGF's very large helicopter force is almost entirely dedicated to the combat assault and fire support needs of the five Soviet Army formations on the former East German territory. It comprises five combat assault regiments of Mi-8 and '17 *Hips* and Mi-24 *Hinds* plus one general purpose transport helicopter unit of Mi-2 *Hoplites*, Mi-8 and '17 *Hips* and Mi-6 *Hooks*. The 15 or so fire support helicop-ter units consist of balanced groups of Mi-2 *Hoplites*, Mi-8 and '17 *Hips* and Mi-24 *Hinds* which provide flexible air support at Divisional level consistent with the ruling Soviet military philosophy of speed of advance and attack. Thus, com-paratively small military formations could prosecute *blitzkrieg* types of attack tak-ing with them their own small, albeit, powerful air-cover force.

While not specifically identified as an integrated component of this force the two regiments of Su-25 *Frogfoots* in the AFWGF are widely assumed to be the responsibility of the Army Air Force (AA). The 80 strong fleet could well be used in *ad hoc* smaller formations according to need, adding punch to the already heavily

■ Left: **MiG-29UB** *Fulcrum* at the 1990 Farnborough display. (Duncan Cubitt)

armed helicopters.

Of the latter part of the above, the majority of these positions remain true today, but following President Gor-bachev's peace initiative in mid-1989 significant changes were made in the front-line composition of what is now the Air Force of the Western Group of Forces. As a result of this bold and unilateral step, the two *Fencer* regiments in Eastern Germany were withdrawn to the Soviet Union in a well publicised ceremony.

As part of this major restructuring exer-cise, probably as many as six of the dual role *Flogger-B, 'G* and *'K* regiments were fairly rapidly swapped for smaller-sized formations of the allegedly single-role MiG-29 *Fulcrum*. The long range offen-sive capability of the Su-24 *Fencer* was substituted by the less capable MiG-27 *Flogger-J* to complete the reshuffle.

Overall objective of this radical 'trans-plant surgery' was to enable the Soviet Union to present a much more defensive-ly-oriented air force organisation in the East Germany which was then inexorably moving towards unification. Thus the AFWGF was converted virtually overnight from a force with at least the theoretical potential for adventurous long-range in-terdiction into Western Europe, spearheaded by *Fencers*, into a visibly less pugilistic package with considerably limited range performance and fire-pow-er. This new force must have facilitated Soviet negotiation of its military position in a Germany which clearly would not wish to embarrass its existing partners by hosting the hitherto more offensive Soviet air force on its territory.

Military Transport Air Force

Military Transport Air Force (VTA) ex-ists to provide the bulk of military air transport support to the Soviet military within the USSR and beyond its State borders. It operates some 100 plus An-12 *Cubs*, around 400 Il-76 *Candids*, 50 plus An-22 *Cocks*, probably around 20 An-124 *Condors* and possibly the small and diminishing number of An-8 *Camp* twin-turboprop transports still noted in service

as recently as December 1989.

The often-quoted reserve pool of all of *Aeroflot's* transport fleet is not always able to satisfy additional demands made upon its resources, and those of VTA, at times of natural disasters, for example, and what looks like on first examination a huge fleet is in fact often sorely stretched to do this job. (This seems to be charac-teristic of all air transport operations!)

A noteworthy feature of VTA is that a very high proportion of its aircraft are actually painted in *Aeroflot* colours with normal civilian-style registration mark-ings. In the case of the *Candid* these colours almost exactly duplicate those of *Aeroflot* whereas the majority of *Cubs* have quite rudimentary *Aeroflot* markings and an overall drab grey paintwork, as do the previously mentioned An-8 *Camps*. Almost all military An-22 *Cocks* are finished in *Aeroflot* colours but it is possi-ble that some, if not all, of the newer An-124 *Condors* carry full Soviet military markings with huge side numbers ('08', '09', '10' seen to date, so possibly half of the delivered total might be in military finish, the others in 'civilian' marks).

There have been no official explana-tions for this extensive 'civilianisation' of their military fleet, but it might simply be a reflection of their own coyness about Soviet military might as presented to the outside world. In 'Old Communist' eyes there was probably some moral kudos to be gained by despatching 'civilian' air-craft to world disaster spots (whenever possible), or for the delivery of arms, whereas most other nations would have to use overtly military aircraft and so concede the moral high ground to a "politically pure and beneficent" Soviet Union. If this is the rationale behind their 'civilian' VTA then it reveals an almost squirming discomfort with their own milit-ary power even when manifested by mundane transport aircraft.

The emergence of VTA *Candids* and other types proudly wearing a proper military 'uniform' would convince us of the 'New Communist' recognition that there is no shame in possessing military strength appropriate to one's status in the World political order. It would also grant more appropriate status to the military personnel who fly and maintain these important aircraft!

It would be more fitting to see the words *Voenno-Transportnaya Aviatsiya* plus the Red Star, in place of *Aeroflot* and a civilian registration on *all* VTA aircraft. Such a measure would help to correct the bizarre spectacle of some IL-78T *Midas* strategic tankers ostensibly being the property of the State Airline! (In the case of the latter aircraft they are probably not the responsibility of VTA, but most likely that of the SA.)

'New Communism' is probably not quite ready to emblazon such emotive titles on its aircraft, but in the present climate of Soviet *glasnost* and joint wil-lingness to be subjected to mutual inspections of military hardware, the external appearance of any weapon system must surely be an important consideration. What easier way could there possibly be to define an aircraft's military status than by the way it is painted?

Army Air Force

Reuse of the wartime title of *Armejskaya Aviatsiya* (AA) in the early 1980s has firmly established the importance of air power to the Soviet Army as it enters a new era of its existence within a radically changing Soviet Union. The precise timing of the reintroduction of this term is unknown, but seems to have surfaced some time post-Afghanistan invasion and probably acknowledged the need for radical reappraisal of the application of air power for the Army in the very demanding circumstances of that conflict.

Probably the best model to use to describe the present day Army Air Force is that attached to the AFWGF in Eastern Germany. There, Army aviation units are organised on a two-tier basis of five combat assault regiments with 40 *Hinds* and 20 *Hips* each, plus a separate logistic regiment of *Hoplites, Hips* and *Hooks*. The second tier consists of around 15 fire support squadrons of Mi-2 *Hoplites*, Mi-8 or '17 *Hips* and Mi-24 *Hinds* consisting of about six helicopters of each type to provide mixed logistics and attack capability.

Essential feature of AA employment is that it can be controlled directly down to at least the Divisional level with a very local, short chain of command. By contrast *all* other Frontal Air Force assets, which are also under the operational control of the local Army commander, operate through a longer and more complex chain of command because of, among other considerations, airspace allocation and control requirements. Flying well below 100 metres the helicopter force will not conflict with ground attack fighters assigned to higher levels. In Eastern Germany the five combat assault regiments are probably used in direct support of each of the five Army formations on Eastern German territory while the logistic regiment and the fire support squadrons are probably assigned to particular Divisions of those armies.

Although the combat employment of these helicopters is probably easy enough to understand the same cannot be said for the more specialised variants of both the *Hip* and the *Hinds*.

It is not known for example if the specialised *Hip-J* and '*K* ECM helicopters are also controlled at the local Divisional level or whether they are more centrally controlled. Equally, the even less familiar *Hind-G* variants are a mystery both in terms of what they do and who actually controls them.

Further question marks are also raised by the impending service introduction of the Mil *Havoc* and the Kamov *Hokum*

'new generation' helicopters. It is by no means certain that *Hinds* will be replaced by *Havocs* on a one-for-one basis, or replaced at all. If they are replaced then it will probably be the fire-support squadron machines which will go first, leaving the combat assault regiments with a supplementary armed troop transport capability for that particular role. If *Hokum* turns out to be the interceptor helicopter it is widely thought to be, then a niche will have to be made for it in AA organisation.

Thus the rejuvenated AA is once again set to undergo a further radical change in the mid-1990s at a time when the armed helicopter is assessed by many military analysts to be ready to oust the tank as the major battlefield weapon. For a country like the Soviet Union which has an impressive history of tank manufacture *and* the distinction of operating the nearest thing to a 'flying tank', in the shape of the existing Mi-24, it is entirely possible that we shall see even more radical designs on this theme emerging towards the end of this decade. Clearly, AA is going to feature largely in the future military development of Soviet air power in particular, and air power in general.

Finally, it is probably appropriate to refer briefly once again to the assumed use of the Su-25 *Frogfoot* by AA. The relationship of *Frogfoot* with the Soviet Army is possibly based more on previous USAF joint helicopter/A-10 operations than on solid evidence of Soviet operations. In a table of systematic tasking responsibilities for individual components of FA in the January 1990 issue of the Soviet 'Air Force' magazine *Aviatsiya i Kosmonautika* the Su-25 was listed under the separate heading of *Shturmovaya Aviatsiya*. This is an almost untrans-

latable description based on the unique characteristics of the Su-25 being the modern day equivalent of the old Il-2 *Shturmovik*. The task described was actually the "suppression of movement and deployment of reserve forces" whilst that for the Army Air Force was "direct fire support of the ground forces". For this reason we do not believe the Su-25 to be an AA asset.

Fighter Air Force

Fighter Air Force of the Air Defence of the Motherland (IA-PVO) is the interceptor component of the very large home defence organisation which also comprises early warning radars and the SAM systems along the periphery of the USSR. It is an entirely separate organisation from any other 'air force' formation in the Soviet Union, and it has its own flying training schools dedicated solely to producing interceptor pilots.

IA-PVO is charged with one major responsibility, that of the protection of the territorial airspace of the USSR. Given that the size of the Soviet landmass and its contiguous airspace is vast, the total number of interceptors assigned to this task is a good deal less than might be imagined. Absolute numbers are once again difficult to establish precisely but the force probably comprises around 800 MiG-23 *Floggers*, 300 plus MiG-25 *Foxbat-As* or '*Es*, 300 MiG-31 *Foxhounds*, 200 plus (and increasing) Su-27 *Flankers*, plus reducing numbers of Su-15 *Flagon-Fs*, and Yak-28P *Firebars*, with probably no operational Tu-128P *Fiddlers* left in service.

It is unlikely that IA-PVO has many more than 1,900 aircraft of all the above types in operational service to cover the

■ **Trial landings by a MiG-29 on the flightdeck of the *Tbilisi* in the Black Sea. *Helix-A* in foreground.** (TASS)

huge peripheral region and the major inland city complexes. While on paper Soviet air power looks impressive, set in the overall context of IA-PVO responsibilities it seems to be only just enough.

Because of the vastness of the Northern periphery of the USSR, and the demands it places upon the air defence task, the Soviet aircraft industry has twice had to arrive at quite unique solutions to the problem of producing a suitable interceptor for this role. First was the enormous Tu-128P *Fiddler* armed with the commensurately huge AA-5 *Ash* air-to-air missile. This airframe/missile combination was the best that Soviet industry could achieve in the late 1950s to satisfy

mics.

Chronological status of the design of the MiG-31 is interesting also in that it follows the aerodynamically more refined MiG-29 – a quantum leap in Soviet fighter technology – so the need to recycle an older design alongside its advanced stablemate is a clear indication of the desperation at the time to field a working design to replace the *Fiddler* as quickly as possible. This is not a criticism of the MiG solution – merely acknowledgement of the nature of the problem and the economically elegant Soviet resolution of it. These two large peripheral air defenders were never expected to engage in close combat dog-fights and both of

Soviet defences against Northern intruders.

Naval Air Force

A fairly large formation of primarily land-based aircraft and helicopters, the Soviet Naval Air Force (AM-AF) deserves deeper treatment than can be given here, particularly in view of the continuing development of their emerging carrier-borne force. It is probably sufficient to say here that like FA, Soviet naval aviation is organised as a well integrated and balanced force of bombers, fighters, fighter-bombers, anti-submarine warfare (ASW), reconnaissance, transport and helicopters. These are distributed among four fleet air forces – the Northern, Baltic, Black Sea and Pacific.

Currently the only operational fixed-wing aircraft deployed at sea with the Soviet Navy is the Yak-38MP *Forger* along with ASW-capable Ka-25 *Hormone-A* and *'B* and Ka-27 *Helix-A* helicopters. The remainder of the large AM-AF force comprises some 200 Tu-22M *Backfires*, 150 *Badgers* (in *'C, 'G* and *G-mod* variants) and reducing numbers of Tu-22 *Blinders* for the maritime strike role. Around 100 carrier capable Yak-38 *Forgers* and 100 plus Su-17 *Fitter-Cs*, *'Hs* and *'Ks* plus increasing numbers of Su-24 *Fencer* light bombers are employed for regional maritime attack.

ASW is handled by 60 plus Tu-142 *Bear-Fs*, 60 plus Il-38 *May* and 90 plus Be-12 *Mails* for open ocean down to local peripheral missions. These are supplemented at sea by 150 plus shipborne Ka-25 *Hormone-As* and *'Bs* (the latter for OTH missile targeting) and 100 plus Ka-27 *Helix-As*. About 120 land-based Mi-14 *Haze-As* augment the ASW capability of the shorter range Be-12 closer to the Soviet coast line.

General maritime reconnaissance is the responsibility of a small force of Tu-95 *Bear-Ds*.

Fifty plus *Badgers* in *'D, 'E, 'F, 'G, 'H, 'J, K'* and *'L* variants provide reconnaissance and ECM facilities within the four fleet areas, along with a small number of Tu-22 *Blinders* (some of which are now modified to carry an under-fuselage recce pod) and An-12 *Cub-Cs* and *'Ds*. Backing up all of these aircraft over the vast territorial spread of the four fleets' locations is a large pool of transport aircraft including the Il-62 *Classic*, An-12 *Cub*, An-26 *Curl* and equally large numbers of helicopters for general transport and more specialised tasks.

For the future there is the prospect of Su-27 *Flanker*, MiG-29K *Fulcrum*, Su-25K *Frogfoot* and the Yak-41 *Fulmar* supersonic V-STOL fighter aircraft being introduced into service. These carrier-borne assets, and the continuing expansion of the Soviet Navy into the realm of 'true' carriers will give the 'new' USSR, for the first time, a global ability without heavy reliance on 'client' states.

■ Yakovlev Ya-38 *Forger-As* on deck. Note lift doors open. (MoD)

■ Troops leave an armed Mi-17 *Hip-H* in the Central Asian Frontier District. (TASS)

the need for a long endurance interceptor with a long range missile armament. Obviously a missile sized to achieve the required range determined the size of the carrier, hence a near *Blinder*-sized interceptor being the solution.

About a quarter of a century later Soviet designers were again called upon to design an aircraft for this unique role, now further complicated by the need to detect and shoot down low flying penetrators including air-launched cruise missiles. Once again the missile determined the design of its carrier and the result was a minimum risk development of the successful MiG-25 *Foxbat*. The MiG-31 *Foxhound*, albeit sophisticated in its electronics and AA-9 *Amos* missile system, at least equal to or better than the fourth generation MiG-29 or Su-27 systems, is unambiguously 1960s in its aerodyna-

them in their respective eras have satisfied the need to extend the air defence 'umbrella' well beyond the boundaries of the Soviet Union.

In the context of extending that 'umbrella' it is appropriate at this point to mention the Il-76 *Mainstay* which is gradually increasing in numbers with the IA-PVO. Probably as many as ten of these airborne radar platforms are already in service and are regularly seen by pilots of Norwegian F-16s around the Northern points of the Kola Peninsula, probably exercising with locally-based Su-27s and MiG-31s. If *Mainstay* proves to be more successful than its predecessor, the Tu-126 *Moss*, which is highly likely, then the combination of its radar performance, allied to the range of the MiG-31 and Su-27 will finally have resulted in the elimination of a huge 'blind-spot' in

■ About 140 Mi-2 *Hoplites* serve the *Magyar Legiaro* as scouts for *Hind* units and for casevac work. (Fred Williamson)

Once the strongest air arm in the Balkans, Hungary took a long time to recover from the shock of 1956. Istvan Nagy examines the *Magar Legiero* as it faces another new era.

ESTABLISHED in 1948, the new Hungarian Air Force (*Magyar Legiero*) operated a mixture of Soviet and German equipment until the early 1950s when the USSR became the sole source of supply. The first MiG-15s arrived in March 1951, followed by a few MiG-15UTI trainers. After delivery of the improved MiG-15bis in April 1958, the early MiG-15s were returned to the Soviet Union. In the ground support role MiG-15s, including the MiG-15UTI, were camouflaged. Some served into the mid-1970s before being withdrawn. The radar equipped MiG-17PF is now allowed to operate day and night, even in bad weather conditions.

The first Mil Mi-4 *Hounds* were supplied to the *Magyar Legiero* in early 1956 followed by the Mi-1 *Hare* for liaison duties. The *Hare* also served with the Hungarian police. Both operated as a single, mixed group.

During the uprising of the Hungarian people against the Russians in October 1956 there was very little air activity although some Mi-4s operated from Budaors, near Budapest. The so-called 'counter-revolution' troops also created a new national insignia.

Before the uprising the *Magyar Leigiero* was the strongest air force in the Balkans, after suppression it was demobilised. Restoration started in 1957, under close Soviet control.

Rebirth began with the same types the Hungarians had flown before the revolution, but reduced in numbers of aircraft, and personnel. In 1959 the supersonic MiG-19PM *Farmer* was added to the inventory followed, in 1967 by a squadron of MiG-21 *Fishbeds*. The *Fishbed* remained the backbone of the Hungarian Air Force up to the mid-1980s and re-

placed most MiG-19s by the early 1970s. MiG-17PFs performed ground support and reconnaissance roles before arrival of the Su-22M-3 *Fitter-H* during the early 1980s.

All major variants of *Fishbed* have served in the *Magyar Legiero*. The MiG-21 F-13 was followed by the MiG-21PF and PFM. Early variants were then replaced by MiG-21MF and MiG-21bis while the inventory also included some-21UM and reconnaissance -21R. A Hungarian pilot defected with this MiG-21 to Italy, bringing a welcome gift of important information. As a result the whole unit had to be moved to another place.

Most *Fishbeds* are now camouflaged in a brown/grey scheme and form two regiments, each comprising three squadrons, based at Kesokemet and Taszar. The *Fishbed* has established itself as a very reliable fighter in the *Magyar Legiero* and will remain in service until conversion to the MiG-29 *Fulcrum*.

In the early 1960s the Hungarians received about 40 L-29 Delphin training aircraft from Czechoslovakia. Due to a change of policy, these will not now be replaced by the advanced L-39 Albatros. Pupils currently receive their practical tuition mainly in the Soviet Union and Czechoslovakia, making the acquisition of a new trainer unnecessary. Most L-29s have been phased out of service, but some are believed to be still based at Papa.

About 12 Ka-26 *Hoodlum* were obtained for the liaison role but apart from the Soviet Union, Hungary is now the sole WarPac country operating them militarily. The type is however, in common agricultural use within many Eastern *bloc* countries and the Agricultural Brigades in Hungary operate a vast number.

Most *Magyar Legiero* Ka-26s were phased out of service by 1987 and assigned to the Air Branch of the Agricultural Brigades, having been overhauled at Budaors, near the Hungarian

■ An-26T transport at Farnborough September 1990. (Peter J Cooper)

HUNGARY

A SIGNATORY of the Anti-Commitern Pact of 1938, Hungary entered World War Two on the side of Hitler's Germany in 1941. Liberated by Soviet troops in February 1945 a coalition government teetered through a series of crises until a Communist government gained control in 1949.

In May 1955 Hungary joined the Warsaw Pact, but unrest continued within its boundaries. On October 23, 1956 a widespread revolution was staged against the Communist government with demands for the removal of Soviet troops and the instigation of free elections — a cry that in the late 1980s was to have a much more widespread, and fruitful, outcome. Swiftly on November 4, 1956, Soviet troops and tanks put down the rebellion and empassioned pleas to the West for help went unanswered. Emphasising the clampdown and the return to hard-line socialism, Hungary was part of the multi-national WarPac force that was sent into Czechoslovakia in August 1968 to put down the liberalist demonstrations in Prague and elsewhere.

With 1956 to the fore in minds within Hungary and without, the demands of the population grew once more towards a more liberal regime in late 1988 and throughout 1989. All of this led on October 23, 1989 to a new constitution and the establishment of a "free and independent legal state". Already it has well outlived the last time that happened — 13 days in 1956.

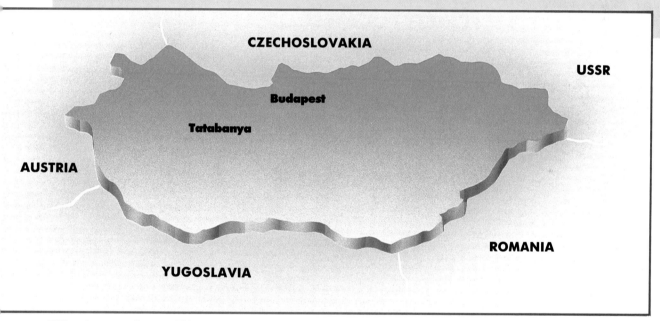

■ Three-tone camouflage on a MiG-21U *Mongol* fighter-capable trainer. (Michel Fournier)

■ Above: **Antonov An-26 carrying a scheme
not dissimilar to Tarom, the national airline.**
(P Heeneman).

■ Below: **Papa-based MiG-23MF *Flogger-B*,
showing two-digit tactical number.** (Michel
Fournier).

■ Above: *Magyar Legiero* operates both the
Hind-D and *Hind-E* in classic battlefield
combination with Mi-8s. This example at Vez
Prem in June 1990. (Michel Fournier).

■ Below: Colourful L.410 Turbolet flight-
checker, note wingtip pod, fuselage 'bubble'
(under serial) and bulged pilot's window.
(Michel Fournier).

capital.

In 1971 the *Magyar Legiero* began operating the Mi-8TB *Hip-C*. First flown in olive-green colour, they now have the Hungarian earth-brown and green camouflage.

About 50 Mi-8s operate in one exclusive *Hip* unit and a mixed Mi-8/24 flight. In 1988 the five-digit tactical number on the tail boom began to be replaced by a three-digit number. These are usually the last digits of the serial.

In 1973 the *Maygar Legiero* received its first 10 Antonov An-24s, followed by some An-26s. As a result, the well-worn Li-2 was sent into retirement. A single transport squadron operates about 20 An-26 *Curls*, which are painted overall grey and are the largest aircraft in the Hungarian Air Force. *Curls* are frequent visitors to Budapest-Ferihegy International Airport.

In early 1980 the *Magyar Legiero* received its first MiG-23MF *Flogger-Bs*. Painted in air superiority grey, they are exclusively used in the intercept and air-defence role. It is believed that some were ex-Soviet Air Force machines and their numbers include a few camouflaged MiG-23UB trainers.

As in other WarPac countries, the attrition of this type is very high and on September 16, 1990 MiG-23 'Red 04' crashed in spectacular manner before the crowd at Papa, killing the pilot.

Hungarian Air Force pilots are noted for exuberant demonstrations at parades. On one occasion a MiG-21 nearly crashed into a VIP area filled with high-ranking Soviet and Hungarian officers. Only the skill of the pilot prevented an embarrassing catastrophe.

Flogger-B units are equipped with the AA-8 *Aphid* and in summer 1988 a medium range missile was added, believed to be a slightly different version of the AA-10 *Alamo*.

Magyar Legiero exclusively operates the MiG-23MF. The more advanced MiG-23MF *Flogger* in use with other War-Pac air forces, has not been operated by Hungary.

The Hungarians have had a change of policy in their tactical numbering of MiG-23s. While on the MiG-21 the four-digit number comprises the last digits of the serial, the two-digit number on MiG-23s relates to the order in which they came into service. '01' is therefore the first in use and '14' or *Flogger* 'Red 14' the 14th etc. In all, the Hungarians operate about 90 *Flogger-Bs*, based at Papa and Szolnok. They do not have the ground attack variant.

Due to the lack of advanced interceptors in neighbouring Austria the *Magyar Legiero* also enjoy local air superiority. Violations of Austrian airspace are quite common and on one occasion a MiG-21 pilot was forced to crash his fighter on Austrian soil after engine failure.

The *Magyar Legiero* operates about 140 Mil Mi-2 *Hoplites* for liaison, observa-

tion, and medevac duties. Mi-2s used in mixed Mi-24 units are used as target guides and most are equipped with a hoist by the port aft door.

Hoplites are also in use with the Hungarian Air Rescue Fleet, based at Budaors, and the *Rendorseg*, the Hungarian Police. Some have a special police paint scheme with Air Force markings and *Rendorseg* lettering, and serals beginning with an R- (Rendorseg/Police).

The police also have some Air Force Mi-2s on loan. They wear camouflage and tactical number plus the lettering *Rendorseg*.

Following the WarPac doctrine to build up front line ground attack power the *Magyar Legiero* established a Su-22M-3 *Fittter-H* unit at Taszar, in southern Hungary, close to the Yugoslavian border. These replaced MiG-17s in 1981 and two squadrons are used for ground attack while the third is a reconnaissance unit. Some two seat trainers, Su-22U *Fitter-G* are also in use.

Hungary and the Soviet Union are the only countries to operate the old Su-22M-3 *Fitter-H*, which lacks an air intake duct at the base of the fin. All other WarPac countries using this large type are equipped with the Su-22M-4 *Fitter-K*. They include Czechoslovakia, Poland and East Germany.

In the early 1980s the *Magyar Legiero* received their first Mi-24 *Hind-Ds* equipping one exclusive Mi-24 regiment and a mixed Mi-24/Mi-8 force. They were delivered from the Soviet Union in grey-green camouflage, which was later replaced by green-light green. The Hungarians can perform all major overhauls on Mi-8/24s at a facility near Budapest.

In 1988 the Hungarians received 80mm rocket launcher pods for their *Hind-Es*. These replace the UB-32 pods which carried Type S-5 rockets. It is believed that Hungary was the first WarPac country outside the Soviet Union to be equipped with this new, more efficient weapon.

The Hungarians have also begun to re-camouflage in an earth-brown/green scheme unique within WarPac. All *Hinds* will be repainted during their next overhauls.

Hungary has deep economic problems and must look to reducing its defence spending. Improved detente between East and West should make the job easier. Recent democratization will doubtless further decrease Hungary's military posture.

Hungary is the only WarPac country to stage an annual airshow held at Budaors Airfield, near Budapest, in the first week of June. These always draw large crowds and in 1988 the Hungarians almost succeeded in attracting an RAF Harrier and Soviet MiG-29s.

Rumours have abounded that the *Magyar Legiero* operates the Sukhoi Su-25 *Frogfoot*, but it has never at any time been equipped with the type and there is no intention of future purchase.

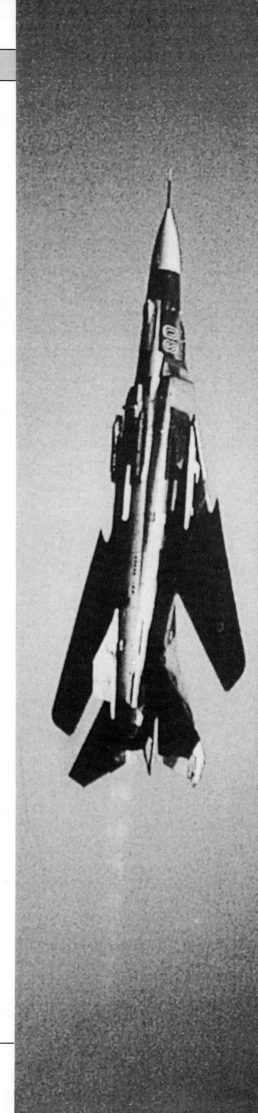

■ Left: Dramatic afterburner aspect of the
MiG-23MF.
■Above: Hungary operates the Mi-8 in
association with the *Hind* force.
■Below: Only Hungary and the Soviet Union
operate the Su-22M-3 *Fitter-H.* Hungary uses
them for both ground attack and
reconnaissance. (All Fred Willemsen)

Flying Tank

■ Frontal aspect of a *Hind* in Afghanistan. Note the sand filters on the intakes and infra-red suppressor 'boxes' on the outlets. (via Guido Potters)

When the West first got wind of the existance of the *Hind* tactics were reviewed and counter-measures instigated. Mike Spick examines the *real* thinking behind this awesome machine at its place on the battlefield

SOVIET BATTLEFIELD doctrine is entirely built on the 'all arms' concept, in which armour, motorised infantry, artillery and air power act in concert to a common plan, the effectiveness of the whole being greater than the sum of its constituent parts. Keynote is shock action, which by its very nature is offensive.

For shock tactics to succeed, maximum mobility must be combined with maximum firepower. The origins of this philosophy date back to the early years of the Great Patriotic War (as the Soviets called their part in World War Two), when the *Blitzkrieg* launched by the *Wehrmacht* cut the Red Armies to pieces. This

method was subsequently adopted by the Soviets, who combined it with overwhelming materiel and manpower to roll the German forces right back to Berlin by 1945.

Little subtlety was involved; concentration of force was achieved by attacks on narrow fronts with greatly superior forces. Tactically little has changed to this day; speed, firepower, and the acceptance of losses are all inherent in current Soviet practice.

All Soviet flying machines, both fixed and rotary wing, are assets of Frontal Aviation, which is an air force subordinated at high level to army control. Battlefield air power is thus subject to the same tactical doctrine as the surface arms. Only against this background can the development and operational usage of the Mi-24/25 battlefield helicopter, codenamed *Hind* by NATO, be understood.

Helicopters promised a whole new dimension to shock action, with their unrivalled speed and total cross-country capability. At first they were seen as troop carriers, but the need to operate in close proximity to, or even behind, the enemy lines, dictated that they carry weapons for defence suppression. This same need highlighted their extreme vulnerability, and the concept of the true battlefield helicopter, capable of taking its place in the front line, was born.

Sometime in 1966, the Mil experimental design bureau (OKB) commenced work on the project, which was designated V-24. High speed, heavy armament, and protection against small arms fire were all specified, plus the

ability to carry a squad of eight fully armed troops.

First prototype flew in 1970, the first production machine was delivered in 1972 as the Mil Mi-24 entering service in 1973. Named *Hind-A*, by NATO it was really neither one thing nor t'other. As an armed transport it had nowhere near the troop-carrying capacity of the earlier Mi-8 *Hip*, while the need to carry even a few troops had compromised its attack capabilities.

On the other hand it *was* fast. A stripped version, designated A-10, set five new world records; three closed circuit speed and two time to altitude in 1975. In September 1978, an uprated engined A-10 set a new absolute helicopter speed record of 228.9mph (368.37km/hr). This really made the West sit up and pay attention!

Although *Hind-A* had retained the engine/reduction gearbox/rotor head layout of the earlier *Hip* with only minor modifications, in appearance it differed greatly from its predecessor. The tail boom was faired into the lines of the fuselage to give a streamlined shape, and the landing gear was retractable, it apparently being considered that the drag reduction of this would more than offset the extra weight and complexity.

More pointed than that of the *Hip,* the front end had a multi-pane greenhouse-type canopy, beneath which a gunner sat centrally in the nose, with the pilot and co-pilot side by side behind him and slightly higher. Below him was mounted a remotely controlled traversable 12.7mm DShK machine gun with a rate of fire of about 16 rounds per second, and an effective range of about 2,450ft (750m).

Forward view for the pilot was not good, being through two very steeply raked flat bullet-proof glass panels. Neither was his view downward very good, as it is partially masked by the gunner and much heavy metal framing.

Eight fully armed troops seated, or sixteen lightly armed troops in conditions of great discomfort could be carried. Access to the troop/cargo compartment was via a horizontally split door on each side. Four vision/rifle ports on each side complete with pintle mounts allowed the occupants to give covering fire when landing in a hot zone.

Hip carried its weaponry on tubular sponsons, and some provision was obviously needed for the *Hind*. The Mil OKB made a virtue out of a necessity by using stub wings, which served a dual purpose. Not only providing six hardpoints for weaponry, they gave lift in forward flight, unloading the rotor, making more power available for acceleration and manoeuvre, or giving more economy at cruising speed.

Early *Hind-A*s were powered by two Isotov TV2-117 turboshaft engines, located above the troop cabin. With an emergency rating of 1,500shp each, these gave a power loading unimpressive by Western standards. More power was obviously needed. This was supplied by an improved *Hind-A* which first appeared in 1976, powered by two Isotov TV3-117 turboshafts with an emergency rating of 2,200shp for a maximum of 2½ minutes. This shifted the power loading from moderate to good.

Externally, this model differed little from the earlier one. The tail rotor, originally a pusher located on the right side of the tail boom, became a tractor on the left side. This revision eliminated the blanketing effect of the vertical tail surface.

Sometime after *Hind-A* entered service, an apparently new model was identified by the West, differing from *Hind-A* in that it had straight wings lacking anhedral, with no endplate pylons. Given the reporting name of *Hind-B*, it promptly vanished from Western sight. It consisted in fact of Mi-24 prototype and preproduction machines, from which *Hind-A* had been developed.

Hind-C was a true variant built in small numbers. First appearing in 1974, it lacked the nose gun and missile stations of the '*A*. Often considered to be a dedicated training machine, production ceased in the same year.

At some point in the early 1970s the Soviet Union revised its helicopter priorities. The new list was headed by the destruction of battlefield forces, equipment and reinforcements. Transport of troops and equipment could be relegated to the more commodious *Hip*. In keeping with the Soviet practice of screwing the last ounce out of proven designs – it was the world's fastest helicopter – *Hind* underwent a metamorphosis.

Marat Tishchenko and the Mil OKB took the original machine and grafted on a new nose section, making an ugly helicopter truly hideous in the process. The new nose contained only two crew positions: the gunner, who now became the weapons officer, also responsible for navigation, seated in front, with the pilot

■ Training variant of the *Hind-D* in Czech service – note the lack of weaponry in the nose. (Steve May)

stepped up in tandem behind him.

By any standards *Hind-D* was an enormous improvement over its predecessor. The pilot now had a good view, both forward through a large optically flat windshield, and a reasonable view to either side through a curved transparency. To aim the fixed weaponry he had a reflector gunsight mounted on the instrument panel shroud, although in later models this was moved to the canopy bow.

Sitting low in the nose, the Weapons Operator remotely controlled the machine gun from a central panel. Missiles are operated from a console under his right hand with the missile sighting and guidance system swinging out for use when needed.

Additionally the Weapons Officer has an emergency control column in the right hand corner. This gives a modicum of control, enough to give him a sporting chance of setting the machine down safely if his pilot became incapacitated. Rudder pedals were not included!

Survivability was the next consideration. Titanium structural sheeting lined both cockpits, which were separated by a titanium shield. The Weapons Officer was protected from in front by a thick plate. Inside both crew positions, the armour was lined with nylon sheeting as protection against spalling.

Almost the entire underside of the fuselage was armoured, as were the engines, fuel tanks and reduction gearbox. This made *Hind-D* virtually impervious to rifle calibre fire, extremely resistant to 12.7mm rounds, and tolerant of 20mm hits. This was the limit of the possible if *Hind-D* was not to serve in a tank regiment!

The wing pylons were adequate for the weapons to be carried, but the DShK gun was lacking in weight of fire. It was replaced by a four barrel 12.7mm Gatling-type gun chin mounted in a remotely controlled barbette. Rate of fire was selectable, the maximum cyclic rate being 70 rounds per second, or nearly six times faster than the original. Muzzle velocity was higher, doubling the maximum effective range to 4,900ft (1,500m).

Traverse angles were also better: plus 15° to minus 60° in elevation, and plus/minus 70° in azimuth. A 2,000 round magazine, giving almost 30 seconds of firing time replaced the original 250 round belts.

An attempt was made to give *Hind-D* some night/adverse weather capability, with improved weapon capabilities. A cupola beneath the right hand side carried forward looking infra-red (FLIR) and low light television (LLTV) seekers, while on the left was a pivoting radar director for the *Swatter* C guidance system. A laser designator pod was located on the port wingtip. Various dielectric panels appeared on the fuselage; probably concealing radar warning receiver (RWR) aerials or active jamming emitters.

Next variant to appear was *Hind-E*, first identified in 1977 and entering large scale service four years later. The original *Swatter* anti-tank missiles were slow, relatively short ranged and vulnerable to ECM. *Hind-E* carried a new weapon both faster and longer ranged; the AT-6 *Spiral*. *Spiral* is a tube launched missile, and both outboard pylons were reconfigured to carry them. *Hind-E* carries a large domed radar director in place of the previous *Swatter* pod.

Meanwhile all sorts of modifications were taking place to both '*D* and '*E* models. Apart from navigation and communications kit, these included tail warning radar, chaff and flare dispensers, which were usually just strapped on the underside of the tail boom, and rear warning radar.

Very significantly, modified exhaust stubs angled the hot efflux gases upwards to promote faster mixing with the rotor downwash, reducing the infra-red (IR) signature. To the new stubs can also be fitted an IR suppressor, a large boxy structure, although this was generally only seen in combat areas such as Afghanistan, presumably the extra drag doing nothing for performance.

Another anti-heat seeker device is a pulsating IR emitter mounted under a dome on top of the tail boom, which is intended to distract heat seeking missiles. A further modification, first seen in 1979 are the rather suggestive-looking

■ First major look at the *Hind-F* for western eyes came in 1989 at Redhill. The latter was the venue for Helitech, where this shot was taken. (David Oliver)

vortex-type dust and FOD extractors fitted to the engine intakes. As these must cause a significant pressure loss at the compressor face, with an attendant performance penalty, the need must have been great, although no firm details have been released.

Final gunship variant is the *Hind-F*, the NATO reporting suffix of which was not confirmed until mid-1987. Very similar in most respects to modified *Hind-Es*, its main difference is that the chin turret has been removed, the gun armament now being a twin-barrelled 23mm GSh-23 cannon with a rate of fire of 56 rounds per second.

Although slower than the previous weapon, the GSh-23 greatly increases the *Hind's* hitting power. It had long been recognised by the helo world that anything less than 20mm is barely worth carrying, and if anything, this modification is well overdue. The cannon is at the exclusive disposal of the pilot, who has to point the whole machine to aim. In previous models he could lock the gun to point straight forward for his own use, but this was an optional extra.

To many people, the adoption of a fixed gun was a retrograde step, on the grounds that it lacks flexibility. This overlooks two points. Firstly a larger gun was needed, but both size and recoil constraints prohibit it from being fitted in a chin turret, even on such a large machine as the *Hind*. Secondly, air combat is increasingly becoming a helicopter requirement, and the cannon is a useful air-to-air weapon. In air combat, the advantages of fixed guns over swivelling were proved as far back as 1916.

Hinds have carried a variety of

weapons during their service lives. Area weapons are generally UB-32 rocket pods, each holding 32 S-5 rockets of 57mm calibre, which can be carried on each of the four inboard pylons. The practical range of this weapon is about 1,200m.

Also an area weapon, cluster bombs were widely used in Afghanistan. The same stations can also be used for FAB-250 or FAB-500 iron bombs, or their laser guided equivalents. Larger air-to-surface unguided rockets, with longer range than the S-5 can be carried; either singly or in pairs. These include the S-16, S-21 and S-24, of 160mm, 210mm and 240mm calibre respectively.

Early anti-tank weaponry consisted of two AT-2 *Swatters* carried on each tip station, although the AT-3 *Sagger* has seen limited use in this role. As attacks on armour are typically made in forward flight, rather than the hover as is Western practice, the radio-command guided *Swatter* may have given less problems than the higher performing but wire guided *Sagger*.

In any event, both have given way to the more modern *Spiral*, eight of which can be mounted. It seems that the minimal troop carrying capacity has been put to better use over the past few years in carrying reload weapons, which can be mounted by the crew in the field. This greatly increases combat persistence.

As it became increasingly obvious that air combat between helicopters was not only possible but inevitable, dedicated air-to-air weapons have been carried. The first of these was an adapted version of the shoulder-launched infantry missile, the SA-7 *Grail*. This was followed by the AA-2 *Advanced Atoll*, and in 1989 *Hinds* were seen armed with AA-8 *Aphid*. All IR homers, these missiles are normally carried on the inboard pylons.

Often having an ambivalent attitude towards Soviet weapons systems, the West on the one hand will decry their crudity, but at the same time extol their virtues. The *Hind* has been no exception. For many years it was regarded as some sort of battlefield bogeyman.

To what extent was this justified? Pull up a sandbag and we'll have a look . . .

Outstanding feature of *Hind's* performance has always been its speed. It was undoubtedly the fastest battlefield helicopter of its day, and at high speeds is very manoeuvrable, with a fair rate of

climb. But by Western standards, *Hind* is rather underpowered. This shows up in low speed flight and particularly in the hover.

In the Middle East, *Hinds* have been observed by British helicopter crewmen, needing a long rolling take-off and even then appearing to struggle to get off the ground. A good analogy is that of a heavy lorry, which although it lacks acceleration from a standing start, can still work up high speeds on a motorway.

With a fully articulated head, there is a tendency to slow control responses. This, combined with the lack of power, makes *Hind* unsuited for Western-style nap of the earth flight, which is essentially a low speed mode. Of course, *Hind* was never intended for NOE operations, being designed for the vast open spaces with little natural cover which abound in Eastern Europe, where speed is the over-riding priority.

In close country, it will be less effective, being forced to use speed rather than natural cover to minimise its exposure time to counter-air weapons. This will make it vulnerable to ambush, either by helicopters or by surface-to-air missiles.

In combat against other helicopters it will be effective so long as it can keep its speed, and thus its energy state, high enough to allow it full powers of manoeuvre. Its speed should allow it to force or decline combat at will against all but the latest Western types.

Hind has seen action in many parts of the world; notably the Ogaden, Chad, Angola, Nicaragua, Iraq and Afghanistan. Mainly it has been engaged in counter-insurgency operations, in which it has proved very effective, although when *Stinger* appeared in the hands of the Afghan freedom fighters (which is not what the Soviets called them!), losses increased sharply.

Apart from small scale actions on the Iran/Iraq border, it has never been used as an anti-tank weapon, and it has never seen action in the type of scenario for which it was originally envisaged. Any judgment as to its effectiveness must therefore be subjective.

Taken in isolation, *Hind D/E/F* does not look very survivable in the context of modern warfare. Its weapon load, although heavy, is in the main short ranged. Its anti-tank missiles are generally launched in forward flight, which means that it must continue to close the enemy counter-air defences during the guidance phase, and it lacks the ability to make the best use of natural cover.

When it is examined in the combined arms context its true value emerges. In conjunction with artillery fire, armoured columns, fixed wing air, and mobile counter-air assets, *Hind* used in regimental strength with its combination of speed, firepower and ballistic tolerance, adds a new dimension to the battlefield. It is not singly that it is a bogeyman, but *en masse*.

To us in the West, the *Hind* concept is difficult to understand, because it conflicts with our own preconceptions of the battlefield helicopter mission. But this does not necessarily make the Soviets wrong!

■ Polish *Hind-Ds* coming into line. Strapped under the tail boom are flare dispensers. The 'beacon'-like device on the spine above the nationality marking is a pulsating infra-red emitter to distract heat-seeking missiles. (via Guido Potters)

■ Right: **Dramatic view of the business end of a *Hind*.** (David Oliver)

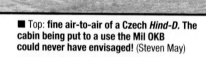

■ Top: **fine air-to-air of a Czech** *Hind-D.* **The cabin being put to a use the Mil OKB could never have envisaged!** (Steven May)

■ Above: **Another air-to-air, this time over Afghanistan, 1988.** (via Guido Potters)

■ Left: **Despite its bulk, the** *Hind* **is an agile performer.**

■ Below: **Close up on the weapon pylon/wing and undercarriage** (Both David Oliver)

ROMANIA

WHILE POLAND and East Germany are most remembered for relatively smooth transitions to democracy, Romania will forever take the burden of history for a vicious and bloody transfer and an equally volatile course since.

Split and segmented during World War Two, with elements being seized by the USSR and other parts going to Bulgaria, the monarchy of Romania was removed in December 1947 when the Romanian People's Republic was established under increasingly Stalinist lines. In May 1955 the country joined the Warsaw Pact, but refused to take part in the invasion of Czechoslovakia to quell unrest there.

In 1967 Nicolae Ceausescu was elected President and his grip on the economy and outlook of the country was to become all the more vice-like and the last bastion of Stalin's iron-fisted approach to communism in Europe. The costly people's revolution and the execution of Ceausescu have proved to be only the start of radical change within the country as reactionary forces continue to try to destabalize the growing democratic institutions.

■ Ignoring the turbulent politics of Romania – which cannot have helped in their own way – development of the IAR-93 (with Yugoslavia) has been protracted. Note: Use of the new roundel (above) is increasing but many aircraft still use the earlier version (below). (Hans Heiri Stapfer)

■ Above: **A pilot accepts his MiG-21PFM from the hands of the ground crew. Until the mid 1970s, national markings were not applied to the top of the wings.** (via Author)

■ Left: **Based on the Alouette III, ICA's IAR-317 Airfox has not yet reached production status.** (David Oliver)

■ Below, left and right: **First delivered in November 1989, pictures of Romanian MiG-29s are rare.** (via Author)

Pictures coming out of Romania of the downfall of the Ceausescu regime stunned the world in 1990. Michael Jones looks at the Romanian Air Force, its varied composition and its prospects.

INCREASINGLY the unruly miscreant in the WarPac line-up, Romania has consistently and openly refused to fulfil its requirement. Compared with the size of the country, Romania only operates a relatively small Air Force under relative independence from *Big Brother* in Moscow. Romania was also the country with the closest links to the Western World.

Nevertheless, it was the USSR that supplied hardware from 1944. In 1952 the first MiG-15s were supplied, shortly followed by the MiG-15bis as well as some Czech licence-built S-102s. The *Fagot* had a very long career in the Romanian Air Force, it was first used as interceptor, then for ground attack duties, where some of the aircraft received a two tone olive drab/earth brown paint scheme. Today, some are still in service for met flights.

First real interception mission for a Romanian fighter took place on October

■ Top: **Checking the UB-16-57 pods on an IAR-330 Puma gunship.** Above: **License-built Alouette III, designated IAR-316B in Romania.** (via Author)

28, 1952 when Major Dumitru Balaur in a Yak-23 intercepted in difficult meteorological conditions a foreign aircraft straying into Romanian airspace.

The MiG-15 was followed by the MiG-17F and MiG-17PF in 1956. The MiG-17F served for a long time in its role as fighter-bomber before being replaced by the Romanian-built IAR-93. In 1959 a few MiG-19PMs were supplied to Romania – the nation's first supersonic aircraft. It was not well liked by either pilots or ground crew, having difficult handling characteristics and being difficult to maintain.

In 1963 the first MiG-21F-13s were supplied to Romania, followed by MiG-21PFMs in 1965. Even nearly 30 years after its introduction the *Fishbed* is numerically still the most important fighter aircraft in the inventory of the Romanian Air Force.

The MiG-21F-13s and 'PFMs were followed by a few MiG-21MFs in the early 1970s. In 1978 the Fighter Interception Group at Kogalniceanu had been equipped with the MiG-23MF. Initially there were two squadrons equipped with the MiG-23MF and a third with the MiG-21. Unlike other WarPac countries, Romania never received the more advanced MiG-23ML *Flogger-G*. Due to the fact that Kogalniceanu is a civil-military used airport the entire Group moves to Ianca during the summer months to avoid the aircraft being spotted by foreign tourists who often use the airport on the way to their vacation on the Black Sea.

In 1988 the first rumours came through aviation circles that Romania was to purchase a new type of fighter aircraft. The Soviet Union offered the Su-27 and the MiG-29 and Romania chose the latter. In early 1989 the first Romanian pilots departed for conversion training at Kiev.

First aircraft were ferried, without national markings, in November 1989 to Romania, where they replaced the MiG-21 at the Kogalniceanu based Group. These aircraft in fact arrived only a

few weeks before the Revolution broke out. The aircraft are state-of-the-art with initial armament of a single GSh-301 cannon as well as the standard types of air-to-air missiles R-27 (AA-10 *Alamo*), R-60 (AA-8 *Aphid*) and R-73 (AA-11 *Archer*).

Fourteen *Fulcrum-A*s and two *Fulcrum-B*s are now on the Romanian inventory with more to follow. It is planned to replace a considerably larger number of uneconomical MiG-21 *Fishbed*s by about 40 MiG-29s.

A *Grup* (the Romanian equivalent for a Soviet regiment) has three *Escadrilâ* (squadrons). This is based on an old pre-war tradition. Although the Soviets also maintain the same structure of a regiment being divided into three squadrons, the nature of this structure is more Romanian than indoctrinated Russian.

A Fighter *Grup* (Group) has about 45 aircraft, 15 for each squadron. All the Groups also have a number of training aircraft assigned.

In addition to the Air Defence Groups there is also a SA-2 *Guideline* Grup with each 24 missiles assigned to each Air Division, based in the Brasov and Hunedoara areas. In all there are about 20 SAM sites with about 135 SA-2s.

The Air Force has 32,000 men in service. There are nine Air Defence Squadrons equipped with various versions of the MiG-21 *Fishbed*, two squadrons with MiG-23MFs and a single squadron with the MiG-29.

Under Ceausescu's leadership, Romania increasingly enjoying more freedom than any other WarPac country. It began to establish its own aviation industry and even to build under licence Western helicopters! Soviet insistence on *Russianization*, Russian language and Soviet methods in every detail has been openly flouted.

During the Party Congress in April 1968, Ceausescu announced the build up of a strong aviation industry. At that time, only Poland and Czechoslovakia

were allowed to produce aircraft within WarPac. Unlike those two countries, it was not intended to build aircraft for other WarPac members as was the case with the Aero L-29 Delphin. Romania sought help in the West for its projects on aircraft and helicopters.

It must be noted that without strong help given by Western companies such as Aerospatiale and British Aerospace, the Romanians would not have a modern aviation industry. It was Western know-how which made the standard

■ Above: **Third IAR-99 Siom carrying four UB-16-57 pods and a GSh-23L cannon fitted in a GP-9 gunpod.** Below, left: **The SA-365 Dauphin that rescued President Ceausescu from his Palace during the revolution. It has since been sold in Australia.** Below, right: **Prototype IAR-823 trainer.** (All via author)

possible. It is probably not surprising that the IAR-93 has a striking resemblance to the SEPE-CAT Jaguar, the IAR-99 to the BAe Hawk as there is a very strong influence on both projects from British consultants.

Apart from know-how, an increasing amount of hardware had been supplied to Romania including Rolls-Royce Viper Mk 632-41 engines, avionics and tyres. For instance, the IAR-93 on exhibit in the Army Museum in Bucharest has a British manufactured nose wheel, but Romanian main wheels!

One of the first demanding projects executed by the *Industria Aeronautica Romana* (IAR) was the IAR-93, a Yugoslavian-Romanian joint venture.

Romanian prototype 'White 001' took-off for the first time on October 31, 1974 at 12.08 hours with test pilot Lt Col Gheorghe Stanica at the controls. The IAR-93 replaced the MiG-17 in the tactical fighter-bomber role and is produced at Craiova. It is also used in training units to train new pilots on the type.

The IAR-99 Soim (Falcon) is an advanced jet trainer as well as capable of use in the ground attack rôle. It is powered by

a single Turbomecanica Viper Mk 632-41M powerplant, licence-built from Rolls-Royce. The prototype, S-001, first flew on December 21, 1985 with Lt Col Stefanel Vagner at the controls from Craiova airfield.

First Soims for ground attack were delivered in the standard Romanian tactical camouflage of olive drab and brown earth. Sub assemblies of the IAR-99 are manufactured at Bacau and then shipped to Craiova for final assembly.

First helicopters supplied to Romania were the Mi-1 and the Mi-4. However, the main part of the rotorcraft force is of Romanian origin. The IAR-316B is a licence-built French Alouette III, the IAR-330 is a licence-built SA.330 Puma, both manufacturing rights given by Aerospatiale. Both aircraft can be also used as assault helicopters equipped with UB-16-57 or UB-32-57 pods on outriggers and they can also carry the AT-2 *Swatter* anti-tank missiles of Soviet origin.

In addition, a few Mi-8TBs as well as Mi-8Ss were in use with the Romanian Air Force. A single SA.365 Dauphin had been acquired for President Ceausescu's VIP flight, but since disposed of.

Transport units have An-24s and An-26s in operation. The An-2 is also used as a *hack* and parachute dropping aircraft. In addition to the regular transport aircraft there is a special VIP flight operated originally for President Ceausescu. This flight has a separate base on the Bucuresti-Baneasa airport. Aircraft used for VIP flights include Tu-154s, Il-62s, Rombac 1-11s and even two Boeing 707-320s – the latter are regularly overhauled in Western Germany.

For initial training the IAR-823 is used. The IAR-28M has replaced the aging Yak-18. For advanced training the Czech-built Aero L-29 and L-39ZO are being supplemented by the IAR-99.

Young pilots receive their theoretical lessons in the *Traian Vuia* (Military Academy). Compared with the education in other WarPac countries the education in Romania is more complex and involves more branches.

Lessons given at *Traian Vuia* include 'flights' on simulators of all current Romanian Air Force aircraft. First flying experience is given to the young pilots at Boboc Air Force Base, where pupils are trained on IAR-823s and later on Aero L-29s or L-39s. An increasing number are also trained on the IAR-99.

The Romanian people have a hard route ahead. The supply of food, warm water and electricity is far better than under Ceausescu, but the new government under Ion Iliescu has shown very little signs of a way towards democracy. Regarding political rights and human rights, surprisingly little had been done. There are a number of voices stating that a second revolution will have to come to bring the country to the circle of democratic countries in Europe.

With this background of mastering the enormous economical troubles in this country, the modernisation of the Romanian Air Force will only slowly progress. It is possible that some projects will be given up in favour of economic efforts.

■ Above: **Disembarking troops from an Mi-8TB, only a few of which were delivered to Romania.** (via Author)

■ Below: **Cockpit of the IAR-99 Siom that attended Farnborough 90. Linked with US manufacturer Jaffe, the Siom is competing for the USAF/USN JPATS requirement.** (Kevin Chevis)

Despite its important position on the southern flank of WarPac, Bulgaria does not possess the latest in Soviet aviation technology. Pavic Burslov looks at this small air arm.

WITH NATO countries Greece and Turkey on its southern flanks, Bulgaria has always occupied a strategic position within the Warsaw Pact. A member of the Pact since it was formulated in May 1955, Bulgaria has received large amounts of Soviet-built or sponsored aircraft.

Although the Air Force *Bulgarski Vozdusny Vojskil* was set up in 1946, the problems of the post-war treaty arrangements meant that it was not until late 1947 that Soviet-supplied aircraft began to arrive and equipment supplied by Nazi Germany could be withdrawn. Since that date, the levels of the Air Force and all other elements of the armed forces, quickly went on to exceed the treaty limitations.

Air Force command comes under the Republic's Army under the Warsaw Pact. Organised into Regiments, backbone of the fighter force are several versions of the MiG-21 *Fishbed* (up to 130 delivered) with over fifty MiG-23 *Floggers* in use in a mixed interceptor/ground-attack role.

Dedicated ground-attack units are five squadrons of ageing MiG-17SF *Frescos*. It is not known if retired interceptor MiG-19 *Farmers* have been transferred to ground-attack or secondary roles. About 30 MiG-15UTI *Mongol* conversion train-ers provide the backbone of operational training.

Up to 40 Mil Mi-24 *Hind* gunships are employed in the anti-armour role. Small numbers of Mi-4 *Hound* and Mi-8 *Hip* provide battlefield transport and liaison. Perhaps a dozen Kamov Ka-26 *Hoodlum* helicopters are also employed.

Basic training is undertaken on Yak-18s with perhaps a small fleet of Yak-11s still in use. Jet training starts on the Czech-built L29 Delfin, upwards of 80 machines have been delivered.

Fixed wing transport is provided by a mixed fleet of Soviet-built types, including the Antonov An-2, An-14, An-24, An-26 and Ilyushin Il-14 (ten delivered)]. Bulgaria is known to have received the An-30 survey aircraft. VIP flights are undertaken by single examples of the Tupolev Tu-134 and a Yakovlev Yak-40.

Bulgaria's Navy operates a small number of anti-submarine helicopters, backed by communications and training types along the country's small Adriatic coastline. An unknown number of Mil Mi-14 *Haze-A* are operated, along with some Mi-4s and Polish-built Mi-2 *Hoplites*.

■ **Polish-built Mi-2 *Hoplites* proliferate in Eastern Europe. The Bulgarian Navy is known to operate the type, but it is likely that the BVV also has some.** (Hanspeter Abt)

■**Ten Il-14s were delivered to Bulgaria for transport use and the survivors are still in service.** (Miroslav Sedy)

BULGARIA

UNIQUE among the WarPac countries in having been very briefly at war with the Soviet Union during World War Two, Bulgaria followed the path of most of the Eastern European states by overthrowing a previous monarchy after liberation. In September 1944 a coalition of left wing groups seized power, but by 1947 Bulgaria was firmly in the grip of the Communist Party and the People's Republic was proclaimed.

Occupied by the Germans in 1941, Bulgaria's location on the Adriatic Sea could not be ignored by the Soviet Union. Bulgaria declared herself to be neutral when war broke out between Hitler and Stalin, but this was not accepted by the USSR. Russia declared war on Bulgaria on September 5, 1944, this 'war' lasting a mere five days until Bulgaria had declared herself at war with Nazi Germany.

It was not to be until February 1947 that the Allied Forces rationalised a separate peace treaty with Bulgaria. This placed major limitations on the size of the country's armed forces. This treaty, and the strictures imposed, has been consistently ignored ever since.

Massive aid has been supplied by the Soviet Union since and the Air Force and Navy reflect this alignment. Bulgaria played her part as a WarPac member in August 1968 by invading Czechoslovakia to suppress the *Prague Spring* rising. Despite her 'front-line' position facing Greece and Turkey, Bulgaria has so far not received state-of-the-art Soviet weaponry, *Floggers* and *Haze-As* representing the current level of supply.

■ Supplying VIP transport for the BVV are a Yak-40 (below) and a Tu-134. They have been known to journey into the West. (Hanspeter Abt)

YUGOSLAVIA

ALWAYS following an independent path, socialist Yugoslavia has grown to encompass a rich mix of ideas and influences. This is certainly reflected in the armed forces which operate Soviet, Western and indigenous products.

Occupied by Nazi Germany, the most effective form of opposition came from the freedom fighters organised by the formidable Josip Broz Tito. With liberation in 1944 Tito's forces were predominant and deposed King Peter, establishing a people's republic later to be formalised as the Socialist Federal Republic of Yugoslavia. Tito became the first President of Yugoslavia and continued so until his death in 1980. Under his rule the country was to make its own way in southern Europe, although since that time the succesion to a wide-based Presidency and continued problems within the nation's nine provinces has led to problems and even open hostility.

Despite its socialist line and being the host to the unifying Cominform from October 1947, relations with the Soviet Union were not good in the early days of the Republic and Yugoslavia was expelled from the organisation in 1948. Relations were not patched up with the USSR until 1956 and have remained cordial but distant since.

■ Known as the L-18 in Yugoslav service, the MiG-29 *Fulcrum* is complementing, not replacing the MiG-21 in the fighter force. Both will give way to the *Novi Avion* in due course. (Pete West)

■ Above: **Yugoslavia is one of the few countries that use the Canadair CL-215 amphibian for search and rescue work – most employ it as a fire-bomber.** (Canadair)

■ Left: **Antonov An-2s serve faithfully as base hacks and for parachute training.** (C J Van Gent)

■ Below: **Seen ready for take-off at Ljubljana, Jastrebs in the colours of the former aerobatic team. The team now fly the Super Galeb – see overleaf.** (David Oliver)

■ **Learjet 35B 70402 was originally acquired for target-towing work. It now serves alongside two Falcon 50s with the VIP flight at Zemen.** (Emil Pozar)

■ **Also serving the needs of VIPs is a fleet of five Yak-40 *Codlings*, again based at Zemen. A further example is used for navaid calibration.** (Emil Pozar)

Emil Pozar and Steve Bond combine to survey Yugoslavian air power, a rich mixture of eastern, western and indigenous types.

OFTEN MISTAKEN as a member of the Warsaw Pact, Yugoslavia is a non-aligned country sandwiched between the states of Bulgaria, Hungary and Romania all of which are, at least on paper, still a part of the Soviet *bloc*, NATO-affiliated Greece and Italy and neutral Albania and Austria. This position has led Yugoslav military strategy to plan for potential threats from both East and West with the air force playing a crucial role in support of the ground forces.

Before World War Two, the Royal Yugoslav Air Force was a small national defence force which relied heavily on the British aircraft industry for its equipment. To counter the ever-growing threat from expansionist Germany, Hurricanes began arriving in December 1938. When the country was finally over-run, free-Yugoslav squadrons continued to fight as part of the RAF.

It was not until 1944 that an air arm of the Yugoslav Liberation Army was again established, this time with a mix of types including Spitfires and captured Messerschmitt Bf 109s. This was the *Jugoslovensko Ratno Vazduhoplovstvo* (JRV) and it adopted a red star superimposed

■ **Current equipment for the national acrobatic team, the Flying Stars, is the Super Galeb.** (Peter Gunti)

■ Left: **Indigenous UTVA 75s are used for primary training at the Air Force Academy.** (Emil Pozar)
■ Below: **Despite many teething problems the Yugoslav/Romanian Orao is now fully operational.** (David Oliver)
■ Bottom: **A small number of light strike Kraguj single seaters still serve, although Jastrebs are due to replace them.** (Emil Pozar)

on an RAF roundel as its emblem.

For the first few years after the end of the war Yugoslavia was totally dominated by the Soviet Union, virtually all aircraft, flying training and operations being controlled by the Soviets. At the start of the 1950s came a shift towards Western influence and for the next decade Yugoslavia relied on the NATO allies for its equipment, including F-84 Thunderjets, F-86D and 'E Sabres and T-33A trainers.

The pendulum swung back in favour of the East at the beginning of the 1960s with the fighter force being updated with MiG-21s and Mi-4s. In addition, Yugoslavia had developed its own aircraft industry which supplied such types as the Aero 2, Aero 3, Soko 522, Type 214-D and Utva 75 trainers and the Utva 66 STOL liaison aircraft. This policy of independence has been pursued with increasing vigour in more recent times with the result that much of the JRV's current front-line strength consists of indigenous types.

JRV is closely linked with the Land Force (KOV). No significant operations involving air power alone are anticipated and some tactical units, especially those equipped with helicopters are directly attached to the KOV.

Largest JRV element is the *Vazduhoplovni Korpus* (Aviation Corps), consisting of a number of *Divizija* (approximating to an RAF Group) and *Puks* (Air Regiments, similar to an RAF Wing). A *Puk* usually consists of three squadrons (*Eskadrila*), with fighter units having an establishment of 16 aircraft plus two two-seaters. JRV organisation is divided into four air regions arranged geographically, with headquarters as follows; No 1 Belgrade, 2 Zagreb, 3 Sarajevo and 4 Scopje.

It is estimated that the JRV has around 200 front-line fighters at its disposal, mainly consisting of MiG-21M, 'MF and 'bis models, with sufficient newly-arrived MiG-29 *Fulcrums* for a single squadron so far. Apart from their primary interception role, all fighter pilots receive ground-attack training as part of the policy of support for the KOV, although it must be said that the MiG-21 especially is not particularly effective in this regard, not being cleared to carry sophisticated air-to-ground weaponry. For air defence,

MiG-21s carry K-13 *Atol*, K-13M Advanced *Atol* and R-3R Radar *Atol* missiles. The MiG-29 has introduced R-60 *Aphid*, R-73 *Archer* and long-range R-27 *Alamo* types. They are backed-up by sophisticated radar systems bought from the UK and Sweden in the 1970s, which replaced Soviet equipment now only used for training purposes.

First MiG-21s acquired were the 'F-13 model, since withdrawn, known in NATO as the *Fishbed* C, which first arrived in October 1962 and operated alongside the elderly F-86 Sabres until they were finally withdrawn in 1974. Elaborate

underground hangarage and maintenance facilities were constructed for MiG-21 operations, unfortunately these are too small to accept the bigger *Fulcrum*, the first two of which were delivered in October 1987. The '21s will therefore be retained, and are currently being updated with new radar and avionics. MiG-21 units are known to be located at Dubrovnik, Lubiljna, Scopje, Zadar and Zagreb, although one of these has since converted to the MiG-29.

Ultimate intention is now to replace *both* the Soviet types with Yugoslavia's own Novi Avion (New Aeroplane), a Dassault Rafale look-alike, reflecting the considerable design assistance coming from France, and intended to be small enough to fit the underground tunnels. The Novi Avion programme was first announced in September 1986 and it is believed that an in-service date of around 1995 is planned.

For many years the prime dedicated

■ Mi-14PL *Hazes* serve the Navy in both anti-submarine and limited AWACS-style roles. (Milan Micevski)

■ Deliveries of the Ka-28 *Helix* were made to the Navy from 1987/early 1988. (Claudio Toselli)

■ Initial anti-submarine helicopter for the Navy was the Ka-25 *Hormone*. (Claudio Toselli)

ground-attack tool was the venerable F-84G, which had a reputation for being robust and reliable with the ability to carry a significant warload. It was replaced in the 1960s by the Soko J-1 Jastreb, a single-seat derivative of the Galeb advanced trainer, which carried far less armament but which could operate from forward unprepared strips. Jastred Air Regiments are located at Beograd, Mostar, Titograd and Zadar.

Yugoslavia then entered into a partnership with neighbouring Romania to produce a more suitable purpose-built strike aircraft, which eventually emerged as the Jaguar-like IAR Orao. This first flew in 1974, the same year that the last Thunderjets were withdrawn. Orao development proceeded painfully slowly, being hampered by problems associated with trying to establish high-quality production techniques in both countries and difficulties in matching a reheat system to the licence-built Rolls-Royce Viper engines. The first unarmed reconnaissance version did not enter service until 1984.

A fully combat-capable model, known as the Orao 2, had to await the reheated Viper 633-41. Orao's introduction into JRV service has proved to be highly successful, carrying a wide variety of weapons including Mk 81 and Mk 82 retarded bombs, Hughes AGM-65 Maverick missiles, Matra Durandal runway-denial bombs and Soviet AS-7 *Kerry* air-to-surface missiles. Oraos are known to be based at Batajnica and Zagreb – the latter having the recce version.

An upgrade of the Orao is planned with a new radar, but attention has now turned towards the replacement of the remaining Jastrebs, which are well over 20 years old. Initial thoughts favoured a similar single-seat derivative of the Soko G-4 Super Galeb, which is very similar-looking to the BAe Hawk. There have been rumours of a Sukhoi Su-25 *Frogfoot* buy, but the local design is now apparently back in the frame. If it goes ahead, the G-4M will feature a nav/attack system and increased weapon load including air-to-air missiles, with a planned production start-up in 1992.

Also operating in a light strike role is the Soko J-20 Kraguj, a single piston-engined aeroplane which is a reminder of the counter-insurgency (COIN) concept so popular with military planners in the late 1960s and early 1970s. Designed to operate from forward grass strips along-

side infantry units of the KOV and armed with small bombs and unguided rockets, the Kraguj is small and manoeuvrable, but is expected to be replaced in the near future by Jastrebs, themselves passed on from other units re-equipping with the Orao or Su-25/G-4M.

For dedicated anti-tank work, the JRV uses Soko-built Aerospatiale SA.342L Gazelle helicopters, known locally as the Gama (for GAZelle-MAljutka). These are armed with four wire-guided AT-3 *Sagger* armour-piercing missiles plus two SA-7B *Grails* for self-defence.

For transport, the JRV relied for many years on the faithful Dakota, plus its Soviet-built Li-2 derivative, together with Ilyushin Il-14s, and for VIP work a few examples of the Il-18, Douglas DC-6, Sud Caravelle and Boeing 727. In the 1970s the fleet was modernized with a pair of Antonov An-12 *Cubs* and numbers of An-26 *Curls*. The An-26 is used both as a vehicle and infantry transport and as a para-dropper. Additionally, they are occasionally used in support of the civilian authorities on casualty evacuation. A lone An-12 and nine An-26s are based at Zagrab with more An-26s based at Beograd/Zemen.

The An-12s have seen little military use, spending most of their time leased out to the national airline JAT on regular freight services around Europe. One of them was destroyed in December 1988 while flying aid to victims of the Armenian earthquake in Soviet Central Asia, tragically killing all on board. Despite rumours that a pair of Ilyushin Il-76 *Candids* may be acquired to replace the surviving An-12, this is considered unlikely for economic reasons, with press reports now speaking of a joint operation of Lockheed C-130 Hercules between the JRV and JAT.

Light transport remains in the hands of the venerable Antonov An-2, used as a base hack and for paratroop training. VIP missions are now carried out by five Yakolev Yak-40 *Codlings*, two Dassault Falcon 50s and a single Gates Learjet 35B originally acquired for target-towing, all based at Beograd/Zemen. A further Yak-40 is used for navaid calibration purposes and a pair of Dornier Do 28D Skyservants carry out various photographic and mapping tasks.

For helicopter transportation, the JRV can call on a considerable number of Mil Mi-8 *Hips* bought in the early 1970s, with aircraft in later batches having the ability to carry four UB-16-57 rocket pods, each carrying 16 S-5 57mm projectiles for suppressive fire in assault operations. Mi-8s are based at Dubrovnik and Pula.

There were plans to replace the armed Mi-8s with licence-built Aerospatiale Super Pumas modified by the addition of clam-shell rear loading doors. This ambitious re-engineering scheme fell through and the Mil Mi-36 will now be acquired instead.

Frequently used for non-military tasks, since there is no large-scale civilian helicopter operator in the country, JRV's helicopter fleet, in particular the Mi-8s, have been used for casualty evacuation, oil rig supply, fire-fighting and in support

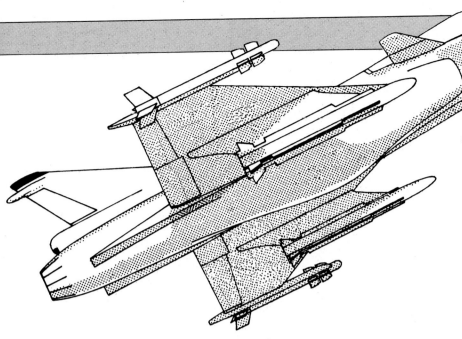

■ JRV places great hopes on the *Novi Avion* project. It will replace both the MiG-21 and MiG-29. (Emil Pozar)

■ Several microlights have been evaluated by the JRV for 'partisan' support and other roles. (M Nikolic)

■ The MiG-21 force will be upgraded with new radar and avionics until *Novi Avion* is ready. MiG-21bis illustrated. (David Oliver)

of construction projects.

Under the direct command of the JRV is the small Navy Air Arm (RV RM). As with many such forces, it is largely dominated by rotorcraft, principally the Kamov Ka-25 *Hormone*, Ka-28 *Helix* and Mil Mi-14PL *Haze*. Despite persistant rumours, the float-equipped UTVA 66s have all long been withdrawn from service, leav-ing the Canadair CL-215s as the only fixed-wing element.

Surface vessels employed by the Navy include two Soviet-built *Koni* class fri-gates with two Yugoslav-built examples coming into use. None of these vessels carry a helicopter landing platform. Accordingly, Navy helicopters operate in a coastal manner in the anti-submarine warfare role, either co-operating with a ship or independently.

During the early 1980s, the Ka-25 was introduced, with the first Ka-28 (export version of the Ka-27) being noted in May 1988 – deliveries having probably been effected in late 1987. Latest deliveries have been a handful of the more capable Mi-14PL.

A typical ASW operation involves at least two helicopters, one acting as an armed 'killer', the other deploying sono-buoys. Attacks are made with anti-sub-marine rocket-assisted torpedoes.

The *Haze* fleet is used in the ASW role, but have also been successfully operated in a 'mini-AWACS' manner, courtesy of the large undernose search radar, pos-sessing a range of 120km (see page 45). With an endurance of up to six hours, the *Haze* is a very useful addition to the fleet.

A few Gazelles and Mi-8s fitted with flotation bags are attached to the Navy for general utility duties. The Navy also has operational control of the fleet of four Zadar-based Canadair CL.215 amphi-bians used primarily for search and res-cue operations.

Remaining operational role of the JRV is tactical reconnaissance, for which it uses a variety of modified versions of other types, with the Orao 1 fitted with an infra-red linescan under-fuselage pod being the most numerous. A single squadron has similarly equipped MiG-21Rs, which still retain an air-to-air mis-sile capability for self-defence. Their rec-ce pods come in three models, daylight photography, day and night photography plus limited electronic countermeasures (ECM), and active radar/radio jamming plus chaff dispensing.

A small number of RJ-1 Jastrebs mounting vertical cameras in a bulged lower fuselage continue in service; these aircraft also carry cameras in the forward sections of their wing-tip fuel tanks. The remaining reconnaissance type is the Gazelle model known as the Hera (HEli-copter-RAdio), which took over the field reconnaissance and gun spotting roles for the KOV from the Utva 66, the latter having been relegated to the light liaison task.

For target-towing the JRV used to employ T-33s replaced by the Galeb in pilot-training units. These have now been supplanted by further Galebs and occa-sionally MiG-21s, carrying SAM-Z80 underwing target pods or expendable target drones.

Another important secondary role is that of refresher flying using the Utva 75. Basic combat training for the light strike and reconnaissance roles is undertaken using Utva 66s, Kragujs and since last year, Galebs. Bases employing Galebs are: Mostar, Niksic, Pula and Scopje.

JRV's pilot training scheme com-mences with four years at the Air Force Academy at Zemunik, which takes stu-dents straight from secondary schools with a large percentage coming from the Marshal Tito military school at Mostar, where they have the opportunity to glide and parachute in affiliated aero clubs and commence powered-flying training in their final year in the Utva 75. All Academy students continue flying instruction in the Utva 75 for a further year, after which they are streamed according to both their preference and ability into fighter, fighter-bomber or helicopter courses.

Potential fighter pilots further their training at Zemunik on the Galeb G-2 and G-4 during the second and third years before moving on to Pula to convert to the MiG-21 in year four. Pilots are not as yet sent to the MiG-29 squadron as first-tourists, but only after a minimum of 500 hours on the '21, although it is intended that this policy will change as more are brought into service.

Those intended for the fighter-bomber or ground attack roles continue with the Galeb during their fourth year, although it is planned to buy two-seat NJ-22 Oraos in the near future to replace this phase of the course. For helicopter students, the third year brings Gazelle and Mi-8 tuition, followed by combat training in the final year.

For the future, the aged Utva 75 is now well overdue for replacement. Current frontrunner is the Embraer Tucano, which would also replace the small number of Zlin Z.526 Trener Masters presently maintained for aerobatic training.

During the 1960s the JRV operated an F-86E aerobatic team, followed by Galeb and Jastreb units, neither of which lasted very long. However, since 1985 the *Letece Zvezde* (Flying Stars) team has been flying a quartet of Jastrebs and last year commenced conversion to the G-4 Super Galeb and an increase in size to six aircraft.

While the *Flogger* family may not be the latest in Soviet technology, the fighter and ground attack versions are numerically Eastern Europe's most important aircraft. Leander Rosenfeld examines their background.

FLOGGER'S roots go back to the early 1960s. Both Sukhoi and the MiG design bureau began to develop a fighter with variable geometry wings. General Designer Rostislav A Belyakov was responsible for this new project.

In parallel with the swept-wing fighter, a delta-winged variant was built. The Ye-23DPD had two Koliesov lift engines in a bay of the centre fuselage. This configuration gave the Ye-23DPD vertical thrust on take-off and landing and the potential to remarkably shorten the take-off and landing length. Both MiG designs, the swing-wing Ye-231 and the delta Ye-23DPD were powered by an uprated Lyulka AL-7F engine, which successfully powered the Sukhoi Su-7 *Fitter*-A.

These two experimental fighters were first tested in late 1966. Evaluation showed that the variable-geometry design was better suited for operational use. On July 9, 1967 the Ye-231 and Ye-23DPD as well as Sukhoi's Su-71G *Fitter*-B swept wing fighter were introduced to the public at Domodedovo.

This was also the first time the NATO military attachés observed the new Soviet design. By that time the Soviet Union had not released an official designation for these new developments. Therefore the ASCC name *Flogger* was allocated to the Ye-231 and *Faithless* to the Ye-23DPD.

Production Ye-231, designated MiG-23S, left the production line in the late 1960s. The production machines were similar to the prototype but received four airbrakes on the tail, improved avionics and a GSh-23 two-barrelled gun on the centreline fuselage behind the nose-wheel bay. A centreline pylon could carry a fuselage fuel tank. Two pylons for various weapon loads were fitted on both the fuselage and wing.

An improved variant of the *Flogger*-A the MiG-23SM had further refinements,

Double-headed spear

■ Comparing nose profiles. East German MiG-23BN *Flogger-H* of JBG-37 'Klement Gottwald' at Drewitz. (David Oliver).

■ MiG-23ML *Flogger-G* of JBG-9 'Heinrich Ran' at Peenemunde on the Baltic. (David Oliver).

but was externally quite similar to the MiG-23S. The MiG-23SM was the last Lyulka AL-7 powered variant of the *Flogger*. Usage of the MiG-23S and 'SM was quite limited in Soviet Regiments and most were soon replaced as the Tumansky-powered MiG-23s became available. None of the *Flogger*-A variants were exported outside of the Soviet Union.

In the meantime, the Tumansky design bureau had developed a new turbojet power-plant. This was a simple two-shaft, 11-stage turbojet with similar performance to the Lyulka engine – but one-third shorter and 40% lighter and more fuel efficient. With full reheat thrust the R-27 produced 22,485lb.

It was a formidable proposition for the MiG-23. To accommodate the Tumansky powerplant in the fuselage of the *Flogger* a major redesign was necessary. The R-27 engine was placed slightly further forward than the AL-7 F-1 but its supporting frames remained unaltered. The tail surfaces were moved aft and the nose was enlarged to accommodate the *Jay Bird* fire control radar as well as some additional avionics and electronic equipment. The missile control radar directing antenna on the port wing glove of the *Flogger*-A was deleted on the new model, called MiG-23M. On this model the wing span remained unchanged from the MiG-23S and 'SM but the wing area was increased and a dogtooth placed at the intermediate sweep angle.

First trials of the Tumansky powered MiG-23M were conducted in 1969. Soon after the type succeeded the MiG-23SM on the production lines. The MiG-23M was soon followed by the MiG-23MS, which was externally quite similar. This was the first variant of the *Flogger* to see large scale production. Armament included the GSh-23 twin barrel cannon. On four weapon pylons K-13A (AA-2 *Atoll*) missiles or UB-16 pods with each 16 Type S-5 unguided rockets could be carried. Allocated to the frontal aviation regiments in the Soviet Union, the MiG-23MS can be regarded as the base model for other developments, the MiG-23MF,

Flogger-B, the MiG-23UM *Flogger*-C, and the MiG-27 *Flogger*-D.

Some MiG-23MS were exported. This variant was first observed by the West when Libya received the MiG-23MS. The ASCC name *Flogger*-E was allocated to this fighter, because it was spotted after the MiG-23MF, and MiG-27. By the time of its discovery by the West it was believed that it was an export model of the *Flogger*-B, but in fact it was the first production variant of the Tumansky powered MiG-23.

From the MiG-23MS emerged the 'ML. This variant had much enhanced electronics and avionics. The *Jay Bird* radar was replaced by a *High Lark* J-Band fire control radar. This system is similar in size and operating mode to the Westinghouse AWG-10 radar. The antenna of the SP-50 ILS-System was repositioned from the centreline to the portside.

The plastic radome was considerably enlarged and in front of the nose wheel bay a TP-23 IR-detector was placed. This all enabled the MiG-23 to operate as an all weather interceptor with stand-off kill capability.

Before the MiG-23 was introduced into the inventory of the other WarPac-countries, it was exported to a number of countries in the Middle East. The following non-WarPac countries are known to operate the *Flogger*-B or 'E: Afghanistan, Algeria, Cuba, Egypt, Iraq, Libya and Syria. MiG-23s of the latter air force saw much combat over the Bekaa Valley in 1982, mostly against Israeli F-16s.

Most of the Egypt MiG-23MF *Flogger*-B and MiG-23BN *Flogger*-H were given to the USA to form a top-secret Aggressor squadron at Nellis AFB, Nevada. At least two *Floggers* found the way from Egypt to the People's Republic of China. It is expected that China will copy the MiG-23.

First WarPac country to receive the MiG-23 *Flogger*-B was Bulgaria. This variant went on to see use with all seven Pact nations. The East German Air Force operated a regiment with 45 *Flogger*-B and 'Gs at Peenemunde. A regiment of Czech *Flogger*-B and 'Gs is based at Zatec. 40 Hungarian MiG-23MF are based at Papa and a further number is based at Szolnok. The Romanian Air Force has a regiment of *Flogger*-B based at Mihail-Kogalniccanu and a further squadron of MiG-23s is operated alongside two MiG-21 squadrons to form another regiment. A single *Flogger*-B regiment belongs to the Polish Air Defence Division at Bydgoszcz. A new variant of the interceptor MiG-23 was observed by the West when six aircraft from Kubinka near Moscow visited Rissala base in Finland in August 1978 – the MiG-23ML, *Flogger*-G. Similar to the *Flogger*-B, this new variant was powered by Tumansky R-29 turbojet with a max rating of 27,500lbs with afterburner. The *Flogger*-G had a shorter, smaller dorsal fin, a redesigned nose undercarriage and new designed IR-detector housing. Within WarPac, *Flogger*-G is also used by East Germany and Czechoslovakia.

Standard armament for interceptor missions includes the AA-7 *Apex* long range air-to-air missile as well as the AA-8 *Aphid* for self defence purposes. On twin missile carrier/launch units two AA-8 *Aphids* can be carried instead of one

■ Polish MiG-23UM *Flogger-C* finished in air superiority grey and lacking underwing pylons. (via Author).

single on a standard pylon.

Latest variant of the interceptor variant of the MiG-23 was observed in 1986. *Flogger*-K features pivoting weapon pylons under the outer wings, which can also carry two 253 gallon fuel tanks, but only usable on the minimum sweep of 16°. *Flogger*-K also has a modified wing glove and a blade-style IFF antenna in front of the cockpit. So far the *Flogger*-K has not been exported outside of the Soviet Union but it can be assumed that it is only a matter of time before this happens.

The trainer variant, MiG-23UM, was developed from the MiG-23MS. *Flogger*-E. It retained the *Jay Bird* radar. Much of the avionics have been moved forward in the nose to make space for the instructor's compartment. The instructor's frontal view is improved by a retractable periscope. The pupil's compartment lacks the rear-view mirror, instead a folding blind flying hood is installed.

NATO allocated the MiG-23UM the name *Flogger*-C. The trainer still retains the centreline mounted GSh-23L cannon and has the same number of armament pylons as the interceptor variants *Flogger*-B and 'G.

In order to meet the requirements for a ground attack aircraft the MiG Design Bureau began to redesign the basic MiG-23MS airframe. The entire nose section to the wings was completely rethought. The wedge-like shape of the nose earned the nickname *Utkanos* (Duck Bill), by Soviet pilots and ground crews. This new nose remarkably improved the view of the pilot. The *High Lark* radar was replaced by a laser range finder and a Doppler navigation radar. Titanium armour plates on both sides of the cockpit should prevent the pilot from rifle and small anti-aircraft fire.

Variable-geometry engine inlets were replaced by smaller ones and the Tumansky R-29-300 engine had a simpler afterburner extension. The new engine has the same dry thrust rating as the R-29 powerplant used in the interceptors. On the rear fuselage two bomb racks were added to accommodate a FAB 100 or 250 bomb. The two fuselage pylons were moved to the air intake ducts.

First trial with the new ground attack aircraft, called MiG-27 was made in about 1972. Three years later the new type had been observed as part of the Group of Soviet forces in Germany and the ASCC name *Flogger*-D was given to this aircraft. On the MiG-27 the GSh-23L cannon was replaced by a 23mm six barrel Gatling-type cannon.

In 1981 a new variant of the *Flogger*-D was first seen in the German Democratic Republic. The MiG-27M included wingroot leading-edge extensions to improve the take-off performance. New sensors in a blister on the nose were added and the ILS-antenna moved on top of the nose. Apart from the Soviet Union the MiG-27M *Flogger*-J is only in service with the Indian Air Force.

Beside the MiG-27 *Flogger*-D or 'J another ground attack variant was developed, this was a mixture of interceptor *Flogger*-B and MiG-27 features. The nose of the MiG-27 had been mated to the MiG-23MS fuselage. The two rear fuselage pylons from the MiG-27 were also added, as well as the missile control directing antenna on the port wing glove. The so-called MiG-23BN uses the same R-29-300 engine as the *Flogger*-D or 'J, but with the well-proven GSh-23L twin cannon instead of the six barrel Gatling cannon.

The MiG-23BN was a step towards simplifying storage of spare parts, since most of the spares and ground equipment could be used for both. This was a major advance for those customers who had already the MiG-23MF *Flogger*-B in service.

MiG-23BNs were exported to Algeria, Cuba, Egypt, Ethiopia, Iraq, Libya, Syria and Vietnam. Only two WarPac countries have the MiG-23BN in service; 30 *Flogger*-H were based at Drewitz as part of the *Jagdbombenfliegerschwader*, 31 *Klement Gottwald*. The Czech Air Force operates a single regiment with three squadrons of each 10 aircraft from Pardubice near Prague. The MiG-23BN is also built under licence by Hindustan Aeronautics at Nasik in India.

Floggers are numerically the most important Soviet Air Force aircraft. About 1,000 interceptor and attack aircraft are based in Europe and the European part of the USSR.

Overtaken by the MiG-29 *Fulcrum* and Su-27 *Flanker*, it no longer represents latest Soviet technology, but *Floggers* are still worthy to serve many years in Air Defence and Attack Regiments of the Soviet Union and WarPac.

Attrition in training and with operational units is generally higher than those units equipped with other aircraft. Due to better flight characteristics and higher weapon load, the Su-22M-4 (*Fitter*-K) would probably be better suited for ground attack duties. Even with these, and other shortcomings, this famous Soviet aircraft will remain a threat to NATO for many years.

MiG-23/27 FLOGGER

■ Top: *Flogger* in natural metal, carrying a mix of *Aphid* and *Atoll* air-to-air missiles. (USAF)
■ Top, right: **MiG-23ML, this type has been seen in France and Finland on good-will visits.** (Guido Buehlmann)
■ Above: **Busy scene at Bydgoszcz, Poland. Line-up of MiG-23MFs, with a TS-11 Iskra being manhandled in the foreground.** (WAF)
■ Right: **Czech MiG-23MF ready for start-up.** (Peter Gunti)
■ Far right: **MiG-27BN of the East German JBG-37 'Klement Gottwald' at Holdzdorf, June 1990.** (David Oliver)

ALBANIA

LIBERATED in November 1944, Albania entered a period of turmoil resulting in the deposing of King Zog in December 1945 and the establishing of a socialist state. A founder member of the Warsaw Pact, relations with the Soviet Union were to change from cordial to outright opposition as the government of Albania crystalised into a fanatically hard-line interpreter of Marxist-Leninist doctrine. These beliefs have kept Albania very much in the background in Eastern Europe.

Increasingly disillusioned with the 'softening' politics of the USSR, Albania turned once more to Mao's China where the adherence to a true party line was applauded. By 1961, China and the Soviet Union were locked into an idealistic war of words and Albania backed China with the result that the country was 'excluded' from WarPac, leading to Albania's official withdrawal in 1968.

Albania's extreme politics have had a drastic effect on the economy and it must be the most backward in Europe. recent political disturbances in the light of the new democratisation of Eastern Europe have arisen within the small country, but have so far only resulted in the expulsion of dissidents.

S TATISTICS relating to most activities in the militantly non-aligned and decidedly isolationist People's Socialist Republic of Albania are thin on the ground. It is therefore not surprising that details of the People's Army Air Force should also be vague.

Formed in 1947, the air arm at first benefited from Albania's status as a founder member of the Warsaw Pact. By 1961, aid from the Soviet Union dried up very quickly and the country was faced with the need to keep equipment running with no form of spares support forthcoming.

Support for China in her idealistic struggle against the USSR found a willing partner and until the late 1970s Chinese equipment–mostly copies of the former Soviet machinery – began to arrive. These have helped to keep some of the Soviet-built machines flying by way of parts commonality. It is therefore difficult to determine how much of the original deliveries from the Soviet Union remain operational.

Combat aircraft strength is put at just over 100 aircraft with the Shenyang J-6 (MiG-19) forming the largest single batch with up to 40 thought delivered. Other combat types include the Xian J-7 (MiG-21), and the Shenyang J-5 (MiG-17). It is thought that the Harbin H-5s (Ilyushin Il-28) delivered are withdrawn from use.

Working hard supplying the only advanced jet training the country has are a mix of Soviet-built and Chinese-built MiG-15UTIs now very much long in the tooth. Basic training is undertaken on a mix of Yakolev Yak-11s and Yak-18s. This small fleet may also include Chinese-built Yak-18s, and the more revised Nanchang CJ-5.

Known Army Air Force bases are Durres, Shijaki, Qytet, Stalin and Valona. Headquartes is located at Tirana.

Transport if provided by a handful of Ilyushin Il-14Ms, and possibly some venerable Lisunov Li-2s (Soviet licence-built Douglas DC-3). The ubiquitous Antonov An-2 also serves, in its Chinese Huabei Y-5 form.

Sole helicopter type known to be operated, with perhaps as many as 30 on strength, is the Harbin Z-4. While Albania no longer merits full-blown aid from China, it would seem that this source will supply hardware for some time to come.

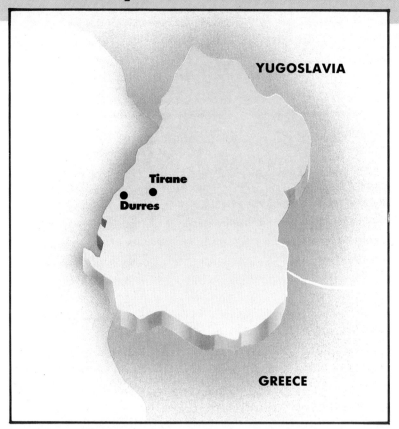

YUGOSLAVIA

Tirane

Durres

GREECE

■ Albanian aircraft are rarely seen outside of the country. Transport workhorse Il-14M starting up. (Bulgar Trevski)

Ilyushin Il-28U *Mascot* – 14.
Ilyushin Il-38 *May* – 14, 61.
Ilyushin Il-40 *Brawny* – 12.
Ilyushin Il-40 *Frosty* – 13.
Ilyushin Il-54 *Blowlamp/Blowpipe/
Blowtorch* – 12.
Ilyushin Il-62 *Classic* – 13, 61, 37, 77.
Ilyushin Il-76 *Candid* – 11, 13, 53, 59, 84.
Ilyushin Il-76 *Mainstay* – 11, 14, 51, 61.
Ilyushin Il-78T *Midas* – 11, 14, 53, 54, 59.
Ilyushin Il-86 *Camber* – 13.
Indian AF – 87.
Iran – 70.
Iraq – 21, 70, 87.
Iraqi AF – 21, 87.
Irkutskin, Soviet Union – 53.
Iryada – see WSK-PZL 1-22.
Isklerka – see WSK PZL M-26.
Iskra – see WSK-PZL Miellc.
Israel – 87.
Israell AF – 87.
Italy – 5, 62, 82.

J

Jaffe – 77.
Jaguar – see SEPECAT.
Jestreb – see SOKO.
JbG31, East German AF – 87.
JbG37, East German AF – 86, 88.
JbG77, East German AF – 21.
JfG9, East German AF – 86.
JG1, East German AF – 22.
JG3, East German AF – 31, 32, 34, 37.
JPATS – 77.

K

Kamenz, East Germany – 37.
Kamov Ka-8 *Hat* – 14.
Kamov Ka-15 *Hen* – 14.
Kamov Ka-18 *Hog* – 14.
Kamov Ka-20 *Harp* – 14.
Kamov K-22 *Hoop* – 14.
Kamov Ka-25 *Hormone* – 14, 45, 61, 84, 85.
Kamov Ka-26 *Hoodlum-A* 13, 14, 62, 78.
Kamov K-27 *Helix* 14, 60, 61, 85.
Kamov Ka-28 *Helix* – 14, 84, 85.
Kamov Ka-29 *Helix B* – 9, 14.
Kamov Ka-32 *Helix* – 14.
Kamov Ka-126 *Hoodlum-B* – 14.
Kamov Ka-136 *Hokum* – 54, 60.
Kampfhubschraubergeschwafder 57, East
German AF – 37.
Karella Wing, Finnish AF – 19.
Kauhava, Finland – 17, 18, 19.
Kbely-Praha, Czechoslovakia – 40, 43.
Kecokemet, Hungary – 62.
Kiev, Russia – 75.
Kiskunkachaza, Hungary – 22.
Kogainiceanu, Romania – 75.
Korea – 7.
. Kosice-Barca, Czechoslovakia – 43, 44.
Kraguj – see SOKO.
Krakow, Poland – 29.
Kubinka, Russia – 87.
Kuopia-Rissala, Finland – 16, 19.
Kuorevesi-Halll, Finland – 19.

L

L18 – 80.
L39 – see Aero.
L-60 – see Omnipol.
L-70 – see Valmet.
La Joys, Peru – 22.
Laage, East Germany – 23, 32, 37.

Lange, East Germany – 22.
Lapland Wing, Finnish AF – 18.
Lavochkin La-7 *Fin* – 13.
Lavotchkin La-9 *Fritz* – 13.
Lavotchkin La-11 *Fang* – 13.
Lavotchkin La-174 *Fantail* – 13.
Learjet – see Gates.
Legnica, Poland – 53.
LET L.410 Turbojet – 36, 37, 43, 44, 65.
Letece Zvezde aerobatic team – see Flying
Stars.
Letov – 44.
Libya – 87.
Libyan AF – 22, 87.
Libyan Navy – 46.
Lightning – see English Electric.
Lisunov Li-2 *Cab* – 13, 66, 84, 90.
Ljubijana, Yugoslavia – 81, 83.
Lockheed C-130 Hercules – 84.
Lockheed F-104 Starfighter – 22.
Lockheed SR-71 – 54.
Lockheed T-33 – 83, 85.
Lockheed U-2 – 6.
Luxembourg – 5.

M

Madge – see Bariev Be-6.
M-26 – see WSK-PZL.
Madcap – see Antonov An-74.
Maestro – see Yakovlev Yak-28U.
Magnet – see Yakovlev Yak-17UTI.
Magnum – see Yakovlev Yak-30.
Malden – see Sukhoi Su-9U.
Mall – see Berlev Be-12.
Mainstay – see Ilyushin Il-76.
Mallow – see Berlev Be-10.
Manching, West Germany – 21.
Mandrake – see Yakovlev Yak-25RD.
Mangrove – see Yakovlev Yak-27.
Mantis – see Yakovlev Yak-32.
Mare – see Yakovlev Yak-14.
Marinehubschraubergeshwader 'Kurt
Barthel', East German AF – 37.
Mark – see Yak-7UTI.
Marshall Tito military school, Yugoslavia –
85.
Mascot – see Ilyushin Il-28U and Yakovlev
Yak-28U.
Max – see Yakovlev Yak-18.
Maxwaide, East Germany – 36, 37.
May – see Ilyushin Il-38.
Maya – see Aero L 29 Delfin.
MBR-2 – see Beriev.
McDonnell-Douglas F-4 Phantom – 8.
McDonnell-Douglas F-18 Hornet – 4, 5.
MDR-6 – see Beriev.
Messerschmitt Bf109 – 18, 82.
MfG-28, East German Navy – 21, 22, 23, 37.
Microlights – 85.
Midas – see Ilyushin Il-78T.
Midget – see MiG-15UTI.
MiG Ye-2A *Faceplate* – 13.
MiG Ye-152 *Flipper* – 13.
MiG-9 *Fargo* – 10, 11, 13.
MiG 15 *Fagot* – 11, 13, 35, 44, 62, 75, 90.
MiG-15 *Falcon* – 11, 13.
MiG-15UTI *Midget* – 10, 11, 14, 37, 62, 78.
MiG-17 *Fresco* – 10, 13, 35, 62, 66, 75, 76,
78, 90.
MiG-19 *Farmer* – 13, 35, 62, 75, 78, 90.
MiG-21 *Fishbed/Mongoi* – 9, 13, 14, 16, 18,
19, 22, 24, 27, 30, 33, 35, 36, 37, 38, 41, 43,

44, 53, 62, 63, 66, 74, 75, 78, 80, 83, 85, 87,
90.
MiG-23 *Flogger* – 11, 13, 22, 26, 28, 36, 38,
43, 53, 54, 59 60, 64, 66, 75, 78, 79, 86, 87, 88,
89.
MiG-23UVP *Faithless* – 13.
MiG-25 *Foxbat* – 13, 54, 59, 60, 61.
MiG-27 *Flogger J* – 13, 59, 86, 87, 88, 89.
MiG-29 *Fulcrum* – 9, 13, 19, 25, 28, 31, 34,
35, 37, 38, 40, 54, 58, 59, 60, 61, 62, 66, 74,
75, 80, 83, 85, 87.
MiG-31 *Foxhound* – 13, 60, 61.
Mihall-Kogainnicoanu, Romania – 87.
Mil A-10 – 68.
Mil Mi-1 *Hare* – 14, 29, 37 43, 62, 76.
Mil Mi-2 *Hoplite* – 11, 14, 29, 30, 37, 43, 44,
59, 60, 62, 66, 76, 78.
Mil Mi-4 *Hound* – 14, 29, 37, 45, 62, 78, 83.
Mil Mi-6 *Hook* – 14, 30, 56, 59, 60.
Mil Mi-8/17 *Hip* – 14, 16, 19, 27, 29, 30, 33,
37, 40, 43, 44, 45, 59, 60, 61, 65, 66, 67, 68,
69, 76, 77, 78, 84, 85.
Mil Mi-9 *Hip-G* – 14.
Mil Mi-10 *Harke* – 14.
Mil Mi-14 *Haze* – 14, 29, 30, 32, 37, 45, 46,
47, 48, 49, 61, 78, 79, 84, 85.
Mil Mi-17 *Hip* – see Mil Mi-8/17.
Mil Mi-24/25/35 *Hind* – 10, 11, 14, 29, 30, 35,
37, 39, 41, 44, 45, 59, 60, 62, 65, 66, 67, 68,
69, 70, 71, 72, 78.
Mil Mi-25 *Hind* – see Mil Mi-24/25/35.
Mil Mi-26 *Halo* – 14.
Mil Mi-28 *Havoc* – 13, 60.
Mil Mi-35 *Hind* – see Mil Mi-24/25/35.
Mil Mi-36 – 84.
Mil V-12 *Homer* – 14.
Mil V-14 – 45, 46.
Mil V-24 – 68.
Military Academy, East German AF – 37.
Milovice, Czechoslovakia – 38.
Mink – see Yakovlev UT-2.
Mirage 2000 – see Dassault.
Mist – see Tsybin Ts-25.
Mole – see Beriev Be-8.
Mongoi – see MiG-21.
Moose – see Yakovlev Yak-11.
Mop – see Consolidated PBN-1 and PBY-6A
and also Taganrog TST.
Morane Sauinier Parasol – 18.
Moscow – 53, 77.
Mosnov, Czechoslovakia – 43, 44.
Moss – see Tupolev Tu-126.
Mostar, Yugoslavia – 84, 85.
Mote – see Beriev MBR-2.
Moujik – see Sukhoi Su-7U/UM.
Mraz-Benes – 44.
Mriya – see Antonov An-225.
Mug – see Beriev MDR-6.
Mule – see Pollkarpov Po2.
Myasishchyev M-4 *Bison* – 12.
Myasishchyev M-17 *Mystic* – 14.
Myasischcyev M-50/M-52 *Bounder* – 12.
Mystic – see Myasishchyev M-17.

N

Namest nad Oslavou, Czechoslovakia – 43.
Nanchang CJ-5 – 90.
Nasik, India – 87.
NATO – 5, 6, 7, 10, 11, 18, 51, 53, 68, 82, 83,
87.
NATO Codes – 10, 11, 12, 13, 14.
Navajo Chieftain – see Piper PA-31.
Nellis AFB, USA – 87.

Continued on Page 96

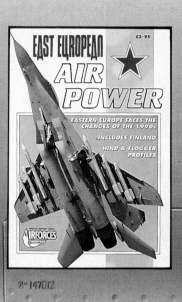